Conversion Tables

Conversion Tables
Volume 1
LC-Dewey

Second Edition

Mona L. Scott

1999
LIBRARIES UNLIMITED, INC.
Englewood, Colorado

Libraries Unlimited, Inc.
P.O. Box 6633
Englewood, CO 80155-6633
1-800-237-6124
www.lu.com

ISBN 1-56308-596-8 (set)
ISBN 1-56308-850-9 (Vol. 1 LC-Dewey)
ISBN 1-56308-848-7 (Vol. 2 Dewey-LC)
ISBN 1-56308-849-5 (Vol. 3 Subject Headings—LC and Dewey)
ISBN 1-56308-597-6 (Disk version)

Contents

Introduction

Analyzing and compiling the first edition of *Conversion Tables: LC-Dewey; Dewey-LC* proved to be an enormous undertaking and the exigencies of publication precluded inclusion of Library of Congress subject headings. For the second edition, however, LC subject headings are included as a separate section comprising Volume 3. Volumes 1 and 2 now consist of the LC-Dewey conversion table and the Dewey-LC conversion table, respectively. It is hoped the division of the book into three separate volumes will facilitate concurrent use of different volumes which, in turn, will facilitate libraries' conversion projects and daily cataloging activities.

Materials referenced in the *Conversion Tables* are the 21st edition of the *Dewey Decimal Classification*; the most current edition of the various volumes of the Library of Congress classification schedules available to me at the NASA/Goddard Space Flight Center Library and the library of the School of Library and Information Science at Catholic University of America in Washington, D.C.; the 1996 edition of *Library of Congress Subject Headings*; and the 1994 edition of *Library of Congress Free-Floating Subdivisions*. Library of Congress subject authority files were consulted regularly to maintain the currency of country or nation names.

Conversion Tables was conceived as a cataloging tool that could be a standard reference in any cataloging department for daily copy cataloging activities, as well as massive projects of converting from one classification system to the other. For the former, the conversion tables most frequently will be used to convert individual MARC records from bibliographic utilities that include only one classification number. With the addition of the LC subject heading table, *Conversion Tables* also can be used as a call number assigning tool.

The LC and Dewey Decimal classification schemes approach the organization of knowledge from different perspectives. This can been seen in how LC and Dewey view language and the literatures of each language. LC classes them together in the Ps while Dewey separates them, placing language in the 400s and literature in the 800s. Similarly, LC places military and naval sciences in stand-alone classes, U for military science and V for naval science; Dewey places both in the so-called megaclass 300s, which includes virtually all of the social sciences.

As the two schemes differ so greatly in basic concepts, it was necessary to analyze the concepts of each order to select the corresponding numbers or alphanumeric notations to construct the tables. Ultimately, it involved assigning more than 52,000 class notations.

Structure of Tables

This cataloging tool is arranged in three sections each in its own volume: LC to Dewey, Volume 1; Dewey to LC, Volume 2; and Subject Headings with corresponding classifications, Volume 3. Thus, each section contains the same lists of classifications in the two systems and corresponding subject headings but in different arrangements.

Example:

LC to Dewey tables

LC	Dewey	Subject Heading
DS109.93	956.9404	Palestine—History—Partition, 1947

Dewey to LC tables

Dewey	LC	Subject Heading
956.9404	DS109.93	Palestine—History—Partition, 1947

Subject Heading tables

Subject Heading	LC	Dewey
Palestine—History—Partition, 1947	DS109.93	956.9404

The notation for a general concept, such as Philosophy which is 100 in Dewey and B in the Library of Congress Classification, will have divisions and subdivisions broken down into smaller concepts and thus more detailed notations (Philosophy—Congresses is 105 in Dewey and B20 in LC).

The differences discussed above also result in more than one notation corresponding to the other, or even a whole range of numbers and alphanumeric notations corresponding to the other. For example, 951.041 in the Dewey schedule under the history of China corresponds to seven LC notations in these tables, in the range DS773.83 to DS777.45.

Dates in the LC and Dewey schemes have been a problem. The two schemes often do not agree on the date that an event occurred. For example, the LC classification indicates that the Time of Troubles in Russian history was from 1598-1613, but the Dewey scheme uses the dates 1605-1613. However, in other places the dates match perfectly, as in the history of Tunisia. To aid in the conversion, I have often used a range of dates from Table 1 in the Dewey Classification to indicate a century, rather than the single date.

The following conventions have been used:

- Diacritics have not been included in the subject headings.

- Within the class numbers and subject headings, "/" indicates a choice and is usually contained within parentheses or brackets.

- As in conventional cataloging rules, brackets [ ] contain words added by the author.

Instructions for Use of the Tables

To convert a classification from LC to Dewey or Dewey to LC, find the section containing the table from which you wish to convert. Locate the classification from which you wish to convert in the left column. As indicated above, it may be included in a range of "numbers" or alphanumeric notations that correspond to the other classification, or it may fall between two classifications. In these cases, locate the class nearest in concept by using the Subject Headings. The classification to which you wish to convert is in the middle column, with the subject heading on the right.

The Subject Heading section provides a shortcut to the call number assigning process. Using that section, you can search for the subject heading that reflects or approximates the subject matter of the item that is being cataloged and note the appropriate classification next to it. This notation may be the classification that is needed, or will lead you to the appropriate one in the schedules.

LC-Dewey Conversion Table

LC	Dewey	Subject Heading	LC	Dewey	Subject Heading
AC1-8	081	American essays	AM141-145	069.53	Museum conservation methods
AC16-19	083	Dutch essays	AM200-401	069.5	Collectors and collecting
AC20-25	084.1	French essays	AM221	069.509	Collectors and collecting—History
AC30-35	083.1	German essays			
AC40-45	085.1	Italian essays	AM237	332.63	Collectibles as an investment
AC70-75	086.(1/9)	[Spanish/Portuguese] essays	AM301-396	069.509(4-9)	Collectors and collecting—[By region or country]
AC80-85	089.945	Finno-Ugric essays			
AC101-102	089.924	Hebrew essays	AM303-311	069.50973	Collectors and collecting—United States
AC103-104	083.91	Yiddish essays			
AC105-106	089.927	Arabic essays	AM313	069.50971	Collectors and collecting—Canada
AC132-133	089.91992	Armenian essays			
AC145-146	089.956	Japanese essays	AM314	069.509728	Collectors and collecting—Mexico
AC149-150	089.951	Chinese essays			
AC168-169	089.99221	Indonesian essays	AM315-322	069.509728	Collectors and collecting—Central America
AC177-189	089.96	African essays			
AC195	089.97	Indian essays	AM323-329	069.509729	Collectors and collecting—West Indies
AC801-895	Varies	Dissertations, Academic			
AC999	Varies	Scrapbooks	AM330-341	069.5098	Collectors and collecting—South America
AG103-190	028.7	Handbooks, vade-mecums, etc.	AM342-371	069.5094	Collectors and collecting—Europe
AG195-196	028.7	Questions and answers			
AG240-243	030	Curiosities and wonders	AM343-347	069.50941	Collectors and collecting—Great Britain
AI	016	Indexes			
AI	050	Periodicals—Indexes	AM349	069.50944	Collectors and collecting—France
AI21	016.07	Newspapers—Indexes			
AM	069	Museums	AM350	069.50943	Collectors and collecting—Germany
AM8	069.083	Chidren's museums			
AM10-101	069.09	Museums—[By region or country]	AM356	069.50947	Collectors and collecting—Russia
AM11-13	069.0973	Museums—United States			
AM21-22	069.0971	Museums—Canada	AM362	069.50946	Collectors and collecting—Spain
AM23-24	069.0972	Museums—Mexico			
AM25-27	069.09728	Museums—Central America	AM363	069.509469	Collectors and collecting—Portugal
AM33-35	069.098	Museums—South America			
AM40-70	069.094	Museums—Europe	AM372-385	069.5095	Collectors and collecting—Asia
AM41-43	069.0941	Museums—Great Britain			
AM46-48	069.0944	Museums—France	AM387-389	069.5096	Collectors and collecting—Africa
AM49-51	069.0943	Museums—Germany			
AM52-53	069.09495	Museums—Greece	AM390-391	069.50994	Collectors and collecting—Australia
AM54-55	069.0945	Museums—Italy			
AM60-61	069.0947	Museums—Russia	AM393	069.50993	Collectors and collecting—New Zealand
AM61.5-64	069.0948	Museums—Scandinavia			
AM65	069.0946	Museums—Spain	AM395-396	069.5099(5-6)	Collectors and collecting—Oceania
AM66	069.09469	Museums—Portugal			
AM69	069.09496	Museums—Balkan Peninsula	AN	070.172	Newspapers
			AP	050	Periodicals
AM71-79	069.095	Museums—Asia	AP2-9	051	English periodicals
AM72	069.0951	Museums—China	AP14-17	053.931	[Dutch/Flemish] periodicals
AM77-78	069.0952	Museums—Japan	AP20-28.7	054.1	French periodicals
AM80-91	069.096	Museums—Africa	AP30-36.7	053.1	German periodicals
AM93-95	069.0994	Museums—Australia	AP37-39	055.1	Italian periodicals
AM96-98	069.0993	Museums—New Zealand	AP85	059.89	Greek periodicals
AM99-100	069.099(5-6)	Museums—Oceania	AP91-93	059.924	Jewish periodicals
AM111-157	069.01	Museums—Methodology	AP200-230	050.835	Youths' periodicals
AM122	069.0681	Museum finance	AS	060	Academies and learned societies

LC	Dewey	Subject Heading	LC	Dewey	Subject Heading
AS	060	Learned institutions and societies	B105.M4	121.68	Meaning (Philosophy)
AS5	060.9	Learned institutions and societies—History	B105.M65	573.701	Movement (Philosophy)
AS6	060	Congresses and conventions	B105.07	117	Order (Philosophy)
			B105.P54	790.01	Play (Philosophy)
AY	030	Almanacs	B105.Q34	119	Quantity (Philosophy)
AY	050	Yearbooks	B105.R4	324.6301	Representation (Philosophy)
AY30-39	030.9	Almanacs—History	B108-708	180	Philosophy, Ancient
AY51-381	031	Almanacs—America	B121-162.7	181	Philosophy, Oriental
AY410-425	031.0971	Almanacs—Canada	B125-128	181.11	Philosophy, Chinese
AY830-839	034.1	Almanacs—Great Britain	B127.C65	181.112	Philosophy, Confucian
AY850-860	033.1	Almanacs—Germany	B127.N4	181.112	Neo-Confucianism
AY890-899	035.1	Almanacs—Italy	B130-133	181.4	Hinduism
AY1000-1009	036.1	Almanacs—Spain	B132.A3	181.482	Advaita
AY1010-1019	036.9	Almanacs—Portugal	B132.Y6	181.45	Yoga
AY1600-1636	032.0994	Almanacs—Australia	B135-138	181.12	Philosophy, Japanese
AY2001	011.7	Directories	B139.1-.4	181.119	Philosophy, Korean
AZ	001.2	Learning and scholarship	B140-143	181.2	Philosophy, Egyptian
AZ101-111	001.201	Learning and scholarship—Philosophy	B145-148	181.6	Philosophy, Babylonian
			B150-153	181.5	Philosophy, Iranian
AZ200-361	001.2090	Learning and scholarship—History	B154-157	181.06	Philosophy, Jewish
			B157.C65	181.06	Jewish cosmology
AZ321	001.20902	Learning and scholarship—History Medieval, 500-1500	B162	181.043	Philosophy, Buddhist
			B162.5	181.044	Jaina philosophy
			B162.6	181.09561	Philosophy, Shinto
			B163	181.114	Philosophy, Taoist
			B193	182	Atomism
AZ501-516	001.2097	Learning and scholarship—North America	B271	186.3	Eclecticism
AZ503-513	001.20973	Learning and scholarship—United States	B279	183	Hedonism
			B285	183.6	Megarians (Greek philosophy)
AZ517-588	001.2098	Learning and scholarship—Latin America	B288	183.1	Sophists (Greek philosophy)
			B398.C34	184	Plato's cave (Allegory)
AZ600-765	001.2094	Learning and scholarship—Europe	B398.G6	184	God (Greek religion)
			B398.I3	184	Idea (Philosophy)
AZ770-795	001.2095	Learning and scholarship—Asia	B398.L9	184	Platonic love
			B491.R44	184	Refutation (Logic)
AZ800-821	001.2096	Learning and scholarship—Africa	B517	186.4	Neoplatonism
			B525	186	Skeptics (Greek philosophy)
AZ850-881	001.2099	Learning and scholarship—Australia	B528	188	Stoics
			B630-708	189	Philosophy, Ancient
AZ999	001.96	Errors, Popular	B645	186.4	Neoplatonism
AZ999	001.96	Superstition	B720-785	189	Philosophy, Medieval
B	100	Philosophy	B728	189.5	Mysticism
B1-8	105	Philosophy—Periodicals	B734	189.4	Scholasticism
B11-18	106	Philosophy—Societies, etc.	B740-753	181.07	Philosophy, Islamic
B20	106	Philosophy—Congresses	B740-753	181.92	Philosophy, Arab
B40-48	103	Philosophy—Dictionaries	B755-759	181.3	Philosophy, Jewish
B49-50	103	Philosophy—Terminology	B770-785	190	Philosophy, Renaissance
B52-.65	107.1	Philosophy—Study and teaching	B778	144	Humanism
			B779	149.73	Skepticism
B65	320	Political science	B790-5739	190	Philosophy, Modern
B69-4695	109	Philosophy—History	B802	190	Enlightenment
B104	109.22	Philosophers	B809.8	146.32	Dialectical materialism
B105.B64	128	Body, Human (Philosophy)	B812	147.4	Dualism
B105.D47	123	Determinism (Philosophy)	B814	148	Eclecticism
B105.D78	362.29201	Drunkenness (Philosophy)	B815	128.37	Emotions
B105.E3	128.37	Emotions (Philosophy)	B816	146.44	Empiricism
B105.E5	392.4	Engagement (Philosophy)	B818	146.7	Evolution
B105.I54	121.4	Innate ideas (Philosophy)	B818.5	142.78	Existential phenomenology
B105.I56	128	Intentionality (Philosophy)	B819	142.78	Existentialism
B105.L54	153.68	Listening (Philosophy)	B820	121.68	General semantics

LC	Dewey	Subject Heading	LC	Dewey	Subject Heading
B820.3	121	Epistemics	BC	160	Logic
B821	144	Humanism	BC1	160.5	Logic—Periodicals
B823	141	Idealism	BC5	160.6	Logic—Congresses
B823	141.3	Transcendentalism	BC11-39	160.9	Logic—History
B823.3	145	Ideology	BC25-32	160	Logic, Ancient
B824	141.4	Individualism	BC34-35	160	Logic, Medieval
B824.6	146.42	Logical positivism	BC38-39	160	Logic, Modern
B828	149.3	Mysticism	BC50-57	160.1	Logic—Methodology
B828.2	146	Naturalism	BC59	160.71	Logic—Study and teaching
B828.36	149.94	Ordinary-language philosophy	BC80-99	161	Induction (Logic)
B828.5	141.5	Personalism	BC131-135	511.3	Logic, Symbolic and mathematical
B829	149.5	Optimism			
B829	149.6	Pessimism	BC137-138	006.3	Logic machines
B829.5	142.7	Phenomenology	BC141	123.3	Chance
B831	146.4	Positivism	BC141	121.63	Probabilities
B831.5	144.3	Pragmatics	BC171-173	121.65	Evidence
B832	144.3	Pragmatism	BC171	121	Truth
B833	149.7	Rationalism	BC175	165	Fallacies (Logic)
B835	149.2	Realism	BC177	160	Reasoning
B836	111	Relationism	BC181	121	Judgment (Logic)
B837	149.73	Skepticism	BC181	160	Proposition (Logic)
B839	149.91	Neo-Scholasticism	BC183	167	Hypothesis
B839	149.91	Scholasticism	BC199.C6	165	Contradiction
B841	133.9	Spiritualism (Philosophy)	BC199.F5	165	Fictions, Theory of
B841.4	149.96	Structuralism	BC199.P2	165	Paradox
B843	144.6	Utilitarianism	BD95-131	110	Metaphysics
B850-945	191	Philosophy, American	BD125	149.91	Scholasticism
B905	141.3	Transcendentalism (New England)	BD143-237	121	Knowledge, Theory of
			BD171	121.63	Certainty
B981-995	191	Philosophy, Canadian	BD181.7	128.3	Memory (Philosophy)
B1015-1019	199.72	Philosophy, Mexican	BD183	121.6	Inquiry (Theory of knowledge)
B1025-1026	199.728	Philosophy, Central American	BD190	169	Analogy
B1028-1029	199.729	Philosophy, West Indian	BD201	121.2	Skepticism
B1030-1084	199.8	Philosophy, South American	BD214	121.35	Senses and sensation
B1111-1674	192	Philosophy, English	BD215	121.(5/6)	Belief and doubt
B1801-2430	194	Philosophy, French	BD220	121.4	Objectivity
B2521-3396	193	Philosophy, German	BD222	121.4	Subjectivity
B3500-3515	199.495	Philosophy, Greek (Modern)	BD232	121.8	Values
B3551-3656	195	Philosophy, Italian	BD236	111.82	Identity
B4041-4095	199.492	Philosophy, Dutch	BD240-241	121.68	Hermeneutics
B4151-4175	199.493	Philosophy, Belgian	BD300-450	111	Ontology
B4201-4279	197	Philosophy, Russian	BD331	110	Spiritualism (Philosophy)
B4325-4395	198.9	Philosophy, Danish	BD331	111.1	Substance (Philosophy)
B4411-4445	198.1	Philosophy, Norwegian	BD331	111	Reality
B4455-4495	198.5	Philosophy, Swedish	BD331	117	Matter
B4561-4568	196.1	Philosophy, Spanish	BD331	126	Personality
B4591-4598	196.9	Philosophy, Portuguese	BD352	111.8	Attribute (Philosophy)
B4628-4651	199.494	Philosophy, Swiss	BD352	142.7	Phenomenalism
B4687-4691	199.438	Philosophy, Polish	BD373	116	Change
B4711-4800	198.8	Philosophy, Finnish	BD394	147.4	Pluralism
B4801-4805	199.437	Philosophy, Czech	BD396	111.82	Whole and parts (Philosophy)
B4811-4815	199.439	Philosophy, Hungarian	BD398	111.5	Nothing (Philosophy)
B4821-4825	199.498	Philosophy, Romanian	BD411	111.6	Finite, The
B4871-4875	199.561	Philosophy, Turkish	BD411	111.6	Infinite
B5000-5295	181	Philosophy, Oriental	BD416	111.6	Absolute, The
B5025-5099	181.(3/6-8)	Philosophy, Middle Eastern	BD417	123.7	Necessity (Philosophy)
B5055-5059	181.3	Philosophy, Israeli	BD418-.5	128.2	Philosophy of mind
B5230-5234	181.11	Philosophy, Chinese	BD419-428	128.1	Soul
B5243-5244	181.12	Philosophy, Japanese	BD430-435	113.8	Life
B5295	181.92	Philosophy, Arab	BD430-435	121.8	Values
B5300-5320	199.6	Philosophy, African	BD436	128.46	Love

LC	Dewey	Subject Heading	LC	Dewey	Subject Heading
BD450	128	Philosophical anthropology	BF295-.5	152.334	Perceptual-motor learning
BD493-708	113	Cosmology	BF299.07	152.1882	Orientation (Psychology)
BD494-497	113.09	Cosmology—History	BF309-499	153	Cognition
BD495	113.0901	Cosmology, Ancient	BF309-499	153	Consciousness
BD495.5	113.0902	Cosmology, Medieval	BF311	153	Cognitive styles
BD530-595	122	Causation	BF311	152.1423	Pattern perception
BD530-595	124	Teleology	BF315	154.2	Subconsciousness
BD555	211.3	Theism	BF315.5	153.44	Intuition (Psychology)
BD581	113	Philosophy of nature	BF318-319.5	153.15	Learning, Psychology of
BD595	123.3	Chance	BF319.5.06	153.1526	Operant conditioning
BD620-655	114-115	Space and time	BF319.5.P34	153.1526	Paired-association learning
BD638	115	Time	BF319.5.R4	153.85	Reinforcement (Psychology)
BD645	113	Harmony of the spheres	BF321-323	153.73	Apperception
BD646	146.5	Atomism	BF321-323	153.733	Attention
BD493-708	117	Matter	BF321.I5	153.1533	Interest (Psychology)
BF	150	Psychology	BF323.L5	153.(68/733)	Listening
BF1-8	150.5	Psychology—Periodicals	BF323.S63	302.12	Social perception
BF20	150.6	Psychology—Congresses	BF323.S8	153.736	Subliminal perception
BF31	150.3	Psychology—Dictionaries	BF327	152.4	Attitude (Psychology)
BF32	150.14	Psychology—Terminology	BF335-337	155.24	Adjustment (Psychology)
BF38.5-39.8	150.1	Psychology—Methodology	BF335-337	152.33	Habit
BF76.4	174.915	Psychologists—Professional ethics	BF337.B74	152.33	Habit breaking
BF76.5-.6	150.72	Psychology—Research	BF337.C62	153	Cognitive balance
BF76.6.E94	150.724	Experiential research	BF353-.5	155.9	Environmental psychology
BF77-80.7	150.71	Psychology—Study and teaching	BF353-.5	155.9	Man—Influence of environment
BF81-105	150.9	Psychology—History	BF353.5.N65	152.15	Noise—Psychological aspects
BF109	150.8996073	Afro-American psychologists	BF353.5.W4	155.915	Weather—Psychological aspects
BF109	150.92	Psychologists			
BF150-172	150	Mind and body	BF357	153.1523	Imitation
BF173-175.5	150.195	Psychoanalysis	BF365-395	153.123	Reproduction (Psychology)
BF175.4.C68	150.195	Psychoanalytic counseling	BF365-395	153.2	Association of ideas
BF175.5.A33	150.1953	Adlerian psychology	BF367	153.32	Eidetic imagery
BF175.5.C37	150.195	Castration complex	BF367	153.32	Imagery (Psychology)
BF175.5.D4	155.937	Death instinct	BF370-387	153.12	Memory
BF175.5.S92	154.24	Sublimation	BF376	153.12	Memory disorders
BF175.5.S93	154.22	Superego	BF378.R4	153.124	Recognition (Psychology)
BF176-.5	150.287	Psychological tests	BF378.R44	153.123	Reminiscing
BF199	150.1943	Behaviorism (Psychology)	BF378.S54	153.12	Short-term memory
BF199	153.8	Motivation (Psychology)	BF380-387	153.14	Mnemonics
BF201	153	Cognitive psychology	BF408-426	153.32	Imagination
BF203	150.1982	Gestalt psychology	BF408-426	153.35	Creation (Literary, artistic, etc.)
BF204	150.198	Humanistic psychology	BF408-426	153.3	Creative thinking
BF204.5	150.192	Existential psychology	BF408	153.3	Creative ability
BF204.5	150.192	Phenomenological psychology	BF410	153.3	Inspiration
BF204.7	150.198	Transpersonal psychology	BF412-426	153.98	Genius
BF205.N6	152.15	Noise	BF431-433	153.93	Ability—Testing
BF209.L9	154.4	LSD (Drug)	BF431-433	153.9	Intellect
BF209.M4	154.4	Mescaline	BF431-432.5	153.93	Intelligence tests
BF210	153.85	Electronic behavior control	BF432.5.D53	153.94	Differential Aptitude Tests
BF231-299	152.1	Senses and sensation	BF432.5.M85	153.94	Multidimensional Aptitude Battery
BF241	152.14	Visual perception			
BF251-.5	152.15	Hearing	BF432.5.N64	153.9324	Non-Verbal Ability Tests
BF261	152.167	Taste	BF432.5.N65	153.9324	Nonverbal intelligence tests
BF271	152.166	Odors	BF441-449.5	153.42	Thought and thinking
BF271	152.166	Smell	BF442	153.43	Reasoning (Psychology)
BF275	152.182	Touch	BF444	153	Human information processing
BF285	152.182	Muscular sense			
BF295-.5	152.3	Movement, Psychology of	BF448	153.83	Decision-making

4

LC	Dewey	Subject Heading	LC	Dewey	Subject Heading
BF455-463	153.6	Speech	BF692-.5	155.3	Sex (Psychology)
BF467-475	153.752	Space and time	BF692.15	155.3	Sexual animosity
BF468	153.753	Time perception	BF692.5	155.332	Masculinity (Psychology)
BF469	153.752	Spatial behavior	BF697-.5	155.2	Self
BF469	153.752	Space perception	BF697-.5	155.2	Individuality
BF475	153.753	Rhythm	BF697-.5	155.2	Self psychology
BF481	158.723	Burn out (Psychology)	BF697.5.S44	155	Self-presentation
BF481	158.7	Work—Psychological	BF697.5.S46	158.1	Self-esteem
		aspects	BF698-.9	158.1	Personality
BF481	158.7	Work	BF698.35.A87	155.232	Authoritarianism (Personality
BF482	152.1886	Fatigue			trait)
BF491-493	154.4	Hallucinations and illusions	BF698.35.C45	155.232	Charisma (Personality trait)
BF501-505	153.8	Achievement motivation	BF698.35.D48	155.234	Determination (Personality
BF505.R48	153.85	Reward (Psychology)			trait)
BF511-593	152.4	Emotions	BF698.35.D64	155.232	Dogmatism
BF515	152.42	Pleasure	BF698.35.I55	155.2	Inner child
BF575.A3	155.232	Aggressiveness (Psychology)	BF698.35.N44	155.232	Negativism
BF575.A45	152.4	Ambivalence	BF698.35.O57	155.232	Optimism
BF575.A5	152.47	Temper	BF698.35.P36	155.232	Passivity (Psychology)
BF575.A5	152.47	Anger	BF698.35.P43	155.232	Pedantry
BF575.A6	152.46	Anxiety	BF698.35.P47	155.232	Perfectionism (Personality
BF575.B3	155.232	Bashfulness			trait)
BF575.D34	155.232	Dependency (Psychology)	BF698.35.P49	155.232	Pessimism
BF575.D35	155.93	Loss (Psychology)	BF698.4-.8	155.28	Personality assessment
BF575.D57	152.4	Disappointment	BF698.7	155.284	Projective techniques
BF575.E53	152.4	Embarrassment	BF698.8.D9	155.283	Dynamic personality
BF575.E55	152.41	Empathy			inventory
BF575.E6	153.1533	Enthusiasm	BF698.8.M5	155.283	Minnesota Multiphasic
BF575.F2	152.46	Fear			Personality Inventory
BF575.F66	158.25	Friendship	BF698.8.P48	155.283	Personality questionnaires
BF575.F7	152.47	Frustration	BF698.8.R5	155.2842	Rorschach Test
BF575.G8	152.4	Guilt	BF699-711	155.7	Genetic psychology
BF575.H27	152.42	Happiness	BF710	155.51	Maturation (Psychology)
BF575.H3	152.4	Hate	BF712-724.85	155	Developmental psychology
BF575.H6	152.47	Hostility (Psychology)	BF719-720	155.422	Infant psychology
BF575.J4	152.48	Jealousy	BF720.A24	155.42239	Ability in infants
BF575.L7	155.92	Loneliness	BF720.A85	155.42221532	Attention in newborn infants
BF575.L8	152.41	Love	BF720.E45	155.42224	Emotions in infants
BF575.S39	155.232	Self-confidence	BF720.E45	155.412	Emotions in children
BF575.S75	155.9042	Stress (Psychology)	BF720.P56	155	Symbolic play
BF575.W8	152.46	Worry	BF720.S45	155.42221	Sensory stimulation in
BF608-635	153.8	Will			newborn infants
BF632	153.8	Self-control	BF721-723	155.4	Child psychology
BF633	153.853	Brainwashing	BF723.A25	155.4139	Ability in children
BF636-637	158	Psychology, Applied	BF723.A4	155.41247	Temper tantrums in children
BF637.B4	153.85	Behavior modification	BF723.A5	155.41246	Anxiety in children
BF637.C45	158.2	Interpersonal	BF723.C5	155.413	Cognition in children
		communication	BF723.C7	155.4133	Creative ability in children
BF637.C56	158.3	Psychological consultation	BF723.D7	155.4133	Drawing ability in children
BF637.C6	158.35	Group counseling	BF723.E6	155.412	Emotions in children
BF637.C6	158.3	Counseling	BF723.F28	155.41332	Fantasy in children
BF637.L4	158.4	Leadership	BF723.F4	155.412	Fear in children
BF637.N4	158.5	Negotiation	BF723.F7	155.41247	Frustration in children
BF637.N66	153.69	Nonverbal communication	BF723.G5	155.455	Gifted children
		(Psychology)	BF723.L68	155.93083	Loss (Psychology) in children
BF637.S4	158.1	Self-actualization	BF723.M54	155.25	Moral development
		(Psychology)	BF723.P4	155.41825	Personality development
BF637.S8	158	Success	BF723.S24	155.4182	Self in children
BF637.T68	158.125	Transcendental Meditation	BF723.S25	155.4138	Self-control in children
BF638-648	299.93	New Thought	BF723.S4	155.3	Psychosexual development
BF660-685	156	Psychology, Comparative	BF723.S42	155.3	Sex role in children

LC	Dewey	Subject Heading	LC	Dewey	Subject Heading
BF723.S43	155.443	Sibling rivalry	BF1371-1389	133.88	Psychokinesis
BF723.S75	155.418	Stress in children	BF1375	133.92	Table-moving (Spiritualism)
BF723.T9	155.444	Twins—Psychology	BF1378	133.92	Materialization
BF724-.3	155.5	Adolescent psychology	BF1385	133.92	Levitation
BF724-.3	155.5	Youthfulness	BF1389.A7	133.95	Astral projection
BF724.3.A34	155.51247	Agressiveness (Psychology) in youth	BF1389.A8	133.892	Aura
BF724.3.A34	155.51247	Agressiveness (Psychology) in adolescence	BF1389.T7	133.9	Transfiguration (Spiritualism)
			BF1404-2050	133	Occultism
BF724.6-.65	155.66	Middle age—Psychological aspects	BF1404	133.06	Occultism—Congresses
			BF1407	133.03	Occultism—Dictionaries
BF724.8-.85	155.67	Aged—Psychology	BF1408-.2	133.092	Occultists
BF724.3.E5	155.512	Emotions in adolescence	BF1409	133.025	Occultism—Directories
BF761-768	158.39	Interviewing	BF1421-1429	133.09	Occultism—History
BF778	153.45	Values	BF1434	133.09(4-9)	Occultism—[By region or country]
BF789.C7	535.6019	Color—Psychological aspects	BF1444-1486	133.1	Apparitions
			BF1444-1486	133.1	Ghosts
BF789.D4	155.937	Death—Psychological aspects	BF1475	133.122	Haunted houses
			BF1483	133.142	Poltergeists
BF789.D5	155.935	Disasters—Psychological aspects	BF1501-1562	133.42	Demonology
			BF1546-1561	133.422	Devil
BF795-811	155.26	Temperament	BF1546-1550	133.422	Satanism
BF818-839	155.2076	Character tests	BF1552	398.21	Fairies
BF818-839	155.2	Character	BF1553	133.425	Evil eye
BF839.8.861	138	Physiognomy	BF1555	133.426	Demoniac possession
BF866-885	139	Phrenology	BF1550	133.423	Vampires
BF889-905	137	Graphology	BF1558	133.44	Incantations
BF908-940	133.6	Hand	BF1559	133.427	Exorcism
BF910-940	133.6	Palmistry	BF1561	133.44	Talismans
BF1001-1999	133	Supernatural	BF1562.5-1584	133.43	Witchcraft
BF1001-1999	001.96	Superstition	BF1585-1623	135.47	Cabala
BF1001-1389	133	Parapsychology	BF1585-1623	133.43	Magic
BF1001-1389	127	Subconsciousness	BF1585-1623	291.144	Shamanism
BF1001-1008	133.05	Parapsychology—Periodicals	BF1623.P9	133.335	Numerology
BF1021	133.06	Parapsychology—Congresses	BF1623.P9	133.3359	Symbolism of numbers
BF1025	133.03	Parapsychology—Dictionaries	BF1623.S9	133.33	Symbolism
BF1026-1027	133.092	Parapsychology—Biography	BF1628	133.323	Dowsing
BF1028-.5	133.09	Parapsychology—History	BF1628	133.323	Dowsers
BF1040.5	133.071	Parapsychology—Study and teaching	BF1651-1729	133.5	Astrology
			BF1714.A6	133.593927	Astrology, Arab
BF1045.A48	154.4	Altered states of consciousness	BF1714.B7	133.59443	Buddhist astrology
			BF1714.H5	133.59445	Hindu astrology
BF1045.D42	133.3	Decision-making—Psychic aspects	BF1714.J28	133.59444	Jaina astrology
			BF1716-.28	133.52	Houses (Astrology)
BF1045.D76	154.4	Drugs—Psychic aspects	BF1716.28	133.52	Eighth house (Astrology)
BF1045.N4	133.9013	Near-death experiences	BF1718	133.5861	Medical astrology
BF1063.D4	133.9013	Deathbed hallucinations	BF1727	133.5262	Aries (Astrology)
BF1068-1073	154.6	Sleep	BF1727.2	133.5263	Taurus (Astrology)
BF1073.S56	154.6	Sleep positions	BF1727.25	133.5264	Gemini (Astrology)
BF1073.S58	154.64	Sleeptalking	BF1727.3	133.5265	Cancer (Astrology)
BF1074-1099	135.3	Dreams	BF1727.35	133.5266	Leo (Astrology)
BF1099.F34	154.63	Family in dreams	BF1727.4	133.5267	Virgo (Astrology)
BF1099.L82	154.63	Lucid dreams	BF1727.45	133.5272	Libra (Astrology)
BF1099.N53	154.63	Nightmares	BF1727.5	133.5273	Scorpio (Astrology)
BF1111-1156	133.89	Hypnotism	BF1727.6	133.5274	Sagittarius (Astrology)
BF1111-1156	154.7	Mesmerism	BF1727.65	133.5275	Capricorn (Astrology)
BF1156.S8	154.7	Mental suggestion	BF1727.7	133.5276	Aquarius (Astrology)
BF1161-1171	133.82	Telepathy	BF1727.75	133.5277	Pisces (Astrology)
BF1228-1389	133.9	Spiritualism	BF1729.P6	133.5832	Astrology and politics
BF1275.G85	133.9	Guides (Spiritualism)	BF1729.S34	133.585	Science and astrology
BF1281-1315	133.91	Channeling (Spiritualism)	BF1745-1779	133.3248	Sibyls

LC	Dewey	Subject Heading	LC	Dewey	Subject Heading
BF1745-1779	133.3248	Oracles	BJ751-759	170.943	Ethics, Germanic
BF1745-1779	133.3	Divination	BJ801-804	170.9495	Ethics, Greek
BF1777	133.334	Omens	BJ847-850	170.9438	Ethics, Polish
BF1779.F4	133.3337	Feng-shui	BJ961-977	170.95	Ethics, Oriental
BF1845-1891	133.3	Fortune-telling	BJ965-968	170.951	Ethics, Chinese
BF1879.T2	133.32424	Tarot	BJ969-971	170.952	Ethics, Japanese
BH	111.85	Aesthetics	BJ973-976	170.9519	Ethics, Korean
BH1-8	111.8505	Aesthetics—Periodicals	BJ991-1185	170	Ethics—Textbooks
BH19	111.8506	Aesthetics—Congresses	BJ1075-1077	170.202	Ethics—Outlines, syllabi, etc.
BH56	111.8503	Aesthetics—Dictionaries			
BH61-62	111.85071	Aesthetics—Study and teaching	BJ1188-1295	291.5	Religious ethics
			BJ1188.5-1278	241	Christian ethics
BH81-208	111.8509	Aesthetics—History	BJ1279-1287	296.36	Ethics, Jewish
BH91-116	111.850901	Aesthetics, Ancient	BJ1286.G64	296.36	Golden rule
BH101-102	111.85095	Aesthetics, Oriental	BJ1289	294.35	Buddhist ethics
BH131-137	111.850902	Aesthetics, Medieval	BJ1289.5.Y6	294.35	Youth, Buddhist—Conduct of life
BH151-208	111.850903	Aesthetics, Modern			
BH161-168	111.8509031	Aesthetics, Modern—16th century	BJ1291-1292	297.5	Islamic ethics
			BJ1298-1335	171.7	Ethics, Evolutionary
BH171-178	111.8509032	Aesthetics, Modern—17th century	BJ1340	171.2	Existential ethics
			BJ1360	171.2	Humanistic ethics
BH181-188	111.8509033	Aesthetics, Modern—18th century	BJ1365-1385	171.2	Ethics, Positivist
			BJ1388	171.7	Socialist ethics
BH191-198	111.8509034	Aesthetics, Modern—19th century	BJ1390-.5	171.7	Communist ethics
			BJ1400-1408.5	170	Good and evil
BH201-208	111.850904	Aesthetics, Modern—20th century	BJ1410-1418	170	Right and wrong
			BJ1420-1428.3	177.3	Truthfulness and falsehood
BH221.B	111.8509495	Aesthetics, Byzantine	BJ1471	170	Conscience
BH221.C	111.850971	Aesthetics, Canadian	BJ1474	171.9	Egoism
BH301.A94	700.411	Avant-garde (Aesthetics)	BJ1474	171.8	Altruism
BH301.C84	153.35	Creation (Literary, artistic, etc.)	BJ1474	171.9	Self-interest
			BJ1475.3	171.2	Humanitarianism
BH301.H3	701.8	Harmony (Aesthetics)	BJ1476	177.7	Forgiveness
BH301.L3	700.42	Landscape	BJ1477-1486	179.9	Cheerfulness
BH301.N3	700.46	Nature (Aesthetics)	BJ1480-1486	170	Happiness
BJ	170	Ethics	BJ1491	171.4	Hedonism
BJ1-8	170.5	Ethics—Periodicals	BJ1491	291.447	Asceticism
BJ10-11	170.6	Ethics—Societies, etc.	BJ1498	175	Leisure
BJ10.E8	171	Ethical culture movement	BJ1498	174	Work
BJ10.M6	267.16	Moral re-armament	BJ1500.P7	177.3	Promises
BJ19	395.06	Ethics—Congresses	BJ1518-1691	179.9	Virtue
BJ37-60	170.1	Ethics—Philosophy	BJ1520-1688	177.1	Courtesy
BJ47	291.5	Religion and ethics	BJ1533.C4	176	Chastity
BJ63	170.3	Ethics—Dictionaries	BJ1533.C5	179.9	Cheerfulness
BJ66-68	170.71	Ethics—Study and teaching	BJ1533.C8	179.6	Courage
BJ71-982	170.9	Ethics—History	BJ1533.C9	177.1	Courtesy
BJ101-214	170.901	Ethics—History	BJ1533.D49	179.9	Self-control
BJ116-118	170.95	Ethics, Chinese	BJ1533.F8	177.62	Friendship
BJ121-123	170.954	Ethics, Indic	BJ1533.G8	179.9	Gratitude
BJ136-138	170.935	Ethics, Assyro-Babylonian	BJ1533.H7	179.9	Honesty
BJ160-224	170.938	Ethics, Greek	BJ1533.K5	177.7	Kindness
BJ231-255	170.902	Ethics, Medieval	BJ1533.M73	179.9	Modesty
BJ271-285	170.90(23-31)	Ethics, Renaissance	BJ1533.P3	179.9	Patience
BJ301-982	170.903	Ethics, Modern	BJ1533.P9	179.9	Prudence
BJ311	170.9033	Ethics, Modern—18th century	BJ1533.S27	179.9	Self-reliance
			BJ1534-1535	179.8	Vices
BJ315	170.9034	Ethics, Modern—19th century	BJ1534-1535	179.8	Vice
			BJ1535.A6	179.8	Anger
BJ319	170.904	Ethics, Modern—20th century	BJ1535.A8	178	Avarice
			BJ1535.C7	179	Cruelty
BJ701-704	170.944	Ethics, French	BJ1535.G6	177.2	Gossip

7

LC	Dewey	Subject Heading	LC	Dewey	Subject Heading
BJ1535.P9	179.8	Pride and vanity	BL263	213	Evolution—Religious aspects
BJ1535.S6	177.3	Slander	BL290	291.22	Soul
BJ1535.S9	179.5	Swearing	BL300-325	291.13	Mythology
BJ1545-1697	170.44	Conduct of life	BL325.D4	222.11	Noah's ark
BJ1725	174	Professional ethics	BL325.H4	291.31	Healing gods
BJ1801-2195	395	Etiquette	BL325.M6	291.2114	Mother goddesses
BJ1801	395.05	Etiquette—Periodicals	BL325.M63	291.212	Mountain gods
BJ1815	395.03	Etiquette—Dictionaries	BL406.C7	291.37	Crosses
BJ1821	395.09	Etiquette—History	BL435-457	291.212	Nature worship
BJ1855	395.142	Etiquette for men	BL438	291.212	Sun worship
BJ1856	395.144	Etiquette for women	BL438	291.212	Moon worship
BJ2018-2019	395.53	Church etiquette	BL439-443	291.212	Animal worship
BJ2021-2078	395.3	Entertaining	BL441	291.212	Serpent worship
BJ2021-2028	395.3	Hospitality	BL444	291.212	Tree worship
BJ2041	395.54	Table etiquette	BL447	291.212	Mountain worship
BJ2051-2065	395.22	Wedding etiquette	BL453	291.212	Fire-worshipers
BJ2071-2075	395.23	Mourning etiquette	BL458	291.178344	Sexism in religion
BJ2100-2115	395.4	Letter writing	BL465	291.213	Emperor worship
BJ2120-2128	395.59	Conversation	BL467	291.213	Ancestor worship
BJ2137-2156	395.5	Travel etiquette	BL473	291.21	Gods
BJ2195	395.59	Telephone etiquette	BL475	291.61	Messiah
BL1-10	200.5	Religion—Periodicals	BL477	291.215	Angels
BL11-21	200.6	Religion—[Societies/ Congresses]	BL480	291.216	Devil
BL29	291.175	Religious literature	BL480	291.216	Satanism
BL35	200.25	Religion—Directories	BL480	291.216	Demonology
BL41	200.71	Religion—Study and teaching	BL485	291.218	Idols and images—Worship
BL48-50	200	Religion	BL500-547	291.23	Eschatology
BL51	210	Religion—Philosophy	BL503	291.23	Resurrection
BL51	210	Knowledge, Theory of (Religion)	BL515	291.237	Reincarnation
			BL525	291.21	Transmigration
BL51	210	Fictions, Theory of	BL535-547	291.23	Future life
BL53	291.175	Psychology, Religious	BL545	291.23	Hell
BL53	291.42	Experience (Religion)	BL550-620	291.3	Worship
BL55	291.17	Religion and civilization	BL560	291.43	Prayer
BL60	291.17	Religion and sociology	BL560	291.43	Prayers
BL65.C58	291.177	Civil rights—Religious aspects	BL570	291.34	Sacrifice
			BL580-586	291.35	Shrines
BL65.C8	291.17	Religion and culture	BL590	291.(447/36)	Fasts and feasts
BL65.E68	291.17834	Equality—Religious aspects	BL600-620	291.37	Symbolism
BL65.J87	291.5622	Religion and justice	BL600-619	291.38	Ritual
BL65.L33	291.177	Religion and law	BL600-619	291.38	Rites and ceremonies
BL65.M4	291.175	Medicine—Religious aspects	BL603	291.37	Emblems
			BL604.C5	291.37	Circle—Religious aspects
BL65.P7	291.177	Religion and politics	BL604.S8	291.37	Swastika
BL65.R3	291.17834	Race—Religious aspects	BL604.V2	291.37	V symbol
BL65.S8	291.177	Religion and state	BL613	291.32	Divination
BL70-71	291.82	Sacred books	BL613	291.32	Oracles
BL74-98	230-299	Religions	BL619.S3	291.36	Sacred meals
BL175-190	210	Natural theology	BL624-627	291.4	Religious life
BL200	211.3	Theism	BL625	291.447	Asceticism
BL210	210	Analogy (Religion)	BL625	291.422	Mysticism
BL215	211	Anthropomorphism	BL626	291.42	Ecstasy
BL217	211.32	Polytheism	BL627	291.435	Meditation
BL218	211.33	Dualism (Religion)	BL632	291.65	Religious communities
BL220	211.2	Pantheism	BL635	291.61	Priests
BL221	211.34	Monotheism	BL640	323.442	Freedom of religion
BL224-226	213	Creation	BL660-687	200.956	Middle East—Religion
BL239-265	291.175	Religion and science	BL689-980	291.13094	Mythology, European
BL256	291.22	Man (Theology)	BL690-980	200.94	Europe—Religion

8

LC	Dewey	Subject Heading	LC	Dewey	Subject Heading
BL700-820	292.13	Mythology, Classical	BL1216	294.52114	Goddesses, Hindu
BL735	292.28	Hell	BL1225.A	294.52113	Aatimna (Hindu deity)
BL740-760	299.9294	Etruscans—Religion	BL1225.A4	294.52114	Aditi (Hindu deity)
BL780-795	292.08	Greece—Religion	BL1225.A42	294.52113	Adityas (Hindu deities)
BL800-820	292.07	Rome—Religion	BL1225.D3	294.52113	Dattatreya (Hindu deity)
BL815.V4	292.61	Vestals	BL1225.D48	294.52113	Devanarayana (Hindu deity)
BL820.A25	292.2113	Adonis (Greek deity)	BL1225.D8	294.52114	Durga (Hindu deity)
BL820.A4	292.2113	Aesculapius (Greek deity)	BL1225.M	294.513	Manus (Hindu mythology)
BL820.A6	292.13	Amazons	BL1226	294.53	Worship (Hinduism)
BL820.A63	292.13	Amycus (Greek mythology)	BL1226.2	294.538	Chants (Hindu)
BL820.A8	292.13	Jason (Greek mythology)	BL1226.82.M3	294.5441	Marriage customs and rites, Hindu
BL820.B2	292.2113	Dionysia			
BL820.C	292.13	Centaurs	BL1228	294.544	Religious life—Hinduism
BL820.C5	292.2114	Demeter (Greek deity)	BL1236.76.S23	294.534	Sacrifice
BL820.C5	292.2114	Ceres (Roman deity)	BL1238	294.5657	Monasticism and religious orders, Hindu
BL820.D	292.13	Dryads			
BL820.D25	292.13	Daedalus (Greek mythology)	BL1239.32	294.5351	Hindu pilgrims and pilgrimages
BL820.D54	292.2114	Diktynna (Greek deity)			
BL820.E5	292.2114	Eileithyia (Greek deity)	BL1239.72-.82	294.538	Fasts and feasts—Hinduism
BL820.F7	292.2114	Fortuna (Roman diety)	BL1241.46	294.5	Brahmans
BL820.F8	292.13	Furies (Roman mythology)	BL1243.72-.78	294.535	Temples, Hindu
BL820.F8	292.13	Erinyes (Greek mythology)	BL1245.A1	294.55	Hindu sects
BL820.G7	292.13	Gorgons (Greek mythology)	BL1282.2-.292	294.5514	Shaktism
BL820.G8	292.13	Graces, The	BL1290.8	299.5145	Taoist ethics
BL820.H5	292.13	Heracles (Greek mythology)	BL1300-1365	294.4	Jainism
BL820.J8	292.2113	Jupiter (Roman deity)	BL1300-1365	294.4	Jains
BL820.L25	292.13	Ladon (Greek mythology)	BL1310-1314.2	294.482	Jainism—Sacred books
BL820.M26	292.2113	Marsyas (Greek diety)	BL1355.5	294.438	Fasts and feasts—Jainism
BL820.M37	292.13	Medea (Greek mythology)	BL1356-1375	294.42	Jainism—Doctrines
BL820.M6	292.2114	Athena (Greek deity)	BL1375.P	294.434	Penance (Jainism)
BL820.M63	292.13	Minotaur (Greek mythology)	BL1375.Y63	294.4436	Yoga (Jainism)
BL820.M65	292.2114	Mother goddesses, Greek	BL1376-1380	294.43	Worship (Jainism)
BL820.06	292.2113	Ops (Roman deity)	BL1377.3	294.437	Jaina mantras
BL820.P	292.13	Pandora (Greek mythology)	BL1378.8	294.4422	Mysticism—Jainism
BL820.P2	292.2113	Pan (Greek deity)	BL1380.D	294.493	Digambara (Jaina sect)
BL820.P4	292.13	Pegasus (Greek mythology)	BL1477.8.D4	294.3435	Temples, Buddhist—Dedication
BL820.P5	292.13	Perseus (Greek mythology)			
BL820.P7	292.2114	Persephone (Greek deity)	BL1477.8.F8	294.3438	Funeral rites and ceremonies, Buddhist
BL820.T6	292.13	Titans (Mythology)			
BL830-875	293	Germanic peoples—Religion	BL1478	294.3657	Profession (Buddhist monastic orders)
BL870.B3	293.2113	Balder (Norse deity)			
BL870.F28	293.13	Fafnir (Germanic mythology)	BL1493	294.3375	Zen Buddhism—Psychology
BL870.S29	292.2113	Saturn (Roman deity)	BL1500-1590	295	Zorastrianism
BL1000-2370	299.5	Mythology, Oriental	BL1500-1590	295	Parsees
BL1100-1270	294.5	Hinduism	BL1510-1525	295.82	Zoroastrianism—Sacred books
BL1100-1245	294.5	Brahmanism			
BL1112.2	294.5921	Vedas	BL1590.R5	299.15	Rider-gods
BL1141.2-1142.6	294.5514	Tantrism	BL1600-1710	299.2	Semites—Religion
			BL1616.E54	299.9295	Enki (Sumarian deity)
BL1171	294.5213	Alvars	BL1625.M37	299.21	Marduk (Babylonian deity)
BL1171	294.5213	Hindu saints	BL1625.P3	299.21	Panbabylonism
BL1200-1225	294.5211	God (Hinduism)	BL1671	299.26	Baal (Deity)
BL1213.32-1215	294.52	Hinduism—Doctrines	BL1695	297.85	Druzes
			BL1800-1975	299.51	China—Religion
BL1213.D87	294.536	Durga-puja (Hindu festival)	BL1830-1875	299.512	Confucianism
BL1214.32.B53	294.5211	Bhakti	BL1900-1940	299.514	Taoism
BL1215.F3	294.5447	Fasting (Hinduism)	BL2000-2030	294.5	Hinduism
BL1215.M3	294.522	Man (Hinduism)	BL2000-2016	294	Mythology, Indic
BL1215.M9	294.5422	Mysticism—Hinduism	BL2015.K3	294.5175	Karma
BL1215.S64	294.517	Sociology, Hindu	BL2017-2018.7	294.6	Sikhism
BL1215.S8	294.522	Soul (Hinduism)	BL2017.2-.4	294.682	Sikhism—Sacred books

LC	Dewey	Subject Heading	LC	Dewey	Subject Heading
BL2018.7	294.69	Sikh sects	BM190-199	296.09033	Judaism—History—Modern period, 1750-
BL2018.7.K44	294.69	Khalsa (Sect)			
BL2020.S5	294.6	Sikhs	BM197.5	296.8342	Conservative Judaism
BL2035	299.14122	Pakistan—Religion	BM197.8	296.834	Humanistic Judaism
BL2050-2150	299.5	Asia, Southeastern—Religion	BM198	296.8332	Hasidism
BL2200-2228	299.56	Japan—Religion	BM199.S3	296.82	Sabbathaians
BL2211.D33	299.56	Daikokuten (Japanese diety)	BM205-225	296.0973	Judaism—United States
BL2211.E24	299.56	Ebisu (Japanese deity)	BM227-229	296.0971	Judaism—Canada
BL2211.E46	299.56	Emperor worship—Japanese	BM230-232	296.0972	Judaism—Mexico
BL2216-2227.8	299.561	Shinto	BM233-247	296.09728	Judaism—Central America
BL2217-.5	299.56182	Shinto—Sacred books	BM248-260	296.09729	Judaism—West Indies
BL2222.H5	299.5619	Hinomoto (Sect)	BM261-289	296.098	Judaism—South America
BL2224.2	299.56138	Shinto—Rituals	BM290-376	296.094	Judaism—Europe
BL2224.3	299.56136	Shinto devotional calendars	BM292-305	296.0941	Judaism—Great Britain
BL2224.9-2225.3	299.56135	Shinto shrines	BM307-309	296.09436	Judaism—Austria
			BM310-312	296.09493	Judaism—Belgium
			BM313-315	296.0944	Judaism—France
BL2230-2240	299.957	Korea—Religion	BM316-318	296.0943	Judaism—Germany
BL2270-2280	299.155	Iran—Religion	BM319-321	296.09495	Judaism—Greece
BL2370.S5	291.144	Shamanism	BM322-324	296.0945	Judaism—Italy
BL2400-2490	299.6	Africa—Religion	BM325-327	296.09492	Judaism—Netherlands
BL2420-2460	299.31	Egypt—Religion	BM328-330	296.09469	Judaism—Portugal
BL2450.A45	299.31	Amon (Egyptian deity)	BM331-333	296.0947	Judaism—Russia
BL2450.A89	299.31	Atum (Egyptian deity)	BM334-336	296.094897	Judaism—Finland
Bl 2450.G6	299.31	Gods, Egyptian	BM337-339	296.09438	Judaism—Poland
BL2450.N45	299.31	Neith (Egyptian deity)	BM340-353	296.0948	Judaism—Scandinavia
BL2450.07	299.31	Osiris (Egyptian deity)	BM342-344	296.09489	Judaism—Denmark
BL2450.S27	299.31	Satis (Egyptian deity)	BM348-350	296.09481	Judaism—Norway
BL2462	299.3	Africa, North—Religion	BM351-353	296.09485	Judaism—Sweden
BL2480.Y6	299.6869	Sopono (Cult)	BM354-356	296.0946	Judaism—Spain
BL2480.Y6	299.6869	Egungun (Cult)	BM357-359	296.09494	Judaism—Switzerland
BL2490	299.675	Voodooism	BM364-366	296.09499	Judaism—Bulgaria
BL2580-2592	299.8	South America—Religion	BM370-372	296.09498	Judaism—Romania
BL2590.B7	299.891	Afro-Brazilian cults	BM373-375	296.094971	Judaism—Yugoslavia
BL2600-2630	299.92	Oceania—Religion	BM377-431	296.095	Judaism—Asia
BL2620.P6	299.924	Mythology, Polynesian	BM386.4-.6	296.09567	Judaism—Iraq
BL2700-2790	211.8	Atheism	BM387-389	296.09569 (1/4)	Judaism—[Syria/Palestine]
BL2700-2790	211.6	Secularism			
BL2700-2790	211.4	Skepticism	BM390-392	296.095694	Judaism—Israel
BL2700-2790	211.4	Rationalism	BM393-395	296.0953	Judaism—Arabia
BM	296	Judaism	BM396-398	296.0955	Judaism—Iran
BM1	296.67	Judaism—Societies, etc.	BM400	296.09581	Judaism—Afghanistan
BM11	296.05	Judaism—Periodicals	BM406-410	296.0954	Judaism—India
BM21-30	296.67	Judaism—Congresses	BM423-425	296.0951	Judaism—China
BM50	296.03	Judaism—Dictionaries	BM426-428	296.0952	Judaism—Japan
BM55-65	296.025	Judaism—Directories	BM432-440	296.096	Judaism—Africa
BM70-135	296.68	Jews—Education	BM434-436	296.0962	Judaism—Egypt
BM150-449	296.09	Judaism—History	BM437	296.0968	Judaism—South Africa
BM165-178	296.09014	Judaism—History—To 70 A.D.	BM443-445	296.099(3/4)	Judaism—[Australia/New Zealand]
BM175	296.8	Jewish sects	BM447-449	296.099(5-6)	Judaism—Oceania
BM175.E8	296.814	Essenes	BM495-532	296.1	Rabbinical literature
BM175.P4	296.812	Pharisees	BM500-509	296.12	Talmud
BM175.S2	296.813	Sadducees	BM511-518	296.14	Midrash
BM177	296.120092	Tannaim	BM516-.5	296.19	Aggada
BM180-185	296.0902	Judaism—History—Medieval and early modern period, 425-1789	BM523.5.S53	340.18	Shaving (Jewish law)
			BM525	296.16	Cabala
			BM600-603	296.3	Judaism—Doctrines
BM184	297.38	Judaism—Liturgy	BM610	296.311	God (Judaism)
BM185-.4	296.81	Karaites	BM612.5	296.31172	Covenants—Judaism

LC	Dewey	Subject Heading	LC	Dewey	Subject Heading
BM615	296.336	Messiah—Judaism	BP133.7.M67	297.122092	Moses (Biblical leader) in the Koran
BM615	296.336	Jewish messianic movements	BP134.E5	297.12209	Egypt in the Koran
BM630	296.32	Sin (Judaism)	BP134.F58	297.12286413	Food in the Koran
BM650-747	296.7	Judaism—Customs and practices	BP135	297.124	Hadith
BM652	296.092	Rabbis	BP137-.5	297.18	Legends, Islamic
BM652.5	296.61	Pastoral counseling (Judaism)	BP140-165	340.59	Islamic law
BM653-655	296.65	Synagogues	BP165.5-166.94	297.2	Islam—Doctrines
BM656-685	296.4	Worship (Judaism)	BP166.2	297.211	Word of God (Islam)
BM657.H3	296.435	Hanukkah lamp	BP166.2	297.211	God (Islam)
BM657.M35	296.435	Menorah	BP166.3	297.227	Predestination—Islam
BM657.T6	296.4615	Torah scrolls	BP166.3	297.227	Free will and determinism (Islam)
BM658.2	296.462	Cantors (Judaism)	BP166.4	297.246	Prophets, Pre-Islamic
BM659.S3	296.4615	Scribes, Jewish	BP166.6	297.2115	Revelation (Islam)
BM669	296.45	Prayer—Judaism	BP166.7	297.22	Man (Islam)
BM675.A8	296.432	Yom Kippur	BP166.73	297.225	Soul (Islam)
BM675.D3	296.45	Siddurim	BP166.75	297.22	Sin (Islam)
BM675.P3	296.437	Passover	BP166.78	297.22	Faith (Islam)
BM685	296.41	Sabbath	BP166.8	297.23	Eschatology, Islamic
BM690-720	296.43	Fasts and feasts—Judaism	BP166.83	297.23	Resurrection (Islam)
BM690	296.43	Religious calendars—Judaism	BP166.85	297.23	Judgment Day (Islam)
BM693.H5	296.431	High Holidays	BP166.87	297.23	Paradise (Islam)
BM693.P5	296.481	Pilgrim Festivals (Judaism)	BP166.89	297.216	Devil (Islam)
BM695.A8	296.432	Yom Kippur	BP166.89	297.216	Demonology, Islamic
BM695.H3	296.435	Hanukkah	BP166.89	297.215	Angels (Islam)
BM695.N5	296.4315	Rosh ha-Shanah	BP166.89	297.21	Spirits (Islam)
BM695.P3	296.437	Passover	BP166.89	297.21	Discernment of spirits (Islam)
BM695.P35	296.437	Seder	BP170.5	297.574	Muslim converts
BM707-.4	296.4424	Confirmation (Jewish rite)	BP170.5	297.574	Muslim converts from Christianity
BM710	296.73	Jews—Dietary laws	BP170.85	297.74	Dawah (Islam)
BM712	296.445	Mourning customs, Jewish	BP173.25-.45	297.27	Sociology, Islamic
BM713	296.444	Marriage customs and rites, Jewish	BP175.S8	297.81	Sunnites
BM720.S2	296.4391	Sabbatical year (Judaism)	BP176	297.31	Pillars of Islam
BM723	296.7	Jewish way of life	BP178	297.382	Prayer—Islam
BM729.C6	296.72	Consolation (Judaism)	BP179	297.53	Fasting (Islam)
BM729.F3	296.32	Faith (Judaism)	BP182	297.72	Jihad
BM729.S85	296.18	Summer (Jewish law)	BP183.6	297.37	Islamic sermons
BM730	296.47	Jewish preaching	BP183.6	297.362	Ramadan sermons
BM746	296.4731	High Holiday sermons	BP184	297.61	Pastoral theology (Islam)
BM747.P3	296.4737	Passover sermons	BP184.2	297.3	Worship (Islam)
BM945	296.3	Samaritan theology	BP184.25	297.37	Islamic preaching
BM970	296.43	Fasts and feasts—Samaritan religion	BP184.4	297.38	Purity, Ritual—Islam
BP1-223	297	Islam	BP184.9.F8	297.385	Funeral rites and ceremonies, Islamic
BP1-9	297.05	Islam—Periodicals	BP186	297.53	Fasts and feasts—Islam
BP10-15	297.65	Islam—Congresses	BP187	297.35	Muslim pilgrims and pilgrimages
BP40	297.03	Islam—Dictionaries	BP187.3	297.352	Muslim pilgrims and pilgrimages—Saudi Arabia—Mecca
BP42-48	297.77	Islamic religious education			
BP62.N4	297.87	Muslims, Black			
BP75-77.5	297.63	Muhammad, Prophet, d. 632	BP188	297.57	Religious life—Islam
BP75.8	297.63	Muhammad, Prophet, d. 632—Miracles	BP188.3.Y6	297.57	Youth, Muslim—Religious life
BP100-134	297.122	Koran	BP189	297.4	Mysticism—Islam
BP133.7.A3	297.122092	Adam (Biblical figure) in the Koran	BP189	297.4	Sufism
			BP189.33	297.4092	Muslim saints
BP133.7.D38	297.122092	David, King of Israel, in the Koran	BP189.62	297.4382	Sufi meditations
			BP190.5.A5	297.39	Amulets (Islam)
			BP190.5.A75	297.576	Asceticism—Islam

11

LC	Dewey	Subject Heading	LC	Dewey	Subject Heading
BP190.5.S4	297.577	Sex—Religious aspects—Islam	BQ4240	294.34	Causation (Buddhism)
BP193	297.82	Shiites	BQ4330	294.344	Bodhisattva stages (Mahayana Buddhism)
BP193.25-.28	297.124	Hadith (Shiites)	BQ4360	294.342	Compassion (Buddhism)
BP194.6	297.35	Shiite shrines	BQ4401-4430	294.35	Virtues (Buddhism)
BP195.A8	297.822	Assassins (Ismailites)	BQ4425-4430	294.35	Vice (Buddhism)
BP221-223	297.87	Black Muslims	BQ4475-4525	294.3423	Eschatology, Buddhist
BP300-395	297.93	Bahai faith	BQ4570.A4	294.3437	Amulets (Buddhism)
BP340	297.92	Babism	BQ4570.A4	294.3437	Charms (Buddhism)
BP380	297.93435	Bahai meditations	BQ4570.P76	294.3375	Buddhism—Psychology
BP500-585	299.934	Theosophy	BQ4570.W6	294.3378344	Woman (Buddhism)
BP573.R5	299.934	Reincarnation	BQ4600-4610	294.3372	Buddhism—Relations
BP595-597	299.935	Anthroposophy	BQ4670-4690	294.363	Buddhas
BP605.G68	299.93	Great White Brotherhood	BQ4690.M3	294.34211	Maitreya (Buddhist deity)
BP605.N48	299.93	New Age movement	BQ4750.D33	294.34211	Dakini (Buddhist deity)
BQ1-9999	294.3	Buddhism	BQ4750.Y35	294.34211	Yama (Buddhist deity)
BQ1-10	294.305	Buddhism—Periodicals	BQ4860.A4	294.34211	Acala (Buddhist deity)
BQ12-93	294.365	Buddhism—Societies, etc.	BQ4890.D33-.D334	294.34211	Dam-tshig-rdo-rje (Buddhist deity)
BQ141-209	294.375	Buddhist education	BQ4965-5030	294.344	Buddhism—Customs and practices
BQ171-199	294.375	Buddhist education of children	BQ4965-5030	294.3438	Buddhism—Rituals
BQ251-799	294.309	Buddhism—History	BQ5005	294.3438	Confirmation (Buddhist rite)
BQ287-296	294.30901	Buddhism—History—To ca. 100 A.D.	BQ5035-5065	294.3438	Chants (Buddhist)
BQ330-349	294.30954	Buddhism—India	BQ5070-5075	294.3437	Buddhism—Liturgical objects
BQ350-379	294.3095493	Buddhism—Sri Lanka			
BQ380-396	294.3095496	Buddhism—Nepal	BQ5070-5075	294.3437	Altars, Buddhist
BQ416-439	294.309591	Buddhism—Burma	BQ5130-5137	294.3435	Temples, Buddhist
BQ440-509	294.30959	Indochina—Religion	BQ5140-5355	294.361	Priests, Buddhist
BQ510-539	294.309598	Buddhism—Indonesia	BQ5360-5680	294.3444	Religious life—Buddhism
BQ540-549	294.309595	Buddhism—Malaysia	BQ5485-5525	294.342	Five Precepts (Buddhism)
BQ550-568	294.309593	Buddhism—Thailand	BQ5485-5530	294.342	Buddhist precepts
BQ570-609	294.30958	Buddhism—Asia, Central	BQ5485-5530	294.342	Buddhism—Doctrines, Central
BQ610-699	294.3095	Buddhism—East Asia	BQ5535-5594	294.34433	Buddhism—Prayer-books and devotions
BQ620-649	294.30951	Buddhism—China	BQ5595-5630	294.344	Devotion (Buddhism)
BQ650-669	294.309519	Buddhism—Korea	BQ5595-5630	294.3443	Prayer—Buddhism
BQ670-699	294.30952	Buddhism—Japan	BQ5700-5720	294.3438	Fasts and feasts—Buddhism
BQ700-709	294.3094	Buddhism—Europe			
BQ710-719	294.3096	Buddhism—Africa	BQ5741-5755	294.333	Mythology, Buddhist
BQ720-760	294.309(7-8)	Buddhism—America	BQ5851-5899	294.33783	Buddhism and social problems
BQ730-739	294.30973	Buddhism—United States	BQ5851-5899	294.3378	Buddhism—Charities
BQ740-749	294.30971	Buddhism—Canada	BQ5901-5975	294.372	Buddhism—Missions
BQ770-799	294.3099(3-6)	Buddhism—Oceania	BQ6001-6160	294.3657	Monasticism and religious orders, Buddhist
BQ840-845	294.3092	Buddhists—Biography	BQ6200-6240	294.34447	Asceticism—Buddhism
BQ922	294.363	Gautama Buddha—Footprints	BQ6300-6388	294.3435	Buddhist shrines
BQ935	294.363	Gautama Buddha—Enlightenment	BQ6400-6495	294.34351	Buddhist pilgrims and pilgrimages
BQ938	294.363	Gautama Buddha—Date of death	BQ6460	294.3435	Gautama Buddha—Shrines
BQ1100-3340	294.382	Tripitaka	BQ7100-7285	294.391	Theravada Buddhism
BQ1100-3340	294.382	Buddhism—Sacred books	BQ7300-7522	294.392	Mahayana Buddhism
BQ4050	294.342	Buddhism—Apologetic works	BQ7530-7950	294.39	Dge-lugs-pa (Sect)
			BQ7530-7950	294.3923	Lamaism
BQ4061-4570	294.342	Buddhism—Doctrines	BQ7669	294.39	Bka'-rgyud-pa (Sect)
BQ4080-4125	294.34209	Buddhism—Doctrines—History	BQ7699.G36	294.3438	Gcod (Buddhist rite)
BQ4170	294.32	Buddhism—Catechisms	BQ7930	294.361	Dalai lamas
BQ4170	294.32	Buddhism—Creeds	BQ7960-7989	294.39	Bonpo (Sect)
BQ4180	294.363	Buddha (The concept)	BQ7982.3	294.3438	Gcod (Bonpo rite)
BQ4195-4250	294.34	Dharma (Buddhism)	BQ7982.4	294.343	Bonpo incantations

LC	Dewey	Subject Heading	LC	Dewey	Subject Heading
BQ8000-9800	294.39	Buddhist sects	BR755-757	274.109031	England—Church history—16th century
BQ8000-8049	294.39	Abhayagiri (Sect)	BR756	274.109032	England—Church history—17th century
BQ8500-8769	294.3926	Pure Land Buddhism			
BQ9250-9519	294.3927	Zen Buddhism	BR758	274.109033	Evangelical Revival
BQ9288	294.3444	Spiritual life—Zen Buddhism	BR759	274.10904	England—Church history—20th century
BR	270	Church history			
BR1-129	230	Christianity	BR794	274.4	Celtic Church
BR1-9	270.05	Church history—Periodicals	BR840-849	274.4	France—Church history
BR21-29	270.06	Church history—Societies, etc.	BR850-856.35	274.3	Germany—Church history
			BR930-939	274.7	Russia—Church history
BR41-43	270.06	Church history—Congresses	BR970-1019	274.8	Scandinavia—Church history
BR60-67	270.1092	Apostolic Fathers	BR1020-1029	274.6	Spain—Church history
BR60-67	270.092	Fathers of the church	BR1060-1357	275	Asia—Church history
BR95	270.03	Church history—Dictionaries	BR1150-1156	275.4	India—Church history
BR97-99	262.009	Ecclesiastical geography	BR1178-1261	275.9	Asia, Southeastern—Church history
BR138	270.01	Church history—Philosophy			
BR110	248.2	Experience (Religion)	BR1280-1297	275.1	China—Church history
BR110	248.24	Conversion	BR1300-1317	275.2	Japan—Church history
BR112	248.2	Enthusiasm	BR1320-1337	275.19	Korea—Church history
BR114	248.2	Fanaticism	BR1359-1470	276	Africa—Church history
BR115.C5	230	Civilization, Christian	BR1369-1415	276.1	Africa, North—Church history
BR115.H5	230	History (Theology)	BR1430	276.7	Africa, Central—Church history
BR115.P85	261.513	Parapsychology—Religious aspects—Christianity	BR1440-1445	276.76	Africa, East—Church history
BR115.W2	241.3	Evil, Non-resistance to	BR1446-1458	276.8	Africa, Southern—Church history
BR127-128	261.2	Christianity and other religions	BR1460-1463	276.6	Africa, West—Church history
BR157	280	Christian sects	BR1480-1483	279.4	Australia—Church history
BR160-481	270.(1-8)	Church history—[By date]	BR1490-1495	279.9(5-6)	Oceania—Church history
BR160-270	270.3	Church history—Middle Ages, 600-1500	BR1600-1609	272	Persecution
BR160-240	270.(1-2)	Church history—Primitive and early church, ca. 30-600	BR1610	241.4	Religious tolerance
			BR1615-1617	230.046	Liberalism (Religion)
BR290-481	270.(5-8)	Church history—Modern period, 1500-	BR1644-.5	270.82	Pentecostalism
BR295	270.6	Reformation—Early movements	BR1650-1653	273.7	Pietism
			BR1690-1725	270.092	Church history—Biography
BR300-420	270.6	Reformation	BR1705	270.092	Fathers of the church
BR307	270.6	Reformation—Causes	BS	220	Bible
BR430	270.6	Counter-Reformation	BS1-3	220.51	Bible. Polyglot
BR500-1500	274-279	[Region or country]—Church history	BS135-198	220.52	Bible. English
			BS405-408	220.5	Bible—Abridgments
BR513-569	277.3	United States—Religion	BS420-429	220.(4-5)	Bible—Concordances
BR520	277.3081	Great Awakening	BS445-460	220.09	Bible—History
BR610-615	277.2	Mexico—Church history	BS450-460	220.(4/5)	Bible—Versions
BR620-625	277.28	Central America—Church history	BS477	220.64	Symbolism in the Bible
			BS478	220.64	Typology (Theology)
BR655	277.29	Caribbean Area—Church history	BS480	220.13	Bible—Inspiration
			BS480	220.1	Bible—Evidences, authority, etc.
BR660-730	278	South America—Church history	BS482-498	220.7	Bible—Commentaries
			BS500-534.8	220.6	Bible—Criticism, interpretation, etc.
BR740-799	274.1	Great Britain—Church history	BS520.5	220.68	Myth in the Bible
BR745-754	274.10902	England—Church history—1066-1485	BS535-537	809.93522	Bible as literature
			BS537	220.(4-5)	Bible—Language, style
BR748	274.4	Celtic Church	BS543	230.041	Bible—Theology
BR749	274.109021	England—Church history—449-1066	BS546-559	220.9505	Bible stories
			BS560	220.49	Hieroglyphic Bibles
BR750	274.10903	England—Church history—1485-	BS569	220.9	Genealogy in the Bible
			BS570-580	220.092	Bible—Biography
			BS573	222.110922	Patriarchs (Bible)

LC	Dewey	Subject Heading
BS580	221.092	Bible. O.T.—Biography
BS580.A3	225.92	Abraham (Biblical patriarch) in the New Testament
BS585-613	220.071	Bible—Study and teaching
BS612	220.076	Bible—Examinatons, questions, etc.
BS617.8	242	Bible—Devotional use
BS635-636	220.9	Bible—History of Biblical events
BS637	220.9	Bible—Chronology
BS646	220.046	Apocalyptic literature
BS646	228	Revelation
BS647-649	220.15	Bible—Prophecies
BS649.J5	909.04924	Jews—Restoration
BS651-652	231.7652	Creationism
BS651-652	231.765	Creation
BS651-652	231.765	Biblical cosmology
BS655	220.852	Astronomy in the Bible
BS658	222.1109505	Noah's ark
BS658	222.11	Deluge
BS660-667	220.85	Nature in the Bible
BS661	220.83058	Ethnology in the Bible
BS661	233	Man (Theology)
BS670	220.8301	Sociology, Biblical
BS670	220.8330	Economics in the Bible
BS680.A34	220.0846	Aged in the Bible
BS680.E3	220.837	Education in the Bible
BS680.E84	220.817	Ethics in the Bible
BS680.F3	220.830685	Family—Biblical teaching
BS680.F32	220.83638	Famines in the Bible
BS680.P3	226.8	Bible—Parables
BS680.P64	242.5	Bible—Prayers
BS680.S5	220.83067	Sex in the Bible
BS701-1013	221.(4-5)	Bible. O.T.—Versions
BS737-765	221.48	Bible. O.T. Greek
BS767-815	221.47	Bible. O.T. Latin
BS1104	221.65	Bible. O.T.—Harmonies
BS1121-1128	221.(4-5)	Bible. O.T.—Concordances
BS1130-1134	221.09	Bible. O.T.—History
BS1143-1158	221.7	Bible. O.T.—Commentaries
BS1160-1191.5	221.6	Bible. O.T.—Criticism, interpetation, etc.
BS1181.17	220.6	D document (Biblical criticism)
BS1181.2	220.6	E document (Biblical criticism)
BS1183	221.68	Myth in the Old Testament
BS1192.5	230.0411	Bible. O.T.—Theology
BS1193-1195	221.071	Bible. O.T.—Study and teaching
BS1199.E38	221.837	Education in the Bible
BS1199.M5	231.73	Miracles
BS1199.P7	221.92	Priests, Jewish
BS1221-1285.5	222.1	Bible. O.T. Pentateuch
BS1225	222.106	Documentary hypothesis (Pentateuchal criticism)
BS1237	222.11	Eden
BS1237	222.11	Forbidden fruit
BS1245	222.12	Manna
BS1281-1285.5	222.16	Ten commandments
BS1401-1405.5	223	Hebrew poetry, Biblical
BS1419-1450	223.2	Bible. O.T. Psalms
BS1445.M4	223.2	Royal Psalms
BS1481-1490	223.9	Bible. O.T. Song of Solomon
BS1501-1675.5	224	Prophets
BS1691-1830	229	Bible. O.T. Apocrypha
BS1901-2970	225-228	Bible. N.T.
BS1901	225.(4-5)	Bible. N.T.—Versions
BS2301-2308	225.(4-5)	Bible. N.T.—Concordances
BS2315-2318	225.09	Bible. N.T.—History
BS2333-2348	225.7	Bible. N.T.—Commentaries
BS2350-2393	225.6	Bible. N.T.—Criticism, interpretation, etc.
BS2378	225.68	Demythologizcation
BS2397	230	Bible. N.T.—Theology
BS2410	270.(1-2)	Christianity—Early church, ca. 30-600
BS2415-2417	232.954	Jesus Christ—Teachings
BS2440	225.92	Apostles
BS2525-2544	225.071	Bible. N.T.—Study and teaching
BS2545.M5	231.73	Miracles
BS2549	226	Bible. N.T. Gospels
BS2620-2628	226.6	Bible. N.T. Acts
BS2630-2815.5	227	Bible. N.T. Epistles
BS2640-2815.5	227	Bible. N.T. Pauline Epistles
BS2820-2827	228	Four Horsemen of the Apocalypse
BS2831-2970	229	Apocryphal books (New Testament)
BT	230	Christian doctrinal theology
BT19-33	230	Dogma
BT20-30	230.09	Theology, Doctrinal—History
BT20-30	262.8	Heresies, Christian
BT40-55	230.01	Philosophical theology
BT65-84	231-239	Theology, Doctrinal
BT82	273.9	Modernism
BT82.2	270.82	Fundamentalism
BT82.25	230.046	Dominion theology
BT82.7	230.08996	Black theology
BT83.55	230.082	Feminist theology
BT83.57	230.0464	Liberation theology
BT88-92	262.8	Authority—Religious aspects
BT91	262.8	Church—Authority
BT94	231.72	Kingdom of God
BT95-97	241.2	Law (Theology)
BT95-96.2	231.5	Providence and government of God
BT97-.2	231.73	Miracles
BT98-180	231	God
BT98-102	231.765	God—Proof, Cosmological
BT98-101	231.042	God—Proof, Ontological
BT98	231.09	God—History of doctrines
BT99	231	God—Biblical teaching
BT109-115	231.044	Trinity
BT117-123	231.3	Holy Spirit
BT122.5	263.94	Pentecost
BT123	234.13	Baptism in the Holy Spirit
BT124	231	Immanence of God
BT126-127.5	231.74	Revelation
BT130-157	231.4	God—Attributes

LC	Dewey	Subject Heading	LC	Dewey	Subject Heading
BT131	231.4	God—Omniscience	BT720	233.14	Sin, Original
BT133	231.4	God—Omnipotence	BT721	241.3	Sin, Unpardonable
BT135	231.5	Providence and government of God	BT725	241.3	Temptation
			BT732.5-.56	234.131	Spiritual healing
BT137	231.8	God—Goodness	BT734-.3	261.8348	Race—Religious aspects—Christianity
BT153.S8	231	Suffering of God			
BT155	231.76	Covenant theology	BT734-.3	261.8348	Race
BT160-162	231.8	Theodicy	BT738-.5	261.5	Sociology, Christian
BT180.G6	231	Glory of God	BT740-743	233.5	Soul
BT198-590	232	Jesus Christ	BT750-810.2	234	Salvation
BT210	232.2	Logos	BT755	234	Salvation outside the Catholic Church
BT220	232.1	Incarnation			
BT225	232.1	Typology (Theology)	BT759	234	Salvation outside the church
BT230-245	232.1	Jesus Christ—Messiahship			
BT232	232.9	Son of Man	BT760-769	234	Grace (Theology)
BT198-590	232.8	Jesus Christ—Person and offices	BT763-764.2	234.7	Justification
			BT767	234.8	Holiness
BT263-268	234.5	Atonement	BT767.3	234.13	Gifts, Spiritual
BT300-302	232.901	Jesus Christ—Biography	BT770-772	234.23	Faith
BT303	242.74	Mysteries of the Rosary	BT773	234	Merit (Christianity)
BT304-.97	232.903	Jesus Christ—Character	BT775	234.3	Redemption
BT306	232	Jesus Christ—Words	BT780	248.24	Conversion
BT315	232.923	Magi	BT790	234.4	Regeneration (Theology)
BT317	232.921	Virgin birth	BT795	234.5	Forgiveness of sin
BT340-500	232.95	Jesus Christ—Biography—Public life	BT800	234.5	Repentance
			BT809-810.2	234.9	Predestination
BT363-367	232.955	Jesus Christ—Miracles	BT809-810.2	234	Election (Theology)
BT373-378	226.8	Jesus Christ—Parables	BT819-891	236	Eschatology
BT378.D5	226.8	Rich man and Lazarus (Parable)	BT830	236.4	Intermediate state
			BT834-838	236.25	Hell
BT378.G6	226.8	Good Samaritan (Parable)	BT840-842	236.5	Purgatory
BT378.G7	226.8	Great supper (Parable)	BT844-849	236.24	Heaven
BT378.M8	226.8	Mustard seed (Parable)	BT844-849	236.24	Paradise
BT378.P	226.8	Pearl of great price (Parable)	BT850-860	235.4	Limbo
BT380-.2	226.9	Sermon on the mount	BT870-872	236.8	Resurrection
BT382	226.93	Beatitudes	BT875-891	236.9	End of the world
BT410	232.956	Jesus Christ—Transfiguration	BT880-882	236.9	Judgment Day
			BT885-886	236.9	Second Advent
BT414	263.925/ 232.96	Holy Week	BT890-891	236.9	Millennium
			BT899-940	236.2	Future life
BT420	232.957	Last Supper	BT910-912	236.21	Eternity
BT430-470	232.96	Jesus Christ—Passion	BT919-925	236.22	Immortality
BT465	232.963	Holy Cross	BT919-925	236.23	Conditional immortality
BT587	232.966	Jesus Christ—Relics	BT930	236.23	Annihilationism
BT587.S4	232.966	Holy Shroud	BT960-968	235.3	Angels
BT595-680	232.91	Mary, Blessed Virgin, Saint	BT960-962	235	Spirits
BT610-660	232.91	Mary, Blessed Virgin, Saint—Theology	BT968.M5	235.3	Michael (Archangel)
			BT972	262.73	Communion of saints
BT620	232.911	Immaculate Conception	BT980-981	235.4	Devil
BT650-660	232.917	Visions	BT985	236	Antichrist
BT650-654	232.917	Mary, Blessed Virgin, Saint—Apparitions and miracles	BT990-1010	238	Creeds
			BT990	238	Creeds, Ecumenical
			BT1010	262	Covenants (Church polity)
BT683-694	235.2	Saints	BT1029-1040	238	Catechisms
BT700-745	233	Man (Christian theology)	BT1095-1255	239	Apologetics
BT700-745	233	Man (Theology)	BT1109-1115	239.09	Apologetics—History
BT704	233	Woman (Christian theology)	BT1115	230.1	Apologetics—Early church, ca. 30-600
BT708	233.5	Sex—Religious aspects—Christianity			
			BT1209-1211	239.7	Rationalism
BT710	233.14	Fall of man	BT1313-1480	270	Theology—History
BT715-722	233.14	Sin	BT1350	273.4	Arianism

15

LC	Dewey	Subject Heading	LC	Dewey	Subject Heading
BT1370	273.4	Donatists	BV283.B7	242.82	Boys—Prayer-books and devotions
BT1390	273.1	Gnosticism			
BT1440	281.8	Nestorians	BV283.G7	242.2	Grace at meals
BV1-4	240-248	Theology, Practical	BV283.S3	242.2	Schools—Prayers
BV5-530	248.3	Worship	BV287	242.2	Prayer groups
BV5-25	264	Public worship	BV301-530	246.75	Hymns
BV5-8	248.309	Worship—History	BV520	246.75	Sunday schools—Hymns
BV6	248.30901	Worship—History—Early church, ca. 30-600	BV590-640	262	Church
			BV600	262.0017	Church renewal
BV30-135	263.9	Fasts and feasts	BV601.3	261	Church—Catholicity
BV30-135	263.9	Church year	BV601.8	261	Mission of the church
BV40	252.61	Advent sermons	BV625	280.042	Interdenominational cooperation
BV50.A4	263.9	All Souls' Day			
BV50.A7	263.97	Feast of the Assumption of the Blessed Virgin	BV626	262.5	Local church councils
			BV629-631	261.7	Church and state
BV50.E7	263.915	Epiphany	BV636	254.7	Church buildings—Interdenominational use
BV50.H6	263.97	Feast of the Holy Innocents			
BV50.I6	263.97	Feast of the Immaculate Conception	BV637	250.91732	City churches
			BV637.5	262.14091732	City clergy
BV53	263.92	Palm Sunday	BV637.7	250.91733	Suburban churches
BV55	263.93	Paschal mystery	BV637.8	250	Small churches
BV55	263.93	Easter	BV638-.8	250.91734	Rural churches
BV57	263.93	Ascension Day	BV652-.9	254	Church management
BV60	263.94	Pentecost Festival	BV652.1	262.1	Christian leadership
BV61-63	263.94	Pentecost season	BV652.25	254.5	Church growth
BV64.J4	263.97	Feast of Jesus Christ the King	BV652.9	250	Church controversies
			BV652.95-657	254.4	Church publicity
BV64.S3	263.97	Feast of the Sacred Heart	BV653	254.4	Advertising—Churches
BV67	263.98	All Saints' Day	BV659-683	262.14	Priests
BV75	263.97	Thanksgiving Day	BV659-683	262.14	Clergy
BV85-95	263.92	Lent	BV669-670.2	262.12	Episcopacy
BV90-95	263.925	Holy Week	BV675	262.14	Group ministry
BV95	263.925	Good Friday	BV675.7	262.14	Clergy couples
BV107-133	263.3	Sunday	BV676	262.14	Women clergy
BV150-168	246.55	Symbolism	BV676	262.14	Ordination of women
BV150-168	246.55	Signs and symbols	BV677	262.15	Lay readers
BV150-168	704.9482	Christian art and symbolism	BV680	262.14	Deacons
BV160	246.558	Crosses	BV685	262.14	Ordination
BV165	246.6	Colors, Liturgical	BV687	262.15	Laity
BV167	391.04204	Church vestments	BV705	262.1	Church officers
BV168.S7	254	Staff, Pastoral	BV710	262.(4-5)	Councils and synods
BV169-199	264	Liturgics	BV741	323.442	Freedom of religion
BV169-199	264	Rites and ceremonies	BV741	323.442	Liberty of conscience
BV180-181	264	Ritualism	BV759-763	262.9	Ecclesiastical law
BV185	264.01	Liturgies, Early Christian	BV761	262.90901	Canon law—Early church, ca. 30-600
BV186.7	264	Ecumenical liturgies			
BV194.D	242.72	Doxology	BV761.A1-.A5	255.00901	Church orders, Ancient
BV195-196	247.1	Altars	BV770-777	254.8	Church finance
BV196.C	264	Censers	BV771	254.8	Tithes
BV197.B5	264.13	Benediction	BV772	254.8	Christian giving
BV197.S5	264.9	Cross, Sign of the	BV772	248.6	Stewardship, Christian
BV198-199	264	Liturgies	BV772.5	254.8	Church fund raising
BV199	265.9	Occasional services	BV800-873	265	Sacraments
BV199.D4	265.92	Dedication services	BV803-814	265.1	Baptism
BV199.F8	265.85	Funeral service	BV813-.2	265.12	Infant baptism
BV199.R5	265	Responsive worship	BV814	265.1	Baptism for the dead
BV200	249	Family—Religious life	BV815	265.2	Confirmation
BV205-287	264.13	Prayer—Christianity	BV820	264.36	Close and open communion
BV228-284	264.13	Prayers	BV820	254.5	Church membership
BV245-283	242.8	Prayer-books	BV823-828	264.36	Lord's Supper
BV250-254	264.13	Pastoral prayers	BV830	262.14	Ordination

LC	Dewey	Subject Heading	LC	Dewey	Subject Heading
BV835-838	265.5	Marriage	BV3780-3785	269.2092	Evangelists
BV840-850	265.6	Penance	BV3793	269.2	Evangelistic invitations
BV845-847	265.62	Confessors	BV3797	252.3	Evangelistic sermons
BV845-847	265.62	Confession	BV3798-3799	269.24	Camp-meetings
BV863.P4	247.1	Pews and pew rights	BV4000-4470	253	Pastoral theology
BV873.E8	265.94	Exorcism	BV4012-.3	253.52	Pastoral psychology
BV873.F7	265.9	Foot washing (Rite)	BV4012.2	253.5	Pastoral counseling
BV873.L3	265.9	Imposition of hands	BV4012.25	253.5	Pastoral counseling centers
BV875-885	264.9	Sacramentals	BV4019-4180	230.071	Theology—Study and teaching
BV890	235.2	Relics			
BV900-1450	267	Church societies	BV4019-4160	230.0711	Theological seminaries
BV950-1220	267	Brotherhoods	BV4163	230.071	Pretheological education
BV1000-1220	267.3	Young Men's Christian associations	BV4164	230.0711	Seminary extension
			BV4200-4317	251	Preaching
BV1300-1393	267.5	Young Women's Christian associations	BV4207-4208	251.009	Preaching—History
			BV4235.B56	251	Biographical preaching
BV1474-1475.2	268.432	Christian education of children	BV4235.E8	251	Extemporaneous preaching
			BV4235.L3	251	Lay preaching
BV1500-1578	268	Sunday schools	BV4235.L43	251	Lectionary preaching
BV1518-1533	241.4	Virtues	BV4235.T65	251	Topical preaching
BV1531	268.3	Directors of religious education	BV4239-4316	252	Sermons
			BV4254.2	252	Occasional sermons
BV1534-1536	268.6	Religious education—Teaching methods	BV4254.3	252.6	Festival-day sermons
			BV4255	252.68	Baccalaureate addresses
BV1534.4	268.67	Drama in Christian education	BV4257	252.615	Christmas sermons
BV1535	268.635	Religious education—Audio-visual aids	BV4257.5	252	Communion sermons
			BV4259	252.63	Easter—Sermons
BV1580-1583	371.071	Week-day church schools	BV4260-4261	252.68	Election sermons
BV1585	268	Vacation schools, Religious	BV4262	252.68	Execution sermons
BV1590	249	Religious education—Home training	BV4270	252.6	Fast-day sermons
			BV4275	252.1	Funeral sermons
BV1650	796.5422	Church camps	BV4282	252.68	New Year sermons
BV2000-3705	266	Missions	BV4290	252.7	Installation (Clergy)
BV2082.A9	266	Aeronautics in missionary work	BV4307.D5	252	Dialogue sermons
			BV4310	252.55	Youth sermons
BV2082.I6	266	Missions—Interdenominational cooperation	BV4315	252.53	Children's sermons
			BV4327	253.2	Clergy—Political activity
BV2130-2300	266.2	Catholic Church—Missions	BV4335	253	Pastoral medicine
BV2350-2595	266	Protestant churches—Missions	BV4382	331.252912532	Clergy—Pensions
			BV4390	253.25	Celibacy
BV2400-2595	266.009	Protestant churches—Missions—History	BV4396	253.22	Clergy—Family relationships
			BV4395.5	253.2	Clergy—Divorce
BV2617	266.0083	Youth in missionary work	BV4405-4408	255.8	Monasticism and religious orders, Protestant
BV2619-2623	266	Missions to Jews			
BV2625-2626.4	266	Missions to Muslims	BV4405-4406	262.26	Christian communities
BV2637	266	Missions to lepers	BV4423-4425	262.14	Deaconesses
BV2650	266.022	Home missions	BV4427-4430	258.0835	Youth in church work
BV2810-2820	266.00971	Missions—Canada	BV4445.5	259.082	Abused women—Pastoral counseling of
BV2855-3145	266.0094	Missions—European			
BV2860-2895	266.00941	Missions—Great Britain	BV4487.E9	269.2	Evangelical academies
BV2940-2945	266.00944	Missions—France	BV4500-4595	248.4	Christian life
BV2950-2957	266.00943	Missions—Germany	BV4501	265.92	Consecration
BV3120-3127	266.00946	Missions—Spain	BV4520	248.5	Witness bearing (Christianity)
BV3149-3487	266.0095	Missions—Asia	BV4523	254.5	Church attendance
BV3440-3457	266.00952	Missions—Japan	BV4530-4579	248.83	Youth—Religious life
BV3500-3630	266.0096	Missions—Africa	BV4560-4579	268.6	Sunday school literature
BV3640-3680	266.0099(3-6)	Missions—Oceania	BV4580	248.85	Aged—Religious life
BV3650-3660	266.00994	Missions—Australia	BV4593	248.88	Working class—Religious life
BV3700-3705	266.0092	Missionaries			
BV3750-3799	269.24	Revivals	BV4615	241.1	Conscience
BV3750-3799	269.2	Evangelistic work	BV4618	241	Human acts

17

LC	Dewey	Subject Heading	LC	Dewey	Subject Heading
BV4625-4780	241	Christian ethics	BV5099	248.47	Quietism
BV4625-4627	241.3	Sins	BX1-9.5	280.042	Christian union
BV4625-4627	241.4	Virtues	BX6.7-.8	262.0011092	Ecumenists
BV4625-4627	241.3	Vices	BX9.5.A37	280.042	Ecumenical movement—
BV4625	241.3	Sin			African influences
BV4625.6-.7	241.31	Sin, Venial	BX9.5.E94	280.042	Evangelicalism and Christian
BV4626	241.3	Deadly sins			union
BV4627.H8	241.3	Hypocrisy	BX9.5.L55	280.042	Liturgics and Christian union
BV4627.Q	241.3	Quarreling	BX9.5.P29	280.042	Papacy and Christian union
BV4627.R4	241.3	Revenge	BX9.5.V45	280.042	Veneration of saints and
BV4627.S6	241.3	Slander			Christian union
BV4627.S9	241.3	Swearing	BX9.5.Y68	280.0420835	Youth in the ecumenical
BV4630-4647	241.3	Vice			movement
BV4630-4647	241.4	Virtue	BX100-189	281.5	Eastern churches
BV4635-4639	241.4	Theological virtues	BX120-129	281.62	Armenian Church
BV4637	241.4	Faith	BX150-159	281.8	Nestorian Church
BV4639	241.4	Charity	BX200-754	281.9	Orthodox Eastern Church
BV4645	241.4	Cardinal virtues	BX303	270.38	Schism—Eastern and
BV4647.C5	241.66	Virginity			Western Church
BV4647.C5	241.66	Chastity	BX350-376	264.019	Orthodox Eastern Church—
BV4647.D6	241.4	Discretion			Liturgy
BV4647.J	241.62	Justice (Virtue)	BX377-378	264.019	Sacraments—Orthodox
BV4647.M2	241.4	Magnanimity			Eastern Church
BV4647.M3	241.4	Meekness	BX380	235.2	Christian saints
BV4647.M4	241.4	Corporal works of mercy	BX382.5	253.53	Spiritual direction
BV4647.M4	241.4	Spiritual works of mercy	BX385-900	255.019	Monasticism and religious
BV4647.M4	241.4	Mercy			orders, Orthodox Eastern
BV4647.P5	241.4	Piety	BX385	255.819	Monasticism and religious
BV4647.S4	241.4	Self-denial			orders
BV4647.T4	241.4	Temperance (Virtue)	BX400-440	262.13	Patriarchs and patriarchate
BV4655-4710	241.52	Ten commandments	BX460-605	281.947	Orthodox Eastern Church
BV4715	241.54	Golden rule	BX485-492	281.94709	Orthodox Eastern Church—
BV4720-4730	241.5	Commandments of the			History
		church	BX520-558	262.01947	Orthodox Eastern Church—
BV4726.S2	241.3	Sacrilege			Government
BV4800-4897	248	Devotional exercises	BX560-563	264.01947	Orthodox Eastern Church—
BV4800-4895	242	Devotional literature			Russia
BV4800-4870	248.34	Meditations	BX575-577.5	235.2	Christian saints
BV4810-4812	242.3	Devotional calendars	BX576	235.24	Canonization
BV4815	242	Devotion	BX577	235.2	Relics
BV4900-4911	242.4	Consolation	BX580-583	255.819	Monasticism and religious
BV4912-4950	248.24	Conversion			orders
BV4912-4915	248.2	Experience (Religion)	BX610-619	281.9495	Orthodox Eastern Church—
BV4930-4935	248.24	Converts			Greece
BV5015-5068	248.47	Asceticism	BX630-639	281.943(6/9)	Orthodox Eastern Church—
BV5023	248.470901	Asceticism—History—			[Austria/Hungary]
		Early church, ca. 30-600	BX800-4795	282	Catholic Church
BV5025	248.470902	Asceticism—History—	BX800-806	282.05	Catholic Church—Periodicals
		Middle Ages, 600-1500	BX808-816	282.06	Catholic Church—Societies,
BV5053	253.53	Spiritual direction			etc.
BV5055	248.47	Fasting	BX820-838	262.52	Councils and synods,
BV5068.R4	269.6	Retreats			Episcopal (Catholic)
BV5070-5095	248.22	Mysticism	BX837.5	262.3	Episcopal conferences
BV5083	248.29	Discernment of spirits			(Catholic)
BV5090-5091	248.29	Trance	BX838	262.3	Diocesan pastoral councils
BV5091.C7	248.34	Contemplation	BX841	282.03	Catholic Church—
BV5091.E3	248.29	Ecstasy			Dictionaries
BV5091.R4	248.29	Private revelations	BX860	262.91	Encyclicals, Papal
BV5091.R4	248.29	Revelation	BX863	262.91	Letters, Papal
BV5091.V6	248.29	Visions	BX895-939	268.82	Catholic Church—Education
BV5095	248.22	Mystics	BX940-1745	282.09/270	Catholic Church—History

LC	Dewey	Subject Heading	LC	Dewey	Subject Heading
BX950-961	262.13	Papacy	BX1939.C665	262.932	Clergy (Canon law)
BX958.A23	262.13	Popes—Abdication	BX1939.C72	262.933	Confirmation (Canon law)
BX958.V7	262.13	Papal visits	BX1939.P47	262.932	Persons (Canon law)
BX965-1263	262.13090(1-23)	Papacy—History—To 1309	BX1939.T65	262.934	Trial practice (Canon law)
BX1001-1378	262.13	Popes	BX1950	254.8	Catholic Church—Finance
BX1301	284.8	Schism, The Great Western, 1378-1417	BX1958-1968	238.2	Catholic Church—Catechisms
BX1407.A5	282.73	Americanism (Catholic controversy)	BX1968	268.82	Catechetics
BX1407.N4	282.08996073	Afro-American Catholics	BX1970	264.02	Liturgical language
BX1404-1418	282.73	Catholic Church—United States	BX1970.A7-.Z	264.02	Catholic Church—Liturgy
BX1419-1424	282.71	Catholic Church—Canada	BX1999.8-2047	264.02 (1-9)	Catholic Church—Liturgy—Texts
BX1427-1431	282.72	Catholic Church—Mexico	BX2000-.68	264.024	Breviaries
BX1432-1447	282.728	Catholic Church—Central America	BX2015-2016	264.023	Missals
BX1448-1459	282.729	Catholic Church—West Indies	BX2015.5.H	264.02	Dog Mass
BX1460-1489	282.8	Catholic Church—South America	BX2037	264.023	Sacramentaries
BX1490-1612	282.4	Catholic Church—Europe	BX2040	264.0274	Stations of the Cross
BX1491-1514	282.41	Catholic Church—Great Britain	BX2045.E96	264.02	Exultets (Liturgy)
BX1528-1533	282.44	Catholic Church—France	BX2045.W34	264.02085	Wake services
BX1534-1539	282.43	Catholic Church—Germany	BX2048.B5	264.13	Benediction
BX1543-1548	282.45	Catholic Church—Italy	BX2050-2155	242.802	Catholic Church—Prayer-books and devotions
BX1558-1560	282.47	Catholic Church—Russia	BX2080	242.802	Books of hours
BX1583-1588	282.46	Catholic Church—Spain	BX2177-2198	242	Devotional literature
BX1615-1673	282.5	Catholic Church—Asia	BX2177-2198	248.34	Meditations
BX1617-1636	282.56	Catholic Church—Middle East	BX2200-2292	264.0208	Sacraments (Liturgy)
BX1662-1670.7	282.5	Catholic Church—East Asia	BX2215-2239	264.02036	Lord's Supper
BX1675-1682	282.6	Catholic Church—Africa	BX2215.A1	264.02036	Eucharistic congresses
BX1685-1692	282.9(3/4)	Catholic Church—[New Zealand/Australia]	BX2220	264.02036	Transubstantiation
BX1700-1745	272.2	Inquisition	BX2230-2234	264.02	Mass
BX1746-1755	230.2	Catholic Church—Doctrines	BX2231.7	264.02036	Private masses
BX1752	230.2	Catholic Church—Apologetic works	BX2237	264.02036	First communion
			BX2240	264.02084	Ordination—Catholic Church
BX1756	252.02	Catholic Church—Sermons	BX2250-2254	264.02085	Marriage service
BX1790-1795	261.7	Church and state—Catholic Church	BX2260-2283	264.02086	Penance
BX1800-1920	262.02	Catholic Church—Government	BX2262-2267	264.020862	Confessors
			BX2262-2267	264.020862	Confession
BX1805-1810	262.13	Popes	BX2279-2283	264.020866	Indulgences
BX1806	262.131	Popes—Infallibility	BX2290	264.0207	Extreme unction
BX1905	262.122	Catholic Church—Bishops	BX2295-2310	264.0209	Sacramentals
BX1910	262.142	Vicars apostolic	BX2305	264.02092	Consecration of virgins
BX1910	262.142	Vicars-general	BX2307.3	264.02036	Baptismal water
BX1911	262.02	Archdeacons	BX2310.A	264.0209	Agnus Dei (Sacramental)
BX1912-1914.5	262.142	Priests	BX2310.R7	242.74	Rosary
BX1912-1914.5	262.142	Catholic Church—Clergy	BX2315	235.2	Relics
BX1912	262.02	Deacons	BX2320-2321	263.042	Christian shrines
BX1912.9	253.252	Catholic Church—Clergy—Sexual behavior	BX2323	263.04	Christian pilgrims and pilgrimages
BX1920	262.152	Laity—Catholic Church	BX2325-2333	270.092	Christian saints
BX1925	390.008822	Church vestments	BX2330	235.24	Canonization
BX1939.A	262.933	Absolution (Canon law)	BX2340	264.02094	Exorcism
BX1939.A	262.932	Abbots (Canon law)	BX2347-2348	264.02	Catholic Church—Liturgy—Theology
BX1939.A3	262.02	Administrators apostolic	BX2350.7	253.53	Spiritual direction
BX1939.B3	262.933	Baptism (Canon law)	BX2375-2376	269.6	Retreats—Catholic Church
BX1939.C3	262.933	Catechetics (Canon law)	BX2375	269.6	Parish missions
			BX2377	241.1	Conscience, Examination of
			BX2400-4560	255.(1-7)	Monasticism and religious orders
			BX2435	255.(1-7)	Monastic and religious life

19

LC	Dewey	Subject Heading	LC	Dewey	Subject Heading
BX2436-2437	255.(1-7)06	Monasticism and religious orders—Rules	BX4843	280.40944	Protestant churches—France
BX2460-2749	255.(1-7)009	Monastic and religious life—History	BX4844-.5	280.40943	Protestant churches—Germany
BX2460-2749	255.(1-7)	Monasteries	BX4847	280.40945	Protestant churches—Italy
BX2505-2525	255.(1-7)00973	Monasticism and religious orders—United States	BX4851	280.40946	Protestant churches—Spain
			BX4857	280.4095	Protestant churches—Asia
BX2527-2529	255.(1-7)00971	Monasticism and religious orders—Canada	BX4872-4883	284.4	Waldenses
			BX4900-4906	284.3	Lollards
BX2530-2532	255.(1-7)00972	Monasticism and religious orders—Mexico	BX4913-4918	284.3	Hussites
			BX4929-4946	284.3	Anabaptists
BX2533-2547	255.(1-7)009728	Monasticism and religious orders—Central America	BX4950-4951	289.(6-7)	Plain People
			BX5001-5009	283	Anglican Communion
BX2561-2589	255.(1-7)0098	Monasticism and religious orders—South America	BX5005	283.09	Anglican Communion—History
BX2631-2676	255.(1-7)0094	Monasticism and religious orders—Europe	BX5008	252.03	Anglican Communion—Sermons
BX2677-2731	255.(1-7)0095	Monasticism and religious orders—Asia	BX5011-5740	283.42	Church of England
BX2732-2740	255.(1-7)0096	Monasticism and religious orders—Africa	BX5011	283.4205	Church of England—Periodicals
BX2743-2745	255.(1-7)0099 (3/4)	Monasticism and religious orders—[New Zealand/ Australia]	BX5031	283.42025	Church of England—Directories
			BX5051-5101	283.4209	Church of England—History
BX2790	390.008822	Church vestments	BX5115-5126	283.42	Church of England—Parties and movements
BX2820	255.(2-3)	Friars	BX5123	264.03	Ritualism
BX2901-2956	255.4	Augustinians	BX5127-5129.8	283.42	Church of England—Relations
BX3501-3556	255.2	Dominicans			
BX3601-3656	255.3	Franciscans	BX5137-5140	230.342	Church of England—Doctrines
BX3651-3653	255.3	Secular Franciscans	BX5140.5-5147	264.0342	Church of England—Liturgy
BX4200-4556	255.9(1-7)	Sisterhoods	BX5145	264.03	Church of England—Prayer-Books and devotions
BX4200-4563	255.9(1-7)	Monasticism and religious orders for women	BX5148-5149	264.035	Sacraments—Church of England
BX4337-.5	255.972	Dominican sisters	BX5149.C5	264.03	Lord's Supper
BX4361-4364	255.973	Franciscans	BX5149.C6	264.03562	Confession
BX4600-4644	282.73	Catholic Church—[By region or country]	BX5150-5182.5	262.0342	Church of England—Government
BX4650-4705	282.092	Catholic Church—Biography	BX5165	248.6	Tithes
BX4654-4662	282.0922	Martyrs—Legends	BX5175-5182.5	262.03	Priests
BX4668.2-.3	255.(1-7)	Ex-monks	BX5175-5182.5	262.03	Church of England—Clergy
BX4718.5-4735	284.84	Jansenists	BX5176-5178	262.12	Episcopacy
BX4800-9999	280.4	Protestant churches	BX5178	255.83	Anglican orders
BX4800-9890	280.4092	Protestants	BX5179	262.(12/03)	Archdeacons
BX4800-4946	280.4	Protestantism	BX5180	390.008823	Church vestments
BX4800	280.405	Protestantism—Periodicals	BX5185	255.983	Sisterhoods
BX4804-4807	280.409	Protestantism—History	BX5197-5199	283.42092	Church of England—Biography
BX4818-.3	280.4	Protestant churches—Relations	BX5200-5207	280.40941	Dissenters, Religious—England
BX4833	280.40972	Protestant churches—Mexico	BX5410-5595	283.415	Church of Ireland
BX4833.5-4834	280.409728	Protestant churches—Central America	BX5500-5510	283.41509	Church of Ireland—History
			BX5590-5595	283.415092	Church of Ireland—Biography
BX4835	280.409729	Protestant churches—West Indies	BX5596-5598	283.429	Church of England—Wales
BX4836	280.4098	Protestant churches—South America	BX5601-5620	283.72	Church of England—Canada
BX4837-4854	280.4094	Protestant churches—Europe	BX5610-5613	283.72	Church of England—Canada—History
BX4838-4840	280.40941	Protestant churches—Great Britain	BX5619-5620	283.0972092	Church of England—Biography

LC	Dewey	Subject Heading	LC	Dewey	Subject Heading
BX5661-5680.7	283.5	Church of England—Asia	BX6330-6331.2	230.6(1-5)	Baptists—Doctrines
BX5681-5700.9	283.6	Church of England—Africa	BX6333	252.06(1-5)	Baptists—Sermons
BX5701-5720.8	283.9(3/4)	Church of England—[New Zealand/Australia]	BX6335	238.6	Baptists—Creeds
			BX6336	238.6(1-5)	Baptists—Catechisms
BX5721-5740	283	Church of England—Oceania	BX6337	264.06(1-5)	Baptists—Liturgy
			BX6340-6346.3	262.06(1-5)	Baptists—Government
BX5800-6093	283.73092	Episcopalians	BX6388.3-.38	286.1	Regular Baptists
BX5850-5876	268.8373	Episcopal Church—Education	BX6390-6408	286.3	Seventh-Day Baptists
			BX6475-6476	269.24	Church camps—Baptists
BX5879-5919	283.7309	Episcopal Church—History	BX6493-6495	286.1092	Baptists—Biography
BX5925	269.2	Evangelicalism—Episcopal Church	BX6751-6793	286.63	General Convention of the Christian Church
BX5926-5928.5	283.73	Episcopal Church—Relations	BX6901-6997	289.5	Christian Science
BX5929-5930.2	230.373	Episcopal Church—Doctrines	BX6903	289.506	Christian Science—Societies, etc.
BX5939	238.373	Episcopal Church—Creeds	BX6905-6907	289.506	Christian Science—Congresses
BX5940-5948	264.03	Episcopal Church—Liturgy	BX6917	268.895	Christian Science—Education
BX5943-5945	264.03	Episcopal Church—Prayer-books and devotions	BX6931-6935	289.509	Christian Science—History
BX5947-5948	264.03	Episcopal Church—Liturgy	BX6958	262.095	Christian Science—Government
BX5949	264.035	Episcopal Church			
BX5949.C6	234.166/265.62	Confession	BX6960	264.095	Christian Science—Liturgy
BX5950-5968	262.0373	Episcopal Church—Government	BX6990-6996	289.5092	Christian Science—Biography
BX5969	266.373	Episcopal Church—Missions	BX7101-7260	285.8	Congregationalism
BX5970-5974	255.83	Monasticism and religious orders, Anglican	BX7101-7260	285.8	Congregational churches
			BX7105	285.806	Congregational churches—Societies, etc.
BX5979	283.7308996073	Afro-American Episcopalians	BX7106-7109	285.806	Congregational churches—Congresses
BX5990-5995	283.73092	Episcopalians—Biography			
BX6051	283.7305	Episcopal Church—Periodicals	BX7119-7127	268.858	Congregational churches—Education
BX6061-6064.5	268.8373	Episcopal Church—Education	BX7131-7228	285.809	Congregational churches—History
BX6065-6069	283.7309	Episcopal Church—History	BX7135-7149	285.873	Congregational churches—United States
BX6074	238.373	Episcopal Church—Creeds			
BX6075	264.03	Episcopal Church—Liturgy	BX7151-7153	285.871	Congregational churches—Canada
BX6076	262.0373	Episcopal Church—Government			
BX6091-6093	283.73092	Episcopalians—Biography	BX7175-7210	285.84	Congregational churches—Europe
BX6101-6193	286.7	Millerite movement	BX7215-7216	285.85	Congregational churches—Asia
BX6101-6193	286.7	Adventists			
BX6115-6117	286.709	Adventists—History	BX7220-7222	285.86	Congregational churches—Africa
BX6123	252.067	Adventists—Sermons			
BX6124.3-.6	264.06708	Sacraments—Adventists	BX7225-7226	285.894	Congregational churches—Australia
BX6151-6155	286.732	Seventh-Day Adventists			
BX6191-6193	286.7092	Adventists—Biography	BX7233	252.058	Congregational churches—Sermons
BX6195-6197	284.9	Arminianism			
BX6201-6495	286.(1-5)	Baptists	BX7235-7236.2	238.58	Congregational churches—Creeds
BX6205	286.(1-5)06	Baptists—Societies, etc.			
BX6211	286.(1-5)03	Baptists—Dictionaries	BX7237	264.058	Congregational churches—Liturgy
BX6219-6227	268.86(1-5)	Baptists—Education			
BX6231-6328	286.(1-5)09	Baptists—History	BX7238-7239	264.05808	Sacraments—Congregational churches
BX6235-6249	286.(1-5)73	Baptists—United States			
BX6251-6253	286.(1-5)71	Baptists—Canada	BX7240-7246	262.058	Congregational churches—Government
BX6271-6273	286.(1-5)8	Baptists—South America			
BX6275-6310	286.(1-5)4	Baptists—Europe	BX7259-7260	285.8092	Congregationalist—Biography
BX6315-6316	286.(1-5)5	Baptists—Asia			
BX6320-6322	286.(1-5)6	Baptists—Africa	BX7301-7343	286.6	Disciples of Christ
BX6325-6326	286.(1-5)94	Baptists—Australia	BX7433	289.9	Dukhobors
BX6327-6328	286.(1-5)9(5-6)	Baptists—Oceania			

LC	Dewey	Subject Heading	LC	Dewey	Subject Heading
BX7601-7795	289.605	Society of Friends	BX8251-8253	287.(1-8)71	Methodist Church—Canada
BX7601	289.605	Society of Friends—Periodicals	BX8271-8273	287.(1-8)8	Methodist Church—South America
BX7606.5-7608	289.606	Society of Friends—Congresses	BX8275-8310	287.(1-8)4	Methodist Church—Europe
BX7619-7627	268.896	Society of Friends—Education	BX8276-8293	287.(1-8)41	Methodist Church—Great Britain
BX7630-7728	289.609	Society of Friends—History	BX8315-8316	287.(1-8)5	Methodist Church—Asia
BX7635-7649	289.673	Society of Friends—United States	BX8320-8322	287.(1-8)6	Methodist Church—Africa
BX7650-7653	289.671	Society of Friends—Canada	BX8325-8326	287.(1-8)9(3/4)	Methodist Church—[Australia/New Zealand]
BX7671-7673	289.68	Society of Friends—South America	BX8330-8331.2	230.7	Methodist Church—Doctrines
BX7675-7710	289.64	Society of Friends—Europe	BX8333	252.7	Methodist Church—Sermons
BX7676-7693	289.641	Society of Friends—Great Britain	BX8335	238.7	Methodist Church—[Catechisms/Creeds]
BX7715-7716	289.65	Society of Friends—Asia	BX8337	264.07	Methodist Church—Liturgy
BX7720-7723	289.66	Society of Friends—Africa	BX8338	264.0708	Sacraments—Methodist Church
BX7725-7726	289.694	Society of Friends—Australia	BX8340-8345.5	262.07	Methodist Church—Government
BX7733	252.096	Society of Friends—Sermons	BX8380-8389	287.63(2/3)	Methodist Episcopal Church
BX7740-7746	262.096	Society of Friends—Government	BX8435-8473	287.8	Afro-American Methodists
BX7790-7795	289.6092	Quakers—Biography	BX8475-8476	269.24	Camp-meetings
BX7990.H6	289.9	Shake cults (Holiness churches)	BX8491-8495	287.092	Methodists—Biography
BX8001-8080	284.1	Lutheran Church	BX8525-8528	289.92	Jehovah's Witnesses
BX8001	284.104	Lutheran Church—Periodicals	BX8551-8593	284.6	Moravians
BX8018-8063	284.109	Lutheran Church—History	BX8553	284.606	Moravians—Societies, etc.
BX8020-8040.5	284.14	Lutheran Church—Europe	BX8561-8564.5	268.846	Moravians—Education
BX8020-8023	284.143	Lutheran Church—Germany	BX8565-8569	284.609	Moravians—History
BX8041-8061	284.173	Lutheran Church—United States	BX8577	252.046	Moravians—Sermons
BX8066	252.041	Lutheran Church—Sermons	BX8591-8593	284.6092	Moravians—Biography
BX8067	264.041	Lutheran Church—Liturgy	BX8601-8695	289.3	Mormon Church
BX8068-8070	238	Catechetics	BX8610	268.893	Mormon Church—Education
BX8071-.2	262.041	Lutheran Church—Clergy	BX8611-8617	289.309	Mormon Church—History
BX8072-8073.5	264.04108	Sacraments—Lutheran Church	BX8621-8631	289.32	Mormon Church—Sacred books
BX8079-8080	284.1092	Lutherans—Biography	BX8627.A3-Z	289.32	Lamanites (Mormon Church)
BX8101-8143	289.7092	Mennonites	BX8628.A5	289.32	Doctrine and covenants stories
BX8115-8119	289.709	Mennonites—History	BX8639	252.093	Mormon Church—Sermons
BX8116-8118	289.773	Mennonites—United States	BX8643.C68	231.765	Mormon cosmology
BX8118.5-.7	289.771	Mennonites—Canada	BX8643.P7	231.745	Prophets (Mormon theology)
BX8127	252.097	Mennonites—Sermons	BX8643.R4	231.74	Revelation (Mormon theology)
BX8129.A1	252.097	Mennonites—Parties and movements	BX8643.T4	246.6	Mormon temples
BX8129.A5-.A6	289.73092	Amish	BX8643.T5	248.6	Tithes—Mormon Church
BX8129.O43	289.7092	Old Order Mennonites	BX8655-.3	264.09308	Sacraments—Mormon Church
BX8141-8143	289.7092	Mennonites—Biography	BX8659.5	262.1	Aaronic Priesthood (Mormon Church)
BX8201-8495	287	Methodist Church	BX8661	266.93	Mormon Church—Missions
BX8201-8495	287	Methodism	BX8701-8749	289.4	New Jerusalem Church
BX8207	287.06	Methodist Church—Societies, etc.	BX8701	289.405	New Jerusalem Church—Periodicals
BX8219-8227	268.87	Methodist Church—Education	BX8705	289.406	New Jerusalem Church—Congresses
BX8231-8328	287.09	Methodist Church—History	BX8714	268.894	New Jerusalem Church—Education
BX8235-8249	287.(1-8)73	Methodist Church—United States			

LC	Dewey	Subject Heading	LC	Dewey	Subject Heading
BX8715-8719	289.409	New Jerusalem Church—History	BX9427-.5	264.042	Reformed Church—Liturgy
BX8724	252.094	New Jerusalem Church—Sermons	BX9430-9480	284.24	Reformed Church—Europe
			BX9430-9439	284.2494	Reformed Church—Switzerland
BX8736	264.09408	Sacraments—New Jerusalem Church	BX9450-9459	284.5	Huguenots
BX8737	262.094	New Jerusalem Church—Government	BX9450-9459	284.244	Reformed Church—France
			BX9470-9479	284.2492	Reformed Church—Netherlands
BX8747-8749	289.4092	New Jerusalem Church—Biography	BX9495-9593	284.273	Reformed Church—United States
BX8762-8780	289.94	Pentecostal churches	BX9551-9593	285.733	Reformed Church in the United States
BX8901-9225	285	Presbyterian Church			
BX8901-9225	287	Calvinistic Methodists	BX9596-9598	284.271	Reformed Church—Canada
BX8901-9225	285.(1-2)	Presbyterianism	BX9615	284.25	Reformed Church—Asia
BX8905	285.(1-2)06	Presbyterian Church—Societies, etc.	BX9618-9640	284.26	Reformed Church—Africa
			BX9680.S3	296.82092	Sabbatarians
BX8917-8925	268.85	Presbyterian Church—Education	BX9701-9743	287.96	Salvation Army
			BX9751-9793	289.8	Shakers
BX8930-9169	285.(1-2)09	Presbyterian Church—History	BX9755	289.806	Shakers—Congresses
			BX9761-9764	268.898	Shakers—Education
BX8960-8968	285.1	Presbyterian Church in the U.S.	BX9765-9769	289.809	Shakers—History
BX8950-8958	285.1	Presbyterian Church in the U.S.A.	BX9766-9768	289.80973	Shakers—United States
			BX9766-9769	289.809(4-9)	Shakers—[By region or country]
BX8990-8998.38	285.136	Reformed Presbyterian Church	BX9776	262.098	Shakers—Government
			BX9777	252.098	Shakers—Sermons
BX9001-9003	285.(1-2)71	Presbyterian Church—Canada	BX9791-9793	289.8092	Shakers—Biography
			BX9801-9869	289.133	Unitarianism
BX9011-9043	285.(1-2)8	Presbyterian Church—Latin America	BX9801-9869	289.1	Unitarian Universalist churches
BX9050-9140	285.(1-2)4	Presbyterian Church—Europe	BX9805-9807	289.106	Unitarian Universalist churches—Congresses
BX9052-9105	285.(1-2)41	Presbyterian Church—Great Britain	BX9817-9823	268.891	Unitarian Universalist churches—Education
BX9075-9095	285.233	Church of Scotland	BX9831-9835	289.109	Unitarian Universalist churches—History
BX9150-9151	285.(1-2)5	Presbyterian Church—Asia			
BX9160-9162	285.(1-2)6	Presbyterian Church—Africa	BX9833-9835	289.1(4-9)	Unitarianism—[By region or country]
BX9168-9169	285.(1-2)9(3-6)	Presbyterian Church—(New Zealand/Australia/Oceania]	BX9833	289.173	Unitarianism—United States
BX9178	252.05	Presbyterian Church—Sermons	BX9843	252.091	Unitarian Universalist churches—Sermons
BX9185-9187	264.05	Presbyterian Church—Liturgy	BX9850	262.091	Unitarian Universalist churches—Government
BX9188-9189	264.05	Sacraments—Presbyterian Church			
			BX9854	264.0913308	Sacraments—Unitarianism
BX9190-9195	262.05	Presbyterian Church—Government	BX9867-9869	289.1092	Unitarians
			BX9901-9969	289.134	Universalism
BX9220-9225	285.092	Presbyterians—Biography	BX9901-9996	289.134	Restorationism
BX9301-9359	285.9	Puritans	BX9905-9907	289.13406	Universalism—Congresses
BX9331-9359	285.909(4-9)	Puritans—[By region or country]	BX9917-9923	268.89134	Universalism—Education
			BX9931-9935	289.13409	Universalism—History
BX9401-9640	284.2	Calvinism	BX9943	252.09134	Universalism—Sermons
BX9401-9640	284.2	Reformed Church	BX9954	264.0913408	Sacraments—Universalism
BX9401	284.205	Calvinism—Periodicals	BX9967-9969	289.134092	Universalists
BX9403	284.206	Reformed Church—Societies, etc.	C	900	Auxiliary sciences of history
			C2	906	Auxiliary sciences of history—Societies, etc.
BX9415	284.209	Reformed Church—History			
BX9420-9422.2	230.42	Reformed Church—Doctrines	C3	906	Auxiliary sciences of history—Congresses
BX9425	262.042	Reformed Church—Government	C4	905	Auxiliary sciences of history—Periodicals
BX9426	252.042	Reformed Church—Sermons			

LC	Dewey	Subject Heading	LC	Dewey	Subject Heading
C20	907.1	Auxiliary sciences of history—Study and teaching	CC600-605	320.12	Boundary stones
CB	909	Civilization	CD1-724	327.2	Diplomatics
CB	306	Culture	CD50-79	327.2090(1-5)	Diplomatics—[By region or country]
CB3	905	Civilization—Periodicals	CD101-392	025.173409 (1-9)	Government publications—[By region or country]
CB9	903	Civilization—Dictionaries			
CB13	902.22	Civilization—Pictoral works	CD101-215	025.1734094	Government publications—Europe
CB15-18	907.2	Civilization—Historiography			
CB19	901	Civilization—Philosophy	CD221-254	025.1734095	Government publications—Asia
CB20	907.1	Civilization—Study and teaching	CD255-269	025.1734096	Government publications—Africa
CB155	303.44	Progress			
CB156	001.94	Civilization—Extraterrestrial influences	CD271-272	025.1734094	Government publications—Australia
CB158-161	003.2	Forecasting	CD291	025.1734099 (5-6)	Government publications—Oceania
CB160-161	003.20904	Twentieth century—Forecasts			
CB195-281	909.04	Race	CD309-311	025.17340973	Government publications—United States
CB195-197	305.8	National characteristics	CD331-332	025.17340971	Government publications—Canada
CB203-231	940.(288-559)	Europe—Intellectual life—20th century			
CB204	940.2(7-87)	Europe—Civilization—19th century	CD333-334	025.17340972	Government publications—Mexico
CB204	940.2(7-87)	Europe—Intellectual life—19th century	CD335-350	025.173409728	Government publications—Central America
CB213-214	943	Civilization, Germanic	CD351-362	025.173409729	Government publications—Caribbean Area
CB216-220	941.0042	Anglo-Saxon race	CD365-392	025.1734098	Government publications—South America
CB245	909.09812	Civilization, Western			
CB253-256	950	Civilization, Oriental	CD921-4280	027	Archives
CB305	930	Protohistory	CD921	027.005	Archives—Periodicals
CB311	930	Civilization, Ancient	CD941	027.0025	Archives—Directories
CB351-369	909.07	Renaissance	CD945	027.003	Archives—Dictionaries
CB351-355	909.07	Civilization, Medieval	CD947	027.001	Archives—Philosophy
CB351-355	909.07	Middle Ages	CD973	027.0028	Archives—Methodology
CB353	909.1	Twelfth century	CD977	027.1	Personal archives
CB357-430	909.08	Civilization, Modern	CD981-986.5	725.15	Archive buildings
CB367-401	909.5	Sixteenth century	CD987-988	027.0071	Archives—Study and teaching
CB411	940.2(526-7)	Europe—Civilization—18th century	CD995-4280	027.009	Archives—History
CB415-417	909.81	Nineteenth century	CD1000-4280	027.0(1-9)	Archives—[By region or country]
CB425-430	909.82	Twentieth century			
CB481	909	War and civilization	CD1000-2000	027.04	Archives—Europe
CC	930.1	Archaeology	CD1040-1199.5	027.041	Archives—Great Britain
CC1-15	930.105	Archaeology—Periodicals	CD1120-1149.5	027.0436	Archives—Austria
CC20-39	930.106	Archaeology—Societies, etc.	CD1150-1169.5	027.0437	Archives—Czechloslovakia
CC70	930.103	Archaeology—Dictionaries	CD1170-1189.5	027.0439	Archives—Hungary
CC72-81	930.101	Archaeology—Philosophy	CD1190-1219.5	027.044	Archives—France
CC73-75	930.101	Archaeology—Methodology	CD1220-1378.195	027.043	Archives—Germany
CC73-75	930.1028	Archaeological surveying			
CC75	930.10283	Excavations (Archaeology)	CD1400-1658	027.045	Archives—Italy
CC77.U5	930.102804	Underwater archaeology	CD1670-1689.5	027.0493	Archives—Belgium
CC77.5	930.1028	Archaeological geology	CD1690-1733.3	027.0492	Archives—Netherlands
CC110-115	930.1092	Archaeologists	CD1710-1739.5	027.047	Archives—Russia
CC120-125	930.1025	Archaeology—Directories	CD1740-1759.5	027.0438	Archives—Poland
CC135-137	930.10288	Antiquities—Collection and preservation	CD1770-1789.5	027.0489	Archives—Denmark
			CD1790-1809.5	027.04912	Archives—Iceland
CC140	364.163	Forgery of antiquities	CD1810-1829.5	027.0481	Archives—Norway
CC165	930.10283	Excavations (Archaeology)	CD1830-1849.5	027.0485	Archives—Sweden
CC200-255	786.8848	Bells	CD1850-1879.5	027.046	Archives—Spain
CC300-350	246.558	Crosses	CD1880-1899.5	027.0469	Archives—Portugal
CC400	611.718	Fibula (Archaeology)	CD1900-1929.5	027.0494	Archives—Switzerland

LC	Dewey	Subject Heading	LC	Dewey	Subject Heading
CD1930-1989.5	027.0496	Archives—Balkan Peninsula	CE75	529.42	Calendar, Julian
CD2001-2291	027.05	Archives—Asia	CE81-83	529.44	Church calendar
CD2010-2919.5	027.05694	Archives—Israel	CE81	263.9	Fasts and feasts
CD2030-2059.5	027.051	Archives—China	CE83	529.44	Easter
CD2080-2099.5	027.054	Archives—India	CE91-92	529.3	Perpetual calendars
CD2160-2189.5	027.052	Archives—Japan	CJ	737	Numismatics
CD2300-2491	027.06	Archives—Africa	CJ1-4625	737.4	Coins
CD2500-2529.5	027.09(3/4)	Archives—[New Zealand/ Australia]	CJ1-9	737.405	Coins—Periodicals
			CJ14-23	737.406	Coins—Societies, etc.
CD2795	027.09(5-6)	Archives—Oceania	CJ27	737.406	Coins—Congresses
CD3020-3615	027.073	Archives—United States	CJ39-41	737.4074	Coins—Exhibitions
CD3070-3609	027.07(4-9)	Archives—[United States, By state]	CJ53	737.401	Coins—Philosophy
			CJ59	737.409	Coins—History
CD3620-3649.6	027.071	Archives—Canada	CJ101	737.4	Coins—Grading
CD3650-3679.5	027.072	Archives—Mexico	CJ125	737.4	Coins—Errors
CD3690-3859.5	027.0728	Archives—Central America	CJ161.F3	737.4	Facing heads (Numismatics)
CD3860-3985	027.0729	Archives—Caribbean area	CJ201-1397	737.493	Coins, Ancient
CD4000-4279.5	027.08	Archives—South America	CJ301-763	737.4938	Coins, Greek
CD5001-6471	737.6	Seals (Numismatics)	CJ359	737.4938	Decadrachma
CD5001	737.605	Seals (Numismatics)— Periodicals	CJ425-763	737.4938	Coins, Greek
			CJ517-542	737.4937	Coins, Italian
CD5005	737.606	Seals (Numismatics)— Societies, etc.	CJ801-1147	737.4937	Coins, Roman
			CJ937	737.4937	AS (Coin)
CD5009	737.606	Seals (Numismatics)— Congresses	CJ1021-1144	737.49(3-9)	Coins, Ancient [By region or country]
CD5017-5018	737.6074	Seals (Numismatics)— Exhibitions	CJ1021-1070	737.4937	Coins, Ancient—Italy
			CJ1071-1085	737.496	Coins, Ancient—Africa
CD5045	737.6071	Seals (Numismatics)— Study and teaching	CJ1087-1099	737.49396	Coins, Ancient—Asian
			CJ1101-1147	737.493(6/98)	Coins, Ancient—Europe
CD5049	737.609	Seals (Numismatics)— History	CJ1201-1291	737.49398	Coins, Byzantine
			CJ1301-1397	737.49396	Coins, Oriental
CD5051-5052	737.6092	Seals (Numismatics)— Biography	CJ1601-1715	737.40902	Coins, Medieval
CD5085-5175	737.6028	Seals (Numismatics)— Techniques	CJ1800-4625	737.49(4-9)	Coins, Medieval—[By region or country]
			CJ1800-2449	737.4973	Coins, American
CD5592-6471	737.609(4-9)	Seals (Numismatics)—[By region or country]	CJ1835	737.4973	Half-dollar
			CJ1860-1879	737.4971	Coins, Canadian
CD5601-5617	737.60973	Seals (Numismatics)— United States	CJ1889-2449	737.498	Coins, Latin American
			CJ2450-3369	737.494	Coins, European
CD5610	737.60973	United States—Seal	CJ2484	737.4941	Guinea (Coin)
CD5619	737.0971	Seals (Numismatics)— Canada	CJ3188	737.4946	Doubloons
			CJ3189	737.4946	Piece of eight
CD5620	737.0972	Seals (Numismatics)— Mexico	CJ3370-3893	737.495	Coins, Oriental
			CJ3920-4389	737.496	Coins, African
CD5621-5700	737.09728	Seals (Numismatics)— Central America	CJ3948	737.4968	Krugerrand (Coin)
			CJ4400-4419	737.4994	Coins, Australian
CE	529	Chronology	CJ4801-5450	737.3	Tokens
CE1	529.05	Chronology—Periodicals	CJ4801	737.305	Tokens—Periodicals
CE1.5	529.06	Chronology—Congresses	CJ4805-4808	737.3074	Tokens—Exhibitions
CE4	529.03	Chronology—Dictionaries	CJ4805-4806	737.3074	Tokens—Museums
CE6	529.09	Chronology—History	CJ4901-5336	737.309(4-9)	Tokens—[By region or country]
CE31-39.5	529.325	Chronology, Oriental			
CE33	529.0935	Calendar, Assyro-Babylonian	CJ4901-4906	737.30973	Tokens—United States
			CJ5501-6661	737.22	Medals
CE33	529.30935	Chronology, Assyro-Babylonian	CJ5501	737.2205	Medals—Periodicals
			CJ5525	737.22071	Medals—Study and teaching
CE35	529.326	Calendar, Jewish			
CE42	529.30938	Chronology, Greek	CJ5581-5690	737.22093	Medals, Ancient
CE46	529.309376	Calendar, Roman	CJ5625	737.220938	Medals, Greek
CE59	529.327	Calendar, Islamic	CJ5641-5685	737.220937	Medals, Roman
CE73	529.3	Calendars	CJ5793.R34	737.224	Religious medals

LC	Dewey	Subject Heading	LC	Dewey	Subject Heading
CJ5795-6661	737.2209(3-9)	Medals—[By Region or country]	CR	929.71	Knights and knighthood
			CR	394.7	Chivalry
CJ5801-5812	737.220973	Medals—United States	CR	929.6	Heraldry
CJ5806	737.223	Campaign insignia	CR1	929.605	Heraldry—Periodicals
CJ5841-5905	737.2209728	Medals—Central America	CR2	929.606	Heraldry—Congresses
CJ6091-6380	737.22094	Medals—Europe	CR9	929.6074	Heraldry—Exhibitions
CJ6381-6485	737.22095	Medals—Asia	CR11	929.6025	Heraldry—Directories
CJ6491-6559	737.22096	Medals—Africa	CR13	929.603	Heraldry—Dictionaries
CJ6561-6569	737.220994	Medals—Australia	CR14-16	929.601	Heraldry—Philosophy
CN	411.7	Inscriptions	CR29-69	929.6	Heraldry, Ornamental
CN1	411.705	Inscriptions—Periodicals	CR41.C5	929.6	Collars in heraldry
CN15	411.706	Inscriptions—Congresses	CR41.F6	929.6	Flowers in heraldry
CN25-30	411.7074	Inscriptions—Collectors and collecting	CR55-57	929.6	Crests
CN40-42	411.701	Inscriptions—Philosophy	CR67-69	929.6	Badges
CN50	411.7071	Inscriptions—Study and teaching	CR67-69	929.6	Devices (Heraldry)
			CR73-75	929.6	Mottoes
CN55	411.709	Inscriptions—History	CR91-93	929.6	Shields
CN70	411.703	Inscriptions—Dictionaries	CR101-115	929.92	Flags
CN120-730	411.7	Inscriptions, Ancient	CR151-159	929.609	Heraldry—History
CN350-455	481.1	Inscriptions, Greek	CR183-185	929.6	Heralds
CN375.E6	929.50938	Epitaphs	CR3499-4420	929.7	Titles of honor and nobility
CN380-455	481.109(3-9)	Inscriptions, Greek—[By region or country]	CR3575	929.7	Precedence
CN400	481.1095	Inscriptions, Greek—Asia	CR4480-4485	929.9	Insignia
CN410-415	481.109561	Inscriptions, Greek—Turkey	CR4480.C7	929.7	Crowns
CN420	481.1094959	Inscriptions, Greek—Crete	CR4485.07	929.7	Orbs
CN430	481.1095693	Inscriptions, Greek—Cyprus	CR4501-6305	929.71	Orders of knighthood and chivalry
CN440-441	481.10953	Inscriptions, Greek—Middle East	CR4501-6305	929.81	Decorations of honor
CN440-441	481.0932	Inscriptions, Greek—Egypt	CR4553	929.6	Tournaments
CN455	487.311	Inscriptions, Byzantine	CR4571-4595	394.8	Dueling
CN479	499.9411	Inscriptions, Etruscan	CR4701-4731	255.791	Orders of knighthood and chivalry, Papal
CN510-740	471	Inscriptions, Latin	CR4759-4775	255.7914	Teutonic Knights
CN528.E6	929.50937	Epitaphs	CR4801-6305	929.7(2-3/094)	Orders of knighthood and chivalry—[By region or country]
CN745	492.411	Inscriptions, Jewish			
CN750-753	487.4	Inscriptions, Christian	CR4801-4917	929.72	Orders of knighthood and chivalry—Great Britain
CN870-1355	411.709	Inscriptions—[By region or country]	CR4951-5005	929.736	Orders of knighthood and chivalry—Austria
CN870-872	411.70973	Inscriptions—United States	CR5025-5085	929.74	Orders of knighthood and chivalry—France
CN877-878	411.70972	Inscriptions—Mexico	CR5100-5475	929.73	Orders of knighthood and chivalry—Germany
CN882-884	411.709728	Inscriptions—Central America			
CN886-888	411.7098	Inscriptions—South America	CR5351	929.8143	Iron Cross
CN900-1130	411.7094	Inscriptions—Europe	CR5485-5489	929.795	Orders of knighthood and chivalry—Greece
CN910-915	411.709436	Inscriptions—Austria			
CN945-948	411.70944	Inscriptions—France	CR5500-5580	929.75	Orders of knighthood and chivalry—Italy
CN950-957	411.70943	Inscriptions—Germany			
CN960-997	411.70941	Inscriptions—Great Britain	CR5547-5577	255.791	Papal decorations
CN1000-1005	481.1	Inscriptions, Greek	CR5547-5577	262.13	Nobility, Papal
CN1010-1015	411.70945	Inscriptions—Italy	CR5547-5575	255.7	Orders of knighthood and chivalry, Papal
CN1060-1065	411.70947	Inscriptions—Russia			
CN1090-1095	411.70946	Inscriptions—Spain			
CN1150-1230	411.7095	Inscriptions—Asia	CR5657-5703	929.77	Orders of knighthood and chivalry—Russia
CN1153	492.71	Inscriptions, Islamic			
CN1160-1161	411.70951	Inscriptions—China	CR5713-5737	929.738	Orders of knighthood and chivalry—Poland
CN1170-1175	411.70954	Inscriptions—India			
CN1180-1181	411.70952	Inscriptions—Japan	CR5745-5809	929.78	Orders of knighthood and chivalry—Scandinavia
CN1193-1194	411.7095694	Inscriptions—Israel			
CN1300-1320	411.7096	Inscriptions—Africa	CR5819-5889	929.76	Orders of knighthood and chivalry—Spain
CN1340-1345	411.70994	Inscriptions—Australia			

LC	Dewey	Subject Heading	LC	Dewey	Subject Heading
CR5900-5925	929.769	Orders of knighthood and chivalry—Portugal	D3	906	History—Congresses
			D9	903	History—Dictionaries
CR6253.Y	929.8173	Young American Medal for Bravery	D11-.5	900	Chronology, Historical
			D13-15	907.2	Historiography
CS	929.1	Genealogy	D14-15	907.202	Historians
CS1	929.105	Genealogy—Periodicals	D16-.18	901	History—Methodology
CS2	929.106	Genealogy—Congresses	D16	902.28	Historical models
CS5	929.1025	Genealogy—Directories	D16.16	901.9	Psychohistory
CS6	929.103	Genealogy—Dictionaries	D16.2-.5	907.1	History—Study and teaching
CS42-2209	929.10720(4-9)	[Region or country]—Genealogy	D16.7-.9	901	History—Philosophy
			D16.9	901	Historicism
CS42-71	929.1072073	United States—Genealogy	D17-24.5	909	World history
CS80-90	929.1072071	Canada—Genealogy	D25-.4	355.009	Military history
CS100-110	929.372	Mexico—Genealogy	D25	355.4	Battles
CS120-199	929.10720(72-8)	Central America—Genealogy	D25.5	355.0218	Guerrillas
CS200-261	929.3729	West Indies—Genealogy	D27	359.009	Naval history
CS270-409	929.38	South America—Genealogy	D27	359.4	Naval battles
CS410-1059	929.107204	Europe—Genealogy	D31-34	909	World politics
CS410-479.5	929.1072041	Great Britain—Genealogy	D51-95	930	History, Ancient
CS610-699	929.1072043	Germany—Genealogy	D51	930.05	History, Ancient—Periodicals
CS780-839	929.10720492	Benelux countries—Genealogy	D54	930.03	History, Ancient—Dictionaries
CS840-869	929.347	Russia—Genealogy	D55	920.00901	Biography—To 500
CS890-939	929.1072048	Scandinavia—Genealogy	D56-.52	930.072	History, Ancient—Historiography
CS1080-1549.5	929.107205	Asia—Genealogy			
CS1550-1779	929.107206	Africa—Genealogy	D70	936.4	Celts—History
CS2000-2009	929.1072094	Australia—Genealogy	D90.D	949.8004	Dacians
CS2170-2179	929.393	New Zealand—Genealogy	D95	359.00901	Naval history, Ancient
CS2191-2209	929.39(5-6)	Oceania—Genealogy	D101-110.5	909.08	History, Modern
CS2300-3090	929.4	Names, Personal	D107-110.5	920.00902	Biography—Middle Ages, 500-1500
CS2395-3090	929.409(4-9)	Names, Personal—[By region or country]	D111-203	909.07	Middle Ages—History
CS2970	929.42971	Names, Personal—Islamic	D115	920.00902	Biography—Middle Ages, 500-1500
CS3010	929.4296	Names, Personal—Jewish			
CT	920	Biography	D127	394.4	Coronations
CT	001.2092	Scholars	D128	355.00902	Military history—Medieval
CT21-22	809.93592	Biography as a literary form	D131	321.3	Feudalism
CT25	920	Autobiography	D134	307.760902	Cities and towns, Medieval
CT101	920	Autobiographies	D135-149	304.8	Migrations of nations
CT108	929.44	Nicknames	D139	304.808939	Vandals
CT280-310	920.071	Canada—Biography	D145	304.8	Lombards
CT329-448	920.0729	West Indies—Biography	D151-173	909.07	Crusades
CT550-558	920.072	Mexico—Biography	D156-.5	909.07092	Crusades—Biography
CT570-638	920.0728	Central America—Biography	D156.58	909.07072	Crusades—Historiography
CT640-758	920.08	South America—Biography	D161-.5	909.07	Crusades—First, 1096-1099
CT759-1495	920.04	Europe—Biography	D162-.5	909.07	Crusades—Second, 1147-1149
CT770-858	920.041	Great Britain—Biography	D163-.5	909.07	Crusades—Third, 1189-1192
CT1050-1099.8	920.043	Germany—Biography			
CT1240-1328	920.048	Scandinavia—Biography	D164-.5	909.07	Crusades—Fourth, 1202-1204
CT1399-1458	920.0496	Balkan Peninsula—Biography	D165	909.07	Crusades—Fifth, 1218-1221
CT1498-1919	920.05	Asia—Biography	D166	909.07	Crusades—Sixth, 1228-1229
CT1870-1919	920.056	Middle East—Biography			
CT1920-2750	920.06	Africa—Biography	D167	909.07	Crusades—Seventh, 1248-1250
CT2800-2808	920.0994	Australia—Biography			
CT2880-2888	920.0993	New Zealand—Biography	D168	909.07	Crusades—Eighth, 1270
CT2900-3090	920.099(5-6)	Oceania—Biography	D171-173	909.07	Crusades—Later, 13th, 14th, and 15th centuries
CT3200-3830	920.72	Women—Biography			
CT9970-9971	904	Adventure and adventurers	D175-195	956.944203	Jerusalem—History—Latin Kingdom, 1099-1244
D	900	History			
D1	905	History—Periodicals			

LC	Dewey	Subject Heading	LC	Dewey	Subject Heading
D201.7-.8	909.1	Twelfth century	D548-549.5	940.4144	World War, 1914-1918—Campaigns—France
D205-1075	909.8	History, Modern	D550-569.5	940.4147	World War, 1914-1918—Campaigns—Eastern front
D205	909.0803	History, Modern—Dictionaries	D557.L5	940.422	Limanova, Battle of, 1914
D206	909.08072	Historiography	D566-568.9	940.415	World War, 1914-1918—Campaigns—Turkey
D214	355.00903	Military history—Modern	D568.7	940.433	Gaza, Battles of, 1917
D217	327.112	Balance of power	D569	940.4145	World War, 1914-1918—Campaigns—Italy
D219-234	909.5	History, Modern—16th century	D580-589	940.45	World War, 1914-1918—Naval operations
D220-271	943.03	Counter-Reformation	D580	940.45	Freedom of the seas
D226.7	321.6	Royal houses	D582.F2	940.423	Falkland Islands, Battle of the, 1914
D242-283.5	940.2 (3-5)	Seventeenth century	D600-607	940.44	World War, 1914-1918—Aerial operations
D242-283.5	909.6	History, Modern—17th century	D609	940.467	World War, 1914-1918—Registers of dead
D251-271	940.24	Thirty Years' War, 1618-1648	D613-614	940.439	World War, 1914-1918—Peace
D274.5-.6	940.252	Anglo-French War, 1666-1667	D625-626	940.405	World War, 1914-1918—Atrocities
D277-278.5	940.252	Dutch War, 1672-1678	D625-626	364.13809041	War crimes
D279-280.5	940.2525	Grand Alliance, War of the, 1689-1697	D642-651	940.439	World War, 1914-1918—Peace
D281-283.5	940.2526	Spanish Succession, War of, 1701-1714	D650.T4-651	940.31426	Mandates
D283.5	940.253	Hague, Treaty of, 1717	D652-659	940.5 (1-2)	Reconstruction (1914-1939)
D287.5	940.253	Quadruple Alliance, 1718	D731-838	940.53	World War, 1939-1945
D291-294	940.2532	Austrian Succession, War of, 1740-1748	D736	940.53092	World War, 1939-1945—Biography
D295	940.253	Neutrality, Armed	D741	940.5311	World War, 1939-1945—Causes
D301-309	940.27	Europe—History—1789-1815	D743.2	940.5300222	World War, 1939-1945—Pictorial works
D351-400	940.2(7-87)	Nineteenth century	D745-.7	940.5400222	World War, 1939-1945—Caricatures and cartoons
D352.1	321.03094	Royal houses	D748-754	940.532	World War, 1939-1945—Diplomatic history
D383	940.27	Quadruple Alliance, 1815	D753.2	940.531	Lend-lease operations (1941-1945)
D410-893	940.(288-5)	Twentieth century			
D410-893	909.82	History, Modern—20th century	D755-769.87	940.54	World War, 1939-1945—Campaigns
D412.7	321.03094	Royal houses	D756-763	940.5421	World War, 1939-1945—Campaigns—Western front
D436	359.0094	Naval history, Modern—20th century	D756.5.A7	940.542131	Ardennes, Battle of the, 1944-1945
D443	940.288	Triple Entente, 1907	D756.5.D5	940.54214	Dieppe Raid, 1942
D501-680	940.3	World War, 1914-1918	D756.5.D8	940.5421428	Dunkerque (France), Battle of, 1940
D507	940.3092	World War, 1914-1918—Biography	D756.5.V3	940.54214	Verdun, Battle of, 1940
D507	940.3092	Generals	D757-.9	940.54213	World War, 1939-1945—Campaigns—Germany
D511	940.288	Triple Entente, 1907	D759-760.8	940.54211	World War, 1939-1945—Campaigns—Great Britain
D529-578	940.4	World War, 1914-1918—Campaigns	D761-762	940.54214	World War, 1939-1945—Campaigns—France
D530-549.5	940.4144	World War, 1914-1918—Campaigns—Western front	D763.N4	940.54219218	Arnhem, Battle of, 1944
D531-538.5	940.4143	World War, 1914-1918—Campaigns—Germany	D764-766.7	940.5425	World War, 1939-1945—Campaigns—Eastern front
D541-542	940.414	World War, 1914-1918—Campaigns—Belgium			
D544-545	940.4144	World War, 1914-1918—Campaigns—France			
D545.A6	940.424	Argonne, Battle of the, 1915			
D545.A63	940.434	Argonne, Battle of the, 1918			
D545.L3	940.421	Le Cateau, Battle of, 1914			
D545.V25	940.421	Verdun, Battle of, 1914			
D545.V3	940.4272	Verdun, Battle of, 1916			

LC	Dewey	Subject Heading	LC	Dewey	Subject Heading
D764.3	940.5421772	Odessa (Ukraine), Battle of, 1941	D803-804.35	940.5405	World War, 1939-1945—Atrocities
D764.3.M	940.5421731	Moscow, Battle of, 1941-1942	D804.S65	940.5405	Katyn Forest Massacre, 1940
D764.3.S7	940.5421721	Stalingrad, Battle of, 1942-1943	D805	940.5472	World War, 1939-1945—Prisoners and prisons
D765-.2	940.542138	World War, 1939-1945—Campaigns—Poland	D805.G3	940.5318	Dachau (Germany : Concentration camp)
D765.2.W3	940.5421384	Warsaw, Battle of, 1945	D805.G3	940.5318	Flossenburg (Germany : Concentration camp)
D766.3-.32	940.5421495	World War, 1939-1945—Campaigns—Greece	D805.G3	940.5318	Neuengamme (Hamburg, Germany: Concentration camp)
D766.6-.62	940.5421497	World War, 1939-1945—Campaigns—Yugoslavia			
D766.82	940.5423	World War, 1939-1945—Campaigns—Africa, North	D805.G3	940.5318	Buchenwald (Germany : Concentration camp)
D766.9	940.5423	El Alamein, Battle of, Egypt, 1942	D805.G3	940.5318	Bergen-Belsen (Germany : Concentration camp)
D767-.99	940.5426	World War, 1939-1945—Campaigns—Pacific Ocean	D805.P5	940.5317599	O'Donnell Camp (Philippines : Concentration camp)
D767.2-.25	940.5425	World War, 1939-1945—Campaigns—Japan			
D767.917	940.5426	Tarawa, Battle of, 1943	D805.P7	940.53170943	Auschwitz (Poland : Concentration camp)
D767.92	940.5426	Pearl Harbor (Hawaii), Attack on, 1941	D806-807	940.5475	World War, 1939-1945—Medical care
D767.99.I9	940.5426	Iwo Jima, Battle of, 1945	D808-809	940.5308691	World War, 1939-1945—Refugees
D767.99.O45	940.5425	World War, 1939-1945—Campaigns—Japan—Okinawa Island	D808-809	940.5477	World War, 1939-1945—Civilian relief
D769.346	940.541273	United States. Army—Airborne troops	D810.J4	940.5318	World War, 1939-1945—Jews
D769.347	940.541273	United States. Army—Parachute troops	D810.P6-.P7	940.5488	World War, 1939-1945—Propaganda
D770-784	940.545	World War, 1939-1945—Naval operations	D811-.5	940.548(1-2)	World War, 1939-1945—Personal narratives
D770-784	940.5452	World War, 1939-1945—Blockades	D812	940.5312	World War, 1939-1945—Armistice
D772.G7	940.5428	Rio de la Plata, Battle of the, 1939	D818-819	940.531422	World War, 1939-1945—Reparations
D774.C	940.5426	Coral Sea, Battle of the, 1942	D824-829	940.53144	Reconstruction (1939-1951)
D774.J	940.5426	Java Sea, Battle of the, 1942	D839-850	909.08	History, Modern—1945-
D774.M5	940.5426	Midway, Battle of, 1942	D839	909.8(24-3)05	History, Modern—1945- —Periodicals
D780-784	940.5451	World War, 1939-1945—Naval operations—Submarine	D847-.2	940.54217	Communist countries
			D880-888	909.09724	Developing countries—History
D785-792	940.544	World War, 1939-1945—Aerial operations	D890-893	909.09811	Eastern Hemisphere—History
D793	940.541	World War, 1939-1945—Tank warfare	D900-1075	940	Europe—History
			D901-980	914	Europe—Description and travel
D797	940.54021	World War, 1939-1945—Casualties (Statistics, etc.)	D1050-1075	940.5(5-6)	Europe—History—1945-
D797	940.5467	World War, 1939-1945—Registers of dead	D1050	940.(55-56)005	Europe—History—1945- —Periodicals
D802	940.5336	World War, 1939-1945—Underground movements	D1050.8-.82	940.(55-56)0071	Europe—History—1945- —Study and teaching
D802.A2	940.5336	World War, 1939-1945—Occupied territories	D1056-.2	940.55004	Ethnology—Europe
D802.Y8	949.7022	Yugoslavia—History—Axis occupation, 1941-1945	D1058-1065	320.94090 (44-511)	Europe—Politics and government—1945-
			D1060	321.04094	European federation
			D1070-1075	920.00904	Biography—20th century

LC	Dewey	Subject Heading
D2009	320.940948	Europe—Politics and government—1989-
D2009	327.4	Europe—Foreign relations—1989-
DA	941/936.1	Great Britain
DA10-18.2	909.0971241	Commonwealth countries—History
DA20-690	936.2/942	England
DA20	936.2005/ 942.005	England—Periodicals
DA28-690	936.1/942	Great Britain—History
DA28-.9	920.0361/ 920.041	Great Britain—Biography
DA49-69.3	355.30942	Great Britain—History, Military
DA70-89.1	359.30942	Great Britain—History, Naval
DA86.22.D7	941.055	Lisbon Expedition, 1589
DA87.5 1794	941.073	First of June, 1794, Battle of
DA87.7 1797	942.073	Spithead Mutiny, 1797
DA88.5 1805	942.073	Trafalgar, Battle of, 1805
DA89.5	358.400942	England. Royal Air force
DA110-115	936.1/942	Great Britain—Civilization
DA120-125	936.1004/ 942.004	Ethnology—Great Britain
DA134-162	936.2/941.01	Great Britain—History—To 1066
DA140-143	941.089916	Celts
DA150-162	942.017	Saxons
DA150-162	941.0892/ 942.017	Anglo-Saxons
DA170-260	941.0(2-46)	Great Britain—History—To 1485
DA196	941.021	Hastings, Battle of, 1066
DA300-591	941.0(5-8)	Great Britain—History—Modern period, 1485-
DA310-360	941.05	Great Britain—History—Tudors, 1485-1603
DA331-339	941.052	Great Britain—History—Henry VIII, 1509-1547
DA350-360	941.055	Great Britain—History—Elizabeth, 1558-1603
DA370-419.5	941.06	Great Britain—History—Early Stuarts, 1603-1649
DA392-.1	941.061	Gunpowder Plot, 1605
DA410-429	941.062	Great Britain—History—Civil War, 1642-1649
DA420-429	941.063	Fifth Monarchy Men
DA430-463	942.06(6-9)	Great Britain—History—1660-1714
DA499	941.071	Great Britain—History—George I, 1714-1727
DA500	941.072	Great Britain—History—George II, 1727-1760
DA505-522	941.073	Great Britain—History—George III, 1760-1820
DA535	941.073	Luddites
DA537-538	941.074	Great Britain—History—George IV, 1820-1830
DA539-542	941.075	Great Britain—History—William IV, 1830-1837
DA550-565	941.081	Great Britain—History—Victoria, 1837-1901
DA566-592	941.082	Great Britain—History—20th century
DA600-632	913.6204/ 914.204	England—Description and travel
DA640	914.2003	Great Britain—Gazetteers
DA675-689	942.1	London (England)—History
DA700-745	942.9	Wales
DA700	942.9005	Wales—Periodicals
DA710	920.0429	Wales—Biography
DA711.5	942.9	Wales—Civilization
DA714-722.1	942.9	Wales—History
DA725-731.2	914.2904	Wales—Description and travel
DA750-890	936.1/941.1	Scotland
DA750	936.1005/ 941.1005	Scotland—Periodicals
DA777-778.9	941.101	Scotland—History—To 1057
DA779-790	941.10(2-5)	Scotland—History—1057-1603
DA784.6	941.104	Flodden, Battle of, 1513
DA803.8	941.1063	Scotland—History—1649-1660
DA809-814.5	941.10(69-73)	Scotland—History—18th century
DA813-814	941.10(69-72)	Jacobites
DA815-818	941.1081	Scotland—History—19th century
DA821-826	941.1082	Scotland—History—20th century
DA850-878	914.1104	Scotland—Description and travel
DA900-995	936./941.5	Ireland—History
DA900	936.1005/ 941.5005	Ireland—Periodicals
DA930-932.6	936.1/ 941.50(1-2)	Ireland—History—To 1172
DA933-937.5	941.50(3-5)	Ireland—History—1172-1603
DA940-946	941.506	Ireland—History—17th century
DA947-949.5	941.507	Ireland—History—18th century
DA949.7-958	941.5081	Ireland—History—19th century
DA954	941.7081	Fenians
DA959-965	941.5082	Ireland—History—20th century
DA969-988	913.6104/ 914.1504	Ireland—Description and travel
DAW	943	Europe, Central
DAW1001	943.0005	Europe, Central—Periodicals
DAW1004	943.0006	Europe, Central—Congresses
DAW1014-1015	914.304	Europe, Central—Description and travel
DAW1024	943	Europe, Central—Civilization
DAW1026-1028	943.004	Ethnology—Europe, Central
DAW1031-1051	943	Europe, Central—History

LC	Dewey	Subject Heading	LC	Dewey	Subject Heading
DB1-879	936.3/943.6	Austria	DB931.94-932.48	943.9041	Hungary—History—Turkish occupation, 1529-1699
DB1	936.3005/943.6005	Austria—Periodicals	DB932.3-934	943.9043	Hungary—History—1699-1848
DB14	913.63003/914.36003	Austria—Gazetteers	DB940-953	943.9042	Hungary—History—Francis Joseph, 1848-1916
DB21-27.5	913.6304/914.3604	Austria—Description and travel	DB947-957	943.90(43-54)	Hungary—History—20th century
DB30	936.3/943.6	Austria—Civilization	DB955	943.905(1-2)	Hungary—History—1918-1945
DB33-34.5	936.3004/943.6004	Ethnology—Austria	DB956-957	943.905(3-4)	Hungary—History—1945-
DB36-.7	920.0363/920.0436	Austria—Biography	DB957	943.9052	Hungary—History—Revolution, 1956
DB36.8-.9	936.30072/943.60072	Austria—Historiography	DB981-999	943.912	Budapest (Hungary)
DB42-44	355.309436	Austria—History, Military	DB2000-3150	943.7	Czechoslovakia
DB45	359.309436	Austria—History, Naval	DB2000	943.7	Czechoslovakia—Periodicals
DB46-99.2	936.3/943.602	Austria—History	DB2003	943.7006	Czechoslovakia—Congresses
DB51-57	936.3	Austria—History—To 1273	DB2007	914.37003	Czechoslovakia—Gazetteers
DB57-59	943.60(25-3)	Austria—History—1273-1519	DB2009	943.70025	Czechoslovakia—Directories
DB65.2-77	943.603	Austria—History—1519-1740	DB2018-2022	914.37(04)	Czechoslovakia—Description and travel
DB72	940.2532	Austrian Succession, War of, 1740-1748	DB2035	943.7	Czechoslovakia—Civilization
DB83	940.284	Austria—History—Revolution, 1848-1849	DB2040-2043	943.7004	Ethnology—Czechoslovakia
DB96-99.2	943.6051	Austria—History—1918-1938	DB2044-2232	943.7	Czechoslovakia—History
DB99	943.6052	Austria—History—1938-1945	DB2080-2133	943.71023	Bohemia (Czech Republic)—History—To 1526
DB99.2	943.6053	Austria—History—1955-	DB2135-2151	943.710232	Bohemia (Czech Republic)—History—1526-1618
DB841-860	943.613	Vienna (Austria)	DB2155-2162	943.7102	Bohemia (Czech Republic)—History—1618-1848
DB881-898	936.3/943.648	Liechtenstein	DB2165-2182	943.71024	Bohemia (Czech Republic)—History—1848-1918
DB881	936.3005/943.648005	Liechtenstein—Periodicals	DB2185-2232	943.7	Czechoslavakia—History
DB888	913.6304/914.364804	Liechtenstein—Description and travel	DB2195-2202	943.7032	Czechoslovakia—History—1918-1939
DB891-894	936.3/943.648	Liechtenstein—History	DB2205-2211	943.7033	Czechoslovakia—History—1938-1945
DB901-999	939.8/943.9	Hungary	DB2215-2232	943.704	Czechoslovakia—History—1945-1992
DB901	939.8005/943.9005	Hungary—Periodicals	DB2222	943.7042	Czechoslovakia—History—Coup d'etat, 1948
DB904	913.98003/914.39003	Hungary—Gazetteers	DB2225-2232	943.7043	Czechoslovakia—History—1968-1989
DB906.9-917.3	913.9804/914.3904	Hungary—Description and travel	DB2232	943.7042	Czechoslovakia—History—Intervention, 1968
DB919-.2	939.8004/943.9004	Ethnology—Hungary	DB2300-2421	943.72	Moravia
DB919	943.900494511	Magyars	DB2335	943.72	Moravia—Civilization
DB920.5	939.8/943.9	Hungary—Civilization	DB2340-2342	943.72004	Moravia—Ethnography
DB922	920.0398/920.0439	Hungary—Biography	DB2345-2421	943.72	Moravia—History
DB927-928.9	939.8/943.901	Hungary—History—To 896	DB2385-2391	943.72021	Moravia (Czech Republic)—History—To 906
DB929-.9	943.902	Hungary—History—896-1301	DB2600-2650	943.712	Prague (Czech Republic)
DB930.2	943.903	Hungary—History—Charles Robert, 1308-1342	DB2700-3150	943.73	Slovakia
DB930.3	943.903	Hungary—History—Louis I, 1342-1382	DB2707	914.373003	Slovakia—Gazetteers
DB930.4	943.903	Hungary—History—Sigismund, 1387-1437	DB2718-2722	914.37304	Slovakia—Description and travel

LC	Dewey	Subject Heading	LC	Dewey	Subject Heading
DB2735	943.73	Slovakia—Civilization	DC116-118	944.0(29-3)	France—History—War of the Huguenots, 1562-1598
DB2740-2743	943.73004	Ethnology—Slovakia	DC116-118	944.029	France—History—Charles IX, 1560-1574
DB2744-3000	943.73	Slovakia—History			
DB2795-2801	943.7302(34-4)	Slovakia—History—1800-1918	DC118	944.028	Saint Bartholomew's Day, Massacre of, France, 1572
DB2795-2801	943.73023	Slovakia—History—1526-1800	DC119-120	944.029	France—History—Henry III, 1574-1589
DB2795-2791	943.7302	Slovakia—History—To 1526	DC120.8-138	944.03	France—History—Bourbons, 1589-1789
DB2805-2841	943.730(3-5)	Slovakia—History—1918-1993	DC122-.9	944.031	France—History—Henry IV, 1589-1610
DB2822	943.73033	Slovakia—History—Uprising, 1944	DC123-.9	944.032	France—History—Louis XIII, 1610-1643
DB2842	943.73042	Slovakia—History—Intervention, 1968	DC124.45	944.033	Dunes, Battle of the, 1658
DC	936.4/944	France	DC124.45	944.03(2-3)	Franco-Spanish War, 1635-1659
DC1	936.4005/ 944.005	France—Periodicals	DC124.5-130	944.033	France—History—Louis XIV, 1643-1715
DC14	913.64003/ 914.4003	France—Gazetteers	DC133-135	944.034	France—History—Louis XV, 1715-1774
DC15	944.0025	France—Directories	DC136-137.5	944.035	France—History—Louis XVI, 1774-1793
DC21-29.3	913.6404/ 914.404	France—Description and travel	DC139-190.8	944.04(1-2)	France—History—Revolution, 1789-1799
DC29	914.4040904	France—Description and travel—1945-1974			
DC33.0	936.4/944	France—Civilization	DC107	394.2635	Bastille Day
DC34-.5	936.4004/ 944.004	Ethnology—France	DC191.2-249	944.0(46-5)	France—History—Consulate and First Empire, 1799-1815
DC35-423	936.4/944	France—History			
DC36-.8	920.0364/ 920.044	France—Biography	DC222.F6	940.27	Fleurus, Battle of, 1794
DC44-47	355.30944	France—History, Military	DC226.N5	940.27	Nile, Battle of the, 1798
DC49-53	359.30944	France—History, Naval	DC227.5.D8	940.27	Durnstein, Battle of, 1805
DC60-81.5	944.01	France—History—To 987	DC231-233.5	940.27	Peninsular War, 1807-1814
DC62-63	936.4	Gaul—History	DC234.65	940.27	Graz (Austria), Battle of, 1809
DC62	936.402	Gergovie, Battle of, 52 B.C.			
DC62	936.402	Gaul—History—Gallic Wars, 58-51 B.C.	DC236-238.5	940.27	Wars of Liberation, 1813-1814
DC96-105	944.025	Hundred Years War, 1339-1453	DC236.7.D8	940.27	Dresden, Battle of, 1813
			DC241-244.7	940.27	Waterloo, Battle of, 1815
DC97.5-101.7	944.02(4-6)	France—History—14th century	DC256-260	944.05	France—History—Louis XVIII, 1814-1824
DC101-.7	944.026	France—History—Charles VI, 1380-1422	DC261-262	944.063	France—History—July Revolution, 1830
DC101.5.A2	944.026	Agincourt, Battle of, 1415	DC265-269	944.063	France—History—Louis Philip, 1830-1848
DC101.5.C33	944.026	France—History—Cabochien Uprising, 1413	DC271.5-274.5	944.07	France—History—Second Republic, 1848-1852
DC102-105.9	944.026	France—History—Charles VII, 1422-1461	DC274-.5	944.07	France—History—Coup d'etat, 1851
DC106-.9	944.027	France—History—Louis XI, 1461-1483	DC275-292	944.07	France—History—Second Empire, 1852-1870
DC107-.2	944.027	France—History—Charles VIII, 1483-1498	DC281-326.5	944.0812	Franco-Prussian War, 1870-1871
DC108-109	944.027	France—History—Louis XII, 1498-1515	DC309.E8	944.0812	Epinal (France), Battle of, 1870
DC113-.5	944.028	France—History—Francis I, 1515-1547	DC342.8-396	944.081	France—History—Third Republic, 1870-1940
DC114-.5	944.028	France—History—Henry II, 1547-1559	DC385	944.0814	France—History—German occupation, 1914-1918
DC115	944.029	France—History—Francis II, 1559-1560	DC397	944.0816	France—History—German occupation, 1940-1945

LC	Dewey	Subject Heading	LC	Dewey	Subject Heading
DC398-423	944.08(2-4)	France—History—1945-	DD207-209	940.284	Germany—History—Revolution, 1848-1849
DC421	944.083(6-7)	France—Politics and government—1969-1974	DD214-216	943.081	Germany—History—1866-1871
DC422	944.083(7-8)	France—Politics and government—1974-1981	DD217-231	943.08(3-4)	Germany—History—1871-1918
DC423	944.0838	France—Politics and government—1981-	DD223-.9	943.083	Germany—History—William I, 1871-1888
DC608.1-.9	944.9	Riviera (France)	DD224-226	943.084	Germany—History—Frederick III, 1888
DC611.C8-.C839	944.945	Corsica (France)—History	DD228-231	943.084	Germany—History—William II, 1888-1918
DC611.P961	396.70944	Courts of love	DD232-257.4	943.08(4-79)	Germany—History—20th century
DC701-790	944.36	Paris (France)			
DC921-930	946.79	Andorra	DD247.R56	943.086	Germany—History—Night of the Long Knives, 1934
DC941-947	944.949	Monaco	DD248	943.085	Germany—History—Revolution, 1918
DD	936.3/943	Germany			
DD14	913.63003/914.3003	Germany—Gazetteers	DD249	943.085	Germany—History—Kapp Putsch, 1920
DD15.5	943.0025	Germany—Directories	DD249	943.085	Germany—History—Beer Hall Putsch, 1923
DD21.5-43	913.6304/914.304	Germany—Description and travel	DD249	943.085	Germany—History—March Uprising, 1921
DD60-68	936.3/943	Germany—Civilization	DD253-256.5	943.086	Germany—History—1933-1945
DD73-78	943.004	Ethnology—Germany			
DD84-257.4	936.3/943	Germany—History	DD253-256.5	943.086	National socialism
DD85-.8	920.0363/920.043	Germany—Biography	DD256.3-.4	943.086	Anti-Nazi movement
DD86-.7	936.30072/943.0072	Germany—Historiography	DD257-.4	943.0879	Germany—History—Unification, 1990
DD99-104	355.30943	Germany—History, Military	DD257-.4	943.087(4-5)	Germany—History—1945-1955
DD106	355.30943	Germany—History, Naval	DD257.4	943.09(79-8)	Germany—History—1990-
DD121-134.2	936.3/943.01(1-4)	Germany—History—To 843	DD258-262	943.087	Germany (West)
DD125-198.7	943.02	Holy Roman Empire—History	DD280-289	943.1087	Germany (East)
DD126.5	943.0(13-25)	Donation of Pepin	DD301-491	936.3/943	Prussia (Germany)
DD128	943.013	Merovingians	DD301	936.3005/943.005	Prussia (Germany)—Periodicals
DD129-134.9	943.014	Carolingians	DD308	913.63003/914.3003	Prussia (Germany)—Gazetteers
DD134.3-135	943.021	Germany—History—843-918			
DD135.G3315	943.086	Germany—History—Kristallnacht, 1938	DD314-320	913.6304/914.304	Prussia (Germany)—Description and travel
DD136-140.7	943.022	Germany—History—Saxon House, 919-1024	DD331	936.3/943	Prussia (Germany)—Civilization
DD141-144	943.023	Germany—History—Franconian House, 1024-1125	DD341-454	936.3/943	Prussia (Germany)—History
DD145-155	943.024	Germany—History—Hohenstaufen, 1138-1254	DD343-.8	920.043/920.043	Prussia (Germany)—Biography
DD156-174.6	943.02(6-9)	Germany—History—1273-1517	DD345	936.30072/943.0072	Prussia (Germany)—Historiography
DD176-189	943.03	Counter-Reformation	DD354	355.30943	Prussia (Germany)—History, Military
DD188-.5	943.041	Germany—History—1618-1648	DD358	359.30943	Prussia (Germany)—History, Naval
DD190-.8	943.0(43-52)	Germany—History—1648-1740	DD394-399.8	943.0(41-52)	Prussia (Germany)—History—1640-1740
DD191-199	943.05	Germany—History—18th century	DD394.3	943.044	Fehrbellin, Battle of, 1675
DD197-231	943.0(57-84)	Germany—History—1789-1900	DD399-.8	943.052	Prussia (Germany)—History—Frederick William I, 1713-1740
DD206-214	943.07	Germany—History—1815-1866			

LC	Dewey	Subject Heading	LC	Dewey	Subject Heading
DD401-413.2	943.053	Prussia (Germany)—History—Frederick II, 1740-1786	DF225.3	938.03	Greece—History—Ionian Revolt, 499-494 B.C.
DD406-413.2	943.05(3-7)	Prussia (Germany)—History—1740-1789	DF225.4	938.03	Marathon, Battle of, 490 B.C.
DD407.5	943.054	Dresden, Peace of, 1745	DF227-228	938.04	Greece—History—Athenian supremacy, 479-431 B.C.
DD409-412.8	940.2534	Seven Years' War, 1756-1763	DF229-230	938.05	Greece—History—Peloponnesian War, 431-404 B.C.
DD414-416	943.06	Prussia (Germany)—History—Frederick William II, 1786-1797	DF231-232	938.0(5-6)	Greece—History—Spartan and Theban Supremacies, 404-362 B.C
DD424	940.284	Prussia (Germany)—History—Revolution, 1848-1849	DF231.32	938.05	Greece—History—Expedition of Cyrus, 401 B.C.
DD424-.9	943.07	Prussia (Germany)—History—Frederick William IV, 1840-1861	DF232.5-234.9	938.07	Greece—History—Macedonian Expansion, 359-323 B.C.
DD425-446	943.0(76-83)	Prussia (Germany)—History—William I, 1861-1888	DF233-238	938.0(1-8)	Macedonia—History—To 168 B.C.
DD446-454	943.08(2-8)	Prussia (Germany)—History—1870-	DF233.2	938.0(1-8)	Corinthian League
DD650.M5	943.085	Germany—History—Allied occupation, 1918-1930	DF233.4	938.07	Greece—History—Third Sacred War, 355-346 B.C.
DD801.S31 .S59	943.21	Saxony (Germany)—History	DF234.5	938.07	Gaugamela, Battle of, 331 B.C.
DD851-900	943.155	Berlin (Germany)	DF235.3-.85	938.08	Greece—History—Macedonian Hegemony, 323-281 B.C.
DE	937/938	Classical antiquities	DF236-238.9	938.08	Greece—History—281-146 B.C.
DE	938	Greece			
DE1	93(7/8).005	Classical antiquities—Periodicals	DF236.4	938.08	Greece—History—Galatian Invasion, 279-278 B.C.
DE7	920.093(7/8)	Classical biography	DF236.5	938.08	Greece—History—Chremonidean War, 267-262 B.C.
DE8-9	907.201822	Mediterranean Region—Historiography			
DE15-.5	93(7/8).0071	Classical antiquities—Study and teaching	DF239-241	938.09	Greece—History—146 B.C.-323 A.D.
DE23-31	913.(7-8)	Classical geography	DF261.A2	938.3	Aetolia (Greece)
DE46-61	937/938	Civilization, Classical	DF261.D35	133.32480938	Delphian oracle
DF	938/949.5	Greece	DF261.E65	949.53	Epirus (Greece and Albania)
DF	938	Classical antiquities	DF261.O5	938.8	Olympia (Greece : Ancient sanctuary)
DF10	938.005/ 949.5005	Greece—Periodicals	DF501-649	949.50(13-3)	Byzantine Empire
DF27-30	913.804/ 914.9504	Greece—Description and travel	DF501	949.50(13-3) 005	Byzantine Empire—Periodicals
DF125	133.32480938	Oracles, Greek	DF501.5	949.50(13-3) 006	Byzantine Empire—Congresses
DF135	938.004/ 949.5004	Ethnology—Greece	DF505-.7	949.50(13-3) 0072	Byzantine Empire—Historiography
DF218-238.9	938.0(1-8)	Greece—History—To 146 B.C.	DF505.8-.82	949.50(13-3) 0071	Byzantine Empire—Study and teaching
DF221-.3	938.01	Greece—History—Dorian Invasions, ca. 1125-1025 B.C.	DF506-.5	920.0495	Byzantine Empire—Biography
DF221.5	938.01	Greece—History—Geometric period, ca. 900-700 B.C.	DF506-.5	949.50(13-3) 0099	Emperors—Byzantine Empire
DF222-224	938.01	Greece—History—Age of Tyrants, 7th-6th centuries, B.C.	DF518	914.95	Byzantine Empire—Geography
DF225-226	938.03	Greece—History—Persian Wars, 500-449 B.C.	DF542-.4	949.50(13-3)004	Ethnology—Byzantine Empire
			DF543	355.309495	Byzantine Empire—History, Military

LC	Dewey	Subject Heading	LC	Dewey	Subject Heading
DF544	359.309495	Byzantine Empire—History, Naval	DF721-728	914.9504	Greece—Description and travel
DF550-649	949.50(13-3)	Byzantine Empire—History	DF745-747	949.50(4-9)004	Ethnology—Greece
DF553.5-568	949.5013	Byzantine Empire—History—To 527	DF750-854.32	949.50(4-9)	Greece—History
			DF765	355.309495	Greece—History, Military
DF559	949.501	Adrianople, Battle of, 378	DF801-.9	949.505	Greece—History—1453-1821
DF561	949.5013	Byzantine Empire—History—Arcadius, 395-408	DF802-854.32	949.50(6-76)	Greece—History—1821-
DF562	949.5013	Byzantine Empire—History—Theodosius II, 408-450	DF823-.7	949.5072	Greece—History—Otho I, 1832-1862
DF564	949.5013	Byzantine Empire—History—Leo I, 457-474	DF823.6	949.5072	Greece—History—Acarnanian Revolt, 1836
DF565	949.5013	Byzantine Empire—History—Leo II, 474	DF823.65	940.284	Greece—History—Revolution, 1848
DF566	949.5013	Byzantine Empire—History—Zeno, 474-491	DF823.68	949.5072	Greece—History—Arta Revolt, 1854
DF572-.8	949.5013	Byzantine Empire—History—Justinian I, 527-565	DF825-832	949.5072	Greece—History—George I, 1863-1913
DF573	949.5013	Byzantine Empire—History—Justine II, 565-578	DF831.5	949.5072	Greece—History—Coup d'etat, 1909
DF573.2	949.5013	Byzantine Empire—History—Tiberius II, 578-582	DF837-841	949.5072	Greece—History—Constantine I, 1913-1917
DF573.5	949.5013	Byzantine Empire—History—Maurice, 582-602	DF849.5-.58	949.5074	Greece—History—Civil War, 1944-1949
DF574	949.5013	Byzantine Empire—History—Heraclius, 610-641	DF850-852.5	959.5074	Greece—History—1950-1967
DF575.3	949.5013	Byzantine Empire—History—Constans II, 641-668	DF853-.5	949.5075	Greece—History—1967-1974
DF582	949.502	Byzantine Empire—History—Leo III the Isaurian, 717-741	DF853	949.5075	Greece—History—Coup d'etat, 1967 (April 21)
DF583	949.502	Byzantine Empire—History—Constantine V Copronymus, 741-775	DF853	949.5075	Greece—History—Coup d'etat, 1967 (December 13)
DF586	949.502	Byzantine Empire—History—Irene, 797-802	DF853	949.5075	Greece—History—Coup d'etat, 1973 (May 22-23)
DF589	949.502	Byzantine Empire—History—Basil I, 867-886	DF854-.32	949.5076	Greece—History—1974-
			DF901.C78-.C89	949.59	Crete (Greece)—History
DF592	949.502	Byzantine Empire—History—Leo VI, 886-911	DF901.I57-.I69	949.55	Ionian Islands (Greece)
			DF915-936	949.512	Athens (Greece)
DF594	949.502	Byzantine Empire—History—Romanus II, 959-963	DG	937/945	Italy
			DG	937	Classical antiquities
DF604-649	949.50(3-4)	Byzantine Empire—History—1081-1453	DG11-365	937	Rome
			DG11	937.005	Rome—Periodicals
DF605	949.503	Byzantine Empire—History—Alexius I Comnenus, 1081-1118	DG12.5	937.006	Rome—Congresses
			DG27-31	913.7	Rome—Geography
			DG28-29	388.10937	Roads, Roman
DF606	949.503	Byzantine Empire—History—John II Comnenus, 1118-1143	DG59.D3	937.07	Dacian War, 1st, 101-102
			DG59.D3	937.07	Dacian War, 2nd, 105-106
			DG61-365	937	Rome—History
DF607	949.503	Byzantine Empire—History—Manuel I Comnenus, 1143-1180	DG75-142	937	Rome—Civilization
			DG124	291.2130937	Emperor worship, Rome
			DG124	937.0099	Roman emperors
DF610-629	949.504	Latin Empire, 1204-1261	DG203-204	920.037	Rome—Biography
DF625	949.504	Byzantine Empire—History—Lascarid dynasty, 1208-1259	DG205	937.0072	Rome—Historiography
			DG206.5	937.0071	Rome—Study and teaching
DF638	949.504	Byzantine Empire—History—John V Palaeologus, 1341-1391	DG221-233.9	937.0(1-2)	Rome—History—To 510 B.C.
			DG235-269	937.0(2-5)	Rome—History—Republic, 510-30 B.C.
DF701-854.32	949.50(4-9)	Greece	DG243-244	937.04	Punic War, 1st, 264-241 B.C.
DF701	949.5(4-9)005	Greece—Periodicals			

LC	Dewey	Subject Heading	LC	Dewey	Subject Heading
DG247-249.4	937.04	Punic War, 2nd, 218-201 B.C.	DG315	937.08	Rome—History—Constantine I, the Great, 306-337
DG251	937.04	Macedonian War, 1st, 215-205 B.C.	DG315-317	937.08	Rome—History—Constantines, 306-363
DG251	937.04	Macedonian War, 2nd, 200-196 B.C.	DG330-338	937.06	Rome—History—Theodosians, 379-455
DG251.6	937.04	Macedonian War, 3rd, 171-168 B.C.	DG365	937.09	Rome—History—Romulus Augustulus, 475-476
DG252.6	937.04	Punic War, 3rd, 149-146 B.C.	DG401-583	937/945	Italy
DG252.9	937.05	Rome—History—Servile Wars, 135-71 B.C.	DG401	937.005/945.005	Italy—Periodicals
DG263	937.05	Rome—History—First Triumvirate, 60-53 B.C.	DG413	945.0025	Italy—Directories
DG264	937.05	Gaul—History—Gallic Wars, 58-51 B.C.	DG415	913.7003/914.5003	Italy—Gazetteers
DG266	937.05	Durazzo, Battle of, 48 B.C.	DG421.5-430.2	913.704/914.504	Italy—Description and travel
DG268-269	937.05	Rome—History—Civil War, 43-31 B.C.	DG441-453	937/945.006	Italy—Civilization
DG269	937.05	Actium, Battle of, 31 B.C.	DG455-457	937.004/945.004	Ethnology—Italy
DG269.5-365	937.06	Rome—History—Empire, 30 B.C.-476 A.D.	DG461-583	937/945	Italy—History
DG270-365	937.0099	Emperors—Rome	DG463-.8	920.037/920.045	Italy—Biography
DG279	937.06	Rome—History—Augustus, 30 B.C.-14 A.D.	DG465-.7	937.0072/945.0072	Italy—Historiography
DG282.5	937.07	Rome—History—Tiberius, 14-37	DG465.8	937.001/945.0071	Italy—Study and teaching
DG283	937.07	Rome—History—Caligula, 37-41	DG480-484	355.30945	Italy—History, Military
DG284	937.07	Rome—History—Claudius, 41-54	DG503-514.7	945.01	Italy—History—476-774
DG285	937.07	Rome—History—Nero, 54-68	DG509	945.02	Italy—History—Gothic War, 535-555
DG286	937.07	Rome—History—Civil War, 68-69	DG511-514.7	945.01	Lombards
DG288	937.07	Rome—History—Revolt of Civilis, 69-70	DG515-517	945.02	Italy—History—Carolingian rule, 774-887
DG289	937.07	Rome—History—Vitellius, 69	DG515-519	945.02	Franks
DG290	937.07	Rome—History—Titus, 79-81	DG517.5-518	945.02	Italy—History—Period of the Italian Kings, 887-962
DG291	937.07	Rome—History—Domitian, 81-96	DG520-529	945.0(3-4)	Italy—History—Germanic rule, 962-1268
DG292-299	937.07	Rome—History—Antonines, 96-192	DG530-537.8	945.0(4-5)	Italy—History—1268-1492
DG294	937.07	Parthian War, 113-117	DG538-551.8	945.0(5-84)	Italy—History—1492-1870
DG294	937.07	Rome—History—Trajan, 98-117	DG539-541.8	945.0(6-7)	Italy—History—16th century
			DG541	945.06	Fornovo, Battle of, 1495
DG295	937.07	Rome—History—Hadrian, 117-138	DG546-549	945.0(7-83)	Italy—History—1789-1815
			DG550.5-551.8	945.0(7-8)	Italy—History—1789-1870
DG300-304	937.07	Rome—History—Severans, 193-235	DG551	945.083	Italy—History—Uprising, 1831
DG306	937.07	Rome—History—Maximimus, 235-238	DG552-554.5	945.08(3-4)	Italy—History—1849-1870
			DG554.5.E96	945.083	Expedition of the Thousand, Italy, 1860
DG307.5	937.07	Rome—History—Gallienus, 260-268	DG554.5	945.083	Italy—History—War of 1860-1861
DG310-365	937.06	Rome—History—Empire, 284-476	DG555-569	945.0(84-91)	Italy—History—1870-1915
			DG570-572	945.091	Italy—History—1914-1945
DG314	937.08	Rome—History—Conference of Carnuntum, 308	DG571	945.091	Fascism
			DG571.75	945.091	Italy—History—March on Rome, 1922
			DG572	945.091	Italy—History—Grand Council, 1943
			DG572	945.091	Italy—History—German occupation, 1943-1945

LC	Dewey	Subject Heading	LC	Dewey	Subject Heading
DG572	945.09(1-24)	Italy—History—Allied occupation, 1943-1947	DH431-435	913.6404/ 914.9304	Belgium—Description and travel
DG577.5-579	945.09(1-27)	Italy—History—1945-1976	DH471	936.4/949.3	Belgium—Civilization
DG581-583	945.092(7-9)	Italy—History—1976-	DH491-492	936.4004/ 949.3004	Ethnology—Belgium
DG600-609	945.(1-3)	Italy, Northern			
DG631-645	945.182	Genoa (Italy)	DH513-516	920.0364/ 920.0493	Belgium—Biography
DG651-664.5	945.2	Lombardy (Italy)			
DG670-684.72	945.31	Venice (Italy)	DH540-545	355.309493	Belgium—History, Military
DG691-694	945.6	Italy, Central	DH551	359.309493	Belgium—History, Naval
DG731-759.3	945.5	Tuscany (Italy)	DH571-584	936.4/ 949.30(1-2)	Belgium—History—To 1555
DG737.42	945.05	Medici, House of			
DG791-800	945.6	Papal States	DH584	949.302	Belgium—History—Charles V, 1506-1555
DG796-800	945.6	Papal States—History			
DG803-818	945.632	Rome (Italy)—History	DH585-606	949.302	Belgium—History—1555-1648
DG819-831	945.7	Italy, Southern			
DG845.8-851	945.73	Naples (Kingdom)—History	DH607-619	949.302	Belgium—History—1648-1794
DG861-875	945.8	Sicily (Italy)—History			
DG975.R6	945.18	Riviera (Italy)	DH616-618.5	949.302	Belgium—History—Revolution, 1789-1790
DG987-999	945.85	Malta			
DG989.8-994.8	945.85	Malta—History	DH620-631	949.302	Belgium—History—1794-1814
DH	936.3/949.2	Benelux countries			
DH	936.3/949.2	Netherlands	DH650-665	949.303	Belgium—History—Revolution, 1830-1839
DH1	936.3005/ 949.2005	Netherlands—Periodicals			
DH14	913.63003/ 914.92003	Netherlands—Gazetteers	DH671-676	949.303	Belgium—History—Leopold II, 1865-1909
DH31-40	913.6304/ 914.9204	Netherlands—Description and travel	DH681-685	949.3041	Belgium—History—Albert I, 1909-1934
DH71	936.3/949.2	Netherlands—Civilization	DH682	949.3041	Belgium—History—German occupation, 1914-1918
DH91-92	936.3004/ 949.2004	Ethnology—Netherlands	DH687	949.3042	Belgium—History—German occupation, 1940-1945
DH95-207	936.3/949.2	Netherlands—History	DH690-692	949.304(3-4)	Belgium—History—Baudoiun I, 1951-
DH103	920.0363/ 920.0492	Netherlands—Biography	DH802-809.95	949.332	Brussels (Belgium)
DH113	355.309492	Netherlands—History, Military	DH901-925	949.35	Luxembourg (Luxembourg)
DH121	359.309492	Netherlands—History, Naval	DH901	949.35005	Luxembourg (Luxembourg)—Periodicals
DH141-162	936.3/949.201	Netherlands—History—To 1384	DH903	914.935003	Luxembourg (Luxembourg)—Gazetteers
DH171-177	949.201	Netherlands—History—House of Burgundy, 1384-1477	DH904	920.04935	Luxembourg (Luxembourg)—Biography
DH179-184	949.202	Netherlands—History—House of Habsburg, 1477-1556	DH906-907	914.93504	Luxembourg (Luxembourg)—Description and travel
			DH908-918.5	949.35	Luxembourg (Luxembourg)—History
DH182	949.202	Netherlands—History—Charles V, 1506-1555	DH913	949.3502	Luxembourg (Luxembourg)—History—Siege, 1684
DH185-207	949.20(2-3)	Netherlands—Wars of Independence, 1556-1648	DJ	936.3/949.2	Netherlands
DH199.D4	949.203	Deventer, Surrender of, 1587	DJ1	936.3005/ 949.2005	Netherlands—Periodicals
DH201	949.203	Netherlands—History—Twelve Years' Truce, 1609-1621	DJ14	913.63003/ 914.92003	Netherlands—Gazetteers
			DJ33-41	913.6304/ 914.9204	Netherlands—Description and travel
DH401-811	936.4/949.3	Belgium	DJ71	936.3/949.2	Netherlands—Civilization
DH401	936.4005/ 949.3005	Belgium—Periodicals	DJ91-92	936.3004/ 949.2004	Ethnology—Netherlands
DH414	913.64003/ 914.93003	Belgium—Gazetteers	DJ95-292	936.3/949.2	Netherlands—History
			DJ103-106	920.0363/ 920.0492	Netherlands—Biography

LC	Dewey	Subject Heading	LC	Dewey	Subject Heading
DJ124	355.309492	Netherlands—History, Military	DJK35-36	947.00071	Europe, Eastern—Study and teaching
DJ130-138	359.309492	Netherlands—History, Naval	DJK49	947.000904 (1-4)	Europe, Eastern—History—1918-1945
DJ151-152	936.3/949.201	Netherlands—History—To 1384	DJK50	947.000904 (4-8)	Europe, Eastern—History—1945-1989
DJ151-152	949.202	Netherlands—History—House of Habsburg, 1477-1556	DJK50	947.00090 (44-5)	Europe, Eastern—History—1945-
DJ151-152	949.202	Netherlands—History—Charles V, 1506-1555	DJK51	947.00090 (48-5)	Europe, Eastern—History—1989-
DJ170	949.203	Netherlands—History—Twelve Years' Truce, 1609-1621	DJK61-66	947.7	Black Sea Coast
			DJK71-76	947.79	Carpathian Mountains
DJ180-209	949.204	Netherlands—History—1648-1795	DJK76.2-.8	943.3	Danube River Valley
			DJK77	939.8	Pannonia Region
DJ180-182	949.204	Anglo-Dutch War, 1664-1667	DK1-290.3	947	Russia
			DK1	947.005	Russia—Periodicals
DJ190-191	949.204	Dutch War, 1672-1678	DK2.5	947.006	Russia—Congresses
DJ205-206	949.204	Anglo-Dutch War, 1780-1784	DK14	914.7003	Russia—Gazetteers
			DK19-29	914.7(04)	Russia—Description and travel
DJ211	949.205	Netherlands—History—Batavian Republic, 1795-1806	DK32-.7	947	Russia—Civilization
DJ241	949.205	Netherlands—History—1815-1830	DK33-35	947.004	Ethnology—Russia (Federation)
			DK34.K13	947.52004	Kabardians
DJ241-251	949.206	Netherlands—History—1830-1849	DK34.K14	947.48	Kalmyks
			DK50-54	355.30947	Soviet Union—History, Military
DJ251	949.206	Netherlands—History—William II, 1840-1849	DK55-59	359.00947	Russia—History, Naval
DJ261	949.206	Netherlands—History—William III, 1849-1890	DK65-290.3	947	Russia—History
			DK70-104	947.0(1-42)	Russia—History—To 1533
DJ281-287	949.20(6-71)	Netherlands—History—Wilhelmina, 1898-1948	DK106-107	947.043	Russia—History—Ivan IV, 1533-1584
DJ287	949.2071	Netherlands—History—German occupation, 1940-1945	DK111-112	947.045	Russia—History—Time of Troubles, 1598-1613
DJ288-292	949.207(1-3)	Netherlands—History—1945-	DK112.8-126	947.04(6-9)	Russia—History—1613-1689
DJ288-289	949.2072	Netherlands—History—Juliana, 1948-1980	DK112.8-264.8	947.0(47-83)	Russia—History—1613-1917
DJ290-292	949.2073	Netherlands—History—Beatrix, 1980-	DK116-122.5	947.048	Russia—History—Aleksei Mikhailovich, 1645-1676
DJ401.F5-.F59	949.213	Frisians	DK118.5	947.048	Russia—History—Rebellion of Stenka Razin, 1667-1671
DJ411.A5-59	949.2352	Amsterdam (Netherlands)	DK125	947.049	Russia—History—Sofia Alekseevna, 1682-1689
DJK	947	Europe, Eastern			
DJK1	947.0005	Europe, Eastern—Periodicals	DK128-148	947.05	Russia—History—Peter I, 1689-1725
DJK1.5	947.0006	Europe, Eastern—Congresses	DK133	947.05	Russia—History—Streltsy Revolt, 1698
DJK6	914.70003	Europe, Eastern—Gazetteers	DK168-183	947.063	Russia—History—Catherine II, 1762-1796
DJK11-18	914.704	Europe, Eastern—Description and travel	DK183	947.063	Russia—History—Rebellion of Pugachev, 1773-1775
DJK24	947	Europe, Eastern—Civilization	DK190-201	947.072	Russia—History—Alexander I, 1801-1825
DJK26-28	947.0004	Ethnology—Europe, Eastern	DK188-264.8	947.0(72-83)	Russia—History—1801-1917
DJK31	920.047	Europe, Eastern—Biography	DK212	947.073	Russia—History—December Uprising, 1825
DJK32-34	947.00072	Europe, Eastern—Historiography	DK209-215.97	947.073	Russia—History—Nicholas I, 1825-1855

LC	Dewey	Subject Heading	LC	Dewey	Subject Heading
DK214-215	947.0738	Crimean War, 1853-1856	DK588-609	947.31	Moscow (Russia)
DK219-223	947.081	Russia—History—Alexander II, 1855-1881	DK670-679.5	947.58	Georgia (Republic)
DK234-243	947.082	Russia—History—Alexander III, 1881-1894	DK680-689.5	947.56	Armenia (Republic)
			DK690-699.5	947.54	Azerbaijan
DK251-264.8	947.083	Russia—History—Nicholas II, 1894-1917	DK751-781	957	Siberia (Russia)
			DK845-860	958	Asia, Central
DK263-264.7	947.083	Russia—History—Revolution, 1905-1907	DK901-909.5	958.45	Kazakhstan
			DK911-919.5	958.43	Kyrgyzstan
DK265.19	947.0841	Russia—History—February Revolution, 1917	DK921-929.5	958.6	Tajikistan
			DK931-939.5	958.5	Turkmenistan
DK265-272.7	947.084(1-2)	Soviet Union—History—1917-1936	DK941-949.5	958.7	Uzbekistan
			DK4010-4800	943.8	Poland
DK265-.95	947.0841	Soviet Union—History—Revolution, 1917-1921	DK4010	943.8005	Poland—Periodicals
			DK4018	943.8006	Poland—Congresses
DK265.42.F8	947.0841	Black Sea Mutiny, 1919	DK4030	914.38003	Poland—Gazetteers
DK265.8.R85	947.084	Russia (Federation)—History—Revolution, 1917-1921	DK4047-4081	914.3804	Poland—Description and travel
			DK4110-4115	943.8	Poland—Civilization
DK266-.5	947.0841	Soviet Union—History—Allied interventon, 1918-1920	DK4120-4122	943.8004	Ethnology—Poland
			DK4130-4138.5	920.0438	Poland—Biography
DK266.A2	947.084005	Soviet Union—Periodicals	DK4139-.25	943.80072	Poland—Historiography
DK266.A33	947.0840072	Soviet Union—Historiography	DK4186-4348	943.802	Poland—History—To 1795
			DK4186-4289	943.802(2-3)	Poland—History—To 1572
DK267-273	947.0842	Soviet Union—History—1925-1953	DK4210-.7	943.8022	Poland—History—To 960 (ca.)
DK273	947.0842	Soviet Union—History—1939-1945	DK4211-4249.5	943.8022	Poland—History—Piast period, 960-1386
DK273	947.0842	Soviet Union—History—German occupation, 1941-1944	DK4222	943.8022	Poland—History—Mieszko II, 1025-1034
DK274-282	947.085	Soviet Union—History—1953-1985	DK4223	943.8022	Poland—History—Casimir I, 1040-1058
DK285-290.3	947.0854	Soviet Union—History—1985-1991	DK4227-4246.5	943.8022	Poland—History—1138-1305
			DK4245.7	943.8022	Poland—History—Mongol Invasion, 1241
DK285-290.3	947.086	Soviet Union—History—Attempted coup, 1991	DK4249.7-4289	943.8023	Poland—History—Jagellons, 1386-1572
DK502.3-.7	947.9	Baltic States	DK4276	943.802(3-4)	Poland—History—16th century
DK502.7	947.9	Baltic States—History	DK4289.5-4328	943.802(4-5)	Poland—History—Elective monarchy, 1572-1763
DK503-.95	947.98	Estonia			
DK503.18	914.798003	Estonia—Gazetteers	DK4314.5	943.80(25-3)	Poland—History—18th century
DK503.75-.77	947.98	Estonia—History—1944-1991	DK4328.9-4348	943.8025	Poland—History—Paritition period, 1763-1796
DK503.8-.85	947.9808	Estonia—History—1991-	DK4330-4348	943.8025	Poland—History—Stanislaus II Augustus, 1764-1795
DK504-.95	947.96	Latvia			
DK504.18	914.796003	Latvia—Gazetteers	DK4338-4345	943.8025	Poland—History—Revolution of 1794
DK504.37-.79	947.95	Latvia—History			
DK505-.95	947.93	Lithuania	DK4359-4363	943.8032	Poland—History—Revolution, 1830-1832
DK505.18	914.793003	Lithuania—Gazetteers			
DK507-.95	947.8	Belarus	DK4363.2	943.8032	Poland—History—Partisan Campaign, 1833
DK507.18	914.78003	Belarus—Gazetteers			
DK507.37-.78	947.8	Belarus—History	DK4364	943.8032	Poland—History—Revolution, 1846
DK505.37-.79	947.93	Lithuania—History			
DK508-.95	947.7	Ukraine	DK4366-4378	943.8033	Poland—History—Revolution, 1863-1864
DK508.92-.939	947.77	Kiev (Ukraine)			
DK509.1-.95	947.(6-7)	Bessarabia (Moldova and Ukraine)	DK4379.5-4395	943.8033	Poland—History—1864-1918
DK510-651	947	Russia			
DK511.G44	947.02	Didgora Mountain (Georgia), Battle of, 1121	DK4383-4389	943.8033	Poland—History—Revolution, 1905-1907

LC	Dewey	Subject Heading	LC	Dewey	Subject Heading
DK4390-4395	943.8033	Poland—History—German occupation, 1914-1918	DL179	948.9701	Kalmar, Union of, 1397
DK4394-4395	943.8033	Poland—History—Austrian occupation, 1915-1918	DL182-192.3	948.90(2-3)	Denmark—History—1448-1660
DK4397-4420	943.804(4-53)	Poland—History—1918-1945	DL185-192.8	948.903	Denmark—History—Frederick I, 1523-1533
DK4404-4409	943.804	Poland—History—Wars of 1918-1921	DL186	948.903	Denmark—History—Frederick I, 1523-1533
DK4409.4	943.804	Poland—History—Coup d'etat, 1926	DL187	948.903	Denmark—History—Christian III, 1534-1559
DK4410-4415	943.8053	Poland—History—Occupation, 1939-1945	DL187	948.903	Denmark—History—The Count's War, 1534-1536
DK4429-4442	943.805(4-7)	Poland—History—1945-	DL187	948.903	Denmark—History—Coup d'etat, 1536
DK4442	943.8057	Poland—History—1989-	DL188-.8	948.903	Denmark—History—Frederick II, 1559-1588
DK4443	943.8056	Poland—History—1980-1989	DL189-.5	948.903	Denmark—History—Christian IV, 1588-1648
DK4600.P77	255.7914	Teutonic Knights	DL190	948.9701	Dano-Swedish War, 1643-1645
DK4600.S44	943.85	Silesia, Lower (Poland and Germany)	DL190	948.9701	Fehmarn, Battle of, 1644
DK4600.S46	943.(72/85)	Silesia, Upper (Poland and Czech Republic)—History	DL191.8	948.903	Denmark—History—Frederick III, 1648-1670
DK4610-4645	943.84	Warsaw (Poland)	DL192	948.9701	Dano-Swedish Wars, 1657-1660
DK4650-4685	943.82	Gdansk (Poland)			
DK4700-4735	943.86	Krakow (Poland)	DL192.3	948.903	Denmark—History—Coup d'etat, 1660
DL	936.3/948	Scandinavia			
DL1	936.3005/948.005	Scandinavia—Periodicals	DL195-.8	948.903	Denmark—History—Christian V, 1670-1699
DL1.5	936.3006/948.006	Scandinavia—Congresses	DL196-.8	948.903	Denmark—History—Fredrick IV, 1699-1730
DL4	913.63003/914.8003	Scandinavia—Gazetteers	DL197-199	948.903	Denmark—History—18th century
DL6.7-11.5	913.6304/914.804	Scandinavia—Description and travel	DL199-.8	948.903	Denmark—History—Coup d'etat, 1784
DL30-33	936.3/948	Scandinavia—Civilization	DL201-249	948.90(3-4)	Denmark—History—19th century
DL41-42	936.3004/948.004	Ethnology—Scandinavia	DL205-208	948.90(3-4)	Denmark—History—Frederick VI, 1808-1839
DL43-87	936.3/948	Scandinavia—History	DL206	948.903	Denmark—History—War of 1807-1814
DL61-65	948.03	Scandinavia—History—15th century			
DL65	948.5014	Vikings	DL209-212	948.904	Denmark—History—Christian VIII, 1839-1848
DL83-87	948.08	Scandinavia—History—20th century	DL213-228	948.904	Denmark—History—Frederick VII, 1848-1863
DL75-81	948.04	Scandinavia—History—The Count's War, 1534-1536	DL217-241	948.904	Denmark—History—1849-1866
DL101-291	936.3/948.9	Denmark—History	DL234-249	948.904	Denmark—History—Christian IX, 1863-1906
DL101	936.3005/948.9005	Denmark—Periodicals	DL248-263	948.90(4-7)	Denmark—History—1900-
DL105	913.63003/914.89003	Denmark—Gazetteers	DL255-257	948.905(1-5)	Denmark—History—Christian X, 1912-1947
DL115-120	913.6304/914.8904	Denmark—Description and travel	DL256.5-257	948.9051	Denmark—History—German occupation, 1940-1945
DL131-133	936.3/948.9	Denmark—Civilization			
DL141-142	936.3004/948.9004	Ethnology—Denmark			
DL162-173.8	948.901	Denmark—History—To 1241	DL276	948.913	Copenhagen (Denmark)
DL174-183.9	948.90(1-2)	Denmark—History—1241-1397	DL301-398	949.12	Iceland
			DL301	949.12005	Iceland—Periodicals
DL176	948.9015	Denmark—History—Waldemar IV, 1340-1375	DL304	914.912003	Iceland—Gazetteers
DL179-181.6	948.902	Denmark—History—1397-1448	DL309-315	914.91204	Iceland—Description and travel
			DL331-334	949.12004	Ethnology—Iceland

LC	Dewey	Subject Heading	LC	Dewey	Subject Heading
DL351-380	949.12	Iceland—History	DL660-700.9	936.3/948.501	Sweden—History—To 1397
DL357-360	949.1201	Iceland—History—To 1262	DL689	948.501	Sweden—History—Magnus II Ericksson, 1319-1363
DL375	949.120(4-5)	Iceland—History—1918-1945	DL694	948.5018	Kalmar, Union of, 1397
DL401-596	936.3/948.1	Norway—History	DL696-700.9	948.5018	Sweden—History—1397-1523
DL401-403	936.3005/948.1005	Norway—Periodicals	DL701-879	948.50(2-5)	Sweden—History—1523-1718
DL405	913.63003/914.81003	Norway—Gazetteers	DL703	948.502	Sweden—History—Gustavus I Vasa, 1523-1560
DL415-419.2	913.6304/914.8104	Norway—Description and travel	DL703.8	948.502	Sweden—History—Eric XIV, 1560-1568
DL431-433	936.3/948.1	Norway—Civilization	DL704.6-.7	948.50(2-3)	Sweden—History—17th century
DL441-442	936.3004/948.1004	Ethnology—Norway	DL704.8	948.502	Sweden—History—Charles IX, 1604-1611
DL444	920.0363/920.0481	Norway—Biography	DL705.A2-715	948.502	Sweden—History—Gustavus II, Adolphus, 1611-1632
DL445	936.30072/948.10072	Norway—Historiography	DL710	948.502	Kalmar War, 1611-1613
DL460-478	936.3/948.101	Norway—History—To 1030	DL725.7	948.503	Sweden—History—Charles X Gustavus, 1654-1660
DL480-502	948.101	Norway—History—1030-1397			
DL485-502	948.102	Norway—History—1397-1814	DL727-729	948.503	Sweden—History—Charles XI, 1660-1697
DL485	948.9701	Kalmar, Union of, 1397	DL730-743	948.503	Sweden—History—Charles XII, 1697-1718
DL490	948.102	Norway—History—Frederick III, 1648-1670	DL733-743	947.05	Northern War, 1700-1721
DL490	948.102	Norway—History—Hannibal's War, 1644-1645	DL747-805	948.503	Sweden—History—1718-1814
DL490	948.102	Norway—History—Scottish Expedition, 1612	DL753	948.503	Sweden—History—Ulrika Eleonora, 1718-1720
DL490	948.102	Norway—History—Christian IV, 1588-1648	DL755-759	948.503	Sweden—History—Frederick I, 1720-1751
DL495-.8	948.102	Norway—History—Christian V, 1670-1699	DL757	948.503	Sweden—History—Insurrection, 1743
DL499	948.102	Norway—History—War of 1807-1814	DL766-770	948.503	Sweden—History—Gustavus III, 1771-1792
DL500-502	948.10(2-3)	Norway—History—Christian Frederick, 1814	DL766	948.503	Sweden—History—Revolution, 1772
DL503-526	948.103	Norway—History—1814-1905	DL807-859	948.50(3-4)	Sweden—History—1814-1905
DL525	948.1041	Norway—History—Separation from Sweden, 1905	DL860-879	948.505	Sweden—History—20th century
DL530-532	948.1041	Norway—History—1905-1940	DL867-870	948.505(1-5)	Sweden—History—Gustavus V, 1907-1950
DL532	948.1041	Norway—History—German Occupation, 1940-1945	DL868	948.5051	Sweden—History—Farmers' Demonstration, 1914
DL533	948.104(5-9)	Norway—History—1945-	DL872-876	948.505(5-7)	Sweden—History—Gustavus VI Adolphus, 1950-1973
DL601-991	936.3/948.5	Sweden—History	DL877-879	948.505(7-6)	Sweden—History—Carl XVI Gustav, 1973-
DL601	936.3005/948.5005	Sweden—Periodicals	DL976	948.73	Stockholm (Sweden)
DL605	913.63003/914.85003	Sweden—Gazetteers	DL1002-1180	948.97	Finland
DL614.55-619.5	913.6304/914.8504	Sweden—Description and travel	DL1002	948.97005	Finland—Periodicals
			DL1004	948.97006	Finland—Congresses
DL631-635	936.3/948.5	Sweden—Civilization	DL1007	914.897003	Finland—Gazetteers
DL639-641	936.3004/948.5004	Ethnology—Sweden	DL1015-.4	914.89704	Finland—Description and travel
DL644	920.0363/920.0485	Sweden—Biography			
DL645	936.30072/948.50072	Sweden—Historiography	DL1017	948.97	Finland—Civilization

LC	Dewey	Subject Heading	LC	Dewey	Subject Heading
DL1018-1020	948.97004	Ethnology—Finland	DP184-185.9	946.052	Spain—History—Philip IV, 1621-1665
DL1024	920.04897	Finland—Biography	DP186-189	946.053	Spain—History—Charles II, 1665-1700
DL1025	948.970072	Finland—Historiography	DP192-200.8	946.054	Spain—History—Bourbons, 1700-
DL1050-1052.9	948.9701	Finland—History—To 1523	DP194-200.8	946.054	Spain—History—18th century
DL1055-1141.6	948.9701	Finland—History—1523-1611	DP195	946.055	Spain—History—Louis I, 1724
DL1058-1063	948.9701	Finland—History—Gustavus II Adolphus, 1611-1632	DP196	940.2526	Spanish Succession, War of, 1701-1714
DL1060-.5	948.9701	Finland—History—Charles X Gustavus, 1654-1660	DP198-.7	946.056	Spain—History—Ferdinand VI, 1746-1759
DL1063-.9	948.9701	Finland—History—18th century	DP199-.9	946.057	Spain—History—Charles III, 1759-1788
DL1065-.8	948.9702	Finland—History—1809-1917	DP200-.8	946.058	Spain—History—Charles IV, 1788-1808
DL1066-1141.6	948.970(2-3)	Finland—History—20th century	DP201-232.6	946.0(58-7)	Spain—History—19th century
DL1070-1075	948.97031	Finland—History—Revolution, 1917-1918	DP204-208	940.27	Spain—History—Napoleonic Conquest, 1808-1813
DL1084	948.97031	Finland—History—1918-1939	DP212-220	946.072	Spain—History—Bourbon Restoration, 1814-1868
DL1090-1105	948.9703(2-4)	Finland—History—1939-	DP214-215.9	946.072	Spain—History—Ferdinand VII, 1813-1833
DL1095-1105	948.97032	Russo-Finnish War, 1939-1940	DP215	946.072	Spain—History—Revolution, 1820-1823
DL1175-.95	948.971	Helsinki	DP216-220	946.072	Spain—History—Isabella II, 1833-1868
DP1-402	936.6/946	Spain	DP217	946.072	Spain—History—Revolution, 1854
DP1	936.6005/ 946.005	Spain—Periodicals	DP219-.2	946.072	Spain—History—Carlist War, 1833-1840
DP2	936.6006/ 946.006	Spain—Congresses	DP222-232.6	946.073	Spain—History—Revolutionary period, 1868-1875
DP11	946.0025	Spain—Directories	DP228-231.5	946.07(3-4)	Spain—History—Carlist War, 1873-1876
DP12	913.66003/ 914.6003	Spain—Gazetteers	DP230-231.5	946.073	Spain—History—Republic, 1873-1875
DP27-43.2	913.6604/ 914.604	Spain—Description and travel	DP232-.6	946.074	Spain—History—Alfonso XII, 1875-1885
DP48-.9	936.6/946	Spain—Civilization	DP233-272.4	946.074	Spain—History—Alfonso XIII, 1886-1931
DP52-53	936.6004/ 946.004	Ethnology—Spain	DP247	946.074	Spain—History—Dictatorship, 1923-1930
DP58	920.0366/ 920.046	Spain—Biography	DP250-269.9	946.081	Spain—History—Republic, 1931-1939
DP63-.83	936.60072/ 946.0072	Spain—Historiography	DP250	946.08	Spain—History—Revolution, 1931
DP76-78	355.30946	Spain—History, Military	DP269.A1-.9	946.081	Spain—History—Civil War, 1936-1939
DP80-81	359.30946	Spain—History, Naval	DP270-271	946.082	Spain—History—1939-1975
DP91-96	936.6/946.01	Spain—History—To 711	DP272-.4	946.083	Spain—History—1975-
DP94-95	936.603	Spain—History—Roman period, 218 B.C.-414 A.D.	DP272	946.083	Spain—History—Coup d'etat, 1981
DP96	946.01	Spain—History—Gothic period, 414-711	DP350-374	946.41	Madrid (Spain)
DP97.3-160.8	946.0(2-3)	Spain—History—711-1516	DP501-900	936.6/946.9	Portugal—History
DP115-118	946.82	Granada (Kingdom)—History			
DP161.5-166	946.03	Spain—History—Ferdinand and Isabella, 1479-1516			
DP170-189	946.04	Spain—History—House of Austria, 1516-1700			
DP172-175	946.042	Spain—History—Charles I, 1516-1556			
DP176-181	946.043	Spain—History—Philip II, 1556-1598			
DP182-183.9	946.051	Spain—History—Philip III, 1598-1621			

LC	Dewey	Subject Heading	LC	Dewey	Subject Heading
DP501	936.6005/ 946.9005	Portugal—Periodicals	DP628	946.902	Portugal—History—Revolution, 1640
DP514	913.66003/ 914.69003	Portugal—Gazetteers	DP634-.8	946.9032	Portugal—History—John IV, 1640-1656
DP520-526.5	913.6604/ 914.6904	Portugal—Description and travel	DP635	946.9032	Portugal—History—Alfonso VI, 1656-1683
DP532-.7	936.6/946.9	Portugal—Civilization	DP635	946.9032	Elvas, Linhas de, Battle of, 1659
DP533-534.5	936.6004/ 946.9004	Ethnology—Portugal	DP636-.8	946.9032	Portugal—History—Peter II, 1683-1706
DP536	920.0366/ 920.0469	Portugal—Biography	DP638	946.9032	Portugal—History—John V, 1706-1750
DP536.8-.96	936.60072/ 946.90072	Portugal—Historiography	DP639-641.9	946.9033	Portugal—History—Joseph I, 1750-1777
DP547	355.309469	Portugal—History, Military	DP642-644.9	946.903(3-4)	Portugal—History—Maria I, 1777-1816
DP550-551	359.309469	Portugal—History, Naval			
DP558-618	936.6/946.901	Portugal—History—To 1385	DP650-651	946.903(4-5)	Portugal—History—John VI, 1816-1826
DP570	946.90(1-2)	Portugal—History—Alfonso Henriques, 1139-1185	DP650	946.9034	Portugal—History—Conspiracy of 1817
DP571	946.902	Portugal—History—Sancho I, 1185-1211	DP650	946.9035	Portugal—History—Revolution, 1820
DP572	946.902	Portugal—History—Alfonso II, 1211-1223	DP653-660	946.903(5-6)	Portugal—History—1826-1853
DP573	946.902	Portugal—History—Sancho II, 1223-1248	DP659	946.9035	Portugal—History—Civil War, 1846-1847
DP574	946.902	Portugal—History—Alfonso III, 1248-1279	DP659	946.9035	Portugal—History—Uprising, 1846
DP575-.3	946.902	Portugal—History—Denis, 1279-1325	DP662	946.9036	Portugal—History—Revolution, 1891
DP576	946.902	Portugal—History—Alfonso IV, 1325-1357	DP665-.5	946.9036	Portugal—History—Peter V, 1853-1861
DP577	946.902	Portugal—History—Pedro I, 1357-1367	DP668-669	946.9036	Portugal—History—Charles I, 1889-1908
DP578	946.902	Portugal—History—Fernando, 1367-1383	DP670-682.2	946.904	Portugal—History—20th century
DP580	946.902	Portugal—History—Interregnum, 1383-1385	DP674-682.2	946.9041	Portugal—History—Revolution, 1910
DP582-618	946.902	Portugal—History—Period of discoveries, 1385-1580	DP675-680.5	946.904(1-3)	Portugal—History—1910-1974
DP585-590	946.902	Portugal—History—John I, 1385-1433	DP680	946.9042	Portugal—History—Revolution, 1926
DP592-594	946.902	Portugal—History—Edward, 1433-1438	DP680	946.9044	Portugal—History—1974-
DP596-598	946.902	Portugal—History—Alfonso V, 1438-1481	DP681	946.9044	Portugal—History—Revolution, 1974
DP600-602	946.902	Portugal—History—John II, 1481-1495	DP681	946.9044	Portugal—History—Coup d'etat, 1975
DP604-606	946.902	Portugal—History—Manual, 1495-1521	DP752-776	946.9425	Lisbon (Portugal)
DP608-610	946.902	Portugal—History—John III, 1521-1557	DQ	936.4/949.4	Switzerland—History
			DQ1	936.4005/ 949.4005	Switzerland—Periodicals
DP612-616	946.902	Portugal—History—Sebastian, 1557-1578	DQ2	936.4006/ 949.4006	Switzerland—Congresses
DP614	946.902	Kassr-el-Kebir, Battle of, 1578	DQ14	913.64003/ 914.94003	Switzerland—Gazetteers
DP618	946.902	Portugal—History—Henry I, 1578-1580	DQ20-26	913.6404/ 914.9404	Switzerland—Description and travel
DP620-682.2	946.90(2-4)	Portugal—History—Modern, 1580-	DQ36-39	936.4/949.4	Switzerland—Civilization
DP622-629	946.902	Portugal—History—Spanish dynasty, 1580-1640	DQ48-49	936.4004/ 949.4004	Ethnology—Switzerland

LC	Dewey	Subject Heading	LC	Dewey	Subject Heading
DQ52-.7	920.0364/ 920.0494	Switzerland—Biography	DR51	939.8005/ 949.9005	Bulgaria—Periodicals
DQ52.8-.95	936.40072/ 949.40072	Switzerland—Historiography	DR53	913.98003/ 914.99003	Bulgaria—Gazetteers
DQ59	355.309494	Switzerland—History, Military	DR53.7	949.90025	Bulgaria—Directories
DQ79-84	936.4/ 949.40(1-3)	Switzerland—History—To 1648	DR57-61	913.9804/ 914.9904	Bulgaria—Description and travel
DQ85-87	936.4/949.401	Switzerland—History—To 1032	DR63	939.8/949.9	Bulgaria—Civilization Ethnology—Bulgaria
DQ85-87	949.401	Carolingians	DR64	939.8004/ 949.9004	
DQ88-110	949.40(1-2)	Switzerland—History—1032-1499	DR65-93.34	939.8/949.9	Bulgaria—History
DQ90-91	949.402	Switzerland—History—Perpetual League, 1291	DR66	920.0398/ 920.0499	Bulgaria—Biography
DQ104-118	949.403	Switzerland—History—1499-1648	DR66.7-.97	939.80072/ 949.90072	Bulgaria—Historiography
DQ107.S8	949.403	Dornach, Battle of, 1499	DR70	355.309499	Bulgaria—History, Military
DQ111-123	949.404	Switzerland—History—1648-1798	DR74.3	939.8/949.901	Bulgaria—History—To 681
DQ124	949.40(5-6)	Switzerland—History—19th century	DR74.5	949.9013	Bulgaria—History—681-1018
DQ131-151	949.405	Switzerland—History—Helvetic Republic, 1798-1803	DR79	949.9014	Bulgaria—History—1018-1185
DQ131-151	949.40(4-5)	Switzerland—History—1789-1815	DR82-.5	949.9015	Bulgaria—History—1393-1878
			DR84.9-.8	949.902	Bulgaria—History—1878-1944
DQ154-191	949.40(6-74)	Switzerland—History—1815-	DR80.0 03.34	949.90(2-3)	Bulgaria—History—1944-
DQ154	949.4062	Switzerland—History—1815-1830	DR97	949.99	Sofia (Bulgaria)
DQ156	949.4062	Switzerland—History—1830-1848	DR201-296	939.8/949.8	Romania
			DR201	939.8005/ 949.8005	Romania—Periodicals
DQ158-161	949.4062	Switzerland—History—Sonderbund, 1845-1847	DR204	913.98003/ 914.98003	Romania—Gazetteers
DQ171-210	949.40(63-74)	Switzerland—History—1848-	DR207-210	913.9804/ 914.9804	Romania—Description and travel
DQ201-210	949.407	Switzerland—History—20th century	DR212	939.8/949.8	Romania—Civilization Ethnology—Romania
DQ458	949.451	Geneva (Switzerland)—History—1536-1603	DR213-214	939.8004/ 949.8004	
DQ820-829	949.47	Alps	DR215-267.5	939.8/949.8	Romania—History
DR	949.6	Balkan Peninsula	DR216.7-.92	939.80072/ 949.80072	Romania—Historiography
DR1	949.6005	Balkan Peninsula—Periodicals	DR219	355.309498	Romania—History, Military
DR1.5	949.6006	Balkan Peninsula—Congresses	DR225	359.309498	Romania—History, Naval
DR5	914.96003	Balkan Peninsula—Gazetteers	DR238-241	939.8/ 949.801(3-5)	Romania—History—To 1711
DR11-16	914.9604	Balkan Peninsula—Description and travel	DR241	949.8016	Romania—History—Revolution, 1821
DR22-23	949.6	Balkan Peninsula—Civilization	DR241	949.8015	Romania—History—1711-1821
DR24-27	949.6004	Ethnology—Balkan Peninsula	DR242-250	949.8016	Romania—History—1821-1859
DR32-48.5	949.6	Balkan Peninsula—History	DR244	940.284	Romania—History—Revolution, 1848
DR33	920.0496	Balkan Peninsula—Biography	DR244	949.80(16-2)	Romania—History—1859-1866
DR50-.84	949.61	Thrace	DR248	949.802	Romania—History—War of Independence, 1876-1878
DR51-98	939.8/949.9	Bulgaria	DR250-266	949.802	Romania—History—Charles I, 1866-1914
			DR252-258	949.802	Romania—History—Peasants' Uprising, 1907

LC	Dewey	Subject Heading	LC	Dewey	Subject Heading
DR256	949.802	Romania—History—Peasants' Uprising, 1888	DR542-545	956.1015	Turkey—History—Ahmed III, 1703-1730
DR263	949.802	Romania—History—1914-1918	DR542	956.1015	Turkey—History—Rebellion, 1703
DR264-266	949.802	Romania—History—Uprising, 1941	DR547-548	956.1015	Turkey—History—Mahmud I, 1730-1754
DR267-.5	949.8031	Romania—History—1989-	DR551-553	956.1015	Turkey—History—Mustafa III, 1757-1773
DR267	949.80(2-31)	Romania—History—1944-1989	DR555	956.1015	Turkey—History—Abdul Hamid I, 1774-1789
DR269.5-.6	949.8032	Romania—History—Revolution, 1989	DR559-.5	956.1015	Turkey—History—Selim III, 1789-1807
DR279-280.74	949.84	Transylvania (Romania)	DR562-564	956.1015	Turkey—History—Mahmud II, 1808-1839
DR343	949.71014	Serbia—History—Insurrection, 1804-1813	DR564-573.7	956.1015	Turkey—History—1829-1878
DR343	949.71	Serbia—History	DR565	956.1015	Turkey—History—Tanzimat, 1839-1876
DR414	939.2003/ 956.1003	Turkey—Gazetteers	DR567	956.1015	Crimean War, 1853-1856
DR421-429.4	913.9204/ 915.6104	Turkey—Description and travel	DR573.7-584.5	956.1015	Turkey—History—1878-1909
DR432	939.2/956.1	Turkey—Civilization	DR583-588	956.1015	Turkey—History—Mehmed V, 1909-1918
DR434-435	939.2004/ 956.1004	Ethnology—Turkey	DR583	956.1015	Turkey—History—Revolution, 1909
DR436-603	939.2/956.1	Turkey—History			
DR438.8-.95	939.20072/ 956.10072	Turkey—Historiography	DR589-590	956.10(23-36)	Turkey—History—1918-1960
DR448	355.309561	Turkey—History, Military	DR589	956.1023	Turkey—History—Revolution, 1918-1923
DR451	359.309561	Turkey—History, Naval			
DR481	939.2/ 956.101(3-5)	Turkey—History—To 1453	DR589	956.1023	Turkey—History—Mehmed VI, 1918-1922
DR485-486	956.101(4-5)	Turkey—History—Ottoman Empire, 1288-1918	DR593-603	956.10(36-4)	Turkey—History—1960-
DR493-502	956.101(4-5)	Turkey—History—1288-1453	DR593	956.1036	Turkey—History—Revolution, 1960
DR496	956.1015	Turkey—History—Bayezid I, 1389-1403	DR600	956.1037	Turkey—History—Coup d'etat, 1971
DR496	956.1015	Turkey—History—Invasion of Timur, 1402	DR601	956.1038	Turkey—History—Coup d'etat, 1980
DR501-.7	956.1015	Turkey—History—Mehmed II, 1451-1481	DR701.M13-.M14	949.76	Macedonia—History
DR502-536	956.1015	Turkey—History—1453-1683	DR716-741	949.618	Istanbul (Turkey)—History
DR503	956.1015	Turkey—History—Bayezid II, 1481-1512	DR901-998	939.8/949.65	Albania
			DR901	939.8005/ 949.65005	Albania—Periodicals
DR505-506	956.1015	Turkey—History—Suleyman I, 1520-1566	DR903.5	939.8006/ 949.65006	Albania—Congresses
DR523	956.1015	Turkey—History—Wars with Persia, 1576-1639	DR907	913.98003/ 914.965003	Albania—Gazetteers
DR525	956.1015	Turkey—History—Mehmed III, 1595-1603	DR914-918	913.9804/ 914.96504	Albania—Description and travel
DR529	956.1015	Turkey—History—Murad IV, 1623-1640	DR922	939.8/949.65	Albania—Civilization
DR534-536.5	956.1015	Turkey—History—Mehmed IV, 1648-1687	DR923-925	939.8004/ 949.65004	Ethnology—Albania
DR534.5.D3	956.1015	Dardanelles, Battle of the, 1656	DR927-977.25	939.8/949.65	Albania—History
			DR928-934	920.0398/ 920.04965	Albania—Biography
DR536-562	956.1015	Turkey—History—1683-1829	DR954-960.5	939.8/949.6501	Albania—History—To 1501
DR537	956.1015	Turkey—History—Suleyman II, 1687-1691	DR959-960.5	949.6501	Albania—History—Turkish War, 15th century
DR541.3	956.1015	Turkey—History—Mustafa II, 1695-1703	DR961-969	949.6501	Albania—History—1501-1912

LC	Dewey	Subject Heading	LC	Dewey	Subject Heading
DR965.9-969	949.6501	Albania—History—1840-1912	DR2004.8	949.71013	Serbia—History—Great Emigration, 1690
DR966	949.6501	Albania—History—1878-1912	DR2005	949.71013	Serbia—History—Insurrection, 1788
DR969	949.6502	Albania—History—Uprising, 1912	DR2006-2032	949.7101(4-5)	Serbia—History—1804-1918
DR970-975	949.6502	Albania—History—1912-1944	DR2016	949.71014	Serbia—History—Milos Obrenovic, 1814-1839
DR972	949.6502	Albania—History—Peasant Uprising, 1914-1915	DR2026.8	949.71015	Serbia—History—Revolt, 1883
DR973	949.6502	Albania—History—June Revolution, 1924	DR2033-2047	949.710(2-3)	Serbia—History—1918-
DR975	949.6502	Albania—History—Axis occupation, 1939-1944	DR2033-2040	949.7102	Serbia—History—1918-1945
DR976-977.25	949.650(2-3)	Albania—History—1944-1990	DR2041-2047	949.710(2-3)	Serbia—History—1945-1992
DR976-977.25	949.650(3-4)	Albania—History—1990-	DR2047	949.7103	Serbia—History—1992-
DR1202-2285	939.8/949.7	Yugoslavia	DR2152-2285	949.76	Macedonia
DR1202	939.8005/ 949.7005	Yugoslavia—Periodicals	DR2211	949.98	Macedonia—History—Karpos Uprising, 1689
DR1205	939.8006/ 949.7006	Yugoslavia—Congresses	DS	950	Asia
			DS1	950.05	Asia—Periodicals
DR1209	913.98003/ 914.97003	Yugoslavia—Gazetteers	DS4	915.03	Asia—Gazetteers
			DS5.95-10	915.04	Asia—Description and travel
DR1218-1224	913.9804/ 914.9704	Yugoslavia—Description and travel	DS11	950	Oriental antiquities
			DS13-28	950.04	Ethnology—Asia
DR1228	939.8/949.7	Yugoslavia—Civilization	DS19-23	950.04942	Mongols
DR1229-1230	939.8004/ 949.7004	Ethnology—Yugoslavia	DS22.7	304.82/ 950.04942	Golden Horde
DR1232-1321	939.8/949.7	Yugoslavia—History	DS25	950.04	Hsiung-nu
DR1233-1235	920.0398/ 920.0497	Yugoslavia—Biography	DS25	950.0494387	Tatars
			DS31-35.2	950	Asia—History
DR1239-1243	939.80072/ 949.70072	Yugoslavia—Historiography	DS35-.2	950.4	Asia—History—20th century
DR1250-1251	355.309497	Yugoslavia—History, Military	DS35.2	950.4(2-3)	Asia—History—1945-
DR1252-1253	359.309497	Yugoslavia—History, Naval	DS35.62	909.097671	Civilization, Islamic
DR1281-1312	949.70(2-3)	Yugoslavia—History—1918-1945	DS36-39.2	909.0974927	Arab countries
			DS36.77-.88	909.0974927	Arab countries—Civilization
DR1297-1298	949.7022	Yugoslavia—History—Coup d'etat, 1941	DS36.77-.88	909.0974927	Civilization, Arab
DR1300	949.7023	Yugoslavia—History—1945-1980	DS37-39.2	909.0974927	Arab countries—History
DR1306-1313.8	949.70(24-3)	Yugoslavia—History—1980-1992	DS38	939.4	Middle East—History—To 622
			DS38	320.5409174927	Panarabism
DR1306-1312	949.7103	Yugoslavia—History—1992-	DS38.1	956.013	Dhat al-Sawari, Battle of, 655
DR1352-1485	939.8/949.73	Slovenia			
DR1376-1450	939.8/949.73	Slovenia—History	DS38.5	956.013	Islamic Empire—History—661-750
DR1444-1450	949.7302	Slovenia—History—1945-1990	DS38.6	956.01(3-4)	Islamic Empire—History—750-1258
DR1452-1457.5	949.730(2-3)	Slovenia—History—1990-	DS38.7	956.01(4-5)	Islamic Empire—History—1258-1517
DR1502-1645	939.8/949.72	Croatia			
DR1547-1598	939.8/949.72	Croatia—History	DS38.8	909.09749270 (5-821)	Arab countries—History—1517-1918
DR1652-1785	939.8/949.742	Bosnia and Hercegovina	DS38.9	909.097492708	Arab countries—History—1798-
DR1697-1785	949.742	Bosnia and Hercegovina—History			
DR1802-1928	949.745	Montenegro	DS39	909.09749270821	Arab countries—History—Arab Revolt, 1916-1918
DR1827-1928	949.745	Montenegro—History			
DR1932-2125	949.71	Serbia	DS39	909.0974927082	Arab countries—History—20th century
DR1977-1999.5	949.71013	Serbia—History—To 1456			
DR2000-2005	949.71013	Serbia—History—1456-1804	DS41-66	939.4/956	Middle East

LC	Dewey	Subject Heading	LC	Dewey	Subject Heading
DS43	913.94003/ 915.6003	Middle East—Gazetteers	DS109.913	956.9402	Palestine—History—70-638
DS44.98-49.7	913.9404/ 915.604	Middle East—Description and travel	DS109.913	933.05/ 956.9402	Jews—History—Rebellion, 66-73
DS54.A4-Z	913.93704/ 915.69304	Cyprus—Description and travel	DS109.916-.925	956.9403	Palestine—History—638-1917
DS54.35	939.37/956.93	Cyprus—Civilization	DS109.92-.93	956.940(3-4)	Jews—History—1789-1945
DS54.4-.44	939.37004/ 956.93004	Ethnology—Cyprus	DS109.93	956.9404	Palestine—History—Proposed partition, 1937
DS54.5-.9	939.37/956.93	Cyprus—History	DS109.93	956.9404	Palestine—History—Arab riots, 1920
DS67.8	913.5003/ 915.67003	Iraq—Gazetteers	DS109.93	956.9404	Palestine—History—Partition, 1947
DS69-70.5	935	Iraq—Antiquities	DS110.S3	933/956.953	Samaria Region
DS70.7	935/956.7	Iraq—Civilization	DS112-113	933/956.94	Jews—Civilization
DS70.7	935	Civilization, Assyro-Babylonian	DS113.2-.8	933.004/ 956.94004	Ethnology—Israel
DS70.8	935.004/ 956.7004	Ethnology—Iraq	DS114-128.19	933/956.94	Israel—History
DS70.82-79.66	935/956.7	Iraq—History	DS119.7	956.94054	Entebbe Airport Raid, 1976
DS72	935.01	Sumerians	DS121.4	933.004926/ 956.004926	Canaanites
DS79.72	956.70442	Persian Gulf War, 1991			
DS80.A5	913.944003/ 915.692003	Lebanon—Gazetteers	DS121.55	933.02	Jews—History—1200-953 B.C.
DS80.2	913.94404/ 915.69204	Lebanon—Description and travel	DS121.6	933.03	Jews—History—953-586 B.C.
DS80.3	939.44	Phoenician antiquities	DS121.7-.8	933.0(4-5)/ 956.9402	Jews—History—168 B.C.-135 A.D.
DS80.4	939.44/956.92	Lebanon—Civilization	DS122.8	956.9402	Jerusalem—History—Siege, 70 A.D.
DS80.5	939.44004/ 956.92004	Ethnology—Lebanon	DS122.9	956.9402	Jews—History—Bar Kokhba Rebellion, 132-135
DS80.7-87.53	939.44/956.92	Lebanon—History			
DS81-89	939.44	Phoenicians	DS123.5	956.9402	Jews—History—70-638
DS83	939.44/ 956.9232	Lebanon—History—635-1516	DS125	956.9403	Palestine—History—1799-1917
DS84	956.9203(2-4)	Lebanon—History—1516-1918	DS125.5-126.4	956.9404	Palestine—History—1917-1948
DS87.5	956.92044	Lebanon—History—Civil War, 1975-	DS126-.4	956.9404	Palestine—History—1929-1948
DS87.53	956.92044	Lebanon—History—Israeli intervention, 1982-1984	DS126	956.9404	Palestine—History—Arab riots, 1929
DS92.6	913.943003/ 915.691003	Syria—Gazetteers	DS126	956.9404	Palestine—History—Arab rebellion, 1936-1939
DS94	913.94304/ 915.69104	Syria—Description and travel	DS126.5-126.99	956.94052	Israel—History—1948-1949
DS94.6	939.43/956.91	Syria—Civilization	DS126.5	956.9405	Israel—History—Declaration of Independence, 1948
DS94.7-.8	939.43004/ 956.91004	Ethnology—Syria			
DS94.9-98.3	939.43/956.91	Syria—History	DS126.9-.99	956.042	Israel-Arab War, 1948-1949
DS101-151	933/956.94	Jews—History	DS127-.9	956.046	Israel-Arab War, 1967
DS101-151	933/956.94	Israel	DS128.1-.19	956.048	Israel-Arab War, 1973
DS103-108.5	913.304/ 915.69404	Israel—Description and travel	DS149-151	320.54095694	Zionism
			DS153-154.9	933/956.95	Jordan
DS109-.94	933/956.9442	Jerusalem	DS153.2	913.304/ 915.69504	Jordan—Description and travel
DS109.85-.94	933/956.9442	Jerusalem—History			
DS109.912	933.03	Jews—History—Babylonian captivity, 598-515 B.C.	DS153.4	933/956.95	Jordan—Civilization
			DS153.5-.55	933.004/ 956.95004	Ethnology—Jordan
DS109.912	933.01	Jews—History—To 1200 B.C.			
DS109.912	933.02	Jews—History—To 953 B.C.	DS153.7-154.55	933/956.95	Jordan—History
			DS154.5-.55	956.950(3-44)	Jordan—History—20th century
DS109.912	933.0(3-5)	Jews—History—586 B.C.-70 A.D.			

LC	Dewey	Subject Heading	LC	Dewey	Subject Heading
DS154.55	956.95043	Jordan—History—Intervention, 1958	DS307.5	955.04	Iran—History—War with Great Britain, 1856-1857
DS161-195.5	947.56	Armenia	DS313	955.0(4-51)	Iran—History—1905-1911
DS165	914.75604	Armenia—Description and travel	DS316.2-318.7	955.05(2-3)	Iran—History—Paklavi dynasty, 1925-1979
DS171	947.56	Armenia—Civilization	DS318-.7	955.053	Iran—History—Mohammed Reza Pahlavi, 1941-1979
DS172	947.56004	Ethnology—Armenia			
DS173-195.5	947.56	Armenia—History	DS318.72-.85	955.054	Iran—History—Revolution, 1979
DS181-184	947.56	Armenia—History—To 428			
DS181-184	947.56	Armenia—History—Arsacid (Arshakuni) dynasty, 66-428	DS318.72-.85	955.054	Iran—History—1979-
			DS318.85	955.0542	Iran-Iraq War, 1980-1988
DS186-188	947.56	Armenia—History—428-640	DS327-329.4	939.6/958	Asia, Central
DS186-188	947.56	Armenia—History—Turkic Mongol Domination, 1045-1522	DS351	913.96003/ 915.81003	Afghanistan—Gazetteers
			DS352	913.9604/ 915.8104	Afghanistan—Description and travel
DS186-188	947.56	Armenia—History—428-1522	DS354	939.6/958.1	Afghanistan—Civilization
DS186-188	947.56	Armenia—History—Arab period, 640-885	DS354.5-.6	939.6004/ 958.1004	Ethnology—Afghanistan
DS191-193	947.5607	Armenia—History—1522-1800	DS355-371.2	939.6/958.1	Afghanistan—History
DS194-.5	947.560(7-83)	Armenia—History—1801-1900	DS371.2	958.1045	Afghanistan—History—Soviet occupation, 1979-1989
DS195-.3	947.5608(3-6)	Armenia—History—1901-			
DS195.5	947.560 (83-841)	Armenian massacres, 1915-1920	DS371.3	958.104(5-6)	Afghanistan—History—1989-
			DS376.8	934/ 915.491(003)	Pakistan—Gazetteers
DS195.5	947.560841	Armenia (Republic)—History—Uprising, 1921	DS377	913.4/ 915.491(04)	Pakistan—Description and travel
DS195.5	947.560841	Armenia—History—Revolution, 1917-1920	DS379	934/954.91	Pakistan—Civilization
DS201-248	939.49/953.8	Saudi Arabia	DS380.A1-.A2	934.004/ 954.91004	Ethnology—Pakistan
DS204.5-208	913.94904/ 915.3804	Saudi Arabia—Description and travel	DS381.7-388.2	934/954.91	Pakistan—History
DS215	939.49/953.8	Saudi Arabia—Civilization	DS385.9	954.904	India-Pakistan Conflict, 1947-1949
DS218-219	939.49004/ 953.8004	Ethnology—Saudi Arabia	DS393.3	934.003/ 915.492003	Bangladesh—Gazetteers
DS221-244.63	939.49/953.8	Saudi Arabia—History	DS393.8	934/954.92	Bangladesh—Civilization
DS232	953.8	Ditch, Battle of the, 627	DS393.82-.83	934.004/ 954.92004	Ethnology—Bangladesh
DS234-238	953.80099	Abbasids			
DS234-238	953.80099	Caliphs	DS394.5-395.7	934/954.92	Bangladesh—History
DS251-326	935/955	Iran	DS395.5	954.92051	Bangladesh—History—Revolution, 1971
DS253	913.5003/ 915.5003	Iran—Gazetteers			
DS255-259.2	913.504/ 915.504	Iran—Description and travel	DS421-486.8	934/954	India
			DS421-428.2	934/954	India—Civilization
DS268-269	935.004/ 955.004	Ethnology—Iran	DS422.C3	305.51220954	Caste
			DS423-425	909.097645	Civilization, Hindu
DS270-318.85	935/955	Iran—History	DS425	934.02	Indo-Aryans
DS276	935	Iran—History—To 640	DS430-432.5	934.004/ 954.004	Ethnology—India
DS276	935.06	Iran—History—Macedonian Conquest, 334-325 B.C.	DS432.B4	954.0049144	Bengali (South Asian people)
DS281-284.7	935.05	Achaemenid dynasty, 559-330 B.C.	DS451-.9	934/ 954.0(2-223)	India—History—324 B.C.-1000 A.D.
DS287.8-288.9	955.02	Iran—History—640-1256	DS451.8	954.02	Gurjara-Pratihara dynasty
DS288-290	955.02	Iran—History—640-1500	DS452-462.8	954.02(23-96)	India—History—1000-1765
DS288.95-289.8	955.02	Iran—History—1256-1500	DS457-460	954.02(23-25)	India—History—1000-1526
			DS459.2	954.0234	Khilji dynasty
DS292-297	955.03	Iran—History—16th-18th centuries	DS461-.9	954.025	Mogul Empire
			DS463-480.83	954.0(296-4)	India—History—British occupation, 1765-1947
DS298-316	955.04	Iran—History—Qajar dynasty, 1794-1925	DS473	954.029	Maratha War, 1775-1782

48

LC	Dewey	Subject Heading	LC	Dewey	Subject Heading
DS474.1	954.0311	India—History—Mysore War, 1790-1792	DS538-539	959.1004	Ethnology—Burma
DS475.3	954.0312	India—History—Mysore War, 1799	DS553.3	959.7041	Dong Khe (Vietnam), Battle of, 1950
DS475.5	954.0313	India—History—Mutiny, 1809	DS553.3.D5	959.7042	Dien Bien Phu (Vietnam), Battle of, 1954
DS475.6	954.0313	Maratha War, 1816-1818	DS554.25	915.96003	Cambodia—Gazetteers
DS478-.3	954.0317	India—History—Sepoy Rebellion, 1857-1858	DS554.34-.382	915.9604	Cambodia—Description and travel
DS480.5	954.0357	Massacres—India—Amritsar	DS554.42	959.6	Cambodia—Civilization
			DS554.44-.46	959.6004	Ethnology—Cambodia
DS480.82	954.0359	India—History—Quit India movement, 1942	DS554.5-.842	959.6	Cambodia—-History
DS480.832-481	954.0(4-5)	India—History—1947-	DS554.6-.64	959.603	Cambodia—History—To 800
DS480.85	954.042	Sino-Indian Border Dispute, 1957-	DS554.6-.64	959.603	Cambodia—History—800-1444
DS485.N4	954.0313	Nepalese War, 1814-1816	DS554.6-.64	959.603	Cambodia—History—1444-1863
DS488-490	954.93	Sri Lanka			
DS488.9	915.493003	Sri Lanka—Gazetteers	DS554.7-.73	959.60(3-41)	Cambodia—History—1863-1953
DS489-.15	915.49304	Sri Lanka—Description and travel	DS554.8-.83	959.604	Cambodia—History—1953-1975
DS489.2-.25	954.93004	Ethnology—Sri Lanka	DS554.84-.842	959.6042	Cambodia—History—1975-
DS489.5-490	954.93	Sri Lanka—History	DS554.84	959.6042	Cambodia—History—Civil War, 1970-1975
DS489.6-.63	954.9301	Sri Lanka—History—To 1505	DS555.25	915.94003	Laos—Gazetteers
DS489.7-.73	954.930(1-2)	Sri Lanka—History—1505-1948	DS555.34-.382	915.9404	Laos—Description and travel
DS489.7	954.9302	Sri Lanka—History—Rebellion, 1848	DS555.42	959.4	Laos—Civilization
			DS555.44-.45	959.4004	Ethnology—Laos
DS489.7	954.9302	Sri Lanka—History—Rebellion, 1818	DS555.5-86	959.4	Laos—History
			DS555.84-.86	959.4042	Laos—History—1975-
DS489.8-.86	954.9303	Sri Lanka—History—1948-	DS556-559.916	959.7	Vietnam
DS489.8	954.93031	Sri Lanka—History—Rebellion, 1971	DS556.25	915.97003	Vietnam—Gazetteers
			DS556.34-.39	915.9704	Vietnam—Description and travel
DS493.3	915.496003	Nepal—Gazetteers	DS556.42	959.7	Vietnam—Civilization
DS493.5-.53	915.49604	Nepal—Description and travel	DS556.44-.45	959.7004	Ethnology—Vietnam
DS493.7	954.96	Nepal—Civilization	DS556.6-.63	959.703	Vietnam—History—To 939
DS493.8-.9	954.96004	Ethnology—Nepal	DS556.7-.73	959.703	Vietnam—History—Later Le dynasty, 1428-1787
DS494.4-495.592	954.96	Nepal—History	DS556.8-.83	959.70(3-4)	Vietnam—History—19th century
DS495	954.96	Nepal—History—To 1768			
DS495.3	954.96	Nepal—History—1768-1951	DS556.815	959.703	Vietnam—History—August Revolution, 1945
DS501-519	950	East Asia	DS556.9-.93	959.704(2-44)	Vietnamese reunification question (1954-1976)
DS516-517.9	952.031	Russo-Japanese War, 1904-1905	DS557-559.8	959.7043	Vietnamese Conflict, 1961-1975
DS518.1	950.4(2-3)	East Asia—History—1945-	DS557.8.E23	959.704342	Easter Offensive, 1972
DS524-526.7	959	Asia, Southeastern—History	DS557.8.I	959.704342	Ia Drang Valley (Vietnam), Battle of, 1965
DS527.5-.7	915.9104	Burma—Description and travel	DS557.8.K5	959.704342	Khe Sanh, Battle of, 1968
DS528-.2	959.1004	Ethnology—Burma	DS557.8.S6	959.704342	Sontay Raid, 1970
DS527.2-.3	959.102	Burma—History—To 1824	DS563	915.93003	Thailand—Gazetteers
DS527.9	959.1	Burma—Civilization	DS564-566.2	915.9304	Thailand—Description and travel
DS529.7-530.32	959.10(2-4)	Burma—History—1824-1948	DS568	959.3	Thailand—Civilization
DS530	959.104	Burma—History—Japanese occupation, 1942-1945	DS569-570	959.3004	Ethnology—Thailand
DS530	959.104	Burma—History—Peasant Uprising, 1931	DS570.95-586	959.3	Thailand—History
			DS591.5	915.95003	Malaysia—Gazetteers
DS530.4	959.105	Burma—History—1948-			

LC	Dewey	Subject Heading	LC	Dewey	Subject Heading
DS592.4-.6	915.9504	Malaysia—Description and travel	DS676	959.9027	Philippines—History—Insurrection, 1896-1898
DS594	959.5	Malaysia—Civilization	DS679	959.9031	Philippines—History—Insurrection, 1899-1901
DS595-.2	959.5004	Ethnology—Malaysia			
DS595.8-597.215	959.5	Malaya—History	DS685	959.9032	Dajo, Mount, Battle of, 1906
DS596.6	959.503	Malaya—History—Japanese occupation, 1942-1945	DS686.4	959.9035	Philippines—History—Japanese occupation, 1942-1945
DS597	959.504	Malaya—History—Malayan Emergency, 1948-1960	DS686.5-.6	959.904(1-6)	Philippines—History—1946-1986
DS614	915.98003	Indonesia—Gazetteers			
DS617-620	915.9804	Indonesia—Description and travel	DS686.6	959.9047	Philippines—History—Attempted coup, 1987
DS625	959.8	Indonesia—Civilization	DS686.6	959.9047	Philippines—History—Coup d'etat, 1989
DS631-632	959.8004	Ethnology—Indonesia			
DS633-644.4	959.8	Indonesia—History	DS686.614	959.904(7-8)	Philippines—History—1986-
DS641	959.8012	Indonesia—History—To 1478	DS686.62	959.9047	Philippines—History—Revolution, 1986
DS641.5-642.22	959.80(15-21)	Indonesia—History—1478-1798	DS701-799.9	931/951	China
DS643-.22	959.8022	Indonesia—History—1798-1942	DS705	931.003/915.1003	China—Gazetteers
DS643	959.8022	Indonesia—History—British occupation, 1811-1816	DS707-712	913.104/915.104	China—Description and travel
DS643	959.8022	Indonesia—History Java War, 1825-1830	DS721-727	931/951	China—Civilization
			DS730-731	931.004/951.004	Ethnology—China
DS643	959.8022	Indonesia—History—Achinese War, 1873-1904	DS740.6-.63	950.(3-41)	Eastern question (Far East)
			DS741-747.23	931.0(1-3)	China—History—To 221 B.C.
DS643.5	959.8022	Indonesia—History—Japanese occupation, 1942-1945	DS747.15	931.01	China—History—Spring and Autumn period, 722-481 B.C.
DS644-.1	959.803(5-6)	Indonesia—History—1950-1966	DS747.2	931.01	China—History—Warring States, 403-221 B.C.
DS644	959.8035	Indonesia—History—Revolution, 1945-1949	DS747.28-749.76	931.04/951.01	China—History—221 B.C.-960 A.D.
DS644.32	959.8036	Indonesia—History—Coup d'etat, 1965	DS747.5-.9	931.004	China—History—Ch'in dynasty, 221-207 B.C.
DS644.4	959.8036	Indonesia—History—1966-	DS748-.164	931.04	China—History—Han dynasty, 202 B.C.-220 A.D.
DS650.2	915.955003	Brunei—Gazetteers			
DS650.35	915.95504	Brunei—Description and travel	DS748.17-.76	931.04	China—History—220-589
			DS748.2-.29	931.04	China—History—Three Kingdoms, 220-265
DS650.4	959.55	Brunei—Civilization			
DS650.42-.43	959.55004	Ethnology—Brunei	DS748.4-.44	931.04	China—History—Chin dynasty, 265-419
DS650.44-.83	959.55	Brunei—History			
DS651-689	959.9	Philippines	DS748.45-.48	931.04	China—History—Five Hu and the Sixteen kingdoms, 304-439
DS654	915.99003	Philippines—Gazetteers			
DS658-660	915.9904	Philippines—Description and travel	DS748.5-.76	951.01	China—History—Northern and Southern dynasties, 386-589
DS663-664	959.9	Philippines—Civilization			
DS673.8	959.901	Philippines—History—To 1521	DS748.6-.66	951.015	China—History—Ch'i dynasty, 479-502
DS674-.9	959.90(1-27)	Philippines—History—1521-1898	DS748.6-.66	951.015	China—History—Liang dynasty, 502-557
DS674	959.90(1-2)	Philippines—History—1521-1812	DS748.6-.66	951.015	China—History—Liu Sung dynasty, 420-479
DS675	959.902	Philippines—History—1812-1898	DS748.7-.76	951.01(5-6)	China—History—Ch'en dynasty, 557-589
DS675.5	959.902	Philippines—History—Cavite Mutiny, 1872	DS748.7-.76	951.015	China—History—Northern Chou dynasty, 557-581

LC	Dewey	Subject Heading
DS748.7-.76	951.015	China—History—Northern Ch'i dynasty, 550-577
DS748.7-.76	931.04/ 951.015	China—History—Northern Wei dynasty, 386-534
DS749.46	951.017	China—History—An Lu shan Rebellion, 755-763
DS749.47	951.017	China—History—Huang Ch'ao Rebellion, 874-884
DS749.5-.76	951.0(18-24)	China—History—Five dynasties and the Ten kingdoms, 907-979
DS749.7-.76	951.0(18-24)	China—History—Later Shu kingdom, 934-965
DS749.7-.76	951.0(18-24)	China—History—Southern T'ang kingdom, 937-975
DS749.7-.76	951.018	China—History—Earlier Shu kingdom, 907-925
DS749.7-.76	951.0(18-24)	China—History—Southern Han kingdom, 917-971
DS751.72.-.78	951.0(18-24)	China—History—Liao dynasty, 947-1125
DS751.82-.88	951.024	China—History—Hsi Hsia dynasty, 1038-1227
DS751.92-.98	951.024	China—History—Chin dynasty, 1115-1234
DS753.65	951.026	China—History—Li Tzu ch'eng Rebellion, 1628-1645
DS753.82-773.6	951.03	Manchus
DS756.3-.37	951.033	China—History—White Lotus Rebellion, 1796-1804
DS757.4-.7	951.033	China—History—Opium War, 1840-1842
DS758.7-759.4	951.034	China—History—Taiping Rebellion, 1850-1864
DS759.5	951.03(4-5)	China—History—Nien Rebellion, 1853-1868
DS763.5-773.6	951.03(4-6)	China—History—1861-1912
DS763.65	951.03(4-5)	China—History—Self strengthening movement, 1861-1895
DS764.4-767.6	951.035	Chinese-Japanese War, 1894-1895
DS770-772.3	951.035	China—History—Boxer Rebellion, 1899-1901
DS771.5	951.035	German Expedition to China, 1900-1901
DS773-.6	951.03(5-6)	China—History—Hsuan t'ung, 1908-1912
DS773.32-.6	951.036	China—History—Revolution, 1911-1912
DS773.83-777.544	951.04	China—History—Republic, 1912-1949
DS774	951.0(35-59)	China—History—20th century
DS775	951.042	China—History—December Ninth Movement, 1935
DS775.4	355.30951	China—History, Military—1912-1949
DS776.4-777.46	951.04(1-2)	China—History—1912-1928
DS777.2	951.041	China—History—Revolution, 1913
DS777.25	951.041	China—History—Revolution, 1915-1916
DS777.36	951.04(1-2)	China—History—Warlord period, 1916-1928
DS777.38	951.041	China—History—Ch'ing Dynasty Restoration Attempt, 1917
DS777.43	951.041	China—History—May Fourth movement, 1919
DS777.45	951.041	China—History—May Thirtieth movement, 1925
DS777.462	951.042	China—History—Tsinan Incident, 1928
DS777.47-.514	951.042	China—History—1928-1937
DS777.5132-.5139	951.042	China—History—Long March, 1934-1935
DS777.51393	951.042	China—History—December Ninth Movement, 1935
DS777.514	951.042	China—History—Sian Incident, 1936
DS777.518-.5316	951.042	China—History—1937-1945
DS777.534	951.042	China—History—Southern Anhui Incident, 1941
DS777.535-.544	951.042	China—History—Civil War, 1945-1949
DS777.545-779.29	941.0(5-6)	China—History—1949-
DS777.55	951.05(5-7)	China—History—1949-1976
DS777.65	355.30951	China—History, Military
DS777.7	359.30951090(45-5)	China—History, Naval—1949-
DS778.4	951.055	China—History—Hundred Flowers Campaign, 1956
DS778.5	951.055	China—History—Antirightist Campaign, 1957-1958
DS778.7	951.056	China—History—Cultural Revolution, 1966-1969
DS779.15-.29	951.0(57-6)	China—History—1976-
DS779.32	951.058	China—History—Tiananmen Square Incident, 1989
DS781-784.2	951.8	Manchus
DS781-784.2	951.8	Manchuria (China)
DS798.96	931.003/ 915.1249003	Taiwan—Gazetteers
DS799.15-.24	913.104/ 915.124904	Taiwan—Description and travel
DS799.4	931/951.249	Taiwan—Civilization
DS799.42-.43	931.004/ 951.249004	Ethnology—Taiwan
DS799.64-.66	931/ 951.2490(2-3)	Taiwan—History—To 1895
DS799.69-.72	951.2490(3/4)	Taiwan—History—1895-1945
DS799.69	951.24904	Taiwan—History—Insurrection, 1895
DS799.77-.833	951.24905	Taiwan—History—1945-

LC	Dewey	Subject Heading	LC	Dewey	Subject Heading
DS799.823	951.24905	Taiwan—History—February Twenty Eighth Incident, 1947	DS881.98-884	952.031	Japan—History—Meiji period, 1868-1912
DS799.83-.833	951.24905	Taiwan—History—1975-	DS882.5	952.031	Japan—History—Takehashi Incident, 1878
DS799.834	951.24905	Taiwan—History—Kaohsiung Incident, 1979	DS882.5	952.031	Japan—History—Kioizaka Incident, 1878
DS799.99-.833	931/951.249	Taiwan—History	DS884.5-890.3	952.0(31-49)	Japan—History—20th century
DS801-897	952	Japan			
DS805	915.2003	Japan—Gazetteers	DS885.8-888	952.032	Japan—History—Taisho period, 1912-1926
DS807-811	915.204	Japan—Description and travel	DS888.15-890.3	952.033	Japan—History—Showa period, 1926-1989
DS820.8-827	952	Japan—Civilization	DS888.4-.5	952.033	Japan—History—February Incident, 1936 (February 26)
DS830-832	952.004	Ethnology—Japan			
DS832	952.004946	Ainu	DS888.4-.5	952.033	Japan—History—1926-1945
DS850-856.72	952.01	Japan—History—To 1185			
DS854	952.01	Japan—History—Earlier Nine Years' War, 1051-1062	DS888.5	952.033	Japan—History—March and October Incidents, 1931
DS855-.73	952.01	Japan—History—To 794	DS888.5	952.033	Japan—History—May Incident, 1932 (May 15)
DS855.6	952.01	Japan—History—Taika Reform, 645-710			
DS855.7-.73	952.01	Japan—History—Nara period, 710-794	DS888.84-890.3	952.0(33-5)	Japan—History—1945-
			DS889.16	952.04(4-5)	Japan—History—Allied occupation, 1945-1952
DS855.87-856.72	952.01	Japan—History—Heian period, 794-1185	DS890.3	952.0(48-5)	Japan—History—Heisei period, 1989-
DS856.3	952.01	Japan—History—Later Three Years' War, 1083-1087	DS895.R97	952.29	Ryukyu Islands—History
DS856.75-869.6	952.02(1-4)	Japan—History—1185-1600	DS901.8	915.10003	Korea—Gazetteers
			DS902.2-.4	915.1904	Korea—Description and travel
DS858-861	952.021	Japan—History—Kamakura period, 1185-1333	DS904	951.9	Korea—Civilization
DS861	952.021	Japan—History—Jokyu Revolt, 1221	DS904.5-.7	951.9004	Ethnology—Korea
			DS911-.78	951.901	Korea—History—To 935
DS861	952.021	Japan—History—Attempted Mongol Invasions, 1274-1281	DS912-.43	951.901	Korea—History—Koryo period, 935-1392
DS861	952.021	Japan—History—Genko Incident, 1331-1333	DS912.4-.43	951.901	Korea—History—Mongolian Invasions, 1231-1270
DS863	952.02(1-2)	Japan—History—Kenmu Restoration, 1333-1336	DS913-915.5	951.902	Korea—History—Yi dynasty, 1392-1910
DS863.75-869.6	952.02(2-3)	Japan—History—Muromachi period, 1336-1573	DS913-.45	951.902	Korea—History—Japanese Invasions, 1592-1598
DS868-869.6	952.02(3-4)	Japan—History—Period of civil wars, 1480-1603	DS913.615-.675	951.902	Korea—History—Manchu Invasions, 1627-1637
DS870-881.84	952.02(4-5)	Japan—History—Tokugawa period, 1600-1868	DS915-.5	951.902	Korea—History—1864-1910
DS871.5	952.025	Japan—History—Keicho Peasant Uprising, 1614-1615	DS915.56-922.42	951.90(2-3)	Korea—History—20th century
DS871.5	952.025	Japan—History—Ako Vendetta, 1703	DS916.525-.58	951.903	Korea—History—Japanese occupation, 1910-1945
DS881-.84	952.0(25-31)	Japan—History—19th century	DS916.6-922.42	951.904	Korea—History—1945-
DS881.2-.84	952.0(25-3)	Japan—History—Restoration, 1853-1870	DS917.5-.55	951.9041	Korea—History—Allied occupation, 1945-1948
DS881.4	952.031	Japan—History—Kobe Incident, 1868	DS918-921.8	951.9042	Korean War, 1950-1953
DS881.4	952.025	Japan—History—Sakai Incidnet, 1868	DS918.2	951.904242	Korean War, 1950-1953—Campaigns
			DS918.2	951.904242	Naktong River (Korea), Battle of, 1950
DS881.83-.84	952.025	Japan—History—Civil War, 1868	DS920.2	951.904248	Korean War, 1950-1953—Aerial operations
DS881.85-890.3	952.0(3-5)	Japan—History—1868-	DS920.8-.9	951.90428	Korean War, 1950-1953—Atrocities

LC	Dewey	Subject Heading	LC	Dewey	Subject Heading
DS921-.2	951.90427	Korean War, 1950-1953—Prisoners and prisons	DT106	962.03	Egypt—History—Ismail, 1863-1879
DS921.7	951.90422	Korean Demilitarized Zone (Korea)	DT107-.4	962.0(3-4)	Egypt—History—Tewfik, 1879-1892
DS921.7	951.90422	Korean War, 1950-1953—Armistices	DT107.3-.8	962.0(4-51)	Egypt—History—British occupation, 1882-1936
DS922-.42	951.95	Korea (South)—History—April Revolution, 1960	DT107.8-.87	962.0(4-55)	Egypt—History—1919-
			DT107.8	962.0(4-51)	Egypt—History—Fuad, 1917-1936
DS922.44	951.95	Korea (South)—May Revolution, 1961	DT107.8	962.04	Egypt—History—Insurrection, 1919
DS922.445	951.95	Kwangju Uprising, Kwangju-si, Korea, 1980	DT107.82	962.052	Egypt—History—Revolution, 1952
DS930-937	951.93	Korea (North)	DT107.821-.87	962.05(3-5)	Egypt—History—1952-
DT	960	Africa	DT107.83	962.053	Egypt—History—Intervention, 1956
DT2	916.003	Africa—Gazetteers	DT154.1-159.9	962.4	Sudan
DT6.5-12.25	916.04	Africa—Description and travel	DT154.4	916.24003	Sudan—Gazetteers
DT14	960	Africa—Civilization	DT154.7-.75	916.2404	Sudan—Description and travel
DT15-16	960.04	Ethnology—Africa	DT154.9	962.4	Sudan—Civilization
DT17-39	960	Africa—History	DT155-.2	962.4004	Ethnology—Sudan
DT24-28	960.(1-23)	Africa—History—To 1884	DT155.3-157.67	962.4	Sudan—History
DT25	960.(1-21)	Africa—History—To 1498	DT156-.3	962.40(1-2)	Sudan—History—To 1820
DT29-30.2	960.(23-326)	Africa—History—1884-1960	DT156.4-157.67	962.40(3-4)	Sudan—History—1820-
DT29	960.(23-314)	Africa—History—1884-1918	DT156.6	962.403	Sudan—History—1862-1899
DT30.5	960.3(26-3)	Africa—History—1960-	DT156.6	962.403	Fashoda Crisis, 1898
DT43-154	932/962	Egypt—History	DT156.7-157.67	962.403	Sudan—History—1899-1956
DT45	913.2003/ 916.2003	Egypt—Gazetteers	DT156.7	962.404	Sudan—History—Coup d'etat, 1985
DT49.98-56	913.204/ 916.204	Egypt—Description and travel	DT157.67	962.40(3-4)	Sudan—History—Civil War, 1955-1972
DT63-.5	932.01	Pyramids	DT160-177	939.7/961	Africa, North
DT70	932/962	Egypt—Civilization	DT160-176	939.7/961	Africa, North—History
DT71-72	932.004/ 962.004	Ethnology—Egypt	DT163-165.2	913.9704/ 916.104	Africa, North—Description and travel
DT83-93	932	Egypt—History—To 640 A.D.	DT168-171	939.7	Africa, North—History—To 647
DT83-91	932.0(1-2)	Egypt—History—To 332 B.C.			
DT87-.5	932.014	Egypt—History—Eighteenth dynasty, ca. 1570-1320	DT172	961.0(22-45)	Africa, North—History—647-1517
DT92-93	932.02	Egypt—History—Greco Roman period, 332 B.C.-640 A.D.	DT176	961.0(3-5)	Africa, North—History—1882-
DT92-.7	932.021	Egypt—History—332 - 30 B.C.	DT179.2-.9	939.71/964	Africa, Northwest
DT92-.7	932.021	Alexandrine War, 48-47 B.C.	DT211-239	939.74/961.2	Libya
DT93	932.02(2-3)	Egypt—History—30 B.C.-640 A.D.	DT218-220.2	913.97404/ 916.1204	Libya—Description and travel
DT95-107.4	962.0(2-3)	Egypt—History—640-1882	DT222	939.74/961.2	Libya—Civilization
DT95-.88	962.02	Egypt—History—640-1250	DT223-.2	961.2004	Ethnology—Libya
DT95.8-.88	962.02	Egypt—History—Saladin, 1171-1193	DT223.2-236	939.74/961.2	Libya—History
			DT228	939.74	Libya—History—To 642
DT95.8	962.02	Egypt—History—Invasion of Saint Louis, 1249	DT229	939.74/961.202	Libya—History—642-1551
DT96-.7	962.02	Egypt—History—1250-1517	DT231	961.202	Libya—History—1551-1912
DT97-107.4	962.03	Egypt—History—1517-1882	DT235	961.203	Libya—History—1912-1951
DT100-107.87	962.0(3-55)	Egypt—History—1798-	DT235.5	961.20(3-41)	Libya—History—1951-1969
DT103	962.03	Egypt—French occupation, 1798-1801	DT236	961.2042	Libya—History—1969-
			DT236	961.2042	Libya—History—Coup d'etat, 1969
DT104	962.03	Egypt—History—Mohammed Ali, 1805-1849	DT236	961.2042	Libya—History—Bombardment, 1986

LC	Dewey	Subject Heading	LC	Dewey	Subject Heading
DT241-269	939.73/961.1	Tunisia	DT313.7-325.92	939.71/964	Morocco—History
DT244	913.973003/	Tunisia—Gazetteers	DT318	939.71	Morocco—History—To 647
	916.11003		DT319	964.02	Morocco—History—647-
DT248-250.2	913.97304/	Tunisia—Description and			1516
	916.1104	travel	DT321-323.5	964.02	Morocco—History—1516-
DT252	939.73/961.1	Tunisia—Civilization			1830
DT253-.2	939.73004/	Ethnology—Tunisia	DT322	964.02	Kassr-el-Kabir, Battle of,
	961.1004				1578
DT253.4-264.49	939.73/961.1	Tunisia—History	DT324-325.92	964.0(4-5)	Morocco—History—20th
DT258	939.73	Tunisia—History—To 647			century
DT259	961.102	Tunisia—History—647-1516	DT324	964.0(2-3)	Morocco—History—19th
DT261-263.76	961.103	Tunisia—History—1516-			century
		1881	DT331-346	966	Sahara
DT262	961.103	Tunisia—History—	DT352.65	967.0(1-2)	Africa, Central—History—
		Expedition of Charles V,			To 1884
		1535	DT352.7	967.03(1-25)	Africa, Central—History—
DT262	961.103	Tunisia—History—			1884-1960
		Conquest, 1573	DT363	967.0312	Emin Pasha Relief
DT263.9-264.3	961.104	Tunisia—History—French			Expedition, 1887-1889
		occupation, 1881-1956	DT365-469	967.6	Africa, East
DT264.35-.49	961.105	Tunisia—History—1956-	DT365.5-.8	967.6	Africa, East—History
DT271-299	939.71/965	Algeria	DT365.65	967.601	Africa, East—History—
DT274	913.971003/	Algeria—Gazetteers			To 1886
	916.5003		DT371-398	963	Ethiopia
DT277.8-280.2	913.97104/	Algeria—Description and	DT371.5	916.3003	Ethiopia—Gazetteers
	916.504	travel	DT375-378.3	916.304	Ethiopia—Description and
					travel
DT282	939.71/965	Algeria—Civilization	DT379.5	963	Ethiopia—Civilization
DT283-299	939.71/965	Algeria—History	DT380-.4	963.004	Ethnology—Ethiopia
DT283-.6	939.71004/	Ethnology—Algeria	DT380.5-387.954	963	Ethiopia—History
	965.004		DT383	963.0(1-2)	Ethiopia—History—To 1490
DT288	939.71	Algeria—History—To 647	DT384-386.73	963.0(2-4)	Ethiopia—History—1490-
DT289	965.02	Algeria—History—647-			1889
		1516	DT387-.92	963.0(43-6)	Ethiopia—History—1889-
DT291-292	965.02	Algeria—History—1516-			1974
		1830	DT387.7-.8	963.054	Ethiopia—History—
DT291	965.02	Algeria—History—English			Rebellion, 1928-1930
		expedition, 1620-1621	DT387.9	963.06	Ethiopia—History—Coup
DT291	965.02	Algeria—History—Spanish			d'etat, 1960
		Expedition, 1775	DT401-409	967.73	Somalia
DT291	965.02	Algeria—History—English	DT401.2	916.773003	Somalia—Gazetteers
		Expedition, 1816	DT401.8	916.77304	Somalia—Description and
DT292	965.02	Algeria—History—			travel
		Expedition of Charles V,	DT402.2	967.73	Somalia—Civilization
		1541	DT402.3-.45	967.73004	Ethnology—Somalia
DT294-295.3	965.03	Algeria—History—1830-	DT402.5-407.3	967.73	Somalia—History
		1962	DT407-.3	967.7305	Somalia—History—1960-
DT294	965.03	Algeria—History—French			1991
		Expedition, 1830	DT407	967.73053	Somalia—History—1991-
DT295-.3	965.03	Algeria—History—1945-	DT411-.9	967.71	Djibout
		1962	DT411.15	916.771003	Djibouti—Gazetteers
DT295	965.046	Algeria—History—	DT411.27	916.77104	Djibouti—Description and
		Revolution, 1954-1962			travel
DT295.5-.55	965.05	Algeria—History—1962-	DT411.4	967.71	Djibouti—Civilization
DT301-330	939.71/964	Morocco	DT411.42-.45	967.71004	Ethnology—Djibouti
DT304	913.971003/	Morocco—Gazetteers	DT411.5-.83	967.71	Djibouti—History
	916.4003		DT433.215	916.761003	Uganda—Gazetteers
DT307-310.2	913.97104/	Morocco—Description and	DT433.227	916.76104	Uganda—Description and
	916.404	travel			travel
DT312	939.71/964	Morocco—Civilization	DT433.24	967.61	Uganda—Civilization
DT313-.6	939.71004/	Ethnology—Morocco	DT433.242-.245	967.61004	Ethnology—Uganda
	964.004				

LC	Dewey	Subject Heading	LC	Dewey	Subject Heading
DT433.252-.287	967.61	Uganda—History	DT469.M39	969.8	Mascarene Islands
DT433.265-.267	967.6101	Uganda—History—To 1890	DT469.M415	916.982003	Mauritius—Gazetteers
DT433.27-.273	967.610(1-3)	Uganda—History—1890-1962	DT469.M429	916.98204	Mauritius—Description and travel
DT433.282	967.61042	Uganda—History—1971-1979	DT469.M44	969.82	Mauritius—Civilization
DT433.284-.286	967.6104(2-4)	Uganda—History—1979-	DT469.M442-.M445	969.82004	Ethnology—Mauritius
DT433.515	916.762003	Kenya—Gazetteers	DT469.M45-.M497	969.82	Mauritius—History
DT433.527	916.76204	Kenya—Description and travel	DT469.M465-.M467	969.8201	Mauritius—History—To 1810
DT433.54	967.62	Kenya—Civilization	DT469.R32	916.981003	Reunion—Gazetteers
DT433.542-.545	967.62004	Ethnology—Kenya	DT469.R35	916.98104	Reunion—Description and travel
DT433.552-.584	967.62	Kenya—History	DT469.R37	969.81	Reunion—Civilization
DT433.565-.567	967.6201	Kenya—History—To 1895	DT469.R38-.R39	969.81004	Ethnology—Reunion
DT433.565-.577	967.620(1-3)	Kenya—History—To 1963	DT469.R42-.R458	969.81	Reunion—History
DT433.57-.577	967.6203	Kenya—History—1895-1963	DT469.R44-.R443	969.8102	Reunion—History—To 1764
DT433.58-.584	967.6204	Kenya—History—1963-	DT469.R45-.R453	969.8102	Reunion—History—1764-1946
DT437	916.78003	Tanzania—Gazetteers	DT469.R45	969.8102	Reunion—History—British occupation, 1810-1815
DT439-440.5	916.7804	Tanzania—Description and travel	DT469.R455-.R458	969.8104	Reunion—History—1946-
DT442.5	967.8	Tanzania—Civilization	DT469.S415	916.96003	Seychelles—Gazetteers
DT443-.3	967.8004	Ethnology—Tanzania	DT469.S427	916.9604	Seychelles—Description and travel
DT443.5-448.25	967.8	Tanzania—History	DT469.S44	969.6	Seychelles—Civilization
DT443.5-448.25	967.8	Tanzania—History—To 1964	DT469.S442-.S443	969.6004	Ethnology—Seychelles
DT450.115	916.7571003	Rwanda—Gazetteers	DT469.S452-.S483	969.6	Seychelles—History
DT450.2	916.757104	Rwanda—Description and travel	DT469.S48	969.6	Seychelles—History—Coup d'etat, 1977
DT450.22	967.571	Rwanda—Civilization	DT469.S48	969.6	Seychelles—History—Coup d'etat, 1981
DT450.24-.25	967.571004	Ethnology—Rwanda	DT470-671	966	Africa, West
DT450.26-.437	967.571	Rwanda—History	DT476	966.0(1-2)	Africa, West—History—To 1884
DT450.435	967.57104	Rwanda—History—Civil War, 1994	DT476.2-.23	966.0(23-326)	Africa, West—History—1884-1960
DT450.515	916.7572003	Burundi—Gazetteers	DT476.5-.523	966.03(26-3)	Africa, West—History—1960-
DT450.6	916.757204	Burundi—Description and travel	DT509.27	916.65104	Gambia—Description and travel
DT450.63	967.572	Burundi—Civilization	DT509.4	966.51	Gambia—Civilization
DT450.64-.65	967.572004	Ethnology—Burundi	DT509.42-.45	966.51004	Ethnology—Gambia
DT450.66-.855	967.572	Burundi—History	DT509.5-.83	966.51	Gambia—History
DT463-.3	967.903	Mozambique—History—Revolution, 1964-1975	DT509.8	966.51031	Gambia—History—Coup d'etat, 1981
DT469.M24	916.91003	Madagascar—Gazetteers	DT510.2	916.6704	Ghana—Description and travel
DT469.M274	969.1	Madagascar—Civilization	DT510.4	966.7	Ghana—Civilization
DT469.M276-.M277	969.1004	Ethnology—Madagascar	DT510.42-.43	966.7004	Ethnology—Ghana
DT469.M282-.M345	969.1	Madagascar—History	DT510.5-512.34	966.7	Ghana—History
DT469.M31-.M313	969.101	Madagascar—History—To 1810	DT511-.3	966.70(1-3)	Ghana—History—To 1957
DT469.M32-.M335	969.101	Madagascar—History—Hova rule, 1810-1885	DT511	966.7016	Ghana—History—Portuguese rule, 1469-1637
DT469.M34-.M342	969.10(1-3)	Madagascar—History—1885-1960	DT511	966.701(6-8)	Ghana—History—Danish Settlements, 1659-1850
DT469.M34	969.103	Madagascar—History—French Invasion, 1895	DT512-.34	966.705	Ghana—History—1957-
DT469.M34	969.103	Madagascar—History—Menalamba Rebellion, 1895-1899			
DT469.M34	969.103	Madagascar—History—Revolution, 1947			

LC	Dewey	Subject Heading	LC	Dewey	Subject Heading
DT512	966.705	Ghana—History—Coup d'etat, 1966	DT545.52-.83	966.68	Cote d'Ivoire—History
DT512	966.705	Ghana—History—Coup d'etat, 1972	DT546.115	916.721003	Gabon—Gazetteers
DT512.32	966.705	Ghana—History—Coup d'etat, 1979	DT546.127-.128	916.72104	Gabon—Description and travel
DT512.32	966.705	Ghana—History—Coup d'etat, 1981	DT546.14	967.21	Gabon—Civilization
DT515.15	916.69003	Nigeria—Gazetteers	DT546.142-.145	967.21004	Ethnology—Gabon
DT515.27	916.6904	Nigeria—Description and travel	DT546.15-.183	967.21	Gabon—History
DT515.4	966.9	Nigeria—Civilization	DT546.165	967.2101	Gabon—History—To 1839
DT515.42-.45	966.9004	Ethnology—Nigeria	DT546.165-.175	967.2102	Gabon—History—1839-1960
DT515.53-.84	966.9	Nigeria—History	DT546.18-.183	967.2104	Gabon—History—1960-
DT515.65-.67	966.901	Nigeria—History—To 1851	DT546.215	916.724003	Congo (Brazzaville)—Gazetteers
DT515.7-.72	966.90(1-3)	Nigeria—History—1851-1899	DT546.227	916.72404	Congo (Brazzaville)—Description and travel
DT515.7-.77	966.903	Nigeria—History—1900-1960	DT546.24	967.24	Congo (Brazzaville)—Civilization
DT515.8-.84	966.905	Nigeria—History—1960-	DT546.242-.245	967.24004	Ethnology—Congo (Brazzaville)
DT515.832	966.9051	Nigeria—History—Coup d'etat, 1966 (January 15)	DT546.25-.283	967.24	Congo (Brazzaville)—History
DT515.832	966.9051	Nigeria—History—Coup d'etat, 1966 (July 29)	DT546.265-.275	967.240(1-3)	Congo (Brazzaville)—History—To 1960
DT515.836	966.9052	Nigeria—History—Civil War, 1967-1970	DT546.315	916.741003	Central African Republic—Gazetteers
DT515.84	966.9053	Nigeria—History—Coup d'etat, 1983	DT546.327	916.74104	Central African Republic—Description and travel
DT516.15	916.64003	Sierra Leone—Gazetteers	DT546.34	967.41	Central African Republic—Civilization
DT516.2	916.6404	Sierra Leone—Description and travel	DT546.342-.345	967.41004	Ethnology—Central African Republic
DT516.4	966.4	Sierra Leone—Civlization	DT546.348-.384	967.41	Central African Republic—History
DT516.42-.45	966.4004	Ethnology—Sierra Leone	DT546.365-.37	967.410(1-3)	Central African Republic—History—To 1960
DT516.5-.82	966.4	Sierra Leone—History	DT546.37	967.4103	Kongo Wars, 1928-1931
DT516.65-.72	966.40(1-2)	Sierra Leone—History—To 1896	DT546.375-.384	967.4105	Central African Republic—History—1960-
DT532.12	966.68	Denkyira (Kingdom)	DT546.38	967.4105	Central African Republic—History—Coup d'etat, 1979
DT532.128	966.(3/51)	Fuladu (Kingdom)			
DT532.23	966.(3/51)	Niumi (Kingdom)	DT546.427	916.74304	Chad—Description and travel
DT541.27	916.68304	Benin—Description and travel	DT546.44	967.43	Chad—Civilization
DT541.4	966.83	Benin—Civilization	DT546.422-.445	967.43004	Ethnology—Chad
DT541.42-.45	966.83004	Ethnology—Benin	DT546.457-.483	967.43	Chad—History
DT541.5-.845	966.83	Benin—History	DT546.48-.483	967.4304	Chad—History—1960-
DT541.65-.67	966.8301	Benin—History—To 1894	DT546.48	967.4304(1-4)	Chad—History—Civil War, 1965-
DT541.845	966.83051	Benin—History—Coup d'etat, 1977	DT547.27	916.62604	Niger—Description and travel
DT543.27	916.65204	Guinea—Description and travel	DT547.4	966.26	Niger—Civilization
DT543.4	966.52	Guinea—Civilization	DT547.42-.45	966.26004	Ethnology—Niger
DT543.42-.45	966.52004	Ethnology—Guinea	DT547.5-.83	966.26	Niger—History
DT543.5-.827	966.52	Guinea—History	DT547.65-.75	966.260(1-3)	Niger—History—To 1960
DT543.8	966.5205	Guinea—History—Portuguese Invasion, 1970	DT549.15	916.63003	Senegal—Gazetteers
DT543.822	966.5205	Guinea—History—Coup d'etat, 1984	DT549.27	916.6304	Senegal—Description and travel
DT545.15	916.668003	Cote d'Ivoire—Gazetteers	DT549.4	966.3	Senegal—Civilization
DT545.27	916.66804	Cote d'Ivoire—Description and travel	DT549.42-.45	966.3004	Ethnology—Senegal
DT545.4	966.68	Cote d'Ivoire—Civilization	DT549.47-.83	966.3	Senegal—History
DT545.42-.45	966.68004	Ethnology—Cote d'Ivoire	DT549.7-.73	966.30(1-3)	Senegal—History—To 1960

LC	Dewey	Subject Heading	LC	Dewey	Subject Heading
DT549.8-.83	966.305	Senegal—History—1960-	DT620.4	967.18	Equatorial Guinea—Civilization
DT549.8	966.305	Senegal—History—Coup d'etat, 1962	DT620.42-.45	967.18004	Ethnology—Equatorial Guinea
DT551.15	916.623003	Mali—Gazetteers	DT620.46-.83	967.18	Equatorial Guinea—History
DT551.27	916.62304	Mali—Description and travel	DT623	916.662003	Liberia—Gazetteers
DT551.4	966.23	Mali—Civilization	DT625-627	916.66204	Liberia—Description and travel
DT551.42-.45	966.23004	Ethnology—Mali	DT629	966.62	Liberia—Civilization
DT551.45.S	966.23	Songhai Empire	DT630-.5	966.62004	Ethnology—Liberia
DT551.5-.82	966.23	Mali—History	DT630.8-636.53	966.62	Liberia—History
DT551.8	966.23051	Mali—History—Coup d'etat, 1968	DT633-.3	966.6201	Liberia—History—To 1847
DT554.15	916.61003	Mauritania—Gazetteers	DT634-.3	966.6202	Liberia—History—1847-1944
DT554.27	916.6104	Mauritania—Description and travel	DT635-636	966.620(2-3)	Liberia—History—1944-1971
DT554.4	966.1	Mauritania—Civilization	DT636.2-.4	966.6203	Liberia—History—1971-1980
DT554.42-.45	966.1004	Ethnology—Mauritania			
DT554.52-.83	966.1	Mauritania—History	DT636.5-.53	966.6203	Liberia—History—1980-
DT554.8-.83	966.105	Mauritania—History—1960-	DT636.5	966.6203	Liberia—History—Coup d'etat, 1980
DT555.15	916.625003	Burkina Faso—Gazetteers			
DT555.27	916.62504	Burkina Faso—Description and travel	DT636.5	966.6203	Liberia—History—Civil War, 1989-
DT555.4	966.25	Burkina Faso—Civilization	DT645-647.5	916.75104	Zaire—Description and travel
DT555.42-.45	966.25004	Ethnology—Burkina Faso			
DT555.52-.83	966.25	Burkina Faso—History	DT649	967.51	Zaire—Civilization
DT555.8	966.2505	Burkina Faso—History—Coup d'etat, 1987	DT649.5-650	967.51004	Ethonology—Zaire
			DT650.2-663	967.51	Zaire—History
DT563	916.711003	Cameroon—Gazetteers	DT654-655.2	967.510(1-22)	Zaire—History—To 1908
DT566-568	916.71104	Cameroon—Description and travel	DT657-.2	967.51024	Zaire—History—1908-1960
DT569.5	967.11	Cameroon—Civilization	DT658-.25	967.5103	Zaire—History—1960-
DT570-571	967.11004	Ethnology—Cameroon	DT658	967.51031	Zaire—History—Civil War, 1960-1965
DT572-578.4	967.11	Cameroon—History			
DT578	967.1104	Cameroon—History—Coup d'etat, 1984	DT658.25	967.51033	Zaire—History—Shaba Invasion, 1977
DT582.15	916.681003	Togo—Gazetteers	DT658.25	967.51033	Zaire—History—Shaba Uprising, 1978
DT582.27	916.68104	Togo—Description and travel	DT671.C22	916.65804	Cape Verde—Description and travel
DT582.4	966.81	Togo—Civilization	DT671.C23	966.58	Cape Verde—Civilization
DT582.42-.45	966.81004	Ethnology—Togo	DT671.C242-.C245	966.58004	Ethnology—Cape Verde
DT582.5-.82	966.81	Togo—History			
DT582.75	966.8103	Togo—History—1922-1960	DT671.C25-.C28	966.58	Cape Verde—History
DT613.2	916.65704	Guinea-Bissau—Description and travel	DT671.C265	966.580(1-2)	Cape Verde—History—To 1975
DT613.4	966.57	Guinea-Bissau—Civilization	DT671.C28	966.5803	Cape Verde—History—1975-
DT613.42-.45	966.57004	Ethnology—Guinea-Bissau			
DT613.5-.83	966.57	Guinea-Bissau—History	DT1123	968.0009034	Africa, Southern—History—Mfecane period, 1816-ca. 1840
DT613.78	966.5702	Guinea-Bissau—History—Revolution, 1963-1974			
DT613.8	966.5703	Guinea-Bissau—History—Coup d'etat, 1980	DT1264	916.73003	Angola—Gazetteers
DT615.2	916.71504	Sao Tome and Principe—Description and travel	DT1282-1286	916.7304	Angola—Description and travel
DT615.42-.45	967.15004	Ethnology—Sao Tome and Principe	DT1302	967.3	Angola—Civilization
			DT1304-1308	967.3004	Ethnology—Angola
DT615.5-.8	967.15	Sao Tome and Principe—History	DT1314-1436	967.3	Angola—History
			DT1357-1369	967.301	Angola—History—1482-1648
DT620.15	916.718003	Equatorial Guinea—Gazetteers			
			DT1357	967.301	Angola—History—To 1482
DT620.27	967.1804	Equatorial Guinea—Description and travel	DT1373-1382	967.302	Angola—History—1648-1885

LC	Dewey	Subject Heading	LC	Dewey	Subject Heading
DT1385-1396	967.30(2-3)	Angola—History—1885-1961	DT2554	916.885003	Lesotho—Gazetteers
			DT2572	916.88504	Lesotho—Description and travel
DT1398-1417	967.303	Angola—History—Revolution, 1961-1975			
			DT2582	968.85	Lesotho—Civilization
DT1428	967.304	Angola—History—Civil War, 1975-	DT2592-2596	968.85004	Ethnology—Lesotho
			DT2604-2660	968.85	Lesotho—History
DT1514	916.881003	Namibia—Gazetteers	DT2630-2648	968.850(1-2)	Lesotho—History—To 1966
DT1532-1536	916.88104	Namibia—Description and travel	DT2652-2660	968.8503	Lesotho—History—1966-
			DT2714	916.887003	Swaziland—Gazetteers
DT1552	968.81	Namibia—Civilization	DT2732	916.88704	Swaziland—Description and travel
DT1554-1558	968.81004	Ethnology—Namibia			
DT1564-1648	968.81	Namibia—History	DT2742	968.87	Swaziland—Civilization
DT1587-1601	968.8101	Namibia—History—To 1884	DT2744-2746	968.87004	Ethnology—Swaziland
DT1603-1622	968.8102	Namibia—History—1884-1915	DT2754-2806	968.87	Swaziland—History
			DT2884	916.891003	Zimbabwe—Gazetteers
DT1618	968.8103	Namibia—History—Herero Revolt, 1904-1907	DT2900-2904	916.89104	Zimbabwe—Description and travel
DT1625-1636	968.8103	Namibia—History—1915-1946	DT2908	968.91	Zimbabwe—Civilization
			DT2910-2913	968.91004	Ethnology—Zimbabwe
DT1638-1648	968.8103	Namibia—History—1946-1990	DT2914-3000	968.91	Zimbabwe—History
			DT2959-2979	968.910(2-4)	Zimbabwe—History—1890-1965
DT1648	968.8104	Namibia—History—1990-			
DT1714	916.8003	South Africa—Gazetteers	DT2968	968.9102	Zimbabwe—History—Ndebele Insurrection, 1896
DT1730-1738	916.804	South Africa—Description and travel			
			DT2970	968.9102	Zimbabwe—History—Shona Insurrection, 1896-1897
DT1752	968	South Africa—Civilization			
DT1754-1770	968.004	Ethnology—South Africa	DT2981-2994	968.9104	Zimbabwe—History—1965-1980
DT1760	968.29	Homelands (South Africa)			
DT1772-1969	968	South Africa—History	DT2988	968.9104	Zimbabwe—History—Chimurenga War, 1966-1980
DT1807-1845	968.0(2-42)	South Africa—History—To 1836			
			DT2996-3000	968.9105	Zimbabwe—History—1980-
DT1837	968.0(3-45)	South Africa—History—Frontier Wars, 1811-1878	DT3037	916.894003	Zambia—Gazetteers
			DT3050	916.89404	Zambia—Description and travel
DT1848-1922	968.04(2-9)	South Africa—History—1836-1909			
			DT3052	968.94	Zambia—Civilization
DT1853	968.044	South Africa—History—Great Trek, 1836-1840	DT3054-3058	968.94004	Ethnology—Zambia
			DT3064-3119	968.94	Zambia—History
DT1863	968.045	South Africa—History—Xhosa Cattle-Killing, 1856-1857	DT3079-3089	968.9401	Zambia—History—To 1890
			DT3091-3101	968.9402	Zambia—History—1890-1924
DT1875-1882	968.045	Zulu War, 1879			
DT1888	968.045	South Africa—History—Usutu Uprising, 1888	DT3103-3106	968.9402	Zambia—History—1924-1953
DT1889	968.045	Jameson's Raid, 1895-1896	DT3108-3111	968.940(3-4)	Zambia—History—1953-1964
DT1924-1941	968.0(49-5)	South Africa—History—1906-1961			
			DT3113-3119	968.9404	Zambia—History—1964-
DT1933	968.052	South Africa—History—Rebellion, 1914-1915	DT3169	916.897003	Malawi—Gazetteers
			DT3182	916.89704	Malawi—Description and travel
DT1945-1970	968.06	South Africa—History—1961-			
			DT3187	968.97	Malawi—Civilization
DT1959	968.0627	South Africa—History—Soweto Uprising, 1976	DT3189-3192	968.97004	Ethnology—Malawi
			DT3194-3237	968.97	Malawi—History
DT2434	916.883003	Botswana—Gazetteers	DT3211-3214	968.9701	Malawi—History—To 1891
DT2448	968.8304	Botswana—Description and travel	DT3216-3225	968.9702	Malawi—History—1891-1953
DT2452	968.83	Botswana—Civilization	DT3225	968.9702	Malawi—History—Chilembwe Rebellion, 1915
DT2454-2458	968.83004	Ethnology—Botswana			
DT2464-2502	968.83	Botswana—History	DT3227-3230	968.970(3-4)	Malawi—History—1953-1964
DT2483-2493	968.830(1-2)	Botswana—History—To 1966			
			DT3232-3240	968.9704	Malawi—History—1964-
DT2496-2502	968.8303	Botswana—History—1966-	DT3294	916.79003	Mozambique—Gazetteers

LC	Dewey	Subject Heading	LC	Dewey	Subject Heading
DT3308-3312	916.7904	Mozambique—Description and travel	DU600	996.11	Fiji
DT3320	967.9	Mozambique—Civilization	DU615	996.81	Kiribati
DT3324-3328	967.9004	Ethnology—Mozambique	DU622	919.69003	Hawaii—Gazetteers
DT3330-3398	967.9	Mozambique—History	DU624.5	996.9	Hawaii—Civilization
DT3345-3348	967.901	Mozambique—History—To 1505	DU624.6-.7	996.9004	Ethnology—Hawaii
DT3350-3359	967.90(1-2)	Mozambique—History—1505-1698	DU625-629	996.9	Hawaii—History
			DU640-648	996.7	Mariana Islands
			DU650	996.4	Line Islands
DT3361-3374	967.902	Mozambique—History—1698-1891	DU700-701	996.31	Marquesas Islands
			DU710	996.83	Marshall Islands
DT3376-3387	967.90(2-3)	Mozambique—History—1891-1975	DU720	995.97	New Caledonia
			DU739-747	995	New Guinea
DT3381	967.902	Mozambique—History—War of 1894-1895	DU740	995.3	Papua New Guinea
			DU760	995.95	Vanuatu
DT3389-3398	967.905	Mozambique—History—1975-	DU790	996.81	Phoenix Islands (Kiribati)
			DU800	996.18	Pitcairn Island
DU	995/996	Oceania	DU810-819	996.1(3-4)	Samoan Islands
DU10	919.5003	Oceania—Gazetteers	DU817	996.1(3-4)	Samoan question
DU19-23.5	919.(5-6)04	Oceania—Description and travel	DU819.A1	996.13	American Samoa
DU28.11-66	995-996	Oceania—History	DU819.A2	996.14	Western Samoa
DU90	919.4003	Australia—Gazetteers	DU850	995.93	Solomon Islands
DU97-5-105.2	919.404	Australia—Description and travel	DU870	996.21	Society Islands
DU98.1	994.01	Australia—History—To 1788	DU870	996.211	Tahiti
DU108-117.2	994	Australia—History	DU880	996.12	Tonga
DU114-115.2	994.0(2-3)	Australia—History—1788-1900	DU910	996.15	Tokelau
DU115	994.02	Australia—History—1788-1851	DU920	996.16	Wallis and Futuna Islands
			DX	909.0491497	Gypsies
DU116-117.2	994.0(4-65)	Australia—History—20th century	DX125-127	920.009291497	Gypsies—Biography
DU120-125	994.004	Ethnology—Australia	DX135-145	909.0491497	Gypsies—History
DU405	919.3003	New Zealand—Gazetteers	E	970/980	America
DU409-413	919.304	New Zealand—Description and travel	E11	970.005/980.005	America—Periodicals
DU418	993	New Zealand—Civilization	E14	917.003/918.003	America—Gazetteers
DU419-422	993	New Zealand—History	E16-18.85	970/980	America—History
DU420.12-.14	993.01	New Zealand—History—To 1840	E17	920.07/920.08	America—Biography
DU420.16-.18	993.02(1-2)	New Zealand—History—1840-1876	E31-45	970	North America
			E31	970.005	North America—Periodicals
DU420.16	993.021	New Zealand—History—Maori War, 1845-1847	E35	917.003	North America—Gazetteers
			E36	920.07	North America—Biography
DU420.22-.34	993.022	New Zealand—History—Taranaki War, 1860-1861	E40	970	North America—Civilization
DU420.22-.24	993.0(23-31)	New Zealand—History—1876-1918	E41	917.04	North America—Description and travel
			E45-46	970	North America—History
DU420.26-.28	993.032	New Zealand—History—1918-1945	E51-73	970.00497	Indians
			E58	970.00497	Indians—History
DU420.32-.34	993.03(5-7)	New Zealand—History—1945-	E59.C6	391.08997	Indians—Costume
			E59.F6	398.08997	Indians—Folklore
DU422.5-424.5	993.004	Ethnology—New Zealand	E75-99	973.1	United States—Antiquities
DU490	995	Melanesia	E75-99	973.0497	Indians of North America
DU500	996.5	Micronesia	E78	973.04974	Pueblo Indians—Antiquities
DU510	996	Polynesia	E99.P9	973.04974	Pueblos
DU560-568	996.6	Caroline Islands	E78.I5	973.0497(3/55)	Five Civilized Tribes
DU565-567	996.6	Caroline Islands—History	E78.045	973.0497(3/55)	Five Civilized Tribes
			E81-83.895	973.(1-8)	Indians of North America—Wars
			E81	973.(26-53)	Indians of North America—Wars—1750-1815
			E81	973.(53-82)	Indians of North America—Wars—1815-1875

DT - E

LC	Dewey	Subject Heading	LC	Dewey	Subject Heading
E82	973.(1-26)	Indians of North America—Wars—1600-1750	E99.A12	973.04971	Abitibi Indians
E83.655	973.23	Esopus Indians—Wars, 1655-1660	E99.A13	973.04973	Abnaki Indians
			E99.A349	973.04973	Algonquin Indians
E83.663	973.23	Esopus Indians—Wars, 1663-1664	E99.A35	973.04973	Algonquian Indians
			E99.A6	973.04972	Apache Indians
E83.67	973.24	Falls Fight, 1676	E99.A7	973.04973	Arapaho Indians
E83.72	974-975 + .02	Eastern Indians, Wars with, 1722-1726	E99.C5	973.049755	Cherokee Indians
			E99.C53	973.04973	Cheyenne Indians
E83.77	975.502	Dunmore's Expedition, 1774	E99.C6	973.04973	Ojibwa Indians
E83.775	973.3	Indians of North America—Wars—1775-1783	E99.C85	973.049745	Comanche Indians
			E99.C92	973.049752	Crow Indians
E83.79	973.41	Indians of North America—Wars—1790-1794	E99.D1	973.049752	Dakota Indians
			E99.D1	978.303	Wounded Knee Massacre, S.D., 1890
E83.812	973.52	Indians of North America—Wars—1812-1815	E99.D5	973.049757	Diegueno Indians
E83.813	975.903	Creek War, 1813-1814	E99.E7	973.04971	Eskimos
E83.817	975.03	Seminole War, 1st, 1817-1818	E99.E7	973.04971	Nunamiut Eskimos
			E99.E7	973.04971	Yupik Eskimos
E83.83	973.56	Black Hawk War, 1832	E99.E7	973.04971	Koniagmiut Eskimos
E83.835	973.57	Seminole War, 2nd, 1835-1842	E99.H7	973.049745	Hopi Indians
			E99.I69	973.049755	Iroquoian Indians
E83.84	979.02	Pacific Coast Indians, Wars with, 1847-1865	E99.M12	973.04973	Mahican Indians
			E99.M44	973.04973	Menominee Indians
E83.86	978.02	Dakota Indians—Wars, 1862-1865	E99.M77	973.049757	Mohave Indians
			E99.M8	973.049755	Mohawk Indians
			E99.M83	973.04973	Mohegan Indians
E83.863	973.7	Indians of North America—Wars—1862-1865	E99.M95	973.04973	Muskogean Indians
			E99.N3	973.04972	Navajo Indians
E83.863	978.802	Sand Creek Massacre, Colo., 1864	E99.N5	973.049741	Nez Perce Indians
			E99.O3	973.049752	Oglala Indians
E83.863	973.7	Shoshoni Indians—Wars, 1863-1865	E99.O8	973.049752	Osage Indians
			E99.P244	976.481	Panhandle culture
E83.866	973.81	Indians of North America—Wars—1868-1869	E99.P3	973.04979	Pawnee Indians
			E99.P6	973.049745	Pima Indians
E83.866	973.8(1-7)	Indians of North America—Wars—1866-1895	E99.P9	973.04974	Cliff-dwellers
			E99.P9	973.04974	Pueblo Indians
E83.876	978.602	Little Bighorn, Battle of the, Mont., 1876	E99.S28	973.04973	Seminole Indians
			E99.S35	973.04973	Shawnee Indians
E83.876	978.02	Dakota Indians—Wars, 1876	E99.S39	973.049745	Shoshonean Indians
			E99.S4	973.049745	Shoshoni Indians
E83.89	978.02	Dakota Indians—Wars, 1890-1891	E99.T2	973.049749	Taos Indians
			E99.T34	973.049752	Teton Indians
E83.89	978.3031	Wounded Knee Massacre, S.D., 1890	E99.U8	973.049745	Ute Indians
			E99.Z9	973.04979	Zuni Indians
E98.C8	391.413008997	Moccasins	E101-135	970.01/980.01	America—Discovery and exploration
E98.D2	299.74	Eagle dance			
E98.D2	299.74	Sun dance	E151-887	973	United States
E98.E6	331.125008997	Indians of North America—Employment	E151	973.05	United States—Periodicals
			E154	917.3003	United States—Gazetteers
E98.M7	332.4089973	Wampum	E154.5-.7	973.025	United States—Directories
E98.P6	497	Picture-writing, Indian	E159.5	973.1	United States—Antiquities
E98.P86	394.2608997	Powwows	E160	333.780973	National parks and reserves—United States
E98.P95	155.8497	Indians of North America—Psychology	E161.5-169.04	917.304	United States—Description and travel
E98.R2	299.74	Wolf ritual	E162-168	973	United States—Civilization
E98.R3	299.7	Indians of North America—Religion	E169.1-.12	973	United States—Civilization
			E171-183.9	973	United States—History
E98.S5	419	Sign language	E175-.7	973.072	United States—Historiography
E98.S7	973.0497/ 390.08997	Indians of North America—Social life and customs			
E98.W2	399.08997	Scalping	E176	920.073	United States—Biography

LC	Dewey	Subject Heading
E176.4	321.80420973	Presidents—United States—Mistresses
E179.5	973	United States—Territorial expansion
E181	355.30973	United States—History, Military
E181	355.30973	United States. Army—History
E182	359.30973	United States. Navy—History
E182	359.30973	United States—History, Naval
E184-185.98	973.04	Ethnology—United States
E184-185.98	305.8073	United States—Race relations
E184.A1	305.8073	United States—Ethnic relations
E184.D6	973.04687293073	Dominican Americans
E184.D9	973.043931073	Dutch Americans
E184.E17	973.04917073	East European Americans
E184.E2	973.04914073	East Indian Americans
E184.E95	973.04(2-8)073	European Americans
E184.F4	973.049921073	Filipino Americans
E184.F5	973.0494541073	Finnish Americans
E184.M5	973.046872073	Mexican Americans
E184.S19	973.043981073	Danish Americans
E184.S75	973.0468073	Hispanic Americans
E185.18-.98	973.0496073	Afro-Americans—History
E185.18	973.(1-7)0496073	Afro-Americans—History—To 1863
E185.2	973.(7-82)0496073	Afro-Americans—History—1863-1877
E185.6	973.(83-923)0496073	Afro-Americans—History—1877-1964
E185.61	305.896073	Afro-Americans—Segregation
E185.61	323.1196073	Afro-Americans—Civil rights
E185.615	973.92(3-9)0496073	Afro-Americans—History—1964-
E185.62	306.846	Miscegenation
E185.625	155.8496073	Afro-Americans—Psychology
E185.63	355.3008996073	United States—Armed Forces—Afro-Americans
E185.8	338.790896073	Afro-Americans in business
E185.8	330.9730896073	Afro-Americans—Economic conditions
E185.86	306.850896073	Afro-American families
E185.86	305.2308996073	Afro-American children
E185.86	973.0496073/390.08996073	Afro-Americans—Social life and customs
E185.86	973.0496073	Afro-Americans—Social conditions
E185.96-.97	920.009296073	Afro-Americans—Biography
E186-199	973.(1-2)	United States—History—Colonial period, ca. 1600-1775
E196	973.25	United States—History—King William's War, 1689-1697
E196	974.702	New York (State)—History—King William's War, 1689-1697
E197	973.25	United States—History—Queen Anne's War, 1702-1713
E197	974.403	Massachusetts—History—Queen Anne's War, 1702-1713
E197	974.702	New York (State)—History—Queen Anne's War, 1702-1713
E197	975.702	South Carolina—History—Queen Anne's War, 1702-1713
E198	973.26	United States—History—King George's War, 1744-1748
E198	974.202	New Hampshire—History—King George's War, 1744-1748
E198	974.502	Rhode Island—History—King George's War, 1744-1748
E198	974.402	Massachusetts—History—King George's War, 1744-1748
E199	973.26	United States—History—French and Indian War, 1755-1763
E199	973.26	Fort William Henry (N.Y.)—Capture, 1757
E199	973.26	Forbes Expedition against Fort Duquesne, 1758
E199	973.26	Ticonderoga, Battle of, 1758
E199	973.26	Fort Oswego (Oswego, N.Y.)—Capture, 1756
E199	973.26	Necessity, Fort, Battle of, 1754
E199	974.402	Massachusetts—History—French and Indian War, 1755-1763
E199	974.02	New England—History—French and Indian War, 1755-1763
E201-298	973.3	United States—History—Revolution, 1775-1783
E215.3	973.3112	Non-importation agreements, 1768-1769
E215.4	973.3113	Boston Massacre, 1770
E215.7	973.3115	Tea tax (American colonies)
E215.7	973.3115	Boston Tea Party, 1773
E230-241	973.33	United States—History—Revolution, 1775-1783—Campaigns
E231	973.33(1-2)	Canadian Invasion, 1775-1776
E231	394.26973	Patriots' Day
E235	973.335	Sullivan's Indian Campaign, 1779

LC	Dewey	Subject Heading	LC	Dewey	Subject Heading
E239	973.339	Evacuation Day, Nov. 25, 1783	E312.6	394.26973	Washington's Birthday
E241.B9	973.3312	Bunker Hill, Battle of, 1775	E315	973.43	Whiskey Rebellion, Pa., 1794
E241.C7	973.3311	Concord, Battle of, 1775	E326	973.44	Fries Rebellion, 1798-1799
E241.E	973.337	Eutaw Springs, Battle of, 1781	E328	973.44	Kentucky and Virginia resolutions of 1798
E241.G9	973.337	Guilford Court House, Battle of 1781	E333	973.46	Louisiana Purchase
E241.K48	973.335	Kettle Creek (Ga.), Battle of, 1779	E334	973.48	Burr Conspiracy, 1805-1807
E241.L6	973.3311	Lexington, Battle of, 1775	E335	973.47	United States—History—Tripolitan War, 1801-1805
E241.M7	973.334	Monmouth, Battle of, 1778	E336.5	973.48	Embargo, 1807-1809
E241.P2	973.333	Paoli Massacre, 1777	E331-337	973.4(6-8)	United States—History—1801-1809
E259	973.34(4-5)	United States. Continental Army—History	E338	973.(51-68)	United States—History—1815-1861
E263.D3	975.210(2-3)	Delmarva Peninsula—History—Revolution, 1775-1783	E341-370	973.5(1-4)	United States—History—1809-1817
E263.D3	975.10(2-3)	Delaware—History—Revolution, 1775-1783	E351-364.9	973.52	United States—History—War of 1812
E263.G3	975.80(2-3)	Georgia—History—Revolution, 1775-1783	E356.B2	973.523	Baltimore, Battle of, 1814
E263.L	976.30(2-3)	Louisiana—History—Revolution, 1775-1783	E356.B5	973.523	Bladensburg, Battle of, 1814
E263.M3	975.20(2-3)	Maryland—History—Revolution, 1775-1783	E356.D4	973.523	Detroit (Mich.)—Surrender to the British, 1812
E263.M4	974.40(2-3)	Massachusetts—History—Revolution, 1775-1783	E356.D8	973.523	Dudley's Defeat, 1813
			E356.E6	973.5254	Erie, Lake, Battle of, 1813
E263.N4	974.20(2-3)	New Hampshire—History—Revolution, 1775-1783	E356.N5	973.5239	New Orleans (La.), Battle of, 1815
E263.N5	974.90(2-3)	New Jersey—History—Revolution, 1775-1783	E356.W3	975.302	Washington (D.C.)—History—Capture by the British, 1814
E263.N6	974.70(2-3)	New York (State)—History—Revolution, 1775-1783	E357-359	974.03	New England—History—War of 1812
E263.N8	975.70(2-3)	North Carolina—History—Revolution, 1775-1783	E357.2-.3	973.525	Impressment
E263.O	977.102	Ohio—History—Revolution, 1775-1783	E359.5.D3	975.103	Delaware—History—War of 1812
E263.R4	974.50(2-3)	Rhode Island—History—Revolution, 1775-1783	E359.5.G4	975.803	Georgia—History—War of 1812
E263.S7	975.70(2-3)	South Carolina—History—Revolution, 1775-1783	E359.5.L8	976.304	Louisiana—History—War of 1812
E263.V5	974.30(2-3)	Vermont—History—Revolution, 1775-1783	E359.5.M2	975.203	Maryland—History—War of 1812
E263.V8	975.50(2-3)	Virginia—History—Revolution, 1775-1783	E359.5.M3	974.403	Massachusetts—History—War of 1812
E263.W5	972.9722	Virgin Islands of the United States—History—1775-1783	E359.5.N6	974.703	New York (State)—History—War of 1812
E263.W5	972.9722	Virgin Islands of the United States—History—1775-1793	E359.5.O2	977.103	Ohio—History—War of 1812
			E359.5.V3	974.303	Vermont—History—War of 1812
E271	973.35	Dominica, Battle of, 1782	E359.5.V8	975.503	Virginia—History—War of 1812
E277	973.343	American loyalists	E365	973.53	United States—History—War with Algeria, 1815
E301-655	973.3	United States—History—1783-1865	E371-375	973.54	United States—History—1817-1825
E303-309	973.318	United States—History—Confederation, 1783-1789	E373	973.7113	Missouri compromise
E310-337	973.4	United States—History—Constitutional period, 1789-1809	E376-380	973.55	United States—History—1825-1829
			E384.3	973.561	Nullification
			E401-415.2	973.62	Mexican War, 1846-1848

LC	Dewey	Subject Heading
E405.2	973.623	Doniphan's Expedition, 1846-1847
E405.2	973.623	Kearny's Expedition, 1846
E406.M7	973.623	Monterrey (Mexico), Battle of, 1846
E415.6-680	973.(63-82)	United States—History—1849-1877
E415.7	973.711	Squatter sovereignty
E423	973.(64/7113)	Compromise of 1850
E441-453	973.711	Slavery
E450	973.7115	Underground railroad
E456-655	973.7	United States—History—Civil War, 1861-1865
E456-459	973.7	Lincoln, Abraham, 1809-1865
E458-459	973.713	Secession—Southern States
E470.2	973.742	Confederate States of America—History, Military
E470.9	978	West (U.S.)—History—Civil War, 1861-1865
E471.1	975.703	South Carolina—History—Civil War, 1861-1865
E472.18	973.731	Bull Run, 1st Battle of, Va., 1861
E472.96	973.731	Fort Henry (Tenn.), Battle of, 1862
E473.2	973.752	Hampton Roads (Va.), Battle of, 1862
E473.54	973.731	Shiloh, Battle of, 1862
E473.6-.68	973.73(1-2)	Peninsular Campaign, 1862
E473.68	973.732	Seven Days' Battles, 1862
E473.7	973.732	Shenandoah Valley Campaign, 1862
E473.77	973.732	Bull Run, 2nd Battle of, Va., 1862
E474.61	973.7336	Maryland Campaign, 1862
E474.65	973.73(2-3)	Antietam, Battle of, Md., 1862
E474.85	973.733	Fredericksburg (Va.), Battle of, 1862
E475.3	973.734	Kelly's Ford (Va.), Battle of, 1863
E475.35	973.733	Chancellorsville (Va.), Battle of, 1863
E475.53	973.7349	Gettysburg (Pa.), Battle of, 1863
E476.52	973.736	Spotsylvania Court House, Battle of, Va., 1864
E476.65	973.736	Lynchburg (Va.), Battle of, 1864
E476.66	973.736	Maryland Campaign, 1864
E476.66	973.73(6-7)	Shenandoah Valley Campaign, 1864 (May-August)
E476.69	973.7378	Sherman's March to the Sea
E476.7	973.7371	Atlanta Campaign, 1864
E476.85	973.75	Mobile Bay (Ala.), Battle of, 1864

LC	Dewey	Subject Heading
E477.21	973.737	Fort Harrison (Va), Battle of, 1864
E477.33	973.737	Shenandoah Valley Campaign, 1864 (August-November)
E477.65	973.738	Shenandoah Valley Campaign, 1865
E477.67	973.738	Dinwiddie Court House, Battle of, Dinwiddie, Va., 1865
E477.67	973.738	Appomattox Campaign, 1865
E482-489	973.713/975	Confederate States of America
E487-488	973.713/975	Confederate States of America—History
E487	973.713/975	Confederate States of America—Social conditions
E500	975.103	Delaware—History—Civil War, 1861-1865
E503	975.803	Georgia—History—Civil War, 1861-1865
E507	977.702	Iowa—History—Civil War, 1861-1865
E508	978.1031	Kansas—History—Civil War, 1861-1865
E510	976.305	Louisiana—History—Civil War, 1861-1865
E513	974.403	Massachusetts—History—Civil War, 1861-1865
E516	976.205	Mississippi—History—Civil War, 1861-1865
E517	977.803	Missouri—History—Civil War, 1861-1865
E520	974.203	New Hampshire—History—Civil War, 1861-1865
E521	974.903	New Jersey—History—Civil War, 1861-1865
E522	978.904	New Mexico—History—Civil War, 1861-1865
E524	975.603	North Carolina—History—Civil War, 1861-1865
E525	977.103	Ohio—History—Civil War, 1861-1865
E528	974.503	Rhode Island—History—Civil War, 1861-1865
E529	975.703	South Carolina—History—Civil War, 1861-1865
E531	976.804	Tennessee—History—Civil War, 1861-1865
E532	976.405	Texas—History—Civil War, 1861-1865
E532.95	979.202	Utah—History—Civil War, 1861-1865
E533	974.303	Vermont—History—Civil War, 1861-1865
E534	975.503	Virginia—History—Civil War, 1861-1865
E536	975.403	West Virginia—History—Civil War, 1861-1865

LC	Dewey	Subject Heading	LC	Dewey	Subject Heading
E537	977.503	Wisconsin—History—Civil War, 1861-1865	E835-837.7	973.921	United States—History—1953-1961
E545	973.742	Confederate States of America—History, Military	E838-851	973.92(2-3)	United States—History—1961-1969
E558.1-.9	975.905	Florida—History—Civil War, 1861-1865	E860	973.924	Watergate Affair, 1972-1974
E559	975.803	Georgia—History—Civil War, 1861-1865	E865	973.925	Mayaguez Incident, 1975
			F	970-989	America—History
E565	976.305	Louisiana—History—Civil War, 1861-1865	F1-15	974	New England—History
			F1	974.005	New England—Periodicals
E568	976.205	Mississippi—History—Civil War, 1861-1865	F2	917.4003	New England—Gazetteers
E569	977.803	Missouri—History—Civil War, 1861-1865	F7-.75	974.0(1-2)	New England—History—Colonial period, ca. 1600-1775
E571	978.904	New Mexico—History—Civil War, 1861-1865	F7	974.02008825	Puritans
E573	975.603	North Carolina—History—Civil War, 1861-1865	F8	974.0(2-3)	New England—History—1775-1865
E577	975.703	South Carolina—History—Civil War, 1861-1865	F8	974.0(2-3)	New England—History—Revolution, 1775-1783
E579	976.804	Tennessee—History—Civil War, 1861-1865	F16-30	974.1	Maine—History
			F16	974.1005	Maine—Periodicals
E580	976.405	Texas—History—Civil War, 1861-1865	F17	917.41003	Maine—Gazetteers
E581	975.503	Virginia—History—Civil War, 1861-1865	F23	974.10(1-2)	Maine—History—Colonial period, ca. 1600-1775
E582	975.403	West Virginia—History—Civil War, 1861-1865	F23	974.102	Maine—History—King William's War, 1689-1697
			F23	974.102	Maine—History—King George's War, 1744-1748
E591-600	359.30975	Confederate States of America—History, Naval	F24	974.10(1-3)	Maine—History—1775-1865
E591-600	359.30975	Confederate States of America. Navy—History	F24	974.103	Maine—History—War of 1812
E611-612	973.771	Confederate States of America. Army—Prisons	F31-45	974.2	New Hampshire—History
E642	394.26973	Memorial Day	F31	974.2005	New Hampshire—Periodicals
E645	394.26975	Confederate Memorial Day	F32	917.42003	New Hampshire—Gazetteers
E660-887	973.(8-9)	United States—History—1865-	F37	974.20(1-2)	New Hampshire—History—Colonial period, ca. 1600-1775
E660-783	973.(8-913)	United States—History—1865-1921			
E660-735	973.8(1-8)	United States—History—1865-1898	F38	974.203	New Hampshire—History—1775-1865
E671-680	973.(63-82)	United States—History—1849-1877	F40	974.2043	New Hampshire—History—1951-
E717.1	973.893	El Caney, Battle of, 1898	F46-60	974.3	Vermont—History
			F46	974.3005	Vermont—Periodicals
E717.7	973.895	Manila Bay, Battle of, 1898	F47	917.43003	Vermont—Gazetteers
E740-887	973.91	United States—History—20th century	F52	974.303	Vermont—History—To 1791
			F61-75	974.4	Massachusetts—History
E740-760	973.911	United States—History—1901-1909	F61	974.4005	Massachusetts—Periodicals
E761-765	973.912	United States—History—1909-1913	F62	917.44003	Massachusetts—Gazetteers
E766-783	973.913	United States—History—1913-1921	F67	974.40(1-2)	Massachusetts—History—Colonial period, ca. 1600-1775
E784-805	973.91(3-6)	United States—History—1919-1933	F68	974.402	Massachusetts—History—New Plymouth, 1620-1691
E806-812	973.917	United States—History—1933-1945	F68	974.402008825	Pilgrims (New Plymouth Colony)
E813-816	973.918	United States—History—1945-1953	F69	974.40(2-3)	Massachusetts—History—1775-1865
			F70-71	974.404	Massachusetts—History—1865-
			F73-.9	974.461	Boston (Mass.)

LC	Dewey	Subject Heading	LC	Dewey	Subject Heading
F76-90	974.5	Rhode Island—History	F161	975.1005	Delaware—Periodicals
F76	974.5005	Rhode Island—Periodicals	F162	917.51003	Delaware—Gazetteers
F77	917.45003	Rhode Island—Gazetteers	F169	975.14(1-3)	Delaware—History—1865-
F82	974.50(1-2)	Rhode Island—History— Colonial period, ca. 1600-1775			1950
			F170	975.104(3-4)	Delaware—History—1951-
			F176-190	975.2	Maryland—History
F83.4	974.503	Dorr Rebellion, 1842	F176	975.2005	Maryland—Periodicals
F91-105	974.6	Connecticut—History	F179	917.52003	Maryland—Gazetteers
F91	974.6005	Connecticut—Periodicals	F184	975.20(1-2)	Maryland—History—
F92	917.46003	Connecticut—Gazetteers			Colonial period, ca. 1600-
F97	974.60(1-2)	Connecticut—History—			1775
		Colonial period, ca. 1600-1775	F189.A6	975.256	Annapolis (Md.)
			F189.B1	975.26	Baltimore (Md.)
F99	974.60(2-3)	Connecticut—History— 1775-1865	F191-205	975.3	Washington (D.C.)
			F191	975.3005	Washington (D.C.)—
F100	974.604(1-3)	Connecticut—History— 1865-1950			Periodicals
			F192	917.53003	Washington (D.C.)—
F101	974.604(3-4)	Connecticut—History—1951-			Gazetteers
F106	974	Middle Atlantic States	F206-220	975	Southern States—History
F116-130	974.7	New York (State)—History	F221-235	975.5	Virginia—History
F116	974.7005	New York (State)— Periodicals	F221	975.5005	Virginia—Periodicals
			F224	917.55003	Virginia—Gazetteers
F117	917.47003	New York (State)— Gazetteers	F229	975.50(1-2)	Virginia—History—Colonial period, ca. 1600-1775
F122-.1	974.70(1-2)	New York (State)—History— Colonial period, ca. 1660-1775	F229	975.502	Bacon's Rebellion, 1676
			F230	975.50(2-3)	Virginia—History— 1775-1865
F123	974.702	New York (State)—History— French and Indian War, 1755-1763	F234.E	975.503	Emporia (Va.)—History— Civil War, 1861-1865
			F236-250	975.4	West Virginia
F123	974.70(2-3)	New York (State)—History— 1775-1865	F236	975.4005	West Virginia—Periodicals
			F239	917.54003	West Virginia—Gazatteers
F124-125	974.74	New York (State)—History— 1865-	F245-.42	975.404(3-4)	West Virginia—History— 1951-
F128.44	974.703	Draft Riot, New York, N.Y., 1863	F251-265	975.6	North Carolina
			F251	975.6005	North Carolina—Periodicals
F128-.9	974.71	New York (N.Y.)	F252	917.56003	North Carolina—Gazetteers
F131-145	974.9	New Jersey—History	F257	975.60(1-2)	North Carolina—History—
F131	974.9005	New Jersey—Periodicals			Colonial period, ca. 1600-
F132	917.49003	New Jersey—Gazetteers			1775
F137	974.90(1-2)	New Jersey—History— Colonial period, ca. 1600-1775	F257	975.602	North Carolina—History— Regulator Insurrection, 1766-1771
F138	974.90(2-3)	New Jersey—History— 1775-1865	F258	975.60(2-3)	North Carolina—History— 1775-1865
F138	974.903	New Jersey—History—War of 1812	F259-260.42	975.604	North Carolina—History— 1865-
F139-140.22	974.904	New Jersey—History—1865-	F266-280	975.7	South Carolina—History
F146-160	974.8	Pennsylvania—History	F266	975.7005	South Carolina—Periodicals
F146	974.8005	Pennsylvania—Periodicals	F267	917.57003	South Carolina—Gazetteers
F147	917.48003	Pennsylvania—Gazetteers	F272	975.70(1-2)	South Carolina—History—
F152-.2	974.80(1-2)	Pennsylvania—History— Colonial period, ca. 1600-1775			Colonial period, ca. 1600-1775
			F273	975.70(2-3)	South Carolina—History— 1775-1865
F153	974.803	Buckshot War, Harrisburg, Pa., 1838	F274-275.42	975.704	South Carolina—History— 1865-
F154-155.3	974.804	Pennsylvania—History— 1865-	F281-295	975.8	Georgia
F158.1-.9	974.811	Philadelphia (Pa.)	F281	975.8005	Georgia—Periodicals
F160.G3	974.8004310748	Pennsylvania Dutch	F284	917.58003	Georgia—Gazetteers
F161-175	975.1	Delaware—History			

LC	Dewey	Subject Heading	LC	Dewey	Subject Heading
F290	975.80(2-3)	Georgia—History—1775-1865	F391	976.40(5-63)	Texas—History—1846-1950
F291-.3	975.804	Georgia—History—1865-	F391.2-.4	976.406(3-4)	Texas—History—1951-
F294.A8	975.8231	Atlanta (Ga.)	F394.D21	976.42812	Dallas (Tex.)
F296	976	Gulf States—History	F394.H8	976.41411	Houston (Tex.)
F306-320	975.9	Florida—History	F396	976	Southwest, Old
F306	975.9005	Florida—Periodicals	F406-420	976.7	Arkansas
F309	917.59003	Florida—Gazetteers	F406	976.7005	Arkansas—Periodicals
F314	975.901	Florida—History—To 1565	F409	917.67003	Arkansas—Gazetteers
F314	975.903	Florida—History—Cession to the United States, 1819	F431-445	976.8	Tennessee
F314	975.90(1-3)	Florida—History—To 1821	F431	976.8005	Tennessee—Periodicals
F314	975.901	Florida—History—Huguenot colony, 1562-1565	F434	917.68003	Tennessee—Gazetteers
			F446-460	976.9	Kentucky—History
F314	975.901	Florida—History—Spanish colony, 1565-1763	F446	976.9005	Kentucky—Periodicals
			F449	917.69003	Kentucky—Gazetteers
F314	975.90(2-3)	Florida—History—English colony, 1763-1784	F454	976.90(1-2)	Kentucky—History—To 1792
			F454	976.902	Estill's Defeat, 1782
F314	975.903	Florida—History—Spanish colony, 1784-1821	F455	976.903	Kentucky—History—1792-1865
F315	975.90(4-5)	Florida—History—1821-1865	F456-.26	976.904	Kentucky—History—1865-
			F456	976.9041	Black Patch War, 1906-1909
F316-.23	975.906	Florida—History—1865-			
F316.2-.23	975.906(3-4)	Florida—History—1951-	F461-475	977.8	Missouri
F321-355	976.1	Alabama	F461	977.8005	Missouri—Periodicals
F321	976.1005	Alabama—Periodicals	F464	917.78003	Missouri—Gazetteers
F324	917.61003	Alabama—Gazetteers	F474.S2	977.866	Saint Louis (Mo.)
F326	976.105	Alabama—History—To 1819	F476-485	977	Northwest, Old
F326	976.10(5-63)	Alabama—History—1819-1950	F486-500	977.1	Ohio
			F486	977.1005	Ohio—Periodicals
F330-.3	976.106(3-4)	Alabama—History—1951-	F489	917.71003	Ohio—Gazetteers
F336-350	976.2	Mississippi	F495	977.10(1-2)	Ohio—History—To 1787
F336	976.2005	Mississippi—Periodicals	F495	977.103	Ohio—History—1787-1865
F339	917.62003	Mississippi—Gazetteers	F496-.2	977.104	Ohio—History—1865-
F341	976.20(1-4)	Mississippi—History—To 1803	F516-520	977	Ohio River Valley
			F521-535	977.2	Indiana
F347.A25	976.202	Ackia, Battle of, 1736	F521	977.2005	Indiana—Periodicals
F350.5-358.2	977	Mississippi River Valley	F524	917.72003	Indiana—Gazetteers
F351-353	976.204	Louisiana Purchase	F526	977.20(1-2)	Indiana—History—To 1787
F366-380	976.3	Louisiana	F530-.22	977.204(3-4)	Indiana—History—1951-
F366	976.3005	Louisiana—Periodicals	F534.I3	977.252	Indianapolis (Ind.)
F367	917.63003	Louisiana—Gazetteers	F536-550	977.3	Illinois
F372-373	976.30(1-3)	Louisiana—History—To 1803	F536	977.3005	Illinois—Periodicals
			F539	917.73003	Illinois—Gazetteers
F374	976.30(4-5)	Louisiana—History—1803-1865	F544	977.30(1-2)	Illinois—History—To 1778
			F545	977.30(2-3)	Illinois—History—1778-1865
F375	976.306(1-3)	Louisiana—History—1865-1950			
			F546-.4	977.304	Illinois—History—1865-
F376-.3	976.306(3-4)	Louisiana—History—1951-	F546.2-.4	977.304(3-4)	Illinois—History—1951-
F379.N5	976.335	New Orleans (La.)	F548-.9	977.311	Chicago (Ill.)
F381-395	976.4	Texas	F551	977	Northern boundry of the United States
F381	976.4005	Texas—Periodicals			
F384	917.64003	Texas—Gazetteers	F561-575	977.4	Michigan
F389-390	976.40(1-4)	Texas—History—To 1846	F561	977.4005	Michigan—Periodicals
F389	976.402	Texas—History—1810-1821	F564	917.74003	Michigan—Gazetteers
			F566	977.40(1-3)	Michigan—History—To 1837
F390	976.403	Texas—History—Revolution, 1835-1836	F566	977.40(3-4)	Michigan—History—1837-
			F570-.2	977.404(3-4)	Michigan—History—1951-
F390	976.404	Texas—History—Republic, 1836-1846	F574.D4	977.434	Detroit (Mich.)
			F576-590	977.5	Wisconsin
			F576	977.5005	Wisconsin—Periodicals
			F579	917.75003	Wisconsin—Gazetteers

LC	Dewey	Subject Heading	LC	Dewey	Subject Heading
F584	977.50(1-3)	Wisconsin—History—To 1848	F771-785	978.8	Colorado
			F771	978.8005	Colorado—Periodicals
F586-.42	977.50(3-4)	Wisconsin—History—1848-	F774	917.88003	Colorado—Gazetteers
F589.M6	977.595	Milwaukee (Wi.)	F780	978.80(1-2)	Colorado—History—To 1876
F590.3-596.3	978	West(U.S.)—History			
F592-.7	978.0(1-2)	West(U.S.)—History—To 1848	F781	978.803(1-3)	Colorado—History—1876-1950
F593	978.02	West(U.S.)—History—1848-1860	F781.2-.3	978.803(3-4)	Colorado—History—1951-
			F784.D4	978.883	Denver (Colo.)
F594	978.02	West(U.S.)—History—1860-1890	F786-790	979	Southwest, New
			F791-805	978.9	New Mexico
F595	978.0(2-32)	West(U.S.)—History—1890-1945	F791	978.9005	New Mexico—Periodicals
			F794	917.89003	New Mexico—Gazetteers
F595-.3	978.033	West(U.S.)—History—1945-	F799-800	978.90(1-3)	New Mexico—History—To 1848
F598	978	Missouri River			
F601-615	977.6	Minnesota	F801-.2	978.90(4-5)	New Mexico—History—1848-
F601	977.6005	Minnesota—Periodicals			
F604	917.76003	Minnesota—Gazetteers	F806-820	979.1	Arizona
F606	977.60(1-4)	Minnesota—History—To 1858	F806	979.1005	Arizona—Periodicals
			F809	917.91003	Arizona—Gazetteers
F606	977.60(4-5)	Minnesota—History—1858-	F811	979.10(1-4)	Arizona—History—To 1912
F614.M5	977.6579	Minneapolis (Minn.)	F811	979.105(2-3)	Arizona—History—1912-1950
F616-630	977.7	Iowa			
F616	977.7005	Iowa—Periodicals	F815-.3	979.105(3-4)	Arizona—History—1951-
F619	917.77003	Iowa—Gazetteers	F819.P57	979.173	Phoenix (Ariz.)
F625-.42	977.703(3-4)	Iowa—History—1951-	F821-835	979.2	Utah
F631-645	978.4	North Dakota	F821	979.2005	Utah—Periodicals
F631	978.4005	North Dakota—Periodicals	F824	917.92003	Utah—Gazetteers
F634	917.84003	North Dakota—Gazetteers	F826	979.202	Morrisite War, 1862
F646-660	978.3	South Dakota	F836-850	979.3	Nevada
F646	978.3005	South Dakota—Periodicals	F836	979.3005	Nevada—Periodicals
F649	917.83003	South Dakota—Gazetteers	F839	917.93003	Nevada—Gazetteers
F661-675	978.2	Nebraska—History	F851.7	979.5	Cascade Range
F661	978.2005	Nebraska—Periodicals	F853	979.7	Columbia River Valley
F664	917.82003	Nebraska—Gazetteers	F856-870	979.4	California
F676-690	978.1	Kansas—History	F856	979.4005	California—Periodicals
F676	978.1005	Kansas—Periodicals	F859	917.94003	California—Gazetteers
F679	917.81003	Kansas—Gazetteers	F864	979.40(1-3)	California—History—To 1846
F685	978.102	Kansas—History—1854-1861			
			F865	979.40(3-4)	California—History—1846-1850
F691-705	976.6	Oklahoma			
F691	976.6005	Oklahoma—Periodicals	F866	979.40(4-53)	California—History—1850-1950
F692	917.66003	Oklahoma—Gazetteers			
F699	976.604	Oklahoma—History—Land Rush, 1889	F866.2-.4	979.405(3-4)	California—History—1950-
			F867	979.49	California, Southern
F699	976.604	Oklahoma—History—Land Rush, 1893	F869.L8	979.494	Los Angeles (Calif.)
			F869.S3	979.461	San Francisco (Calif.)
F721-722	978	Rocky Mountains	F871-885	979.5	Oregon
F722	978.752	Yellowstone National Park	F871	979.5005	Oregon—Periodicals
F726-740	978.6	Montana	F874	917.95003	Oregon—Gazetteers
F726	978.6005	Montana—Periodicals	F879-880	979.50(1-3)	Oregon—History—To 1859
F729	917.86003	Montana—Gazetteers	F880	979.503	Oregon Trail
F735-.2	978.603(3-4)	Montana—History—1951-	F881-.35	979.504	Oregon—History—1859-
F741-755	979.6	Idaho	F881.2-.35	979.504(3-4)	Oregon—History—1951-
F741	979.6005	Idaho—Periodicals	F886-900	979.7	Washington (State)
F744	917.96003	Idaho—Gazetteers	F886	979.7005	Washington (State)—Periodicals
F750-.22	979.603(3-4)	Idaho—History—1951-			
F756-770	978.7	Wyoming	F889	917.97003	Washington (State)—Gazetteers
F756	978.7005	Wyoming—Periodicals			
F759	917.87003	Wyoming—Gazetteers	F891	979.70(1-3)	Washington (State)—History—To 1889
F761	978.701	Fetterman Fight, Wyo., 1866			

LC	Dewey	Subject Heading	LC	Dewey	Subject Heading
F891	979.704	Washington (State)—History—1889-	F1056	971.3005	Ontario—Periodicals
F899.S4	979.7772	Seattle (Wash.)	F1056.4	917.13003	Ontario—Gazetteers
F901-951	979.8	Alaska	F1060-.97	971.92	Northwest, Canadian
F901	979.8005	Alaska—Periodicals	F1061-1065	971.27	Manitoba—History
F902	917.98008	Alaska—Gazetteers	F1061	971.27005	Manitoba—Periodicals
F907	979.80(1-2)	Alaska—History—To 1867	F1061.4	917.127003	Manitoba—Gazetteers
F908-909	979.80(3-4)	Alaska—History—1867-1959	F1070-1074.7	971.24	Saskatchewan—History
F910-.7	979.805	Alaska—History—1959-	F1070	971.24005	Saskatchewan—Periodicals
F951	979.84	Aleutian Islands (Alaska)	F1070.4	917.124003	Saskatchewan—Gazetteers
F1001-1040	971	Canada	F1075-1080	971.23	Alberta—History
F1001	971.005	Canada—Periodicals	F1075	971.23005	Alberta—Periodicals
F1004	917.1003	Canada—Gazetteers	F1975.4	917.123003	Alberta—Gazetteers
F1012-1017	917.104	Canada—Description and travel	F1086-1089.7	971.1	British Columbia—History
F1021-.2	971	Canada—Civilization	F1086	971.1005	British Columbia—Periodicals
F1027	971.004114	French-Canadians	F1086.4	917.11003	British Columbia—Gazetteers
F1028	355.30971	Canada—History, Military	F1091-1095.5	971.91	Yukon Territory—History
F1028.5	359.30971	Canada—History, Naval	F1091.A1	971.91005	Yukon Territory—Periodicals
F1030-.9	971.01	Canada—History—To 1763 (New France)	F1092	917.191003	Yukon Territory—Gazetteers
F1030	971.018	Lake of the Woods Massacre, 1736	F1106-1110.5	971.94	Keewatin—History
F1030.9	971.0188	Canada—History—1755-1763	F1106.A1	971.94005	Keewatin—Periodicals
			F1121-1124	971.8	Newfoundland—History
			F1121	971.8005	Newfoundland—Periodicals
			F1121.4	917.18003	Newfoundland—Gazetteers
			F1135-1139	971.82	Labrador (Nfld.)—History
F1031	971.02	Canada—History—1763-1791	F1135	971.82005	Labrador (Nfld.)—Periodicals
F1032	971.02(2-49)	Canada—History—1763-1867	F1135.4	917.182003	Labrador (Nfld.)—Gazetteers
F1032	971.024	Canada—History—1775-1783	F1201-1392	972	Mexico
			F1201	972.005	Mexico—Periodicals
F1032	971.03	Canada—History—1791-1841	F1204	917.2003	Mexico—Gazetteers
			F1210	972	Mexico—Civilization
F1032	971.038	Canada—History—Rebellion, 1837-1838	F1211-1216.5	917.204	Mexico—Description and travel
F1032	971.04	Canada—History—1841-1867	F1219-1221	972.00497	Indians of Mexico
			F1219.73-.75	972.00497452	Aztecs
F1033	971.048	Canada—History—Fenian Invasions, 1866-1870	F1219.73-.75	972.00497452	Nahuas
			F1228.98	972.01	Mexico—History—To 1519
F1033	971.05	Canada—History—Confederation, 1867	F1229-1231	972.0(1-2)	Mexico—History—To 1810
F1034	971.06(12-32)	Canada—History—1914-1945	F1230	972.02	Mexico—History—Conquest, 1519-1540
F1034.2-.3	971.063(2-48)	Canada—History—1945-	F1231	972.02	Mexico—History—Spanish colony, 1540-1810
F1035.8	971.5	Maritime Provinces—History	F1231.5-1236.6	972.0(3-83)	Mexico—History—1810-
F1036-1040	971.6	Nova Scotia—History	F1232	972.03	Mexico—History—Wars of Independence, 1810-1821
F1036	971.6005	Nova Scotia—Periodicals			
F1036.4	917.16003	Nova Scotia—Gazetteers	F1232-.5	972.0(3-6)	Mexico—History—1821-1861
F1041	971.51005	New Brunswick—Periodicals			
F1041.4	917.151003	New Brunswick—Gazetteers	F1233	972.07	Mexico—History—European intervention, 1861-1867
F1046-1049.7	971.7	Prince Edward Islands—History	F1233.5	972.081(2-4)	Mexico—History—1867-1910
F1046	971.7005	Prince Edward Islands—Periodicals	F1234	972.08(16-21)	Mexico—History—Revolution, 1910-1920
F1051-1055	971.4	Quebec (Province)—History	F1234	972.0816	El Ebano, Battle of, 1915
F1051	971.4005	Quebec (Province)—Periodicals	F1234	972.08(16-26)	Mexico—History—1910-1946
F1051.4	917.14003	Quebec (Province)—Gazetteers	F1234	972.0816	Mexico—History—Decena Tragica, 1913
F1056-1059.7	971.3	Ontario—History	F1234	972.0822	Mexico—History—Revolution, 1923-1924

LC	Dewey	Subject Heading	LC	Dewey	Subject Heading
F1235-.5	972.08(27-31)	Mexico—History—1946-1970	F1488.3-.53	972.84053	El Salvador—History—1979-
F1236	972.083(2-4)	Mexico—History—1970-1988	F1488.3	972.84053	El Salvador—History—1979-1992
F1236	972.083(5-6)	Mexico—History—1988-	F1488.5-.53	972.84053	El Salvador—History—1992-
F1401	980.005	Latin America—Periodicals			
F1406	918.003	Latin America—Gazetteers	F1501-1517	972.83	Honduras
F1408.3-.4	980	Latin America—Civilization	F1501	972.83005	Honduras—Periodicals
F1409-.3	918.04	Latin America—Description and travel	F1502	917.283003	Honduras—Gazetteers
			F1503.8	972.83	Honduras—Civilization
F1421-1577	972.8	Central America	F1504	917.28304	Honduras—Description and Travel
F1421	972.8005	Central America—Periodicals	F1505.5-1508.33	972.83	Honduras—History
F1424	917.28003	Central America—Gazetteers			
F1430	972.8	Central America—Civilization	F1507	972.830(1-4)	Honduras—History—To 1838
F1431-1433.2	917.2804	Central America—Description and travel	F1507.5	972.8305(1-2)	Honduras—History—1838-1933
F1434-1435.3	972.800497	Indians of Central America	F1507.5	972.83051	Honduras—History—Coup d'etat, 1904
F1435.4-1439.5	972.8	Central America—History	F1507.5	972.83051	Honduras—History—Revolution, 1919
F1441-1457	972.82	Belize			
F1441	972.82005	Belize—Periodicals	F1508-.22	972.8305(2-3)	Honduras—History—1933-1982
F1443.8	972.82	Belize—Civilization	F1508.3-.33	972.83053	Honduras—History—1982-
F1444-.3	917.28204	Belize—Description and travel	F1521-1537	972.85	Nicaragua
F1445.5-1448	972.82	Belize—History	F1521	972.85005	Nicaragua—Periodicals
F1461-1477	972.81	Guatemala	F1522	917.285003	Nicaragua—Gazetteers
F1461	972.81005	Guatemala—Periodicals	F1523.8	972.85	Nicaragua—Civilization
F1462	917.281003	Guatemala—Gazetteers	F1524-.3	917.28504	Nicaragua—Description and travel
F1463.5	972.81	Guatemala—Civilization	F1525.5-1528.22	972.85	Nicaragua—History
F1464-.3	917.28104	Guatemala—Description and travel			
F1465-1466.7	972.81	Guatemala—History	F1526.25	972.850(1-42)	Nicaragua—History—To 1838
F1466.4	972.810(1-3)	Guatemala—History—To 1821	F1526.25	972.8503	Nicaragua—History—English Invasion, 1780-1781
F1466.45	972.810(4-52)	Guatemala—History—1821-1945	F1526.27	972.850(44-51)	Nicaragua—History—1838-1909
F1466.5	972.81052	Guatemala—History—1945-1985	F1526.27	972.85044	Nicaragua—History—Filibuster War, 1855-1860
F1466.7	972.8105(2-3)	Guatemala—History—1985-	F1526.3	972.85051	Nicaragua—History—Revolution, 1909-1910
F1481-1497	972.84	El Salvador	F1526.3	972.8505(1-2)	Nicaragua—History—1909-1937
F1481	972.84005	El Salvador—Periodicals	F1526.3	972.85051	Nicaragua—History—Revolution of 1912
F1482	917.284003	El Salvador—Gazetteers	F1526.3	972.85051	Nicaragua—History—Revolution, 1926-1929
F1483.8	972.84	El Salvador—Civilization			
F1484-.3	917.28404	El Salvador—Description and travel	F1527	972.85052	Nicaragua—History—1937-1979
F1485.5-1488.53	972.84	El Salvador—History	F1527	972.85052	Nicaragua—History—San Carlos Barracks Attack, 1977
F1487	972.840(1-42)	El Salvador—History—To 1838	F1527	972.85052	Nicaragua—History—Uprising, 1978
F1487.5	972.840(4-52)	El Salvador—History—1838-1944			
F1487.5	972.84052	El Salvador—History—Revolution, 1944	F1528	972.85052	Nicaragua—History—Revolution, 1979
F1488	972.84052	El Salvador—History—1944-1979	F1528	972.85053	Nicaragua—History—1979-1990
F1488	972.84052	El Salvador—History—Revolution of 1948			
F1488	972.84052	El Salvador-Honduras Conflict, 1969			

LC	Dewey	Subject Heading
F1528	972.85054	Nicaragua—History—1990-
F1541-1557	972.86	Costa Rica
F1541	972.86005	Costa Rica—Periodicals
F1542	917.286003	Costa Rica—Gazetteers
F1543.8	972.86	Costa Rica—Civilization
F1544	917.28604	Costa Rica—Description and travel
F1547	972.860(1-3)	Costa Rica—History—To 1821
F1547.5	972.8604	Costa Rica—History—1821-1948
F1547.5	972.86044	Costa Rica—History—Uprising, 1932
F1548	972.8605	Costa Rica—History—1948-1986
F1548.2-.23	972.8605	Costa Rica—History—1986-
F1561-1577	972.87	Panama
F1561	972.87005	Panama—Periodicals
F1562	917.287003	Panama—Gazetteers
F1563.8	972.87	Panama—Civilization
F1564-.3	917.28704	Panama—Description and travel
F1565.5-1567	972.87	Panama—History
F1566.45	972.870(1-3)	Panama—History—To 1903
F1566.5	972.87051	Panama—History—Revolution, 1903
F1566.5	972.87051	Panama—History—1903-1946
F1566.5-1567	972.8705(1-3)	Panama—History—1946-1981
F1566.5	972.87051	Panama—History—Coup d'etat, 1968
F1567	972.87053	Panama—History—1981-
F1567	972.87053	Panama—History—American Invasion, 1989
F1601-1629	972.9	West Indies
F1601	972.9005	West Indies—Periodicals
F1604	917.29003	West Indies—Gazetteers
F1609.5	972.9	West Indies—Civilization
F1610-1613	917.2904	West Indies—Description and travel
F1619	972.900497	Indians of the West Indies
F1620-1623	972.9	West Indies—History
F1621	972.903	English West Indian Expedition, 1793-1794
F1621	972.903	English West Indian Expedition, 1654-1655
F1621	972.903	English West Indian Expedition, 1695
F1621	972.903	English West Indian Expedition, 1795-1796
F1630-1640	972.99	Bermuda Islands
F1630	972.99005	Bermuda Islands—Periodicals
F1630.7	917.299003	Bermuda Islands—Gazetteers
F1631	917.29904	Bermuda Islands—Description and travel
F1633	972.99	Bermuda Islands—Civilization
F1635-1637	972.99	Bermuda Islands—History
F1650-1660	972.96	Bahamas
F1650	972.96005	Bahamas—Periodicals
F1650.7	917.296003	Bahamas—Gazetteers
F1651	917.29604	Bahamas—Description and travel
F1654	972.96	Bahamas—Civilization
F1655.3-1657.2	972.96	Bahamas—History
F1741-1991	972.9(1-5)	Antilles, Greater
F1751-1854.9	972.91	Cuba
F1751-1849	972.91	Cuba—History
F1751	972.91005	Cuba—Periodicals
F1754	917.291003	Cuba—Gazetteers
F1760	972.91	Cuba—Civilization
F1761-1765.3	917.29104	Cuba—Description and travel
F1779	972.910(1-4)	Cuba—History—To 1810
F1781	972.9103	Cuba—History—British occupation, 1762-1763
F1783	972.9105	Cuba—History—1810-1899
F1783	972.9105	Cuba—History—Black Eagle Conspiracy, 1830
F1783	972.9105	Cuba—History—Negro Conspiracy, 1844
F1783	972.9105	Cuba—History—Insurrection, 1849-1851
F1785	972.9105	Cuba—History—Insurrection, 1868-1878
F1785	972.9105	Cuba—History—1878-1895
F1785	972.9105	Cuba—History—Revolution, 1879-1880
F1786-1788.22	972.910(5-6)	Cuba—History—1895-
F1786	972.9105	Cuba—History—Revolution, 1895-1898
F1787	972.9106(1-2)	Cuba—History—1899-1906
F1787	972.91062	Cuba—History—American occupation, 1906-1909
F1787	972.91062	Cuba—History—1909-1933
F1787.5	972.91063	Cuba—History—Revolution, 1933
F1787.5	972.91063	Cuba—History—Moncada Barracks Attack, 1953
F1787.5	972.91063	El Jigue (Cuba), Battle of, 1958
F1788	972.91064	Cuba—History—Revolution, 1959
F1788	972.91064	Cuba—History—Invasion, 1961
F1861-1896	972.92	Jamaica
F1861-1896	972.92005	Jamaica—Periodicals
F1864	917.292003	Jamaica—Gazetteers
F1870-1872.2	917.29204	Jamaica—Description and travel
F1874	972.92	Jamaica—Civilization
F1878-1887	972.92	Jamaica—History
F1884-1886	972.920(1-5)	Jamaica—History—To 1962
F1884	972.92034	Jamaica—History—Maroon War, 1795-1796
F1886	972.92034	Jamaica—History—Slave Insurrection, 1831

LC	Dewey	Subject Heading	LC	Dewey	Subject Heading
F1886	972.9204	Jamaica—History—Insurrection, 1865	F1960	972.95	Puerto Rico—Civilization
F1887	972.9206	Jamaica—History—1962-	F1961-1965.3	917.29504	Puerto Rico—Description and travel
F1900-1930	972.94	Haiti	F1970-1976.3	972.95	Puerto Rico—History
F1900	972.94005	Haiti—Periodicals	F1973	972.950(1-4)	Puerto Rico—History—To 1898
F1913	917.294003	Haiti—Gazetteers	F1973	972.9504	Puerto Rico—History—Insurrection, 1868
F1916	972.94	Haiti—Civilization			
F1917	917.29404	Haiti—Description and travel	F1975	972.950(4-52)	Puerto Rico—History—1898-1952
F1918-1939	972.94	Haiti—History			
F1923	972.940(1-3)	Haiti—History—To 1791	F1975	972.95052	Puerto Rico—History—Nationalist Insurrection, 1950
F1923	972.9403	Haiti—History—Revolution, 1791-1804			
F1924	972.9404	Haiti—History—1804-1844	F1976-.3	972.95053	Puerto Rico—History—1952-
F1926	972.9404	Haiti—History—1844-1915			
F1927	972.9405	Haiti—History—American occupation, 1915-1934	F2001-2151	972.9(7-8)	Antilles, Lesser
			F2006	972.97	Leeward Islands (West Indies)
F1927-1928	972.940(6-72)	Haiti—History—1934-1986			
F1928.2-.23	972.94073	Haiti—History—1986-	F2011	972.98	Windward Islands
F1928.2	972.94073	Haiti—History—Coup d'etat, 1991	F2033	972.973	Anguilla
			F2035	972.974	Antigua
F1931-1941	972.93	Dominican Republic	F2041	972.981	Barbados
F1931	972.93005	Dominican Republic—Periodicals	F2048	972.986	Bonaire
			F2048.5	972.921	Cayman Islands
F1932	917.293003	Dominican Republic—Gazetteers	F2049	972.986	Curacao
			F2050	972.976	Desirade (Guadeloupe)
F1935	972.93	Dominican Republic—Civilization	F2051	972.9841	Dominica
			F2056	972.9845	Grenada
F1936-.3	917.29304	Dominican Republic—Description and travel	F2061	972.9844	The Grenadines
			F2066	972.976	Guadeloupe
F1937-1938.58	972.93	Dominican Republic—History	F2070	972.976	Saintes Islands (Guadeloupe)
F1938.3	972.9404	Haiti—History—Revolution, 1843	F2076	972.976	Marie Galante
			F2081	972.982	Martinique
F1938.3	972.930(1-4)	Dominican Republic—History—To 1844	F2082	972.975	Montserrat
			F2088	972.977	Saba (Netherlands Antilles)
F1938.4	972.930(4-52)	Dominican Republic—History—1844-1930	F2091	972.973	Saint Kitts and Nevis
			F2096	972.9722	Saint Croix (V.I.)
F1938.45	972.93052	Dominican Republic—History—American occupation, 1916-1924	F2097	972.977	Saint Eustatius (Netherlands Antilles)
			F2098	972.9722	Saint John (V.I.)
F1938.5	972.93053	Dominican Republic—History—1930-1961	F2100	972.9843	Saint Lucia
			F2103	972.976	Saint Martin
F1938.5-.58	972.9305(3-4)	Dominican Republic—History—1930-	F2105	972.9722	Saint Thomas (V.I.)
F1938.5	972.93053	Dominican-Haitian Conflict, 1937	F2116-2123	972.983	Trinidad and Tobago
			F2129	972.9725	British Virgin Islands
F1938.5	972.93053	Dominican Republic—History—Invasion, 1959	F2136	972.9722	Virgin Islands of the United States
F1938.55-.58	972.93054	Dominican Republic—History—1961-	F2151	972.903	English West Indian Expedition, 1759
F1938.55	972.93054	Dominican Republic—History—Coup d'etat, 1963	F2155-2191	972.9	Caribbean Area
			F2161	910.45092	Buccaneers
F1938.55	972.93054	Dominican Republic—History—Revolution, 1965	F2173-2191	972.9	Caribbean Area—History
			F2201-3799	980	South America
F1938.55	972.93054	Dominican Republic—History—Revolution, 1973	F2201-2239	980	South America—History
			F2217	980.0099	Gauchos
F1938.55	972.93054	Dominican Republic—History—Uprising, 1984	F2229-2290	980.00498	Indians of South America
			F2251-2299	986.1	Colombia
F1951-1983	972.95	Puerto Rico	F2251	986.1005	Colombia—Periodicals
F1951	972.95005	Puerto Rico—Periodicals	F2254	918.61003	Colombia—Gazetteers
F1954	917.295003	Puerto Rico—Gazetteers	F2260	986.1	Colombia—Civilization

LC	Dewey	Subject Heading	LC	Dewey	Subject Heading
F2261-2264.2	918.6104	Colombia—Description and travel	F2325	987.0631	Venezuela—History—Anglo German Blockade, 1902
F2270.3-2279.22	986.1	Colombia—History	F2325	987.0631	Venezuela—History—Revolution, 1902-1903
F2272	986.10(1-2)	Colombia—History—To 1810	F2325	987.06313	Venezuela—History—1908-1935
F2272	986.102	Colombia—History—Insurrection of the Comuneros, 1781	F2326-2327	987.063(2-3)	Venezuela—History—1935-1974
F2272.5	986.102	English West Indian Expedition, 1739-1742	F2326	987.0632	Venezuela—History—1935-1958
F2273	986.1(2-62)	Colombia—History—19th century	F2326	987.0632	Venezuela—History—Revolution, 1945
F2273	986.10(3-6)	Colombia—History—1810-	F2326	987.0632	Venezuela—History—Coup d'etat, 1948
F2274	986.10(3-4)	Colombia—History—War of Independence, 1810-1822	F2326	987.0632	Venezuela—History—Revolution, 1958
F2275	986.104	Colombia—History—1822-1832	F2328-.52	987.0633	Venezuela—History—1974-
F2276	986.105(2-61)	Colombia—History—1832-1886	F2328	987.0633	Venezuela—History—Attempted coup, 1992 (February 4)
F2276	986.1053	Colombia—History—Civil War, 1860-1862	F2328	987.0633	Venezuela—History—Attempted coup, 1992 (November 27)
F2276.5	986.1062	Colombia—History—1886-1903	F2361-2391	988.1	Guyana
F2276.5	986.1062	Colombia—History—Revolution, 1899-1903	F2361	988.1005	Guyana—Periodicals
			F2364	918.81003	Guyana—Gazetteers
F2277	986.106(2-31)	Colombia—History—1903-1946	F2369.8	988.1	Guyana—Civilization
			F2380.3-2391	988.1	Guyana—History
F2278	986.1063(2-3)	Colombia—History—1946-1974	F2383	988.101	Guyana—History—To 1803
F2278	986.10632	Colombia—History—Coup d'etat, 1953	F2384	988.10(1-31)	Guyana—History—1803-1966
F2279-.22	986.1063(4-5)	Colombia—History—1974-	F2385	988.1032	Guyana—History—1966-
F2301-2349	987	Venezuela	F2401-2431	988.3	Surinam
F2301	987.005	Venezuela—Periodicals	F2401	988.3005	Surinam—Periodicals
F2304	918.7003	Venezuela—Gazetteers	F2404	918.83003	Surinam—Gazetteers
F2310	987	Venezuela—Civilization	F2409.8	988.3	Surinam—Civilization
F2311-2315	918.704	Venezuela—Description and travel	F2410-2413	918.8304	Surinam—Description and travel
F2319.5-2328.52	987	Venezuela—History	F2420.3-2425.23	988.3	Surinam—History
			F2423	988.301	Surinam—History—To 1814
F2322	987.0(1-3)	Venezuela—History—To 1556	F2424	988.30(1-31)	Surinam—History—1814-1950
F2322	987.0(1-3)	Venezuela—History—To 1810	F2425-.23	988.303(1-2)	Surinam—History—1950-
F2322	987.03	Venezuela—History—1556-1810	F2425	988.3032	Surinam—History—Coup d'etat, 1980
F2322	987.03	Venezuela—History—Insurrection of the Comuneros, 1781	F2425	988.3032	Surinam—History—Coup d'etat, 1982
F2322	987.03	Venezuela—History—Miranda's Expedition, 1806	F2441-2471	988.2	French Guiana
			F2441	988.2005	French Guiana—Periodicals
F2322.8	987.0(4-6)	Venezuela—History—1810-	F2444	918.82003	French Guiana—Gazetteers
F2324	987.0(4-5)	Venezuela—History—War of Independence, 1810-1823	F2449.8	988.2	French Guiana—Civilization
			F2450-2452	918.8204	French Guiana—Description and travel
F2324	987.0(4-5)	Venezuela—History—1810-1830	F2460.3-2464	988.2	French Guiana—History
F2325	987.061	Venezuela—History—1830-1935	F2501-2656	981	Brazil
			F2501	981.005	Brazil—Periodicals
			F2504	918.1003	Brazil—Gazetteers
F2325	987.061	Venezuela—History—Federal Wars, 1858-1863	F2510	981	Brazil—Civilization
			F2511-2517	918.104	Brazil—Description and travel
			F2520.3-2538.5	981	Brazil—History

LC	Dewey	Subject Heading	LC	Dewey	Subject Heading
F2526-2534	981.0(1-33)	Brazil—History—To 1822	F2683	989.203	Paraguay—History—Revolution of the Comuneros, 1721-1735
F2526	981.03(1-2)	Brazil—History—1500-1548			
F2528	981.032	Brazil—History—1548-1580			
F2528	981.032	Brazil—History—1549-1762	F2683	989.203	Paraguay—History—War of Independence, 1810-1811
F2528	981.032	Brazil—History—War of the Emboabas, 1707-1709	F2686-2687	989.20(4-5)	Paraguay—History—1811-1870
F2529	981.032	Brazil—History—French colony, 1555-1567	F2688-.5	989.20(6-71)	Paraguay—History—1870-1938
F2530	981.032	Brazil—History—1580-1640	F2688	989.20(6-7)	Paraguay—History—20th century
F2532	981.032	Brazil—History—Dutch Conquest, 1624-1654	F2688	989.2071	Paraguay—History—Revolution, 1904
F2534	981.033	Brazil—History—1763-1822			
F2534	981.033	Brazil—History—United Kingdom, 1815-1822	F2688	989.2071	Paraguay—History—Revolution, 1922-1923
F2535-2538.5	981.0(4-6)	Brazil—History—1822-	F2688	989.2071	Paraguay—History—Revolution, 1936
F2536	981.033	Brazil—History—Declaration of Independence, 1822	F2689	989.207(1-3)	Paraguay—History—1938-1989
F2536	981.04	Brazil—History—Empire, 1822-1889	F2689	989.2072	Paraguay—History—Revolution, 1947
F2536	981.04	Brazil—History—Revolution, 1842	F2689.2-.23	989.2073	Paraguay—History—1989-
F2536	981.04	Brazil—History—Quebra Quilos' Revolt, 1874	F2689.2	989.2073	Paraguay—History—Coup d'etat, 1989
F2537	981.05	Brazil—History—1889-1930			
F2537	981.05	Brazil—History—Naval Revolt, 1893-1894	F2701-2799	989.5	Uruguay
			F2701	989.5005	Uruguay—Periodicals
F2537	981.05	Brazil—History—Canudos Campaign, 1893-1897	F2704	918.95003	Uruguay—Gazetteers
			F2710	989.5	Uruguay—Civilization
F2537	981.05	Brazil—History—Naval Revolt, 1910	F2711-2715	918.9504	Uruguay—Description and travel
F2537	981.05	Brazil—History—Contestado Insurrection, 1912-1916	F2720-2729.52	989.5	Uruguay—History
			F2723	989.50(1-3)	Uruguay—History—To 1810
F2537	981.05	Brazil—History—Revolution, 1922	F2725	989.50(1-4)	Uruguay—History—1810-1830
F2537	981.05	Brazil—History—Revolution, 1924-1925	F2726	989.505	Uruguay—History—1830-1875
F2538	981.05	Brazil—History—Revolution, 1930	F2726	989.505	Uruguay—History—Great War, 1843-1852
F2538	981.061	Brazil—History—1930-1945	F2726	989.50(5-61)	Uruguay—History—1875-1904
F2538	981.061	Brazil—History—Uprising, 1935	F2726	989.5061	Uruguay—History—Revolution, 1886
F2538	981.061	Brazil—History—Revolution, 1938	F2726	989.5061	Uruguay—History—Revolution, 1897
F2538	981.061	Brazil—History—1945-1954	F2728	989.506(1-5)	Uruguay—History—1904-1973
F2538.2-.22	981.062	Brazil—History—1954-1964			
F2538.2	981.063	Brazil—History—Revolution, 1964	F2728	989.5063	Uruguay—History—Revolution, 1935
F2538.25-.27	981.063	Brazil—History—1964-1985	F2729	989.5066	Uruguay—History—Coup d'etat, 1973
F2538.3-.5	981.064	Brazil—History—1985-			
F2661-2699	989.2	Paraguay	F2729	989.5066	Uruguay—History—1973-1985
F2661	989.2005	Paraguay—Periodicals			
F2664	918.92003	Paraguay—Gazetteers	F2729	989.5067	Uruguay—History—1985-
F2670	989.2	Paraguay—Civilization	F2801-3021	982	Argentina
F2671-2676	918.9204	Paraguay—Description and travel	F2801	982.005	Argentina—Periodicals
			F2804	918.2003	Argentina—Gazetteers
F2679.35-2689.23	989.2	Paraguay—History	F2810	982	Argentina—Civilization
			F2811-2817	918.204	Argentina—Description and travel
F2683-2684	989.20(1-3)	Paraguay—History—To 1811	F2827-2849.22	982	Argentina—History

73

LC	Dewey	Subject Heading	LC	Dewey	Subject Heading
F2841	982.0(1-24)	Argentina—History—To 1810	F3095	983.061	Chile—History—War with Spain, 1865-1866
F2841	982.0(1-22)	Argentina—History—1515-1535	F3098	983.062	Chile—History—Revolution, 1891
F2841	982.023	Argentina—History—1535-1617	F3099	983.06(3-6)	Chile—History—20th century
F2841	982.023	Argentina—History—1617-1776	F3099	983.06(3-45)	Chile—History—1920-1970
F2841	982.023	Argentina—History—1776-1810	F3099	983.0641	Chile—History—Naval Revolt, 1931
F2843	982.0(24-5)	Argentina—History—19th century	F3099	983.0642	Chile—History—Uprising, 1938
F2843	982.0(3-6)	Argentina—History—1810-	F3100	983.0646	Chile—History—1970-1973
F2845	982.024	Argentina—History—English Invasions, 1806-1807	F3100	983.065	Chile—History—Coup d'etat, 1973
F2845	982.03	Argentina—History—War of Independence, 1810-1817	F3100	983.065	Chile—History—1973-1988
			F3100	984.06(5-6)	Chile—History—1988-
F2846	982.0(3-4)	Argentina—History—1817-1860	F3169	996.18	Easter Island
F2846	982.04	Argentina—History—Revolution, 1833	F3301-3359	984	Bolivia
			F3301	984.005	Bolivia—Periodicals
F2847	982.0(4-5)	Argentina—History—1860-1910	F3304	918.4003	Bolivia—Gazetteers
F2847	982.05	Argentina—History—Revolution, 1890	F3310	984	Bolivia—Civilization
			F3311-3315	918.404	Bolivia—Description and travel
F2848	982.061	Argentina—History—1910-1943	F3320.3-3327	984	Bolivia—History
			F3322	984.0(1-3)	Bolivia—History—To 1809
F2848	982.061	Argentina—History—Revolution, 1930	F3323	984.041	Bolivia—History—Wars of Independence, 1809-1825
F2849-.22	982.06(1-4)	Argentina—History—1943-	F3324-3325	984.0(45-51)	Bolivia—History—1879-1938
F2849	982.06(1-2)	Argentina—History—1943-1955	F3324	984.04(2-5)	Bolivia—History—1825-1879
F2849.2	982.063	Argentina—History—Revolution, 1955	F3326-3327	984.05(1-2)	Bolivia—History—1938-
			F3326	984.05(1-2)	Bolivia—History—1938-1982
F2849.2	982.06(3-4)	Argentina—History—1955-1983	F3326	984.051	Bolivia—History—Coup d'etat, 1943
F2849.2	982.063	Argentina—History—Peronist Revolt, 1956	F3326	984.051	Bolivia—History—Revolution, 1946
F2849.2	982.063	Argentina—History—Coup d'etat, 1966	F3326	984.052	Bolivia—History—Revolution, 1952
F2849.2	982.064	Argentina—History—1983-	F3326	984.052	Bolivia—History—Revolution, 1964
F3051-3285	983	Chile	F3326	984.052	Bolivia—History—Coup d'etat, 1979
F3051	983.005	Chile—Periodicals			
F3054	918.3003	Chile—Gazetteers	F3326	984.052	Bolivia—History—Coup d'etat, 1980
F3060	983	Chile—Civilization			
F3061-3065	918.304	Chile—Description and travel	F3327	984.052	Bolivia—History—1982-
			F3401-3619	985	Peru
F3081-3098	983	Chile—History	F3401	985.005	Peru—Periodicals
F3091	983.0(1-3)	Chile—History—To 1565	F3404	918.5003	Peru—Gazetteers
F3091	983.0(1-3)	Chile—History—To 1810	F3410	985	Peru—Civilization
F3091	983.03	Chile—History—1565-1810	F3410.5-3425	918.504	Peru—Description and travel
F3093	983.0(4-6)	Chile—History—1810-			
F3094	983.04	Chile—History—War of Independence, 1810-1824	F3430.3-3448.4	985	Peru—History
			F3442-3444	985.0(1-4)	Peru—History—To 1820
F3095	983.0(4-63)	Chile—History—1824-1920	F3442	985.0(1-2)	Peru—History—To 1548
F3095	983.05	Chile—History—Insurrection, 1851	F3442	985.02	Peru—History—Conquest, 1522-1548
F3095	983.05	Chile—History—Insurrection, 1859	F3444	985.0(2-4)	Peru—History—1548-1820
			F3444	985.03	Peru—History—Insurrection of Tupac Amaru, 1780-1781

LC	Dewey	Subject Heading
F3446	985.0(4-5)	Peru—History—War of Independence, 1820-1829
F3447	985.0(5-631)	Peru—History—1829-1919
F3447	985.05	Peru—History—Spanish question, 1864
F3447	985.061	Peru—History—Revolution of 1872
F3448	985.063(1-2)	Peru—History—1919-1968
F3448	985.0631	Peru—History—Revolution, 1930
F3448.2	985.0633	Peru—History—Coup d'etat, 1968
F3448.2	985.0633	Peru—History—1968-1980
F3448.2	985.0633	Peru—History—1980-
F3701-3799	986.6	Ecuador
F3701	986.6005	Ecuador—Periodicals
F3704	918.66003	Ecuador—Gazetteers
F3710	986.6	Ecuador—Civilization
F3711-3716	918.6604	Ecuador—Description and travel
F3723.3-3738.4	986.6	Ecuador—History
F3733	986.60(1-2)	Ecuador—History—To 1809
F3734	986.60(2-4)	Ecuador—History—Wars of Independence, 1809-1830
F3736	986.60(5-6)	Ecuador—History—1830-1895
F3736	986.606	Ecuador—History—Revolution, 1895
F3737	986.60(6-72)	Ecuador—History—1895-1944
F3737	986.607	Ecuador—History—20th century
F3737	986.6072	Ecuador—History—Coup d'etat, 1925
F3737	986.6072	Ecuador-Peru Conflict, 1941
F3738	986.607(2-4)	Ecuador—History—1944-
F3738	986.6072	Ecuador—History—Coup d'etat, 1944
F3738	986.6074	Ecuador-Peru Conflict, 1981
G-GF	910	Geography
G2-55	910.6	Geography—Societies, etc.
G67-69	910.92	Geographers—Biography
G70-.4	910.01	Geography—Methodology
G72-76.5	910.71	Geography—Study and teaching
G80-99	910.9	Geography—History
G83-88	913	Geography, Ancient
G86	530.8	Mile, Roman
G87	913.(7-8)	Classical geography
G89-95	911.0902	Geography, Medieval
G109-110	910.21	Distances—Tables
G141	911	Historical geography
G149-922	910	Voyages and travels
G149-180	910	Travel
G153	910.202	Travel—Guidebooks
G154.9	338.4791	Tourist trade
G156.5.Y6	910.83	Youth—Travel
G200-336	910.9	Discoveries in geography
G200-336	910.92	Travelers
G420-445	910.41	Voyages around the world
G445	910.41	Flights around the world
G516	916.04	Safaris
G521-539	904	Adventure and adventurers
G521-539	910.452	Shipwrecks
G535-537	910.45092	Buccaneers
G535-537	910.45092	Pirates
G539	355.354	Soldiers of fortune
G540-550	910.45	Seafaring life
G540-550	910.45	Ocean travel
G545	910.45	Whaling
G575-597	910.0211	Polar regions
G600-839	919.8	Arctic regions
G640-665	910.0216327	Northwest Passage
G680-700	910.021811	Eastern Hemisphere
G725-770	917.98(6-7)	Arctic regions—American
G778-787	914.843	Arctic regions—Norwegian
G820-839	915.7	Arctic regions—Siberian
G845-890	919.89	Antarctica
G850	919.890409034	Expedition antarctique belge, 1897-1899
G905-910	910.0213	Tropics
G912-916	910.021813	Northern Hemisphere
G918-922	910.021814	Southern Hemisphere
G1000.3-.5	912.991	Moon—Maps
G1001-1046	912	World maps
G1050	912.19813	Northern Hemisphere—Maps
G1052	912.19814	Southern Hemisphere—Maps
G1053	912.193	Tropics—Maps
G1054-1055	912.191	Polar regions—Maps
G1059-1061	912.1962	Nautical charts
G1100-1779	912.19812	Western Hemisphere—Maps
G1105-1692	912.7	North America—Maps
G1110-1114	912.982	Greenland—Maps
G1115-1193	912.71	Canada—Maps
G1200-1534.24	912.73	United States—Maps
G1535-1537	912.729	Caribbean Area—Maps
G1545-1549	912.72	Mexico—Maps
G1550-1594	912.728	Central America—Maps
G1600-1692	912.729	West Indies—Maps
G1700-1779	912.8	South America—Maps
G1780-2799	912.19811	Eastern Hemisphere—Maps
G1791-1799	911.4	Europe—Historical geography—Maps
G1805-1829.24	912.41	Great Britain—Maps
G1837-1844.24	912.44	France—Maps
G1850-1874	912.492	Benelux countries
G1895-1899	912.494	Switzerland—Maps
G1907-1924	912.43	Germany—Maps
G1935-1939	912.436	Austria—Maps
G1940-1944	912.439	Hungary—Maps
G1945-1949	912.437	Czechoslovakia—Maps
G1950-1954	912.438	Poland—Maps
G1965-1969	912.46	Spain—Maps
G1975-1979	912.469	Portugal—Maps
G1983-1989.53	912.45	Italy—Maps
G2000-2004	912.495	Greece—Maps
G2015-2017	912.4971	Serbia—Maps
G2020-2022	912.49745	Montenegro—Maps

LC	Dewey	Subject Heading	LC	Dewey	Subject Heading
G2025-2027	912.4972	Dalmatia (Croatia)—Maps	G3410-3444	912.715	Maritime Provinces—Maps
G2030-2032	912.4972	Croatia—Maps	G3420-3424	912.716	Nova Scotia—Maps
G2035-2039	912.498	Romania—Maps	G3430-3434	912.7151	New Brunswick—Maps
G2040-2044	912.499	Bulgaria—Maps	G3440-3444	912.717	Prince Edward Islands—Maps
G2055-2059	912.489	Denmark—Maps			
G2060-2064	912.4912	Iceland—Maps	G3450-3454	912.714	Quebec (Province)—Maps
G2065-2069	912.481	Norway—Maps	G3460-3464	912.713	Ontario—Maps
G2070-2074	912.485	Sweden—Maps	G3470-3504	912.712	Prairie Provinces—Maps
G2075-2079	912.4897	Finland—Maps	G3480-3484	912.7127	Manitoba—Maps
G2110-2193	912.47	Russia—Maps	G3490-3494	912.7124	Saskatchewan—Maps
G2200-2444	912.5	Asia—Maps	G3500-3504	912.7123	Alberta—Maps
G2210-2214	912.561	Turkey—Maps	G3510-3514	912.711	British Columbia—Maps
G2215-2219	912.5693	Cyprus—Maps	G3520-3524	912.7191	Yukon Territory—Maps
G2220-2224	912.5691	Syria—Maps	G3530-3564	912.7192	Northwest Territories—Maps
G2225-2229	912.5692	Lebanon—Maps			
G2235-2239	912.5694	Israel—Maps	G3600-3604	912.718	Newfoundland—Maps
G2240-2244	912.5695	Jordan—Maps	G3610-3612	912.7182	Labrador (Nfld.)—Maps
G2249.3-.34	912.538	Saudi Arabia—Maps	G3690-3691	912.73	United States—Territories and possessions—Maps
G2250-2254	912.567	Iraq—Maps			
G2255-2259	912.55	Iran—Maps	G3690-4383	912.73	United States—Maps
G2265-2269	912.581	Afghanistan—Maps	G3701	911.73	United States—Historical geography—Maps
G2270-2274	912.5491	Pakistan—Maps			
G2275-2279	912.5492	Bangladesh—Maps	G3709.3-3933	912.7(4-5)	Atlantic States—Maps
G2280-2284	912.54	India—Maps	G3720-3784	912.74	New England—Maps
G2285-2289	912.591	Burma—Maps	G3730-3734	912.741	Maine—Maps
G2290-2294	912.5493	Sri Lanka—Maps	G3740-3744	912.742	New Hampshire—Maps
G2295-2299	912.5496	Nepal—Maps	G3750-3754	912.743	Vermont—Maps
G2305-2321	912.51	China—Maps	G3760-3764	912.744	Massachusetts—Maps
G2330-2334.34	912.519	Korea—Maps	G3770-3774	912.745	Rhode Island—Maps
G2340-2344	912.51249	Taiwan—Maps	G3780-3784	912.746	Connecticut—Maps
G2355-2359	912.52	Japan—Maps	G3790-3854	912.74	Middle Atlantic States—Maps
G2370-2374	912.597	Vietnam—Maps			
G2374.3-.34	912.596	Cambodia—Maps	G3800-3804	912.747	New York (State)—Maps
G2374.5-.54	912.594	Laos—Maps	G3810-3814	912.749	New Jersey—Maps
G2375-2379	912.593	Thailand—Maps	G3820-3824	912.748	Pennsylvania—Maps
G2445-2739	912.6	Africa—Maps	G3830-3834	912.751	Delaware—Maps
G2455-2499	912.61	Africa, North—Maps	G3840-3844	912.752	Maryland—Maps
G2500-2559	912.676	Africa, East—Maps	G3850-3854	912.753	Washington (D.C.)—Maps
G2590-2639	912.67	Africa, Central—Maps	G3870-3933	912.75	South Atlantic States—Maps
G2640-2714	912.66	Africa, West—Maps			
G2750-2793	912.94	Australia—Maps	G3880-3884	912.755	Virginia—Maps
G2795-2799	912.93	New Zealand—Maps	G3890-3894	912.754	West Virignia—Maps
G2805-2839	912.1963	Atlantic Ocean—Maps	G3900-3904	912.756	North Carolina—Maps
G2860-2867	912.1964	Pacific Ocean—Maps	G3910-3914	912.757	South Carolina—Maps
G2870-2894	912.95	Melanesia—Maps	G3920-3924	912.758	Georgia—Maps
G2905-2934	912.965	Micronesia—Maps	G3930-3934	912.759	Florida—Maps
G2970-2984	912.96	Polynesia—Maps	G3950-3954	912.769	Kentucky—Maps
G3055-3064	912.19632	Arctic Ocean—Maps	G3960-3964	912.768	Tennessee—Maps
G3100-3102	912.989	Antarctica—Maps	G3970-3974	912.761	Alabama—Maps
G3195-3199	912.991	Moon—Maps	G3980-3984	912.762	Mississippi—Maps
G3200-9980	912	Maps	G4000-4004	912.767	Arkansas—Maps
G3210-3212	912.19813	Northern Hemisphere—Maps	G4010-4014	912.763	Louisiana—Maps
			G4020-4024	912.766	Oklahoma—Maps
G3220-3222	912.19814	Southern Hemisphere—Maps	G4030-4034	912.764	Texas—Maps
			G4050-4052	912.78	West (U.S.)—Maps
G3240-3241	912.193	Tropics—Maps	G4080-4084	912.771	Ohio—Maps
G3260-3272	912.191	Polar regions—Maps	G4090-4094	912.772	Indiana—Maps
G3290-5669	912.7	America—Maps	G4100-4104	912.773	Illinois—Maps
G3300-4884	912.7	North America—Maps	G4110-4114	912.774	Michigan—Maps
G3380-3384	912.982	Greenland—Maps	G4120-4124	912.775	Wisconsin—Maps
G3400-3612	912.71	Canada—Maps	G4140-4144	912.776	Minnesota—Maps

LC	Dewey	Subject Heading	LC	Dewey	Subject Heading
G4150-4154	912.777	Iowa—Maps	G5260-5264	912.883	Surinam—Maps
G4160-4164	912.778	Missouri—Maps	G5270-5274	912.882	French Guiana—Maps
G4170-4174	912.784	North Dakota—Maps	G5280-5284	912.87	Venezuela—Maps
G4180-4184	912.783	South Dakota—Maps	G5290-5294	912.861	Colombia—Maps
G4190-4194	912.782	Nebraska—Maps	G5300-5304	912.866	Ecuador—Maps
G4200-4204	912.781	Kansas—Maps	G5310-5314	912.85	Peru—Maps
G4230-4232	912.79	Pacific States—Maps	G5320-5324	912.84	Bolivia—Maps
G4250-4254	912.786	Montana—Maps	G5330-5334	912.83	Chile—Maps
G4260-4264	912.787	Wyoming—Maps	G5350-5354	912.82	Argentina—Maps
G4270-4274	912.796	Idaho—Maps	G5370-5374	912.895	Uruguay—Maps
G4280-4284	912.797	Washington (State)—Maps	G5380-5384	912.892	Paraguay—Maps
G4290-4294	912.795	Oregon—Maps	G5400-5404	912.81	Brazil—Maps
G4310-4314	912.788	Colorado—Maps	G5700-7153	912.4	Europe—Maps
G4320-4324	912.789	New Mexico—Maps	G5740-5814	912.41	Great Britain—Maps
G4330-4334	912.791	Arizona—Maps	G5741	911.41	Great Britain—Historical geography—Maps
G4340-4344	912.792	Utah—Maps			
G4350-4354	912.793	Nevada—Maps	G5750-5754	912.42	England—Maps
G4360-4364	912.794	California—Maps	G5760-5764	912.429	Wales—Maps
G4370-4374	912.798	Alaska—Maps	G5770-5774	912.411	Scotland—Maps
G4380-4384	912.969	Hawaii—Maps	G5780-5784	912.415	Ireland—Maps
G4390-4392	912.729	Caribbean Area—Maps	G5790-5794	912.416	Northern Ireland—Maps
G4410-4414	912.72	Mexico—Maps	G5830-5834	912.44	France—Maps
G4800-4884	912.728	Central America—Maps	G5980-5984	912.44949	Monaco—Maps
G4810-4814	912.7281	Guatemala—Maps	G6000-6004	912.492	Netherlands—Maps
G4820-4824	912.7282	Belize—Maps	G6010-6014	912.493	Belgium—Maps
G4830-4834	912.7283	Honduras—Maps	G6020-6024	912.4935	Luxemburg—Maps
G4840-4844	912.7284	El Salvador—Maps	G6035-6036	912.4947	Alps—Maps
G4850-4854	912.7285	Nicaragua—Maps	G6040-6044	912.494	Switzerland—Maps
G4860-4864	912.7286	Costa Rica—Maps	G6050-6054	912.43648	Liechtenstein—Maps
G4870-4874	912.7287	Panama—Maps	G6080-6428	912.43	Germany—Maps
G4900-5184	912.729	West Indies—Maps	G6490-6494	912.436	Austria—Maps
G4920-4924	912.7291	Cuba—Maps	G6500-6504	912.439	Hungary—Maps
G4940-4944	912.7294	Haiti—Maps	G6510-6514	912.437	Czechoslovakia—Maps
G4950-4954	912.7293	Dominican Republic—Maps	G6520-6524	912.438	Poland—Maps
G4960-4964	912.7292	Jamaica—Maps	G6560-6564	912.46	Spain—Maps
G4965-4969	912.72921	Cayman Islands—Maps	G6690-6694	912.469	Portugal—Maps
G4970-4974	912.7295	Puerto Rico—Maps	G6710-6714	912.45	Italy—Maps
G4980-4984	912.7296	Bahamas—Maps	G6760-6763	912.458	Sicily (Italy)—Maps
G5010-5014	912.729722	Virgin Islands of the United States—Maps	G6810-6814	912.495	Greece—Maps
			G6840-6844	912.497	Yugoslavia—Maps
G5020-5024	912.729725	British Virgin Islands—Maps	G6850-6853	912.4971	Serbia—Maps
G5030-5059	912.7297	Leeward Islands (West Indies)—Maps	G6860-6863	912.49742	Bosnia and Hercegovina—Maps
G5040-5044	912.72973	Saint Kitts (Island)—Maps	G6870-6873	912.4972	Croatia—Maps
G5045-5049	912.72973	Anguilla—Maps	G6875-6878	912.4973	Slovenia—Maps
G5050-5054	912.72974	Antigua—Maps	G6880-6884	912.498	Romania—Maps
G5055-5059	912.72975	Montserrat—Maps	G6890-6894	912.499	Bulgaria—Maps
G5070-5074	912.72976	Guadeloupe—Maps	G6910-6963	912.48	Scandinavia—Maps
G5080-5084	912.72982	Martinique—Maps	G6920-6924	912.489	Denmark—Maps
G5090-5184	912.7298	Windward Islands—Maps	G6930-6934	912.4912	Iceland—Maps
G5100-5104	912.729841	Dominica—Maps	G6940-6944	912.481	Norway—Maps
G5110-5114	912.729843	Saint Lucia—Maps	G6950-6954	912.485	Sweden—Maps
G5120-5124	912.729844	Saint Vincent—Maps	G6960-6964	912.4897	Finland—Maps
G5130-5134	912.729845	Granada—Maps	G7030-7033	912.4798	Estonia—Maps
G5140-5144	912.72981	Barbados—Maps	G7040-7043	912.4796	Latvia—Maps
G5150-5162	912.72983	Trinidad and Tobago—Maps	G7060-7342	912.47	Russia—Maps
G5170-5174	912.72986	Aruba—Maps	G7400-8198.54	912.5	Asia—Maps
G5175-5179	912.72986	Bonaire—Maps	G7420-7624	912.56	Middle East—Maps
G5180-5184	912.72986	Curacao—Maps	G7430-7434	912.561	Turkey—Maps
G5200-5668	912.8	South America—Maps	G7450-7454	912.5693	Cyprus—Maps
G5250-5254	912.881	Guyana—Maps	G7460-7464	912.5691	Syria—Maps

LC	Dewey	Subject Heading	LC	Dewey	Subject Heading
G7470-7474	912.5692	Lebanon—Maps	G8675-8679	912.6715	Sao Tome and Principe
G7500-7504	912.5694	Israel—Maps	G8690-8694	912.6721	Gabon—Maps
G7510-7514	912.5695	Jordan—Maps	G8700-8704	912.6724	Congo (Brazzaville)—Maps
G7530-7534	912.538	Saudi Arabia—Maps	G8710-8714	912.6741	Central African Republic—
G7550-7554	912.533	Yemen—Maps			Maps
G7560-7564	912.5353	Oman—Maps	G8720-8724	912.6743	Chad—Maps
G7580-7584	912.5363	Qatar—Maps	G8730-8734	912.6711	Cameroon—Maps
G7590-7594	912.5365	Bahrain—Maps	G8750-8754	912.6683	Benin—Maps
G7600-7604	912.5367	Kuwait—Maps	G8760-8764	912.6681	Togo—Maps
G7610-7614	912.567	Iraq—Maps	G8770-8774	912.6626	Niger—Maps
G7620-7624	912.55	Iran—Maps	G8780-8784	912.6668	Cote d'Ivoire—Maps
G7630-7634	912.581	Afghanistan—Maps	G8790-8794	912.6652	Guinea—Maps
G7640-7644	912.5491	Pakistan—Maps	G8800-8804	912.6623	Mali—Maps
G7645-7649	912.5492	Bangladesh—Maps	G8805-8809	912.6625	Burkina Faso—Maps
G7650-7654	912.54	India—Maps	G8810-8814	912.663	Senegal—Maps
G7720-7724	912.591	Burma—Maps	G8820-8824	912.661	Mauritania—Maps
G7750-7754	912.5493	Sri Lanka—Maps	G8840-8844	912.669	Nigeria—Maps
G7760-7764	912.5496	Nepal—Maps	G8850-8854	912.667	Ghana—Maps
G7780-7784	912.5498	Bhutan—Maps	G8860-8864	912.664	Sierra Leone—Maps
G7820-7824	912.51	China—Maps	G8870-8874	912.6651	Gambia—Maps
G7895-7899	912.517	Mongolia—Maps	G8880-8884	912.6662	Liberia—Maps
G7940-7944	912.5125	Hong Kong—Maps	G8890-8894	912.6657	Guinea-Bissau—Maps
G7945-7947	912.5126	Macao—Maps	G8960-8964	912.94	Australia—Maps
G7960-7964	912.52	Japan—Maps	G9080-9084	912.93	New Zealand—Maps
G8000-8198.54	912.59	Indochina—Maps	G9130-9134	912.4699	Azores—Maps
G8010-8014	912.596	Cambodia—Maps	G9140-9144	912.4698	Madeira Islands—Maps
G8015-8019	912.594	Laos—Maps	G9150-9154	912.649	Canary Islands—Maps
G8020-8024	912.597	Vietnam—Maps	G9160-9164	912.6658	Cape Verde—Maps
G8025-8029	912.593	Thailand—Maps	G9170-9174	912.973	Saint Helena—Maps
G8030-8034	912.595	Malaysia—Maps	G9175-9179	912.9711	Falkland Islands—Maps
G8040-8044	912.5957	Singapore—Maps	G9185-9189	912.6982	Mauritius—Maps
G8060-8064	912.599	Philippines—Maps	G9190-9194	912.6981	Reunion—Maps
G8070-8074	912.598	Indonesia—Maps	G9200-9204	912.696	Seychelles—Maps
G8140-8142	912.95	New Guinea—Maps	G9210-9214	912.694	Comoro Islands—Maps
G8200-8202	912.6	Africa—Maps	G9215-9219	912.5495	Maldives—Maps
G8220-8222	912.61	Africa, North—Maps	G9260-9262	912.95	Melanesia—Maps
G8230-8234	912.64	Morocco—Maps	G9280-9284	912.9593	Solomon Islands—Maps
G8240-8244	912.65	Algeria—Maps	G9295-9297	912.9595	Vanuatu—Maps
G8250-8254	912.611	Tunisia—Maps	G9340-9344	912.9597	New Caledonia—Maps
G8260-8264	912.612	Libya—Maps	G9380-9384	912.9611	Fiji—Maps
G8300-8304	912.62	Egypt—Maps	G9400-9494	912.965	Micronesia—Maps
G8330-8334	912.63	Ethiopia—Maps	G9410-9414	912.967	Mariana Islands—Maps
G8350-8354	912.6773	Somalia—Maps	G9420-9424	912.966	Caroline Islands—Maps
G8410-8414	912.6762	Kenya—Maps	G9460-9464	912.9683	Marshall Islands—Maps
G8420-8424	912.6761	Uganda—Maps	G9480-9484	912.9681	Kiribati—Maps
G8430-8434	912.67571	Rwanda—Maps	G9500-9652	912.96	Polynesia—Maps
G8435-8439	912.67572	Burundi—Maps	G9515-9517	912.9616	Wallis and Futuna Islands—
G8440-8444	912.678	Tanzania—Maps			Maps
G8450-8454	912.679	Mozambique—Maps	G9530-9534	912.964	Line Islands—Maps
G8460-8464	912.691	Madagascar—Maps	G9550-9554	912.9615	Tokelau—Maps
G8500-8504	912.68	South Africa—Maps	G9555-9557	912.961(3-4)	Samoan Islands—Maps
G8530-8533	912.684	Natal (South Africa)—Maps	G9570-9574	912.9612	Tonga—Maps
G8540-8543	912.682	Transvaal—Maps	G9600-9604	912.9623	Cook Islands—Maps
G8580-8584	912.6885	Lesotho—Maps	G9620-9624	912.9631	Marquesas Islands—Maps
G8590-8594	912.6887	Swaziland—Maps	G9640-9644	912.9621	Society Islands—Maps
G8600-8604	912.6883	Botswana—Maps	G9660-9664	912.9618	Pitcairn Island—Maps
G8610-8614	912.6897	Malawi—Maps	G9800-9804	912.989	Antartica—Maps
G8620-8624	912.6881	Namibia—Maps	GA1-87	526	Mathematical geography
G8640-8644	912.673	Angola—Maps	GA4	526.021	Mathematical geography—
G8650-8654	912.6751	Zaire—Maps			Tables
G8660-8664	912.6718	Equatorial Guinea—Maps	GA23	526.3	Area measurement

LC	Dewey	Subject Heading	LC	Dewey	Subject Heading
GA51-87	526.9	Surveys	GB1207	551.483	Streamflow
GA101-1999	526	Cartography	GB1399-.5	551.489	Floods
GA101-130	912	Outline maps	GB1399.2	551.4890112	Flood forecasting
GA109.8	310.0223	Maps, Statistical	GB1401-1597	551.484	Waterfalls
GA110-115	526.8	Map projection	GB1601-1798.9	551.482	Lakes
GA130	526.0221	Map drawing	GB2201-2398	551.482	Lagoons
GA201-246	526.09	Cartography—History	GB2401-2598	551.343	Sea ice drift
GA405	526.0973	Cartography—United States	GB2401-2598	551.312	Glaciers
GA409-460	526.097(4-9)	Cartography—[United States, By state]	GB2401-2598	551.31	Ice sheets
			GB2401-2597	551.31	Ice
GB	910.02	Physical geography	GB2401-2597	551.342	Icebergs
GB400-649	551.41	Geomorphology	GB2401.72.A37	551.31028	Aerial photography in glaciology
GB400-649	551.41	Landforms			
GB400.42.A35	551.41028	Aerial photography in geomorphology	GB2801-2998	551.57	Hydrometeorology
			GC	551.46	Oceanography
GB448	551.43	Slopes (Physical geography)	GC41	551.460284	Oceanographic instruments
GB451-460	551.458	Seashore	GC57-59	551.46072	Oceanography—Research
GB454.F5	551.44	Fjords	GC65-78	551.4607	Underwater exploration
GB454.I54	551.44	Inlets	GC66	551.46072	Manned undersea research stations
GB461-468	551.424	Reefs			
GB461-468	551.424	Coral reefs and islands	GC67	387.2045	Oceanographic submersibles
GB471-478	551.42	Islands	GC83-87.6	551.46084	Submarine topography
GB501-555	551.432	Mountains	GC87-.6	551.46083	Ocean bottom
GB561-568	551.442	Arroyos	GC87.6	551.4608	Submarine trenches
GB561-568	551.442	Floodplains	GC96-97.8	551.4609	Estuarine oceanography
GB561-568	551.442	Valleys	GC96-97.8	551.4609	Estuaries
GB561-568	551.45	Watersheds	GC100-103	551.4601	Seawater
GB561-568	551.453	Savannas	GC109-149	551.4601	Chemical oceanography
GB571-578	551.434	Plateaus	GC121-127	551.4601	Salinity
GB571-578	551.453	Prairies	GC160-177	551.4601	Ocean temperature
GB571-578	551.434	Mesas	GC175	551.4601	Deep-sea temperature
GB571-578	551.453	Plains	GC190-.5	551.5246	Ocean-atmosphere interation
GB571-578	551.453	Steppes	GC205-226	551.4702	Ocean waves
GB581-588	551.315	Glacial landforms	GC211-222	551.4702	Waves
GB591-598	551.453	Alluvial plains	GC225-226	551.47022	Storm surges
GB591-598	551.456	Deltas	GC228.5-.6	551.47	Ocean circulation
GB599-609.2	551.447	Karst	GC229-299	551.4701	Ocean currents
GB601-608	551.447	Caves	GC296.8.E	551.4701	El Nino Current
GB609.2	551.447	Sinkholes	GC296.G9	551.4701	Gulf Stream
GB611-618	551.415	Arid regions	GC300-376	551.4708	Tides
GB611-618	551.415	Desertification	GC308-309	551.4708	Tidal currents
GB611-618	551.415	Desertification—Control	GC376	551.4708	Bores (Tidal phenomena)
GB611-618	551.415	Deserts	GC380-399	551.46083	Marine sediments
GB621-628	551.41	Bogs	GC401-455	551.468	Oceanography—Arctic Ocean
GB621-628	551.41	Swamps			
GB631-638	551.375	Sand dunes	GC461-462	551.469	Oceanography—Antarctic Ocean
GB641-648	551.312	Rock glaciers			
GB649.S3	551.375	Sand waves	GC481-711	551.461	Oceanography—Atlantic Ocean
GB651-2998	551.48	Hydrology			
GB651-2998	551.48	Water	GC721-761	551.467	Oceanography—Indian Ocean
GB651-2998	551.48	Water-supply			
GB656.2.A37	551.48028	Aerial photography in hydrology	GC771-871	551.465	Oceanography—Pacific Ocean
GB855	546.22	Water chemistry	GC1000-1023	333.9164	Marine resources
GB1001-1199.8	551.49	Groundwater	GC1018	333.916416	Marine resources conservation
GB1198-.4	551.23	Hot springs			
GB1198-.4	551.498	Springs	GC1080-1581	363.7394	Marine pollution
GB1198.5-.8	551.23	Geysers	GE70-90	333.7071	Environmental education
GB1201-1399.5	551.483	Rivers	GE140-160	639.9	Environmental degradation
GB1201-1398	551.4830287	Stream measurements	GE195-199	333.72	Green movement
GB1203	551.489	Flood routing	GF1-900	304.2	Human ecology

G - GF

LC	Dewey	Subject Heading	LC	Dewey	Subject Heading
GF24	304.2	Applied human geography	GN285	569.9	Neanderthals
GE70-90	333.7071	Environmental education	GN301-673	305.8	Ethnology
GF51-71	304.2	Man—Influence of environment	GN307-499	569.9	Man, Primitive
GF71	304.25	Man—Influence of climate	GN345.2	305.8009	Ethnohistory
GF101-127	307.14	Human settlements	GN345.6	303.482	Intercultural communication
GF125	910.021732	Urban geography	GN345.65	303.482	Cross-cultural orientation
GF127	910.021734	Rural geography	GN365.9	304.5	Sociobiology
GF500-895	304.209(4-9)	Human ecology—[By region or country]	GN370	304.8	Man—Migrations
GF503-504	304.20973	Human ecology—United States	GN372	305.4	Wild women
			GN372	305.31	Wild men
GF895	304.20913	Human ecology—Tropics	GN372	155.4567	Feral children
GN	301	Anthropology	GN380	306.08	Indigenous peoples
GN	301	Man	GN387	305.90691	Nomads
GN20-21	301.092	Anthropologists	GN395	307.76	Urban anthropology
GN33-34.3	301.01	Anthropology—Methodology	GN400-406	306	Culture
GN33.5	304.6	Demographic anthropology	GN406-498	301.7	Society, Primitive
GN34.3.A35	301.028	Aerial photography in anthropology	GN407-411.5	641.592	Food
			GN407.4-.8	630	Traditional farming
GN35-41	305.80074	Ethnological museums and collections	GN407.6-.7	636	Domestic animals
			GN414	722	Architecture, Primitive
GN42-46	301.072	Anthropology—Research	GN415.C8	645.4	Cradles
GN49-298	599.9	Physical anthropology	GN418-419	391	Clothing and dress
GN51-59	599.94	Anthropometry	GN419.15	391.65	Body marking
GN59.A35	599.940040	Aged—Anthropometry	GN419.2	391.65	Mutilation
GN63	612.65	Child development	GN419.5	391.434	Masks
			GN431	746.412	Basket making
GN63	599.90835	Adolescence	GN432	641.812	Tapa
GN63.6	306.875	Quintuplets	GN432	677.028242	Weaving
GN63.6	306.875	Quadruplets	GN432	677.028242092	Weavers
GN63.6	306.875	Twins	GN432	677.02822	Spinning
GN63.6	306.875	Triplets	GN435.7-450.5	332.4	Shell money
GN66-69	599.949	Proportion (Anthropometry)	GN436.2	332.4	Stone money
GN66	599.949	Somatotypes	GN436.8-437	621.9	Tools
GN69.3-.5	599.949	Midgets	GN440.1	387.2	Ships
GN69.3-.5	599.949	Dwarfs	GN440.2	386.229	Outrigger canoes
GN70	599.947	Skeleton	GN440.2	386.229	Dugout canoes
GN70	599.947	Ribs	GN440.2	386.229	Canoes and canoeing
GN71-131	599.948	Craniology	GN448-450.7	306.3	Economic anthropology
GN71-131	599.948	Skull	GN451-477.7	306.42	Intellectual life
GN131	599.948	Eye-sockets	GN454-455	306.483	Sports
GN181-190.5	599.948	Brain	GN454-456	394.3	Toys
GN191-199	599.945	Skin	GN454.6	306.482	Gambling
GN192	599.945	Dermatoglyphics	GN454.8-455	394.3	Games
GN192	599.945	Fingerprints	GN468	305.8001	Ethnophilosophy
GN197	599.945	Color of man	GN470-474	291.3	Worship
GN199	599.945	Albinos and albinism	GN471	291.21	Animism
GN209	599.943	Dental anthropology	GN472	291.21	Fetishism
GN209	599.943	Teeth	GN473	291.38	Rites and ceremonies
GN231-232	599.947	Posture	GN475.3	291.3/133.43	Magic
GN254	306.846	Miscegenation	GN475.6	133.425	Evil eye
GN270-279	155.82	Ethnopsychology	GN476.1	513	Arithmetic
GN281-289	599.938	Human evolution	GN476.4	910	Geography
GN281-.4	599.938	Man—Origin	GN477-.7	615.882	Traditional medicine
GN282-286.7	569.9	Fossil man	GN477.5-.7	617.0901	Surgery, Primitive
GN282.5	569.9	Missing link	GN478-491.7	305	Social structure
GN283.9	569.9	Homo habilis	GN479.6	321.1	Patriarchy
GN284-.7	569.9	Homo erectus	GN480-.65	306.85	Family
GN284.4	569.9	Solo man	GN480-.65	306.83	Kinship
GN284.6	569.9	Java man	GN480	306.83	Double descent (Kinship)
GN284.7	569.9	Peking man	GN480	306.81	Marriage
			GN480.1	392.4	Bridal price

LC	Dewey	Subject Heading	LC	Dewey	Subject Heading
GN480.3	306.82	Endogamy and exogamy	GN700-890	930.1	Archaeology
GN480.3	306.877	Incest	GN750-751	001.94	Lost continents
GN480.33-.36	306.8423	Polygamy	GN771	930.12	Paleolithic period, Lower
GN480.4	306.81	Cross-cousin marriage	GN775-776	930.11	Eoliths
GN480.6	306.8423	Polyandry	GN775-768	930.1(2-4)	Stone age
GN482.1	392.12	Birth customs	GN777-778	930.15	Bronze age
GN483-484	305.235	Adolescence	GN777-778	930.15	Copper age
GN484	392.1	Circumcision	GN783-784	930.1	Cave dwellings
GN484.3	392.6	Sex customs	GN783-.5	930.1	Caves
GN484.43	392.4	Betrothal	GN785-786	569.9	Lake-dwellers and lake-dwellings
GN486	393.1	Burial			
GN486	393	Funeral rites and ceremonies	GN789	930.1028	Earthworks (Archaeology)
			GN795-796	930.1	Mounds
GN486.3	302.34	Friendship	GN799.A	700.901	Art, Prehistoric
GN489	291.211	Totemism	GN799.A4	630.901	Agriculture—Origin
GN491	291.211	Totems	GN799.A4	630.901	Agricultural implements, Prehistoric
GN491.4	305.5122	Caste			
GN492-495	306.2	Political anthropology	GN799.A8	520.901	Astronomy, Prehistoric
GN492.3	398.27	Political customs and rites	GN799.B62	623.821	Boats, Prehistoric
GN492.5	306.08	Tribes	GN799.C49	623.8620901	Cordage, Prehistoric
GN492.6	320.11	State, The—Origin	GN799.H84	639.0901	Hunting, Prehistoric
GN492.7	321	Kings and rulers	GN799.P5	646.2040284	Pins and needles, Prehistoric
GN493.3	306	Social norms			
GN494	390	Taboo	GN799.R4	291.13	Religion, Prehistoric
GN495.2	366.(1-5)	Secret societies	GN799.S4	732	Sculpture, Prehistoric
GN495.4	305.8	Ethnic groups	GN799.T73	302.2	Communication, Prehistoric
GN495.5	321.60901	Kings and rulers, Ancient	GN799.T75	790.1330901	Toys
GN495.6	305.8	Ethnicity	GN799.W3	623.441	Weapons, Prehistoric
GN496-498	305.8	Ethnic relations	GN799.W66	569.9	Women, Prehistoric
GN496-498	305.8	Race relations	GN871-875	994.01	Australian aborigines—Antiquities
GN497.5	306.859	Matriarchy			
GN498	623.441	Spears	GR	398	Folklore
GN498.B78	623.441	Arrowheads	GR50	398.092	Folklorists
GN498.B78	623.441	Bow and arrow	GR72-390	398.2	Folk literature
GN498.S5	623.441	Shields	GR72.3	398	Folklore—Performance
GN498.S55	623.441	Slings	GR72.3	808.543	Storytelling
GN502-517	155.82	Ethnopsychology	GR74-76	398.2	Tales
GN510	303.32	Socialization	GR75.L56	398.245	Little Red Riding Hood (Tale)
GN537	305.8034	Caucasian race	GR75.S6	398.21	Snow White (Tale)
GN547	305.8924	Jews	GR81	398.41	Superstition
GN547	305.892	Semites	GR100-390	398.09(3-9)	Folklore—[By region or country]
GN548	305.8942	Mongols			
GN549.G4	305.83	Germanic peoples	GR101-118	398.097	Folklore—North America
GN549.T4	305.83	Teutonic race	GR103	394.308996073	Afro-American children's games
GN550-560	305.80097	Ethnic groups—North America			
			GR130-133	398.098	Folklore—South America
GN562-564	305.80098	Ethnic groups—South America	GR135-263	398.094	Folklore—Europe
			GR265-345	398.095	Folklore—Asia
GN575-585	305.80094	Ethnic groups—Europe	GR350-360	398.096	Folklore—Africa
GN625-635	305.80095	Ethnic groups—Asia	GR365-385	398.099(3-6)	Folklore—[New Zealand/Australia/Oceania]
GN643-661	305.80096	Ethnic groups—Africa			
GN645	305.8044	Mulattoes	GR455	393	Dead
GN662-671	305.80099(5-6)	Ethnic groups—Oceania	GR455	393	Death
GN664.N3	305.8096	Negritos	GR462	398.354	Sex—Folklore
GN664.P2	305.89912	Papuans	GR465	392.5	Marriage
GN666	305.89915	Australian aborigines—Ethnic identity	GR480-485	394.3	Games
			GR485	398.8	Counting-out rhymes
GN669	305.89952	Micronesians	GR490-497	392.36	Dwellings
GN671.B5	305.8995	Gunantuna (Melanesian people)	GR500-510	398.45	Supernatural
			GR525	398.45	Ghouls and ogres
GN700-890	569.9	Man, Prehistoric	GR530	398.45	Witchcraft

LC	Dewey	Subject Heading	LC	Dewey	Subject Heading
GR540	398.45	Demonology	GT251-252	392.360097291	Dwellings—Cuba
GR540	398.45	Exorcism	GT253-254	392.360097294	Dwellings—Haiti
GR540	398.45	Incantations	GT255-256	392.360097292	Dwellings—Jamaica
GR549-552	398.45	Fairies	GT257-.5	392.360097295	Dwellings—Puerto Rico
GR550-552	398.2	Fairy tales	GT261-262	392.3600982	Dwellings—Argentina
GR555	398.45	Trolls	GT263-264	392.3600984	Dwellings—Bolivia
GR560	398.45	Ghouls and ogres	GT265-266	392.3600981	Dwellings—Brazil
GR580	398.47	Ghosts	GT267-268	392.3600983	Dwellings—Chile
GR600	398.45	Amulets	GT269-270	392.36009861	Dwellings—Colombia
GR600	398.45	Charms	GT271-272	392.36009866	Dwellings—Ecuador
GR660	398.3209143	Mountains	GT275-276	392.36009892	Dwellings—Paraguay
GR600	398.45	Talismans	GT277-278	392.3600985	Dwellings—Peru
GR625	398.362	Sun	GT279-280	392.36009895	Dwellings—Uruguay
GR625	398.362	Stars	GT281-282	392.3600987	Dwellings—Venezuela
GR630	398.363	Lightning	GT285-294	392.3600941	Dwellings—Great Britain
GR630	398.363	Thunderstorms	GT294.5-.6	392.36009415	Dwellings—Ireland
GR650-690	398.32	Geographical myths	GT295-296	392.36009436	Dwellings—Austria
GR680	398.32091693	Rivers	GT296.5-.6	392.36009439	Dwellings—Hungary
GR690	398.364	Springs—Folklore	GT297-298	392.3600944	Dwellings—France
GR690	398.364	Wells	GT298.9-300.5	392.3600943	Dwellings—Germany
GR720	398.3699772	Dogs	GT301-302	392.36009495	Dwellings—Greece
GR740	398.36979	Reptiles	GT303-304	392.3600945	Dwellings—Italy
GR745	398.3697	Fishes—Folklore	GT307-308	392.36009492	Dwellings—Netherlands
GR750	398.36957	Insects	GT311-312	392.3600947	Dwellings—Russia
GR780	398.368	Botany—Folklore	GT315-316	392.36009489	Dwellings—Denmark
GR780-790	302.222	Flower language	GT317-318	392.360094912	Dwellings—Iceland
GR780-790	398.368	Plants	GT319-320	392.36009481	Dwellings—Norway
GR785	398.368216	Trees—Folklore	GT321-322	392.36009485	Dwellings—Sweden
GR800	398.365	Rocks	GT323-324	392.3600946	Dwellings—Spain
GR820-830	398.369	Animals, Mythical	GT325-326	392.36009469	Dwellings—Portugal
GR825-830	398.45	Monsters	GT327-328	392.36009494	Dwellings—Switzerland
GR830.D7	398.469	Dragons	GT331-341	392.36009496	Dwellings—Balkan
GR830.U6	398.469	Unicorns			Peninsula
GR830.V3	398.45	Vampires	GT343-372	392.360095	Dwellings—Asia
GR880	615.882	Traditional medicine	GT344-.2	392.360095691	Dwellings—Syria
GR890-910	398.355	Occupations—Folklore	GT345-346	392.36009561	Dwellings—Turkey
GR910	398.45	Mermaids	GT346.5-.6	392.36009567	Dwellings—Iraq
GR930	398.33	Days	GT347-348	392.3600955	Dwellings—Iran
GR930	398.33	Seasons	GT349-350	392.360095	Dwellings—Asia
GR933	398.41	Thirteen (The number)	GT351-352	392.3600954	Dwellings—India
GR940-941	398.32	Geographical myths	GT352.5-.6	392.360095493	Dwellings—Sri Lanka
GR950.L4	398.355	Lanterns	GT355-356	392.36009593	Dwellings—Thailand
GT	390	Manners and customs	GT357-358	392.36009595	Dwellings—Malaysia
GT	390	Rites and ceremonies	GT359-360	392.36009598	Dwellings—Indonesia
GT49	391	Beauty, Personal	GT361-362	392.36009599	Dwellings—Philippines
GT165-476	392.36	Dwellings	GT365-366	392.3600951	Dwellings—China
GT170	392.36	Dwellings—Social aspects	GT367-368	392.3600952	Dwellings—Japan
GT201-384	392.36009(4-9)	Dwellings—[By region or country]	GT369-370	392.36009519	Dwellings—Korea
			GT373-377	392.360096	Dwellings—Africa
GT205-227	392.3600973	Dwellings—United States	GT375-376	392.3600962	Dwellings—Egypt
GT2220	391.44	Staffs (Sticks, canes, etc.)	GT379-380	392.3600994	Dwellings—Australia
GT228-229	392.3600971	Dwellings—Canada	GT381-382	392.3600993	Dwellings—New Zealand
GT231-232	392.3600972	Dwellings—Mexico	GT383-384	392.360099(5-6)	Dwellings—Oceania
GT235-236	392.360097282	Dwellings—Belize	GT420-425	392.36	Heating
GT237-238	392.360097286	Dwellings—Costa Rica	GT440-445	392.36	Lighting
GT239-240	392.360097281	Dwellings—Guatemala	GT445	392.36	Lanterns
GT241-242	392.360097283	Dwellings—Honduras	GT445	392.36	Lamps
GT243-244	392.360097285	Dwellings—Nicaragua	GT450	392.36	Furniture
GT245-.5	392.360097287	Dwellings—Panama	GT472	392.36	Sanitation, Household
GT246-.5	392.360097284	Dwellings—El Salvador	GT476	392.36	Toilets
GT249-250	392.360097296	Dwellings—Bahamas	GT500-2350	391	Clothing and dress

LC	Dewey	Subject Heading	LC	Dewey	Subject Heading
GT500-2370	391	Fashion	GT2680	392.50902	Marriage customs and rites, Medieval
GT500-2370	391	Costume			
GT525	391	Clothing and dress—Social aspects	GT2695.M8	392.50882971	Marriage customs and rites, Islamic
GT529	391	Cold weather clothing	GT2701-2796	392.509(3-9)	Marriage customs and rites—[By region or country]
GT530-596	391.0090(1-5)	Costume—History			
GT530-560	391.00901	Costume—History—To 500	GT2797	392.5	Wedding cakes
GT540	391.0088296	Costume, Jewish	GT2800	394.2	Wedding anniversaries
GT575	391.00902	Costume—History—Medieval, 500-1500	GT2810	392.5	Chastity belts
			GT2850-2960	394.1	Food habits
GT585	391.00903(1-3)	Costume—History—[16th/18th] century	GT2850-2930	394.1	Drinking customs
			GT2865-2866	394.12	Food of animal origin
GT601-1605	391.009(3-9)	Costume—[By region or country]	GT2870	394.12	Condiments
			GT2870	394.12	Salt
GT603-648	391.0097	Costume—North America	GT2870	394.12	Spices
GT675-716	391.0098	Costume—South America	GT2905-2916	394.12	Tea
GT720-1330	391.0094	Costume—Europe	GT2910-2916	394.120952	Japanese tea ceremony
GT1370-1570	391.0095	Costume—Asia	GT2918	394.12	Coffee
GT1560	391.00952	Kimonos	GT2940-2947	394.1(2/3)	Drinking cups
GT1580-1589	391.0096	Costume—Africa	GT2952	394.12	Toothpicks
GT1590-1599	391.0099(3-6)	Costume—[New Zealand/ Australia/Oceania]	GT2955	394.15	Picnicking
			GT2995	394.12	Lying down position
GT1747-1748	391	Disguise	GT3000.3-.5	392	Sleeping customs
GT1747-1748	391.434	Masks	GT3005.3-.4	392	Sitting customs
GT1850	391.024	Peasantry	GT3010	394.14	Narcotics
GT2073	391.42	Underwear	GT3020-3030	394.14	Tobacco
GT2075	391.42	Crinolines	GT3020	394.14	Smoking
GT2075	391.42	Corsets	GT3030	394.14	Snuff
GT2110	391.43	Head-gear	GT3050	394	Salutations
GT2110	391.43	Hats	GT3050	394	Gifts
GT2112	391.43	Veils	GT3080	394	Swearing
GT2120	391.44	Neckties	GT3085	394	Oaths
GT2128	391.413	Hosiery	GT3150-3390.5	393.1	Burial
GT2150	391.44	Fans	GT3150-3390.5	393	Death
GT2170	391.412	Gloves	GT3150-3390.5	393	Funeral rites and ceremonies
GT2190	391.412	Muffs			
GT2210	391.44	Umbrellas and parasols	GT3150-3390	393	Dead
GT2220	391.44	Staffs (Sticks, canes, etc.)	GT3170	393.0901	Funeral rites and ceremonies, Ancient
GT2250-2281	391.7	Jewelry			
GT2250-2280	391.7	Gems	GT3320	393.1	Cemeteries
GT2260	391.7	Necklaces	GT3330	393.2	Cremation
GT2265	391.7	Earrings	GT3340	393.3	Embalming
GT2270	391.7	Rings	GT3350	393.4	Scaffold burial
GT2280	391.44	Pins and needles	GT3353	393	Body snatching
GT2310	391.5	Wigs	GT3370	393.9	Sati
GT2318	391.5	Mustache	GT3370	393.9	Widow suicide
GT2320	391.5	Beard	GT3380	393.1	Ship burial
GT2340-2341	391.63	Cosmetics	GT3412	390.0952	Geishas
GT2340	391.63	Perfumes	GT3470	390.091734	Country life
GT2370	391.44	Eyeglasses	GT3490	390.09143	Mountain life
GT2420	392	Family	GT3510-3530	390.23	Courts and courtiers
GT2420	392.3	Home	GT3650	390.478	Minstrels
GT2460-2465	392.12	Birth customs	GT3650	390.478	Troubadours
GT2520-2540	390.082	Women	GT3770-3896	395.53	Hotels
GT2540	390.08342	Girls	GT3920-4995	394.2	Fasts and feasts
GT2600-2640	392.4	Love	GT3930-4995	394.26	Festivals
GT2620	392.4	Courtly love	GT3930-4995	394.26	Holidays
GT2640	394	Kissing	GT3980-4096	394.5	Parades
GT2650	392.4	Betrothal	GT3980-4099	394.5	Processions
GT2660-2800	392.5	Marriage customs and rites	GT3980-4099	394.5	Pageants
			GT4180-4299	394.25	Carnivals

LC	Dewey	Subject Heading	LC	Dewey	Subject Heading
GT4380-4499	394.26	Harvest festivals	GV200.2	796.5223	Rock climbing
GT4403	394.26	Kwanzaa	GV200.3	796.52	Snow and ice climbing
GT4580-4699	394.6	Fairs	GV200.4	796.58	Orienteering
GT4905-4908	394.2614	New Year	GV200.5-.56	796.5	Wilderness survival
GT4930	394.2667	Holy Week	GV200.6-.66	796.525	Caving
GT4935	394.2667	Easter	GV201-555	796.07	Physical education and training
GT4945	394.2627	May Day			
GT4945	394.2627	May-pole	GV346-350	796.043	College sports
GT4965	394.2646	Halloween	GV346	796.042	School sports
GT4975	394.2649	Thanksgiving Day	GV350.5	796.043	College athletes—Recruiting
GT4985	394.2663	Christmas			
GT4987.5	394.2667	Advent calendars	GV401-433	796.068	Sports facilities
GT4989	394.2663	Christmas trees	GV403-405	796.068	Gymnasiums
GT4995.A4	394.264	All Souls' Day	GV411-416	796.068	Athletic fields
GT4995.A6	394.262	April Fools' Day	GV415-416	796.068	Stadiums
GT4995.A8	394.266	Ascension Day	GV421-433	796.068	Playgrounds
GT4995.G	394.261	Groundhog Day	GV426-.5	796.0680284	Playgrounds—Equipment and supplies
GT4995.P3	394.262	Saint Patrick's Day			
GT4995.P45	394.266	Pentecost Festival	GV428-433	613.706	Physical fitness centers
GT4504-.995	394.262	Spring festivals	GV436	613.70287	Physical fitness—Testing
GT5010-5090	390.23	Nobility—Social life and customs	GV443	613.7042	Physical education for children
GT5020	394.23	Heralds	GV450	613.194	Nudism
GT5050	394.4	Coronations	GV451-.4	613.19406	Nudist camps
GT5220-5285	394.53	Travel	GV454.B3	796.53	Beaches
GT5220	394.53	Transportation	GV461-475	796.44	Gymnastics
GT5350-5490	390.23	Nobility—Social life and customs	GV460-548	613.71	Exercise
			GV464	613.714	Musico-callisthenics
GT5650-5680	390.24	Peasantry—Social life and customs	GV482.5	613.71081	Exercise for men
			GV501.5	613.71	Step aerobics
GT5810-5895	395.5	Hunting	GV536	613.714	Uneven parallel bars
GT5810-5850	394.3	Hunting customs	GV539	613.714	Rings (Gymnastics)
GT5810-5856.995	390.463	Harvesting	GV546.3	613.713	Weight lifting
			GV546.5-.56	646.75	Bodybuilding
GT5870-5899	392.3	Domestication	GV547.4	613.7130284	Dumbbells
GT5904-5905	394.3	Fishing	GV551-553	796.47	Acrobatics
GT6010-6070	395.52	Commerce	GV561-1198.995	796	Sports
GT6110-6390	395.52	Professions	GV561-749.5	796	Athletics
GT6550-6710	390.406927	Criminals	GV563	796.068	Athletic clubs
GV1-200	790.0135	Leisure	GV697	796.092	Athletes
GV14.5	790.092	Recreation leadership	GV709.3	796.087	Sports for the handicapped
GV33	798	Chariot racing	GV710	796.042	Intramural sports
GV35	796.8092	Gladiators	GV711	796.077	Coaching (Athletics)
GV182-.5	790.068	Recreation centers	GV713	796.06	Sports administration
GV182.8	790.191	Family recreation	GV716	796.0681	Sports—Economic aspects
GV184	790.1926	Aged—Recreation	GV721.8	796.48	Olympics—Records
GV191.2-200.56	796.5	Outdoor life	GV743-749	796.0284	Sporting goods
GV191.67.F6	333.784	Forest reserves—Recreational use	GV743-749	796.0284	Athletics—Equipment and supplies
GV191.68-198.9	796.54	Camping	GV749.B34	796.30284	Balls (Sporting goods)
GV192-198	796.54	Camps	GV749.M6	796.0284	Mouth protectors
GV197.H3	796.542087	Camps for the handicapped	GV750-770	797.5	Aeronautical sports
GV198.9	796.54	Snow camping	GV761.5	796.154	Model airplane racing
GV198.945-.975	796.56	Dude ranches	GV762-763	797.51	Ballooning
GV198.95	796.54	Swamp camping	GV763	797.51	Balloon racing
GV198.L3	796.54	Camp sites, facilities, etc.	GV764-766	797.55	Gliding and soaring
GV199-.5	796.51	Hiking	GV769.5-770	797.56	Skydiving
GV199.6	796.51	Backpacking	GV769.5-770.2	797.56	Parachuting
GV199.7	796.54	Packhorse camping	GV770.27	797.5	Bungee jumping
GV199.8-200.3	796.522	Mountaineering	GV771-840	797	Aquatic sports
GV200.19.R34	796.522	Rappelling	GV771-836.15	797.1	Boats and boating

LC	Dewey	Subject Heading	LC	Dewey	Subject Heading
GV775	797.14	Regattas	GV881.5	796.3578	T-ball
GV777.7	643.2	Boat living	GV884	796.323092	Basketball players
GV781-790.3	797.1224	Kayaking	GV885	796.323	Basketball
GV781-785	797.122	Canoes and canoeing	GV891-899	794.73	Pool (Game)
GV788.5	797.1224	Sea kayaking	GV901-909	794.6	Bowling
GV790.9-807.5	797.123	Rowing	GV910.5.D8	794.6	Duckpin bowling
GV811	797.124	Sailing, Single-handed	GV937-960	796.332	Football
GV811	797.124	Sailing	GV939	796.332092	Football players
GV811.53-.58	797.1246	Multihull sailboats	GV942.7	796.3343	Soccer referees
GV811.57	797.1246	Catamarans	GV943-944	796.334	Soccer
GV811.63.W56	797.33	Windsurfing	GV943.45-.54	796.33464	Soccer—Tournaments
GV811.65	643.2	Sailboat living	GV943.5	796.33466	Europa Cup (Soccer)
GV811.8-833	797.1246	Yachting	GV945	796.333	Rugby football
GV826.5-832	797.14	Yacht racing	GV951.18	796.3322	Football—Defense
GV832	797.14091631	Fastnet Yacht Race	GV951.25	796.3322	End play (Football)
GV833.5-835.9	797.125	Motorboats	GV951.8	796.3322	Football—Offense
GV835	797.125	Launches	GV955	796.33202022	Football—Rules
GV836	797.129	Houseboats	GV959.55.C45	796.332083	Football for children
GV837	797.24	Diving	GV961-987	796.352	Golf
GV837	797.21	Swimming	GV989	796.347	Lacrosse
GV837.9-838	797.23092	Skin divers	GV990-1005	796.342	Tennis
GV838.5	797.21	Swimming—Records	GV1003.2	796.34	Paddleball
GV838.52.C73	797.21	Swimming—Crawl stroke	GV1005	796.346	Table tennis
GV838.53.E94	613.716	Aquatic exercises	GV1006	796.346	Paddle tennis
GV838.53.L65	797.21	Long distance swimming	GV1015-.57	796.325	Volleyball
GV838.62.M45	797.24081	Diving for men	GV1015.5.B43	796.325	Beach volleyball
GV838.62.W65	797.24082	Diving for women	GV1018	796	Racing
GV838.65.J32	797.24	Diving—Jackknife dive	GV1021-1025	796.7	Automobile travel
GV838.65.S84	797.24	Diving—Swan dive	GV1029	796.73	Grand Prix racing
GV838.67.S65	797.24	Springboard diving	GV1029.2	796.73	Automobile rallies
GV838.68-.76	797.21	Life-saving	GV1029.3	796.72	Drag racing
GV838.76	797.21	Survival swimming	GV1029.7	796.6	Soap box derbies
GV840.S5	797.35	Water skiing	GV1029.9.D8	796.72	Dune buggy racing
GV840.S78	797.23	Deep diving	GV1032	796.72092	Automobile racing drivers
GV841-857	796.9	Winter sports	GV1033.5.D	796.72068759	Daytona International Speedway Race
GV843	796.97	Ice-boats	GV1040-1058	796.6(2-4)	Bicycles
GV847	796.962	Hockey	GV1040-1058	796.6(2-4)	Tricycles
GV848.9-852	796.91	Skating	GV1040-1059	796.6	Cycling
GV853	796.92	Snowshoes and showshoeing	GV1044-1046	796.64	Bicycle touring
GV854	796.93	Skis and skiing	GV1049	796.62	Bicycle racing
GV854-.87	796.935	Downhill skiing	GV1056	796.63	All terrain cycling
GV854.35	796.93068	Ski resorts	GV1060.14	796.75	Sidecar motocycle racing
GV854.9.R3	796.935	Downhill ski racing	GV1060.5-1098	796.42	Track-athletics
GV854.9.R3	796.935	Ski racing	GV1061-1069	796.42	Running
GV856	796.95	Bobsledding	GV1065-.23	796.4252	Marathon running
GV856	796.95	Tobogganing	GV1071	796.51	Walking (Sports)
GV855-.5	796.932	Cross-country skiing	GV1079-1080	796.434	Vaulting
GV857.S57	796.95	Snowboarding	GV1099	796.2	Shuffleboard
GV857.S6	796.94	Snowmobiling	GV1107-1108.6	791.82	Bullfights
GV858.2-859.7	796.21	Roller-skating	GV1111-1141	796.81	Hand-to-hand fighting
GV861	796.3	Ball games	GV1111	613.66	Self-defense
GV862-880.6	796.357	Baseball	GV1113	796.8092	Martial artists
GV865	796.357092	Baseball players	GV1114	796.8152	Judo
GV870	796.35724	Fielding (Baseball)	GV1114.3	796.8153	Karate
GV875.3	796.357075	Baseball cards	GV1114.35	796.8154	Aikido
GV877	796.357	Baseball—Records	GV1114.7	796.8159	Kung fu
GV879.5	976.357068	Baseball fields	GV1115-1137	796.83	Boxing
GV880.5	796.357083	Little League baseball	GV1143-1150.6	796.86	Fencing
GV881	796.3578	Slow pitch softball	GV1143-1150.6	796.86	Swordplay
GV881-.4	796.3578	Softball	GV1144-.2	796.86092	Fencers

LC	Dewey	Subject Heading	LC	Dewey	Subject Heading
GV1151-1181.3	799.31	Shooting	GV1788	792.84	Ballet dancing
GV1167-1172	799.31	Shooting contests	GV1789.2	792.8026	Ballet—Costume
GV1175	799.31	Pistol shooting	GV1794	792.78	Tap dancing
GV1175.5	799.31	Fast draw pistol shooting	GV1796.D57	793.33	Disco dancing
GV1177	799.31	Rifle practice	GV1796.H8	792.319969	Hula (Dance)
GV1181-.3	799.3132	Trapshooting	GV1796.J6	793.33	Jitterbug (Dance)
GV1181.3	799.3132	Skeet shooting	GV1796.L5	793.33	Lindy (Dance)
GV1185-1189	799.32	Archery	GV1796.M5	793.3	Minuet
GV1191-.75	790.134	Tournaments	GV1796.P55	793.31	Polka (Dance)
GV1195	796.812	Wrestling	GV1796.S9	793.35	Sword-dance
GV1196.5	796.812	Arm wrestling	GV1799	793.083	Dance for children
GV1199-1570	790.1	Games	GV1799.2	793.087	Dance for the handicapped
GV1201	790.13	Hobbies	GV1799.3	793.0846	Dance for the aged
GV1201.42	790.102022	Games—Rules	GV1800-1831	791.3	Circus
GV1205	793.21	Children's parties	GV1811	791.33	Clowns
GV1213	796.2	Marbles (Game)	GV1829-1831	791.32	Animal training
GV1219	790.133	Dolls	GV1834	791.84	Rodeos
GV1220	790.133	Dollhouses	GV1834.45.B35	791.84	Barrel racing
GV1220.7	790.133	Teddy bears	GV1834.7-1835.56	791.1	Carnivals
GV1221-1229	793	Indoor games			
GV1232-1299	795.4	Card games	GV1835	791.1	Carnivals
GV1251-1255	795.412	Poker	GV1838	791.3	Amateur circus
GV1282.8.D86	795.415	Duplicate contract bridge	GV1851-1860	791.068	Amusement parks
GV1283	795.413	Duplicate whist	H	300	Social sciences
GV1295.P6	795.416	Double pinochle	H1-8	300.5	Social sciences—Periodicals
GV1295.R8	795.418	Rummy (Game)			
GV1299.M3	795.34	Mah jong	H21-29	300.6	Social sciences—Congresses
GV1301-1311	795	Gambling			
GV1302	795	Gambling systems	H51-53	300.9	Social sciences—History
GV1303	795.1	Dice	H57-59	300.92	Social sciences—Biography
GV1303	795.1	Dice games	H61-.4	300.1	Social sciences—Methodology
GV1309	795.23	Roulette			
GV1312-1469	794	Board games	H61.28	361.322	Focused group interviewing
GV1313-1457	794.1	Chess	H62-.5	300.71	Social sciences—Study and teaching
GV1461-1463	794.2	Checkers			
GV1467	795.32	Dominoes	H62-.5	300.72	Social sciences—Research
GV1469.15-.25	794.8	Computer games	H62	300.724	Social sciences—Experiments
GV1469.2	794.8	Electronic games			
GV1469.3	794.8	Video games	HA	310	Statistics
GV1470-1521	793.2	Entertaining	HA1	310.5	Statistics—Periodicals
GV1491-1507	793.73	Puzzles	HA17	310.3	Statistics—Dictionaries
GV1493	790.138	Literary recreations	HA19	310.9	Statistics—History
GV1507.A5	793.734	Anagrams	HA29-32	310.1	Statistics—Methodology
GV1507.C7	793.732	Crossword puzzles	HA30.6	310.1	Spatial analysis (Statistics)
GV1541-1561	793.8	Conjuring	HA31	001.4226	Statistics—Graphic methods
GV1541-1561	793.8	Tricks	HA31.2	310.0723	Sampling (Statistics)
GV1545	793.8092	Magicians	HA31.3	310.72	Correlation (Statistics)
GV1549	793.85	Card tricks	HA35	310.72	Statistics—Research
GV1557	793.89	Ventriloquism	HA154-4737	310	Vital statistics
GV1564-1565	794.3	Darts (Game)	HA175-4737	310	Census
GV1570	796.156	Model car racing	HA201-730	317.3	United States—Census
GV1580 1799.4	792.8	Dance	HA201-214	317.3	United States—Statistics, Vital
GV1580-1799	793.31	Folk dancing			
GV1600	792.809	Dance criticism	HA201-214	317.3	United States—Statistics [United States, By state]—Census
GV1746-1750	793.38	Balls (Parties)	HA221-730	317.(4-7.9)	
GV1751	793.33	Ballroom dancing			
GV1757	793.38	Balls (Parties)	HA740	319.82	Greenland—Census
GV1761	793.33	Waltz	HA741-750	317.1	Canada—Census
GV1783	792.8	Modern dance	HA761-770	317.2	Mexico—Census
GV1785	792.8092	Dance—Biography	HA791-800	317.282	Belize—Census
GV1787	792.84	Ballet	HA801-810	317.286	Costa Rica—Census

LC	Dewey	Subject Heading	LC	Dewey	Subject Heading
HA811-820	317.281	Guatemala—Census	HA1541-1560	314.6	Spain—Census
HA821-830	317.283	Honduras—Census	HA1571-1580	314.69	Portugal—Census
HA831-840	317.285	Nicaragua—Census	HA1591-1610	314.94	Switzerland—Census
HA841-850	317.284	El Salvador—Census	HA1620.5	314.965	Albania—Census
HA851-854	317.287	Panama—Census	HA1621-1630	314.99	Bulgaria—Census
HA861	317.296	Bahamas—Census	HA1631-1635	314.97	Yugoslavia—Census
HA865	317.2981	Barbados—Census	HA1641-1650	314.98	Romania—Census
HA866-.9	317.297	Leeward Islands (West Indies)—Census	HA2280	314.699	Azores—Census
			HA2285	314.698	Madeira Islands—Census
HA867	317.2983	Trinidad and Tobago—Census	HA2287	316.49	Canary Islands—Census
			HA2289	316.658	Cape Verde—Census
HA871-880	317.291	Cuba—Census	HA2291	319.73	Saint Helena—Census
HA881-885	317.294	Haiti—Census	HA2295	319.71	Falkland Islands—Census
HA886-890	317.293	Dominican Republic—Census	HA2300	315.495	Maldives—Census
			HA2301	316.96	Seychelles—Census
HA891-900	317.292	Jamaica—Census	HA2303	316.94	Comoro Islands—Census
HA901-910	317.295	Puerto Rico—Census	HA2305	316.982	Mauritius—Census
HA911-915	317.29722	Virgin Islands of the United States—Census	HA2307	316.981	Reunion—Census
			HA2309	316.99	Kerguelen Islands—Census
HA917-.78	317.2986	Netherlands Antilles—Census	HA3001-3010	319.4	Australia—Census
			HA3171-3190	319.3	New Zealand—Census
HA918.7	317.2976	Guadeloupe—Census	HA4012	319.67	Guam—Census
HA918.9	317.2982	Martinique—Census	HA4013	319.53	Papua New Guinea—Census
HA921-930	317.299	Bermuda Islands—Census	HA4014	319.593	Solomon Islands—Census
HA941-960	318.2	Argentina—Census	HA4015	319.597	New Caledonia—Census
HA961-970	318.4	Bolivia—Census	HA4015.5	319.595	Vanuatu—Census
HA971-990	318.1	Brazil—Census	HA4016	319.611	Fiji—Census
HA991-1010	318.3	Chile—Census	HA4016.7	319.681	Kiribati—Census
HA1011-1020	318.61	Colombia—Census	HA4017	319.612	Tonga—Census
HA1021-1030	318.66	Ecuador—Census	HA4017.5	319.623	Cook Islands—Census
HA1033	318.81	Guyana—Census	HA4018.5	319.613	American Samoa—Census
HA1035	318.83	Surinam—Census	HA4020-.5	319.89	Antarctica
HA1037	318.82	French Guiana—Census	HA4556.5	315.61	Turkey—Census
HA1041-1050	318.92	Paraguay—Census	HA4557	315.693	Cyprus—Census
HA1051-1070	318.5	Peru—Census	HA4558	315.691	Syria—Census
HA1071-1090	318.95	Uruguay—Census	HA4559	315.692	Lebanon—Census
HA1091-1100	318.7	Venezuela—Census	HA4560	315.694	Israel—Census
HA1107-1650	314	Europe—Census	HA4561	315.695	Jordan—Census
HA1121-1170	314.1	Great Britain—Census	HA4563	315.38	Saudi Arabia—Census
HA1141-1150	314.16	Northern Ireland—Census	HA4564	315.33	Yemen—Census
HA1151-1160	314.11	Scotland—Census	HA4565	315.353	Oman—Census
HA1161-1170	314.29	Wales—Census	HA4566	315.357	United Arab Emirates—Census
HA1170.1-.5	314.15	Ireland—Census			
HA1171-1190	314.36	Austria—Census	HA4567	315.363	Qatar—Census
HA1191-1200	314.37	Czechoslovakia—Census	HA4568	315.365	Bahrain—Census
HA1201-1210	314.39	Hungary—Census	HA4569	315.67	Iraq—Census
HA1210.5	314.3648	Liechtenstein—Census	HA4570.2	315.5	Iran—Census
HA1211-1230	314.4	France—Census	HA4570.6	315.81	Afghanistan—Census
HA1231-1349	314.3	Germany—Census	HA4570.7	315.91	Burma—Census
HA1351-1359	314.95	Greece—Census	HA4570.8	315.493	Sri Lanka—Census
HA1361-1379	314.5	Italy—Census	HA4570.9	315.496	Nepal—Census
HA1381-1390	314.92	Netherlands—Census	HA4581-4590	315.4	India—Census
HA1391-1410	314.93	Belgium—Census	HA4590.3	315.498	Bhutan—Census
HA1411-1420	314.935	Luxembourg—Census	HA4590.5	315.491	Pakistan—Census
HA1431-1450.12	314.7	Russia—Census	HA4590.6	315.492	Bangladesh—Census
HA1450.5	314.897	Finland—Census	HA4600.3	315.96	Cambodia—Census
HA1451-1460	314.38	Poland—Census	HA4600.4	315.94	Laos—Census
HA1471-1490	314.89	Denmark—Census	HA4600.5	315.97	Vietnam—Census
HA1491-1500	314.912	Iceland—Census	HA4600.55	315.93	Thailand—Census
HA1501-1520	314.81	Norway—Census	HA4600.6	315.95	Malaysia—Census
HA1521-1540	314.85	Sweden—Census	HA4601-4610	315.98	Indonesia—Census

LC	Dewey	Subject Heading	LC	Dewey	Subject Heading
HA4611-4620	315.99	Philippines—Census	HB21	330.06	Economics—Congresses
HA4621-4630	315.2	Japan—Census	HB61	330.03	Economics—Dictionaries
HA4630.5-.6	315.19	Korea—Census	HB63	330.025	Economics—Directories
HA4630.8	315.17	Mongolia—Census	HB131	330.01	Economics—Methodology
HA4631-4640	315.1	China—Census	HB75-130	330.09	Economics—History
HA4641-4645	315.126	Macao—Census	HB77-83	330.090(1-33)	Economics—History—To 1800
HA4646-4650	315.1249	Taiwan—Census			
HA4651-4655	315.125	Hong Kong—Census	HB85	330.09034	Economics—History—19th century
HA4682	316.4	Morocco—Census			
HA4683	316.5	Algeria—Census	HB87	330.0904	Economics—History—20th century
HA4684	316.11	Tunisia—Census			
HA4685	316.12	Libya—Census	HB91	330.1513	Mercantile system
HA4686	316.2	Egypt—Census	HB95	330.122	Free enterprise
HA4687	316.24	Sudan—Census	HB97.5	335.4	Marxian economics
HA4689	316.3	Ethiopia—Census	HB137	330.0727	Economics—Statistical methods
HA4690	316.773	Somalia—Census			
HA4691	316.771	Djibouti—Census	HB139-141	330.015195	Econometrics
HA4693	316.762	Kenya—Census	HB141	330.011	Econometric models
HA4694	316.761	Uganda—Census	HB142	339.23	Input-output analysis
HA4695	316.7571	Rwanda—Census	HB143	338.52	Shadow prices
HA4696	316.7572	Burundi—Census	HB145	339.5	Equilibrium (Economics)
HA4697	316.78	Tanzania—Census	HB201-205	330.157	Marginal utility
HA4698	316.79	Mozambique—Census	HB201-206	338.521	Value
HA4699	316.91	Madagascar—Census	HB201-206	338.521	Supply and demand
HA4701	316.8	South Africa—Census	HB206	335.412	Labor theory of value
HA4702	316.80	Rhodesia—Census	HB221-236	338.52	Prices
HA4703	316.894	Zambia—Census	HB236	330.526	Prices—Government policy
HA4704	316.885	Lesotho—Census	HB238	338.6048	Competition, Imperfect
HA4705	316.887	Swaziland—Census	HB241	330.15	Supply-side economics
HA4706	316.883	Botswana—Census	HB401	333.5/339.21	Rent
HA4707	316.897	Malawi—Census	HB501	332.041	Capital
HA4708	316.881	Namibia—Census	HB522-715	331.21	Income
HA4710	316.73	Angola—Census	HB531-549	332.6323	Interest rates
HA4711	316.751	Zaire—Census	HB551	332.83	Usury
HA4712	316.718	Equatorial Guinea—Census	HB601	338.516	Profit
HA4713	316.715	Sao Tome and Principe—Census	HB615	338.04	Entrepreneurship
			HB615	338.5	Risk
HA4715	316.721	Gabon—Census	HB701-715	330.17	Property
HA4716	316.724	Congo (Brazzaville)—Census	HB801-843	339.47	Consumption (Economics)
HA4717	316.741	Central African Republic—Census	HB848-3697	304.6	Demography
			HB848-3697	304.6	Population
HA4718	316.743	Chad—Census	HB848	304.605	Demography—Periodicals
HA4719	316.711	Cameroon—Census	HB850-.5	304.6072	Population Research
HA4722	316.683	Benin—Census	HB851-853	304.609	Population—History
HA4723	316.681	Togo—Census	HB855-865	304.6092	Demography—Biography
HA4724	316.626	Niger—Census	HB883.5	363.9	Population policy
HA4725	316.668	Cote d'Ivoire—Census	HB884	304.6091724	Developing countries—Population
HA4726	316.652	Guinea—Census			
HA4727	316.623	Mali—Census	HB884.5	363.96091724	Population assistance
HA4728	316.625	Burkina Faso—Census	HB887	304.6	Demographic transition
HA4729	316.63	Senegal—Census	HB901-1108	304.632	Fertilily, Human
HA4730	316.61	Mauritania—Census	HB901-1108	304.63209(1-9)	Fertility, Human—[By region or country]
HA4731	316.69	Nigeria—Census			
HA4732	316.67	Ghana—Census	HB1108	304.632091724	Fertility, Human—Developing countries
HA4733	316.64	Sierra Leone—Census			
HA4734	316.651	Gambia—Census	HB1111-1317	306.81021	Marital status—Statistics
HA4735	316.662	Liberia—Census	HB1121-1317	306.8109	Marital status—[By region or country]
HA4736	316.657	Guinea-Bissau—Census			
HA4737	316.48	Western Sahara—Census	HB1125-1126	306.810973	Marital status—United States
HB1-130	330	Economics			
HB1-9	330.05	Economics—Periodicals			

LC	Dewey	Subject Heading	LC	Dewey	Subject Heading
HB1145	306.81097(4-9)	Marital status—[United States, By state]	HB2007-2008	304.6097296	Population geography—Bahamas
HB1147	306.81097(4-9)	Marital status—[United States, By city]	HB2009-2010	304.6097291	Population geography—Cuba
HB1321-1528	304.64	Mortality	HB2011	304.6097294	Population geography—Haiti
HB1322	304.64021	Mortality—Tables			
HB1323.B5	304.6408996073	Afro-Americans—Mortality	HB2012	304.6097293	Population geography—Dominican Republic
HB1323.C5	304.64083	Children—Mortality			
HB1323.S8	362.28021	Suicide—Statistics	HB2013-2014	304.6097292	Population geography—Jamaica
HB1335-1526	304.645(4-9)	Mortality—[By region or country]	HB2016.3	304.609729722	Population geography—Virgin Islands of the United States
HB1528	304.6451724	Mortality—Developing countries			
HB1531-1738	305.2	Age distribution (Demography)	HB2016.57	304.60972981	Population geography—Barbados
HB1541-1737	305.209(4-9)	Age distribution (Demography)—[By region or country]	HB2016.72	304.60972973	Population geography—Anguilla
			HB2016.74	304.60972974	Population geography—Antigua
HB1545-1567	305.20973	Age distribution (Demography)—United States	HB2016.76	304.60972975	Population geography—Monserrat
HB1565	305.2097(4-9)	Age distribution (Demography)—[United States, By state]	HB2016.78	304.60972973	Population geography—Saint Kitts and Nevis
HB1741-1948	305.3	Sex distribution (Demography)	HB2016.93	304.609729841	Population geography—Dominica
HB1755-1777	305.30973	Sex distribution (Demography)—United States	HB2016.95	304.609729845	Population geography—Grenada
HB1775	305.3097(4-9)	Sex distribution (Demography)—[United States, By state]	HB2016.97	304.609729843	Population geography—Saint Lucia
HB1777	305.3097(4-9)	Sex distribution (Demography)—[United States, By city]	HB2016.99	304.609729844	Population geography—Saint Vincent
			HB2017	304.60972983	Population geography—Trinidad and Tobago
HB1953	304.61	Population density	HB2017.35	304.60972986	Population geography—Aruba
HB1955	307.24	Rural-urban migration			
HB1956-2157	307.26	Urban-rural migration	HB2017.36	304.60972986	Population geography—Bonaire
HB1965-1987	304.60973	Population geography—United States	HB2017.37	304.60972986	Population geography—Curacao
HB1985	304.6097(4-9)	Population geography—[United States, By state]	HB2017.385	304.60972977	Population geography—Saint Eustatius (Netherlands Antilles)
HB1987	304.6097(4-9)	Population geography—[United States, By city]	HB2017.39	304.60972977	Population geography—Saint Martin
HB1989-1990	304.60971	Population geography—Canada			
HB1991-1992	304.60972	Population geography—Mexico	HB2017.7	304.60972976	Population geography—Guadeloupe
HB1995-1996	304.6097282	Population geography—Belize	HB2017.9	304.60972982	Population geography—Martinique
HB1997-1998	304.6097286	Population geography—Costa Rica	HB2019-2020	304.60982	Population geography—Argentina
HB1999	304.6097281	Population geography—Guatemala	HB2021-2022	304.60984	Population geography—Bolivia
HB2000	304.6097283	Population geography—Honduras	HB2023-2024	304.60981	Population geography—Brazil
HB2001	304.6097285	Population geography—Nicaragua	HB2025-2026	304.60983	Population geography—Chile
HB2002-2003	304.6097287	Population geography—Panama	HB2027-2028	304.609861	Population geography—Colombia
HB2004	304.6097284	Population geography—El Salvador	HB2029-2030	304.609866	Population geography—Ecuador

LC	Dewey	Subject Heading	LC	Dewey	Subject Heading
HB2032.3	304.609881	Population geography—Guyana	HB2083-2084	304.609494	Population geography—Switzerland
HB2032.5	304.609883	Population geography—Surinam	HB2086.5	304.6094965	Population geography—Albania
HB2032.7	304.609882	Population geography—French Guiana	HB2087-2088	304.609499	Population geography—Bulgaria
HB2033-2034	304.609892	Population geography—Paraguay	HB2088.5	304.609497	Population geography—Yugoslavia
HB2035-2036	304.60985	Population geography—Peru	HB2091-2092	304.609498	Population geography—Romania
HB2037-2038	304.609895	Population geography—Uruguay	HB2092.5	304.609495	Population geography—Greece
HB2039-2040	304.60987	Population geography—Venezuela	HB2093.4	304.609561	Population geography—Turkey
HB2045-2046	304.60942(9)	Population geography—England and Wales	HB2093.5	304.6095693	Population geography—Cyprus
HB2047-2048	304.609411	Population geography—Scotland	HB2093.7	304.6095691	Population geography—Syria
HB2048.5	304.609416	Population geography—Northern Ireland	HB2093.9	304.6095692	Population geography—Lebanon
HB2049-2050	304.609415	Population geography—Ireland	HB2094	304.6095694	Population geography—Israel
HB2051-2052	304.609436	Population geography—Austria	HB2094.3	304.6095695	Population geography—Jordan
HB2052.3	304.609437	Population geography—Czuuhoslovakia	HB2094.7	304.609538	Population geography—Saudi Arabia
HB2052.5	304.609439	Population geography—Hungary	HB2094.9-2095	304.609533	Population geography—Yemen
HB2052.9	304.60943648	Population geography—Liechtenstein	HB2095.3	304.6095353	Population geography—Oman
HB2053-2054	304.60944	Population geography—France	HB2095.5	304.6095357	Population geography—United Arab Emirates
HB2055-2056	304.60944949	Population geography—Germany	HB2095.7	304.6095363	Population geography—Qatar
HB2059-2060	304.60945	Population geography—Italy	HB2095.9	304.6095365	Population geography—Bahrain
HB2063-2064	304.609493	Population geography—Belgium	HB2096	304.6095367	Population geography—Kuwait
HB2065-2066	304.609492	Population geography—Netherlands	HB2096.3	304.609567	Population geography—Iraq
HB2066.5	304.6094935	Population geography—Luxembourg	HB2096.4	304.60955	Population geography—Iran
HB2067-2068.2	304.60947	Population geography—Russia	HB2096.6	304.609581	Population geography—Aghanistan
HB2068.3	304.6094897	Population geography—Finland	HB2096.7	304.609591	Population geography—Burma
HB2068.7	304.609438	Population geography—Poland	HB2096.8	304.6095493	Population geography—Sri Lanka
HB2071-2072	304.609489	Population geography—Denmark	HB2096.9	304.6095496	Population geography—Nepal
HB2073-2074	304.6094912	Population geography—Iceland	HB2099-2100	304.60954	Population geography—India
HB2075-2076	304.609481	Population geography—Norway	HB2100.3	304.6095498	Population geography—Bhutan
HB2077-2078	304.609485	Population geography—Sweden	HB2100.5	304.6095491	Population geography—Pakistan
HB2079-2080	304.60946	Population geography—Spain	HB2100.6	304.6095492	Population geography—Bangladesh
HB2081-2082	304.609469	Population geography—Portugal	HB2104.3	304.609596	Population geography—Cambodia

LC	Dewey	Subject Heading	LC	Dewey	Subject Heading
HB2104.4	304.609594	Population geography—Laos	HB2123.6	304.6096894	Population geography—Zambia
HB2104.5	304.609597	Population geography—Vietnam	HB2123.7	304.6096885	Population geography—Lesotho
HB2104.55	304.609593	Population geography—Thailand	HB2123.8	304.6096887	Population geography—Swaziland
HB2104.6	304.609595	Population geography—Malaysia	HB2123.9	304.6096883	Population geography—Botswana
HB2107-2108	304.609598	Population geography—Indonesia	HB2124	304.6096897	Population geography—Malawi
HB2109-2110	304.609599	Population geography—Philippines	HB2124.2	304.6096881	Population geography—Namibia
HB2111-2112	304.60952	Population geography—Japan	HB2124.4	304.609673	Population geography—Angola
HB2112.5-.6	304.609519	Population geography—Korea	HB2124.5	304.6096751	Population geography—Zaire
HB2112.8	304.609517	Population geography—Mongolia	HB2124.6	304.6096718	Population geography—Equatoria Guinea
HB2114	304.60951	Population geography—China	HB2124.7	304.6096715	Population geography—Sao Tome and Principe
HB2115	304.6095126	Population geography—Macao	HB2124.9	304.6096721	Population geography—Gabon
HB2116	304.60951249	Population geography—Taiwan	HB2125	304.6096724	Population geography—Congo (Brazzaville)
HB2117	304.6095125	Population geography—Hong Kong	HB2125.2	304.6096741	Population geography—Ubangi-Shari
HB2121.3	304.60964	Population geography—Morocco	HB2125.3	304.6096743	Population geography—Chad
HB2121.4	304.60965	Population geography—Algeria	HB2125.4	304.6096711	Population geography—Cameroon
HB2121.5	304.609611	Population geography—Tunisia	HB2125.7	304.6096683	Population geography—Benin
HB2121.6	304.609612	Population geography—Libya	HB2125.8	304.6096681	Population geography—Togo
HB2121.7	304.60962	Population geography—Egypt	HB2125.9	304.6096626	Population geography—Niger
HB2121.8	304.609624	Population geography—Sudan	HB2126	304.6096668	Population geography—Cote d'Ivoire
HB2122	304.60963	Population geography—Ethiopia	HB2126.2	304.6096652	Population geography—Guinea
HB2122.2	304.6096773	Population geography—Somalia	HB2126.3	304.6096623	Population geography—Mali
HB2122.3	304.6096771	Population geography—Djibouti	HB2126.4	304.6096625	Population geography—Burkina Faso
HB2122.5	304.6096762	Population geography—Kenya	HB2126.5	304.609663	Population geography—Senegal
HB2122.6	304.6096761	Population geography—Uganda	HB2126.6	304.609661	Population geography—Mauritania
HB2122.7	304.60967571	Population geography—Rwanda	HB2126.7	304.609669	Population geography—Nigeria
HB2122.8	304.60967572	Population geography—Burundi	HB2126.8	304.609667	Population geography—Ghana
HB2122.9	304.609678	Population geography—Tanzania	HB2126.9	304.609664	Population geography—Sierra Leone
HB2123	304.609679	Population geography—Mozambique	HB2127	304.6096651	Population geography—Gambia
HB2123.2	304.609691	Population geography—Madagascar	HB2127.2	304.6096662	Population geography—Liberia
HB2123.4	304.60968	Population geography—South Africa	HB2127.3	304.6096657	Population geography—Guinea-Bissau

LC	Dewey	Subject Heading	LC	Dewey	Subject Heading
HB2127.4	304.609648	Population geography—Western Sahara	HB2160	304.6091724	Population geography—Developing countries
HB2127.5	304.6094699	Population geography—Azores	HB2371-2578	304.6091734	Rural population
			HB2581-2787	331.7	Occupations—Statistics
HB2128	304.6097299	Population geography—Bermuda Islands	HB3505-3527	304.60973	Demography—United States
HB2128.5	304.6094698	Population geography—Madeira Islands	HB3525	304.6097(4-9)	Demography—[United States, By State]
HB2129	304.609649	Population geography—Canary Islands	HB3527	304.6097(4-9)	Demography—[United States, By City]
HB2129.5	304.6096658	Population geography—Cape Verde	HB3529-3530	304.60971	Demography—Canada
			HB3531-3532	304.60972	Demography—Mexico
HB2130	304.609973	Population geography—Saint Helena	HB3535-3536	304.6097282	Demography—Belize
HB2130.5	304.609973	Population geography—Tristan da Cunha	HB3537-3538	304.6097286	Demography—Costa Rica
			HB3539	304.6097281	Demography—Guatemala
HB2131	304.6099711	Population geography—Falkland Islands	HB3540	304.6097283	Demography—Honduras
			HB3541	304.6097285	Demography—Nicaragua
HB2131.5	304.6095495	Population geography—Maldives	HB3542-3543	304.6097287	Demography—Panama
			HB3544	304.6097284	Demography—El Salvador
HB2132	304.609696	Population geography—Seychelles	HB3547-3548	304.6097296	Demography—Bahamas
			HB3549-3550	304.6097291	Demography—Cuba
HB2132.5	304.609694	Population geography—Comoro Islands	HB3551	304.6097294	Demography—Haiti
			HB3552	304.6097293	Demography—Dominican Republic
HB2133	304.6096982	Population geography—Mauritius	HB3553-3554	304.6097292	Demography—Jamaica
HB2133.5	304.6096981	Population geography—Reunion	HB3556.3	304.609729722	Demography—Virgin Islands of the United States
			HB3556.57	304.60972901	Demography—Barbados
HB2134	304.609699	Population geography—Kerguelen Islands	HB3556.72	304.60972973	Demography—Anguilla
			HB3556.74	304.60972974	Demography—Antigua
HB2135-2136	304.60994	Population geography—Australia	HB3556.76	304.60972975	Demography—Montserrat
			HB3556.78	304.60972973	Demography—Saint Kitts and Nevis
HB2152.5	304.60993	Population geography—New Zealand	HB3556.93	304.609729841	Demography—Dominica
HB2152.7	304.609967	Population geography—Guam	HB3556.95	304.609729845	Demography—Grenada
			HB3556.97	304.609729843	Demography—Saint Lucia
HB2152.8	304.609953	Population geography—Papua New Guinea	HB3556.99	304.609729844	Demography—Saint Vincent
			HB3557	304.60972983	Demography—Trinidad and Tobago
HB2152.9	304.6099681	Population geography—Kiribati	HB3557.35	304.60972986	Demography—Aruba
			HB3557.36	304.60972986	Demography—Bonaire
HB2153	304.6099593	Population geography—Solomon Islands	HB3557.37	304.60972986	Demography—Curacao
			HB3557.38	304.60972977	Demography—Saba (Netherlands Antilles)
HB2153.3	304.6099597	Population geography—New Caledonia	HB3557.385	304.60972977	Demography—Saint Eustatius (Netherlands Antilles)
HB2153.4	304.6099595	Population geography—Vanuatu			
HB2153.5	304.6099611	Population geography—Fiji	HB3557.39	304.60972977	Demography—Saint Martin
HB2153.6	304.6099612	Population geography—Tonga	HB3557.7	304.60972976	Demography—Guadeloupe
			HB3557.9	304.60972982	Demography—Martinique
HB2153.65	304.6099623	Population geography—Cook Islands	HB3559-3560	304.60982	Demography—Argentina
			HB3561-3562	304.60984	Demography—Bolivia
HB2153.7	304.6099613	Population geography—American Samoa	HB3563-3564	304.60981	Demography—Brazil
			HB3565-3566	304.60983	Demography—Chile
HB2153.8	304.6099614	Population geography—Western Samoa	HB3567-3568	304.609861	Demography—Colombia
			HB3569-3570	304.609866	Demography—Ecuador
HB2153.9	304.609962	Population geography—French Polynesia	HB3572.3	304.609881	Demography—Guyana
			HB3572.5	304.609883	Demography—Surinam
HB2155	304.60998(1-8)	Population geography—Arctic regions	HB3572.7	304.609882	Demography—French Guiana
HB2156	304.609982	Population geography—Greenland	HB3573-3574	304.609892	Demography—Paraguay
			HB3575-3576	304.60985	Demography—Peru

LC	Dewey	Subject Heading	LC	Dewey	Subject Heading
HB3577-3578	304.609895	Demography—Uruguay	HB3644.5	304.609597	Demography—Vietnam
HB3579-3580	304.60987	Demography—Venezuela	HB3644.55	304.609593	Demography—Thailand
HB3585-3586	304.60942(9)	Demography—England and Wales	HB3644.6	304.609595	Demography—Malaysia
			HB3647-3648	304.609598	Demography—Indonesia
HB3587-3588	304.609411	Demography—Scotland	HB3649-3650	304.609599	Demography—Philippines
HB3588.5	304.609416	Demography—Northern Ireland	HB3651-3652	304.60952	Demography—Japan
			HB3652.5-.6	304.609519	Demography—Korea
HB3589-3590	304.609415	Demography—Ireland	HB3652.8	304.609517	Demography—Mongolia
HB3591-3592	304.609436	Demography—Austria	HB3654	304.60951	Demography—China
HB3592.3	304.609437	Demography—Czechoslovakia	HB3655	304.6095126	Demography—Macao
			HB3656	304.60951249	Demography—Taiwan
HB3592.5	304.609439	Demography—Hungary	HB3657	304.6095125	Demography—Hong Kong
HB3592.9	304.60943648	Demography—Liechtenstein	HB3661.3	304.60964	Demography—Morocco
HB3593-3594	304.60944	Demography—France	HB3661.4	304.60965	Demography—Algeria
HB3594.5	304.60944949	Demography—Monaco	HB3661.5	304.609611	Demography—Tunisia
HB3595-3596.5	304.60943	Demography—Germany	HB3661.6	304.609612	Demography—Libya
HB3599-3600	304.60945	Demography—Italy	HB3661.7	304.60962	Demography—Egypt
HB3603-3604	304.609493	Demography—Belgium	HB3661.8	304.609624	Demography—Sudan
HB3605-3606	304.609492	Demography—Netherlands	HB3662	304.60963	Demography—Ethiopia
HB3606.5	304.6094935	Demography—Luxembourg	HB3662.2	304.6096773	Demography—Somalia
HB3607-3608.2	304.60947	Demography—Russia	HB3662.3	304.6096771	Demography—Djibouti
HB3608.3	304.6094897	Demography—Finland	HB3662.5	304.6096762	Demography—Kenya
HB3608.7	304.609438	Demography—Poland	HB3662.6	304.6096761	Demography—Uganda
HB3611-3612	304.609489	Demography—Denmark	HB3662.7	304.60967571	Demography—Rwanda
HB3613-3614	304.6094912	Demography—Iceland	HB3662.8	304.60967572	Demography—Burundi
HB3615-3616	304.609481	Demography—Norway	HB3662.9	304.609678	Demography—Tanzania
HB3617-3618	304.609485	Demography—Sweden	HB3663	304.609679	Demography—Mozambique
HB3619-3620	304.60946	Demography—Spain	HB3663.2	304.609691	Demography—Madagascar
HB3621-3622	304.609469	Demography—Portugal	HB3663.4	304.60968	Demography—South Africa
HB3623-3624	304.609494	Demography—Switzerland	HB3663.6	304.6096894	Demography—Zambia
HB3626.5	304.6094965	Demography—Albania	HB3663.7	304.6096885	Demography—Lesotho
HB3627-3628	304.609499	Demography—Bulgaria	HB3663.8	304.6096887	Demography—Swaziland
HB3628.5	304.609497	Demography—Yugoslavia	HB3663.9	304.6096883	Demography—Botswana
HB3631-3632	304.609498	Demography—Romania	HB3664	304.6096897	Demography—Malawi
HB3632.5	304.609495	Demography—Greece	HB3664.2	304.6096881	Demography—Namibia
HB3633.4	304.609561	Demography—Turkey	HB3664.4	304.609673	Demography—Angola
HB3633.5	304.6095693	Demography—Cyprus	HB3664.5	304.6096751	Demography—Zaire
HB3633.7	304.6095691	Demography—Syria	HB3664.6	304.6096718	Demography—Equatorial Guinea
HB3633.9	304.6095692	Demography—Lebanon			
HB3634	304.6095694	Demography—Israel	HB3664.7	304.6096715	Demography—Sao Tome and Principe
HB3634.3	304.6095695	Demography—Jordan			
HB3634.7	304.609538	Demography—Saudi Arabia	HB3664.9	304.6096721	Demography—Gabon
HB3634.9-3635	304.609533	Demography—Yemen	HB3665	304.6096724	Demography—Congo (Brazzaville)
HB3635.3	304.6095353	Demography—Oman			
HB3635.5	304.6095357	Demography—United Arab Emirates	HB3665.2	304.6096741	Demography—Ubangi-Shari
			HB3665.3	304.6096743	Demography—Chad
HB3635.7	304.6095363	Demography—Qatar	HB3665.4	304.6096711	Demography—Cameroon
HB3635.9	304.6095365	Demography—Bahrain	HB3665.7	304.6096683	Demography—Benin
HB3636	304.6095367	Demography—Kuwait	HB3665.8	304.6096681	Demography—Togo
HB3636.3	304.609567	Demography—Iraq	HB3665.9	304.6096626	Demography—Niger
HB3636.4	304.60955	Demography—Iran	HB3666	304.6096668	Demography—Cote d'Ivoire
HB3636.6	304.609581	Demography—Afghanistan	HB3666.2	304.6096652	Demography—Guinea
HB3636.7	304.609591	Demography—Burma	HB3666.3	304.6096623	Demography—Mali
HB3636.8	304.6095493	Demography—Sri Lanka	HB3666.4	304.6096625	Demography—Burkina Faso
HB3636.9	304.6095496	Demography—Nepal	HB3666.5	304.609663	Demography—Senegal
HB3639-3640	304.60954	Demography—India	HB3666.6	304.609661	Demography—Mauritania
HB3640.3	304.6095498	Demography—Bhutan	HB3666.7	304.609669	Demography—Nigeria
HB3640.5	304.6095491	Demography—Pakistan	HB3666.8	304.609667	Demography—Ghana
HB3640.6	304.6095492	Demography—Bangladesh	HB3666.9	304.609664	Demography—Sierra Leone
HB3644.3	304.609596	Demography—Cambodia	HB3667	304.6096651	Demography—Gambia
HB3644.4	304.609594	Demography—Laos	HB3667.2	304.6096662	Demography—Liberia

LC	Dewey	Subject Heading	LC	Dewey	Subject Heading
HB3667.3	304.6096657	Demography—Guinea-Bissau	HC59-60.5	330.09044	Economic history—1945-
HB3667.4	304.609648	Demography—Western Sahara	HC79.C3	332.041	Capital
			HC79.C6	339.47092	Consumers
HB3667.5	304.6094699	Demography—Azores	HC79.C6	339.47	Consumption (Economics)
HB3668	304.6097299	Demography—Bermuda Islands	HC79.D5	338.7	Business relocation
			HC79.F3	363.8	Famines
HB3668.5	304.6094698	Demography—Madeira Islands	HC79.I55	303.4833	Information technology
			HC79.P6	339.46	Poverty
HB3669	304.609649	Demography—Canary Islands	HC79.P7	338.516	Profit
			HC101-110	330.973	United States—Economic conditions
HB3669.5	304.6096658	Demography—Cape Verde	HC110.5	330.9982	Greenland—Economic conditions
HB3670	304.609973	Demography—Saint Helena			
HB3670.5	304.609973	Demography—Tristan da Cunha	HC111-120	330.971	Canada—Economic conditions
HB3671	304.6099711	Demography—Falkland Islands	HC131-140	330.972	Mexico—Economic conditions
HB3671.5	304.6095495	Demography—Maldives	HC141-148	330.9728	Central America—Economic conditions
HB3672	304.609696	Demography—Seychelles			
HB3672.5	304.609694	Demography—Comoro Islands	HC151-158.6	330.9729	West Indies—Economic conditions
HB3673	304.6096982	Demography—Mauritius	HC161-239.5	330.98	South America—Economic conditions
HB3673.5	304.6096981	Demography—Reunion			
HB3674	304.609699	Demography—Kerguelen Islands	HC171-180	330.982	Argentina—Economic conditions
HB3675-3676	304.60994	Demography—Australia	HC181-185	330.984	Bolivia—Economic conditions
HB3692.5	304.60993	Demography—New Zealand			
HB3692.7	304.609967	Demography—Guam	HC186-190	330.981	Brazil—Economic conditions
HB3692.8	304.609953	Demography—Papua New Guinea	HC191-195	330.983	Chile—Economic conditions
			HC196-200	330.9861	Colombia—Economic conditions
HB3692.9	304.6099681	Demography—Kiribati			
HB3693	304.6099593	Demography—Solomon Islands	HC201-204.5	330.9866	Ecuador—Economic conditions
HB3693.3	304.6099597	Demography—New Caledonia	HC221-225	330.9892	Paraguay—Economic conditions
HB3693.4	304.6099595	Demography—Vanuatu	HC226-230	330.985	Peru—Economic conditions
HB3693.5	304.6099611	Demography—Fiji	HC231-235	330.9895	Uruguay—Economic conditions
HB3693.6	304.6099612	Demography—Tonga			
HB3693.65	304.6099623	Demography—Cook Islands	HC236-239.5	330.987	Venezuela—Economic conditions
HB3693.7	304.6099613	Demography—American Samoa	HC240-407	330.94	Europe—Economic conditions
HB3693.8	304.6099614	Demography—Western Samoa	HC241.2-.25	341.2422	European Economic Community literature
HB3693.9	304.609962	Demography—French Polynesia	HC246	330.917241	Commonwealth countries—Economic conditions
HB3695	304.60998	Demography—Arctic Regions	HC251-260	330.942	England—Economic conditions
HB3696	304.609982	Demography—Greenland	HC261-270	330.9436	Austria—Economic conditions
HB3711-3840	338.542	Business cycles			
HB3711-3840	338.542	Depressions	HC270.2-.295	330.9437	Czechoslovakia—Economic conditions
HB3722-3725	338.542	Financial crises			
HB3729	338.542	Long waves (Economics)	HC271-280	330.944	France—Economic conditions
HB3730	330.0112	Economic forecasting			
HB3732	339.5	Economic stabilization	HC275	330.944	Famine compact, 1765
HB3741-3840	338.54209(4-9)	Business cycles—[By region or country]	HC281-290.795	330.943	Germany—Economic conditions
HC	330.9	Economic history	HC291-300	330.9495	Greece—Economic conditions
HC41-42	330.0902	Economic history—Medieval, 500-1500			
HC54-60.5	330.0904	Economic history—20th century	HC301-310	330.945	Italy—Economic conditions

LC	Dewey	Subject Heading	LC	Dewey	Subject Heading
HC311-320	330.9493	Belgium—Economic conditions	HC426-430	330.951	China—Economic conditions
HC321-329.5	330.9492	Netherlands—Economic conditions	HC430.5	330.951249	Taiwan—Economic conditions
HC330	330.94935	Luxembourg—Economic conditions	HC431-440	330.954	India—Economic conditions
HC331-340	330.947	Russia—Economic conditions	HC440.5	330.95491	Pakistan—Economic conditions
HC340.3	330.9438	Poland—Economic conditions	HC440.8	330.95492	Bangladesh—Economic conditions
HC341-380	330.948	Scandinavia—Economic conditions	HC442	330.9596	Cambodia—Economic conditions
HC351-360	330.9489	Denmark—Economic conditions	HC443	330.9594	Laos—Economic conditions
HC361-370	330.9481	Norway—Economic conditions	HC444	330.9597	Vietnam—Economic conditions
HC371-380	330.9485	Sweden—Economic conditions	HC445	330.9593	Thailand—Economic conditions
HC381-390	330.946	Spain—Economic conditions	HC446-450	330.9598	Indonesia—Economic conditions
HC391-394.5	330.9469	Portugal—Economic conditions	HC451-460	330.9599	Philippines—Economic conditions
HC395-400	330.9494	Switzerland—Economic conditions	HC461-465	330.952	Japan—Economic conditions
HC401-407	330.9496	Balkan Peninsula—Economic conditions	HC466-470.2	330.9519	Korea—Economic conditions
HC402	330.94965	Albania—Economic conditions	HC471-480	330.955	Iran—Economic conditions
HC403	330.9499	Bulgaria—Economic conditions	HC491-495	330.9561	Turkey—Economic conditions
HC405	330.9498	Romania—Economic conditions	HC585-595.5	330.997	Islands of the Atlantic—Economic conditions
HC407	330.9497	Yugoslavia—Economic conditions	HC601-610	330.994	Australia—Economic conditions
HC411-495	330.95	Asia—Economic conditions	HC661-670	330.993	New Zealand—Economic conditions
HC415.23	330.95691	Syria—Economic conditions	HC681-688	330.99(5-6)	Islands of the Pacific—Economic conditions
HC415.24	330.95692	Lebanon—Economic conditions	HC731-740	330.998(1-8)	Arctic regions
HC415.25	330.95694	Israel—Economic conditions	HC800-1085	330.96	Africa—Economic conditions
HC415.26	330.95695	Jordan—Economic conditions	HC810	330.964	Morocco—Economic conditions
HC415.33	330.9538	Saudi Arabia—Economic conditions	HC815	330.965	Algeria—Economic conditions
HC415.34	330.9533	Yemen—Economic conditions	HC820	330.9611	Tunisia—Economic conditions
HC415.35	330.95353	Oman—Economic conditions	HC825	330.9612	Libya—Economic conditions
HC415.36	330.95357	United Arab Emirates—Economic conditions	HC830	330.962	Egypt—Economic conditions
HC415.37	330.95363	Qatar—Economic conditions	HC835	330.9624	Sudan—Economic conditions
HC415.38	330.95365	Bahrain—Economic conditions	HC845	330.963	Ethiopia—Economic conditions
HC415.39	330.95367	Kuwait—Economic conditions	HC850	330.96773	Somalia—Economic conditions
HC415.4	330.9567	Iraq—Economic conditions	HC865	330.96762	Kenya—Economic conditions
HC416-420	330.9581	Afghanistan—Economic conditions	HC870	330.96761	Uganda—Economic conditions
HC422	330.9591	Burma—Economic conditions	HC875	330.967571	Rwanda—Economic conditions
HC424	330.95493	Sri Lanka—Economic conditions	HC880	330.967572	Burundi—Economic conditions
HC425	330.95496	Nepal—Economic conditions	HC885	330.9678	Tanzania—Economic conditions
			HC890	330.9679	Mozambique—Economic conditions

LC	Dewey	Subject Heading	LC	Dewey	Subject Heading
HC895	330.9691	Madagascar—Economic conditions	HD62.27	338.7	Couple-owned business enterprises
HC905	330.968	South Africa—Economic conditions	HD66-.2	658.4013	Quality circles
			HD66-.2	658.402	Work groups
HC910	330.9689	Rhodesia—Economic conditions	HD69.C6	658.46	Business consultants
			HD72-88	338.9	Economic development
HC915	330.96894	Zambia—Economic conditions	HD82-85	338.9	Autarchy
			HD87-88	338.9	Economic policy
HC925	330.96887	Swaziland—Economic conditions	HD101-1131	333.73	Land use
			HD101-1131	333.76	Land capability for agriculture
HC950	330.9673	Angola—Economic conditions	HD108-.8	338.901	Economic development—Methodology
HC955	330.96751	Zaire—Economic conditions	HD113-156	333.7309	Land use—History
HC975	330.96721	Gabon—Economic conditions	HD170-279	333.730973	Land use—United States
			HD241	333.740973	Grazing
HC980	330.96724	Congo (Brazzaville)—Economic conditions	HD242.5	333.850973	Mineral lands
			HD251-279	333.30973	Real property
HC990	330.96743	Chad—Economic conditions	HD311-320	333.730971	Land use—Canada
HC995	330.96711	Cameroon—Economic conditions	HD321-330	333.730972	Land use—Mexico
			HD336-340	333.73097282	Land use—Belize
HC1020	330.96626	Niger—Economic conditions	HD341-350	333.73097286	Land use—Costa Rica
HC1025	330.96668	Cote d'Ivoire—Economic conditions	HD351-360	333.73097281	Land use—Guatemala
			HD361-370	333.73097283	Land use—Honduras
HC1030	330.96652	Guinea—Economic conditions	HD371-380	333.73097285	Land use—Nicaragua
HC1055	330.9660	Nigeria—Economic conditions	HD381-385	333.73097287	Land use—Panama
			HD386-390	333.730972875	Land use—Panama Canal Zone
HD	338	Production (Economic theory)	HD391-400	333.73097284	Land use—El Salvador
HD28-70	658	Management	HD406-410	333.73097296	Land use—Bahamas
HD30.22	338.068	Managerial economics	HD411-420	333.73097291	Land use—Cuba
HD30.23	658.403	Decision-making	HD421-425	333.73097294	Land use—Haiti
HD30.28	658.4012	Strategic planning	HD426-430	333.73097293	Land use—Dominican Republic
HD38.2-.25	658.409	Executive ability			
HD38.5	658.5	Business logistics	HD431-440	333.73097292	Land use—Jamaica
HD38.7	658.47	Business intelligence	HD441-450	333.73097295	Land use—Puerto Rico
HD39-40.7	658.152	Capital	HD450.3	333.7309729722	Land use—Virgin Islands of the United States
HD39.5	658.72	Industrial procurement			
HD41	338.6048	Competition	HD451.5	333.730972981	Land use—Barbados
HD47.3	658.1552	Cost control	HD453.2	333.730972973	Land use—Anguilla
HD47.4	658.1554	Cost effectiveness	HD453.4	333.730972974	Land use—Antigua
HD50-.5	658.402	Delegation of authority	HD453.6	333.730972975	Land use—Montserrat
HD50	658.402	Decentralization in management	HD453.8	333.730972973	Land use—Saint Kitts and Nevis
HD56-57.5	338.06	Industrial productivity	HD454.3	333.7309729841	Land use—Dominica
HD57.7	658.4	Leadership	HD454.5	333.7309729845	Land use—Grenada
HD58.6	658.4052	Negotiation in business	HD454.7	333.7309729843	Land use—Saint Lucia
HD58.7	658.019	Organizational behavior	HD454.9	333.7309729844	Land use—Saint Vincent
HD58.8	658.406	Organizational change	HD455	333.730972983	Land use—Trinidad and Tobago
HD59	338.74	Corporations—Investor relations			
HD59-.6	659.2	Public relations	HD456.5	333.730972986	Land use—Aruba
HD59.2	338.74	Corporate image	HD456.6	333.730972986	Land use—Bonaire
HD59.3	659.1	Advocacy advertising	HD456.7	333.730972986	Land use—Curacao
HD60-.5	658.408	Social responsibility of business	HD456.8	333.730972977	Land use—Saba (Netherlands Antilles)
HD61	658.155	Risk management	HD456.85	333.730972977	Land use—Saint Eustatius (Netherlands Antilles)
HD62	658.562	Standardization			
HD62.15	658.4013	Total quality management	HD456.9	333.730972977	Land use—Saint Martin
HD62.25	338.7	Family-owned business enterprises	HD458	333.730972976	Land use—Guadeloupe
			HD459	333.730972982	Land use—Martinique
			HD471-480	333.730982	Land use—Argentina

96

LC	Dewey	Subject Heading	LC	Dewey	Subject Heading
HD481-490	333.730984	Land use—Bolivia	HD860.9	333.73095496	Land use—Nepal
HD491-500	333.730981	Land use—Brazil	HD871-880	333.730954	Land use—India
HD501-510	333.730983	Land use—Chile	HD880.3	333.73095498	Land use—Bhutan
HD511-520	333.7309861	Land use—Colombia	HD880.5	333.73095491	Land use—Pakistan
HD521-530	333.7309866	Land use—Ecuador	HD880.6	333.73095492	Land use—Bangladesh
HD540.3	333.7309881	Land use—Guyana	HD890.3	333.7309596	Land use—Cambodia
HD540.5	333.7309883	Land use—Surinam	HD890.4	333.7309594	Land use—Laos
HD540.7	333.7309882	Land use—French Guiana	HD890.5	333.7309597	Land use—Vietnam
HD541-550	333.7309892	Land use—Paraguay	HD890.55	333.7309593	Land use—Thailand
HD551-560	333.730985	Land use—Peru	HD890.6	333.7309595	Land use—Malaysia
HD561-570	333.7309895	Land use—Uruguay	HD891-900	333.7309598	Land use—Indonesia
HD571-580	333.730987	Land use—Venezuela	HD901-910	333.7309599	Land use—Philippines
HD601-610	333.730942	Land use—England	HD911-920	333.730952	Land use—Japan
HD611-620	333.7309411	Land use—Scotland	HD920.5-.6	333.7309519	Land use—Korea
HD620.5	333.7309416	Land use—Northern Ireland	HD920.8	333.7309517	Land use—Mongolia
HD621-630	333.7309415	Land use—Ireland	HD921-930	333.730951	Land use—China
HD631-640	333.7309436	Land use—Austria	HD931-935	333.73095126	Land use—Macao
HD640.3	333.7309437	Land use—Czechoslovakia	HD936-940	333.730951249	Land use—Taiwan
HD640.5	333.7309439	Land use—Hungary	HD941-945	333.73095125	Land use—Hong Kong
HD640.9	333.730943648	Land use—Liechtenstein	HD972	333.730964	Land use—Morocco
HD641-650	333.730944	Land use—France	HD973	333.730965	Land use—Algeria
HD650.5	333.730944949	Land use—Monaco	HD974	333.7309611	Land use—Tunisia
HD651-660.5	333.730943	Land use—Germany	HD975	333.7309612	Land use—Libya
HD671-680	333.730945	Land use—Italy	HD976	333.730962	Land use—Egypt
HD691-700	333.7309493	Land use—Belgium	HD977	333.7309624	Land use—Sudan
HD701-710	333.7309492	Land use—Netherlands	HD979	333.730963	Land use—Ethiopia
HD710.5	333.73094935	Land use—Luxembourg	HD980	333.73096773	Land use—Somalia
HD711-720	333.730947	Land use—Russia	HD981	333.73096771	Land use—Djibouti
HD721-725	333.73094897	Land use—Finland	HD983	333.73096762	Land use—Kenya
HD726-729.5	333.7309438	Land use—Poland	HD984	333.73096761	Land use—Uganda
HD731-740	333.7309489	Land use—Denmark	HD985	333.730967571	Land use—Rwanda
HD741-750	333.73094912	Land use—Iceland	HD986	333.730967572	Land use—Burundi
HD751-760	333.7309481	Land use—Norway	HD987	333.7309678	Land use—Tanzania
HD761-770	333.7309485	Land use—Sweden	HD988	333.7309679	Land use—Mozambique
HD771-780	333.730946	Land use—Spain	HD989	333.7309691	Land use—Madagascar
HD781-790	333.7309469	Land use—Portugal	HD991	333.730968	Land use—South Africa
HD791-800	333.7309494	Land use—Switzerland	HD992	333.7309689	Land use—Rhodesia
HD810.5	333.73094965	Land use—Albania	HD993	333.73096894	Land use—Zambia
HD811-820	333.7309499	Land use—Bulgaria	HD994	333.73096885	Land use—Lesotho
HD821-825	333.7309497	Land use—Yugoslavia	HD995	333.73096887	Land use—Swaziland
HD831-840	333.7309498	Land use—Romania	HD996	333.73096883	Land use—Botswana
HD840.5	333.7309495	Land use—Greece	HD997	333.73096897	Land use—Malawi
HD846.5	333.7309561	Land use—Turkey	HD998	333.73096881	Land use—Namibia
HD847	333.73095693	Land use—Cyprus	HD1000	333.7309673	Land use—Angola
HD848	333.73095691	Land use—Syria	HD1001	333.73096751	Land use—Zaire
HD849	333.73095692	Land use—Lebanon	HD1002	333.73096718	Land use—Equatorial Guinea
HD850	333.73095694	Land use—Israel			
HD851	333.73095695	Land use—Jordan	HD1003	333.73096715	Land use—Sao Tome and Principe
HD853	333.7309538	Land use—Saudi Arabia			
HD854-.5	333.7309533	Land use—Yemen	HD1005	333.73096721	Land use—Gabon
HD855	333.73095353	Land use—Oman	HD1006	333.73096724	Land use—Congo (Brazzaville)
HD856	333.73095357	Land use—United Arab Emirates			
HD857	333.73095363	Land use—Qatar	HD1007	333.73096741	Land use—Central African Republic
HD858	333.73095365	Land use—Bahrain	HD1008	333.73096743	Land use—Chad
HD859	333.73095367	Land use—Kuwait	HD1009	333.73096711	Land use—Cameroon
HD860	333.7309567	Land use—Iraq	HD1012	333.73096683	Land use—Benin
HD860.2	333.730955	Land use—Iran	HD1013	333.73096681	Land use—Togo
HD860.6	333.7309581	Land use—Afghanistan	HD1014	333.73096626	Land use—Niger
HD860.7	333.7309591	Land use—Burma	HD1015	333.73096668	Land use—Cote d'Ivoire
HD860.8	333.73095493	Land use—Sri Lanka	HD1016	333.73096652	Land use—Guinea

LC	Dewey	Subject Heading	LC	Dewey	Subject Heading
HD1017	333.73096623	Land use—Mali	HD1401-2210	338.16	Farms
HD1018	333.73096625	Land use—Burkina Faso	HD1478	333.335563	Sharecropping
HD1019	333.7309663	Land use—Senegal	HD1483-1491.5	334.683	Agriculture, Cooperative
HD1020	333.7309661	Land use—Mauritania	HD1492-.5	334.683	Collective farms
HD1021	333.7309669	Land use—Nigeria	HD1493-.5	334.683	State farms
HD1022	333.7309667	Land use—Ghana	HD1521-1542	331.763	Agricultural laborers
HD1023	333.7309664	Land use—Sierra Leone	HD1521-1542	331.544	Migrant agricultural laborers
HD1024	333.73096651	Land use—Gambia	HD1521-1542	331.763	Peasantry
HD1025	333.73096662	Land use—Liberia	HD1549	338.163	Gleaning
HD1026	333.73096657	Land use—Guinea Bissau	HD1665-1671	333.73137	Waste lands
HD1027	333.7309648	Land use—Western Sahara	HD1690-1702	333.91	Water resources development
HD1028	333.73094699	Land use—Azores			
HD1028.3	333.73097299	Land use—Bermuda Islands	HD1711-1741	333.736153	Desert reclamation
HD1028.5	333.73094698	Land use—Madeira Islands	HD2321-4730.9	338	Industries
HD1028.7	333.7309649	Land use—Canary Islands	HD2329	338	Industrialization
HD1028.9	333.73096658	Land use—Cape Verde	HD2331-2336.35	338.634	Home labor
HD1029	333.7309973	Land use—Saint Helena	HD2331-2336.35	338.634	Home-based businesses
HD1029.3	333.7309973	Land use—Tristan da Cunha	HD2331-2336.35	331.25	Telecommuting
HD1029.5	333.7309971	Land use—Falkland Islands	HD2337-2339	331.117	Sweatshops
HD1029.7	333.73095495	Land use—Maldives	HD2336.2-.25	338.634	Cottage industries
HD1029.9	333.7309696	Land use—Seychelles	HD2350.8-2356	338.644	Big business
HD1030	333.7309694	Land use—Comoro Islands	HD2350.8-2356	338.65	Factory system
HD1030.3	333.73096982	Land use—Mauritius	HD2365-2385	331.542	Contracting out
HD1030.5	333.73096981	Land use—Reunion	HD2709-2932	338.82	Monopolies
HD1030.7	333.7309699	Land use—Kerguelen Islands	HD2709-2932	338.86	Stock companies
			HD2709-2932	338.74	Corporations
HD1031-1040	333.730994	Land use—Australia	HD2741-2749	658.4	Corporate governance
HD1120.5	333.730993	Land use—New Zealand	HD2746.5-.55	338.83	Consolidation and merger of corporations
HD1121.5	333.7309967	Land use—Guam			
HD1122	333.7309953	Land use—Papau New Guinea	HD2747	658.1	Liquidation
			HD2753	336.207	Corporations—Taxation
HD1122.3	333.73099681	Land use—Kiribati	HD2756-.2	338.6	Diversification in industry
HD1123	333.73099593	Land use—Solomon Islands	HD2756-.2	338.8042	Conglomerate corporations
HD1124	333.73099597	Land use—New Caledonia	HD2757-2768	338.82	Oligopolies
HD1125	333.73099595	Land use—Vanuatu	HD2757.5	338.87	Cartels
HD1126	333.73099611	Land use—Fiji	HD2763-2768	363.6	Public utilities
HD1127	333.73099612	Land use—Tonga	HD2770-2930.7	338.7409	Corporations—[By region or country]
HD1127.5	333.73099623	Land use—Cook Islands			
HD1128	333.73099613	Land use—American Samoa	HD2771-2798.5	338.740973	Corporations—United States
HD1129.5	333.7309962	Land use—French Polynesia			
HD1130	333.730998(1-8)	Land use—Arctic regions	HD2807-2810	338.740971	Corporations—Canada
HD1130.5	333.7309982	Land use—Greenland	HD2811	338.740972	Corporations—Mexico
HD1241-1339	333.3	Land tenure	HD2813.5-2819	338.7409728	Corporations—Central America
HD1286-1289	333.2	Commons			
HD1301-1339	333.14	Land, Nationalization of	HD2820.5-2825.9	338.7409729	Corporations—West Indies
HD1311-1313	330.155	Single tax			
HD1332-1333.5	333.31	Land reform	HD2827-2843	338.74098	Corporations—South America
HD1334-1335	333.33	Consolidation of land holdings			
			HD2844-2891.84	338.74094	Corporations—Europe
HD1336-1339	333.32	Peasantry	HD2845-2847.5	338.740941	Corporations—Great Britain
HD1361-1395.5	333.33	Real estate business	HD2853-2856	338.740944	Corporations—France
HD1393	333.76	Farms—Valuation	HD2857-2860.5	338.740943	Corporations—Germany
HD1393.5	333.77	Industrial districts	HD2862-2865	338.740945	Corporations—Italy
HD1428-1431	338.181	Agriculture—International cooperation	HD2865.5-2873.5	338.7409492	Corporations—Benelux countries
			HD2874-2877	338.740947	Corporations—Russia
HD1439-1440	332.71	Agricultural credit	HD2885-2888	338.740946	Corporations—Spain
HD1443	332.72	Mortgages	HD2889	338.7409469	Corporations—Portugal
HD1447	338.13	Agricultural prices	HD2891.83	338.7409495	Corporations—Greece
HD1470-1476	338.16	Farms, Size of	HD2891.93	338.7409561	Corporations—Turkey
HD1471	333.335	Haciendas	HD2892.2	338.74095694	Corporations—Israel
HD1471	338.16	Farms			

LC	Dewey	Subject Heading	LC	Dewey	Subject Heading
HD2892.55	338.7409567	Corporations—Iraq	HD4928.E4	331.255	Employee discounts
HD2892.56	338.740955	Corporations—Iran	HD4928.G34	331.2164	Gain sharing
HD2897-2900	338.740954	Corporations—India	HD4928.H	331.2576	Holiday pay
HD2904	338.7409598	Corporations—Indonesia	HD4928.N6	331.255	Cafeteria benefit plans
HD2905	338.7409599	Corporations—Philippines	HD4928.N6	331.255	Employee fringe benefits
HD2907	338.740952	Corporations—Japan	HD4928.P5	331.2164	Piece-work
HD2910	338.740951	Corporations—China	HD4928.S74	331.2164	Employee stock options
HD2917-2929.3	338.74096	Corporations—Africa	HD4928.T93	331.216	Two-tier wage payment
HD2930	338.740994	Corporations—Australia			systems
HD2951-3575	334	Cooperation	HD4966.A29	331.283	Agricultural wages
HD2952	334.06	Cooperation—Societies, etc.	HD4966.C82	331.287482	Coopers and cooperage
			HD4967	331.21091724	Wages—Developing countries
HD2956	334.09	Cooperation—History	HD4973-4976	331.210973	Wages—United States
HD2970-3110.9	331.2164	Profit-sharing	HD4977-4980	331.210971	Wages—Canada
HD2981-3110.9	331.216409 (4-9)	Profit-sharing—[By region or country]	HD4981	331.210972	Wages—Mexico
			HD4983-4989	331.2109728	Wages—Central America
HD3120-3260.9	334.6	Producer cooperatives	HD4990-4995.9	331.2109729	Wages—West Indies
HD3131-3260.9	334.609(4-9)	Producer cooperatives—[By region or country]	HD4996-5013	331.21098	Wages—South America
			HD5014-5061.84	331.21094	Wages—Europe
HD3271-3575	334.5	Consumers' leagues	HD5106-5267	331.25723	Eight-hour movement
HD3271-3575	334.5	Consumer cooperatives	HD5106-5267	331.257	Hours of labor
HD3281-3410.9	334.509	Consumer cooperatives—[By region or country]	HD5108-.2	331.257	Hours of labor, Staggered
			HD5109-.2	331.2572	Hours of labor, Flexible
HD3611-4730.9	321.94	Corporate state	HD5110-.2	331.2572	Part-time employment
HD3656-3790.9	658.568	Factory inspection	HD5110.5-.6	331.2572	Work sharing
HD3661-3790.9	658.56809(4-9)	Factory inspection—[By region or country]	HD5111	331.2162	Overtime
			HD5111.5-.6	331.2572	Shift systems
HD3840-4420.8	352.266	Government ownership	HD5112	331.2576	Rest periods
HD3840-4420.8	363	Public works	HD5113-.2	331.2574	Night work
HD3850	352.266	Corporations, Government	HD5114	331.2576	Weekly rest-day
HD3860-3861	346.023	Public contracts	HD5115.5-.6	331.25762	Sick leave
HD3881-4420.8	352.2660973	Corporations, Government—United States	HD5255-5257.3	331.25763	Leave of absence
			HD5257-.2	331.25763	Educational leave
HD4001-4420.7	352.26609(4-9)	Corporations, Government—[Other regions or countries]	HD5260-5267	331.2576	Vacations, Employee
			HD5306-5474	331.892	Strikes and lockouts
HD4421-4730.9	352.266	Municipal ownership	HD5307	331.8925	General strikes
HD4801-8943	331.11	Proletariat	HD5309	331.8923	Strikes and lockouts, Sympathetic
HD4801-8943	331	Work			
HD4801-8943	331	Labor	HD5311	331.8924	Wildcat strikes
HD4801-8943	331.11	Working class	HD5321-5450.7	331.892(4-9)	Strikes and lockouts—[By region or country]
HD4801-4854	331.8	Labor movement			
HD4861-4865	331.11734	Slave labor	HD5366	331.89250941	General strike, Great Britain, 1926
HD4871-4875	331.542	Contract labor			
HD4871-4875	331.1173	Service, Compulsory non-military	HD5368	331.892509416	General strike, Northern Ireland, 1974
HD4871-4875	306.363	Indentured servants	HD5379.C6	331.89290943	Eles (Firm) Strike, Bleidenstadt, Ger., 1975
HD4881-4885	331.55	Apprentices			
HD4903-.5	331.702	Free choice of employment	HD5427	331.89290952	Daiichi Togyo Kabushiki Kaisha Strike, 1970-1975
HD4903-.5	331.133	Discrimination in employment			
HD4903-.5	331.8892	Right to labor	HD5461	331.893	Boycotts
HD4904.7	331.11	Human capital	HD5468	331.8927	Picketing
HD4905-.3	306.3613	Work ethic	HD5473	331.893	Sabotage
HD4905.5	331.1173	Service, Compulsory non-military	HD5481-5630.7	331.89143	Arbitration, Industrial
			HD5501-5630.7	331.8914309 (4-9)	Arbitration, Industrial—[By region or country]
HD4909-5100.7	331.21	Wages			
HD4917-4924	331.23	Minimum wage	HD5650-5660	338.7	Employee ownership
HD4918-4924	331.2309(4-9)	Minimum wage—[By region or country]	HD5650-5660	331.0112	Management—Employee particpation
HD4928.A5	331.21	Guaranteed annual wage	HD5701-5852	331.123	Labor demand
HD4928.B6	331.2164	Bonus system	HD5701-5852	331.12	Labor market
HD4928.D5	331.216	Severance pay			

LC	Dewey	Subject Heading	LC	Dewey	Subject Heading
HD5701-5852	331.12	Labor supply	HD6091-6220.7	331.409(4-9)	Working class women—[By region or country]
HD5701.5-.75	331.125	Employment (Economic theory)	HD6228-6250.5	331.31	Children—Employment
HD5707.5-5710.2	331.137	Unemployed	HD6270-6276	331.34	Youth—Employment
HD5707.5-5710.2	331.137	Unemployment	HD6271-.2	331.137044	Summer employment
HD5708.4-.45	331.2596	Job security	HD6276.5-.52	331.34	College students—Employment
HD5708.46-.47	331.137041	Structural unemployment	HD6279-6283	331.398	Aged—Employment
HD5708.5-.55	338.6042	Plant shutdowns	HD6300	331.62	Alien labor
HD5708.7-.75	331.137	Disguised unemployment	HD6304	331.6	Minorities—Employment
HD5708.8-.85	331.137	Hard-core unemployed	HD6331-.2	331.25	Employees—Effect of technological innovations on
HD5709-.2	331.13	Underemployment			
HD5710.5	331.124	Job vacancies	HD6331-.2	331.137042	Technological unemployment
HD5713.5-.6	352.63	Public service employment	HD6350-6940.7	331.88	Trade-unions
HD5715-.2	331.2598	Abenteeism (Labor)	HD6451-6481.2	331.8809	Trade-unions—History
HD5715-.5	370.113	Occcupational training	HD6477	335.82	Syndicalism
HD5723-5851	331.1209(4-9)	Labor market—[By region or country]	HD6479	335.15	Guild socialism
			HD6488-.2	331.8892	Open and closed shop
HD5723-5726	331.120973	Labor market—United States	HD6490.07	331.8912	Trade-unions—Organizing
			HD6490.R4	331.8912	Trade-unions—Recognition
HD5727-5729	331.120971	Labor market—Canada	HD6500-6940.7	331.8809(4-9)	Trade-unions—[By region or country]
HD5731	331.120972	Labor market—Mexico			
HD5733-5739	331.1209728	Labor market—Central America	HD6500-6519	331.880973	Trade-unions—United States
			HD6951-6957	306.36	Industrial sociology
HD5740-5745.9	331.1209729	Labor market—West Indies	HD6951-6957	306.361	Quality of work life
HD5746-5763	331.12098	Labor market—South America	HD6958.5-6976	331	Industrial relations
HD5764-5811.84	331.12094	Labor market—Europe	HD6971.5-.85	331.89	Collective bargaining
HD5765-5767.5	331.120941	Labor market—Great Britain	HD6971.8	331.011	Employee rights
HD5773-5776	331.120944	Labor market—France	HD6972.5	331.8896	Grievance procedures
HD5777-5780.5	331.120943	Labor market—Germany	HD6977-7080	339.42	Cost and standard of living
HD5782-5785	331.120945	Labor market—Italy	HD6977-7080	338.52	Prices
HD5785.5-5793.5	331.1209492	Labor market—Benelux countries	HD7088-7250.7	368.4	Social security
			HD7095-7096	331.2550973	Insurance, Unemployment
HD5794-5797	331.120947	Labor market—Russia	HD7105-7108.4	331.252	Retirement age
HD5805-5808	331.120946	Labor market—Spain	HD7105.2-.25	368.382	Insurance, Disability
HD5810	331.1209494	Labor market—Switzerland	HD7105.3-.35	331.252	Old age pensions
HD5811.83	331.1209495	Labor market—Greece	HD7110-.5	306.38	Early retirement
HD5811.93	331.1209561	Labor market—Turkey	HD7121-7250.7	368.4009	Social security—[By region or country]
HD5812.2	331.12095694	Labor market—Israel			
HD5812.55	331.1209567	Labor market—Iraq	HD7123-7126	368.400973	Social security—United States
HD5812.56	331.120955	Labor market—Iran			
HD5812.6	331.1209581	Labor market—Afghanistan	HD7255-7256	362.0425	Rehabilitation counselors
HD5817-5820	331.120954	Labor market—India	HD7260-7780.8	331.25	Work environment
HD5825	331.1209599	Labor market—Philippines	HD7262-.5	363.11	Industrial accidents
HD5827	331.120952	Labor market—Japan	HD7273	363.107	Safety appliances
HD5830	331.120951	Labor market—China	HD7285-7391	363.5	Housing
HD5837-5849.3	331.12096	Labor market—Africa	HD7287.7-.72	334.1	Housing, Cooperative
HD5850	331.120994	Labor market—Australia	HD7287.8-.82	363.506	Homeowners' associations
HD5855-5856	331.544	Casual labor	HD7287.8-.82	363.5	Home ownership
HD5855-5856	331.544	Migrant labor	HD7288.72U	363.5908996073	Afro-Americans—Housing
HD5855-5856	331.137044	Seasonal unemployment	HD7289	363.5091734	Housing, Rural
HD5860-6000.7	331.128	Employment agencies	HD7289.4-.42	363.5091732	Urban homesteading
HD5871-6000.7	331.12809(4-9)	Employment agencies—[By region or country]	HD7291-7391	363.509(4-9)	Housing—[By region or country]
HD6060-.5	331.4133	Sex discrimination in employment	HD7293-7304	363.50973	Housing—United States
			HD7305	363.50971	Housing—Canada
HD6061-.2	331.2153	Pay equity	HD7306	363.50972	Housing—Mexico
HD6065-.5	331.25763	Parental leave	HD7307-7313	363.509728	Housing—Central America
HD6072-.2	640.46	Domestics	HD7314-7319.9	363.509729	Housing—West Indies
HD6073.M7	746.92092	Models (Persons)	HD7320-7331	363.5098	Housing—South America
			HD7332-7357.7	363.5094	Housing—Europe

LC	Dewey	Subject Heading
HD7333-7335.5	363.50941	Housing—Great Britain
HD7338	363.50944	Housing—France
HD7339-.5	363.50943	Housing—Germany
HD7341	363.50945	Housing—Italy
HD7342-7344.5	363.509492	Housing—Benelux countries
HD7345	363.50947	Housing—Russia
HD7351	363.50946	Housing—Spain
HD7353	363.509494	Housing—Switzerland
HD7357.5	363.509495	Housing—Greece
HD7358.25	363.509561	Housing—Turkey
HD7358.45	363.5095694	Housing—Israel
HD7359	363.509567	Housing—Iraq
HD7359.2	363.50955	Housing—Iran
HD7359.6	363.5095	Housing—Asia
HD7361	363.50954	Housing—India
HD7366	363.509599	Housing—Philippines
HD7367	363.50952	Housing—Japan
HD7368	363.50951	Housing—China
HD7372-7378.4	363.5096	Housing—Africa
HD7379	363.50994	Housing—Australia
HD7391	363.5091724	Housing—Developing countries
HD7395.C5	363.1172	Protective clothing
HD7406-7510	338.4767	Factories
HD7651-7780.8	613.6209(4-9)	Industrial hygiene—[By region or country]
HD7795-8013	331.12042	Labor policy
HD8001-8013	352.63	Civil service
HD8038	331.712	Professional employees
HD8039.A425	629.1366092	Air traffic controllers
HD8039.B2	641.815	Bakers and bakeries
HD8039.B7-.B72	685.310092	Shoemakers
HD8039.D5	640.46	Domestics
HD8039.D7	615.1092	Drugstore employees
HD8039.F65	639.2092	Fishers
HD8039.G5	666.1092	Glass-workers
HD8039.L8	387.5092	Stevedores
HD8039.M39	381.1092	Clerks (Retail trade)
HD8039.M39	331.792	White collar workers
HD8039.M6-.M7	331.7622	Miners
HD8039.M9	338.47355092	Defense industries—Employees
HD8039.P496	630.92	Plantation workers
HD8039.R1-.R45	385.092	Railroads—Employees
HD8039.S4	387.5092	Sailors
HD8039.T4	677.028242092	Weavers
HD8045-8942.5	331.09(4-9)	Labor—[By region or country]
HD8051-8085	331.0973	Labor—United States
HD8101-8110	331.0971	Labor—Canada
HD8111-8120	331.0972	Labor—Mexico
HD8126-8190	331.09728	Labor—Central America
HD8191-8250	331.09729	Labor—West Indies
HD8251-8370	331.098	Labor—South America
HD8371-8650.7	331.094	Labor—Europe
HD8381-8400	331.0941	Labor—Great Britain
HD8421-8440	331.0944	Labor—France
HD8441-8460.5	331.0943	Labor—Germany
HD8471-8490	331.0945	Labor—Italy
HD8491-8520.5	331.09492	Labor—Benelux countries
HD8521-8530	331.0947	Labor—Russia
HD8581-8590	331.0946	Labor—Spain
HD8601-8610	331.09494	Labor—Switzerland
HD8650.5	331.09495	Labor—Greece
HD8656-8669	331.0956	Labor—Middle East
HD8660	331.095694	Labor—Israel
HD8670	331.09567	Labor—Iraq
HD8670.2	331.0955	Labor—Iran
HD8670.6	331.09581	Labor—Afghanistan
HD8681-8690	331.0954	Labor—India
HD8711-8720	331.09599	Labor—Philippines
HD8721-8730	331.0952	Labor—Japan
HD8731-8740	331.0951	Labor—China
HD8771-8837	331.096	Labor—Africa
HD8841-8850	331.0994	Labor—Australia
HD9000-9019	338.17	Farm produce
HD9000-9019	363.8	Food supply
HD9000-9019	380.141	Farm produce—Marketing
HD9000.9	363.192	Food adulteration and inspection
HD9019.A43-.A434	633.577	Agave products industry
HD9030-9049	380.1431	Grain trade
HD9049.W3-.W5	633.11	Durum wheat industry
HD9057-9058	641.815	Bakers and bakeries
HD9070-9093	338.17351	Cotton growing
HD9070-9089	380.141351	Cotton trade
HD9130-9149	336.27863371	Tobacco industry
HD9210-9211	380.141383	Spice trade
HD9220-9235	380.1415	Vegetable trade
HD9275-9283.7	380.1417	Dairy products—Marketing
HD9275-9283.7	338.47637143	Dairy products industry
HD9282	338.7637143	Dried milk industry
HD9330.B2-.B23	664.68	Baking powder
HD9390-9395	338.4766316	Distilling industries
HD9433	380.14162	Cattle trade
HD9486-.6	338.76313	Agricultural machinery industry
HD9490-.5	338.476655	Oil industries
HD9502-.5	333.79	Energy policy
HD9506-9624	380.1424	Metal trade
HD9536	622.3423	Silver mines and mining
HD9536	622.3422	Gold mines and mining
HD9540-9559	380.14224	Coal trade
HD9540-9559	338.2724	Coal
HD9579.D5-.D54	338.476655384	Diesel fuels industry
HD9585.B67-.B674	338.27633	Borax
HD9650-9660	338.4766	Chemical industry
HD9660.D84-.D844	338.4754786	Dye industry
HD9660.G58-.G6	338.476682	Glycerin
HD9662.E42-.E423	338.47678	Elastomer industry
HD9665-9675	338.476151	Nonprescription drug industry
HD9675.A7-.A74	338.476153137	Aspirin
HD9681	333.7923	Solar energy industries
HD9685-9695	333.7932	Electric utilities
HD9696.D36-.D364	338.4702504	Database industry
HD9696.D54-.D544	338.47004	Digital computer industry

LC	Dewey	Subject Heading	LC	Dewey	Subject Heading
HD9698-.5	333.7924	Nuclear industry	HE374-377	388.132	Bridges
HD9705-9705.5	338.476218	Machinery industry	HE380.8-560	386	Waterways
HD9705.5.F35-.F354	338.4762161	Fans (Machinery) industry	HE392.8-398	386.0973	Waterways—United States
			HE399-401.25	386.0971	Waterways—Canada
HD9709.5	388.341	Wagons	HE401.5-402	386.098	Waterways—Latin America
HD9710-.37	380.145388342	Automobiles—Marketing	HE403.5-520.9	386.09(4-9)	Waterways—[Other regions or countries]
HD9711-.2	338.4738773	Aircraft industry			
HD9711.5	338.4762912	Aerospace industries	HE526	386.4	Canals
HD9715-9717.5	338.47624	Construction industry	HE528-545	386.42	Canals, Interoceanic
HD9716.C3-.C33	694	Carpentry	HE550-560	387.1	Harbors
HD9720-9739	338.4767	Manufactures	HE550-560	387.15	Docks
HD9743-9744	338.47355	Defense industries	HE561-971	387.5	Shipping
HD9744.F55-.F554	338.476834	Firearms industry and trade	HE561	387.505	Shipping—Periodicals
			HE562	387.506	Shipping—Congresses
HD9750-9769	634.98	Forest products	HE564	387.506	Shipping—Societies, etc.
HD9750-9769	674.82	Coopers and cooperage	HE565-566	387.20216	Ship registers
HD9778-.5	675.2	Hides and skins	HE565	387.2	Tonnage
HD9801	338.476816	Electronic office machine industry	HE566.P3	387.2044	Paddle steamers
			HE566.R64	387.5442	Roll-on/roll-off ships
HD9870-9889	380.141351	Cotton trade	HE566.T3	387.245	Tankers
HD9929.5.A27-.A274	338.476774742	Acrylic fiber industry	HE593-597	387.544	Freight and freightage
			HE594	387.54	Shipping—Rates
HD9939	338.476453	Drapery industry	HE595.L7	387.5448	Cattle—Transportation
HD9940-9949.5	380.145391	Fashion merchandising	HE599-601	387.2044	Steamboats—Passenger accommodation
HD9948.3	338.4739142	Lingerie industry			
HD9971.5.T32-.T324	338.4767634	Disposal tableware industry	HE603-605	387.54	Shipping—Finance
			HE617-720	623.89229	Inland navigation
HD9975	658.567	Waste products	HE623-720	623.89229(4-9)	Inland navigation—[By region or country]
HD9980-9990	338.4	Service industries			
HD9993-.D65-.D654	338.476887221	Doll industry	HE623-633	623.8922973	Inland navigation—United States
HD9995.D54-.D544	338.47681761	Diagnostic equipment industry	HE635-720	623.89229(4-9)	Inland navigation—[Other regions or countries]
HD9999.A4-.A44	338.476683	Adhesives industry	HE730-943	387.5	Merchant marine
HD9999.T34-.T344	651.73	Telephone answering services	HE740-743	387.50681	Shipping bounties and subsidies
HD9999.U5-.U54	363.75	Undertakers and undertaking	HE745-943	387.509(4-9)	Merchant marine—[By region or country]
HE	388	Transportation			
HE1-8	388.05	Transportation—Periodicals	HE745-767	387.50973	Merchant marine—United States
HE11	388.06	Transportation—Congresses			
HE147.5-149	388.01	Transportation—Theory	HE769-937	387.509(4-9)	Merchant marine—[Other regions and countries]
HE151.4-.5	388.092	Transportation—Biography			
HE159-181	388.09	Transportation—History	HE943	387.5091724	Merchant marine—Developing countries
HE191.4-.5	388.021	Transportation—Statistics			
HE191.9-192	388.071	Transportation—Study and teaching	HE945	387.2044	Steamboat lines
			HE951-953	387.15	Docks
HE195.4-.5	388.049	Transportation—Rates	HE961-971	368.2(2/3)	Insurance, Marine
HE199-.5	388.044	Freight and freightage	HE971	387.55	Salvage
HE305-311	388.4	Urban transportation	HE1001-5600	385	Railroads
HE331-380	388.1	Roads	HE1001	385.05	Railroads—Periodicals
HE331-380	388.411	Streets	HE1003	385.06	Railroads—Societies, etc.
HE336.B8	388.12	Bus lanes	HE1009	385.025	Railroads—Directories
HE336.B8	388.12	High occupancy vehicle lanes	HE1021	385.09	Railroads—History
			HE1062	385.0979	Pacific railroads
HE336.C64	388.314	Traffic congestion	HE1613-1614	385.314	Railroad stations
HE336.H48	388.314	Highway capacity	HE1617-1618	385.312	Railroads—Crossings
HE336.R68	388.1	Route choice	HE1621-1813	385.068	Railroads—Management
HE336.R85	388.12091734	Rural roads	HE1741-1759	331.761385	Railroads—Employees
HE336.T64	388.122	Toll roads	HE1779-1795	363.122	Railroad accidents
HE369-373	388.312	Traffic regulations	HE1811	385.092	Railroad conductors
HE369-373	388.310723	Traffic surveys	HE1821-2591	385.2	Railroads—Traffic

LC	Dewey	Subject Heading	LC	Dewey	Subject Heading
HE1826	385.22	Demurrage (Car service)	HE3191-3200	385.0946	Railroads—Spain
HE1830	385.37	Railroads—Cars	HE3201-3210	385.09469	Railroads—Portugal
HE1831-2220	388.042	Transportation—Rates	HE3211-3220	385.09494	Railroads—Switzerland
HE1951-2100	385.22	Railroads—Fares	HE3231-3240	385.09499	Railroads—Bulgaria
HE2231-2261	385.1	Railroads—Finance	HE3241-3245	385.09497	Railroads—Yugoslavia
HE2271-2273	385.021	Railroads—Statistics	HE3251-3260	385.09498	Railroads—Romania
HE2301-2547	385.24	Freight and freightage	HE3281-3290	385.0951	Railroads—China
HE2301-2547	385.24	Railroads—Freight	HE3291-3300	385.0954	Railroads—India
HE2321.E8	385.24	Explosives—Transportation	HE3300.3	385.095493	Railroads—Sri Lanka
HE2321.L7	385.24	Railroads—Livestock transportaton	HE3300.5	385.095491	Railroads—Pakistan
			HE3300.6	385.095492	Railroads—Bangladesh
HE2321.L7	385.24	Cattle—Transportation	HE3320.3	385.09597	Railroads—Vietnam
HE2556	385.22	Railroads—Baggage handling	HE3320.4	385.09594	Railroads—Laos
			HE3321-3330	385.09595	Railroads—Malaysia
HE2561-2591	385.22	Railroads—Passenger traffic	HE3331-3340	385.09598	Railroads—Indonesia
			HE3341-3350	385.09599	Railroads—Philippines
HE2701-3560	385.09(4-9)	Railroads—[By region or country]	HE3351-3360	385.0952	Railroads—Japan
			HE3360.5	385.09519	Railroads—Korea
HE2704-2791	385.0973	Railroads—United States	HE3380.3	385.09538	Railroads—Saudi Arabia
HE2763	385.0979	Pacific railroads—Early projects	HE3401-3410	385.0962	Railroads—Egypt
			HE3411	385.0964	Railroads—Morocco
HE2763	385.0979	Pacific railroads	HE3412	385.0965	Railroads—Algeria
HE2801-2810	385.0971	Railroads—Canada	HE3413	385.09611	Railroads—Tunisia
HE2811-2820	385.0972	Railroads—Mexico	HE3414	385.09612	Railroads—Libya
HE2825.5	385.097282	Railroads—Belize	HE3415	385.09624	Railroads—Sudan
HE2831-2835	385.097286	Railroads—Costa Rica	HE3416	385.0963	Railroads—Ethiopia
HE2836-2840	385.097281	Railroads—Guatemala	HE3417	385.096773	Railroads—Somalia
HE2841-2845	385.097283	Railroads—Honduras	HE3419	385.096762	Railroads—Kenya
HE2846-2850	385.097285	Railroads—Nicaragua	HE3420	385.096761	Railroads—Uganda
HE2851-2855	385.097284	Railroads—El Salvador	HE3421	385.0967571	Railroads—Rwanda
HE2856-2889	385.09729	Railroads—West Indies	HE3422	385.0967572	Railroads—Burundi
HE2891-3000	385.098	Railroads—South America	HE3423	385.09678	Railroads—Tanzania
HE2901-2910	385.0982	Railroads—Argentina	HE3424	385.09679	Railroads—Mozambique
HE2911-2920	385.0984	Railroads—Bolivia	HE3425	385.09691	Railroads—Madagascar
HE2921-2930	385.0981	Railroads—Brazil	HE3426	385.0968	Railroads—South Africa
HE2931-2940	385.0983	Railroads—Chile	HE3428	385.096894	Railroads—Zambia
HE2941-2950	385.09861	Railroads—Colombia	HE3429	385.096885	Railroads—Lesotho
HE2951-2960	385.09866	Railroads—Ecuador	HE3430	385.096887	Railroads—Swaziland
HE2962	385.09881	Railroads—Guyana	HE3431	385.096883	Railroads—Botswana
HE2963	385.09883	Railroads—Surinam	HE3432	385.096897	Railroads—Malawi
HE2964	385.09882	Railroads—French Guiana	HE3432.3	385.096881	Railroads—Namibia
HE2966-2970	385.09892	Railroads—Paraguay	HE3433	385.09673	Railroads—Angola
HE2971-2980	385.0985	Railroads—Peru	HE3434	385.096751	Railroads—Zaire
HE2981-2990	385.09895	Railroads—Uruguay	HE3435	385.096718	Railroads—Equatoria Guinea
HE2991-3000	385.0987	Railroads—Venezuela			
HE3011-3040	385.0941	Railroads—Great Britain	HE3436	385.096715	Railroads—Sao Tome and Principe
HE3041-3050	385.09415	Railroads—Ireland			
HE3051-3059.2	385.09436	Railroads—Austria	HE3438	385.096721	Railroads—Gabon
HE3059.3	385.09437	Railroads—Czechoslovakia	HE3439	385.096724	Railroads—Congo (Brazzaville)
HE3059.5	385.09439	Railroads—Hungary			
HE3060.5	385.09438	Railroads—Poland	HE3441	385.096743	Railroads—Chad
HE3061-3070	385.0944	Railroads—France	HE3442	385.096711	Railroads—Cameroon
HE3071-3080.5	385.0943	Railroads—Germany	HE3444	385.096683	Railroads—Benin
HE3091-3100	385.0945	Railroads—Italy	HE3445	385.096681	Railroads—Togo
HE3111-3120	385.09493	Railroads—Belgium	HE3446	385.096626	Railroads—Niger
HE3121-3130	385.09492	Railroads—Netherlands	HE3447	385.096668	Railroads—Cote d'Ivoire
HE3131-3140.2	385.0947	Railroads—Russia	HE3448	385.096652	Railroads—Guinea
HE3151-3160	385.09489	Railroads—Denmark	HE3449	385.096623	Railroads—Mali
HE3161-3170	385.094912	Railroads—Iceland	HE3450	385.096625	Railroads—Burkina Faso
HE3171-3180	385.09481	Railroads—Norway	HE3451	385.09663	Railroads—Senegal
HE3181-3190	385.09485	Railroads—Sweden	HE3452	385.09661	Railroads—Mauritania

LC	Dewey	Subject Heading	LC	Dewey	Subject Heading
HE3453	385.09669	Railroads—Nigeria	HE6184.A35	383.144	Aerogrammes
HE3454	385.09667	Railroads—Ghana	HE6184.D4	769.56	Essays and proofs (Philately)
HE3455	385.09664	Railroads—Sierra Leone	HE6184.D56	769.56	Disinfection markings
HE3456	385.096651	Railroads—Gambia			(Philately)
HE3457	385.096662	Railroads—Liberia	HE6184.F57	769.56	First day covers (Philately)
HE3458	385.096657	Railroads—Guinea-Bissau	HE6184.P65	383.122	Postcards
HE3458.2	385.09648	Railroads—Western Sahara	HE6187-6230	769.56	Stamp collecting
HE3461-3550	385.0994	Railroads—Australia	HE6221	769.56075	Postage-stamp albums
HE3550.5	385.0993	Railroads—New Zealand	HE6238	383.144	Air mail service
HE3601-4043	388.42	Railroads, Local and light	HE6246-6278	383.41	Postal service—
HE3601	388.4205	Railroads, Local and light—			International cooperation
		Periodicals	HE6300-7496	383.49(4-9)	Postal service—[By region
HE3651-4043	388.4209(4-9)	Railroads, Local and light—			or country]
		[By region or country]	HE6300-6500	383.4973	Postal service—United
HE4051-4071	385.6	Mountain railroads			States
HE4201-5300	388.44	Railroads, Elevated	HE6448	383.12020973	Franking privilege—United
HE4341-4345	388.46	Street-railroads—Fares			States
HE4351	388.46	Street-railroads—Finance	HE6455-6456	383.1450973	Rural free delivery—United
HE4401-5260	388.4409(4-9)	Railroads, Elevated—[By			States
		region or country]	HE6471-6473	383.1250973	Parcel post—United States
HE4401-4491	388.440973	Railroads, Elevated—	HE6475-.3	383.1430973	Railway mail service—
		United States			United States
HE4500-5260	388.4409(4-9)	Railroads, Elevated—	HE6651-7496	383.49(4-9)	Postal service—[Other
		[Other regions or countries]			regions and countries]
HE5351-5600	388.42	Electric railroads	HE7601-8635	384.1	Telegraph
HE5601-5725	388.322	Bus lines	HE7603	384.106	Telegraph—Societies, etc.
HE5601-5725	388.413214	Cab and omnibus service	HE7621	384.1025	Telegraph—Directories
HE5601-5725	388.34232	Taxicabs	HE7669-7679	384.14	Cipher and telegraph codes
HE5601-5725	388.324	Trucking	HE7681-7691	384.13	Telegraph—Rates
HE5613.5-5614.6	363.125	Traffic safety	HE7709-7741	384.1	Cables, Submarine
HE5620.C3	388.413212	Car pools	HE7761-8630.7	384.109(4-9)	Telegraph—[By region or
HE5620.D7	363.12514	Drinking and traffic accidents			country]
HE5620.R53	388.413212	Ridesharing	HE7761-7798	384.10973	Telegraph—United States
HE5623-5725	388.32409(4-9)	Trucking—[By region or	HE8660-8688	384.52	Telegraph, Wireless
		country]	HE8689.7.F34	384.54	Fairness doctrine
HE5736-5739	388.3472	Bicycles			(Broadcasting)
HE5746-5749	388.228	Coaching	HE8690-8699	384.54	Radio broadcasting
HE5751-5870	386.6	Ferries	HE8697.P57	384.54	Pirate radio broadcasting
HE5880-5990	388.044	Express service	HE8700-.95	384.55	Television broadcasting
HE5893-5990	388.04409(4-9)	Express service—[By	HE8700.65-.66	384.5532	Television programs—
		region or country]			Rating
HE5893-5904.5	388.0440973	Express service—United	HE8700.7-.72	384.555	Satellite master antenna
		States			television
HE5905-5990	388.04409(4-9)	Express service—[Other	HE8700.7-.72	384.55	Low power television
		regions and countries]	HE8701-9685	384.6	Telephone companies
HE5999	383.1	Mail receiving and	HE8701-9685	384.6	Telephone
		forwarding services	HE8801-9685	384.609(4-9)	Telephone companies—
HE6000-7500	383.1	Postal service			[By region or country]
HE6031	383.1025	Postal service—Directories	HE8801-8846	384.60973	Telephone companies—
HE6036	383.1071	Postal service—Study and			United States
		teaching	HE8861-9685	384.609(4-9)	Telephone companies—
HE6041-6055	383.49	Postal service—History			[Other regions or countries]
HE6061	383.492	Postal service—Biography	HE9713-9715	384.53	Cellular radio
HE6125-6148	383.23	Postal rates	HE9719-9721	384.51	Artificial satellites in
HE6148	383.1202	Franking privilege			telecommunication
HE6149	383.1	Postal service—Unclaimed	HE9723-9737	384	Signals and signaling
		mail	HE9751-9756	651.3743	Messengers
HE6171-6173	383.125	Parcel post	HE9761-9900	387.7	Aeronautics, Commercial
HE6175-.5	383.143	Railway mail service	HE9761-.9	387.705	Aeronautics, Commercial—
HE6182-6228	383.1	Postmarks			Periodicals
HE6182-6228	383.23	Postage stamps			

LC	Dewey	Subject Heading	LC	Dewey	Subject Heading
HE9774-9775	387.709	Aeronautics, Commercial—History	HE9882-9888.4	387.7096	Aeronautics, Commercial—Africa
HE9783-.75	387.712	Airlines—Rates	HE9889	387.70994	Aeronautics, Commercial—Australia
HE9785	387.7	Local service airlines			
HE9787-.5	387.742	Aeronautics, Commercial—Passenger traffic	HF	380.1	Commerce
			HF1-53	380.105	Commerce—Periodicals
HE9795-9796	387.7	Airplanes, Company	HF54	380.1025	Commerce—Directories
HE9797-.5	387.736	Airports	HF294-343	380.106	Commercial associations
HE9797.4.S56	387.7364	Airport slot allocation	HF294-343	380.106	Boards of trade
HE9801-9900	387.709(4-9)	Aeronautics, Commercial—[By region or country]	HF351-499	380.109	Boards of trade—History
			HF370	380.1089926	Phoenicians
HE9803-9814	387.70973	Aeronautics, Commercial—United States	HF1001-1002.5	380.103	Commerce—Encyclopedias
			HF1014	382.17	Balance of trade
HE9815	387.70971	Aeronautics, Commercial—Canada	HF1016-1017	380.1021	Commercial statistics
			HF1021-1027	330.9	Commercial geography
HE9816	387.70972	Aeronautics, Commercial—Mexico	HF1021-1027	330.9	Economic geography
			HF1040-1054	338	Primary commodities
HE9817-9823	387.709728	Aeronautics, Commercial—Central America	HF1040-1044	380.1	Commercial products
			HF1051-1054	333.7	Raw materials
HE9824-9829.9	387.709729	Aeronautics, Commercial—West Indies	HF1101-1186	380.1071	Business education
			HF1131-1186	380.10710(4-9)	Business education—[By region or country]
HE9830-9841	387.7098	Aeronautics, Commercial—South America			
			HF1131-1134	380.1071073	Business education—United States
HE9842-9867.7	387.7094	Aeronautics, Commercial—Europe			
			HF1135	380.107108	Business education—Latin America
HE9843-9845.5	387.70941	Aeronautics, Commercial—Great Britain			
			HF1140-1165	380.107104	Business education—Europe
HE9848	387.70944	Aeronautics, Commercial—France			
			HF1171	380.107105	Business education—Asia
HE9849-.5	387.70943	Aeronautics, Commercial—Germany	HF1176	380.107106	Business education—Africa
			HF1181-1182	380.1071094	Business education—Australia
HE9851	387.70945	Aeronautics, Commercial—Italy			
			HF1351-1532.935	337	International economic relations
HE9852-9854.5	387.709492	Aeronautics, Commercial—Benelux countries	HF1371-1385	382	International trade
			HF1410-1411	380.13	Commercial policy
HE9855	387.70947	Aeronautics, Commercial—Russia	HF1413.5	327.117	Economic sanctions
			HF1414	338.6048	Competition
HE9861	387.70946	Aeronautics, Commercial—Spain	HF1414.4-1417.3	382.6	Exports
			HF1414.5-.55	382.64	Export controls
HE9863	387.709494	Aeronautics, Commercial—Switzerland	HF1417.5	382	Foreign trade promotion
			HF1418-.5	387.13	Free ports and zones
HE9867.5	387.709495	Aeronautics, Commercial—Greece	HF1419-1420	382.5	Imports
HE9868.2-.95	387.70956	Aeronautics, Commercial—Middle East	HF1425	382.6	Dumping (International trade)
HE9868.45	387.7095694	Aeronautics, Commercial—Israel	HF1430	382.9	Nontariff trade barriers
			HF1451-1647	337.(4-9)	International economic relations—[By region or country]
HE9869	387.709567	Aeronautics, Commercial—Iraq			
HE9869.2	387.70955	Aeronautics, Commercial—Iran	HF1701-2701	382.7	Tariff
			HF1715-1718	382.7	Drawbacks
HE9869.22-9869.27	387.7095	Aeronautics, Commercial—Asia	HF1721-1733	382.7	Tariff preferences
			HF1721-1733	382.9	Reciprocity
HE9871	387.70954	Aeronautics, Commercial—India	HF1745-2580.9	382.709(4-9)	Tariff—[By region or country]
			HF1750-1757	382.70973	Tariff—United States
HE9876	387.709599	Aeronautics, Commercial—Philippines	HF1761-2580.9	382.709(4-9)	Tariff—[Other regions or countries]
HE9877	387.70952	Aeronautics, Commercial—Japan	HF2651.G8	380.14133	Grain trade
			HF2701	382.63	Export subsidies
HE9878	387.70951	Aeronautics, Commercial—China	HF3000-3163	380.10973	United States—Commerce

LC	Dewey	Subject Heading	LC	Dewey	Subject Heading
HF3001-3006	380.10973	United States—Commerce—Statistics	HF5416	380.1	Product coding
			HF5416.5-5417	658.816	Pricing
HF3021-3031	380.10973	United States—Commerce—History	HF5417	658.816	Price maintenance
			HF5417	658.816	Price fixing
HF3221-3230	380.10971	Canada—Commerce	HF5417	338.52	Price cutting
HF3231-3240	380.10972	Mexico—Commerce	HF5419-5422	381.2092	Brokers
HF3241-3310	380.109728	Central America—Commerce	HF5419-5422	381.2	Wholesale trade
			HF5422	381.2092	Commission merchants
HF3311-3369	380.109729	West Indies—Commerce	HF5428-5429.6	381.1	Retail trade
HF3371-3480	380.1098	South America—Commmerce	HF5429.2-.215	381.149	Discount houses (Retain trade)
HF3491-3750.7	380.1094	Europe—Commerce	HF5429.2-.215	381.15	Outlet stores
HF3501-3530.5	380.10941	Great Britain—Commerce	HF5429.7-5430.6	381.1	Shopping centers
HF3551-3560	380.10944	France—Commerce	HF5429.7-5430.6	381.1	Shopping malls
HF3561-3570.5	380.10943	Germany—Commerce	HF5438-5439	380.1	Selling
HF3581-3590	380.10945	Italy—Commerce	HF5438.8.M4	658.8106	Sales meetings
HF3591-3620.5	380.109492	Benelux countries—Commerce	HF5438.8.P74	658.82	Sales presentations
			HF5439.25-.8	381.092	Sales executives
HF3621-3630	380.10947	Russia—Commerce	HF5439.25-.8	381.092	Sales personnel
HF3681-3690	380.10946	Spain—Commerce	HF5439.A8	380.145388342	Selling—Automobiles
HF3701-3710	380.109494	Switzerland—Commerce	HF5439.D75	380.1456151	Selling—Drugs
HF3750.5	380.109495	Greece—Commerce	HF5441-5444	381.092	Traveling sales personnel
HF3756-3770.2	380.10956	Middle East—Commerce	HF5446-5456	380.1	Canvassing
HF3760	380.1095694	Israel—Commerce	HF5457-5459	381.092	Peddlers and peddling
HF3770	380.109567	Iraq—Commerce	HF5460-5469.5	381.141	Department stores
HF3770.2	380.10955	Iran—Commerce	HF5465.5-5467	381.142	Mail-order business
HF3770.22-.27	380.10958	Asia, Central—Commerce	HF5468	381.12	Chain stores
HF3781-3790	380.10954	India—Commerce	HF5468.2	380.145004	Computer stores
HF3811-3820	380.109599	Philippines—Commerce	HF5469.25-.55	381.147	Convenience stores
HF3821-3830	380.10952	Japan—Commerce	HF5469.7-5481	381.18	Markets
HF3831-3840	380.10951	China—Commerce	HF5469.7-5481	381.18	Fairs
HF3871-3937	380.1096	Africa—Commerce	HF5476-5477	381.17	Auctions
HF3941-3950	380.10994	Australia—Commerce	HF5481	381.18	Fairs
HF4050	382	East-West trade	HF5482.15	381.192	Flea markets
HF5001-6182.2	338.7	Business	HF5482.3	381.195	Garage sales
HF5371	651.29	Business—Forms	HF5484-5495	380.1	Warehouses
HF5381-5382.5	650.1	Career development	HF5495	381.1	Stores or stock-room keeping
HF5381-5382.5	331.702	Vocational guidance	HF5546-5548	651.3	Office Management
HF5382.7-.75	650.14	Job hunting	HF5548-.115	651.2	Office equipment and supplies
HF5383	650.14	Applications for positions			
HF5383	650.14	Resumes (Employment)	HF5548	651.74	Dictating machines
HF5384.5	650.1	Career plateaus	HF5548	651.74	Dictograph
HF5386	650.1	Success in business	HF5548.125-.6	651.8	Office practice—Automation
HF5387	174.4	Business ethics	HF5548.115	652.5	Word processing
HF5389	395.52	Business etiquette	HF5548.33	651.8	Electronic data interchange
HF5410-5417.5	380.1	Marketing	HF5548.7-.85	158.7	Psychology, Industrial
HF5415	381.3	Rationing	HF5548.85	158.72	Job stress
HF5415.126	381.1	Direct marketing	HF5549-.5	658.3	Personnel management
HF5415.126	380.14502504	Database marketing	HF5549.12	658.302	Supervision of employees
HF5415.126	381.1	Multilevel marketing	HF5549.5.A4	658.3822	Alcoholism and employment
HF5415.1265	381.1	Telemarketing	HF5549.5.C35	658.3	Career development
HF5415.15-.157	658.5	Product management	HF5549.5.C8	658.3151	Employees—Counseling of
HF5415.2-5415.34	380.1072/658.83	Marketing research	HF5549.5.D7	658.3822	Drugs and employment
HF5415.3	380.1/658.83	Market surveys	HF5549.5.D7	658.3112	Employees—Drug testing
HF5415.5-.55	658.812	Customer relations	HF5549.5.E43	658.473	Employee theft
HF5415.5	381.3	Consumer affairs departments	HF5549.5.E5	658.3112	Employment tests
			HF5549.5.G7	658.3155	Grievance procedures
HF5415.6-.9	380.1	Physical distribution of goods	HF5549.5.I5	658.3142	Incentives in industry
			HF5549.5.I53	658.31242	Employee orientation
HF5415.9	363.19	Product recall	HF5549.5.I6	658.31124	Employment interviewing

LC	Dewey	Subject Heading	LC	Dewey	Subject Heading
HF5549.5.J6	658.306	Job analysis	HF5845-5849	659.152	Display of merchandise
HF5549.5.J613	658.306	Job descriptions	HF5845-5849	659.157	Show-windows
HF5549.5.M3	658.301	Manpower planning	HF5851	659.132	Advertising cards
HF5549.5.M63	658.314	Employee motivation	HF5861-5863	659.133	Commercial catalogs
HF5549.5.P7	658.3126	Promotions	HF5861-5863	659.133	Advertising, Direct-mail
HF5549.5.R3	658.3125	Employees-Rating of	HF5871-6141	659.132	Advertising, Newspaper
HF5549.5.R44	658.3111	Employees—Recruiting	HF5901-6097	659.13209(4-9)	Advertising, Newspaper—
HF5549.5.S4	658.312	Seniority, Employee			[By region or country]
HF5549.5.T8	331.126	Labor turnover	HF6125.5	659.19658311	Help-wanted advertising
HF5601-5689.8	657	Accounting	HF6146.D75	659.13	Advertising drinking glasses
HF5601-5689.8	657.2	Bookkeeping	HF6146.P75	659.17	Prize contests in advertising
HF5630	657.071	Accounting—Study and	HF6146.T42	659.143	Television advertising
		teaching (Internship)	HF6161.A38	659.193877	Advertising—Airlines
HF5657.4	658.1511	Managerial accounting	HF6178-6182	659.1125	Advertising agencies
HF5667-5668.25	657.45	Auditing	HG	332	Finance
HF5667.65	657.3	Financial statements,	HG1-9999	332	Financial institutions
		Unaudited	HG1-61	332.05	Finance—Periodicals
HF5668-.25	657.458	Auditing, Internal	HG63	332.06	Finance—Congresses
HF5679	657.0284	Accounting machines	HG64-96	332.025	Finance—Directories
HF5680-5681	657	Account books	HG151	332.03	Finance—Encyclopedias
HF5681.A2	657.72	Accounts current	HG152-.5	332.071	Finance—Study and
HF5681.A27	657.74	Accounts payable			teaching
HF5681.A3	657.72	Accounts receivable	HG171	332.09	Finance—History
HF5681.B2	657.3	Funds-flow statements	HG176-.5	332.021	Finance—Statistics
HF5681.B2	657.3	Financial statements	HG177-.5	658.15224	Fund raising
HF5681.D39	657.46	Deferred tax	HG179	332.024	Finance, Personal
HF5681.D5	657.73	Depreciation	HG179.5	332.024092	Financial planners
HF5681.G55	657	Going concern (Accounting)	HG201-1496	332.4	Money
HF5681.N65	657.74	Employee fringe benefits—	HG223	332.41	Value
		Accounting	HG226.5	332.414	Demand for money
HF5681.V3	657.73	Valuation	HG226.6	332.401	Quantity theory of money
HF5686.C7	657.95	Corporations—Accounting	HG229-.5	332.41	Purchasing power
HF5686.C8	657.42	Cost accounting	HG229-.5	332.41	Prices
HF5686.C8	657.42	Direct costing	HG235	332.4	Shell money
HF5688-5689	681.145	Calculators	HG258-312	332.4042	Precious metals
HF5691-5716	650.01513	Business mathematics	HG261-315	332.4042	Coinage
HF5705-5707	658.32021	Wages—Tables	HG289	332.4042	Gold
HF5717-5734.7	651.7	Business communication	HG297	332.4222	Gold standard
HF5718.3-5734	651.74	Business writing	HG301-309	332.4223	Silver
HF5719	651.74	Business report writing	HG321-329	332.4	Mints
HF5721-5734	651.75	Commercial correspondence	HG321	332.4042	Gold—Minting
HF5735-5746	651	Filing systems	HG325-329	669.92	Assaying
HF5735-5746	651.53	Card system in business	HG335-341	332.90973	Counterfeits and
HF5738	651.53	Electronic filing systems			counterfeiting
HF5761-5780	658.788	Delivery of goods	HG348-353.5	332.4044	Paper money
HF5761-5780	658.788	Shipment of goods	HG348-353.5	332.4044	Bank notes
HF5770	658.7884	Cartons	HG353.5	332.4	Military currency
HF5801-6182	659.1	Advertising	HG361-363	332.42042	Legal tender
HF5801-5802	659.105	Advertising—Periodicals	HG381-421	332.45	Coinage, International
HF5803	659.103	Advertising—Encyclopedias	HG393	332.4048	Decimal system
HF5804-5808	659.1122	Advertising departments	HG451-1496	332.49(4-9)	Money—[By region or
HF5804-5808	659.1025	Advertising—Directories			country]
HF5811-5813	659.109	Advertising—History	HG451-645	332.4973	Money—United States
HF5814-5815	659.1071	Advertising—Study and	HG551-566	332.40420973	Coinage
		teaching	HG551	332.40420973	Gold
HF5825	659.132	Advertising layout and	HG604	332.40440973	Greenbacks
		typography	HG607-610	332.40440973	Bank notes
HF5826.5	659.111	Advertising media planning	HG641-645	332.490973	Counterfeits and
HF5828	659.157	Advertising, Point-of-sale			counterfeiting
HF5833	343.082	Advertising laws	HG1501-3550	332.1	Banks and banking
HF5843-.5	659.132	Posters	HG2070-2106	332.34	Pawnbrokers

LC	Dewey	Subject Heading	LC	Dewey	Subject Heading
HG1616.C34	332.1	Bank capital	HG3691-3769	332.7	Credit
HG1616.C87	332.17	Banks and banking—Customer services	HG3705-3711	332.75	Credit control
			HG3745	332.77	Letters of credit
HG1616.I5	332.1754	Bank investments	HG3746	332.7	Documentary credit
HG1621-1623	332.82	Interest rates	HG3751-3754.5	332.742	Commercial credit
HG1641-1643	332.1753	Commercial loans	HG3751.5-.9	332.7	Credit ratings
HG1641-1643	332.1753	Bank loans	HG3752.3	332.7	Accounts receivable loans
HG1641-1643	332.1753	Term loans	HG3753-3754	332.742	Export credit
HG1643	332.178	Bank credit cards	HG3755-3756	332.743	Consumer credit
HG1643	332.178	Affinity credit cards	HG3755-3756	332.743	Loans, Personal
HG1643	332.178	Check credit plans	HG3755.5	332.743	Installment plan
HG1651-1654	332.84	Discount houses (Finance)	HG3760-3769	332.75	Bankruptcy
HG1651-1654	332.84	Discount	HG3773	332.75	Receivers
HG1655	332	Acceptances	HG3810-4000	332.45	Foreign exchange
HG1656	332.1	Bank reserves	HG3810.5	332.4503	Foreign exchange—Encyclopedias
HG1660	332.1752	Bank deposits			
HG1660	332.1752	Bank accounts	HG3811-3815	332.4509	Foreign exchange—History
HG1660	332.1752	Savings accounts	HG3853	332.645	Foreign exchange futures
HG1662	368.854	Deposit insurance	HG3854-3858	332.4021	Money—Tables
HG1685-1704	332.55	Drafts	HG3879-4000	332.042	International finance
HG1691-1704	332.1752	Checking accounts	HG3882-3890	332.152	Balance of payments
HG1692	332.76	Check collection systems	HG3891	332.042	Capital movements
HG1692	332.76	Check float	HG3896	337.14	Euro-bond market
HG1696-1698	332.9	Forgery	HG3901-4000	332.4509(4-9)	Foreign exchange—[By region or country]
HG1706-1708	657.8333	Banks and banking—Accounting	HG4001-4285	338.6041	Business enterprises—Finance
HG1709	332.10285	Banks and banking—Computer programs	HG4001-4285	338.74	Corporations—Finance
HG1710-.5	332.10285	Electronic funds transfer	HG4027.7	338.6420681	Small business—Finance
HG1710.5	332.76	Debit cards	HG4028.B6	332.6323	Bond transfer
HG1711-1712	332.17	Home banking services	HG4028.C4	332.0414	Capital investments
HG1722	332.16	Bank mergers	HG4028.C45	658.15244	Cash management
HG1723	332.6722	Bank stocks	HG4028.D5	332.63221	Dividend reinvestment
HG1725-1778	346.082	Banking law	HG4028.M4	338.83	Consolidation and merger of corporations
HG1881-1966	332.21	Savings banks			
HG1951-1956	332.22	Postal savings banks	HG4028.S7	658.15224	Going public (Securities)
HG1970-1971	332.37	Merchant banks	HG4028.T4	332.6322	Tender offers (Securities)
HG1975-1976	332.28	Development banks	HG4028.V3	332.63221	Valuation
HG1978-2031	332.123	Private banks	HG4301-4480.9	332.26	Trust companies
HG2032-2039	334.22	Credit unions	HG4307	332.26025	Trust companies—Directories
HG2032-2039	334.2	Banks and banking, Cooperative	HG4311	332.2609	Trust companies—History
HG2039.5-2040.5	332.32	Mortgage banks	HG4341-4480.9	332.2609(4-9)	Trust companies—[By region or country]
HG2039.5-2040.5	332.72	Mortgage loans, Reverse	HG4341-4356	332.260973	Trust companies—United States
HG2040.4	332.722	Home improvement loans	HG4357-4480.9	332.2609(4-9)	Trust companies—[Other regions or countries]
HG2040.45	332.722	Home equity loans			
HG2041-2051	332.31	Agricultural cooperative credit associations	HG4501-6051	332.6	Investments
HG2041-2051	332.31	Land banks	HG4529.5	332.6	Portfolio management
HG2070-2106	332.34	Pawnbroking	HG4530	332.6	Investment clubs
HG2121-2156	332.32	Savings and loan associations	HG4530	332.6327	Mutual funds
			HG4538	332.673	Investments, Foreign
HG2251-2256	332.178	Safe-deposit boxes	HG4551-4598	332.642	Stock-exchanges
HG2301-2351	332.12	Clearinghouses (Banking)	HG4571-4575.3	332.64273	Wall Street
HG2401-3542.7	332.109(4-9)	Banks and banking—[By region or country]	HG4621	332.62	Discount brokers
			HG4621	332.642	Floor traders (Finance)
HG2401-2626	332.10973	Banks and banking—United States	HG4621	332.62	Stockbrokers
			HG4651	332.6323	Bonds
HG2559-2565	332.110973	Federal Reserve banks	HG4650-4930.5	332.632	Securities
			HG4655	332.63244	Mortgages

LC	Dewey	Subject Heading	LC	Dewey	Subject Heading
HG4661	332.6322	Stocks	HG9751-9899	368.11009(4-9)	Insurance, Fire—[By region or country]
HG4701-4726	332.63232	Government securities			
HG4726	332.63233	Municipal bonds	HG9751-9780	368.1100973	Insurance, Fire—United States
HG4901-5993	332.609(4-9)	Investments—[By region or country]			
			HG9781-9866	368.11009(4-9)	Insurance, Fire—[Other regions or countries]
HG4905-5131	332.60973	Investments—United States			
HG4931-4955	332.632320973	Government securities—United States	HG9903-9905	368.23	Insurance, Inland marine
			HG9956-9969	368.5	Insurance, Casualty
HG4951-4953	379.130973	School bonds	HG9966-9969	368.121	Insurance, Agricultural
HG5151-5993	332.609(4-9)	Investments—[Other regions or countries]	HG9970	368.092	Insurance, Automobile
			HG9970.A4-.A68	368.5728	Insurance, No-fault automobile
HG6001-6051	332.645	Speculation			
HG6024-6051	332.645	Futures	HG9972	368.093	Insurance, Aviation
HG6024.3-.9	332.645	Financial futures	HG9979	368.122	Insurance, Disaster
HG6042	332.63228	Stock options	HG9981	368.1226	Insurance, Earthquake
HG6043	332.63228	Stock index futures	HG9983	368.1222	Insurance, Flood
HG6046-6051	332.6328	Commodity futures	HG9986	368.096	Homeowner's insurance
HG6046-6051	332.644	Commodity exchanges	HG9990	368.5	Insurance, Liability
HG6105-6270.9	336.17	Lotteries	HG9992	368.852	Mortgage guarantee insurance
HG6126-6134	336.170973	Lotteries—United States			
HG7920-7933	332.0415	Saving and thrift	HG9995	368.562	Insurance, Products liability
HG8011-9999	368	Insurance	HG9997	368.8(3/4)	Insurance, Surety and fidelity
HG8053.5-8054.45	368.564	Insurance, Malpractice	HG9999	368.88	Insurance, Title
			HJ	336	Finance, Public
HG8054	368.5642	Insurance, Physicians' liability	HJ9-99.8	336.005	Finance, Public—Periodicals
			HJ210-240	336.09(4-9)	Finance, Public—History
HG8054.5	368	Risk (Insurance)	HJ241-785	336.73	Finance, Public—United States
HG8058	368.3	Insurance, Group			
HG8059	368.094	Insurance, Business	HJ285-785	336.7(4-9)	Finance, Public—[United States, By state]
HG8075-8107	368.0065	Insurance companies			
HG8082	368	Self-insurance	HJ2005-2216	352.48	Budget
HG8205-8220	368.4	Insurance, Government	HJ2050-2053	352.530973	United States—Appropriations and expenditures
HG8501-8745	368.9(4-9)	Insurance—[By region or country]			
			HJ2054-2216	352.5309(4-9)	[Other regions or countries]—Appropriations and expenditures
HG8501-8540	368.973	Insurance—United States			
HG8550-8740.5	368.9(4-9)	Insurance—[Other regions or countries]			
			HJ2240-7395	336	Taxation
HG8751-9271	368.32	Insurance, Life	HJ2240-7395	336.02	Revenue
HG8779-8793	368.3200151	Insurance, Life—Mathematics	HJ2250-2279	336.2009	Taxation—History
			HJ2321-2323	336.294	Tax incidence
HG8783-8785	368.3201	Mortality—Tables	HJ2326-2327	336.293	Progressive taxation
HG8790-8793	368.37	Annuities	HJ2336-2337	336.206	Tax exemption
HG8901-8914	346.08632	Insurance, Life—Law and legislation	HJ2351.4	336.20015195	Tax revenue estimating
			HJ2361-3192.7	336.2009(4-9)	Taxation—[By region or country]
HG8941-9200.5	368.32009(4-9)	Insurance, Life—[By region or country]			
			HJ2361-2442	336.200973	Taxation—United States
HG9201-9245	334.7	Friendly societies	HJ2361	336.200973	Internal revenue—United States
HG9251-9262	368.362	Industrial life insurance			
HG9271	368.32	Insurance, Child	HJ2391-2442	336.20097(4-9)	Taxation—[United States, By state]
HG9291-9295	368.424	Insurance, Maternity			
HG9301-9343	368.384	Insurance, Accident	HJ2449-3192.7	336.2009(4-9)	Taxation—[Other regions or countries]
HG9371-9399	368.382	Insurance, Health			
HG9389	368.3827	Insurance, Hospitalization	HJ3241	336.2	Tax assessment
HG9466-9479	368.366	Insurance, Burial	HJ3863-3925	336.294	Direct taxation
HG9651-9899	368.11	Insurance, Fire	HJ3925.A-.Z	336.29409(4-9)	Direct taxation—[By region or country]
HG9660	368.11009	Insurance, Fire—History			
HG9663	368.110021	Insurance, Fire—Statistics	HJ4101-4936	336.22	Property tax
HG9711-9715	368.11014	Fire insurance claims adjusters	HJ4120-4460	336.2309(4-9)	Property tax—[By region or country]
HG9733-9735	346.086	Insurance, Fire—Law and legislation	HJ4581-4601	336.23	Taxation of personal property

LC	Dewey	Subject Heading	LC	Dewey	Subject Heading
HJ4621-4830	336.24	Income tax	HM101-121	306	Culture
HJ4653.C3	336.24240973	Capital gains tax	HM101-121	303.44	Progress
HJ4653.E8	336.24320973	Excess profits tax	HM104	301.09	Historical sociology
HJ5250-5255	336.294	Indirect taxation	HM121	304.5	Heredity
HJ5301-5508	336.16	Licenses	HM131-134	307	Community life
HJ5315	336.272	Revenue-stamps	HM131-134	305	Social groups
HJ5321-5510	336.1609(4-9)	Licenses—[By region or country]	HM132	302	Interpersonal relations
			HM132.5	302.34	Friendship—Sociological aspects
HJ5321-5374	336.160973	Licenses—United States			
HJ5711-5721	336.2713	Sales tax	HM136-146	302.54	Individualism
HJ5711-5715	336.27	Turnover tax	HM141	303.34	Leadership
HJ5711-5715	336.2714	Value-added tax	HM146	305	Equality
HJ5730-5731	336.271	Excise tax	HM206-208	304.2	Social ecology
HJ5771-5797	336.271	Luxuries—Taxation	HM213	306.42	Intellectuals
HJ5801-5823	336.276	Inheritance and transfer tax	HM216	303.372	Social ethics
HJ6603-7390	352.448	Customs administration	HM221	306.46	Technology—Sociological aspects
HJ6619	364.133	Smugglers			
HJ6622-7390	352.44809(4-9)	Customs administration—[By region or country]	HM251-291	302	Social psychology
			HM253	302.015195	Sociometry
HJ6622-6731	352.4480973	Customs administration—United States	HM258	303.482	Intercultural communication
			HM259	303.34	Social influence
HJ6690-6710	364.1330973	Smugglers—United States	HM261	303.380723	Public opinion polls
HJ6750-7390	352.44809(4-9)	Customs administration—[Other regions or countries]	HM261	303.38	Public opinion
			HM263	303.375	Propaganda
HJ7461-7977	336.39	Expenditures, Public	HM271-276	303.36	Authority
HJ7537-7977	336.3909(4-9)	Expenditures, Public—[By region or country]	HM281-283	302.33	Crowds
			HM281-283	303.625	Riots
HJ7537-7654	336.390973	Expenditures, Public—United States	HM281-283	302.33	Mobs
			HM281-283	303.64	Revolutions
HJ7663-7977	336.3909(4-9)	Expenditures, Public—[Other regions or countries]	HM281-283	303.6	Violence
			HM291	302.(3/4)	Social interaction
HJ8001-8899	336.3	Debts, Public	HN	361.1	Social problems
HJ8003-8899	336.3	Debts, External	HN1	361.105	Social problems—Periodicals
HJ8052	336.363	Sinking-funds			
HJ8061	336.368	State bankruptcy	HN3	361.106	Social problems—Congresses
HJ8101-8899	336.3409(4-9)	Debts, Public—[By region or country]	HN8-19	361.109	Social problems—History
			HN25	306	Quality of life
HJ9103-9695	336.014	Local finance	HN29	361.10723	Social surveys
HJ9103	336.01405	Local finance—Periodicals	HN30-39	261.83	Church and social problems
HJ9115-9123	336.2014	Municipal revenue	HN41-46	790.068	Community centers
HJ9141-9695	336.014(4-9)	Local finance—[By region or country]	HN43-46	790.068(4-9)	Community centers—[By region or country]
HJ9141-9343	336.01473	Local finance—United States	HN43-45	790.06873	Community centers—United States
HJ9350-9695	336.014(4-9)	Local finance—[Other regions or countries]	HN49.C6	307.14	Community development
HJ9701-9995	657.61	Finance, Public—Accounting	HN49.V64	302.14	Voluntarism
HM	301	Sociology	HN51-90	973	United States—Social conditions
HM1-7	301.05	Sociology—Periodicals			
HM13	301.06	Sociology—Congresses	HQ12-449	306.7	Sex
HM17	301.03	Sociology—Dictionaries	HQ12-18	306.73	Sex customs
HM19-22	301.09	Sociology—History	HQ19-30.7	306.7	Sexual instinct
HM24-37	301.01	Sociology—Methodology	HQ27-.5	306.70835	Young adults—Sexual behavior
HM24	305.8001	Ethnomethodology			
HM33	320	Political science	HQ27	306.7088375	Students—Sexual behavior
HM35	306.3	Economics—Sociological aspects	HQ29	306.7082	Women—Sexual behavior
			HQ30	306.70846	Aged—Sexual behavior
HM45-47	301.071	Sociology—Study and teaching	HQ30.5	306.70816	Handicapped—Sexual behavior
HM101	909	Civilization	HQ31-64	176	Sexual ethics
HM101-121	303.4	Social change	HQ35	176.0835	Sexual ethics for teenagers

LC	Dewey	Subject Heading	LC	Dewey	Subject Heading
HQ46	176.082	Sexual ethics for women	HQ679-680	306.8109599	Marriage—Philippines
HQ51	613.9071	Sex instruction for girls	HQ681-682	306.810952	Marriage—Japan
HQ53	613.9071	Sex instruction for children	HQ684	306.810951	Marriage—China
HQ41	613.9071	Sex instruction for boys	HQ691-697.4	306.81096	Marriage—Africa
HQ54-.4	613.9071	Sex instruction for the handicapped	HQ705-706	306.810994	Marriage—Australia
			HQ745	392.5/395.22	Marriage service
HQ55	613.9071	Sex instruction for the aged	HQ750-755.5	363.92	Eugenics
HQ56-59	613.9071	Sex instruction	HQ755.7-759.92	306.874	Parenting
HQ60	613.9072	Sexology—Research	HQ755.7-759.92	306.874	Parenthood
HQ71-72	364.153	Sex offenders	HQ755.85	306.874	Abused parents
HQ71-72	364.153	Sex crimes	HQ755.86	306.874084	Parent and adult child
HQ71	306.877	Incest	HQ756-.7	306.8742	Fatherhood
HQ74-.2	306.765	Bisexuality	HQ756-.7	306.8742	Fathers
HQ75-76.95	306.766	Homosexuality	HQ756	306.874208653	Divorced fathers
HQ75.3-.6	305.489664	Abused lesbians	HQ756	306.8742	Stepfathers
HQ75.3-.6	306.7663	Lesbianism	HQ756.6	640.92	Househusbands
HQ75.8	305.389664	Gay men	HQ759-.6	306.8743	Motherhood
HQ76.5-.8	305.90664	Gay liberation movement	HQ759-.6	306.8743	Mothers
HQ76.97-77.2	306.77	Transvestites	HQ759.2	394.262	Mother's Day
HQ77.7-.95	305.3	Transsexualism	HQ759.3	306.8743	Absentee mothers
HQ79	306.775	Sadism	HQ759.4	306.87430835	Teenage mothers
HQ79	306.77	Fetishism (Sexual behavior)	HQ759.48	306.8743	Working mothers
HQ79	306.775	Sadomasochism	HQ759.5	306.8743	Surrogate mothers
HQ101-440.7	306.74	Prostitution	HQ759.64	306.8740835	Teenage parents
HQ111-117	306.7409	Prostitution—History	HQ759.9	306.8745	Grandparenting
HQ141-270.7	306.7409(4-9)	Prostitution—[By region or country]	HQ759.912	306.874087	Handicapped parents
			HQ759.913	306.874	Parents of exceptional children
HQ301-440.7	362.809(4-9)	Church work with prostitutes			
HQ447	306.772	Masturbation	HQ759.913	306.874	Parents of handicapped children
HQ450-472	809.933538	Erotic literature			
HQ471-472	363.47	Pornography	HQ759.98	304.634	Family demography
HQ471	363.47	Pornography—Social aspects	HQ760-767.7	304.634	Family size
			HQ762	304.63409(1-9)	Family size—[By region or country]
HQ503-1064	306.81	Marriage			
HQ503-1064	306.8	Family	HQ763-767.52	304.666	Birth control
HQ503-1064	306.8	Home	HQ766.2-.4	363.96	Birth control—Moral and ethical aspects
HQ503-518	306.8109	Marriage—History			
HQ531-727.9	306.8109(4-9)	Marriage—[By region or country]	HQ767-.4	363.46	Abortion
			HQ767.8-792.2	305.23	Children
HQ535-557	306.810973	Marriage—United States	HQ767.87	305.2309	Children—History
HQ559-560	306.810971	Marriage—Canada	HQ768-777.95	392.13/649.1	Child rearing
HQ561-562	306.810972	Marriage—Mexico	HQ769.5	649.10248	Babysitting
HQ563-574	306.8109728	Marriage—Central America	HQ770.4	364.67	Corporal punishment
HQ575-587.9	306.8109729	Marriage—West Indies	HQ770.4	649.64	Discipline of children
HQ588-610	306.81098	Marriage—South America	HQ773.5	649.155	Gifted children
HQ611-662.7	306.81094	Marriage—Europe	HQ774	305.232	Infants
HQ613-618.5	306.810941	Marriage—Great Britain	HQ774	305.232	Infants—Development
HQ623-624	306.810944	Marriage—France	HQ774.5	305.233	Preschool children
HQ625-626.5	306.810943	Marriage—Germany	HQ774.5	305.232	Toddlers
HQ629-630	306.810945	Marriage—Italy	HQ775	649.132	Boys
HQ631-636.5	306.8109492	Marriage—Benelux Countries	HQ777.2	306.87	First-born children
			HQ777.22	306.87	Second-born children
HQ637-638	306.810947	Marriage—Russia	HQ777.9	306.843083	Children of interracial marriage
HQ649-650	306.810946	Marriage—Spain			
HQ653-654	306.8109494	Marriage—Switzerland	HQ778.5-.7	362.712	Day care centers
HQ662.5	306.8109495	Marriage—Greece	HQ778.6	305.234	School-age child care
HQ663-690.5	306.81095	Marriage—Asia	HQ779-.5	305.232	Baby books
HQ664	306.81095694	Marriage—Israel	HQ783	303.32	Socialization
HQ666.3	306.8109567	Marriage—Iraq	HQ784.F7	302.34083	Friendship in children
HQ666.4	306.810955	Marriage—Iran	HQ784.S45	306.7083	Children—Sexual behavior
HQ669-670	306.810954	Marriage—India	HQ793-799.9	305.235	Youth

LC	Dewey	Subject Heading	LC	Dewey	Subject Heading
HQ798	305.23508352	Teenage girls	HQ1871-2030.7	305.4(06/8)/ 367	Women—Societies and clubs
HQ799	305.23509(4-9)	Youth—[By region or country]	HS	366	Societies
HQ799.15	306.874	Parent and teenager	HS1	366.005	Societies—Periodicals
HQ799.5-.9	305.235	Young adults	HS5	366.006	Societies—Congresses
HQ799.95-.97	305.24	Adulthood	HS12	366.003	Societies—Encyclopedias
HQ803	306.84	Temporary marriage	HS17	366.0025	Societies—Directories
HQ800-.4	305.90652	Single people	HS25-35	366.009	Societies—History, organization, etc.
HQ800.15	306.732	Celibacy			
HQ800.2	305.489652	Single women	HS101-330.7	366.(1-5)	Secret societies
HQ800.3	305.389652	Bachelors	HS101-106	366.(1-5)05	Secret societies—Periodicals
HQ801-.83	306.7	Man-woman relationships			
HQ801.8	306.73	Interracial dating	HS110	366.(1-5)06	Secret societies—Congresses
HQ801.83	306.73	Dating violence			
HQ803	306.84	Marriage, Companionate	HS121-123	366.(1-5)03	Secret societies—Directories
HQ805	306.88	Desertion and non-support			
HQ806	306.736	Adultery	HS125-148	366.(1-5)09	Secret societies—History, organization, etc.
HQ811-960.7	306.89	Divorce			
HQ831-960.7	306.8809(4-9)	Divorce—[By region or country]	HS155-158	366.(1-5)	Secret societies—Rituals Insignia
			HS159-160	366.6027	
HQ833-836	306.880973	Desertion—United States	HS201-330.7	366.(1-5)09(4-9)	Secret societies—[By region or country]
HQ837-960.9	306.8809(4-9)	Desertion—[Other regions and countries]	HS203-206	366.(1-5)0973	Secret societies—United States
HQ961-967	306.735	Free love			
HQ970-975.7	307.774	Communal living	HS207-330.7	366.(1-5)09(4-9)	Secret societies—[Other regions or societies]
HQ981-996	306.842	Group marriage			
HQ981-996	306.8423	Polygamy	HS351-929	336.1	Freemasons
HQ998-999	305.906945	Illegitimacy	HS351-929	366.1	Freemasonry
HQ1017	392.4	Dowry	HS351-359	366.105	Freemasons—Periodicals
HQ1018-1019	306.84	Remarriage	HS381-390	366.1025	Freemasons—Directories
HQ1028	306.84	Marriage with deceased wife's sister	HS403-420	366.109	Freemasons—History
			HS455-459	366.12	Freemasonry—Rituals
HQ1031	306.843	Interfaith marriage	HS501-680.7	366.109(4-9)	Freemasons—[By region or country]
HQ1031	306.846	Interracial marriage			
HQ1036-1043	306.81087	Handicapped—Marriage	HS503-539	366.10973	Freemasons—United States
HQ1040	306.810872	Deaf—Marriage	HS557-680.7	366.109(4-9)	Freemasons—[Other regions or countries]
HQ1058-.5	305.389654	Widowers			
HQ1058-.5	305.489654	Widows	HS875-895	366.108996073	Afro-American freemasonry
HQ1059.4-.5	305.244	Middle age	HS951-1179	366.3	Independent Order of Odd Fellows
HQ1060-1064	305.26	Aged—Government policy			
HQ1060-1064	305.26091734	Rural aged	HS951-953	366.305	Independent Order of Odd Fellows—Periodicals
HQ1060-1064	305.26	Aged			
HQ1073-.5	306.9	Thanatology	HS963-975	366.3025	Independent Order of Odd Fellows—Directories
HQ1073-.5	306.9	Death			
HQ1075-.5	305.3	Sex role	HS987-991	366.309	Independent Order of Odd Fellows—History
HQ1088-1090.7	305.31	Men's studies			
HQ1101-2030.7	305.4	Women	HS1019-1021	728.4	Independent Order of Odd Fellows—Rituals
HQ1121-1870.5	305.42	Women—Social conditions			
HQ1121-1172	305.409	Women—History	HS1041-1051	366.309(4-9)	Independent Order of Odd Fellows—[By region or country]
HQ1139	305.409	Amazons			
HQ1170	305.486971	Muslim women			
HQ1172	305.48696	Jewish women	HS1041-1045	366.30973	Independent Order of Odd Fellows—United States
HQ1180-1186	305.407	Women's studies			
HQ1190	305.42	Feminist theory	HS1501-1510	334.7	Friendly societies
HQ1201-1216	302.32082	Women—Socialization	HS2301-2460.7	369	Patriotic societies
HQ1206-1216	155.633	Women—Psychology	HS2321-2330	369.1	Patriotic societies—United States
HQ1229	155.533	Young women—Psychology			
HQ1236-.5	323.34	Women's rights	HS2501-3371	367	Clubs
HQ1400-1870.5	305.409(4-9)	Women—[By region or country]	HS2501-2503	367.05	Clubs—Periodicals
			HS2507-2515	367.025	Clubs—Directories
HQ1402-1439	305.40973	Women—United States	HS2721-3200	367.9(4-9)	Clubs—[By region or country]

LC	Dewey	Subject Heading	LC	Dewey	Subject Heading
HS2721-2725	367.973	Clubs—United States	HT607	305.509	Social classes—History
HS2731-3200	367.9(4-9)	Clubs—[Other regions or countries]	HT608	305.5072	Social classes—Research
			HT647-653	305.52	Aristocracy (Social class)
HS3250-3270	367.4	Youth—Societies and clubs	HT647-653	305.5223	Nobility
HS3301-3325	369.42	Boys—Societies and clubs	HT657	305.5232	Gentry
HS3312-3316	369.43	Boy Scouts	HT680-690	305.55	Middle class
HS3353.G5	369.463	Girl Scouts	HT690	305.5509(4-9)	Middle class—[By region or country]
HS3359	369.463	Daisy Girl Scouts			
HT51-65	307	Human settlements	HT713-725	305.5122	Caste
HT101-395	307	Cities and towns	HT751-815	306.365	Serfdom
HT101-395	307.76	Sociology, Urban	HT781-815	306.36509(4-9)	Serfdom—[By region or country]
HT110	307.76072	Sociology, Urban—Research			
HT111-150	307.7609	Sociology, Urban—History	HT781	306.3650941	Serfdom—Great Britain
HT114	307.76093	Cities and towns, Ancient	HT785	306.3650944	Serfdom—France
HT115	307.760902	Cities and towns, Medieval	HT791-801	306.3650943	Serfdom—Germany
HT123-.5	307.760973	Sociology, Urban—United States	HT803	306.3650943 (6/9)	Serfdom—Austria
HT127	307.760971	Sociology, Urban—Canada	HT807-809	306.3650947	Serfdom—Russia
HT127.7	307.760972	Sociology, Urban—Mexico	HT851-1444	305.567	Slavery
HT128	307.7609728	Sociology, Urban—Central America	HT863-867	305.56709	Slavery—History
			HT910-921	261.8	Slavery and the church
HT129	307.76098	Sociology, Urban—South America	HT975-1445	380.144	Slave-trade
			HT1025-1037	326.8	Slaves—Emancipation
HT131-145	307.76094	Sociology, Urban—Europe	HT1051-1052	305.5670971	Slavery—Canada
HT133	307.760941	Sociology, Urban—Great Britain	HT1053-1054	305.5670972	Slavery—Mexico
			HT1055-1056	305.56709728	Slavery—Central America
HT135	307.760944	Sociology, Urban—France	HT1071-1119	305.56709729	Slavery—West Indies
HT137	307.760943	Sociology, Urban—Germany	HT1121-1152	305.567098	Slavery—South America
HT147	307.76095	Sociology, Urban—Asia	HT1155-1240	305.567094	Slavery—Europe
HT148	307.76096	Sociology, Urban—Africa	HT1161-1165	305.5670941	Slavery—Great Britain
HT149	307.760994	Sociology, Urban—Australia	HT1176-1180	305.5670944	Slavery—France
HT149.5	307.76091724	Sociology, Urban—Developing countries	HT1181	305.5670943	Slavery—Germany
			HT1191-1194	305.5670945	Slavery—Italy
HT156	307.76	Inner cities	HT1196-1203	305.56709492	Slavery—Benelux countries
HT161-165	307.76	Garden cities	HT1206-1209	305.5670947	Slavery—Russia
HT165.5-169.5	307.1216	City planning	HT1216-1220	305.5670946	Slavery—Spain
HT167-169.54	307.121609(4-9)	City planning—[By region or country]	HT1227-1228	305.56709494	Slavery—Switzerland
			HT1234	305.56709495	Slavery—Greece
HT167-168	307.12160973	City planning—United States	HT1240.5-1315	305.567095	Slavery—Asia
			HT1241-1244	305.5670951	Slavery—China
HT169.55-.57	307.768	Planned communities	HT1271	305.56709599	Slavery—Philippines
HT169.55-.57	307.768	New towns	HT1276	305.5670952	Slavery—Japan
HT169.6-.9	333.7717	Zoning	HT1321-1427	305.567096	Slavery—Africa
HT170-178	307.3416	Urban renewal	HT1431	305.5670994	Slavery—Australia
HT175-177	307.34160973	Urban renewal—United States	HT1501-1595	305.8	Race
			HT1501-1595	305.8	Race relations
HT178	307.341609(4-9)	Urban renewal—[Other regions or countries]	HT1507	305.8009	Race relations—History
			HT1575-1577	305.8034	Caucasian race
HT206	305.23091732	City children	HT1581-1589	305.8(036/93)	Black race
HT241-243	577.56	Urban ecology	HV	361.6	Public welfare
HT321-325	330.91732	Urban economics	HV1-4959	361.7	Charities
HT351-352	307.74	Suburban life	HV1-4630	362.5	Poverty
HT381	307.26	Urban-rural migration	HV1-696	361	Social service
HT392-395	307.1209(4-9)	Regional planning—[By region or country]	HV6	361.006	Social service—Societies, etc.
HT392-394	307.120973	Regional planning—United States	HV7	361.025	Social service—Directories
			HV10.5	361.3023	Social service—Vocational guidance
HT401-485	307.72	Sociology, Rural			
HT415	307.7209	Sociology, Rural—History	HV11-.8	361.3071	Social work education
HT421	305.555	Farm life	HV16-25	361.709	Social service—History
HT601-1444	305.5	Social classes			

LC	Dewey	Subject Heading	LC	Dewey	Subject Heading
HV29.2-.5	361.10285	Information storage and retrieval systems—Social service	HV835-847	362.73	Foundlings
			HV862-866	362.732	Group homes for children
			HV868	363.83	Milk programs
HV40-69	361.7	Charity organization	HV873-887	362.708691	Street children
HV40.54	361.3092	Social workers—Supervision of	HV873-875.7	362.73	Abandoned children
			HV874.8-875.7	362.734	Adoption
HV41.2-.9	361.70681	Fund raising	HV875.5	362.734	Intercountry adoption
HV45	361.4	Social group work	HV877-878	369.42	Boys
HV59-63	361.05	Institutional care	HV878	369.42	Boys—Societies and clubs
HV61	362.585	Almshouses	HV879-887	369.46	Girls
HV67	361.91734	Social service, Rural	HV880-887	362.7309(4-9)	Abandoned children—[By region or country]
HV85-520.5	361.9(4-9)	Social service—[By region or country]			
			HV880-885	362.730973	Abandoned children—United States
HV85-99	361.973	Social service—United States			
			HV888-907	362.(3-4)	Handicapped children—Services for
HV98-99	361.97(4-9)	Social service—[United States, By state or city]			
			HV891-901	362.1968	Developmentally disabled children
HV101-520.5	361.9(4-9)	Social service—[Other regions or countries]	HV891-901	362.38	Day care centers for mentally handicapped children
HV530	361.75	Church charities			
HV544	361.7	Bazaars (Charities)			
HV547	374.22	Self-help groups	HV903-907	362.4083	Disfigured children
HV553-639	363.348	Disaster relief	HV959-1420.5	362.732	Orphanages
HV555	363.34809(4-9)	Disaster relief—[By region or country]	HV959-1420.5	362.73	Orphans
			HV971-1420.5	362.73209(4-9)	Orphanages—[By region or country]
HV560-503	361.77	Red Cross			
HV575-580	361.7709(4-9)	Red Cross—[By region or country]	HV971-995	362.7320973	Orphanages—United States
			HV1423	362.7083	Young men
HV599-600	363.3495	Earthquakes	HV1425	362.7083	Young women
HV609-610	363.34938	Floods	HV1442-1448	362.83	Women—Services for
HV620	363.37	Fires	HV1449	361.308664	Social work with gays
HV625-626	363.34929	Droughts	HV1450-1494	362.6091734	Rural aged
HV630-635	363.8	Famines	HV1450-1494	362.6	Aged
HV635.5-636	363.3492	Storms	HV1450-1493	362.6	Old age
HV639	363.34988	War relief	HV1454-.2	362.61	Old age homes
HV640-.5	362.87	Refugees	HV1455-.2	362.68	Day care centers for the aged
HV640-.5	362.87	Refugees, Political			
HV675-677	363.107	Accidents—Prevention	HV1457-1494	362.609(4-9)	Aged—[By region or country]
HV687-694	361.7	Charities, Medical	HV1551-3024	362.(3-4)	Handicapped
HV687-694	362.1	Sick	HV1568.7-.8	362.48	Day care centers for the handicapped
HV687-688	362.10425	Medical social work			
HV689-690	362.20425	Psychiatric social work	HV1570-.5	362.1968	Developmentally disabled
HV694	363.883	Diet kitchens	HV1571-2349	362.41	Blind
HV696.F6	363.883	Food relief	HV1597-.2	362.41	Blind-deaf—Services for
HV696.F6	363.882	Food stamps	HV1597.5	362.6	Blind aged
HV697-700	362.713	Aid to families with dependent children	HV1618-1782	371.911	Blind—Education
			HV1631.5	362.418	Visually handicapped—Means of communication
HV697-700	362.83	Maternal and infant welfare			
HV697-700.5	362.8292	Abused wives—Services for	HV1652-1658	331.1250871	Blind—Employment
HV699-700	362.829209(4-9)	Abused wives—Services for—[By region or country]	HV1701	362.418	Blind, Apparatus for the
			HV1780-.6	362.418071	Guide dog schools
HV700.5	362.8394	Unmarried mothers	HV1783-2220.5	362.4109(4-9)	Blind—[By region or country]
HV700.7	362.8294	Unmarried fathers	HV1783-1796	362.410973	Blind—United States
HV701-1420.5	362.7	Child welfare	HV1801-2220.5	362.4109(4-9)	Blind—[Other regions or places]
HV701	362.705	Child welfare—Periodicals			
HV741-804	362.709(4-9)	Child welfare—[By region or country]	HV2350-2990.5	362.42	Deaf
			HV2350-2990.5	362.42	Hearing impaired
HV741-743	362.70973	Child welfare—United States	HV2402	362.4283	Interpreters for the deaf
			HV2417-2500	371.912	Deaf—Education
HV745-804	362.709(4-9)	Child welfare—[Other regions or countries]	HV2477-2480	419	Finger spelling

LC	Dewey	Subject Heading	LC	Dewey	Subject Heading
HV2503	362.4283	Video recordings for the hearing impaired	HV5001-5720	362.2928	Temperance
			HV5001-5002	362.29205	Alcoholism—Periodicals
HV2510-2990.5	362.4209(4-9)	Deaf—[By region or country]	HV5006	362.292	Temperance—Societies, etc.
HV2510-2561	362.420973	Deaf—United States	HV5020-5025	362.292709	Temperance—History
HV3004-3009.5	362.1968	Day care centers for the developmentally disabled	HV5045	616.8610019	Alcoholism—Psychological aspects
HV3004-3009	362.3	Mental retardation	HV5053-5055	362.292	Alcoholism and crime
HV3004-3008	362.385	Mental retardation facilities	HV5132	362.2923	Children of alcoholics
HV3006-3008	362.30973	Mentally handicapped—[By region or country]	HV5132	362.2923	Alcoholics' spouses
			HV5132	362.2923	Alcoholics—Family relationships
HV3011-3024	362.48	Physically handicapped—Services for	HV5132	362.2923	Adult children of alcoholics
HV3023-3024	362.4809(4-9)	Physically handicapped—[By region or country]	HV5275-5283	362.29286	Alcoholism counseling
			HV5285-5722	362.29209(4-9)	Alcoholism—[By region or country]
HV3023	362.480973	Physically handicapped—United States	HV5285-5298	362.2920973	Alcoholism—United States
HV3024	362.4809(4-9)	Physically handicapped—[Other regions or countries]	HV5301-5722	362.29209(4-9)	Alcoholism—[Other regions or countries]
HV3025-3163	362.858	Sailors—Services for	HV5725-5770	362.296	Smoking
HV3181-3185	362.8496073	Afro-Americans—Services for	HV5725-5770	362.296	Ex-smokers
HV4023-4170.7	307.3364	Slums	HV5725-5770	362.296	Tobacco habit
HV4023-4470.7	362.5091732	Urban poor	HV5740-5745	362.296	Cigarette habit
HV4023-4470.7	362.5	Poor	HV5755-5770	362.29609(4-9)	Smoking—[By region or country]
HV4041-4173	362.509(4-9)	Poor—[By region or country]	HV5755-5768	362.2960973	Smoking—United States
HV4043-4046	362.50973	Poor—United States	HV5770	362.29609(4-9)	Smoking—[Other regions or places]
HV4047-4050	362.50971	Poor—Canada			
HV4051	362.50972	Poor—Mexico	HV5800-5840	362.29(3-8)	Drug abuse
HV4053-4059	362.509728	Poor—Central America	HV5800-5840	362.29(3-8)7	Drug abuse—Prevention
HV4060-4065.9	362.509729	Poor—West Indies	HV5800-5840	362.293	Narcotic habit
HV4066-4083	362.5098	Poor—South America	HV5810	362.298	Cocaine habit
HV4084-4131.84	362.5094	Poor—Europe	HV5813	362.293	Morphine habit
HV4085-4087.5	362.50941	Poor—Great Britain	HV5816	362.293	Opium habit
HV4093-4096	362.50944	Poor—France	HV5822.5.L9	362.294	LSD (Drug)
HV4097-4100.5	362.50943	Poor—Germany	HV5822.G5	362.299	Glue-sniffing
HV4102-4105	362.50945	Poor—Italy	HV5822.H4	362.293	Heroin
HV4105.5-4113.5	362.509492	Poor—Benelux countries	HV5822.M3	362.295	Marihuana
HV4114-4117	362.50947	Poor—Russia	HV5825-5840	362.29(3-8)09(4-9)	Drug abuse—[By region or country]
HV4125-4128	362.50946	Poor—Spain			
HV4131.85-4156.5	362.5095	Poor—Asia	HV5825-5833	362.29(3-8)0973	Drug abuse—United States
HV4137-4140	362.50954	Poor—India	HV5840	362.29(3-8)09(4-9)	Drug abuse—[Other regions or countries]
HV4147	362.50952	Poor—Japan			
HV4150	362.50951	Poor—China	HV6001-7220.5	364	Criminology
HV4157-4169.3	362.5096	Poor—Africa	HV6001-7220.5	364	Crime
HV4170	362.50994	Poor—Australia	HV6001-7220.5	364.3	Criminals
HV4173	362.5091724	Poor—Developing countries	HV6001-6197	364.2	Criminal anthropology
HV4330-4470.7	287.96	Salvation Army	HV6001-6006	364.05	Criminology—Periodicals
HV4480-4630.7	364.148	Vagrancy	HV6021-6023	364.09	Criminology—History
HV4480-4630	362.5	Tramps	HV6024	364.071	Criminology—Study and teaching
HV4701-4959	636.0832	Animal welfare			
HV4701-4890.7	179.3	Animal rights	HV6024.5	364.072	Criminology—Research
HV4746	636.0832	Dog rescue	HV6047	364.24	Criminal behavior—Genetic aspects
HV4749-4755	364.187	Horses			
HV4975-4977	362.2	Insanity	HV6049	364.3	Recidivism
HV4997-5840	362.29	Substance abuse	HV6065-6079	363.258	Criminals—Identification
HV4999.2-5000	362.2909(4-9)	Substance abuse—[By region or country]	HV6071	363.24	Legal photography
			HV6074	363.24	Fingerprints
HV4999.C45	362.290834	School children—Substance use	HV6080-6113	364.3	Criminal psychology
			HV6089	155.962	Prison psychology
HV4999.Y68	362.29083	Youth—Substance use	HV6121-6125	364.24	Heredity
HV5001-5722	362.292	Alcoholism			

LC	Dewey	Subject Heading	LC	Dewey	Subject Heading
HV6133	364.24	Insane, Criminal and dangerous	HV6595-6604	364.154	Kidnapping
HV6163	364.24	Crime and age	HV6618	364.1555	Assault and battery
HV6166	364.25	Education and crime	HV6626-.23	364.1555(3-4)	Family violence
HV6166	364.25	Reading disability and crime	HV6626-.23	364.15553	Wife abuse
HV6174	364.256	Begging	HV6626.5-.54	364.15554	Child abuse
HV6177	364.22	Cities and towns	HV6631	364.156	Libel and slander
HV6189	364.2	War and crime	HV6635-6700	364.16	Offenses against property
HV6250-.4	362.88	Victims of crimes	HV6638-.5	364.164	Arson
HV6250	362.880723	Victims of crimes surveys	HV6638.5	364.16409(4-9)	Arson—[By region or country]
HV6250.4.A34	362.880846	Aged—Crimes against	HV6640	364.164	Bombings
HV6250.4.E75	362.8808996073	Afro-Americans—Crimes against	HV6646-6665	364.162	Burglary
			HV6646-6665	364.1552	Cattle stealing
HV6250.4.S78	362.88088375	Students—Crimes against	HV6646-6665	364.1552	Mugging
HV6250.4.W65	362.88082	Women—Crimes against	HV6653	364.162	Thieves
HV6250.4.Y68	362.88083	Youth—Crimes against	HV6666-6669	364.164	Vandalism
HV6251-6773.3	364	Crime	HV6675-6685	364.163	Forgery
HV6252	364.135	Transnational crime	HV6675-6685	364.162	Embezzlement
HV6254-6322.7	364.131	Political crimes and offenses	HV6688	364.165	Extortion
HV6275	364.1	Conspiracies	HV6691-6699	364.163	Fraud
HV6275	364.131	Treason	HV6705-6738	364.1	Crimes without victims
HV6278	364.1524	Assassination	HV6708-6722	364.172	Gambling
HV6285	364.131	Sedition	HV6711	364.17206	Casinos
HV6301-6321	364.1323	Bribery	HV6763-6771	364.168	Corporations—Corrupt practices
HV6303-6321	364.132309(4-9)	Bribery—[By region or country]	HV6763-6771	364.168	Insurance crimes
HV6306-6316	364.13230973	Bribery—United States	HV6763-6771	364.168	Securities theft
HV6322-.7	362.87	Disappeared persons	HV6763-6771	364.168	Securities fraud
HV6322.7	364.151	Genocide	HV6772-6773.3	364.168	Computer crimes
HV6326	364.134	Perjury	HV6774-7220.5	364.(1/3)09(4-9)	Criminals—[By region or country]
HV6419-6433	364.142	Offenses against public safety	HV6774-6795	364.(1/3)0973	Criminals—United States
HV6422-6425	364.147	Traffic violations	HV6801-7220.5	364.(1/3)09(4-9)	Criminals—[Other regions or countries]
HV6433.I	323.0440951	Red Brigades			
HV6437-6439	364.106	Gangs	HV7231-9960	345.05	Criminal justice, Administration of
HV6441-6453	364.1552	Brigands and robbers			
HV6441-6453	364.106	Mafia	HV7231-9960	364.6	Punishment
HV6441-6453	364.3	Outlaws	HV7245-7400	364.09(4-9)021	Criminal statistics—[By region or country]
HV6441-6453	364.256	Vendetta			
HV6448	364.10660973	Black Hand (United States)	HV7245-7300	364.0973021	Criminal statistics—United States
HV6455-6471	364.134	Lynching			
HV6474-6485	364.143	Riots	HV7250-7300	364.097(4-9)021	Criminal statistics—[United States, By state]
HV6474-6485	364.143	Mobs			
HV6486-6491	364.143	Disorderly conduct	HV7315	364.0971021	Criminal statistics—Canada
HV6493-6633	364.15	Offenses against the person	HV7316	364.0972021	Criminal statistics—Mexico
HV6499-6535	364.1524	Assassination	HV7317-7323	364.09728021	Criminal statistics—Central America
HV6499-6542	364.1523	Murder			
HV6518-6535	364.152309(4-9)	Murder—[By region or country]	HV7324-7329.9	364.09729021	Criminal statistics—West Indies
HV6518-6534	364.15230973	Murder—United States	HV7330-7341	364.098021	Criminal statistics—South America
HV6535	364.152309(4-9)	Murder—[Other regions or countries]	HV7342-7367.7	364.094021	Criminal statistics—Europe
HV6537-6541	364.1523	Infanticide	HV7343-7345.5	364.0941021	Criminal statistics—Great Britain
HV6543-6548	364.1522	Suicide			
HV6547	364.1522	Mass suicide	HV7348	364.0944021	Criminal statistics—France
HV6549-6555	364.1791	Poisoning	HV7349-.5	364.0943021	Criminal statistics—Germany
HV6558-6569	364.1532	Gang rape			
HV6558-6569	364.1532	Rape	HV7351	364.0945021	Criminal statistics—Italy
HV6558-6569	364.153	Sex crimes	HV7355	364.0947021	Criminal statistics—Russia
HV6571-6574	364.154	Abduction	HV7361	364.0946021	Criminal statistics—Spain
HV6584-6589	364.153	Seduction	HV7368-7381	364.0995021	Criminal statistics—Asia

LC	Dewey	Subject Heading	LC	Dewey	Subject Heading
HV7371	364.0954021	Criminal statistics—India	HV8079.N3	363.25977	Drug traffic—Investigation
HV7377	364.0952021	Criminal statistics—Japan	HV8079.O73	363.25906	Organized crime investigation
HV7378	364.0951021	Criminal statistics—China			
HV7382-7388.4	364.096021	Criminal statistics—Africa	HV8079.R35	363.259532	Rape—Investigation
HV7389	364.0994021	Criminal statistics—Australia	HV8079.R62	363.259552	Robbery investigation
			HV8079.S48	363.25953	Sex crimes—Investigation
HV7419.5	345.05072	Criminal justice, Administration of—Research	HV8079.S67	363.2595553	Wife abuse—Investigation
HV7428	361.3	Social work with criminals	HV8079.W47	363.25968	White collar crime investigation
HV7431	364.4	Crime prevention	HV8080.A6	363.232	Arrest (Police methods)
HV7435-7439	363.33	Gun control	HV8080.D54	363.22	Police divers
HV7551-8280.7	363.2	Police	HV8080.P2	363.232	Police patrol—Field interrogation
HV7900	363.2025	Police—Directories			
HV7903-7909	363.209	Police—History	HV8080.P2	363.232	Police patrol—Surveillance operations
HV7923	363.2071	Police—Study and teaching			
HV7935-8025	353.36	Police administration	HV8081-8099	363.289	Private investigators
HV7936.C58	364.4	Crime stoppers programs	HV8130-8280.7	363.209(4-9)	Police—[By region or country]
HV7936.C8	363.24	Police communication systems			
			HV8130-8148	363.20973	Police—United States
HV7936.C88	363.256	Crime analysis	HV8157-8160	363.20971	Police—Canada
HV7936.D78	363.2	Police—Drug testing	HV8161	363.20972	Police—Mexico
HV7936.E7	363.20284	Handcuffs	HV8163-8169	363.209728	Police—Central America
HV7936.E7	363.20284	Riot helmets	HV8170-8175.9	363.209729	Police—West Indies
HV7936.E7	363.20284	Nonlethal weapons	HV8176-8193	363.2098	Police—South America
HV7936.E7	363.20284	Tear gas munitions	HV8194-8261.84	363.2094	Police—Europe
HV7936.E7	363.20284	Truncheons	HV8195-8197.5	363.20941	Police—Great Britain
HV7936.J63	363.22019	Police—Job stress	HV8203-8206	363.20944	Police—France
HV7936.P75	363.22	Police psychiatrists	HV8207-8210	363.20943	Police—Germany
HV7936.P75	363.22	Police psychologists	HV8212-8215	363.20945	Police—Italy
HV7936.R53	363.24	Police reports	HV8215.5-8223.5	363.209492	Police—Benelux countries
HV7961	363.283	Secret service	HV8224-8227	363.20947	Police—Russia
HV7965-7985	363.2091734	Police, Rural	HV8235-8238	363.20946	Police—Spain
HV7981	363.2	Constables	HV8239	363.209469	Police—Portugal
HV8012	363.22	Police chiefs	HV8241.83	363.209495	Police—Greece
HV8023	363.22082	Policewomen	HV8241.85-8263	363.2095	Police—Asia
HV8025	636.70886	Police dogs	HV8241.9-8242.56	363.20956	Police—Middle East
HV8059	683.4	Firearms ownership			
HV8067	363.	Vice control	HV8247-8250	363.20954	Police—India
HV8073-8079.3	363.25	Criminal investigation	HV8255	363.209599	Police—Philippines
HV8073-8077.5	363.25	Chemistry, Forensic	HV8257	363.20952	Police—Japan
HV8073-.8	363.258	Identification	HV8260	363.20951	Police—China
HV8073.4	363.258	Police artists	HV8267-8279.3	363.2096	Police—Africa
HV8074-8076	363.2565	Writing—Identification	HV8280	363.20994	Police—Australia
HV8077	363.2562	Forensic ballistics	HV8290-8291	363.289	Police, Private
HV8077	363.2565	Firearms—Identification	HV8290-8291	363.289	Campus police
HV8077.5.F6	363.2562	Footprints	HV8290-8291	363.289	Private security services
HV8078-.5	363.254	Lie detectors and detection	HV8290-8291	363.289	Watchmen
HV8078	363.254092	Polygraph operators	HV8301-9960	365	Prisons
HV8079.2-.3	363.22	Police social work	HV8482-8488	365.021	Prisons—Statistics
HV8079.5-.55	363.2332	Traffic police	HV8497-8654	365.09	Prisons—History
HV8079.5	363.23320284	Radar in speed limit enforcement	HV8551-8586	364.66	Executions and executioners
			HV8552-8555	364.66	Beheading
HV8079.A98	363.25962	Automobile theft investigation	HV8555	364.66	Guillotine
			HV8569	364.66	Crucifixion
HV8079.C46	363.2595554	Child abuse—Investigation	HV8579-8581	364.66	Hanging
HV8079.C48	363.2595554	Child sexual abuse—Investigation	HV8593-8599	364.67	Torture
			HV8609	364.67	Branding (Punishment)
HV8079.C65	363.25968	Computer crimes—Investigation	HV8609-8621	364.67	Corporal punishment
			HV8613-8621	364.67	Flagellation
HV8079.D76	363.25947	Drunk driving—Investigation	HV8647-8649	365.3	Galleys
HV8079.F7	363.25963	Fraud investigation	HV8657-8658	365.641	Escapes

LC	Dewey	Subject Heading	LC	Dewey	Subject Heading
HV8692	364.65	Pardon	HV9806-9810	365.9599	Prisons—Philippines
HV8696	364.66	Electrocution	HV9811-9815	365.952	Prisons—Japan
HV8705-8749	365	Imprisonment	HV9816-9820	365.951	Prisons—China
HV8708-8719	365	Prison sentences	HV9836-9868.5	365.96	Prisons—Africa
HV8738	365.34082	Reformatories for women	HV9871-9875	365.994	Prisons—Australia
HV8748-8749	365.34	Workhouses	HV9950-9960	345 0509(4-9)	Criminal justice, Administration of— [By region or country]
HV8756-8763	365.068	Prison administration			
HV8766-8778	365.643	Prison discipline	HV9950-9956	345.050973	Criminal justice, Administration of— United States
HV8833-8844	365.66	Prison physicians			
HV8833-8844	365.66	Prison nurses			
HV8884	365.6	Prison visits	HX1-550	335	Socialism
HV8888-8931	365.65	Convict labor	HX19-.2	335.0071	Socialism—Study and teaching
HV8888-8931	365.65	Prison industries			
HV8935-8962	365.64	Prisoners, Transportation of	HX21-54	335.009	Socialism—History
HV8935-8962	365.34	Penal colonies	HX51-54	335.7	Socialism, Christian
HV8971-8978	365.7	Prison reformers	HX77	335.43	Democratic centralism
HV9025	365.6	Prison violence	HX80-517.5	335.009(4-9)	Socialism—[By region or country]
HV9025	365.64	Prison homocide			
HV9051-9230.7	364.36	Juvenile delinquency	HX518.L4	335.4092	Communist leadership
HV9051-9230.7	365.34	Reformatories	HX546	306.735	Free love
HV9051-9230.7	364.36	Juvenile delinquents	HX550.A37	334.683	Communism and agriculture
HV9051-9230.7	364.6	Social work with juvenile delinquents	HX626-632	335.1209	Utopian socialism—History
			HX651-780.7	335.1209(4-9)	Utopian socialism—[By region or country]
HV9051-9230.7	365.6	Status offenders			
HV9068	364.36071	Juvenile delinquency— Study and teaching	HX742.2	335.1209694	Kibbutzim
HV9101-9230.7	364.3609(4-9)	Juvenile delinquency— [By region or country]	HX806-011	321.07	Utopias
			HX821-970.7	335.83	Anarchism
HV9103-9106	364.360973	Juvenile delinquency— United States	HX841-970.7	335.8309(4-9)	Anarchism—[By region or country]
HV9107-9230.7	364.3609(4-9)	Juvenile delinquency— [Other regions or countries]	HX914-917	149.8	Nihilism
			J	320	Political science
HV9261-9430.7	364.601	Criminals—Rehabilitation	J80-82	352.238	Presidents—Messages
HV9276.5	364.68	Alternatives to imprisonment	J82	352.2380973	Presidents—United States—Messages
HV9277	364.68	Fines (Penalties)	JA	320	Political science
HV9277.5	364.68	Community service (Punishment)	JA1-26	320.05	Political science— Periodicals
HV9278	364.63	Parole	JA27-34	320.06	Political science— Societies, etc.
HV9278	364.63	Probation			
HV9279	365.34	Community-based corrections	JA35.5	320.06	Political science— Congresses
HV9441-9649	365.9(4-9)	Prisons—[By region or country]	JA75.8	333.72	Green movement
			JA81-84	320.09	Political science—History
HV9456-9481	365.973	Prisons—United States	JA81-84	320.11	Social contract
HV9501-9510	365.971	Prisons—Canada	JA86-88	320.071	Political science—Study and teaching
HV9511-9515	365.972	Prisons—Mexico			
HV9516-9550	365.9728	Prisons—Central America	JC	320.011	State, The
HV9551-9575.95	365.9729	Prisons—West Indies	JC20-89	321.5	Theocracy
HV9576-9635	365.98	Prisons—South America	JC66	320.932	Egypt—Politics and government
HV9636-9775.7	365.94	Prisons—Europe			
HV9641-9650	365.941	Prisons—Great Britain	JC67	320.933	Jews—Politics and government
HV9661-9670	365.944	Prisons—France			
HV9671-9680.5	365.943	Prisons—Germany	JC71-75	320.938	Greece—Politics and government—To 146 B.C.
HV9686-9695	365.945	Prisons—Italy			
HV9696-9710.5	365.9492	Prisons—Benelux countries	JC75.D	320.938	Deme
HV9711-9715	365.947	Prisons—Russia	JC75.S8	324.620938	Suffrage
HV9741-9745	365.946	Prisons—Spain	JC81-89	320.9376	Rome—Politics and government
HV9776-831	365.9495	Prisons—Greece			
HV9776.5-9785.2	365.956	Prisons—Middle East	JC85.S8	324.6209376	Suffrage
HV9791-9795	365.954	Prisons—India			

LC	Dewey	Subject Heading	LC	Dewey	Subject Heading
JC91-93	320.9495	Byzantine Empire—Politics and government	JF331-341	352.24	Cabinet system
JC109-121	321.3	Feudalism	JF341	352.293	Ministerial responsibility
JC312	323.1	Minorities	JF491-619	328	Legislation
JC311-314	320.54	Nationalism	JF491-497	328.23	Referendum
JC319-323	320.12	Political geography	JF501-619	328	Legislative bodies
JC319-323	320.12	Geopolitics	JF518	328.369	Opposition (Political science)
JC323	320.12	Boundaries	JF519	328.34	Filibusters (Political science)
JC327	320.15	Sovereignty	JF538	328.34	Cloture
JC328	323.6	Allegiance	JF541-549	328.31	Legislative bodies—Upper chambers
JC328	323.6	Treason	JF601-619	328.32	Legislative bodies—Lower chambers
JC328.3	323.044	Government, Resistance to			
JC328.3	322.4	Civil disobedience	JF711	347.012	Judicial review
JC336	320.11	Social contract	JF781	345.052	Extradition
JC345-347	929.(82/92)	Seals (Numismatics)	JF801	323.6	Citizenship
JC352	321.06	City-states	JF825-1141	324.62	Voting
JC355	321.02	Federal government	JF831-851	324.62	Suffrage
JC359	321.030944	Bonapartism	JF841	324.62	Voting age
JC359	325.32	Imperialism	JF847-855	324.623	Women—Suffrage
JC361-363	327.17	Internationalism	JF1001-1048	324	Elections
JC362	327.17	International cooperation	JF1031	324.62	Voting, Compulsory
JC365	321.06	States, Small	JF1033	324.65	Absentee voting
JC374-408	321	Kings and rulers	JF1051-1075	324.63	Representative government and representation
JC375-393	321.6	Monarchy			
JC375-392	321.6	Despotism	JF1051-1075	324.63	Majorities
JC389	321.6	Divine right of kings	JF1071-1075	328.3347	Proportional representation
JC391	321.6	Coronations	JF1081-1083	324.66	Elections—Corrupt practices
JC393	371.82621	Education of princes	JF1081-1083	324.66	Political corruption
JC419	321.5	Oligarchy	JF1091-1177	324.65	Ballot
JC421-423	321.8	Democracy	JF1125	324.65	Polling places
JC421-458	321.86	Republics	JF1128	324.65	Voting-machines
JC474	321.92	Communist state	JF1501-1521	351	Civil service
JC478	321.94	Corporate state	JF1525.D4	352.33	Public administration—Decision making
JC481	320.533	Fascism			
JC480-481	321.9	Totalitarianism	JF1525.P7	352.5	Government property
JC478	321.94	Corporate state	JF1621	352.35	Administrative responsibility
JC491	321.094	Revolutions	JF1621	352.885	Government liability
JC492	321.09	Counterrevolutions	JF1671	353.549	Civil service—Pensions
JC494	321.09	Coups d'etat	JF2011-2112	324.2	Political parties
JC495	321.9092	Dictators	JF2085	324.54	Primaries
JC571-628	323	Human rights	JF2085	324.5	Nominations for office
JC571-628	323	Civil rights	JF2085	324.52	Caucus
JC571-605	323	Individualism	JF2101	324.3	Political clubs
JC575-578	323.42	Equality	JK	342.73029	United States—Constitutional history
JC578	320.011	Justice			
JC585-599	323.044	Political persecution	JK	320.973	United States—Politics and government
JC585-599	323.44	Liberty			
JC609	323.48	Petition, Right of	JK4	353.00074	Freedom Train
JF	350	Public administration	JK54-103	320.9730903	United States—Politics and government—To 1775
JF71-99	342.0292	Constitutional conventions			
JF195	322.5	Civil-military relations	JK301	342.73024	Constitutional conventions
JF225	352.283	Delegation of powers	JK305	342.73044	Separation of powers
JF229	320.404	Separation of powers	JK311-325	342.73042	States rights
JF247.R4	324.68	Recall	JK310-331	342.73042	Secession
JF251-289	321	Heads of state	JK318	346.043	Squatter sovereignty
JF251-289	352.235	Executive power	JK320	320.97309034	United States—Politics and government—Civil War, 1861-1865
JF255	352.23	Presidents			
JF285	324.63	Presidents—Election			
JF285	321.8042	Heads of state—Succession	JK321	320.97309034	United States—Politics and government—1865-1877
JF286	352.23	Heads of state—Term of office			

LC	Dewey	Subject Heading	LC	Dewey	Subject Heading
JK371.P7-.P8	342.0418	Police power	JK2556	320.120973	United States—Territories and possessions
JK404-1685	353	Public administration—United States	JK2701-9593	352.1309(4-9)	State governments—[United States, By state]
JK511-609	352.230973	Presidents—United States			
JK524-529	324.0973	Presidents—United States—Election	JK9661-9993	320.0975	Confederate States of America—Politics and government
JK536	394.40973	Inauguration Day	JK9717-9719	351.75	Executive departments—Confederate States of America
JK609.5	352.2390973	Vice-Presidents—United States			
JK610-616	352.240973	Cabinet officers	JL1-500	351.71	Public administration—Canada
JK631-868	351.73063	Civil service			
JK681	352.630973	Civil service reform	JL1-500	320.971	Canada—Politics and government
JK765-770	352.63	Civil service—Personnel management	JL41-45	320.971090 (1-33)	Canada—Politics and government—To 1763
JK771-794	352.630973	United States—Officials and employees—Salaries, etc.	JL48	320.97109033	Canada—Politics and government—1763-1791
JK1012-1432	328.73	United States. Congress	JL53	320.9710903 (3-4)	Canada—Politics and government—1791-1841
JK1012	328.73025	United States. Congress—Directories	JL55	320.97109034	Canada—Politics and government—1841-1867
JK1033-1059	342.730509	United States. Congress—History	JL65	320.971090 (34-511)	Canada—Politics and government—1867-
JK1118	328.380973	Lobbying	JL87-111	347.71	Executive departments—Canada
JK1154-1259	328.310973	United States. Congress. Senate			
JK1308-1432	328.320973	United States. Congress. House	JL106-111	352.670071	Civil service—Canada
JK1347-1343	328.33455	Gerrymander			
JK1533	324.680973	Recall	JL131-179	354.7299	Canada. Parliament
JK1543	364.1340973	Contempt of court	JL590-599	320.97299	Bermuda Islands—Politics and government
JK1548.P8	345.7301	Public defenders	JL610-619	320.97296	Bahamas—Politics and government
JK1606	347.7301	Courts—United States			
JK1717-2217	323.0973	Political rights—United States	JL629.5	320.972921	Cayman Islands—Politics and government
JK1731	323.480973	Petition, Right of	JL629.6	320.9729845	Grenada—Politics and government
JK1758-1759	323.60973	Patriotism—United States			
JK1758	323.60973	Americanization	JL630-639	320.97292	Jamaica—Politics and government
JK1761	394.26973	Flag Day			
JK1846-1929	324.60973	Suffrage—United States	JL640-649.7	320.97297	Leeward Islands (West Indies)—Politics and government
JK1924-1929	324.6208996073	Afro-Americans—Suffrage			
JK1965-2217	324.620973	Elections	JL650-659	320.972983	Trinidad and Tobago—Politics and government
JK1991-.5	324.780973	Campaign funds			
JK1994	324.66	Elections—Corrupt practices	JL670-679	320.97282	Belize—Politics and government
JK2063-2075	324.273015	Nominations for office	JL680-689	320.9881	Guyana—Politics and government
JK2071-2077	324.2730154	Primaries			
JK2214-2217	324.650973	Ballot	JL690-699	320.99711	Falkland Islands—Politics and government
JK2249	324.660973	Elections—Corrupt practices	JL770-779	320.972986	Curacao—Politics and government
JK2255-2261	324.2730156	Political conventions			
JK2251-2391	324.70973	Campaign literature	JL780-789	320.9883	Surinam—Politics and government
JK2403-9593	352.130973	State governments—United States			
JK2413-2428	342.0297(4-9)	Constitutions, State	JL810-819	320.9882	French Guiana
JK2441	352.133	Interstate agreements			
JK2443-2525	352.1309(4-9)	Public administration—[United States, By state]	JL820-829	320.972976	Guadeloupe—Politics and government
JK2447-2454	352.232130973	Governors—United States	JL830-839	320.972982	Martinique—Politics and government
JK2459	352.2390973	Lieutenant governors—United States	JL1000-1019	320.97291	Cuba—Politics and government
JK2498	328.38097(4-9)	Lobbying			

LC	Dewey	Subject Heading	LC	Dewey	Subject Heading
JL1040-1059	320.97295	Puerto Rico—Politics and government	JN1150-1159	320.9429	Wales—Politics and government
JL1080-1099	320.97294	Haiti—Politics and government	JN1187-1371	320.9411	Scotland—Politics and government
JL1120-1139	320.97293	Dominican Republic—Politics and government	JN1405-1571.5	320.9415	Ireland—Politics and government
JL1200-1299	320.972	Mexico—Politics and government	JN1572	320.9416	Northern Ireland—Politics and government
JL1440-1459	320.97286	Costa Rica—Politics and government	JN1601-2041	320.9436	Austria—Politics and government
JL1480-1499	320.97281	Guatemala—Politics and government	JN2210-2229	320.9437	Czechoslovakia—Politics and government
JL1520-1539	320.97283	Honduras—Politics and government	JN2301-3007	320.944	France—Politics and government
JL1560-1579	320.97284	El Salvador—Politics and government	JN3201-4944	320.943	Germany—Politics and government
JL1600-1619	320.97285	Nicaragua—Politics and government	JN3250.C83	324.630943	Electors (Kurfursten)
JL2000-2099	320.982	Argentina—Politics and government	JN5001-5191	320.9495	Greece—Politics and government
JL2200-2299	320.984	Bolivia—Politics and government	JN5201-5690	320.954	Italy—Politics and government
JL2400-2499	320.981	Brazil—Politics and government	JN5701-5999	320.9492	Netherlands—Politics and government
JL2600-2699	320.983	Chile—Politics and government	JN6101-6371	320.9493	Belgium—Politics and government
JL2800-2899	320.9861	Colombia—Politics and government	JN6500-6598	320.947	Russia—Politics and government
JL3000-3099	320.9866	Ecuador—Politics and government	JN6750-6769	320.9438	Poland—Politics and government
JL3200-3299	320.9892	Paraguay—Politics and government	JN7011-7066	320.948	Scandinavia—Politics and government
JL3400-3499	320.985	Peru—Politics and government	JN7101-7367	320.9489	Denmark—Politics and government
JL3600-3699	320.9895	Uruguay—Politics and government	JN7370-7379	320.94912	Iceland—Politics and government
JL3800-3899	320.987	Venezuela—Politics and government	JN7380-7389	320.9982	Greenland—Politics and government
JN	354.094	Public administration—Europe	JN7390-7399	320.94897	Finland—Politics and government
JN12	320.94	Europe—Politics and government—20th century	JN7401-7695	320.9481	Norway—Politics and government
JN15	321.04094	European federation	JN7721-7995	320.9485	Sweden—Politics and government
JN101-1371	320.941	Great Britain—Politics and government	JN8101-8399	320.946	Spain—Politics and government
JN137-158	320.9410902 (1-4)	Great Britain—Politics and government—1066-1485	JN8423-8661	320.9469	Portugal—Politics and government
JN175-231	320.941090 (3-511)	Great Britain—Politics and government—1485-	JN8701-9599	320.9494	Switzerland—Politics and government
JN309-678	351.41	Public administration—Great Britain	JN9600-9689	320.9496	Balkan Peninsula—Politics and government
JN331-389	352.2330941	Great Britain—Kings and rulers	JQ21-1825	320.95	Asia—Politics and government
JN500-678	328.41	Great Britain. Parliament	JQ200-620	320.954	India—Politics and government
JN900-1088	323.0941	Political rights—Great Britain	JQ629	320.95491	Pakistan—Politics and government
JN1088	324.660941	Elections—Corrupt practices	JQ630-639	320.95492	Bangladesh—Politics and government
JN1111-1129	324.241	Political parties—Great Britain	JQ650-659	320.95493	Sri Lanka—Politics and government
JN1129.T7	324.24102	Tories, English			

LC	Dewey	Subject Heading	LC	Dewey	Subject Heading
JQ751	320.9595	Burma—Politics and government	JS	352.14	Local government
JQ760-779	320.9598	Indonesia—Politics and government	JS42	352.1406	Local government—Societies, etc.
JQ800-899	320.9597	Vietnam—Politics and government	JS49	352.14071	Local government—Study and teaching
JQ930-939	320.9596	Cambodia—Politics and government	JS55-67	352.1409	Local government—History
JQ950-959	320.9594	Laos—Politics and government	JS113	352.283	Decentralization in government
JQ1250-1419	320.9599	Philippines—Politics and government	JS113	320.85	Municipal home rule
			JS143-163	352.23216	Mayors
JQ1500-1519	320.951	China—Politics and government	JS148-155	352.16092	Municipal officials and employees
JQ1520-1539	320.951249	Taiwan—Politics and government	JS148-153	352.63	Civil service
JQ1600-1699	320.952	Japan—Politics and government	JS215	324.62	Suffrage
			JS261	352.16	Boroughs
JQ1720-1729.5	320.9519	Korea—Politics and government	JS300-1583	351.7(4-9)	Local government—United States
JQ1740-1749	320.9593	Thailand—Politics and government	JS342-343	352.250973	Municipal government by commission
JQ1760-1769	320.9581	Afghanistan—Politics and government	JS344.R4	324.680973	Recall
JQ1780-1789	320.955	Iran—Politics and government	JS411	352.150973	County government—United States
JQ1800-1809	320.9501	Turkey—Politics and government	JS422	352.16097(4-9)	Metropolitan government—United States
JQ1811	320.95693	Cyprus—Politics and government	JS426	324.973	Special districts—United States
JQ1826	320.95691	Syria—Politics and government	JS601-1583	352.16097(4-9)	Municipal government—[U.S. by city]
JQ1828	320.95692	Lebanon—Politics and government	JS1701-1800	351.71	Local government—Canada
			JS1840-2058	351.729	Local government—West Indies
JQ1830	320.95694	Israel—Politics and government	JS2101-2143	351.72	Local government—Mexico
JQ1833	320.95695	Jordon—Politics and government	JS2145-2219	351.728	Local government—Central America
JQ1841	320.9538	Saudi Arabia—Politics and government	JS2300-2778	351.8	Local government—South America
JQ1842	320.9533	Yemen—Politics and government	JS3000-6949.8	351.4	Local government—Europe
JQ1843	320.95353	Oman—Politics and government	JS3001-4295	351.41	Local government—Great Britain
JQ1844	320.95357	United Arab Emirates	JS4501-4655	351.436	Local government—Austria
JQ1845	320.95363	Qatar—Politics sand government	JS4661-4696	351.439	Local government—Hungary
			JS4801-5250	351.44	Local government—France
JQ1846	320.95365	Bahrain—Politics and government	JS5301-5598	351.43	Local government—Germany
			JS5701-5925	351.45	Local government—Italy
JQ1848	320.95367	Kuwait—Politics and government	JS5931-5998	351.492	Local government—Netherlands
JQ1849	320.9567	Iraq—Politics and government	JS6001-6048	351.493	Local government—Belgium
			JS6051-6109	351.47	Local government—Russia
JQ1850	320.9174927	Arab countries—Politics and government	JS6151-6185	351.489	Local government—Denmark
			JS6251-6285	351.485	Local government—Sweden
JQ1870-3981	320.96	Africa—Politics and government	JS6301-6335	351.46	Local government—Spain
			JS6341-6375	351.469	Local government—Portugal
JQ5995-6651	320.9(5-6)	Oceania—Politics and government	JS6401-6889	351.494	Local government—Switzerland
			JS6899.5-6949.8	351.496	Local government—Balkan Peninsula
JS	320.85	Municipal corporations	JS6950-7520	351.5	Local government—Asia
JS	320.85	Municipal government	JS7001-7090	351.54	Local government—India
			JS7301-7335	351.599	Local government—Philippines

LC	Dewey	Subject Heading	LC	Dewey	Subject Heading
JS7351-7365	351.51	Local government—China	JV7429	325.(27287/7287)	Panama—Emigration and immigration
JS7371-7385	351.52	Local government—Japan	JV7440-7449	325.(282/82)	Argentina—Emigration and immigration
JS7435-7520	351.056	Local government—Middle East	JV7450-7459	325.(284/84)	Bolivia—Emigration and immigration
JS7525-7819	351.6	Local government—Africa	JV7460-7469	325.(281/81)	Brazil—Emigration and immigration
JS8001-8310	351.94	Local government—Australia	JV7470-7479	325.(283/83)	Chile—Emigration and immigration
JS8331-8399	351.93	Local government—New Zealand	JV7480-7489	325.(2861/861)	Colombia—Emigration and immigration
JS8450-8490	351.9(5-6)	Local government—Oceania	JV7490-7499	325.(2866/866)	Ecuador—Emigration and immigration
JV	321.08	Colonies	JV7500-7509	325.(2892/892)	Paraguay—Emigration and immigration
JV1-5399	325.3	Colonization	JV7510-7519	325.(285/85)	Peru—Emigration and immigration
JV61-151	325.309	Colonies—History	JV7520-7529	325.(2895/895)	Uruguay—Emigration and immigration
JV221-231	325.(7-8)	America—Colonization	JV7530-7539	325.(287/87)	Venezuela—Emigration and immigration
JV246	325.6	Africa—Colonization	JV7600-7699	325.(241/41)	Great Britain—Emigration and immigration
JV412-461	353.15	Colonies—Administration	JV7700-7709	325.(2411/411)	Scotland—Emigration and immigration
JV431	353.15092	Viceroyalty	JV7710-7719	325.(2415/415)	Ireland—Emigration and immigration
JV443	353.15	Civil service, Colonial	JV7800-7899	325.(2436/436)	Austria—Emigration and immigration
JV500-599	325.373	United States—Territories and possessions	JV7900-7999	325.(244/44)	France—Emigration and immigration
JV1000-1099	325.341	Great Britain—Colonies	JV8000-8099	325.(243/43)	Germany—Emigration and immigration
JV1800-1899	325.344	France—Colonies	JV8110-8119	325.(2495/495)	Greece—Emigration and immigration
JV2200-2299	325.345	Italy—Colonies	JV8130-8139	325.(245/45)	Italy—Emigration and immigration
JV2500-2899	325.3492	Benelux countries—Colonies	JV8150-8159	325.(2492/492)	Netherlands—Emigration and immigration
JV3300-3399	325.3489	Denmark—Colonies	JV8160-8169	325.(2493/493)	Belgium—Emigration and immigration
JV4000-4099	325.346	Spain—Colonies	JV8175	325.(24935/4935)	Luxembourg—Emigration and immigration
JV4200-4299	325.3469	Portugal—Colonies	JV8180-8189	325.(247/47)	Russia—Emigration and immigration
JV5200-5299	325.352	Japan—Colonies	JV8195	325.(2438/438)	Poland—Emigration and immigration
JV6001-9500	325.(2/1)	Emigration and immigration	JV8200-8209	325.(2489/489)	Denmark—Emigration and immigration
JV6021-6032	325.(1-2)09	Emigration and immigration—History	JV8210-8219	325.(2481/481)	Norway—Emigration and immigration
JV6118	325.(4-9)	Emigration and immigration—Economic aspects	JV8220-8229	325.(2485/485)	Sweden—Emigration and immigration
JV6342	303.482	Assimilation (Sociology)	JV8250-8259	325.(246/46)	Spain—Emigration and immigration
JV6403-7127	325.(73/273)	United States—Emigration and immigration	JV8260-8269	325.(2469/469)	Portugal—Emigration and immigration
JV7200-7299	325.(71/271)	Canada—Emigration and immigration	JV8280-8289	325.(2494/494)	Switzerland—Emigration and immigration
JV7320-7397	325.(729/2729)	West Indies—Emigration and immigration			
JV7370-7379	325.(7291/27291)	Cuba—Emigration and immigration			
JV7380-7389	325.(7295/27295)	Puerto Rico—Emigration and immigration			
JV7393	325.(7294/27294)	Haiti—Emigration and immigration			
JV7395	325.(7293/27293)	Dominican Republic—Emigration and immigration			
JV7400-7409	325.(72/272)	Mexico—Emigration and immigration			
JV7413	325.(7286/27286)	Costa Rica—Emigration and immigration			
JV7416	325.(27281/7281)	Guatemala—Emigration and immigration			
JV7419	325.(27283/7283)	Honduras—Emigration and immigration			
JV7423	325.(27284/7284)	El Salvador—Emigration and immigration			
JV7426	325.(27285/7285)	Nicaragua—Emigration and immigration			

LC	Dewey	Subject Heading	LC	Dewey	Subject Heading
JV8490-8758	325.(25/5)	Asia—Emigration and immigration	K1960-2000	344.0316	Public welfare—Law and legislation
JV8500-8509	325.(254/54)	India—Emigration and immigration	K2100-2385	347.05	Procedure (Law)
JV8685	325.(2599/599)	Philippines—Emigration and immigration	K2201-2385	347.05	Civil procedure
			K2320	344.01893	Injunctions
JV8700-8709	325.(251/51)	China—Emigration and immigration	K3236-3268	342.085	Civil rights
			K3236-3268	342.085	Human rights
JV8710-8719	325.(251249/51249)	Taiwan—Emigration and immigration	K3220-3225	342.041	Public policy (Law)
			K3252	342.085	Right to life
JV8720-8729	325.(252/52)	Japan—Emigration and immigration	K3150	342	Public law
			K3154-3367	342	Constitutional law
JV8739-8751	325.(256/56)	Middle East—Emigration and immigration	K3161	342.029	Constitutional history
			K3224-3229	342.08	People (Constitutional law)
JV8790-9024.5	325.(26/6)	Africa—Emigration and immigration	K3280-3282	322.1	Church and state
			K3285	321.02	Federal government
JV9100-9199	325.(294/94)	Australia—Emigration and immigration	K3290-3304	342.08	People (Constitutional law)
			K3332-3351	342.062	Executive power
JV9260-9269	325.(293/93)	New Zealand—Emigration and immigration	K3367	347.012	Judicial power
JV9290-9470	325.(29(5-6)/9(5-6))	Oceania—Emigration and immigration	K3375	341.28	Colonies—Law and legislation
			K3400-3431	342.066	Administrative law
K	340-349	Law	K3440-3460	342.068	Civil service
K50-54	340.03	Law—Dictionaries	K3476-3558	343.02	Public domain
K100-103	340.071	Law—Study and teaching	K3478-3486	346.044	Natural resources—Law and legislation
K140-165	340.09	Law—History	K3492	343.0942	Highway law
K170	340.092	Law—Biography	K3496-3501	343.0921	Water supply—Law and legislation
K183-184.7	340.0207	Law—Humor			
K190-195	340.52	Law, Primitive	K3511-3512	343.0252	Eminent domain
K280-286	340.11	Law—Sources	K3531-3544	346.045	Regional planning—Law and legislation
K325-328	340.09	Historical jurisprudence			
K368-380	340.115	Sociological jurisprudence	K3550-3553	344.063635	Public housing—Law and legislation
K540-5570	341	International law			
K540-546	347.07	Trials	K3558-3560	343.02	Government property
K583-591	340.2	Comparative law	K3566-3597	344.04	Public health laws
K623-968	346	Civil law	K3615-3617	344.049	Veterinary hygiene—Law and legislation
K670-709	346.015	Domestic relations			
K783-793	341.48	Personal property	K3626-3633	344.04232	Food law and legislation
K805-821	346.052	Inheritance and succession	K3651-3654	344.042	Alcohol—Law and legislation
K830-968	346.02	Obligations (Law)			
K840-917	346.02	Contracts	K3661	344.0533	Weapons—Law and legislation
K920	346.029	Quasi contracts			
K923-968	346.03	Torts	K3740-3762	344.07	Educational law and legislation
K970	342.03288	Reparation			
K1001-1388	346.07	Commercial law	K3770	344.09	Research—Law and legislation
K1010-1014	346.07	Business law			
K1024-1132	346.02	Contracts	K3840-4375	343.07	Commercial law
K1054-1065	346.096	Negotiable instruments	K3842-3862	343.08	Trade regulation
K1066-1088	346.082	Banking law	K3978-3990	343.09	Public utilities—Law and legislation
K1100-1108	346.092	Security (Law)			
K1112-1116	346.092	Investments—Law and legislation	K4021-4025	343.093	Transportation—Law and legislation
K1241-1287	346.086	Insurance law	K4028-4042	343.0942	Highway law
K1401-1578	346.048	Intellectual property	K4061-4070	343.095	Railroad law
K1411-1485	346.0482	Copyright	K4080	343.098	Local transit—Law and legislation
K1500-1578	346.048	Industrial property			
K1701-2000	344	Social legislation	K4091-4124	343.097	Aeronautics—Law and legislation
K1701-1841	344.01	Labor laws and legislation			
K1861-1929	344.05242	Social security—Law and legislation	K4135	341.47	Space law

124

LC	Dewey	Subject Heading	LC	Dewey	Subject Heading
K4182-4194	343.0967	Inland navigation—Law and legislation	K7340-7512	340.97	Conflict of laws—Commercial law
K4198-4200	343.0967	Harbors—Law and legislation	K7350-7444	340.97	Conflict of laws—Contracts
K4245-4254	343.0992	Postal service—Law and legislation	K7350	340.972	Conflict of laws—Sales
			K7360-7370	340.996	Conflict of laws—Negotiable instruments
K4301-4339	343.0994	Telecommunication—Law and legislation	K7380-7384	340.982	Conflict of laws—Banking
K4360-4375	344.01712	Professions—Law and legislation	K7449-7460	343.096	Conflict of laws—Maritime law
K4430-4675	343.03	Finance, Public—Law and legislation	K7470	340.986	Conflict of laws—Insurance
			K7490-7495	340.966	Conflict of laws—Corporations
K4456-4590	343.04	Taxation—Law and legislation	K7550-7582	340.948	Conflict of laws—Intellectual property
K4501-4550	343.052	Income tax—Law and legislation	K7555-7557	340.9482	Conflict of laws—Copyright licenses
K4560-4564	343.054	Property tax—Law and legislation	K7570-7582	340.948	Conflict of laws—Industrial property
K4568	343.0532	Inheritance and succession	K7680	340.9	Judgments, Foreign
K4572-4580	343.0553	Excise tax—Law and legislation	K7690	347.09	Conflict of laws—Arbitration and award
K4600-4640	343.056	Tariff—Law and legislation	KD	349.42	Law—England
K4650-4675	343.03	Local finance—Law and legislation	KD125-180	328.3742	Legislation—England
			KD125-150	348.42022	Statutes—England
K4720-4760	343.01	Military readiness—Law and legislation	KD187-291	348.42041	Law reports, digests, etc.—England
K5011-5316	345	Criminal law	KD313	349.4203	Law—England—Dictionaries
K5036-5048	345.01	Criminal jurisdiction	KD318	347.42055	Forms (Law)—England
K5064-5083	345.04	Criminal liability	KD327-332	347.42013	Judicial statistics—England
K5401-5570	345.05	Criminal procedure	KD370-379.5	347.4207	Trials—England
K5423	345.01	Criminal jurisidiction	KD392-400	349.42072	Legal research—England
K5425	345.072	Indictments	KD419-452	349.42071	Law—Study and teaching—England
K5460-5492	345.075	Trials			
K5465-5490	345.06	Evidence, Criminal	KD460-472	349.42	Lawyers—England
K5492	345.075	Jury	KD530-632	349.4209	Law—England—History
K5495	347.035	Appellate procedure	KD674	346.42004	Equity—England
K5510-5560	345.0772	Sentences (Criminal procedure)	KD680-685	342.42042	Conflict of laws—England
			KD720-721	347.42	Civil law—England
K5575-5582	345.08	Juvenile courts	KD723-785	346.42012	Persons (Law)—England
K7000-7720	342.042	Conflict of laws	KD750-785	346.42015	Domestic relations—England
K7010-7011	348.022	Statutes			
K7051-7054	341.7	Law—International unification	KD810-815	346.420437	Possession (Law)—England
			KD821-1195	346.42043	Real property—England
K7120-7197	340.912	Conflict of laws—Persons	KD833-960	346.420432	Land tenure—Law and legislation—England
K7145-7148	340.913	Conflict of laws—Juristic persons	KD834-839	340.550942	Feudal law—England
K7155-7197	340.915	Conflict of laws—Domestic relations	KD841-960	346.420432	Estates (Law)—England
			KD1010-1016	346.4204364	Mortgages—England
K7181-7197	340.917	Conflict of laws—Parent and child	KD1034-1107	343.4202	Government property—England
K7197	340.918	Conflict of laws—Guardian and ward	KD1035	346.42046	Natural resources—Law and legislation—England
K7200-7218	340.94	Conflict of laws—Property	KD1040-1048	343.420942	Highway law—England
K7230-7245	340.952	Conflict of laws—Inheritance and succession	KD1070	346.4204691	Water—Law and legislation—England
K7260-7335	340.92	Conflict of laws—Obligations	KD1125-1162	346.42045	Zoning law—England
K7265-7305	340.92	Conflict of laws—Contracts	KD1185-1189	343.420252	Eminent domain—England
K7310	340.929	Conflict of laws—Quasi contracts	KD1195	343.420256	Public works—Law and legislation—England
K7315-7335	340.93	Conflict of laws—Torts	KD1205-1465	346.42047	Personal property—England

LC	Dewey	Subject Heading	LC	Dewey	Subject Heading
KD1238-1450	346.42048	Intangible property—England	KD2405-2430	343.4207833847664	Food law and legislation—England
KD1261-1450	346.42048	Intellectual property—England	KD2435	343.42078624	Construction industry—Law and legislation
KD1281-1325	346.420482	Copyright—England	KD2455-2530	343.4207	Commercial law—England
KD1345	346.420484	Design protection—England	KD2535-2560	343.4209	Public utilities—Law and legislation—England
KD1361-1413.3	346.420486	Patent laws and legislation—England	KD2571-2838	343.42093	Transportation—Law and legislation—England
KD1450	346.42048	Business names—England	KD3000-3315	344.42	Social legislation—England
KD1497	346.4205	Estate planning—England	KD3001-3177	344.4201	Labor laws and legislation—England
KD1500-1534	346.42052	Inheritance and succession—England	KD3241-3250	343.4205242	Social security—Law and legislation—England
KD1554-1920	346.4202	Contracts—England	KD3291-3315	344.420316	Public welfare—Law and legislation
KD1638-1642	344.42201542	Labor contract—England			
KD1679-1685	346.42025	Bailments—England	KD3351-3375	344.4204	Public health laws—England
KD1695-1699	346.42096	Negotiable instruments—England	KD3395-3413	344.4204	Medical laws and legislation—England
KD1715-1737	346.42082	Banking law—England	KD3420-3422	344.42049	Veterinary hygiene—Law and legislation—England
KD1740-1742	346.42073	Loans—Law and legislation—England	KD3460-3462	344.4204233	Drugs—Law and legislation—England
KD1752	346.42074	Suretyship and guaranty—England	KD3466-3480	344.42042	Alcohol—Law and legislation—England
KD1774-1787	346.42092	Investments—Law and legislation—England	KD3402	344.420633	Weapons—Law and legislation—England
KD1800-1847	343.42093	Carriers—Law and legislation—England			
KD1804	343.42097	Aeronautics, Commercial—Law and legislation—England	KD3510	344.42047	Accident law—England
			KD3523	344.42099	Amusements—Law and legislation—England
KD1845-1847	346.420862	Insurance, Marine—England	KD3525	344.42099	Sports—Law and legislation—England
KD1851-1913	346.42086	Insurance law—England			
KD1924	346.42029	Quasi contracts—England	KD3527	344.42099	Gambling—Law and legislation—England
KD1941-1980	346.4203	Torts—England			
KD2022	346.42029	Power of attorney—England	KD3600-3689	344.4207	Educational law and legislation
KD2046-2054	346.42064	Unincorporated societies—England	KD3720-3731	344.42097	Performing arts—Law and legislation—England
KD2049-2054	346.420682	Partnership—England			
KD2057-2127	346.42066	Corporation law—England	KD3736	344.42093	Museums—Law and legislation—England
KD2061-2062	346.42064	Nonprofit organizations—Law and legislation—England	KD3746	344.42092	Library legislation—England
			KD3753-3755	344.42092	Archives—Law and legislation—England
KD2141-2164	346.42078	Bankruptcy—England	KD3931-4645	342.42	England—Constitutional law
KD2204-2231	343.4208	Trade regulation—England			
KD2206	343.42082	Advertising laws—England	KD3931-3966	342.42029	England—Constitutional history
KD2208-2209	343.42082	Labels—Law and legislation—England	KD4000-4010	342.42044	Separation of powers—England
KD2215	343.42083	Price regulation—England	KD4030	342.420412	England—Foreign relations—Law and legislation
KD2218-2220	343.420721	Antitrust law—England			
KD2225-2226	343.42072	Competition, Unfair—England	KD4050-4058	342.42083	Citizenship—England
KD2228	346.4206	Trade associations—Law and legislation—England	KD4080-4119	342.42085	Civil rights—England
			KD4130-4139	342.42083	Aliens—England
KD2230-2231	343.42075	Containers—Law and legislation—England	KD4190-4381	342.4205	Great Britain. Parliament.
			KD4430-4531	342.4206	Monarchy—Great Britain
KD2241-2295	343.42076	Agricultural laws and legislation—England	KD4462	342.4206	Prime ministers—Great Britain
KD2310-2315	343.4207692	Fishery law and legislation—England	KD4645	347.4201	Courts—England
KD2331-2370	343.42077	Mining law—England			

LC	Dewey	Subject Heading	LC	Dewey	Subject Heading
KD4650	344.4209	Emblems, National—England	KDC910-920	345.411	Criminal law—Scotland
			KDE	349.416	Law—Northern Ireland
KD4746-4840	342.4209	Local government—Law and legislation—England	KDE42-50	328.37416	Legislation—Northern Ireland
KD5020-5025	349.42	Commonwealth countries	KDE55-60	348.416041	Law reports, digests, etc.—Northern Ireland
KD5280-5752	343.4203	Finance, Public—Law and legislation—England	KDE90-98	346.416012	Persons (Law)—Northern Ireland
KD5284-5286	343.42032	Money—Law and legislation—England	KDE145-151	346.416052	Inheritance and succession—Northern Ireland
KD5288	343.42032	Foreign exchange—Law and legislation—England	KDE235-282	343.41607	Commercial law—Northern Ireland
KD5292	343.42034	Budget—Law and Legislation—England	KDE320-348	344.416	Social legislation—Northern Ireland
KD5300	343.42037	Debts, Public—Law and legislation—England	KDE410-462	342.416	Northern Ireland—Constitutional law
KD5351-5605	343.4204	Taxation—Law and legislation—England	KDE510-530	347.41605	Procedure (Law)—Northern Ireland
KD5641-5694	343.42056	Tariff—Law and legislation—England	KDE550-557	345.41675	Criminal procedure—Northern Ireland
KD5710-5752	343.42(1-9)03	Local finance—Law and legislation—England	KDG	349.4234	Law—Channel Islands
KD6000-6355	343.4201	Military readiness—Law and legislation—England	KDG26-170	349.4279	Law—Isle of Man
			KDG220-380	349.42341	Law—Jersey (Channel Islands)
KD6340	344.420535	Civil defense—Law and legislation—England	KDG421-440	349.42342	Law—Guernsey (Channel Islands)
KD6850-7640	347.4205	Procedure (Law)—England			
KD7132-7216	347.4203	Appellate courts—England	KDK	349.415	Law—Ireland
KD7645-7647	347.4209	Arbitration and award—England	KDK38-50	328.37415	Legislation—Ireland
			KDK61-80	348.41504	Law reports, digests, etc.—Ireland
KD7850-8090	345.42	Criminal law—England	KDK84	349.41503	Law—Ireland—Dictionaries
KD8220-8464	345.4205	Criminal procedure—England	KDK102-106	347.41507	Trials—Ireland
KD8850-9355	349.42	Statutes—England	KDK120-134	349.415	Lawyers—Ireland
KD8996-9142	342.421	Statutes—London	KDK185-205	346.415012	Persons (Law)—Ireland
KD9400-9500	349.429	Law—Wales	KDK360-365	346.415052	Inheritance and succession—Ireland
KD9407	348.429022	Statutes—Wales			
KD9410-9417	348.429041	Law reports, digests, etc.—Wales	KDK370-437	346.41502	Contracts—Ireland
KD9420	349.42903	Law—Wales—Dictionaries	KDK450-469	346.41503	Torts—Ireland
KD9423	345.42907	Trials—Wales	KDK550-769	343.41507	Commercial law—Ireland
KD9460	344.429071	Law—Wales—Study and teaching	KDK800-895	344.415	Social legislation—Ireland
			KDK926-932	344.415041	Medical laws and legislation—Ireland
KD9480-9484	347.42901	Courts—Wales			
KD9490	345.429	Criminal law—Wales	KDK1200-1350	342.415	Ireland—Constitutional law
KDC	349.411	Law—Scotland	KDK1430-1526	343.41503	Finance, Public—Law and legislation—Ireland
KDC70-90	328.37411	Legislation—Scotland			
KDC110-113	347.41103	Appellate courts—Scotland	KDK1580-1713	347.41505	Procedure (Law)—Ireland
KDC152	349.411003	Law—Scotland—Dictionaries	KDK1750-1782	345.415	Criminal law—Ireland
KDC184-188	347.41107	Trials—Scotland	KDZ	349.7	Law—North America
KDC225-247	349.411	Lawyers—Scotland	KDZ2000-2499	349.7299	Law—Bermuda
KDC350-378	346.411012	Persons (Law)—Scotland	KDZ3000-3499	349.982	Law—Greenland
KDC462-470	346.411052	Inheritance and succession—Scotland	KDZ4000-4499	349.7188	Law—St. Pierre and Miquelon
KDC635-674	344.411	Social legislation—Scotland	KE	349.71	Law—Canada
KDC690-695	344.411041	Medical laws and legislation—Scotland	KE78-125	328.3771	Legislation—Canada
			KE132-156	348.71041	Law reports, digests, etc.—Canada
KDC750-785	342.411	Scotland—Constitutional law			
			KE198-206	347.71013	Judicial statistics—Canada
KDC807-825	343.41103	Finance, Public—Law and legislation—Scotland	KE225-237	347.7107	Trials—Canada
			KE250-259	349.71072	Legal research—Canada
KDC840-915	347.41105	Procedure (Law)—Scotland			

LC	Dewey	Subject Heading	LC	Dewey	Subject Heading
KE273-322	349.71071	Law—Study and teaching—Canada	KE4125-4775	342.71	Canada—Constitutional law
KE335-355	349.71	Lawyers—Canada	KE4310	342.710412	Canada—Foreign relations—Law and legislation
KE457	346.71004	Equity—Canada	KE4381-4430	342.71085	Civil rights—Canada
KE470-474	342.71042	Conflict of laws—Canada	KE4533-4665	342.7105	Canada. Parliament.
KE495	347.71	Civil law—Canada	KE4730	342.7106	Prime ministers—Canada
KE498-606	346.71012	Persons (Law)—Canada	KE4775	347.7101	Courts—Canada
KE531-606	346.71015	Domestic relations—Canada	KE4900-4995	342.7109	Local government—Law and legislation—Canada
KE625-754	346.71043	Real property—Canada			
KE765-781	346.71047	Personal property—Canada	KE5006-5010	342.710418	Police power—Canada
KE806-833	346.71052	Inheritance and succession—Canada	KE5105-5420	343.7102	Government property—Canada
KE850-1225	346.7102	Contracts—Canada	KE5258-5284	346.71045	Regional planning—Law and legislation—Canada
KE928-936	344.710189	Labor contract—Canada			
KE970-972	346.71025	Bailments—Canada	KE5600-6328	343.7103	Finance, Public—Law and legislation—Canada
KE980-986	346.71096	Negotiable instruments—Canada			
			KE6800-7240	343.7101	Military readiness—Law and legislation—Canada
KE991-1026	346.71082	Banking law—Canada			
KE1030-1034	346.71073	Loans—Law and legislation—Canada	KE8200-8605	347.7101	Courts—Canada
			KE8341-8605	347.7105	Procedure (Law)—Canada
KE1042-1056	346.71092	Securities—Canada	KE8618	347.7109	Arbitration and award—Canada
KE1060-1089	346.71092	Investments—Law and legislation—Canada			
			KE8801-9112	345.71	Criminal law—Canada
KE1099-1135	343.71093	Carriers—Law and legislation—Canada	KEA	349.7123	Law—Alberta
			KEB	349.711	Law—British Columbia
KE1141-1220	346.71086	Insurance law—Canada			
KE1232-1309	346.7105	Torts—Canada	KEM	349.7127	Law—Manitoba
KE1328-1332	346.7102	Agency (Law)—Canada	KEN0-599	349.7151	Law—New Brunswick
KE1351-1361	346.71064	Unincorporated societies—Canada	KEN1200-1799	349.718	Law—Newfoundland
			KEN7400-7999	349.716	Law—Nova Scotia
KE1369-1465	346.71066	Corporation law—Canada	KEO	349.713	Law—Ontario
KE1491-1506	346.71078	Bankruptcy—Canada	KEP	349.717	Law—Prince Edward Island
KE1591-1660	343.7108	Trade regulation—Canada	KEQ	349.714	Law—Quebec
KE1610-1614	343.71082	Advertising laws—Canada	KES	349.7124	Law—Sasketchewan
KE1616-1618	343.71082	Labels—Law and legislation—Canada	KEY	349.7191	Law—Yukon Territory
			KEZ	349.71(1-9)	Law—[Canada, cities]
KE1671-1745	343.71076	Agricultural laws and legislation—Canada	KF	349.73	Law—United States
			KF16-22	348.7301	Bills, Legislative—United States
KE1760-1765	343.7107692	Fishery law and legislation—Canada			
			KF50-70	348.73022	Statutes—United States
KE1790-1802	343.71077	Mining law—Canada	KF101-153	347.7301	Courts—United States
KE1867-1906	344.7104232	Food law and legislation—Canada	KF156	349.7303	Law—United States—Dictionaries
KE1915	343.71078624	Construction industry—Law and legislation—Canada	KF165	348.7(4-9)	Uniform state laws
			KF180-185	347.73013	Judicial statistics—United States
KE1935-1999	343.7107	Commercial law—Canada			
KE2020-2061	343.7109	Public utilities—Law and legislation—Canada	KF219-224	345.7307	Trials—United States
			KF221.B74	345.7302	Trials (Bribery)—United States
KE2071-2649	343.71093	Transportation—Law and legislation—Canada			
			KF221.C6	345.730207	Trials (Conspiracy)—United States
KE2771-2998	346.71048	Intellectual property—Canada			
			KF224.W	345.730231	Watergate Trial, Washington, D.C., 1973
KE3098-3542	344.71	Social legislation—Canada			
KE3575-3635	344.71041	Public health laws—Canada	KF240-247	349.73072	Legal research—United States
KE3646-3660	344.71041	Medical laws and legislation—Canada	KF255	348.73041	Law reporting—United States
KE3714-3725	344.7104233	Drugs—Law and legislation—Canada	KF261-292	349.73071	Law—United States—Study and teaching
KE3805-3917	344.7107	Educational law and legislation—Canada			
			KF285	341.0711	Law School Admission Test
KE3968	344.71097	Law and art—Canada			

LC	Dewey	Subject Heading	LC	Dewey	Subject Heading
KF297-338	349.73	Lawyers—United States	KF1480	346.73067	Corporations, Government—
KF299.A35	349.7308996073	Afro-American lawyers			Law and legislation—
KF338	340.0973	Lawyer referral service—			United States
		United States	KF1501-1548	346.73078	Bankruptcy—United States
KF350-374	349.7309	Law—United States—	KF1600-2940	343.7307	Commercial law—United
		History			States
KF382	340.11	Rule of law—United States	KF1601-1611	343.73072	Competition, Unfair—
KF398-400	346.73004	Equity—United States			United States
KF410-418	342.73042	Conflict of laws—United	KF1614-1617	343.73082	Advertising laws—United
		States			States
KF465-553	346.73012	Persons (Law)—United	KF1619-1620	343.73082	Labels—Law and
		States			legislation
KF501-553	346.73015	Domestic relations—United	KF1631-1657	343.73072	Monopolies—United States
		States	KF1659-.1	343.7307	Small business—Law and
KF566-698	346.73043	Real property—United			legislation—United States
		States	KF1661	346.73064	Trade associations—Law
KF701-720	346.73047	Personal property—United			and legislation—United
		States			States
KF753-780	346.73052	Inheritance and	KF1665-1666	343.73075	Weights and measures—
		succession—United States			Law and legislation—
KF801-1241	346.7302	Contracts—United States			United States
KF898-905	344.7301542	Contracts for work and	KF1681-1755	343.73076	Agricultural laws and
		labor—United States			legislation—United States
KF939-951	346.73025	Bailments—United States	KF1770-1773	343.7307692	Fishery law and legislation—
KF956-962	346.73096	Negotiable instruments—			United States
		United States	KF1801-1873	343.73077	Mining law—United States
KF966-1032	346.73082	Banking law—United States	KF1875-1893	343.73078	United States—
KF1035-1040	346.73073	Loans—Law and			Manufactures—Law and
		legislation—United States			legislation
KF1045	346.73074	Suretyship and guaranty—	KF1900-1944	344.7304232	Food law and legislation—
		United States			United States
KF1046-1062	346.73092	Security (Law)—United	KF1950	343.73078624	Construction industry—Law
		States			and legislation—United
KF1066-1084	346.73092	Investments—Law and			States
		legislation—United States	KF1970-2105	346.7307	Business law—United States
KF1085-1087	343.7308	Commodity exchanges—Law	KF2161-2654	343.73093	Transportation—Law and
		and legislation—United			legislation—United States
		States	KF2900-2940	344.7301712	Professions—Law and
KF1091-1137	343.73093	Carriers—Law and			legislation—United States
		legislation—United States	KF2971-3193	346.73048	Intellectual property—
KF1146-1238	346.73086	Insurance law—United			United States
		States	KF2986-3080	346.730482	Copyright—United States
KF1241	344.730542	Contracts, Aleatory—	KF3084	070.520973	Authors and publishers—
		United States			United States
KF1244-.5	346.73029	Quasi contracts—United	KF3086	346.730484	Design protection—United
		States			States
KF1246-1329	346.7303	Torts—United States	KF3091-3193	346.730486	Patent laws and legislation—
KF1341-1348	346.73029	Agency (Law)—United			United States
		States	KF3195-3198	343.73072	Competition, Unfair—
KF1355-1480	346.7306	Associations, institutions,			United States
		etc.—Law and legislation	KF3300-3771	344.73	Social legislation—United
KF1361-1381	346.73064	Unincorporated societies—			States
		United States	KF3301-3580	344.7301	Labor laws and legislation—
KF1384-1480	346.73066	Corporation law—United			United States
		States	KF3641-3664	343.7305242	Social security—United
KF1388-1390	346.73064	Nonprofit organizations—			States
		Law and legislation—	KF3720-3745	344.730316	Public welfare—Law and
		United States			legislation—United States
KF1396-1477	346.73066	Corporations—Law and	KF3750	344.7305348	Disaster relief—Law and
		legislation—United States			legislation—United States

LC	Dewey	Subject Heading	LC	Dewey	Subject Heading
KF3775-3816	344.7304	Public health laws—United States	KF4700-4720	342.73083	Citizenship—United States
KF3821-3829	344.73041	Medical laws and legislation—United States	KF4788	342.73087	Political parties—United States
KF3832	344.73048	Sterilization, Eugenic—Law and legislation—United States	KF4794-.5	342.73082	Passports—United States
			KF4800-4848	342.73083	Aliens—United States
KF3835-3838	344.73049	Veterinary hygiene—Law and legislation—United States	KF4850-4856	344.7305	Internal security—United States
KF3901-3925	344.7305	Alcohol—Law and legislation—United States	KF4865-4869	342.730852	Church and state—United States
KF3941-3942	344.730533	Weapons—Law and legislation—United States	KF4881-4921	342.7308	People (Constitutional law)—United States
KF3945-3965	344.73042	Product safety—Law and legislation—United States	KF4930-5005	342.7305	Legislative bodies—United States
KF3970	344.73047	Accident law—United States	KF5050-5125	342.7306	Executive departments—United States
KF3975-3977	344.7305377	Fire prevention—Law and legislation—United States	KF5130	347.73012	Judicial power—United States
KF3987	344.73099	Amusements—Law and legislation—United States	KF5150	344.7309	Emblems, National—United States
KF3989	344.73099	Sports—Law and legislation—United States	KF5300-5332	342.7309	Local government—Law and legislation—United States
KF3992	344.730542	Lotteries—Law and legislation—United States	KF5336-5398	342.73068	Civil service—United States
			KF5399-.5	342.730418	Police power—United States
KF4101-4257	344.7307	Educational law and legislation—United States	KF5401-5425	342.73066	Administrative law—United States
KF4125-4143	344.73076	Education—Finance—Law and legislation—United States	KF5500-5865	343.7302	Government property—United States
			KF5505-5510	346.73044	Conservation of natural resources—United States
KF4150-4166	344.73079	Students—Legal status, laws, etc.—United States	KF5521-5536	343.730942	Highway law—United States
KF4175-4190	344.73078	Teachers—Legal status, laws, etc.—United States	KF5551-5590	346.7304691	Water resources development—Law and legislation
KF4192-.5	344.7307	School employees—Legal status, laws, etc.—United States	KF5594	344.730655168	Weather control—Law and legislation—United States
			KF5599	343.730252	Eminent domain—United States
KF4195-4223	344.7307	Educational law and legislation—United States	KF5670-5673	343.730253	Homestead law—United States
KF4225-4257	344.73074	Education, Higher—Law and legislation—United States	KF5675-5677	343.730253	Land grants—Law and legislation—United States
KF4305	344.73093	Museums—Law and legislation—United States	KF5691-5710	346.73045	City planning and redevelopment law—United States
KF4310-4312	344.73094	Historic buildings—Law and legislation—United States	KF5721-5740	344.73063635	Housing—Law and legislation—United States
KF4315-4319	344.73092	Library legislation—United States	KF5865	344.7306	Public works—Law and legislation—United States
KF4325	344.73092	Archives—Law and legislation—United States	KF5900-6075.5	343.7301	War and emergency legislation—United States
KF4501-5130	342.73	United States—Constitutional law	KF6200-6795	343.7303	Finance, Public—Law and legislation—United States
KF4546-4554	342.73	United States—Constitutional law	KF6201-6219	343.73032	Money—Law and legislation—United States
KF4555-4558	342.73032	United States—Constitutional law—Amendments	KF6221-6227	343.73034	Budget—Law and legislation—United States
KF4565-4579	342.73044	Separation of powers—United States	KF6231-6239	343.73034	Finance, Public—Auditing—Law and legislation
KF4600-4629	342.73042	Federal government—United States	KF6241-6245	343.73037	Debts, Public—Law and legislation—United States
KF4635	342.730413	Law—United States—Territories and possessions	KF6251-6708	343.73036	Internal revenue law—United States
KF4695	342.730418	Police power—United States			

LC	Dewey	Subject Heading	LC	Dewey	Subject Heading
KF6271-6636	343.7304	Taxation—Law and legislation—United States	KF9725	345.730773	Capital punishment—United States
KF6329-6330	343.7304	Tax exemption—Law and legislation—United States	KF9763	344.7303288	Victims of crimes—United States
KF6334	345.730233	Tax evasion—United States	KFA0-599	349.761	Law—Alabama
KF6351-6499	343.73052	Income tax—Law and legislation—United States	KFA1200-1799	349.798	Law—Alaska
			KFA2400-2999	349.791	Law—Arizona
KF6525-6558	343.73054	Property tax—Law and legislation—United States	KFA3600-4199	349.767	Law—Arkansas
			KFC0-1199	349.794	Law—California
KF6598-6609	343.730526	Indirect taxation	KFC1800-2399	349.788	Law—Colorado
KF6651-6708	343.73056	Tariff—Law and legislation—United States	KFC3600-4199	349.746	Law—Connecticut
			KFD0-599	349.751	Law—Delaware
KF6770-6795	343.73043	Local finance—Law and legislation—United States	KFD1200-1799	349.753	Law—Washington, D.C.
			KFF0-599	349.759	Law—Florida
KF7625-7659	343.730143	Courts-martial and courts of inquiry—United States	KFG0-599	349.758	Law—Georgia
			KFH0-599	349.969	Law—Hawaii
KF7685	344.730535	Civil defense—Law and legislation—United States	KFI0-599	349.796	Law—Idaho
			KFI1200-1799	349.773	Law—Illinois
KF8201-8228	342.730872	Indians of North America—Legal status, laws, etc.	KFI4200-4799	349.777	Law—Iowa
			KFK0-599	349.781	Law—Kansas
KF8700-9075	347.7305	Procedure (Law)—United States	KFK1200-1799	349.769	Law—Kentucky
			KFL0-599	349.763	Law—Louisiana
KF8741-8752	347.7305	Appellate procedure—United States	KFM0-599	349.741	Law—Maine
			KFM1200-1799	349.752	Law—Maryland
KF8771-8807	347.731(4-6)	Courts—United States—Officials and employees	KFM2400-2999	349.744	Law—Massachusetts
			KFM4200-4799	349.774	Law—Michigan
KF8810-9075	347.7305	Civil procedure—United States	KFM5400-5999	349.776	Law—Minnesota
			KFM6600-7199	349.762	Law—Mississippi
KF8816-8821	347.73051	Court rules—United States	KFM7800-8399	349.778	Law—Missouri
KF8858-8861	347.73051	Jurisdiction—United States	KFM9000-9599	349.786	Law—Montana
KF8863-8865	347.73053	Actions and defenses—United States	KFN0-599	349.782	Law—Nebraska
			KFN600-1199	349.793	Law—Nevada
KF8866-8885	347.73072	Pleading—United States	KFN1200-1799	349.742	Law—New Hampshire
KF8890-8896.5	347.73052	Parties to actions—United States	KFN1800-2399	349.749	Law—New Jersey
			KFN3600-4199	349.789	Law—New Mexico
KF8900-8902	347.73072	Pre-trial procedure—United States	KFN5000-6199	349.747	Law—New York (State)
			KFN7400-7999	349.756	Law—North Carolina
KF8910-8986	347.7307	Trials—United States	KFN8600-9199	349.784	Law—North Dakota
KF8911-8925	347.73075	Trial practice—United States	KFO0-599	349.771	Law—Ohio
KF8931-8969	347.7306	Evidence (Law)—United States	KFO1200-1799	349.766	Law—Oklahoma
			KFO2400-2999	349.795	Law—Oregon
KF8971-8984	347.730752	Jury—United States	KFP0-599	349.748	Law—Pennsylvania
KF8990-9002	347.73077	Judgments—United States	KFR0-599	349.745	Law—Rhode Island
KF9085-9086	347.7309	Arbitration and award—United States	KFS1800-2399	349.757	Law—South Carolina
			KFS3000-3599	349.783	Law—South Dakota
KF9201-9479	345.73	Criminal law—United States	KFT0-599	349.768	Law—Tennessee
KF9304-9329	345.73025	Offenses against the person—United States	KFT1200-1799	349.764	Law—Texas
			KFU0-599	349.792	Law—Utah
KF9350-9379	345.73026	Offenses against property—United States	KFV0-599	349.743	Law—Vermont
			KFV2400-2999	349.755	Law—Virginia
KF9625	345.730527	Arrest—United States	KFW0-599	349.797	Law—Washington
KF9630	345.730522	Searches and seizures—United States	KFW1200-1799	349.754	Law—West Virginia
			KFW2400-2999	349.775	Law—Wisconsin
KF9632	345.73056	Bail—United States	KFW4200-4799	349.787	Law—Wyoming
KF9635	345.73052	Extradition—United States	KFX	349.7(4-9)	Law—[United States, cities]
KF9640-9642	345.73072	Indictments—United States			
KF9645-9650	345.73072	Arraignment—United States	KFZ8600-9199	349.75	Law—Confederate States of America
KF9660-9678	345.7306	Evidence, Criminal—United States			
			KGA	349.7282	Law—Belize
KF9680	345.73075	Jury—United States	KGB	349.7286	Law—Costa Rica
KF9695	345.73077	Pardon—United States	KGC	349.7284	Law—El Salvador

LC	Dewey	Subject Heading	LC	Dewey	Subject Heading
KGD	349.7281	Law—Guatemala	KKE	349.495	Law—Greece
KGE	349.7283	Law—Honduras	KKF	349.439	Law—Hungary
KGF	349.72	Law—Mexico	KKG	349.4912	Law—Iceland
KGG	349.7285	Law—Nicaragua	KKH	349.45	Law—Spain
KGH	349.7287	Law—Panama	KKJ	349.43648	Law—Liechtenstein
KGJ-KGZ	349.729	Law—West Indies	KKK0-499	349.4935	Law—Luxembourg
KGJ7000-7499	349.72973	Law—Anguilla	KKK1000-1499	349.4585	Law—Malta
KGK0-499	349.72974	Law—Antiguilla	KKL	349.44949	Law—Monaco
KGK1000-1499	349.72986	Law—Aruba	KKM	349.492	Law—Netherlands
KGL0-499	349.7296	Law—Bahamas	KKN	349.481	Law—Norway
KGL1000-1499	349.72981	Law—Barbados	KKP	349.438	Law—Poland
KGL2000-2499	349.72986	Law—Bonaire	KKQ	349.469	Law—Portugal
KGL4000-4499	349.729725	Law—British Virgin Islands	KKR	349.498	Law—Romania
KGN	349.7291	Law—Cuba	KKT	349.46	Law—Spain
KGP0-499	349.72986	Law—Curacao	KKV	349.485	Law—Sweden
KGP2000-2499	349.729841	Law—Dominica	KKW	349.494	Law—Switzerland
KGQ	349.7293	Law—Dominican Republic	KKX	349.561	Law—Turkey
KGR1000-1499	349.72986	Law—Aruba	KKZ	349.497	Law—Yugoslavia
KGR3000-3499	349.72976	Law—West Indies, French	L	371	Schools
KGR4000-4499	349.729845	Law—Grenada	L	370	Education
KGR5000-5499	349.72976	Law—Guadeloupe	L7-101	370.5	Education—Periodicals
KGS	349.7294	Law—Haiti	L106-107	370.6	Education—Congresses
KGT0-499	349.7292	Law—Jamaica	L111-791	370.9(4-9)	Education—[By region or country]
KGT1000-1499	349.72982	Law—Martinique			
KGT2000-2499	349.72975	Law—Montserrat	L111-219	370.973	Education—United States
KGV	349.7295	Law—Puerto Rico	L116-219	370.97(4-9)	Education—[United States, By state]
KGW0-499	349.72977	Law—Saba (Netherlands Antilles)			
KGW2000-2499	349.72973	Law—Saint Kitts and Nevis	L221-223	370.971	Education—Canada
KGW3000-3499	349.729843	Law—Saint Lucia	L227-229	370.972	Education—Mexico
KGW5000-5499	349.729844	Law—Saint Vincent	L231-249	370.9728	Education—Central America
KGW7000-7499	349.72977	Law—Saint Eustatius	L251-267	370.9729	Education—West Indies
KGW8000-8499	349.72977	Law—Saint Martin	L291-335	370.98	Education—South America
KGX0-499	349.72983	Law—Trinidad and Tobago	L341-359	370.941	Education—Great Britain
KGZ0-499	349.729722	Law—Virginia Islands of the United States	L341-551	370.94	Education—Europe
			L346-348	370.9415	Education—Ireland
KH	349.8	Law—South America	L361-366	370.9436	Education—Austria
KHA	349.82	Law—Argentina	L381-383	370.9439	Education—Hungary
KHC	349.84	Law—Bolivia	L385-387	370.9437	Education—Czechoslovakia
KHD	349.81	Law—Brazil	L391-396	370.944	Education—France
KHF	349.83	Law—Chile	L401-410	370.943	Education—Germany
KHH	349.861	Law—Columbia	L411-416	370.9495	Education—Greece
KHK	349.866	Law—Ecuador	L421-426	370.945	Education—Italy
KHL	349.9711	Law—Falkland Islands	L431-436	370.9493	Education—Belgium
KHM	349.882	Law—French Guiana	L441-446	370.9492	Education—Netherlands
KHP	349.892	Law—Paraguay	L451-466	370.947	Education—Russia
KHQ	349.85	Law—Peru	L471-476	370.9489	Education—Denmark
KHS	349.883	Law—Surinam	L481	370.94912	Education—Iceland
KHU	349.895	Law—Uruguay	L491-496	370.9481	Education—Norway
KHW	349.87	Law—Venezuela	L501-506	370.9485	Education—Sweden
KJA3210	343.37604	Taxation (Roman law)	L511-516	370.946	Education—Spain
KJG	349.4965	Law—Albania	L521-526	370.9469	Education—Portugal
KJJ	349.436	Law—Austria	L531-536	370.9494	Education—Switzerlad
KJK	349.493	Law—Belgium	L539-540	370.9561	Education—Turkey
KJM	349.499	Law—Bulgaria	L541-542	370.9499	Education—Bulgaria
KJN	349.5645	Law—Cyprus	L545-546	370.9498	Education—Romania
KJP	349.437	Law—Czechoslovakia	L549-550	370.9497	Education—Yugoslavia
KJR	349.489	Law—Denmark	L561-642	370.95	Education—Asia
KJT	349.4897	Law—Finland	L571-573	370.951	Education—China
KJV	349.44	Law—France	L577-578	370.954	Education—India
KK	349.43	Law—Germany	L578.5-.6	370.95491	Education—Pakistan
			L585-586	370.959(4-7)	Education—Indochina

LC	Dewey	Subject Heading	LC	Dewey	Subject Heading
L597-598	370.9598	Education—Indonesia	LB1029.S5	371.397	Simulated environment (Teaching method)
L611-612	370.952	Education—Japan			
L613-614	370.9519	Education—Korea	LB1029.S53	371.397	Education—Simulation methods
L615-616	370.955	Education—Iran			
L617-620	370.957	Education—Siberia	LB1029.T6	371.337	Educational toys
L627-628	370.9567	Education—Iraq	LB1029.U6	371.36	Unit method of teaching
L631-632	370.95694	Education—Israel	LB1032	371.148	Team learning approach in education
L651-742	370.96	Education—Africa			
L750-791	370.99(3-6)	Education—[New Zealand/ Australia/Oceania]	LB1033	371.1023	Teacher-student relationships
L797-898	370.74	Education—Museums	LB1033.5	370.14	Nonverbal communication in education
L900-991	373/378.0 + (025)	Education—Directories			
LA	370.9	Education—History	LB1039	371.37	Recitation (Education)
LA23	370.207	Humor in education	LB1042	372.677	Storytelling
LA31-81	370.901	Education, Ancient	LB1043-1044.9	371.335	Audio-visual education
LA37	370.932	Education, Egyptian	LB1043.5-1044	371.335	Visual aids
LA75	370.938	Education, Greek	LB1043.5	371.335	Overhead projection
LA77	370.938	Education, Minoan	LB1043.6	371.33	Displays in education
LA91-98	370.902	Education, Medieval	LB1043.67	371.3352	Pictures in education
LA106-108	370.11209024	Education, Humanistic	LB1043.8	371.3352	Filmstrips in education
LA173-186	378.009	Education, Higher	LB1044.5-.6	371.3331	Radio in education
LA177	378.00902	Education, Medieval	LB1044.7	371.3358	Television in education
LA186	371.81	Student movements	LB1044.75	371.33523	Video tapes in education
LA190-2284	370.9 (4-9)	Education—History	LB1044.75	371.33523	Video tapes
LA2301-2397	370.92	Educators	LB1047	371.384	School field trips
LA2301-2397	370.92	Teachers	LB1047	371.384	Outdoor education
LB41	370.1	Education—Aims and objectives	LB1048	371.30281	Homework
			LB1049	371.3943	Independent study
LB41.5	370.112	Education—Forecasting	LB1050	372.4	Reading
LB45	306.43	Educational anthropology	LB1050.37	372.40284	Reading machines
LB51-875	370.92	Educators	LB1050.43	372.414	Reading readiness
LB125-875	370.1	Education—Philosophy	LB1050.45	372.47	Reading comprehension
LB1025-1050.7	371.1	Teaching	LB1050.46	372.48	Reading—Ability testing
LB1027	371.3	Educational innovations	LB1050.5	372.43	Reading—Remedial teaching
LB1027.3	371.3	Education—Experimental methods	LB1050.5	371.9144	Dyslexia
			LB1050.53	418.4	Developmental reading
LB1027.5-.8	371.4	Educational counseling	LB1050.55	418.4	Silent reading
LB1027.5	371.4047	Peer counseling of students	LB1051-1091	370.15	Educational psychology
LB1027.55	371.713	School psychology	LB1059	153.154	Transfer of training
LB1027.9	379.111	School choice	LB1060-1091	153.15	Learning, Psychology of
LB1028-.25	370.72	Education—Research	LB1060	153.15	Learning
LB1028.24	370.72	Action research in education	LB1060.2	370.153	Behavior modification
			LB1062	370.157	Creative thinking
LB1028.4	371.33	Media programs (Education)	LB1063-1064	370.1522	Memory
			LB1065	153.1533	Interest (Psychology)
LB1028.43	371.334	Education—Data processing	LB1065	153.1532	Attention
LB1028.5-.7	371.334	Computer-assisted instruction	LB1067	153.73	Apperception
			LB1067.5	153.152	Visual learning
LB1028.5	371.334	Programmed instruction	LB1071	153.8	Will
LB1028.75	371.334	Interactive video	LB1075	152.1886	Mental fatigue
LB1029.A85	371.334	Teaching machines	LB1101-1139	155.4	Child development
LB1029.F7	371.04	Free schools	LB1123	152.335	Left- and right-handedness
LB1029.G3	371.337	Educational games	LB1134	153.9	Learning ability
LB1029.L3	371.382	Dalton laboratory plan	LB1135	155.5	Adolescence
LB1029.M7	371.39	Monitorial system of education	LB1139.2-.4	372.21	Early childhood education
			LB1139.L3	153.6	Speech
LB1029.M75	371.392	Montessori method of education	LB1139.S88	370.158	Student adjustment
			LB1140-.5	372.21	Education, Preschool
LB1029.N6	371.255	Nongraded schools	LB1140.5.R4	372.4	Reading (Preschool)
LB1029.06	371.256	Open plan schools	LB1141-1499	372.218	Kindergarten
LB1029.R4	374.012	Remedial teaching	LB1181.2	372.4	Reading (Kindergarten)

LC	Dewey	Subject Heading	LC	Dewey	Subject Heading
LB1501-1547	372	Education, Primary	LB2342	378.106	Universities and colleges—
LB1525-.8	372.4	Reading (Primary)			Finance
LB1525	372.4	Reading (Elementary)	LB2342-.2	378.38	College costs
LB1536	372.634	Penmanship	LB2343	378.194	Faculty advisors
LB1537	372.11	Education, Primary—	LB2351-2359	378.161	Universities and colleges—
		Activity programs			Admission
LB1555-1601	372	Education, Elementary	LB2351-2360	378.1617	Universities and colleges—
LB1570-1571	375	Education—Curricula			Entrance requirements
LB1573	372.4	Reading (Elementary)	LB2351.5-.52	378.1616	College applications
LB1573.3	372.465	Reading—Phonetic method	LB2353	378.1662	Universities and colleges—
LB1573.37	372.462	Reading (Elementary)—			Examinations
		Whole-word method	LB2359.5	378.1618	College credits
LB1573.5	372.452	Oral reading	LB2361-2365	378.199	Universities and colleges—
LB1574	372.632	Spelling ability			Curricula
LB1576	372.6	Language arts (Elementary)	LB2366-2367	378.241	Examinations
LB1590	372.634	Penmanship	LB2367	378.1662	Universities and colleges—
LB1590.3-.5	153.42	Thought and thinking			Examinations
LB1595-1599	372.5	Manual training	LB2369	378.242	Dissertations, Academic
LB1603-1694	373.238	High schools	LB2371	378.155	Universities and colleges—
LB1623	373.236	Middle schools			Graduate work
LB1623	373.236	Junior high schools	LB2372.E3	378.155	Education—Graduate work
LB1627.7	373.238	High school equivalency	LB2375-2378	378.016	Student exchange programs
		certificates	LB2375-2378	378.016	Educational exchanges
LB1705-2286	370.711	Teachers—Training of	LB2381-2391	378.2	Degrees, Academic
LB1731	370.711	Teachers—In-service training	LB2383	378.2	Bachelor of arts degree
LB1755-1779	371.11	Teachers	LB2385	378.2	Master of arts degree
LB1762-1765	370.711	Examinations	LB2386	378.2	Doctor of philosophy degree
LB1771-1773	371.12	Teachers—Certification	LB2389	378.28	Academic costume
LB1775-1785	371.1	Teaching	LB2393	378.1796	Lecture method in teaching
LB1775.5	372.21	Preschool teachers	LB2393.5	378.177	Seminars
LB1775.6	372.11	Early childhood educators	LB2395	378.170281	Note-taking
LB1776	372.11	Elementary school teachers	LB2801-2997	378.1	School management and
LB1777-.4	373.11	High school teachers			organization
LB1778	378.12	College teachers	LB2806.2	371.393	Performance contracts in
LB1805-2151	370.711	Teachers colleges			education
LB2157	370.71	Student teachers	LB2806.22	379.158	Educational accountability
LB2283-2286	370.116	Educational exchanges	LB2806.3	371.2	School management teams
LB2283-2285	370.1163	Teacher exchange programs	LB2806.4	371.203	School supervision
LB2300-2411	378	Universities and colleges	LB2809	379.152	State departments of
LB2328	378.1543	Junior colleges			education
LB2328	378.1543	Community colleges	LB2810-.5	379.158	Accreditation (Education)
LB2328.4	378.052	Urban universities and	LB2813	379.123	County school systems
		colleges	LB2817-.5	379.1535	School districts
LB2329	378.052	Municipal universities and	LB2818	373.241	Magnet schools
		colleges	LB2822.5	372.12	Elementary school
LB2329.5	378.053	State universities and			administration
		colleges	LB2822.75	379.158	Educational evaluation
LB2331.5	378.104	University cooperation	LB2823	370.723	Educational surveys
LB2331.6-.615	353.88284	Universities and colleges—	LB2823.2	379.1535	School closings
		Accreditation	LB2824-2830	371.206	Education—Finance
LB2331.7-.74	378.12	Universities and colleges—	LB2824-2830	379.13	School bonds
		Faculty	LB2825-2826.6	379.121	Federal aid to education
LB2335.95-2337	378.106	Educational fund raising	LB2828	379.32	State aid to private schools
LB2336-2337	378.106	Endowments	LB2831	379.1531	School boards
LB2337.2-2340.8	378.3	Student aid	LB2831.5-	371.201	School personnel
LB2338-2339	378.34	Scholarships	2844.4		management
LB2340-.4	378.362	Student loan funds	LB2831.5-.585	371.201	School employees
LB2341	378.111	College administrators	LB2831.7-.776	371.2011	School superintendents
LB2341	378.161	Student registration	LB2831.8-.876	371.2011	School administrators
LB2341	371.4	Deans (Education)	LB2831.9-.976	371.2012	School principals
			LB2831.9-.976	373.12012	High school principals

LC	Dewey	Subject Heading	LC	Dewey	Subject Heading
LB2831.9-.976	372.12012	Elementary school principals	LB3253	371.61	Campus parking
LB2832-2844.47	371.1	Teachers	LB3261-3281	371.63	Schools—Furniture, equipment, etc.
LB2832.2	379.1535	Public school closings	LB3401-3495	371.71	School hygiene
LB2836	371.104	Teachers—Tenure	LB3401-3495	371.71	School health services
LB2844.1.W6	371.1412	Teachers—Workload	LB3473-3479	371.716	School children—Food
LB2842-2844	331.2813711	Teachers—Salaries, etc.	LB3473-3479	371.716	School milk programs
LB2843.L4	371.104	Teachers—Leaves of absence	LB3473-3479	371.716	School breakfast programs
LB2844.1	371.14	Teachers, Part-time	LB3602-3618	371.8	Students
LB2844.1.P7	371.144	Teachers, Probationary	LB3604-3615	371.8	Hazing
LB2844.52-.53	331.88113711	Teachers' unions	LB3604	371.8	Students—Language
LB2846	370.21	Educational statistics	LB3605	371.8	Student activities
LB2848-2849	371.223	Scholarships	LB3609	174.9375	Student ethics
LB2861	379.1535	Schools—Centralization	LB3613.M3	371.82655	Married students
LB2862	379.1535	Schools—Decentralization	LB3621	371.897	Student publications
LB2864	371.872	School children—Transportation	LB3635	791.64	Cheerleading
LB2864.6.A25	363.119371	School accidents	LC	371.01	Public schools
LB2865	363.1257	School safety patrols	LC40	371.042	Home schooling
LB3011-3095	371.5	School discipline	LC41	371.394	Tutors and tutoring
LB3011-3095	371.2	School management and organization	LC47-57	371.02	Private schools
LB3013	371.1024	Classroom management	LC58-.7	373.222	Preparatory schools
LB3013.2	371.251	Class size	LC71-188	379	Education and state
LB3013.3	371.78	School violence	LC71.2	371.207	Educational planning
LB3013.4	371.46	School social work	LC72-.5	371.104	Academic freedom
LB3013.5	371.46	Visiting teachers	LC72-.5	371.104	Teaching, Freedom of
LB3025	371.5	Discipline of children	LC107-120	379.28	Religion in the public schools
LB3034	371.23	School year	LC129-139	379.23	Education, Compulsory
LB3044.7-.74	027.7	Instructional materials centers	LC130-139	371.219	School enrollment
LB3045-3048	371.32	Textbooks	LC142-145	371.2913	Dropouts
LB3045.6	371.32	Textbook bias	LC142-148.5	371.294	School attendance
LB3045.66	379.156	Sexism in textbooks	LC145.5-.8	372.12913	Elementary school dropouts
LB3050-3060	371.271	Examinations	LC146	373.1219	High school enrollment
LB3051-3059	371.271	Examinations—Questions	LC146.5-.8	373.12913	High school dropouts
LB3051-3060.87	371.271	Educational tests and measurements	LC149-160	379.24	Literacy
LB3051-3063	371.272	Grading and marking (Students)	LC189-214.53	306.43	Educational sociology
			LC201.5-.7	370.117	Native language and education
LB3060.3	371.271	Achievement tests	LC212-.863	379.26	Discrimination in education
LB3060.32.D65	371.271	Domain-referenced tests	LC212.5-.73	379.26	Segregation in education
LB3060.32.M85	371.271	Multiple-choice examinations	LC212.6-.63	379.263	De facto school segregation
LB3060.32.N67	371.271	Norm-referenced tests	LC212.8-.83	379.26	Sex discrimination in education
LB3060.32.O35	371.271	Objective tests	LC213-.3	379.26	Educational equalization
LB3060.57	371.27	Examinations—Study guides	LC213-.3	370.111	Compensatory education
LB3060.65	371.27	Examinations—Design and construction	LC214-.3	379.263	School integration
			LC214.5-.53	379.263	Busing for school integration
LB3060.77	371.27	Examinations—Scoring	LC225.5	371.103	Parent-teacher conferences
LB3061	371.254	Ability grouping in education	LC230-235	371.19206	Parents' and teachers' associations
LB3061.8	371.25	Track system (Education)	LC241-245	371.206	Educational fund raising
LB3064	371.2914	Students, Transfer of	LC251-301	370.114	Character
LB3081-3087	371.294	School attendance	LC251-318	370.114	Moral education
LB3089-.4	371.543	Student suspension	LC427-629	371.071	Church schools
LB3092-3095	371.59	Student government	LC427-629	378.071	Church colleges
LB3205-3295	371.6	School buildings	LC487	378.07122	Catholic universities and colleges
LB3205-3325	371.6	School facilities			
LB3226-3228	371.871	Student housing	LC905.T42	371.100882971	Muslim teachers
LB3226-3229	371.871	Dormitories	LC1001-1024	370.112	Education, Humanistic
LB3249	371.58	School vandalism	LC1001-1021	373.242	Classical education
LB3251	371.61	School grounds	LC1035-.8	370	Basic education

LC	Dewey	Subject Heading	LC	Dewey	Subject Heading
LC1037-.8	370.113	Career education	LC5144-.3	371.826942	Homeless students
LC1041-1047	370.113	Vocational education	LC5146-5148	370.91734	Education, Rural
LC1041-1047	370.113	Technical education	LC5161-5163	370.111	Fundamental education
LC1049-.8	371.28	Educational acceleration	LC5201-6660	374	Adult education
LC1051-1071	378.013	Professional education	LC5201-6660	374	Continuing education
LC1070-1071	378.013076	Examinations	LC5451-5493	371.8246	Aged—Education
LC1099-.5	370.117	Multicultural education	LC5501-5560	374.8	Evening and continuation schools
LC1101-1261	340.0711	Law schools			
LC1401-2571	371.822	Women—Education	LC5701-5760	371.232	Summer schools
LC1500-1506	370.113082	Women—Vocational education	LC5800-5808	371.35	Distance education
			LC6201-6401	378.175	University extension
LC1551-1651	378.19822	Women—Education (Higher)	LC6501-6560.4	080	Lectures and lecturing
LC1660-1666	374.1822	Adult education of women	LC6501-6560	371.396	Forums (Discussion and debate)
LC2601-2611	370.91724	Education—Developing countries			
LC2667-2688	370.8968073	Hispanic Americans—Education	LD	371.00973	Schools—United States
			LD13-7251	378.73	Universities and colleges—United States
LC2699-2913	371.82996073	Blacks—Education			
LC2701-2853	371.82996073	Afro-Americans—Education	LD6501	378.15430973	Junior colleges—United States
LC2707	371.22308996073	Afro-Americans—Scholarships, fellowships, etc.			
LC2771	372.182996073	Afro-Americans—Education (Elementary)	LD7501	373.73	High schools—United States
			LE	378.(7/8)	Universities and colleges—America
LC2779	373.182996073	Afro-Americans—Education (Secondary)	LE3-5	378.71	Universities and colleges—Canada
LC2780	370.11308996073	Afro-Americans—Vocational education	LF	378.4	Universities and colleges—Europe
LC2781	378.1982996073	Afro-Americans—Education (Higher)	LG21-995	378.5	Universities and colleges—Asia
LC2785	378.01308996073	Afro-Americans—Professional education	LG401-681	378.6	Universities and colleges—Africa
LC3001-3501	371.82995	Asians—Education	LJ	371.85	Greek letter societies
LC3503-3520	371.82991497	Gypsies—Education	LT	371.32	Textbooks
LC3701-3743	370.1175	Education, Bilingual	M	780	Music
LC3701-3740	371.829	Minorities—Education	M5-1459	784	Instrumental music
LC3800-3806	371.829	Ethnic schools	M6-14	786.5	Organ music
LC3950-3990.4	371.9	Special education	M14.8	786.59	Electronic organ music
LC3991-4000	371.8279	Gifted children	M15-17	786.55	Reed-organ music
LC4001-4100	371.91	Handicapped children—Education	M20-39	786.3	Clavichord music
			M20-39	786.2	Piano music
LC4051-4100	371.82694	Socially handicapped children—Education	M20-39	786.4	Harpsichord music
			M20-32	786.4	Electronic harpsichord music
LC4165-4184	371.94	Mentally ill children—Education	M20-32	786.66	Player-piano music
LC4201-4580	371.91	Physically handicapped children—Education	M40-44	787.2	Violin music
			M45-49	787.3	Viola music
			M50-54	787.4	Violoncello music
LC4219.7	370.113087	Physically handicapped children—Vocational education	M55-58	787.5	Double-bass music
			M59	787.6	Hardanger fiddle music
			M59	787.6	Baryton music
			M59	787.6	Viol music
LC4601-4700	371.92	Mentally handicapped children—Education	M59.5	787	String instrument music
			M59.V	787.66	Violetta d'amore music
LC4604	371.9573	Mentally handicapped children—Education (Secondary)	M60-64	788.3	Flute music
			M60-62	788.33	Fife music
			M65-69	788.52	Oboe music
LC4661-4700.4	371.926	Slow learning children	M70-74	788.62	Clarinet music
LC4704-4706	371.9	Learning disabilities	M70-74	788.65	Bass clarinet music
LC4708-4710	371.9144	Dyslexic children	M75-79	788.58	Bassoon music
LC4818-.53	371.9	Learning disabled	M85-89	788.92	Trumpet music
LC5001-5060	371.82623	Working class—Education	M85-89	788.96	Cornet music
LC5101-5143	370.91732	Education, Urban	M90-94	788.93	Trombone music
LC5101-5143	370.91732	Urban schools	M90-94	788.975	Baritone music

LC	Dewey	Subject Heading	LC	Dewey	Subject Heading
M95-99	788.98	Tuba music	M955-959	785.43	Wind ensembles
M105-109	788.7	Saxophone music	M955-959	785.8	Woodwind ensembles
M110	788.974	Alto horn music	M955-959	785.9	Brass ensembles
M110	788.92	Alpenhorn music	M1000-1075	784.2	Orchestral music
M110.B33	788.975	Euphonium music	M1001	784.184	Symphonies
M110.E5	788.53	English-horn music	M1004	784.18926	Overtures
M110.P5	788.33	Piccolo music	M1100-1160	784.7	String-orchestra music
M110.R4	788.36	Recorder music	M1200-1268	784	Band music
M111	788	Wind instrument music	M1200-1269	784.9	Brass band music
M111	788.9	Brass instrument music	M1247	784.1897	Marches (Band)
M115-119	787.9	Harp music	M1260	784.1897	Marches (Band)
M120-122	787.88	Banjo Music	M1270	781.599	Military music
M125-129	787.87	Guitar music	M1270	788.92	Trumpet-calls
M125-129	787.87	Bass guitar music	M1350	784.4	Salon-orchestra music
M130-134	787.84	Mandolin music	M1356	784.48	Dance-orchestra music
M135-137	787.7	Zither music	M1365	791.12	Minstrel music
M140-141	787.83	Lute music	M1366	781.65	Jazz
M142.A7	787.75	Appalachian dulcimer music	M1366	781.645	Ragtime music
M142.B2	787.875	Balalaika music	M1366	784.48	Big band music
M142.C44	787.95	Celtic harp music	M1366	781.653	Dixieland music
M142.D8	787.74	Dulcimer music	M1470	781.3	Chance compositions
M142.S5	787.82	Sitar music	M1473	786.74	Synthesizer music
M142.U5	787.89	Ukulele music	M1495-5000	782	Vocal music
M145	788.49	Bagpipe music	M1500-1527.8	782.1	Dramatic music
M146	786.873	Cymbal music	M1500-1508	782.14	Musicals
M146	786.93	Tabla music	M1500-1508	782.14	Revues
M146	786.94	Snare drum music	M1500-1508	782.1	Operas
M146	786.93	Timpani music	M1528-1529.5	782.0438	Vocal ensembles
M146	786.8	Percussion music	M1530-1546.5	782.48	Cantatas, Secular
M147	786.843	Glockenspiel music	M1547-1610	782.5	Choruses, Secular
M147	786.88485	Handbell music	M1578-1600	783.1	Part-songs
M154	788.84	Concertina music	M1609	782.5	Cantatas, Secular (Unison)
M172	786.64	Carillon music	M1621.4	782.47	Song cycles
M172	786.848	Chime music	M1627-1853	781.599	National music
M175.5	785	Solo instrument music	M1627-1844	781.63	Popular music
M175.A4	788.86	Accordion music	M1627	782.42162	Folk songs
M175.A8	787.75	Autoharp music	M1627	782.43	Ballads
M175.B2	788.84	Bandonion music	M1670-1671	782.253	Spirituals (Songs)
M175.C35	786.873	Castanet music	M1977.C5	782.42	Songbooks
M175.C44	786.83	Celesta music	M1977.P75	781.592	Protest songs
M175.H9	787.69	Hurdy-gurdy music	M1977.S2	782.421595	Sea songs
M175.M38	788.863	Melodeon music	M1999-2199	782.3	Sacred vocal music
M175.M8	788.82	Harmonica music	M2000-2007	782.23	Oratorios
M175.T	786.8842	Triangle music	M2010-2014	782.3238	Requiems
M175.T	786.95	Tambourine music	M2018-2019.5	782.221438	Sacred vocal ensembles
M175.X6	786.843	Vibraphone music	M2020-2036	782.24	Cantatas, Sacred
M175.X6	786.843	Marimba music	M2038-2099	782.265	Anthems
M175.X6	786.843	Xylophone music	M2099.5	781.76	Synagogue music
M176	781.542	Silent film music	M2114.3	781.76	Synagogue music
M176.5	781.544	Radio music	M2115-2145	782.27	Hymns
M177-990	785	Chamber music	M2186-2187	781.76	Synagogue music
M177-298.5	785.12	Duets	M2198-2199	782.254	Gospel music
M300-386	785.13	Trios	ML	780.72	Musicology
M349-353	785.13	String trios	ML25-28	780.6	Music—Societies, etc.
M400-486	785.14	Quartets	ML35-38	780.79	Music festivals
M450-454	784.4	String quartets	ML48-49	780	Librettos
M500-586	785.15	Quintets	ML93-98	780.262	Musicians—Autographs
M600-686	785.16	Sextets	ML93-98	780	Music—Manuscripts
M700-786	785.17	Septets	ML100-110	780.3	Music—Dictionaries
M800-886	785.18	Octets	ML105-107	780.12	Music—Bio-bibliography
M900-986	785.19	Nonets	ML108	780.14	Music—Terminology

LC	Dewey	Subject Heading	LC	Dewey	Subject Heading
ML111-158	016.78	Music—Bibliography	ML525-541	784.195	Musical instruments—Asia
ML155	784.190294	Musical instruments—Catalogs, Manufacturers'	ML527	784.19538	Musical instruments—Saudia Arabia
ML159-3799	780.9	Music—History and criticism	ML531	784.195	Musical instruments—China
ML162-169	784.1901	Musical instruments, Ancient	ML533	784.1954	Musical instruments—India
ML196	780.9034	Romanticism in music	ML535	784.1952	Musical instruments—Japan
ML385-403	780.92	Musicians	ML537	784.19519	Musical instruments—Korea
ML385-429	780.92	Music—Bio-bibliography			
ML430-455	781.309	Composition (Music)	ML539	784.1955	Musical instruments—Iran
ML457	780.7809	Music—Performance	ML544	784.196	Musical instruments—Africa
ML457	781.4409	Performance practice (Music)	ML547	784.199(3-6)	Musical instruments—[New Zealand/Australia/Oceania)
ML459-1093	784.1909	Musical instruments			
ML475-1354	784.19(4-9)	Musical instruments—[By region or country]	ML550-649	786.509	Organ
ML476	784.1973	Musical instruments—United States	ML597	786.5509	Reed-organ
			ML597	786.509	Hammond organ
ML478	784.1971	Musical instruments—Canada	ML649.8-747	786.209	Piano
			ML649.8-747	786.309	Clavichord
ML480	784.19729	Musical instruments—West Indies	ML750-927	787.09	Stringed instruments
ML482	784.1972	Musical instruments—Mexico	ML800-897	787.209	Violin
			ML929-990	788.09	Wind instruments
ML484	784.19728	Musical instruments—Central America	ML935-937	788.3309	Piccolo
			ML953	788.5807	Bassoon
ML486	784.198	Musical instruments—South America	ML900	788.4000	Gaita
			ML990.E	788.97509	Euphonium
ML489-522	784.194	Musical instruments—Europe	ML1015-1018	787.7409	Dulcimer
			ML1030-1040	786.809	Percussion instruments
ML491	784.19436	Musical instruments—Austria	ML1035	786.909	Drum
			ML1038.S	786.9409	Snare drum
ML493	784.19437	Musical instruments—Czechoslovakia	ML1055	788.3609	Music recorder
			ML1055	780.26609	Phonograph
ML494	784.19439	Musical instruments—Hungary	ML1058	786.6609	Mechanical organs
			ML1065-1066	786.6509	Music box
ML496	784.19493	Musical instruments—Belgium	ML1083	788.8609	Accordion
			ML1087	786.88709	Jew's harp
ML497	784.1944	Musical instruments—France	ML1088	788.8209	Harmonica
			ML1092	786.7409	Electronic keyboard (Synthesizer)
ML499-500	784.1943	Musical instruments—Germany			
ML501	784.1941	Musical instruments—Great Britain	ML1100-1165	785.009	Chamber music—History and criticism
ML503	784.1945	Musical instruments—Italy	ML1158	784.18509	Suite (Music)
ML505	784.19492	Musical instruments—Netherlands	ML1200-1251	784.209	Orchestra
			ML1258	784.18509	Suite (Music)
ML513-516	784.1948	Musical instruments—Scandinavia	ML1300-1354	784.09	Bands (Music)
			ML1400-3275	782.009	Vocal music—History and criticism
ML514	784.19489	Musical instruments—Denmark	ML1500-1554	782.509	Choral music
ML515	784.19481	Musical instruments—Norway	ML1699-2100	782.109	Dramatic music
			ML1700-1751	782.1409	Musicals—History and criticism
ML516	784.19485	Musical instruments—Sweden	ML1900	782.1209	Operatta
ML518	784.190946	Musical instruments—Spain	ML2500-2862	782.4209	Songs—History and criticism
			ML2900-3275	782.2209	Sacred vocal music
ML519	784.19469	Musical instruments—Portugal	ML3000-3190	781.71009	Church music
			ML3001	782.3209	Music in churches
ML520	784.19494	Musical instruments—Switzerland	ML3002-3051	782.3222009	Church music—Catholic Church

LC	Dewey	Subject Heading	LC	Dewey	Subject Heading
ML3060	782.32215009	Church music—Catholic Church (Byzantine rite)	MT62	784.18307	Sonata
			MT68	781.4707	Songs—Accompaniment
ML3100-3188	782.3224009	Church music—Protestant churches	MT68	781.4707	Musical accompaniment
			MT82	781.426	Music—Memorizing
ML3166	782.3223009	Church music—Episcopal Church	MT85	781.4507	Conducting
			MT88	782.507	Choirs (Music)
ML3166	782.3223009	Church music—Church of England	MT90-145	781.17	Music appreciation
			MT125	784.117	Band music—Analysis, appreciation
ML3300-3354	781.5609	Program music			
ML3400-3451	781.55409	Dance music—History and criticism	MT125	784.2117	Orchestral music—Analysis, appreciation
			MT170-805	784.1907	Musical instruments
ML3460	781.55609	Ballet	MT180-258	786.07	Keyboard instruments
ML3469-3541	781.6309	Popular music	MT180	786.507	Organ—Instruction and study
ML3469-3541	784.16309	Popular instrumental music			
ML3505.8-3509	784.165309	Dixieland music	MT190	786.14707	Musical accompaniment
ML3518	784.4809	Dance-orchestra music	MT208	786.5507	Reed-organ—Methods—Self-instruction
ML3519-3520	784.164209	Bluegrass music			
ML3521	784.164309	Blues (Music)	MT220-255	786.207	Piano—Instruction and study
ML3523-3524	784.164209	Country music			
ML3533.8-3534	784.16609	Rock music	MT236	781.42307	Sight-reading (Music)
ML3535	784.16609	Rockabilly music	MT239	786.214707	Musical accompaniment
ML3541	784.16409	Western swing (Music)	MT259-338	787.07	Stringed instruments
ML3545	781.59909	National music—History and criticism	MT320-334	787.5107	Double bass
			MT340-348	788.307	Flute
ML3795	331.28178	Musicians—Salaries, etc.	MT356	788.3307	Fife
ML3797.7-3799	780.89	Ethnomusicology	MT360-378	788.5207	Oboe
ML3800-3920	780.1	Music—Philosophy and aesthetics	MT380-388	788.6207	Clarinet
			MT418	788.907	Brass instruments
ML3800	780.9	Music, Origin of	MT493	788.9707	Fluegelhorn
ML3807-3809	781.232	Musical pitch	MT560-570	787.8807	Banjo
ML3809	784.1928	Musical temperament	MT580-588	787.8707	Guitar
ML3809	781.246	Musical intervals and scales	MT620-634	787.707	Zither—Instruction and study
ML3815	781.25	Harmony			
ML3830-3838	781.11	Music—Psychology	MT700	786.607	Musical instruments (Mechanical)
ML3834	781.24	Melody			
ML3836	781.25	Harmony	MT710	786.8848507	Handbell ringing
ML3845	781.825	Variation (Music)	MT724	786.707	Musical instruments, Electronic
ML3849	780.0398	Music and mythology			
ML3850	781.22(4/6)	Musical Meter and rhythm	MT728	785.143807	Ensemble playing
ML3851	781.24	Melody	MT733.4	784.8307	Marching bands
ML3852	781.25	Harmony	MT737	781.54207	Silent films—Musical accompaniment
ML3855	781.56	Program music			
ML3857-3862	781.552	Dramatic music	MT825-850	782.001	Singing—Methods
ML3858	782.1	Opera	MT870	782.042307	Sight-singing
ML3869	781.71017	Church music	MT875	782.507	Choral singing
ML3919-3920	615.85154	Music therapy	MT882	782.001	Singing—Methods
ML3920	780.0365	Music in prisons	MT949.5	782.98	Whistling
MT	780.7	Music—Instruction and study	N	700	Art
			N1-9.9	705	Art—Periodicals
MT6-7	781	Music—Theory	N10-17	706	Art—Societies, etc.
MT9	780.76	Music—Examinations, questions, etc.	N21	706	Art—Congresses
			N33	703	Art—Dictionaries
MT35	780.1407	Musical shorthand	N40-43	709.2	Art—Biography
MT35	781.424	Ear training	N50-55	702.5	Art—Directories
MT35	780.14	Musical dictation	N61-79	701.17	Aesthetics
MT35	780.148	Musical notation	N61-79	701.15	Imgination
MT38	780.87107	Blind, Music for the	N61-75	701	Art—Philosophy
MT40-67	781.307	Composition (Music)	N61	701.1709031	Aesthetics, Modern—16th century
MT42	781.2207	Tempo (Music)			
MT47	781.2407	Melody			

LC	Dewey	Subject Heading
N61	701.1709032	Aesthetics, Modern—17th Century
N61	701.1709033	Aesthetics, Modern—18th century
N61	701.170902	Aesthetics, Medieval
N61	701.1709034	Aesthetics, Modern—19th century
N61	701.170904	Aesthetics, Modern—20th century
N70	709.0342	Romanticism in art
N72.P5	770	Art and photography
N81-390	707.1	Art—Study and teaching
N325-335	707.1	Art schools
N328-330	707.1073	Art schools—United States
N332	707.104	Art schools—Europe
N400-3990	708	Art museums
N510-880	708.1(3-9)	Art museums—United States
N1010-3690	708.(2-9)	Art museums—Europe
N1020-1560	708.2	Art museums—Great Britain
N1750-1850	708.93	Art museums—Belgium
N2010-2180	708.4	Art museums—France
N2210-2406	708.3	Art museums—Germany
N2410-2430	708.95	Art museums—Greece
N2450-2505	708.92	Art museums—Netherlands
N2510-3065	708.5	Art museums—Italy
N3310-3382	708.7	Art museums—Russia
N3410-3499	708.6	Art museums—Spain
N4000-4042	779.074	Photograph collections
N4390-5098	707.4	Art—Exhibitions
N5198-5299	708	Art—Private collections
N5215-5220	708.1(3-9)	Art—Private collections—United States
N5240-5280	708.(2-8)	Art—Private collections—Europe
N5300-7418	709	Art—History
N5310-5313	709.011	Art, Primitive
N5310-5313	709.011	Art, Prehistoric
N5312-5313	745	Folk art
N5315-5899	709.01	Art, Ancient
N5343-5345	709.31	Oriental antiquities
N5350-5351	709.32	Art, Egyptian
N5370	709.35	Art, Sumerian
N5460	709.3943	Art, Syrian
N5470	709.394	Art, Arab
N5480-5560	709.392	Art, Turkish
N5603-5896.3	709.38	Art, Classical
N5630-5720	709.38	Art, Greek
N5760-5763	709.37	Art, Roman
N5940-6320	709.02	Art, Medieval
N6280	709.0216	Art, Romanesque
N6350-6494	709.03	Art, Modern
N6370-6375	709.024	Art, Renaissance
N6410-6425	709.03(2-3)	Art, Modern—17th-18th centuries
N6410	709.0332	Art, Rococo
N6450-6465	709.034	Art, Modern—19th century
N6465.N44	709.0345	Neo-impressionism (Art)
N6480-6494	709.04	Art, Modern—20th century Modernism (Art)
N6490	700.4112	
N6490	709.04052	Art, Abstract
N6494.A7	709.04012	Art deco
N6494.D3	709.04062	Dadaism
N6538.N5	700.08996073	Afro-American artists
N6540-6545.5	709.71	Art—Canada—History
N6555-.5	709.72	Art—Mexico—History
N6573.2-6582.5	709.728	Art—Central America—History
N6635-6735.5	709.8	Art—South America—History
N6805-6808.5	709.436	Art—Austria—History
N6819-6820.5	709.439	Art—Hungary—History
N6828-6831.5	709.437	Art—Czechoslovakia—History
N6897-6898.5	709.495	Art—Greece—History
N6915-6923	709.45	Art—Italy—History
N6967-6973	709.493	Art—Belgium—History
N7007-7088	709.48	Art—Scandinavia—History
N7105-7108.5	709.46	Art—Spain—History
N7125-7128.5	709.469	Art—Portugal—History
N7260-7355.5	709.5	Art, Oriental
N7429.7-7433	701.8	Composition (Art)
N7429.7-7433	702.8	Art—Technique
N7436.5-.53	745.8	Panoramas
N7475-7485	701.18	Art criticism
N7572	704.9421	Nude in art
N7574	702.8	Artists' models
N7575-7640	704.042	Portraits
N7616	704.942	Portrait miniatures
N7720	700.4548	Dance of death
N7740-7745	704.946	Symbolism in art
N7760-7763	704.947	Art and mythology
N7810-8189.6	704.9482	Christian art and symbolism
N7832	704.9482	Art, Early Christian
N8205	700.421734	Pastoral art
N8217.D3	704.9497928	Dance in art
N8217.E6	704.9428	Erotic art
N8543	702.84	Artists' tools
N8550-8553	684	Picture frames and framing
N8554-8585	702.88	Art—Conservation and restoration
N8580	702.872	Pictures—Copying
N8600	332.63	Art as an investment
N8610-8660	381.457(3-6)	Art dealers
N8665	707.4	Sidewalk art exhibitions
N8795	364.162	Art thieves
NA	720.92	Architects
NA	720	Architecture
NA1-9	720.5	Architecture—Periodicals
NA10-17	720.6	Architecture—Societies, etc.
NA31	720.3	Architecture—Encyclopedias
NA40	720.92	Architecture—Biography
NA50-60	720.25	Architecture—Directories
NA105-112	720.288	Architecture—Conservation and restoration
NA190-1555.5	722-724	Architecture—History
NA205-207	722	Architecture, Primitive
NA210-340	722	Architecture, Ancient
NA215-216	722.2	Architecture, Egyptian
NA220-221	722.51	Architecture, Assyro-Babylonian
NA270-290	722.8	Architecture, Greek

LC	Dewey	Subject Heading	LC	Dewey	Subject Heading
NA277	728.820938	Palaces	NA1023-1034.5	720.9437	Architecture—Czechoslovakia
NA295-340	722.70937	Architecture, Italian	NA1041-1059	720.944	Architecture—France
NA300-301	722.62	Architecture, Etruscan	NA1061-1089	720.943	Architecture—Germany
NA310-340	722.7	Architecture, Roman	NA1091-1103	720.9495	Architecture—Greece
NA320	728.8209376	Palaces	NA1111-1123.3	720.945	Architecture—Italy
NA350-497	723	Architecture, Medieval	NA1141-1153.3	720.9492	Architecture—Netherlands
NA390-419	723.4	Architecture, Romanesque	NA1161-1173.3	720.9493	Architecture—Belgium
NA423-429	723.4	Architecture, Norman	NA1181-1199	720.947	Architecture—Russia
NA440-489	723.5	Architecture, Gothic	NA1466.P6	720.9438	Architecture—Poland
NA490-497	725.18	Military architecture	NA1455.F5	720.94897	Architecture—Finland
NA500-680	724	Architecture, Modern	NA1201-1293.3	720.948	Architecture—Scandinavia
NA510-575	724.12	Architecture, Renaissance	NA1211-1223.3	720.9489	Architecture—Denmark
NA590	724.16	Architecture, Baroque	NA1241-1253.3	720.94912	Architecture—Iceland
NA590	724.19	Architecture, Rococo	NA1261-1273.3	720.9481	Architecture—Norway
NA600	724.2	Neoclassicism (Architecture)	NA1281-1293.3	720.9485	Architecture—Sweden
NA627-640	724.19	Architecture, Modern—17th-18th centuries	NA1301-1313.3	720.946	Architecture, Spanish
NA630	720.94209033	Architecture, Queen Anne	NA1301-1313.3	720.946	Architecture—Spain
NA640	724.19	Architecture, Georgian	NA1321-1333.3	720.9469	Architecture—Portugal
NA645-670	724.5	Architecture, Modern—19th century	NA1341-1353.3	720.9494	Architecture—Switzerland
NA673-682	724.6	Architecture, Modern—20th century	NA1361-1375	720.9561	Architecture—Turkey
NA702.5-939	720.9(7-8)	Architecture, American	NA1381-1393.3	720.9499	Architecture—Bulgaria
NA705-738	720.973	Architecture—United States	NA1421-1433.3	720.9498	Architecture—Romania
NA707	724.1	Architecture, Colonial	NA1441-1453.3	720.9497	Architecture—Yugoslavia
NA740-749.5	720.971	Architecture—Canada	NA1455.F5	720.94897	Architecture—Finland
NA750-759	720.972	Architecture—Mexico	NA1460-1579	720.95	Architecture, Oriental
NA760-790	720.9728	Architecture—Central America	NA1466.P6	720.9438	Architecture—Poland
NA773-775	720.97286	Architecture—Costa Rica	NA1460-1570.3	720.95	Architecture, Oriental
NA776-778	720.97281	Architecture—Guatemala	NA1467-1469	720.9567	Architecture—Iraq
NA779-781	720.97283	Architecture—Honduras	NA1470-1472	720.9538	Architecture—Saudi Arabia
NA782-784	720.97285	Architecture—Nicaragua	NA1476.6-.8	720.95692	Architecture—Lebanon
NA785-787	720.97287	Architecture—Panama	NA1477-1479	720.95694	Architecture—Israel
NA788-790	720.97284	Architecture—El Salvador	NA1479.6-.8	720.95695	Architecture—Jordan
NA791-815	720.9729	Architecture—West Indies	NA1480-1489	720.955	Architecture—Iran
NA800-802	720.97296	Architecture—Bahamas	NA1489.6-.8	720.95691	Architecture—Syria
NA803-805	720.97291	Architecture—Cuba	NA1492-.3	720.9581	Architecture—Afghanistan
NA806-808	720.97294	Architecture—Haiti	NA1492.6-1499	720.957	Architecture—Asiatic Russia
NA809-811	720.97292	Architecture—Jamaica	NA1501-1510.3	720.954	Architecture—India
NA812-814	720.97295	Architecture—Puerto Rico	NA1510.6-.63	720.95493	Architecture—Sri Lanka
NA820-939	720.98	Architecture—South America	NA1510.7-.73	720.95491	Architecture—Pakistan
NA830-839	720.982	Architecture—Argentina	NA1512-.3	720.9591	Architecture—Burma
NA840-849	720.984	Architecture—Bolivia	NA1514-.63	720.9597	Architecture—Vietnam
NA850-859	720.981	Architecture—Brazil	NA1515-.3	720.9596	Architecture—Cambodia
NA860-869	720.983	Architecture—Chile	NA1516-.3	720.9594	Architecture—Laos
NA870-879	720.9861	Architecture—Colombia	NA1521-1523	720.9593	Architecture—Thailand
NA880-889	720.9866	Architecture—Ecuador	NA1525-.8	720.9595	Architecture—Malaysia
NA895	720.9881	Architecture—Guyana	NA1526-.8	720.9598	Architecture—Indonesia
NA896	720.9883	Architecture—Surinam	NA1527-1529	720.9599	Architecture—Philippines
NA897	720.9882	Architecture—French Guiana	NA1540-1549.6	720.951	Architecture—China
NA900-909	720.9892	Architecture—Paraguay	NA1540-1547	720.951	Pagodas
NA910-919	720.985	Architecture—Peru	NA1550-1559.6	720.952	Architecture—Japan
NA920-929	720.9895	Architecture—Uruguay	NA1560-1570.3	720.9519	Architecture—Korea
NA930-939	720.987	Architecture—Venezuela	NA1580-1599	720.96	Architecture—Africa
NA950-1455	720.94	Architecture—Europe	NA1581-1585.3	720.962	Architecture, Egyptian
NA961-981	720.941	Architecture—Great Britain	NA1586-.3	720.963	Architecture—Ethiopia
NA1001-1011.6	720.9436	Architecture—Austria	NA1588-.3	720.965	Architecture—Algeria
NA1012-1022	720.9439	Architecture—Hungary	NA1589-.3	720.9612	Architecture—Libya
			NA1590-.3	720.964	Architecture—Morocco
			NA1591-.3	720.9611	Architecture—Tunisia
			NA1591.7-1596.6	720.968	Architecture—Southern Africa

LC	Dewey	Subject Heading	LC	Dewey	Subject Heading
NA1597-.6	720.9676	Architecture—Africa, East	NA4415	725.1109(4-9)	[Other countries]—Capital and capitol
NA1598-1599	720.966	Architecture—Africa, West			
NA1600-1605.3	720.994	Architecture—Australia	NA4430-4437	725.13	City halls
NA1606-1608	720.993	Architecture—New Zealand	NA4430-4437	725.13	Municipal buildings
NA1610-1613	720.99(5-6)	Architecture—Oceania	NA4440-4447	725.17	Embassy buildings
NA1995	174.972	Architects—Professional ethics	NA4450-4457	725.16	Post office buildings
			NA4470-4477	725.15	Courthouses
NA2000-2320	720.71	Architecture—Study and teaching	NA4490-4497	725.18	Police stations
			NA4610-4710	726.1	Temples
NA2335-2360	720.79	Architecture—Competitions	NA4670	726.2	Mosques
NA2500	720.1	Architecture—Aesthetics	NA4690	726.3	Synagogue architecture
NA2542.7	720.473	Underground architecture	NA4790-6113	726.5	Church architecture
NA2542.A73	720.9154	Architecture—Arid regions	NA4790-5095	726.5	Church buildings
NA2545	720.87	Architecture and the handicapped	NA4800-6113	726.7	Abbeys
			NA4828.5	726.58(1-9)	Protestant church buildings
NA2545.P5	725.087	Public buildings—Access for the physically handicapped	NA4830	726.6	Cathedrals
			NA4850	726.7	Monasteries
NA2600-2635	720.222	Architecture—Designs and plans	NA4870	726.4	Chapels
			NA4910	726.4	Baptisteries
NA2700-2780	720.222	Architectural drawing	NA5000	726.51	Church decoration and ornament
NA2750-2793	721	Architectural design			
NA2760	729.11	Architecture—Composition, proportion, etc.	NA5060	726.5291	Altars
			NA5070	726.5291	Fonts
NA2790	720.22	Architectural models	NA6120-6199	726.8	Tombs
NA2794	729.28	Daylighting	NA6149-6199	726.809	Tombs—[By region or country]
NA2800	729.29	Architectural acoustics			
NA2835-3060	721	Architecture—Details	NA6210-6290	725.2	Commercial buildings
NA2840-2841	729.1	Facades	NA6225	725.21	Shop fronts
NA2850-2856	729.24	Interior architecture	NA6230-6234	725.23	Office buildings
NA2860-2875	721.3	Columns, Corinthian	NA6230-6234	720.483	Tall buildings
NA2860	721.3	Columns, Ionic	NA6240-6245	725.24	Bank buildings
NA2880	721.41	Arches	NA6300-6307	725.39	Airport buildings
NA2890	721.46	Domes	NA6340-6343	725.35	Warehouses
NA2900	721.5	Roofs, Open-timbered	NA6396-6589	725.4	Industrial buildings
NA2920	721.5	Gables	NA6396-6589	725.4	Factories
NA2930	721.5	Spires	NA6400-6589	725.4	Architecture, Industrial
NA2930	721.5	Towers	NA6598	725.4	Employees' buildings and facilities
NA2940-2942	721.2	Walls			
NA2950	721.7	Ceilings	NA6600-6605	727.3	College buildings
NA2970	721.6	Floors	NA6750-6751	725.91	Exhibition buildings
NA3000-3030	721.823	Windows	NA6815	725.83	Auditoriums
NA3010	721.822	Doorways	NA6820-6846	725.822	Theater architecture
NA3040	721.5	Chimneys	NA6820-6845	725.822	Theaters
NA3050-3055	721.8	Fireplaces	NA6845-6846	725.823	Motion picture theaters
NA3060	721.832	Stairs	NA6860-7010	725.827	Stadiums
NA3070	721.84	Balconies	NA6880-.5	725.91	Convention facilities
NA3310-4050	729	Decoration and ornament, Architectural	NA7100-7882	728	Architecture, Domestic
			NA7100-7884	728	Dwellings
NA3705	721.0443	Tiles	NA7125	721.84	Porches
NA3750-3860	729.7	Pavements, Mosaic	NA7127-7135	728	Architecture, Domestic—Designs and plans
NA3750-3860	729.7	Mosaics			
NA4125	721.0445	Concrete construction	NA7150	728	Brick houses
NA4140	721.04496	Glass construction	NA7160	728	Concrete houses
NA4170-5095	725	Public buildings	NA7160	728	Stucco
NA4201-4385	725.09(4-9)	Public buildings—[By region or country]	NA7175	728	Half-timbered houses
			NA7180	728	Steel houses
NA4205-4228.3	725.0973	Public buildings—United States	NA7195.A4	728.0846	Aged—Dwellings
			NA7201-7333	728.09(4-9)	Architecture, Domestic—[By region or country]
NA4410-4417	725.11	Capitols			
NA4411-4413	725.110973	United States—Capital and capitol	NA7520	728.312	Row houses
			NA7531	728.370473	Earth sheltered houses

LC	Dewey	Subject Heading	LC	Dewey	Subject Heading
NA7551-7555	728.37	Cottages	NB285-287	730.97287	Sculpture—Panama
NA7570-7572.5	728.091733	Suburban homes	NB288-290	730.97284	Sculpture—El Salvador
NA7574-7579	728.7	Vacation homes	NB291-315	730.9729	Sculpture—West Indies
NA7710-7786	728.82	Palaces	NB300-302	730.97296	Sculpture—Bahamas
NA7710-7786	728.81	Castles	NB303-305	730.97291	Sculpture—Cuba
NA7800-7853	728.5	Hotels	NB306-308	730.97294	Sculpture—Haiti
NA7860-7863	728.314	Apartment houses	NB309-311	730.97292	Sculpture—Jamaica
NA7910-7977	728.4	Clubhouses	NB312-314	730.97295	Sculpture—Puerto Rico
NA8200-8260	728.92	Farm buildings	NB320-439	730.98	Sculpture—South America
NA8208-8210	728.6	Farmhouses	NB330-339	730.982	Sculpture—Argentina
NA8230	728.922	Barns	NB340-349	730.984	Sculpture—Bolivia
NA8240	728.92	Granaries	NB350-359	730.981	Sculpture—Brazil
NA8280	728.922	Dairy barns	NB360-369	730.983	Sculpture—Chile
NA8348	725.38	Garages	NB370-379	730.9861	Sculpture—Colombia
NA8375	728.93	Patios	NB380-389	730.9866	Sculpture—Ecuador
NA8390-8392	631.27	Fences	NB395	730.9881	Sculpture—Guyana
NA8470	728.73	Log cabins	NB396	730.9883	Sculpture—Surinam
NA8480	721.04497	Buildings, Prefabricated	NB397	730.9882	Sculpture—French Guiana
NA9000-9428	711.3	Regional planning	NB400-409	730.9892	Sculpture—Paraguay
NA9000-9284	711	City planning	NB410-419	730.985	Sculpture—Peru
NA9050.5	725	Public architecture	NB420-429	730.9895	Sculpture—Uruguay
NA9053.B58	711.41	Blocks (City planning)	NB430-439	730.987	Sculpture—Venezuela
NA9053.N	711.45	New towns	NB450-955	730.94	Sculpture—Europe
NA9070-9072	711.55	Plazas	NB461-481	730.941	Sculpture—Great Britain
NA9101-9285	711.09(4-9)	City planning—[By region or country]	NB501-511.6	730.9436	Sculpture—Austria
			NB512-522.6	730.9439	Sculpture—Hungary
NA9325-9355	725.94	Soldiers' monuments	NB523-534.5	730.9437	Sculpture—Czechoslovakia
NA9325-9330	725.94	War memorials	NB541-553.3	730.944	Sculpture—France
NA9335-9355	725.94	Monuments	NB561-589	730.943	Sculpture—Germany
NA9360-9380	725.96	Triumphal arches	NB591-603	730.9495	Sculpture—Greece
NA9400-9425	714	Fountains	NB611-623.3	730.945	Sculpture—Italy
NB	730	Sculpture	NB641-653.3	730.9492	Sculpture—Netherlands
NB	731.7	Statues	NB661-673.3	730.9493	Sculpture—Belgium
NB1	730.5	Sculpture—Periodicals	NB681-699	730.947	Sculpture—Russia
NB16-17	730.74	Sculpture—Exhibitions	NB955.P6	730.9438	Sculpture—Poland
NB35	730.216	Sculpture—Catalogs	NB955.F5	730.94897	Sculpture—Finland
NB60-615	730.9	Sculpture—History	NB701-793.3	730.948	Sculpture—Scandinavia
NB62-64	732.2	Sculpture, Primitive	NB711-723.3	730.9489	Sculpture—Denmark
NB69-169	732.2	Sculpture, Ancient	NB741-753.3	730.94912	Sculpture—Iceland
NB69-169	732.2	Marble sculpture, Ancient	NB761-773.3	730.9481	Sculpture—Norway
NB90-105	733.3	Sculpture, Greek	NB781-793.3	730.9485	Sculpture—Sweden
NB115-120	733.5	Sculpture, Roman	NB801-813.3	730.946	Sculpture—Spain
NB135-143	731.456	Bronze sculpture	NB821-833.3	730.9469	Sculpture—Portugal
NB144	733.3	Marble sculpture, Classical	NB841-853.3	730.9494	Sculpture—Switzerland
NB145-159	731.2	Terra-cotta sculpture	NB861-873.3	730.9561	Sculpture—Turkey
NB170-180	734	Sculpture, Medieval	NB921-933.3	730.9498	Sculpture—Romania
NB172	734.224	Sculpture, Byzantine	NB941-953.3	730.9497	Sculpture—Yugoslavia
NB185-198.5	735	Sculpture, Modern	NB960-1070.3	730.95	Sculpture—Asia
NB180	734.25	Sculpture, Gothic	NB967-969	730.9567	Sculpture—Iraq
NB190	735.21	Sculpture, Renaissance	NB970-972	730.9538	Sculpture—Saudi Arabia
NB193	735.21	Sculpture, Rococo	NB976.6-.8	730.95692	Sculpture—Lebanon
NB201-1114	730.9(4-9)	Sculpture—[By region or country]	NB977-979	730.95694	Sculpture—Israel
			NB979.6-.8	730.95695	Sculpture—Jordan
NB205-238	730.973	Sculpture—United States	NB980-989	730.955	Sculpture—Iran
NB240-249.5	730.971	Sculpture—Canada	NB989.6-.8	730.95691	Sculpture—Syria
NB250-259	730.972	Sculpture—Mexico	NB992-.3	730.9581	Sculpture—Afghanistan
NB260-290	730.9728	Sculpture—Central America	NB992.4-999	730.957	Sculpture—Asiatic Russia
NB273-275	730.97286	Sculpture—Costa Rica	NB1001-1010.3	730.954	Sculpture—India
NB276-278	730.97281	Sculpture—Guatemala	NB1010.6-.63	730.95493	Sculpture—Sri Lanka
NB279-281	730.97283	Sculpture—Honduras	NB1010.7-.73	730.95491	Sculpture—Pakistan
NB282-284	730.97285	Sculpture—Nicaragua	NB1012-.3	730.9591	Sculpture—Burma

LC	Dewey	Subject Heading	LC	Dewey	Subject Heading
NB1014-.63	730.9597	Sculpture—Vietnam	NC87-.5	741.09033	Drawing—18th century
NB1015-.3	730.9596	Sculpture—Cambodia	NC90-.5	741.09034	Drawing—19th century
NB1016-.3	730.9594	Sculpture—Laos	NC95-.5	741.0904	Drawing—20th century
NB1021-1023	730.9593	Sculpture—Thailand	NC101-377	741.09(3-9)	Drawing—[By region or country]
NB1025-.8	730.9595	Sculpture—Malaysia			
NB1026-.8	730.9598	Sculpture—Indonesia	NC105-139.3	741.0973	Drawing—United States
NB1027-1029	730.9599	Sculpture—Philippines	NC141-143.3	741.0971	Drawing—Canada
NB1040-1049.6	730.951	Sculpture, Chinese	NC144-146	741.0972	Drawing—Mexico
NB1050-1059.6	730.952	Sculpture, Japanese	NC147-167	741.09728	Drawing—Central America
NB1060-1070.6	730.9519	Sculpture—Korea	NC153-155	741.097286	Drawing—Costa Rica
NB1080-1099	730.96	Sculpture—Africa	NC156-158	741.097281	Drawing—Guatemala
NB1081-1085.3	730.962	Sculpture—Egypt	NC159-161	741.097283	Drawing—Honduras
NB1086.3	730.963	Sculpture—Ethiopia	NC162-164	741.097285	Drawing—Nicaragua
NB1088.3	730.965	Sculpture—Algeria	NC165	741.097287	Drawing—Panama
NB1089.3	730.9612	Sculpture—Libya	NC167	741.097284	Drawing—El Salvador
NB1090.3	730.964	Sculpture—Morocco	NC168-186	741.09729	Drawing—West Indies
NB1091.6	730.9611	Sculpture—Tunisia	NC171-173	741.097296	Drawing—Bahamas
NB1091.7-1096.6	730.968	Sculpture—Africa, Southern	NC174-176	741.097291	Drawing—Cuba
NB1097-.6	730.9676	Sculpture—Africa, East	NC177-179	741.097294	Drawing—Haiti
NB1098-1099	730.966	Sculpture—Africa, West	NC180-182	741.097292	Drawing—Jamaica
NB1100-1105.3	730.994	Sculpture—Australia	NC183-185	741.097295	Drawing—Puerto Rico
NB1106-1108	730.993	Sculpture—New Zealand	NC189-224	741.098	Drawing—South America
NB1110-1113	730.99(5-6)	Sculpture—Oceania	NC192-194	741.0982	Drawing—Argentina
NB1115	730.92	Sculptors	NC195-197	741.0984	Drawing—Bolivia
NB1142.5	730.11	Sculpture—Appreciation	NC198-200	741.0981	Drawing—Brazil
NB1170-1195	731.028	Sculpture—Technique	NC204-206	741.09861	Drawing—Colombia
NB1180-1185	731.42	Modelling	NC207-209	741.09866	Drawing—Ecuador
NB1190	731.452	Plaster casts	NC213-215	741.09892	Drawing—Paraguay
NB1199	731.48	Sculpture—Conservation and restoration	NC216-218	741.0985	Drawing—Peru
			NC219-221	741.09895	Drawing—Uruguay
NB1208-1210	731.463	Stone carving	NC222-224	741.0987	Drawing—Venezuela
NB1215	731.2	Concrete sculpture	NC225-312	741.094	Drawing—Europe
NB1218	731.2	Marble sculpture	NC228-242	741.0941	Drawing—Great Britain
NB1220	731.2	Metal sculpture	NC246-248	741.0944	Drawing—France
NB1240.I75	731.2	Iron sculpture	NC249-251.6	741.0943	Drawing—Germany
NB1250	731.2	Driftwood sculpture	NC252-254	741.09495	Drawing—Greece
NB1265	731.2	Terra-cotta sculpture	NC255-257	741.0945	Drawing—Italy
NB1270.G4	731.2	Glass sculpture	NC267-269	741.0947	Drawing—Russia
NB1270.G5	731.2	Fiberglass craft	NC270-284	741.0948	Drawing—Scandinavia
NB1270.P3	731.2	Paper sculpture	NC273-275	741.09489	Drawing—Denmark
NB1270.P5	731.2	Plastic sculpture	NC276-278	741.094912	Drawing—Iceland
NB1280-1291	731.54	Bas-relief	NC279-281	741.09481	Drawing—Norway
NB1293-1310	731.82	Portrait sculpture	NC282-284	741.09485	Drawing—Sweden
NB1300	731.74	Busts	NC285	741.0946	Drawing—Spain
NB1310	731.75	Masks (Sculpture)	NC288-290	741.09469	Drawing—Portugal
NB1312-1313	731.81	Equestrian statues	NC291-293	741.09494	Drawing—Switzerland
NB1315	731.55	Mobiles (Sculpture)	NC294-296	741.09561	Drawing—Turkey
NB1330-1685	731.76	Monuments	NC297-308	741.09496	Drawing—Balkan Peninsula
NB1501-1685	731.7609(4-9)	Monuments—[By region or country]	NC315-359	741.095	Drawing—Asia
			NC318-320	741.0956	Drawing—Middle East
NB1800-1895	736.5	Sepulchral monuments	NC320	741.095694	Drawing—Israel
NB1930-1936	731.82	Figure sculpture	NC321-323	741.0955	Drawing—Iran
NB1940-1942	731.832	Animal sculpture	NC324.6	741.09581	Drawing—Afghanistan
NC	741	Drawing	NC325	741.0957	Drawing—Asiatic Russia
NC1	741.05	Drawing—Periodicals	NC327-329	741.0954	Drawing—India
NC15-17	741.074	Drawing—Exhibitions	NC330	741.095493	Drawing—Sri Lanka
NC30-33	741.074	Drawing—Private collections	NC331	741.095491	Drawing—Pakistan
NC37-38.5	741.0294	Drawing—Catalogs	NC334.C3	741.09596	Drawing—Cambodia
NC70-75	741.0902	Drawing, Medieval	NC334.L3	741.09594	Drawing—Laos
NC85	741.090(24-31)	Drawing, Renaissance	NC334.V5-.V55	741.09597	Drawing—Vietnam
NC86	741.09032	Drawing—17th century	NC335	741.09593	Drawing—Thailand

LC	Dewey	Subject Heading	LC	Dewey	Subject Heading
NC336-338	741.09595	Drawing—Malaysia	ND	750	Painting
NC339-341	741.09598	Drawing—Indonesia	ND34-38	759	Painting—Biography
NC342-344	741.09599	Drawing—Philippines	ND40-45	750.294	Painting—Catalogs
NC348-350	741.0951	Drawing—China	ND49-813	759	Painting—History
NC351-353	741.0952	Drawing—Japan	ND70-130	759.01	Painting, Ancient
NC353.6-.7	741.09519	Drawing—Korea	ND140-146	759.02	Painting, Medieval
NC360-368.6	741.096	Drawing—Africa	ND146	750.882971	Painting, Islamic
NC361-365.6	741.0961	Drawing—Africa, North	ND160-196	759.06	Painting, Modern
NC363-.3	741.0962	Drawing—Egypt	ND170-172	759.03	Painting, Renaissance
NC365.7	741.0963	Drawing—Ethiopia	ND177-188	759.04	Painting, Modern—17th-18th centuries
NC366-6	741.09676	Drawing—Africa, East			
NC367-.6	741.0966	Drawing—Africa, West	ND190-192	759.05	Painting, Modern—19th century
NC368-.6	741.0968	Drawing—Africa, Southern			
NC369-371	741.0994	Drawing—Australia	ND195-196	759.06	Painting, Modern—20th century
NC372-374	741.0993	Drawing—New Zealand			
NC375-376	741.099(5-6)	Drawing—Oceania	ND204-1113	759.(1-9)	Painting—[By region or country]
NC390-670	741.071	Drawing—Study and teaching			
			ND205-238	759.13	Painting—United States
NC703	745.4	Design	ND240-249.5	759.11	Painting—Canada
NC730-758	741.2	Drawing—Technique	ND250-259	759.972	Painting—Mexico
NC745	741.018	Proportion (Art)	ND260-290	759.9728	Painting—Central America
NC749-750	742	Perspective	ND273-275	759.97286	Painting—Costa Rica
NC755	742	Shades and shadows	ND276-278	759.97281	Painting—Guatemala
NC760-783.8	743.49	Anatomy, Artistic	ND279-281	759.97283	Painting—Honduras
NC765-778	743.4	Figure drawing	ND282-284	759.97285	Painting—Nicaragua
NC770	743.42	Face	ND285-287	759.97287	Painting—Panama
NC775	743.5	Drapery in art	ND288-290	759.97284	Painting—El Salvador
NC780-783.8	743.6	Animals in art	ND291-315	759.9729	Painting—West Indies
NC790-800	743.836	Landscape drawing	ND300-302	759.97296	Painting—Bahamas
NC825.E76	743.828	Erotic drawing	ND303-305	759.97291	Painting—Cuba
NC845-915	741.2	Drawing instruments	ND306-308	759.97294	Painting—Haiti
NC850	741.22	Charcoal drawing	ND309-311	759.97292	Painting—Jamaica
NC855-875	741.23	Crayon drawing	ND312-314	759.97295	Painting—Puerto Rico
NC880	741.235	Pastel drawing	ND320-439	759.98	Painting—South America
NC890-895	741.24	Pencil drawing	ND330-339	759.982	Painting—Argentina
NC900-902	741.25	Silverpoint drawing	ND340-349	759.984	Painting—Bolivia
NC905	741.26	Pen drawing	ND350-359	759.981	Painting—Brazil
NC910-.5	741.7	Silhouettes	ND360-369	759.983	Painting—Chile
NC915.R8	760	Rubbing	ND370-379	759.9861	Painting—Colombia
NC960-995.8	741.6	Illustration of books	ND380-389	759.9866	Painting—Ecuador
NC965.85	741.6	Picture books	ND395	759.9881	Painting—Guyana
NC997-1003	741.6	Commercial art	ND396	759.9883	Painting—Surinam
NC997.A1	741.605	Commercial art—Periodicals	ND397	759.9882	Painting—French Guiana
NC1000	741.6071	Commercial art—Study and teaching	ND400-409	759.9892	Painting—Paraguay
			ND410-419	759.985	Painting—Peru
NC1300-1766	741.5	Caricatures and cartoons	ND420-429	759.9895	Painting—Uruguay
NC1300	741.505	Caricatures and cartoons—Periodicals	ND430-439	759.987	Painting—Venezuela
			ND450-955	759.(2-8)	Painting—Europe
NC1310-1312	741.5074	Caricatures and cartoons—Exhibitions	ND461-481	759.2	Painting—Great Britain
			ND501-511.6	759.36	Painting—Austria
NC1400-1762	741.59(4-9)	Caricatures and cartoons—[By region or country]	ND512-522.6	759.39	Painting—Hungary
			ND541-553.3	759.4	Painting—France
NC1470-1479	827.0222	English wit and humor, Pictorial	ND568-589	759.3	Painting—Germany
			ND591-603.3	759.3	Painting—Greece
NC1765-1766	741.58	Animated films	ND611-623.3	759.5	Painting—Italy
NC1800-1850	741.674	Posters	ND681-699	759.7	Painting—Russia
NC1849.T68	741.674	Travel posters	ND701-793.3	759.8	Painting—Scandinavia
NC1870-1879	741.683	Postcards	ND711-723.3	759.89	Painting—Denmark
NC1882-1883.3	741.66	Sound recordings—Album covers	ND761-773.3	759.81	Painting—Norway
			ND781-793.3	759.85	Painting—Sweden
NC1920-1940	741.217	Drawing—Copying	ND801-813.3	759.6	Painting—Spain

LC	Dewey	Subject Heading	LC	Dewey	Subject Heading
ND821-833.3	759.69	Painting—Portugal	ND1309.6	757.0904	Portrait painting—20th century
ND861-873.3	759.9561	Painting—Turkey			
ND955.F5	759.897	Painting—Finland	ND1311-.9	757.0973	Portrait painting—United States
ND960-1070.3	759.95	Painting—Asia			
ND967-969	759.9567	Painting, Iraqi	ND1313-1324	757.0904	Portrait painting—Europe
ND970-972	759.9538	Painting—Saudi Arabia	ND1314-.6	757.0941	Portrait painting—Great Britain
ND976.6-.8	759.95692	Painting—Lebanon			
ND977-979	759.95694	Painting—Israel	ND1316-.6	757.0944	Portrait painting—France
ND979-.8	759.95695	Painting—Jordan	ND1317-.7	757.0943	Portrait painting—Germany
ND980-989	759.955	Painting—Iran	ND1318-.6	757.0945	Portrait painting—Italy
ND989.6-.8	759.95691	Painting—Syria	ND1319-.6	757.09492	Portrait painting—Netherlands
ND992-.3	759.9581	Painting—Afghanistan			
ND992.4-999	759.957	Painting—Asiatic Russia	ND1320-.6	757.0947	Portrait painting—Russia
ND999.P6	759.38	Painting—Poland	ND1322-.6	757.0956	Portrait painting—Spain
ND1001-1010.3	759.954	Painting—India	ND1325-1326.8	757.095	Portrait painting—Asia
ND1010.6-.63	759.95493	Painting—Sri Lanka	ND1328-1329	759	Portrait painting—Biography
ND1010.7-.73	759.95491	Painting—Pakistan	ND1329.8-1337	757.7	Portrait miniatures
ND1012-.3	759.9591	Painting—Burma	ND1340-1367	758.1	Landscape painting
ND1014-.63	759.9597	Painting—Vietnam	ND1351-1367	758.10973	Landscape painting—[By region or country]
ND1015-.3	759.9596	Painting—Cambodia			
ND1016-.3	759.9594	Painting—Laos	ND1351-.6	758.109(3-9)	Landscape painting—United States
ND1021-1023	759.9593	Painting—Thailand			
ND1025-.8	759.9595	Painting—Malaysia	ND1352	758.109(71-8)	Landscape painting—[Other American countries]
ND1026-.8	759.9598	Painting—Indonesia			
ND1027-1029	759.9599	Painting—Philippines	ND1353-1364	758.1094	Landscape painting—Europe
ND1040-1049.6	759.951	Painting—China			
ND1050-1059.6	759.952	Painting—Japan	ND1354-.6	758.109411	Landscape painting—Great Britain
ND1050-1059.6	759.952	Painting, Japanese			
ND1060-1070.3	759.9519	Painting—Korea	ND1356-.6	758.10944	Landscape painting—France
ND1060-1070.3	759.9519	Painting, Korean			
ND1080-1099	759.96	Painting—Africa	ND1357-.6	758.10943	Landscape painting—Germany
ND1081-1085.3	759.962	Painting—Egypt			
ND1086-.3	759.963	Painting—Ethiopia	ND1358-.6	758.10945	Landscape painting—Italy
ND1088-.3	759.965	Painting—Algeria	ND1362-.6	758.10946	Landscape painting—Spain
ND1089-.3	759.9612	Painting—Libya			
ND1090-.3	759.964	Painting—Morocco	ND1365-.96	758.1095	Landscape painting—Asia
ND1091-.3	759.9611	Painting—Tunisia	ND1370-1375	758.2	Marine painting
ND1091.7-1096.6	759.968	Painting—Africa, Southern	ND1380-1383	758.3	Animals in art
ND1097-.6	759.9676	Painting—Africa, East	ND1390-1400	758.4	Still-life painting
ND1098-1099	759.966	Painting—Africa, West	ND1450-1452	754	Genre painting
ND1100-1105.3	759.994	Painting—Australia	ND1505	751.4	Brushwork
ND1106-1108	759.993	Painting—New Zealand	ND1510	751.2	Pigments
ND1110-1113	759.99(5-6)	Painting—Oceania	ND1535	751.426	Acrylic painting
ND1115-1120	750.71	Painting—Study and teaching	ND1630-1662	751.6	Painting—Conservation and restoration
ND1142-1146	750	Pictures	ND1700-2495	751.422	Watercolor painting
ND1159	751.77	Small painting	ND2110-2115	751.422071	Watercolor painting—Study and teaching
ND1265	709.04042	Expressionism (Art)			
ND1267	700.4145	Primitivism in art	ND2190-2192	751.42242	Figure painting
ND1290-1293	757	Figure painting	ND2200-2202	751.42242	Portrait painting
ND1300-1337	757	Portrait painting	ND2240-2243	751.422436	Landscape painting
ND1308	757.090(24-31)	Portrait painting—15th century	ND2270-2272	751.422437	Marine painting
			ND2290-2305	751.422435	Still-life painting
ND1308	757.09031	Portrait painting—16th century	ND2460	741.26	Brush drawing
			ND2480	751.46	Encaustic painting
ND1309.3	757.09032	Portrait painting—17th century	ND2550-2877	751.73	Mural painting and decoration
ND1309.4	757.09033	Portrait painting—18th century	ND2601-2877	751.7309(4-9)	Mural painting—[By region or country]
ND1309.5	757.09034	Portrait painting—19th century	ND2880-2881	751.74	Panoramas
			ND2880-.5	751.74	Diorama

LC	Dewey	Subject Heading	LC	Dewey	Subject Heading
ND2885-2888	751.75	Scene painting	NE1710-1719	760.09033	Engraving—18th century
ND2889-3416	745.67	Illumination of books and manuscripts	NE1720.5-1739	760.09034	Engraving—19th century
			NE1740-1749	760.0904	Engraving—20th century
ND2893	745.67074	Illumination of books and manuscripts—Exhibitions	NE1815-1816.5	766.2	Mezzotint engraving
			NE1843-1844	764.8	Serigraphy
ND2910	745.670901	Illumination of books and manuscripts, Ancient	NE1850-1879	769	Color prints
			NE1940-2232.5	767.2	Etching
ND2920-2980	745.670902	Illumination of books and manuscripts, Medieval	NE1950-1955	767.2074	Etching—Exhibitions
			NE1960	767.20294	Etching—Catalogs
ND2990	745.67090 (24-31)	Illumination of books and manuscripts—Renaissance	NE1980-2055.5	767.209	Etching—History
			NE1990-1992	767.209033	Etching—18th century
ND3001-3294.5	745.6709(4-9)	Illumination of books and manuscripts—[By region or country]	NE1994-1995	767.209034	Etching—19th century
			NE1997-1998	767.20904	Etching—20th century
			NE2001-2096.3	767.209(4-9)	Etching—[By region or country]
NE	760	Engraving			
NE	769	Prints	NE2110	767.2092	Etchers
NE1	769.05	Prints—Periodicals	NE2220-2225	767.3	Dry-point
NE20	769.03	Prints—Encyclopedias	NE2230	766.3	Aquatint
NE57-59	769.12	Prints—Private collections	NE2250-2529	763	Lithography
NE62	380.145769	Prints—Marketing	NE2272-2275	763.074	Lithography—Exhibitions
NE63-75	769.0294	Prints—Catalogs	NE2280	763.0294	Lithography—Catalogs
NE380	769.0288	Prints—Conservation and restoration	NE2295-2396.3	763.09	Lithography—History
			NE2297	763.09034	Lithography—19th century
NE400-773	769.9	Prints—History	NE2298	763.0904	Lithography—20th century
NE501-794.5	769.9(4-9)	Prints—[By region or country]	NE2301-2396.3	763.09(4-9)	Lithography—[By region or country]
NE539.3.A35	769.08996073	Afro-American prints	NE2410	763.092	Lithographers
NE800	769.92	Engravers	NE2500-2529	764.2	Chromolithography
NE820	760.278	Engravers' marks	NE2690	748.62	Glass engraving
NE830-835	760.28	Prints—Technique	NE2700-2710	765	Engraving (Metal-work)
NE880-885	769.12	Prints—Collectors and collecting	NE2800-2890	760	Engraving—Printing
			NK	745.1	Antiques
NE886	760.04	Engraving—Themes, motives	NK	745	Art objects
			NK1-9	745.105	Antiques—Periodicals
NE957-.3	769.437	Naval prints	NK28	745.103	Antiques—Encyclopedias
NE960-.3	769.49796	Sporting prints	NK30	745.103	Antiques—Dictionaries
NE965-.3	741.685	Business cards	NK50-440	745.1071	Antiques—Study and teaching
NE1000-1325	761.2	Wood-engraving			
NE1000	761.205	Wood-engraving—Periodicals	NK492	745.5928	Miniature objects
NE1010-1012	761.2074	Wood-engraving—Exhibitions	NK512-520	745.1074	Antiques—Exhibitions
NE1030-1196.3	761.209	Wood-engraving—History	NK530-570	745.1074	Antiques—Private collections
NE1050-1075	761.209024	Wood-engraving—15th century			
			NK610-685	745.0901	Art objects, Ancient
NE1050-1075	761.209031	Wood-engraving—16th century	NK665-680	745.0938	Art objects, Classical
			NK801-1094.5	745.09(4-9)	Art objects—[By region or country]
NE1050-1075	761.209032	Wood-engraving—17th century			
			NK839.3.A35	745.08996073	Afro-American decorative arts
NE1085-1088	761.209033	Wood-engraving—18th century			
			NK1125-1130	745.075	Art objects—Collectors and collecting
NE1090-1093	761.209034	Wood-engraving—19th century			
			NK1128	745.102872	Antiques—Reproduction
NE1095-1097	761.20904	Wood-engraving—20th century	NK1133-.26	745.0294	Art objects—Catalogs
			NK1135-1149.5	745	Arts and crafts movement
NE1101-1196.3	761.209(4-9)	Wood-engraving—[By region or country]	NK1160-1590	745.4	Design
			NK1160-1590	745.4	Decoration and ornament
NE1410-1412	760.074	Engraving—Exhibitions	NK1170	745.4071	Design—Study and teaching
NE1638	760.09023	Engraving—14th century	NK1177	745.441	Decoration and ornament, Primitive
NE1655-1656	760.09024	Engraving—15th century			
NE1665-1666	760.09031	Engraving—16th century	NK1180-1250	745.442	Decoration and ornament, Ancient
NE1670-1690	760.09032	Engraving—17th century			

LC	Dewey	Subject Heading	LC	Dewey	Subject Heading
NK1260-1295	745.442	Decoration and ornament, Medieval	NK4295-.5	738.37	Delftware
NK1270-1275	745.442088297	Decoration and ornament, Islamic	NK4360-4367	738.3	Stoneware
			NK4370-4584	738.2	Porcelain
NK1285	745.442	Decoration and ornament, Romanesque	NK4660	738.82	Hummel figurines
			NK4695.F6	738.8	Food warmers
NK1295	745.442	Decoration and ornament, Gothic	NK4695.T33	738.38	Ceramic tableware
			NK4870	745.594	Fans
NK1330	745.443	Decoration and ornament, Renaissance	NK4891.3-4894.4	745.5923	Dollhouses
			NK4891.3-4894.4	745.59221	Dolls
NK1345	745.443	Decoration and ornament, Baroque	NK4997-5024	738.4	Enamel and enameling
			NK5100-5440	748	Glass
NK1355	745.443	Decoration and ornament, Rococo	NK5100-5440	748.2	Glassware
			NK5200-5205	748.6	Cut glass
NK1652.25	745.442	Decoration and ornament, Byzantine	NK5300-5430	748.50282	Glass painting and staining
			NK5430	748.50285	Mosaics
NK1676	745.40882943	Decoration and ornament, Buddhist	NK5439.E5	748.6	Enameled glass
			NK5440.D75	748.83	Drinking glasses
			NK5440.D85	748.83	Dwarf ale glasses
NK1700-3505	747	Interior decoration	NK5440.P3	748.84	Paperweights
NK2000-2096.3	747.2(1-9)	Interior decoration—[By region or country]	NK5440.S49	748.8	Glass shoes
			NK5561	736.20932	Scarabs
NK2115.5.D73	747.5	Drapery in interior decoration	NK5720-5722	736.222	Cameos
			NK6020-6022	736.6	Bone carving
NK2117.B33	747.78	Bathrooms	NK6200-6210	745.531	Leatherwork
NK2117.D5	747.76	Dining room furniture	NK6400-8459	739	Art metal-work
NK2117.D5	747.76	Dining rooms	NK6400-8459	739	Metal-work
NK2117.L5	747.75	Living room furniture	NK6600-6999	739.7	Weapons
NK2190-2192	747.86	Church decoration and ornament	NK6700-6799	739.722	Swords
			NK6808	739.752	Shields
NK2200-2750	749	Furniture	NK7100-7695	739.23	Silverwork
NK2210-2211	747.074	Furniture—Exhibitions	NK7234-7235	739.2383	Silver flatware
NK2220	749.074	Furniture—Private collections	NK7300-7695	739.27	Jewelry
			NK7440-7459	739.2782	Rings
NK2235	749	Furniture—Styles	NK7650-7690	739.27	Precious stones
NK2401-2694.5	749.2(1-9)	Furniture—[By region or country]	NK8400-8420	739.533	Pewter
			NK8440-.2	748.8	Mirrors
NK2740	749.3	Shelving (Furniture)	NK8470-8475	745.0228	Miniature objects
NK2775-2898	747.5	Rugs	NK8475.A7	739.70228	Miniature weapons
NK2775-2898	747.5	Carpets	NK8500	738.5	Mosaics
NK2790	747.5074	Rugs—Private collections	NK8643	745.55	Shellcraft
NK2808-2810	746.75095	Rugs, Oriental	NK8800-9505.5	746	Textile design
NK2809.I8	746.70882971	Rugs, Islamic	NK8800-9505.5	746.4	Needlework
NK2910	749.3	Screens	NK9100-9499	746.46	Patchwork
NK2910	746.3	Wall hangings	NK9206.4.H56	746.44	Embroidery, Hmong
NK2975-3049	746.3	Tapestry	NK9510	745.74	Decalcomania
NK3175-3296.3	746.94	Drapery	NK9600-9955	745.51	Woodwork
NK3375-3496.3	747.3	Wallpaper	NK9700-9799	736.4	Wood-carving
NK3600-3640	745.61	Lettering	NK9900-.7	745.726	Lacquer and lacquering
NK3649.5-.55	746.412	Basketwork	NX	700	Arts
NK3650-.5	745.582	Beadwork	NX1-9	700.5	Arts—Periodicals
NK3685	745.5933	Candlesticks	NX70	700.3	Arts—Encyclopedias
NK3700-4695	738	Pottery	NX80	700.3	Arts—Dictionaries
NK3800-3855	738.0901	Pottery, Ancient	NX501-596.3	700.9(3-9)	Arts—[By region or country]
NK3870-3885	738.0902	Pottery, Medieval	NX503-512.3	700.973	Arts—United States
NK4001-4184	738.09(4-9)	Pottery—[By region or country]	NX513-.3	700.971	Arts—Canada
			NX514	700.972	Arts—Mexico
NK4200-4210	738.092	Potters	NX515-522	700.9728	Arts—Central America
NK4230	738.075	Pottery—Collectors and collecting	NX517	700.97286	Arts—Costa Rica
			NX518	700.97281	Arts—Guatemala
NK4277	738.27	Blue and white transfer ware	NX519	700.97283	Arts—Honduras
			NX520	700.97285	Arts—Nicaragua

148

LC	Dewey	Subject Heading	LC	Dewey	Subject Heading
NX521	700.97287	Arts—Panama	NX588.7	700.963	Arts—Ethiopia
NX522	700.97284	Arts—El Salvador	NX588.8-.9	700.9676	Arts—Africa, East
NX523-529	700.9729	Arts—West Indies	NX589-.6	700.966	Arts—Africa, West
NX524	700.97296	Arts—Bahamas	NX589.7-.8	700.968	Arts—Africa, Southern
NX525	700.97291	Arts—Cuba	NX590	700.994	Arts—Australia
NX526	700.97294	Arts—Haiti	NX593	700.993	Arts—New Zealand
NX527	700.97292	Arts—Jamaica	NX595-596	700.99(5-6)	Arts—Oceania
NX528	700.97295	Arts—Puerto Rico	NX600.D3	709.04062	Dadaism
NX530-541	700.98	Arts—South America	NX600.S9	709.04062	Surrealism
NX531	700.982	Arts—Argentina	NX636	702.874	Arts—Forgeries
NX532	700.984	Arts—Bolivia	NX650.E7	704.9428	Pornography
NX533	700.981	Arts—Brazil	NX688	704.9489	Arts, Islamic
NX534	700.983	Arts—Chile	NX700-750	700.79	Arts—Endowments
NX535	700.9861	Arts—Colombia	P1-410	400	Language and languages
NX536	700.9866	Arts—Ecuador	P1-10	405	Language and languages—Periodicals
NX538	700.9892	Arts—Paraguay			
NX539	700.985	Arts—Peru	P29	403	Language and languages—Dictionaries
NX540	700.9895	Arts—Uruguay			
NX541	700.987	Arts—Venezuela	P35	417.7	Linguistic paleontology
NX542-571	700.94	Arts—Europe	P37	401.9	Psycholinguistics
NX543-547.6	700.941	Arts—Great Britain	P40	306.44	Sociolinguistics
NX548	700.9436	Arts—Austria	P47	801.959	Criticism, Textual
NX549	700.944	Arts—France	P51-59	407.1	Language and languages—Study and teaching
NX550-.6	700.943	Arts—Germany			
NX551	700.9495	Arts—Greece	P53.44	407.1	Immersion method (Language teaching)
NX552	700.945	Arts—Italy			
NX554	700.9492	Arts—Netherlands	P87-96	302.2	Communication
NX555	700.9493	Arts—Belgium	P94.5.A37	302.2308996073	Afro-Americans and mass media
NX556	700.947	Arts—Russia			
NX557-561	700.948	Arts—Scandinavia	P94.5.A37	302.2308996073	Afro-Americans in mass media
NX558	700.9489	Arts—Denmark			
NX559	700.94912	Arts—Iceland	P94.5.A37	302.2308996073	Afro-American mass media
NX560	700.9481	Arts—Norway	P94.5.A37	302.208996073	Afro-Americans—Communication
NX561	700.9485	Arts—Sweden			
NX562	700.946	Arts—Spain	P94.5.M55	302.23089	Ethnic mass media
NX563	700.9469	Arts—Portugal	P95.8	302.2	Communication policy
NX564	700.9494	Arts—Switzerland	P95.8	302.23	Mass media policy
NX565	700.9561	Arts—Turkey	P96.A38	305.26	Aged in mass media
NX566-569	700.9496	Arts—Balkan Peninsula	P96.A39	362.1969792	AIDS (Disease) in mass media
NX572-586	700.95	Arts—Asia			
NX573-.7	700.956	Arts—Middle East	P96.A83	302.23	Audiences
NX573.7	700.95694	Arts—Israel	P96.C74	364	Crime in mass media
NX574	700.955	Arts—Iran	P96.D4	363.25092	Detectives in mass media
NX575.6	700.9581	Arts—Afghanistan	P96.E29	370	Education in mass media
NX575.7	700.957	Arts—Asiatic Russia	P96.F36	154.3	Fantasy in mass media
NX576	700.954	Arts—India	P96.M6	567.9	Dinosaurs in mass media
NX576.6	700.95493	Arts—Sri Lanka	P96.S34	808.838762	Science fiction
NX576.7	700.95491	Arts—Pakistan	P96.S48	305.3	Sexism in communication
NX578.6.C3	700.9596	Arts—Cambodia	P96.S5	305.3	Sex role in mass media
NX578.6.L3	700.9594	Arts—Laos	P96.V5	303.6	Violence in mass media
NX578.6.V5-.V55	700.9597	Arts—Vietnam	P99-.4	401.41	Semiotics
NX578.7	700.9593	Arts—Thailand	P99.4.P72	401.9	Pragmatics
NX579	700.9595	Arts—Malaysia	P118-.7	401.93	Language acquisition
NX580	700.9598	Arts—Indonesia	P118.2	401.93	Second language acquisition
NX581	700.9599	Arts—Philippines			
NX583	700.951	Arts—China	P121-149	410.92	Linguists
NX584	700.952	Arts—Japan	P121-143.3	410	Linguistics
NX584.6-.7	700.9519	Arts—Korea	P123	410	Comparative linguistics
NX587-589.8	700.96	Arts—Afria	P140	417.7	Historical linguistics
NX587.6-588.6	700.961	Arts—Africa, North	P128.E94	417.24	Linguistics, Experimental
NX588-.3	700.962	Arts—Egypt	P128.M48	410.1	Metalanguage

LC	Dewey	Subject Heading	LC	Dewey	Subject Heading
P147	410.18	Functionalism (Linguistics)	PA231-241	489.3071	Greek language—Study and teaching
P151-299	415	Grammar, Comparative and general	PA251-379	489.35	Greek language—Grammar
P207	415	Language and languages— Grammars	PA265-281	489.315	Greek language—Phonology
P211-214	411	Alphabets	PA283-287	489.35	Greek language— Morphology
P221-232	414.8	Phonetics	PA303-361	489.35	Greek language—Parts of speech
P223	414.8	Tone (Phonetics)			
P226	411	Transliteration	PA367-379	489.35	Greek language—Syntax
P241-259	415	Morphemics	PA401-407	889.309	Greek language—Style
P270-288	415	Parts of speech	PA421-430	489.32	Greek language—Etymology
P301-.5	808	Rhetoric	PA431-465	489.33028	Greek language— Lexicography
P302-.87	401.41	Discourse analysis			
P305-.18	401.4	Vocabulary	PA441-465	489.33	Greek language— Dictionaries
P307-310	418.020285	Machine translating			
P311	808.1	Versification	PA500-581	489	Greek language—Dialects
P321-324.5	412	Language and languages— Etymology	PA530-539	480	Doric Greek dialect
			PA550-554	480	Aeolic Greek dialect
P325-.5	401.43	Semantics	PA600-895	487.4	Greek language, Hellenistic (300 B.C.-600 A.D.)
P325.5.H57	401.4309	Semantics, Historical			
P326	401.409	Historical lexicology	PA695-895	487.4	Greek language, Biblical
P361	413	Polyglot glossaries, phrase books, etc.	PA813-857	487.45	Greek language, Biblical— Grammar
P361	413	Dictionaries, Polyglot	PA881	487.43	Greek language, Biblical— Dictionaries
P375-381	409	Linguistic geography			
P408	418	Colloquial language	PA1000-1179	489	Greek language, Medieval and late
P409-410	417.2	Slang			
P409	417.2	Jargon (Terminology)	PA1000-1179	489.3	Greek language, Modern
P501-769	410	Indo-European languages	PA1031	489.33	Greek language, Modern— Dictionaries
P501-769	410	Indo-European philology			
P501	413.028	Indo-European philology— Periodicals	PA1041-1049	489.3071	Greek language, Modern— Study and teaching
P505	410.6	Indo-European languages— Congresses	PA1051-1099	489.35	Greek language, Modern— Grammar
P575-769	415	Indo-European languages— Grammar, Comparative	PA1061-1072	489.315	Greek language, Modern— Phonology
P583-610	414	Indo-European languages— Phonology	PA1076	489.35	Greek language, Modern— Morphology
P611-627	415	Indo-European languages— Morphology	PA1081-1089	489.35	Greek language, Modern— Parts of speech
P631-663	415	Indo-European languages— Parts of speech	PA1091-1097	489.35	Greek language, Modern— Syntax
P671-675	415	Indo-European languages— Syntax	PA1111-1114.5	489.32	Greek language, Modern— Etymology
P721-725	412	Indo-European languages— Etymology	PA1123-1145	489.33	Greek language, Modern— Dictionaries
P761-769	413.028	Indo-European languages— Lexicography	PA1151-1159	489.37	Greek language, Modern— Dialects
P943	499.93	Elamite language	PA2001-2995	470	Latin language
P945	491.998	Hittite language	PA2001-2067	470	Latin philology
P1001	491.998	Anatolian languages	PA2061-2067	470.71	Latin language—Study and teaching
P1078	499.94	Etruscan language			
PA	480	Classical languages	PA2071-2310	475	Latin language—Grammar
PA1-199	480	Classical philology	PA2111-2131	475	Latin language—Phonology
PA31	480.03	Classical languages— Dictionaries	PA2133-2158	475	Latin language—Morphology
			PA2161-2281	475	Latin language—Parts of speech
PA47	880.9	Criticism, Textual			
PA111	485	Classical languages— Grammar, Comparative	PA2285-2297	475	Latin language—Syntax
			PA2300-2309	477	Latin language, Postclassical
PA201-1179	489.3	Greek language	PA2329-2340	871.6	Latin language—Metrics and rhythmics

LC	Dewey	Subject Heading	LC	Dewey	Subject Heading
PA2341-2350	472	Latin language—Etymology	PA5290-5294	889.2008	Greek drama, Modern
PA2351-2390	473.028	Latin language—Lexicography	PA5295	889.808	Greek prose literature, Modern
PA2361-2390	473	Latin language—Dictionaries	PA5301-5395	889.08001	Greek literature, Modern—1453-1800
PA2420-2915	470	Italic languages and dialects	PA6001-6098	870.9001	Latin literature—History and criticism
PA2510-2519	477	Latin language, Preclassical to ca. 100 B.C.	PA6045-6063	871.09	Latin poetry
PA2600-2748	477	Latin language, Vulgar	PA6067-6075	872.09	Latin drama—History and criticism
PA3001-3045	880.09	Classical literature—History and criticism	PA6081-6095.5	878.08	Latin prose literature—History and criticism
PA3013	880.01	Classical literature—Appreciation	PA6101-6139	870.8001	Latin literature
PA3019-3022	881.009	Classical poetry	PA6121-6135	871.08	Latin poetry
PA3024-3029	882.009	Classical drama—History and criticism	PA6125	871.032108	Epic poetry, Latin
			PA6137	872.08	Latin drama
PA3051-4505	880	Greek literature	PA6138-6139	878.08	Latin prose literature
PA3081-3084	880	Greek literature, Hellenistic	PA8001-8595	870.900(3-4)	Latin literature, Medieval and modern
PA3092-3125	881.009	Greek poetry	PA8050-8065	871.(3-4)09	Latin poetry, Medieval and modern—History and criticism
PA3105-3107.5	881.03209	Epic poetry, Greek			
PA3131-3239	882.009	Greek drama			
PA3131-3159	882.051209	Greek drama (Tragedy)	PA8073-8079	872.(3-4)09	Latin drama, Medieval and modern
PA3161-3199	882.052309	Greek drama (Comedy)			
PA3255-3273	888.08	Greek prose literature	PA8081-8096	878.08	Latin prose literature, Medieval and modern
PA3265	808.0481	Rhetoric, Ancient			
PA3285	398.2048	Folk literature, Greek	PA8120-8133	871.(3-4)08	Latin poetry, Medieval and modern
PA3300-3516	880.8	Greek literature			
PA3301-3671	880.8	Classical literature	PA8135-8140	872.(3-4)08	Latin drama, Medieval and modern
PA3301-3371	091.09495	Manuscripts, Greek (Papyri)			
PA3431-3459	881	Classical poetry	PA8145-8149	878.08	Latin prose literature, Medieval and modern
PA3437-3439	881.03208	Epic poetry, Greek			
PA3461-3468	882	Greek drama	PB73	418	Polyglot glossaries, phrase books, etc.
PA3461-3466	882.008	Classical drama			
PA3461-3463	882.051208	Greek drama (Tragedy)	PB331	413	Dictionaries, Polyglot
PA3465-3466	882.052308	Greek drama (Comedy)	PB1001-1095	491.6	Celtic philology
PA3473-3475	888.08	Greek prose literature	PB1001-1095	491.6	Celtic languages
PA3479-3842	885.108	Oratory, Ancient	PB1011	491.6071	Celtic languages—Study and teaching
PA3482	885.008	Funeral orations			
PA3520-3564	880.9	Greek literature—Criticism, Textual	PB1019-1071	491.6(2-8)5	Celtic languages—Grammar
			PB1083-1085	491.6(2-8)2	Celtic languages—Etymology
PA3527	880.9	Greek literature, Hellenistic—Criticism, Textual	PB1087-1089	491.6(2-8)3028	Celtic languages—Lexicography
			PB1101-1113	491.6(2/3)	Gaelic philology
PA3537-3543	881.009	Greek poetry, Hellenistic—Criticism, Textual	PB1111	491.6(2-3)071	Gaelic philology—Study and teaching
PA5101-5167	880.9002	Byzantine literature	PB1187-1189	491.6(2-3)3028	Gaelic language—Lexicography
PA5150-5155	881.209	Byzantine poetry			
PA5160-5163	882.209	Byzantine drama	PB1201-1299	491.62	Irish language
PA5165	888.08	Byzantine prose literature	PB1211	491.62071	Irish language—Study and teaching
PA5170-5198	880.8002	Byzantine literature			
PA5180-5189	881.208	Byzantine poetry	PB1218	491.627	Irish language—To 1100
PA5190-5194	882.208	Byzantine drama	PB1218	491.627	Irish language—Middle Irish, 1100-1550
PA5195-5196	888.08	Byzantine prose literature			
PA5201-5660	889	Greek literature, Modern	PB1221-1273	491.625	Irish language—Grammar
PA5230-5269	889.09	Greek literature, Modern—History and criticism	PB1283-1284	491.622	Irish language—Etymology
			PB1287-1295	491.623028	Irish language—Lexicography
PA5259-5255	889.1009	Greek poetry, Modern			
PA5260-5263	889.2009	Greek drama, Modern	PB1299	491.627	Irish language—Slang
PA5265	888.08	Greek prose literature, Modern	PB1306-1449	891.62	Irish literature
PA5280-5289	889.1008	Greek poetry, Modern	PB1321	891.6208001	Irish literature—To 1100

LC	Dewey	Subject Heading	LC	Dewey	Subject Heading
PB1321	891.621009	Fili (Irish poets)	PC911-923	459.95	Raeto-Romance language—Grammar
PB1322	891.6208002	Irish literature—Middle Irish, 1100-1550	PC931	459.92	Raeto-Romance language—Etymology
PB1501-1599	491.6(2-3)	Gaelic language	PC937	459.93	Raeto-Romance language—Dictionaries
PB1511	491.6(2-3)071	Gaelic language—Study and teaching	PC941-949	459.97	Raeto-Romance language—Dialects
PB1521-1573	491.6(2-3)5	Gaelic language—Grammar	PC949	459.97	Raeto-Romance language—Slang
PB1583-1584	491.6(2-3)2	Gaelic language—Etymology			
PB1587-1595	491.6(2-3)3028	Gaelic language—Lexicography	PC951-986	859.9	Raeto-Romance literature
PB1605-1709	891.63	Gaelic literature	PC1001-1977	450	Italian language
PB1801-1847	491.64	Manx language	PC1001-1977	450	Italian philology
PB1851-1867	891.64	Manx literature	PC1065	450.71	Italian language—Study and teaching
PB2001-2060	491.6	Brythonic languages			
PB2005	491.6(2-8)071	Brythonic languages—Study and teaching	PC1099-1400	455	Italian language—Grammar
			PC1300-1766	857.00222	Wit and humor, Pictorial
PB2009-2015	491.6(2-8)5	Brythonic languages—Grammar	PC1571-1580	452	Italian language—Etymology
PB2021	491.6(2-8)2	Brythonic languages—Etymology	PC1620-1693	453.028	Italian language—Lexicography
PB2023	491.6(2-8)3028	Brythonic languages—Lexicography	PC1620-1645	453	Italian language—Dictionaries
PB2101-2199	491.66	Welsh language	PC1700-1977	457	Italian language—Dialects
PB2206-2499	891.66	Welsh literature	PC1851-1874	457	Gallo-Italian dialects
PB2501-2549	491.67	Cornish language	PC1951-1977	457	Italian language—Slang
PB2507	491.67071	Cornish language—Study and teaching	PC2001-3761	440	French language
			PC2001-2071	440	French philology
PB2511-2547	491.675	Cornish language—Grammar	PC2065	440.71	French language—Study and teaching
PB2551-2621	891.67	Cornish literature	PC2101-2400	445	French language—Grammar
PB2800-2849	491.68	Breton language	PC2113-2117	448.6	French language—Readers
PB2807	491.68071	Breton language—Study and teachingx	PC2131-2151	441.5	French language—Phonology
			PC2171-2175	445	French language—Morphology
PB2811-2847	491.685	Breton language—Grammar	PC2201-2321	445	French language—Parts of speech
PB2856-2932	891.68	Breton literature			
PB3001-3029	491.6	Gaulish language	PC2571-2591	442	French language—Etymology
PC	440	Romance languages	PC2620-2693	443.028	French language—Lexicography
PC	440	Romance philology			
PC1-5	440.05	Romance languages—Periodicals	PC2700-3761	447	French language—Dialects
			PC2721-2746	445	French language—Grammar
PC35-39	440.071	Romance languages—Study and teaching	PC2761	442	French language—Etymology
			PC2766	443.028	French language—Lexicography
PC601-872	459	Romanian philology			
PC601-799	459	Romanian language	PC2801-2896	447.0(1-2)	French language—To 1500
PC619	459.071	Romanian language—Study and teaching	PC2821-2873	447.0(1-2)5	French language—To 1500—Grammar
PC631-725	459.5	Romanian language—Grammar	PC2883-2886	447.01(1-2)2	French language—To 1500—Etymology
PC761-767	459.2	Romanian language—Etymology	PC2887-2895	447.0(1-2)3028	French language—To 1500—Lexicography
PC775-784	459.3028	Romanian language—Lexicography	PC3081-3148	449	Franco-Provencal dialects
PC785	459.11	Abbreviations, Romanian	PC3201-3299	449	Provencal language
PC799	459.7	Romanian language—Slang	PC3219-3273	449.5	Provencal language—Grammar
PC800-872	859	Romanian literature			
PC890	457.994972	Dalmatian language (Romance)	PC3283-3286	449.2	Provencal language—Etymology
			PC3287-3295	449.3028	Provencal language—Lexicography
PC901-949	459.9	Raeto-Romance language			
PC907	459.9071	Raeto-Romance language—Study and teaching	PC3296	449.77	Provencal language—Dialects

LC	Dewey	Subject Heading	LC	Dewey	Subject Heading
PC3299	449.7	Provencal language—Slang	PD700-777	430.047	Germanic languages—Dialects
PC3301-3359	849	Provencal literature			
PC3304-3330	849.104	Troubadours	PD1101-1211	439.9	Gothic language
PC3371-3420	449	Langue d'oc	PD1119-1167	439.95	Gothic language—Grammar
PC3381-3420.5	849	Langue d'oc literature	PD1193	439.93	Gothic language—Dictionaries
PC3801-3899	449.9	Catalan language			
PC3819-3873	449.95	Catalan language—Grammar	PD1270	439.9	Vandal language
			PD1501-5929	439.(5-6)	Scandinavian languages
PC3883-3886	449.92	Catalan language—Etymology	PD1501-1541	439.(5-6)	Scandinavian philology
			PD1535-1539	439.(5-6)071	Scandinavian languages—Study and teaching
PC3887-3895	449.93028	Catalan language—Lexicography	PD1559-1701	439.(5-6)5	Scandinavian languages—Grammar
PC3900-3976	849.9	Catalan literature			
PC4001-4977	460	Spanish language	PD1801-1819	439.(5-6)2	Scandinavian languages—Etymology
PC4001-4071	460	Spanish philology			
PC4065	460.71	Spanish language—Study and teaching	PD1823	439.(5-6)3028	Scandinavian languages—Lexicography
PC4099-4400	465	Spanish language—Grammar	PD1850-1893	439.(5-6)7	Scandinavian languages—Dialects
PC4571-4580	462	Spanish language—Etymology	PD2201-2392	439.6	Old Norse language
			PD2201-2392	439.6	Old Norse philology
PC4620-4693	463.028	Spanish language—Lexicography	PD2229-2331	439.65	Old Norse language—Grammar
PC4620-4645	463	Spanish language—Dictionaries	PD2361-2369	439.62	Old Norse language—Etymology
PC4700-4941	467	Spanish language—Dialects	PD2376-2385	439.63028	Old Norse language—Lexicography
PC4951-4977	467	Spanish language—Slang	PD2387-2392	439.67	Old Norse language—Dialects
PC5001-5498	469	Portuguese language	PD2401-2447	439.69	Icelandic language
PC5001-5041	469	Portuguese philology	PD2407	439.69071	Icelandic language—Study and teaching
PC5035-5039	469.0071	Portuguese language—Study and teaching	PD2411-2423	439.695	Icelandic language—Grammar
PC5061-5231	469.5	Portuguese language—Grammar	PD2431	439.692	Icelandic language—Etymology
PC5301-5315	469.2	Portuguese language—Etymology	PD2437	439.693	Icelandic language—Dictionaries
PC5320-5348	469.3028	Portuguese language—Lexicography	PD2447	439.697	Icelandic language—Slang
PC5325-5348	469.3	Portuguese language—Dictionaries	PD2483-2489	439.67	Old Norse Language—Dialects
PC5350-5498	469.7	Portuguese language—Dialects	PD2483	439.699	Faroese language
PC5411-5414	469.794	Galician dialect	PD2501-2999	439.82	Norwegian philology
PC5498	469.709	Portuguese language—Slang	PD2571-2699	439.82	Norwegian language
			PD2611-2612	439.82071	Norwegian language—Study and teaching
PD	430	Germanic languages			
PD1-9	430.05	Germanic languages—Periodicals	PD2619-2673	439.825	Norwegian language—Grammar
PD51-60	437	Germanic languages—History	PD2683-2684	439.822	Norwegian language—Etymology
PD65-69	430.071	Germanic languages—Study and teaching	PD2687-2695	439.823028	Norwegian language—Lexicography
PD99-321	430.045	Germanic languages—Grammar	PD2688-2695	439.823	Norwegian language—Dictionaries
PD571-599	430.042	Germanic languages—Etymology	PD2696-2699	439.827	Norwegian language—Dialects
PD601-660	430.043028	Germanic languages—Lexicography	PD2699	439.827	Norwegian language—Slang
PD625-660	430.043	Germanic languages—Dictionaries	PD3001-3929	439.81	Danish language
			PD3001-3071	439.81	Danish philology
			PD3065	439.81071	Danish—Study and teaching

LC	Dewey	Subject Heading	LC	Dewey	Subject Heading
PD3101-3400	439.815	Danish language—Grammar	PE688	427.027	English language—Middle English, 1100-1500—Dialects
PD3571-3599	439.812	Danish language—Etymology			
PD3601-3693	439.813028	Danish language—Lexicography	PE1001-3729	420	English language
PD3625-3693	439.813	Danish language—Dictionaries	PE1065-1069	420.71	English language—Study and teaching
PD3700-3929	439.817	Danish language—Dialects	PE1079-1087	427.9	English language—History
PD3901-3929	439.817	Danish language—Slang	PE1079-1081	427.00903(1/2)	English language—Early modern, 1500-1700
PD5001-5929	439.7	Swedish language			
PD5001-5071	439.7	Swedish philology	PE1083	427.009033	English language—18th century
PD5065	439.7071	Swedish language—Study and teaching	PE1085	427.009034	English language—19th century
PD5101-5400	439.75	Swedish language—Grammar	PE1097-1105	425	English language—Grammar
PD5571-5599	439.72	Swedish language—Etymology	PE1112	425	English language—Grammar—1950-
PD5611-5693	439.73028	Swedish language—Lexicography	PE1117-1130	428.6	Readers
PD5625-5693	439.73	Swedish language—Dictionaries	PE1133-1168	421.5	English language—Phonology
PD5700-5929	439.77	Swedish language—Dialects	PE1133	421.509	English language—Phonology, Historical
PE	420	English philology	PE1144-1146	428.1	Spellers
PE101-299	429	English language—Old English, ca. 450-1100	PE1151	421	Phonetic alphabet
PE101-123	429	English language—Old English, ca. 450-1100 Philology	PE1151	421	Phonetic spelling
			PE1171	425	English language—Morphology
PE129-231	429.5	English language—Old English, ca. 450-1100—Grammar	PE1199-1359	425	English language—Parts of speech
PE261-269	429.2	English language—Old English, ca. 450-1100—Etymology	PE1402-1497	808.042	English language—Rhetoric
			PE1417	428.6	Readers
PE274-285	429.3028	English language—Old English, ca. 450-1100—Lexicography	PE1425	820.8023	Narration (Rhetoric)
			PE1427	820.8022	Description (Rhetoric)
PE275-285	429.3	English language—Old English, ca. 450-1100—Dictionaries	PE1571-1599	422	English language—Etymology
PE287-299	429.7	English language—Old English, ca. 450-1100—Dialects	PE1591	423.1	English language—Synonyms and antonyms
PE501-685	427.02	English language—Middle English, 1100-1500	PE1601-1693	423.028	English language—Lexicography
PE524-531	427.02	English language—Middle English, 1100-1500—Philology	PE1704	423	English language—Dictionaries
PE529-531	427.025	English language—Middle English, 1100-1500—Grammar	PE1700-3601	427	English language—Dialects
			PE2101-2364	427.9411	Scots language
PE561-569	427.022	English language—Middle English, 1100-1500—Etymology	PE2801-3102	427.73	English language—United States
PE574-585	427.023028	English language—Middle English, 1100-1500—Lexicography	PE3701-3729	427	English language—Slang
			PE3729.U	427	Pig Latin
			PF	430	Germanic languages
PE575-585	427.023	English language—Middle English, 1100-1500—Dictionaries	PF1-979	439.31	Dutch language
			PF1-979	439.31	Dutch philology
			PF51-60	439.3109	Dutch language—History
			PF65-69	439.31071	Dutch language—Study and teaching
			PF97	439.315	Dutch language—Grammar
			PF131-168	439.3115	Dutch language—Phonology
			PF171-197	439.315	Dutch language—Morphology
			PF199-335	439.315	Dutch language—Parts of speech
			PF410-497	808.043931	Dutch language—Rhetoric

LC	Dewey	Subject Heading	LC	Dewey	Subject Heading
PF571-599	439.32	Dutch languages—Etymology	PF4333-4345	437.023	German language—Middle High German, 1050-1500—Dictionaries
PF601-693	439.313028	Dutch language—Lexicography	PF4501-4596	437.09	German language—Early modern, 1500-1700
PF620-693	439.313	Dutch language—Dictionaries	PF5000-5951	437	German language—Dialects
PF700-979	439.317	Dutch language—Dialects	PF5601-5844	439.4	Low German language
PF861-884	439.36	Afrikaans language	PF5971-5999	437	German language—Slang
PF951-979	439.317	Dutch language—Slang	PG1-9198	491.8	Slavic languages
PF1001-1184	439.31	Dutch language	PG1-41	491.8	Slavic philology
PF1015	439.3109	Dutch language—History	PG35-39	491.8071	Slavic languages—Study and teaching
PF1019	439.31071	Dutch language—Study and teaching	PG59-97	491.8045	Slavic languages—Grammar
PF1033-1125	439.315	Dutch language—Grammar	PG301-319	491.8042	Slavic languages—Etymology
PF1161-1167	439.312	Dutch language—Etymology	PG320-335	491.8043028	Slavic languages—Lexicography
PF1175-1184	439.313	Dutch language—Dictionaries	PG331-335	491.83	Slavic languages—Dictionaries
PF1401-1497	439.2	Frisian language	PG350-400	491.877	Slavic languages—Dialects
PF1401-1411	439.2	Frisian language—Philology	PG400	491.877	Slavic languages—Slang
PF1501-1541	839.2	Frisian literature	PG500-585	891.8	Slavic literature
PF3001-5999	430	German language	PG601-698	491.81701	Church Slavic language
PF3051-3060	437	German language—History	PG661-698	491.817015	Church Slavic language—Grammar
PF3065-3069	430.71	German language—Study and teaching	PG700-716	891.81	Church Slavic literature
PF3097-3400	435	German language—Grammar	PG801-993	491.81	Bulgarian language
PF3131-3168	431.5	German language—Phonology	PG801-823	491.81	Bulgarian philology
PF3171-3197	435	German language—Morphology	PG831-925	491.815	Bulgarian language—Grammar
PF3199-3335	435	German language—Parts of speech	PG975-984	491.813	Bulgarian language—Dictionaries
PF3410-3497	808.0431	German language—Rhetoric	PG1000-1146	891.8109	Bulgarian literature
PF3571-3599	432	German language—Etymology	PG1161-1164	491.819	Macedonian language
			PG1201-1223	491.82	Serbo-Croatian philology
PF3601-3693	433.028	German language—Lexicography	PG1224-1399	491.82	Serbo-Croatian language
PF3620-3693	433	German language—Dictionaries	PG1229-1313	491.825	Serbo-Croatian language—Grammar
PF3801-3991	437.01	German language—Old High German, 750-1050	PG1374-1384	491.823	Serbo-Croatian language—Dictionaries
PF3801-3823	437.01	German language—Old High German, 750-1050—Philology	PG1399	491.827	Serbo-Croatian language—Slang
PF3831-3931	437.015	German language—Old High German, 750-1050—Grammar	PG1650-.5	891.821009	Dalmatian poetry
			PG1654-.5	891.821008	Dalmatian poetry
PF3985-3991	839	German literature—Old High German, 750-1050	PG1801-1899	491.84	Slovenian language
PF3992-4000	439.4	Old Saxon language	PG1801-1813	491.84	Slovenian philology
PF4043-4350	437.02	German language—Middle High German, 1050-1500	PG1819-1881	491.845	Slovenian language—grammar
PF4061-4171	437.025	German language—Middle High German, 1050-1500—Grammar	PG1887-1894.5	491.843028	Slovenian language—Lexicography
			PG1888-1894.5	491.843	Slovenian language—Dictionaries
PF4327-4345	437.023028	German language—Middle High German, 1050-1500—Lexicography	PG1900-1962	891.84	Slovenian literature
			PG2001-2847	491.7	Russian language
			PG2001-2069	491.7	Russian philology
			PG2065-2069	491.7071	Russian language—Study and teaching
			PG2097-2127	491.75	Russian language—Grammar
			PG2131-2161	491.715	Russian language—Phonology

155

LC	Dewey	Subject Heading	LC	Dewey	Subject Heading
PG2171-2197	491.75	Russian language—Morphology	PH101-293	494.541	Finnish language
PG2199-2321	491.75	Russian language—Parts of speech	PH101-123	494.541	Finnish philology
PG2571-2591	491.72	Russian language—Etymology	PH131-225	494.5415	Finnish language—Grammar
PG2601-2693	491.73028	Russian language—Lexicography	PH300-405	894.54109	Finnish literature
PG2625-2693	491.73	Russian language—Dictionaries	PH501-509	494.54	Karelian language
PG2700-2850	491.77	Russian language—Dialects	PH541-549	494.54	Veps language
PG2850	491.7709	Russian language—Slang	PH561-569	494.54	Votic language
PG2900-3580	891.7	Russian literature	PH581-589	494.54	Livonian language
PG3801-3899	491.79	Ukrainian language	PH601-629	494.545	Estonian language
PG3819-3881	491.795	Ukrainian language—Grammar	PH630-671	894.545	Estonian literature
PG3887-3894.5	491.793028	Ukranian language—Lexicography	PH701-729	494.55	Lapp language
PG3888-3894.5	491.793	Ukranian language—Dictionaries	PH731-735	894.55	Lapp literature
PG3900-3987	891.79	Ukrainian literature	PH751-779	494.56	Mordvin language
PG4001-4771	491.86	Czech philology	PH781-785	894.56	Mordvin literature
PG4601-4771	491.86	Czech language	PH801-807	494.56	Mari language
PG4625-4693	491.863	Czech language—Dictionaries	PH1001-1004	494.53	Permic languages
PG4700-4771	491.807	Czech language—Dialects	PH1091-1097	493.111	Hieroglyphics
PG5000-5146	891.86	Czech literature	PH1251-1254	494.51	Ob-Ugric languages
PG5201-5399	491.87	Slovak language	PH2001-2800	494.511	Hungarian language
PG5201-5223	491.87	Slovak philology	PH2097-2410	494.5115	Hungarian language—Grammar
PG5231-5325	491.875	Slovak language—Grammar	PH2601-2693	494.5113028	Hungarian language—Lexicography
PG5375-5384	491.873	Slovak language—Dictionaries	PH2625-2693	494.5113	Hungarian language—Dictionaries
PG5400-5546	891.87	Slovak literature	PH2800	494.5117	Hungarian language—Slang
PG5631-5698	491.88	Sorbian languages	PH3001-3445	894.511	Hungarian literature
PG5661-5698	891.88	Sorbian literature	PH5001-5259	499.92	Basque language
PG6001-6790	491.85	Polish language	PH5001-5022	499.92	Basque philology
PG6001-6790	491.85	Polish philology	PH5280-5490	899.92	Basque literature
PG6625-6638	491.853028	Polish language—Lexicography	PJ	490	Oriental languages
PG6700-6790	491.857	Polish language—Dialects	PJ65-69	490.071	Oriental languages—Study and teaching
PG7001-7446	891.85	Polish literature	PJ120-171	490.5	Oriental languages—Grammar
PG8201-8208	491.91	Prussian language	PJ183	490.2	Oriental languages—Etymology
PG8206	491.913	Prussian language—Dictionaries	PJ187	490.3028	Oriental languages—Lexicography
PG8501-8693	491.92	Lithuanian language	PJ306-489	895	Oriental literature
PG8501-8693	491.92	Lithuanian philology	PJ371	895.2008	Oriental drama
PG8701-8772	891.92	Lithuanian literature	PJ990	492	Afroasiatic languages
PG8801-8993	491.93	Latvian language	PJ1001-1479	493.1	Egyptian language
PG8801-8993	491.93	Latvian philology	PJ1001-1109	493.1	Egyptian philology
PG8998-9146	891.93	Latvian literature	PJ1031	493.13	Egyptian language—Dictionaries
PG9501-9599	491.991	Albanian language	PJ1051-1109	493.111	Egyptian language—Writing
PG9501-9513	491.991	Albanian philology	PJ1091-1097	493.111	Egyptian language—Writing, Hieroglyphic
PG9601-9665	891.991	Albanian literature	PJ1091	493.1	Hieroglyphics
PH	494.5	Finno-Ugric languages	PJ1105	493.11	Egyptian language—Writing, Hieratic
PH1-11	494.5	Finno-Ugric philology	PJ1107	493.111	Egyptian language—Writing, Demotic
PH11	494.5071	Finno-Ugric languages—Study and teaching	PJ1121-1201	493.15	Egyptian language—Grammar
PH21-41	494.55	Finno-Ugric languages—Grammar	PJ1350-1371	493.12	Egyptian language—Etymology
PH91-98	494.54	Finnic languages	PJ1401-1439	493.13028	Egyptian language—Lexicography

LC	Dewey	Subject Heading	LC	Dewey	Subject Heading
PJ1423-1439	493.13	Egyptian language—Dictionaries	PJ4051-4075	499.9511	Cuneiform inscriptions, Sumerian
PJ1481-1989	893.1	Egyptian literature	PJ4121-4129	492.047	Semitic languages, Northwest
PJ1487	893.13	Egyptian fiction			
PJ1501-1921	493.111	Egyptian language—Papyri	PJ4149	496.35	Mossi languages
PJ1501-1819	493.111	Egyptian language—Inscriptions	PJ4150	492.67	Ugaritic language
			PJ4171-4187	492.6	Phoenician language
PJ1571	893.12	Egyptian drama	PJ4501-4937	492.4	Hebrew language
PJ1801-1921	493.17	Egyptian language—Demotic, ca. 650 B.C.-450 A.D.	PJ4501-4541	492.4	Hebrew philology
			PJ4553-4731	492.45	Hebrew language—Grammar
PJ2001-2187	493.2	Coptic language	PJ4576-4583	492.415	Hebrew language—Phonology
PJ2019	493.2071	Coptic language—Study and teaching	PJ4601-4677	492.45	Hebrew language—Morphology
PJ2029-2113	493.25	Coptic language—Grammar	PJ4801-4819	492.42	Hebrew language—Etymology
PJ2161	493.22	Coptic language—Etymology			
PJ2181	493.23028	Coptic language—Lexicography	PJ4820-4847	492.43028	Hebrew language—Lexicography
PJ2190-2199	893.2	Coptic literature	PJ4825-4847	492.43	Hebrew language—Dictionaries
PJ2340-2349	493.3	Berber languages			
PJ2345	493.35	Berber languages—Grammar	PJ4855-4937	492.47	Hebrew language—Dialects
PJ2347	493.32	Berber languages—Etymology	PJ4901-4950	492.47	Hebrew language, Talmudic
PJ2349	493.33	Berber languages—Dictionaries	PJ4911-4925	492.475	Hebrew language—Grammar
			PJ4931-4933	492.42	Hebrew language—Etymology
PJ2369-2399	493.3	Berber languages			
PJ2377	493.3	Rif language	PJ4934-4937	492.43028	Hebrew language—Lexicography
PJ2401-2413	493.5	Cushitic languages			
PJ2405	493.55	Cushitic langues—Grammar	PJ4935-4937	492.43	Hebrew language—Dictionaries
PJ2409	493.52	Cushitic languages—Etymology	PJ5001-5060	892.4	Hebrew literature
			PJ5007	892.4071	Hebrew literature—Study and teaching
PJ2413	493.53	Cushitic languages—Dictionaries	PJ5016	892.409002	Hebrew literature, Medieval
PJ2425-2594	493.57	Cushitic languages—Dialects	PJ5017-5021	892.409003	Hebrew literature, Modern
			PJ5034.4-.9	492.411	Inscriptions, Hebrew
PJ2465	493.5	Afar language	PJ5037	892.408002	Hebrew literature, Medieval
PJ2531-2534	493.54	Somali language	PJ5038	892.408003	Hebrew literature, Modern
PJ3001-9278	492	Semitic languages	PJ5048	398.204924	Folk literature, Hebrew
PJ3004	492.043	Semitic languages—Dictionaries	PJ5111-5119	439.1	Yiddish language
			PJ5115-5116.5	439.15	Yiddish language—Grammar
PJ3011-3013	492.04071	Semitic languages—Study and teaching	PJ5117	439.13	Yiddish language—Dictionaries
PJ3021-3041	492.045	Semitic languages—Grammar	PJ5120-5192	839.09	Yiddish literature
			PJ5201-5329	492.2	Aramaic language
PJ3065	492.042	Semitic languages—Etymology	PJ5208-5209	492.211	Inscriptions, Aramaic
			PJ5271-5279	492.29	Samaritan Aramaic language
PJ3071-3075	492.043028	Semitic languages—Lexicography	PJ5401-5411	492.3	Syriac philology
PJ3081-3095	492.0411	Inscriptions, Semitic	PJ5401	492.37	Mandailing dialect
PJ3097	892.009	Semitic literature	PJ5419-5471	492.35	Syriac langue—Grammar
PJ3101	492.1	Akkadian language	PJ5483	492.32	Syriac language—Etymology
PJ3191-3225	492.111	Cuneiform writing	PJ5490-5493	492.33	Syriac language—Dictionaries
PJ3601-3953	892.1	Assyro-Babylonian literature			
PJ4001-4041	499.95	Sumerian language	PJ5601-5695	892.3	Syriac literature
PJ4011-4025	499.955	Sumerian language—Grammar	PJ5701-5809	492.3	Syriac language
			PJ6001-7144	492.7	Arabic language
PJ4037	499.953	Sumerian language—Dictionaries	PJ6001-6071	492.7	Arabic philology
PJ4045-4083	899.95	Sumerian literature	PJ6031	492.73	Arabic language—Dictionaries

157

LC	Dewey	Subject Heading
PJ6065-6069	492.7071	Arabic language—Study and teaching
PJ6101-6599	492.75	Arabic language—Grammar
PJ6123	492.711	Arabic alphabet
PJ6172-6199	492.72	Arabic language—Etymology
PJ6701-6901	492.77	Arabic language—Dialects
PJ6751-6760	492.77	Arabic language—Dialects—Spain
PJ6771-6799	492.77	Arabic language—Dialects—Egypt
PJ6805-6808	492.77	Arabic language—Dialects—Palestine
PJ6810	492.77	Arabic language—Dialects—Lebanon
PJ6811-6820	492.77	Arabic language—Dialects—Syria
PJ6821-6830	492.77	Arabic language—Dialects—Iraq
PJ6841-6880	492.77	Arabic language—Dialects—Arabian Peninsula
PJ7501-8518	892.7	Arabic literature
PJ7541-7561	892.71009	Arabic poetry
PJ7565	892.72009	Arabic drama
PJ7571-7577	892.7808	Arabic prose literature
PJ7580	398.204927	Folk literature, Arabic
PJ7593-7600	492.711	Inscriptions, Arabic
PJ7639-7660	892.71009	Arabic poetry
PJ7665	892.72008	Arabic drama
PJ7671-7677	892.7808	Arabic prose literature
PJ7680	398.204927	Folk literature, Arabic
PJ8025-8190	892.7	Arabic literature—Asia
PJ8030-8129	892.7	Arabic literature—Middle East
PJ8195-8390	892.7	Arabic literature—Africa
PJ8395-8490	892.7	Arabic literature—Europe
PJ8500-8517	892.7	Arabic literature—America
PJ8991-8999	492.8	Ethiopian languages
PJ9001-9087	492.81	Ethiopic language
PJ9090-9101	892.81	Ethiopic literature
PK1-9201	491.1	Indo-Iranian languages
PK1-17	491.1	Indo-Iranian philology
PK11-13	491.1071	Indo-Iranian philology—Study and teaching
PK14	491.13	Indo-Iranian languages—Dictionaries
PK21-41	491.15	Indo-Iranian languages—Grammar
PK75-77	491.13	Indo-Iranian languages—Dictionaries
PK80-85	891.1	Indo-Iranian literature
PK101-2899	491.(2-4)	Indo-Aryan languages
PK101-119	491.(2-4)	Indo-Aryan philology
PK119	491.(2-4)	Devanagari alphabet
PK201-379	491.29	Vedic language
PK231-313	491.295	Vedic language—Grammar
PK361-369	491.292	Vedic language—Etymology
PK375-379	491.293	Vedic language—Dictionaries
PK401-976	491.2	Sanskrit language
PK401-418	491.2	Sanskrit philology
PK501-811	491.25	Sanskrit language—Grammar
PK901-919	491.22	Sanskrit language—Etymology
PK920-969	491.23028	Sanskrit language—Lexicography
PK925-969	491.23	Sanskrit language—Dictionaries
PK1001-1095	491.37	Pali language
PK1001-1095	491.37	Pali philology
PK1017-1073	491.375	Pali language—Grammar
PK1083-1086	491.372	Pali language—Etymology
PK1087-1093	491.373028	Pali language—Lexicography
PK1089-1095	491.373	Pali language—Dictionaries
PK1201-1429	491.3	Prakrit languages
PK1206-1215	491.35	Prakrit languages—Grammar
PK1223-1225	491.33	Prakrit languages—Dictionaries
PK1231-1239	491.1	Maharashtri language
PK1501-2845	491.4	Indo-Aryan languages, Modern
PK1511-1523	491.15	Indo-Aryan languages, Modern—Grammar
PK1537	491.13	Indo-Aryan languages, Modern—Dictionaries
PK1539-1542	491.4(1-9)	Indo-Aryan languages, Modern—Dialects
PK1550-1599	491.451	Assamese language
PK1651-1695	491.44	Bengali language
PK1821-1824	491.454	Magahi language
PK1836	491.487	Divehi language
PK1841-1847	491.47	Gujarati language
PK1850-1888	891.47	Gujarati literature
PK1931-1937	491.43	Hindustani language
PK1931-1939	491.43	Hindi language
PK1975-1987	491.439	Urdu language
PK2030-2142	891.43	Hindustani literature
PK2030-2058	891.439	Urdu literature
PK2351-2378	491.46	Marathi language
PK2561-2569	491.45	Oriya language
PK2591-2610	491.49	Pahari languages
PK2595-2599	491.495	Nepali language
PK2631-2639	491.42	Panjabi language
PK2701-2709	491.479	Rajasthani language
PK2781-2794	491.41	Sindhi language
PK2896-2899	491.497	Romany language
PK2911	891.29	Vedic literature
PK3591-4485	891.2	Sanskrit literature
PK4501-4681	891.37	Pali literature
PK4990-5001.8	891.309	Prakrit literature
PK5003-5009	891.308	Prakrit literature
PK6001-6996	491.5	Iranian languages
PK6001-6996	491.5	Iranian philology
PK6101-6109	491.52	Avestan language
PK6121-6129	491.51	Old Persian language
PK6128	491.5111	Old Persian inscriptions
PK6135	491.53	Iranian languages, Middle
PK6201-6399	491.55	Persian language
PK6395	491.5511	Abbreviations, Persian
PK6400-6599	891.55	Persian literature

LC	Dewey	Subject Heading	LC	Dewey	Subject Heading
PK6416-6420	891.551009	Persian poetry	PL410-419	894.23	Mongolian literature
PK6421-6422	891.552009	Persian drama	PL450	494.1	Tungus-Manchu languages
PK6423	891.55808	Persian prose literature	PL451-459	494.1	Evenki language
PK6426	398.2049155	Folk literature, Persian	PL471-479	494.1	Manchu language
PK6443	891.55808	Persian prose literature	PL481.E92	494.1	Even language
PK6871-6879	491.56	Dari language	PL491-494	895	East Asian literature
PK7001-7070	491.499	Dardic languages	PL495	494.6	Ainu language
PK7021-7029	491.499	Kashmiri language	PL501-700	495.6	Japanese language
PK7031-7037	891.499	Kashmiri literature	PL525-.6	495.67	Japanese language—Meiji period, 1868-1912
PK7045.M3	491.499	Maiya language			
PK7070	491.499	Khowar language	PL525.2	495.67	Japanese language—To 794
PK8001-8454	491.992	Armenian language	PL525.5	495.67	Japanese language—Edo period, 1600-1868
PK8451-8499	491.9927	East Armenian dialect			
PK8501-8835	891.992	Armenian literature	PL525.2	495.67	Japanese language—To 794
PK8601-8661	891.992	Armenian literature— Europe	PL525.5	495.67	Japanese language—Edo period, 1600-1868
PK8681-8689	891.992	Armenian literature— United States	PL525-.6	495.67	Japanese language—Meiji period, 1868-1912
PK9001-9201	499.96	Caucasian languages	PL531.3-532.5	495.65	Japanese language— Grammar
PK9051	499.962	Abkhazo-Adyghian languages			
			PL674.5-677.6	495.63	Japanese language— Dictionaries
PK9051	499.964	Daghestan languages			
PK9051.5-.8	899.964	Daghestan literature	PL700-889	895.6	Japanese literature
PK9101-9151	499.969	Georgian language	PL726.12	895.609001	Japanese literature—To 794
PK9106-9115	499.965	Georgian language— Grammar	PL726.1185- .1186	895.609001	Japanese literature—To 1185
PK9160-9169	899.969	Georgian literature	PL727-733	895.61009	Japanese poetry
PK9201.A2	499.962	Abazin language	PL734-739	895.62009	Japanese drama
PK9201.A3	499.9623	Abkhaz language	PL740-747	895.63009	Japanese fiction
PK9201.A35- .A39	899.9623	Abkhaz literature	PL742-.83	895.6009	Japanese essays
			PL748-749	398.204956	Folk literature, Japanese
PK9201.A45- .A49	899.9625	Adygei literature	PL750-751	495.611	Inscriptions, Japanese
			PL755.12	895.608	Japanese literature
PK9201.D3	499.964	Dargwa language	PL757-763	895.61008	Japanese poetry
PK9201.D35- .D39	899.964	Dargwa literature	PL764-769	895.62008	Japanese drama
			PL770-777	895.63008	Japanese fiction
PK9201.K3	499.9624	Kabardian language	PL772-.83	895.408	Japanese essays
PK9201.K35- .K39	899.9624	Kabardian literature	PL787-789	895.6108001	Japanese literature—Heian period, 794-1185
PL1-9	494	Altaic lanugages	PL790-792	895.608002	Japanese literature— 1185-1600
PL21-29	494.3	Turkic languages			
PL31	494.31	Old Turkic language	PL793-799	895.608003	Japanese literature—Edo period, 1600-1868
PL41-45	494.37	Turkic languages, Northeast			
			PL800-820	895.6080042	Japanese literature—Meiji period, 1868-1912
PL51-56	494.357	Turkic languages, Southeast			
			PL821-866	895.60800(44-5)	Japanese literature— Showa period, 1926-1989
PL61-65	494.37	Turkic languages, Northwest			
			PL901-949	495.7	Korean language
PL65.B2	494.38	Karachay-Balkar language	PL935-.6	495.73	Korean language— Dictionaries
PL65.C74	494.388	Crimean Tatar language			
PL65.T3	494.387	Tatar language	PL950-998	895.7	Korean literature
PL65.T35-.T39	894.387	Tatar literature	PL959-961.4	895.71009	Korean poetry
PL101-199	494.35	Turkish language	PL962-964	895.72009	Korean drama
PL201-272	894.35	Turkish literature	PL965-967	895.73009	Korean fiction
PL221	894.352009	Turkish drama	PL968.2-.4	398.204957	Folk literature, Korean
PL237-238	894.352008	Turkish drama	PL969.2-.4	495.711	Inscriptions, Korean
PL311-314	494.361	Azerbaijani language	PL974-976.4	895.71008	Korean poetry
PL331-334	494.364	Turkmen language	PL977-979	895.72008	Korean drama
PL364.Z9.D	494.332	Dolgan dialect	PL980-981.5	895.73008	Korean fiction
PL400-431	494.23	Mongolian languages	PL1001-2244	495.1	Chinese language
PL401-409	494.23	Mongolian language	PL1077	495.17	Chinese language—To 600

LC	Dewey	Subject Heading	LC	Dewey	Subject Heading
PL1079	495.17	Chinese language—Ancient chinese, 600-1200	PL4051-4054	495	Karen language
PL1081	495.17	Chinese language—Middle Chinese, 1200-1919	PL4111-4251	495.91	Thai language
			PL4200-4209	895.911	Thai literature
PL1083	495.17	Chinese language—Modern Chinese, 1919-	PL4281-4587	495.93	Austroasiatic languages
			PL4301-4309	495.93	Mon-Khmer languages
PL1099-1241	495.15	Chinese language—Grammar	PL4371-4379	495.922	Vietnamese language
			PL4378	895.922	Vietnamese literature
PL1201-1219	495.115	Chinese language—Phonology	PL4501-4509	495.95	Munda languages
			PL4601-4794	494.8	Dravidian languages
PL1281-1315	495.12	Chinese language—Etymology	PL4601	494.8	Dravidian philology
			PL4627	494.82	Gadaba language (Dravidian)
PL1401-1498	495.13028	Chinese language—Lexicography	PL4641-4649	494.814	Kannada language
			PL4711-4719	494.812	Malayalam language
PL1420-1498	495.13	Chinese language—Dictionaries	PL4751-4759	494.811	Tamil language
			PL4771-4779	494.827	Telugu language
PL1501-1940	495.17	Chinese language—Dialects	PL5021-6571	499.2	Austronesian languages
			PL5071-5079	499.221	Indonesian langue
PL1731-1740	495.17	Cantonese dialects	PL5101-5129	499.28	Malay language
PL1861-1870	495.17	Hsiang dialects	PL5161-5169	499.222	Javanese language
PL1891-1900	495.1	Mandarin dialects	PL5170-5179	899.222	Javanese literature
PL1931-1940	495.17	Wu dialects	PL5221-5224	499.22	Balinese language
PL2250-3207	895.1	Chinese literature	PL5501-6135	499.21	Philippine languages
PL2280	895.1109	Chinese literature—To 221 B.C.	PL5530-5547	899.21	Philippine literature
			PL6051-6059	499.211	Tagalog language
PL2283	895.10900(2-3)	Chinese literature—221 B.C.-960 A.D.	PL6058	899.211	Tagalog literature
			PL6191-6195	499.52	Micronesian languages
			PL6201-6209	499.5	Melanesian languages
PL2284.5	895.109002	Chinese literature—220-589	PL6235	499.5	Fijian language
			PL6401-6551	499.4	Polynesian languages
PL2285	895.109002	Chinese literature—Three kingdoms, 220-265	PL6465	499.442	Maori language
			PL6515	499.444	Tahitian language
PL2286	895.109002	Chinese literature—Chin dynasty, 265-419	PL6531	499.48	Tonga language (Tonga Islands)
PL2287	895.109002	Chinese literature—Liu Sung dynasty, 420-479	PL6601-6621	499.12	Papuan languages
			PL7001-7101	499.15	Australian languages
PL2290	895.1090024	Chinese literature—Sui dynasty, 581-618	PL8000-8008	496	African languages
			PL8004	496.071	African languages—Study and teaching
PL2294	895.1090044	Chinese literature—Yuan dynasty, 1260-1368	PL8008	496.5	African languages—Grammar
PL2296	895.1090046	Chinese literature—Ming dynasty, 1368-1644	PL8010-8014	896	African literature
PL2297	895.1090048	Chinese literature—Ch'ing dynasty, 1644-1912	PL8024.A33	496.361	Adamawa languages
			PL8025	496.391	Bisa language
PL2306-2355.8	895.11009	Chinese poetry	PL8025	496.39	Bantu languages
PL2356-2393	895.12009	Chinese drama	PL8026.N44	496.3	Niger-Congo languages
PL2395-2413	895.14009	Chinese essays	PL8041	496.5	Acoli language
PL2415-2443	895.13009	Chinese fiction	PL8046.A63	496.3385	Akan language
PL2445-2446	398.204951	Folk literature, Chinese	PL8117	493.7	Daba language
PL2517-2565.8	895.11008	Chinese poetry	PL8123.5-.9	896.34	Dan literature
PL2566-2603	895.12008	Chinese drama	PL8127	496.5	Daza language
PL2606-2623	895.14008	Chinese essays	PL8131	496.5	Dinka language
PL2625-2653	895.13008	Chinese fiction	PL8134	496.32	Diola language
PL3521-3529	495	Sino-Tibetan languages	PL8141	496.3962	Duala language
PL3551-4001	495.4	Tibeto-Burman languages	PL8147	496.3642	Efik language
PL3601-3651	495.4	Tibetan language	PL8161-8164	496.3374	Ewe language
PL3651.D96	495.4	Dzongkha language	PL8164.Z9	496.337	Fon dialect
PL3701-3775	895.4	Tibetan literature	PL8167.F3	496.396	Fang language
PL3881-3884	495.4	Naga languages	PL8167.F4	496.3385	Fanti language
PL3921-3969	495.8	Burmese language	PL8181-8184	496.322	Fula language
PL3970-3988	895.8	Burmese literature	PL8191	496.3378	Ga language
PL4001.G2	495.4	Garo language	PL8197	496.5	Gambai dialect

LC	Dewey	Subject Heading	LC	Dewey	Subject Heading
PL8201	496.3957	Ganda language	PN49	808.804291	Mysticism in literature
PL8204	496.348	Gbandi language	PN56.A5	808.8015	Allegory
PL8205	496.361	Gbaya language	PN56.C6	808.80142	Classicism
PL8207.G55	496.395	Gisu language	PN56.M94	808.8015	Myth in literature
PL8221	496.33	Grebo language	PN56.M95	808.8037	Mythology in literature
PL8541	496.1	Nama langue	PN56.R3	808.8012	Realism in literature
PL8571-8574	496.5	Nubian languages	PN56.R3	808.8012	Naturalism in literature
PL8689	496.3977	Sotho language	PN56.R7	808.80145	Romanticism
PL8701-8704	496.392	Swahili language	PN56.S87	808.801163	Surrealism (Literature)
PL8771	496.397	Venda language	PN56.S9	808.8015	Symbolism in literature
PL8801-8804	496.397	Yao language	PN57.D4	808.8038291216	Devil in literature
PL8841-8844	496.3986	Zulu language	PN59-72	807.1	Literature—Study and teaching
PM1-7356	497	Indians of North America—Languages			
			PN75-99	809	Literature—History and criticism
PM1-95	494.6	Hyperborean languages			
PM31-34	497.19	Aleut language	PN83	808.54509	Reading
PM50-94	497.1	Eskimo languages	PN101-249	808.02	Authorship
PM50-64	497.12	Inuit language	PN154	174.98	Literary ethics
PM600-609	497.3	Algonquian languages	PN161	380.145808	Authorship—Marketing
PM635	497.3	Arapaho language	PN161	380.14580802	Queries (Authorship)
PM781-784	497.55	Cherokee language	PN162	808.027	Editing
PM851-854	497.3	Ojibwa language	PN163	070.52	Literary agents
PM1001	497.52	Crow language	PN167-168	808	Plagiarism
PM1021-1024	497.52	Dakota language	PN171.4-229	808	Rhetoric
PM1343	497.57	Hokan-Coahuiltecan languages	PN171.F6-.F7	098.3	Literary forgeries and mystifications
PM1351	497.45	Hopi language	PN171.Q6	808.882	Quotation
PM1381-1384	497.55	Iroquoian languages	PN203	808	Style, Literary
PM1881-1884	497.55	Mohawk language	PN205	808.066	Exposition (Rhetoric)
PM1885	497.3	Mohegan language	PN441-595	809	Literature—History and criticism
PM1971-1974	497.3	Muskogean languages			
PM2006-2009	497.2	Navajo language	PN597	809.91	Literary movements
PM2175	497.45	Pima languages	PN601	808.8012	Naturalism in literature
PM2321	497.45	Shoshonean languages	PN603	808.80145	Romanticism
PM2515	497.45	Ute language	PN611-630	809.01	Literature, Ancient
PM2711	497.9	Zuni language	PN665-694	808.8002	Literature, Medieval
PM3001-4566	497.9	Indians of Central America—Languages	PN683-687	398.20902	Legends
			PN688-691	808.82	Poetry, Medieval
PM3961-3969	497.4152	Mayan lanuagages	PN691	808.814	Lyric poetry
PM4061-4069	497.452	Nahuatl Language	PN695-779	808.800(3-4)	Literature, Modern
PM5001-7356	497/498	Indians of South America—Languages	PN715-749	808.800(24-32)	Renaissance
			PN750-759	808.80145	Romanticism
PM5071-5079	497	Indians of the West Indies—Languages	PN816	808.80145	Romance fiction
			PN836	839.3009	Germanic fiction
PM7171-7179	498.38	Tupi languages	PN849.G	820	British literature
PM7801-7895	417.22	Pidgin languages	PN849.026	899	Pacific Island literature
PM7801-7895	401.3	Lingua francas	PN849.R9-.R92	891.708004	Soviet literature
PM7831-7875	447.9	Creole dialects	PN905-1008	398.209	Folk literature—History and criticism
PM7875.G8	427.9	Sea Islands Creole dialect			
PM7891	427.9	Pidgin English	PN931-937	827	English wit and humor
PM8001-9021	499.99	Languages, Artificial	PN1010-1525	808.1	Poetry
PM8008	401.3	Language, Universal	PN1031-1035	808.1	Versification
PM8201-8298	499.992	Esperanto	PN1039-1049	808.1	Poetics
PM9001-9021	417.2	Languages, Secret	PN1101	808.81071	Poetry—Study and teaching
PN1-9	805	Literature—Periodicals	PN1105-1279	809.1	Poetry—History and criticism
PN20-29	806	Literature—Societies, etc.	PN1301-1333	808.8132	Epic poetry
PN44	808.8024	Literature—Stories, plots, etc.	PN1341-1347	398.2	Folk poetry
			PN1351-1389	808.14	Lyric poetry
PN45	801.93	Literature—Aesthetics	PN1441	808.882	Epigrams
PN45	801	Literature—Philosophy	PN1514	808.8142	Sonnet
PN48	808.8036	Nature in literature	PN1530	808.8245	Monologue

LC	Dewey	Subject Heading	LC	Dewey	Subject Heading
PN1551	808.8026	Dialogue	PN2181-2193	792.09034	Theater—History—20th century
PN1560-1590	790.2	Performing arts			
PN1581	790.209	Performing arts—History	PN2205-2217	792.028092	Actors
PN1585-1589	725.83	Centers for the performing arts	PN2205-2217	792.028092	Actresses
			PN2219.08	792.022	Theater, Open-air
PN1600-1861	808.2	Drama	PN2220-2298	792.0973	Theater—United States
PN1660-1692	808.2	Drama—Technique	PN2267	792.02230973	Little theater movement
PN1701	808.20071	Drama—Study and teaching	PN2270.A35	792.08996073	Afro-American theater
PN1707	809.2	Dramatic criticism	PN2660-2668	792.09495	Theater—Greece
PN1720-1861	809.2	Drama—History and criticism	PN2870-2878	792.0951	Theater—China
			PN2920-2928	792.0952	Theater—Japan
PN1761	809.2527	Mysteries and miracle-plays	PN2924.5.K3	792.0952	Kabuki
PN1910-1919	808.82527	Melodrama	PN3151-3171	792.0222	Amateur theater
PN1940-1949	808.825232	Farce	PN3202-3299	791.62	Pageants
PN1960-1969	792.7	Music-halls (Variety-theaters, cabarets, etc.)	PN3203-3299	792.16	Passion-plays
			PN3311-3503	808.3	Fiction
PN1960-1969	792.7	Vaudeville	PN3329-3503	809.3	Fiction—History and criticism
PN1970-1979	791.53	Puppets			
PN1979.S5	791.53	Shadow shows	PN3355-3383	808.3	Fiction—Technique
PN1990-1992.92	384.54	Broadcasting	PN3373	809.31	Short story
PN1991-.9	791.44	Radio broadcasting	PN3377.5.D4	809.3872	Detective and mystery stories—Technique
PN1991.73	808.222	Radio plays—Technique			
PN1991.8.C65	791.44617	Radio comedies	PN3378	809.924	Plots (Drama, novel, etc.)
PN1991.8.E84	384.54089	Ethnic radio broadcasting	PN3433-.8	808.838762	Science fiction
PN1991.8.S4	791.446	Soap operas	PN3441	809.381	Historical fiction
PN1992-.92	384.5532	Television programs	PN3448.A3	809.387	Adventure stories
PN1992.4	791.45028092	Television actors and actresses	PN3448.D4	809.3872	Detective and mystery stories
PN1992.8.C66	791.45617	Television comedies	PN4001-4355	808.85	Oratory
PN1992.8.S4	791.456	Soap operas	PN4021-4055	809.5	Oratory—History
PN1992.95	791.45	Video recordings	PN4096	809	Rhetorical criticism
PN1993-1999	791.43	Motion pictures	PN4121-4130	808.851	Public speaking
PN1995	791.4375	Motion pictures—Reviews	PN4142	808.5	Speechwriting
PN1995.5	791.43682	Motion pictures—Religious aspects	PN4145-4151	808.54	Oral interpretation
			PN4177-4191	808.53	Debates and debating
PN1995.5	175	Motion pictures—Moral and ethical aspects	PN4199-4355	808.54	Recitations
			PN4305.M6	808.8245	Monologues
PN1995.9.D78	791.43655	Drugs in motion pictures	PN4400	809.6	Letters
PN1995.9.E77	791.4092	Entertainers in motion pictures	PN4500	808.4	Essay
			PN4700-5650	070.4	Journalism
PN1995.9.F67	791.43	Foreign films	PN4700-5650	070.172	Press
PN1995.9.M86	791.43657	Musical films	PN4700-5650	050	Periodicals
PN1995.9.N4	791.4308996073	Blacks in motion pictures	PN4720	070.4074	Journalism—Exhibitions
PN1995.9.S7	791.43028092	Stunt performers	PN4749	070.4	Journalism—Social aspects
PN1996-1997	791.437	Motion picture plays	PN4751	070.44932	Journalism—Political aspects
PN1997.5	741.58	Animated films			
PN2000-3299	792	Theater	PN4778	070.41	Journalism—Editing
PN2055	792.023	Acting—Vocational guidance	PN4781	070.43	Reporters and reporting
PN2056	174.97914	Actors—Professional ethics	PN4784.A18	363.46	Abortion in the press
PN2061-2071	792.028	Acting	PN4784.D57	904	Disasters in the press
PN2071.G4	792.3	Mime	PN4784.E53	070.435	Electronic news gathering
PN2071.I5	792.028	Improvisation (Acting)	PN4784.N5	070.175	Newsletters
PN2091.A	792.028	Theaters—Accidents	PN4784.S6	070.449796	Sports journalism
PN2091.S8	792.025	Theaters—Stage-setting and scenery	PN4785-4823	070.4071	Journalism—Study and teaching
PN2100-2193	792.09	Theater—History	PN4823	070.4333092	War correspondents
PN2131-2145	792.0901	Theater—History—To 500	PN4840-4900	071	American periodicals
PN2152-2160	792.0902	Theater—History—Medieval, 500-1500	PN4840-4899	051	American newspapers
			PN4882.5	070.484	Afro-American press
PN2171-2179	792.09033	Theater—History—18th century	PN4882.5	070.484	Afro-American newspapers
			PN4888.A2	363.460973	Abortion in the press

LC	Dewey	Subject Heading	LC	Dewey	Subject Heading
PN4901-4920	051	Canadian periodicals	PN6366-6377	793.73	Acrostics
PN4930.5-4959	079.72	Journalism—West Indies	PN6400-6525	398.9	Proverbs
PN5000-5106	079.8	South American periodicals	PN6700-6790	070.444	Comic books, strips, etc.
PN5110-5355	073-078	European periodicals	PQ1-3999	840	French literature
PN5111-5130	052	English periodicals	PQ51-65	840.71	French literature—Study and teaching
PN5111-5129	072.(1-8)	English newspapers			
PN5171-5790	054.1	French periodicals	PQ151-221	840.900(1-2)	French literature—To 1500
PN5201-5220	053.1	German periodicals	PQ151-216	848.08	French prose literature—To 1500
PN5241-5250	055.1	Italian periodicals			
PN5271-5280	059.9171	Russian periodicals	PQ201-205	841.03209	Epic literature, French
PN5280.5-5310	058	Scandinavian periodicals	PQ230-239	840.9003	French literature—16th century
PN5281-5290	058.81	Danish periodicals			
PN5281-5289	078.489	Danish newspapers	PQ241-251	840.9004	French literature—17th century
PN5317.P4	056.1	Spanish periodicals			
PN5321-5330	056.9	Portuguese periodicals	PQ261-276	840.9005	French literature—18th century
PN5360-5449	079.5	Asian periodicals			
PN5450-5499	079.6	African periodicals	PQ281-299	840.9007	French literature—19th century
PN5510-5590	079.94	Australian periodicals			
PN6010-6078	808	Literature—Collections	PQ301-307	840.90091	French literature—20th century
PN6010-6065	808.8	Anthologies			
PN6071.E7	808.803538	Erotic literature	PQ400-491	841.009	French poetry
PN6080-6095	808.882	Quotations	PQ416-418	841.309	French poetry—16th century
PN6081-6084	820.802	Quotations, English			
PN6086-6089	840.802	Quotations, French	PQ421-423	841.409	French poetry—17th century
PN6090-6093	830.802	Quotations, German			
PN6099-6110	808.108	Poetry—Collections	PQ426-428	841.509	French poetry—18th century
PN6110.5-6120	808.82	Drama—Collections			
PN6110.C4	398.8	Nursery rhymes	PQ431-439	841.709	French poetry—19th century
PN6110.E6	808.8132	Epic poetry			
PN6110.N17	808.813	Narrative poetry	PQ441-443	841.9109	French poetry—20th century
PN6110.O4	808.8143	Odes			
PN6110.P3	808.87	Parodies	PQ601-657	848.08	French prose literature
PN6111-6120	808.820512	Tragedy	PQ631-671	843.009	French fiction
PN6119.9	792.0222	Amateur plays	PQ671	843.909	French fiction—20th century
PN6120.95.A38	808.8387	Adventure stories			
PN6120.95.S33	808.838762	Science fiction	PQ781-841	398.20441	Folk literature, French
PN6120.F3	808.825232	Farces	PQ1121-1125	840.8003	French literature—16th century
PN6120.M9	808.82527	Detective and mystery plays			
PN6120.P3-.P4	792.3	Pantomines	PQ1126-1130	840.8004	French literature—17th century
PN6120.R2	808.8222	Radio plays			
PN6121-6129	808.85	Speeches, addresses, etc.	PQ1131-1135	840.8005	French literature—18th century
PN6130-6140	808.86	Letters			
PN6141-6145	808.84	Essays	PQ1136-1139	840.8007	French literature—19th century
PN6147-6231	808.87	Wit and humor			
PN6147	808.87092	Humorists	PQ1141	840.80091	French literature—20th century
PN6149.P3	808.87	Parody			
PN6157-6162	817.008	American wit and humor	PQ1160-1193	841.008	French poetry
PN6173-6175	827.008	English wit and humor	PQ1211-1241	842.008	French drama
PN6222.N	839.317008	Dutch wit and humor	PQ1243-1279	848.08	French prose literature
PN6222.S	839.367	Afrikaans wit and humor	PQ1261-1279	843.008	French fiction
PN6231.B84	792.7	Burlesques	PQ1281-1283	845.008	Speeches, addresses, etc., French
PN6231.L5	808.8175	Limericks			
PN6231.S2	808.87	Satire	PQ1300-1595	840.800(1-2)	French literature—To 1500
PN6259-6268	808.882	Anecdotes	PQ1300-1391	841.(1-2)08	French poetry—To 1500
PN6269-6278	398.9	Aphorisms and apothegms	PQ1341-1385	842.(1-2)08	French drama—To 1500
PN6279-6288	808.882	Epigrams	PQ3809	840	French literature—Foreign countries
PN6282	848.02	Epigrams, French			
PN6299-6308	398.9	Maxims	PQ3810-3858	840	Belgian literature (French)
PN6340-6348	808.851	Toasts	PQ3870-3888	840	Swiss literature (French)
PN6366-6377	793.24	Charades	PQ3900-3919.2	840	French-Canadian literature
PN6366-6377	808.882	Riddles			

LC	Dewey	Subject Heading
PQ3940-3949	840	West Indian literature (French)
PQ3960-3979	840	Vietnamese literature (French)
PQ3980-3989.2	840	African literature (French)
PQ3998.5.N	840	New Caledonian literature (French)
PQ4001-5999	850	Italian literature
PQ4001-4199	850.9	Italian literature—History and criticism
PQ4013-4023	850.71	Italian literature—Study and teaching
PQ4075	850.9003	Italian literature—15th century
PQ4079-4080	850.9004	Italian literature—16th century
PQ4081-4082	850.9005	Italian literature—17th century
PQ4083-4084	850.9006	Italian literature—18th century
PQ4085-4086	850.9007	Italian literature—19th century
PQ4087	850.90091	Italian literature—20th century
PQ4091-4131	851.009	Italian poetry
PQ4133-4160	852.009	Italian drama
PQ4161-4165	858.08	Italian prose literature
PQ4183.E8	854.009	Italian essays
PQ4183.L4	856.009	Italian letters
PQ4186-4199	398.20451	Folk literature, Italian
PQ6001-8929	860	Spanish literature
PQ6013-6020	860.71	Spanish literature—Study and teaching
PQ6022-6167	860.009	Spanish literature—History and criticism
PQ6057-6060	860.900(1-2)	Spanish literature—To 1500
PQ6063-6072	860.900(2-3)	Spanish literature—Classical period, 1500-1700
PQ6075-6098	861.009	Spanish poetry
PQ6099-6129	862.009	Spanish drama
PQ6131-6153	868.08	Spanish prose literature
PQ6138-6147	863.009	Spanish fiction
PQ6155-6167	398.20461	Folk literature, Spanish
PQ6174.95-6215	861.008	Spanish poetry
PQ6217-6241	862.008	Spanish drama
PQ6247-6264	868.08	Spanish prose literature
PQ6251-6257	863.008	Spanish fiction
PQ7020-8921	860	Spanish literature—Foreign countries
PQ7100-7298.36	860	Mexican literature
PQ7370-7390	860	Cuban literature
PQ7400-7409.2	860	Dominican literature
PQ7402	861.009	Dominican poetry
PQ7406	861.008	Dominican poetry
PQ7420-7440	860	Puerto Rican literature
PQ7480-7489.2	860	Costa Rican literature
PQ7490-7499.2	860	Guatemalan literature
PQ7500-7509.2	860	Honduran literature
PQ7510-7519.2	860	Nicaraguan literature
PQ7520-7529.2	860	Panamanian literature
PQ7530-7539.2	860	Salvadoran literature
PQ7600-7798.36	860	Argentine literature
PQ7801-7820	860	Bolivian literature
PQ7900-8098.36	860	Chilean literature
PQ8160-8180.36	860	Colombian literature
PQ8200-8220.36	860	Ecuadorian literature
PQ8210	861	Ecuadorian poetry
PQ8212	863	Ecuadorian fiction
PQ8214-.5	861	Ecuadorian poetry
PQ8216.F5	863	Ecuadorian fiction
PQ8250-8259	860	Paraguayan literature
PQ8300-8498.36	860	Peruvian literature
PQ8510-8519	860	Uruguayan literature
PQ8530-8550.36	860	Venezuelan literature
PQ8700-8899	860	Philippine literature
PQ9000-9999	869	Portuguese literature
PQ9008-9009.5	869.071	Portuguese literature—Study and teaching
PQ9061-9081	869.1009	Portuguese poetry
PQ9083-9095	869.2009	Portuguese drama
PQ9097-9119	869.808	Portuguese prose literature
PQ9121-9128	398.20469	Folk literature, Portuguese
PQ9149-9163	869.1008	Portuguese poetry
PQ9164-9170	869.2008	Portuguese drama
PQ9172-9188	869.808	Portuguese prose literature
PQ9421	869	Portuguese literature—Foreign countries
PQ9450-9460.2	860	Galician literature
PQ9500-9699	869	Brazilian literature
PQ9900-9948	869	African literature (Portuguese)
PR1-9680	820	English literature
PR1-978	820.9	English literature—History and criticism
PR19	820.3	English literature—Dictionaries
PR31-55	820.71	English literature—Study and teaching
PR57-78	820.9	English literature—Criticism, Textual
PR87	820.0202	English literature—Outlines, syllabi, etc.
PR111-119	821.0099287	English poetry—Women authors
PR111-119	820.99287	English literature—Women authors
PR171-236	829.009	English literature—Old English, ca. 450-1100
PR201-217	829.1009	English poetry—Old English, ca. 450-1100
PR221-236	829.808	English prose literature—Old English, ca. 450-1100
PR251-369	820.900(1-2)	English literature—Middle English, 1100-1500
PR311-369	821.(1-2)09	English poetry, Middle English, 1100-1500
PR321-347	821.03209	Epic poetry, English
PR401-439	820.900(2-4)	English literature—Early modern, 1500-1700
PR441-449	820.9005	English literature—18th century

LC	Dewey	Subject Heading
PR451-469	820.9008	English literature—19th century
PR471-479	820.9009	English literature—20th century
PR500-611	821.009	English poetry
PR500-609	821.009	English poetry—History and criticism
PR521-549	821.(2-4)09	English poetry—Early modern, 1500-1700
PR551-579	821.509	English poetry—18th century
PR581-599	821.809	English poetry—19th century
PR601-609	821.909	English poetry—20th century
PR621-739	822.009	English drama
PR631	822.052309	English drama (Comedy)
PR633	822.051209	English drama (Tragedy)
PR635.D45	822.009	Domestic drama, English
PR641-644	822.(1-2)09	English drama—To 1500
PR646-658	822.(2-3)09	English drama—Early modern and Elizabethan, 1500-1600
PR671-698	822.409	English drama—17th century
PR701-719	822.509	English drama—18th century
PR721-734	822.809	English drama—19th century
PR736-739	822.909	English drama—20th century
PR750-888	828.08	English prose literature
PR767-769	828.08	English prose literature—Early modern, 1500-1700
PR769	828.08	English prose literature—18th century
PR821-888	823.009	English fiction
PR881-888	823.909	English fiction—20th century
PR901-907	825.009	Speeches, addresses, etc., English
PR908	828.03	English diaries
PR911-917	826.009	English letters
PR921-927	824.009	English essays
PR931-937	827.009	English wit and humor
PR951-981	398.2042	Folk literature, English
PR1110.C3	820.809222	English literature—Catholic authors
PR1110.W6	820.809287	English literature—Women authors
PR1119-1131	820.8001	English literature—Middle English, 1100-1500
PR1119-1131	820.800(3-4)	English literature—Early modern, 1500-1700
PR1134-1139	820.8005	English literature—18th century
PR1143-1145	820.8008	English literature—19th century
PR1149	820.8008	English literature—20th century
PR1170-1227	821	English poetry
PR1177	821.00809287	English poetry—Women authors
PR1195.M2	782.43	Madrigals
PR1203	821.(1-2)08	English poetry—Middle English, 1100-1500
PR1204-1213	821.(3-4)08	English poetry—Early modern, 1500-1700
PR1215-1219	821.508	English poetry—18th century
PR1221-1224	821.808	English poetry—19th century
PR1224-1227	821.908	English poetry—20th century
PR1241-1273	822.008	English drama
PR1248	822.052308	English drama (Comedy)
PR1257	822.051208	English drama (Tragedy)
PR1260	822.(1-2)08	English drama—To 1500
PR1262-1263	822.(2-3)08	English drama—Early modern and Elizabethan, 1500-1600
PR1265.3-1266	822.408	English drama—17th century
PR1269	822.508	English drama—18th century
PR1271	822.808	English drama—19th century
PR1272	822.908	English drama—20th century
PR1281-1300	828.08	English prose literature
PR1281-1309	823.008	English fiction
PR1285	820.8022	Description (Rhetoric)
PR1293-1295	828.08	English prose literature—Early modern, 1500-1700
PR1297	828.08	English prose literature—18th century
PR1301-1304	820.8008	English literature—19th century
PR1321-1329	825.008	Speeches, addresses, etc., English
PR1330	828.03	English diaries
PR1341-1349	826.008	English letters
PR1361-1369	824.008	English essays
PR1490-1508	829.1	English poetry—Old English, ca. 450-1100
PR2750-3112	822.33	Shakespeare, William, 1564-1616
PR8500-8621	820.99411	English literature—Scottish authors
PR8510-8553	820.9	Scottish literature
PR8561-8581	821.0089411	English poetry—Scottish authors
PR8597-8607	828.08	English prose literature—Scottish authors
PR8631-8693	820.809411	English literature—Scottish authors
PR8631-8644	820	Scottish literature
PR8649-8663	821.00809411	English poetry—Scottish authors
PR8672-8687	828.08	English prose literature—Scottish authors

LC	Dewey	Subject Heading	LC	Dewey	Subject Heading
PR8700-8821	820.99415	English literature—Irish authors	PS335	812.0071	American drama—Study and teaching
PR8831-8893	820.809415	English literature—Irish authors	PS336.C7	812.052309	American drama (Comedy)
			PS336.T7	812.051209	American drama (Tragedy)
PR8848-8863	821.00809415	English poetry—Irish authors	PS360-379	818.08	American prose literature
			PS366	818.08	American prose literature—Colonial period, ca. 1600-1775
PR8900-8997	820.809429	English literature—Welsh authors			
PR8926-8932	821.00909429	English poetry—Welsh authors	PS367-369	818.08	American prose literature—Revolutionary period, 1775-1783
PR8955-8969	821.00809429	English poetry—Welsh authors	PS371-379	813.009	American fiction
PR9320-.9	820	Guyanese literature	PS400-408	815.009	Speeches, addresses, etc., American
PR9340-9408	820.9	African literature (English)			
PR9342	821.009	African poetry (English)	PS409	818.03	American diaries
PR9343	822	African drama (English)	PS410-418	816.009	American letters
PR9344	823	African fiction (English)	PS420-428	814.009	American essays
PR9346-.5	821.008	African poetry (English)	PS430-438	817.009	American wit and humor
PR9347	822.008	African drama (English)	PS451-478	398.20973	Folk literature, American
PR9347.5	823.009	African fiction (English)	PS508.N3	810.80896073	American literature—Afro-American authors
PR9600-9619.3	820	Australian literature			
PR9632.2-.6	828.08	New Zealand prose literature	PS508.W7	810.809287	American literature—Women authors
PR9637.25-.92	828.08	New Zealand prose literature	PS589	811.00809287	American poetry—Women authors
PR9900.J	820.80952	English literature—Japanese authors	PS591.N4	811.0080896073	American poetry—Afro-American authors
PS	810	American literature	PS623-635	812.008	American drama
PS	811	American poetry	PS642-659.2	818.08	American prose literature
PS147-151	810.99287	American literature—Women authors	PS660-668	815.008	Speeches, addresses, etc., American
PS153-490	810.9	American literature—History and criticism	PS669	818.3	American diaries
			PS670-678	816.008	American letters
PS153.N5	810.9896073	Afro-American authors	PS680-688	814.008	American essays
PS185-191	810.9001	American literature—Colonial period, ca. 1600-1775	PT1-1021	830	German literature
			PT31	830.6	German literature—Congresses
PS193	810.9002	American literature—Revolutionary period, 1775-1783	PT41	830.3	German language dictionaries
PS201-214	810.9003	American literature—19th century	PT51-65	830.71	German literature—Study and teaching
PS208	810.900(2-3)	American literature—1783-1850	PT175-230	830.9002	German literature—Middle High German, 1050-1500
PS221-228	810.9005	American literature—20th century	PT175-227	831.209	German poetry—Middle High German, 1050-1500
PS306-.5	811.071	American poetry—Study and teaching	PT183	830.9001	German literature—Old High German, 750-1050
PS312	811.109	American poetry—Colonial period, ca 1600-1775	PT238-281	830.900(3-5)	German literature—Early modern, 1500-1700
PS314	811.209	American poetry—Revolutional period, 1775-1783	PT285-321	830.9006	German literature—18th century—History and criticism
PS316-321	811.309	American poetry—19th century	PT341-395	830.9007	German literature—19th century—History and criticism
PS319	811.209	American poetry—1783-1850	PT401-403	830.9009	German literature—20th century
PS324	811.509	American poetry—20th century	PT412-418	839.69808	Icelandic prose literature
			PT500-597	831.009	German poetry
PS330-351	812.009	American drama	PT525-531	831.(4-5)09	German poetry—Early modern, 1500-1700

LC	Dewey	Subject Heading	LC	Dewey	Subject Heading
PT533-535	831.609	German poetry—18th century	PT3808-3809	830	German literature—Foreign countries
PT541-547	831.709	German poetry—19th century	PT3830-3837.5	830	German literature—Czechoslovakia
PT551-553	831.909	German poetry—20th century	PT3840-3848	830	Hungarian literature (German)
PT605-709	832.009	German drama	PT3860-3878	830	Swiss literature (German)
PT711-871	838.08	German prose literature	PT3900-3919	830	German American literature (German)
PT741-772	833.009	German fiction			
PT753-756	833.(3-5)09	German fiction—Early modern, 1500-1700	PT4801-4897	839.4	Low German literature
PT759	833.609	German fiction—18th century	PT4803	839.4071	Low German literature—Study and teaching
PT763-771	833.709	German fiction—19th century	PT4813	839.409001	Low German literature—To 1500
PT772	833.909	German fiction—20th century	PT4817-4820	839.41009	Low German poetry
PT801	835.009	Speeches, addresses, etc., German	PT4821	839.42009	Low German drama
			PT4829-4830	398.204394	Folk literature, Low German
PT811	836.009	German letters	PT4834-4836	839.41008	Low German poetry
PT831	834.009	German essays	PT4837-4838	839.42008	Low German drama
PT881-951	398.20431	Folk literature, German	PT5001-5980	839.31	Dutch literature
PT1100-1479	830.8	German literature	PT5040-5044	839.31071	Dutch literature—Study and teaching
PT1121-1126	830.800(3-5)	German literature—Early modern, 1500-1700	PT5121-5137	839.3109001	Dutch literature—To 1500
PT1131	830.8006	German literature—18th century	PT5141-5165	839.310900 (2-4)	Dutch literature—1500-1800
PT1136	830.8007	German literature—19th century	PT5170-5175	839.3109005	Dutch literature—19th century
PT1141	830.8009	German literature—20th century	PT5180-5185	839.3109006	Dutch literature—20th century
PT1151-1241	831.008	German poetry	PT5201-5245	839.311009	Dutch poetry
PT1163-1165	831.(3-5)08	German poetry—Early modern, 1500-1700	PT5250-5295	839.312009	Dutch drama
PT1167-1169	831.608	German poetry—18th century	PT5300-5336	839.31808	Dutch prose literature
			PT5320-5336	839.313009	Dutch fiction
PT1171-1173	831.708	German poetry—19th century	PT5346	839.317009	Dutch wit and humor
			PT5351-5395	398.2043931	Folk literature, Dutch
PT1174-1175	831.908	German poetry—20th century	PT5470-5488	839.311008	Dutch poetry
			PT5490-5515	839.312008	Dutch drama
PT1251-1299	832.008	German drama	PT5517-5547	839.31808	Dutch prose literature
PT1271-1273	832.051208	German drama (Tragedy)	PT5520-5530	839.313008	Dutch fiction
PT1275-1277	832.052308	German drama (Comedy)	PT5539	839.314008	Dutch essays
PT1301-1340	838.08	German prose literature	PT5541	839.317008	Dutch wit and humor
PT1315	833.608	German fiction—18th century	PT6000-6466.36	839.31	Flemish literature
PT1321-1340	833.008	German fiction	PT6040	839.31071	Flemish literature—Study and teaching
PT1332	833.708	German fiction—19th century	PT6140	839.311009	Flemish poetry
PT1334	833.908	German fiction—20th century	PT6200-6230	398.2043931	Folk literature, Flemish
			PT6330-6348	839.311008	Flemish poetry
PT1337-1340	833.0108	Short stories, German	PT6350-6360	839.312008	Flemish drama
PT1344-1345	835.008	Speeches, addresses, etc., German	PT6365-6397	839.31808	Flemish prose literature
			PT6500-6593.36	839.36	Afrikaans literature
PT1348-1352	836.008	German letters	PT6515	839.361009	Afrikaans poetry
PT1354	834.008	German essays	PT6520	839.362009	Afrikaans drama
PT1375-1479	830.8002	German literature—Middle High German, 1050-1700	PT6525	839.363009	Afrikaans fiction
			PT6525	839.36808	Afrikaans prose literature
PT1391-1429	831.(1-3)08	German poetry—Middle High German, 1050-1500	PT6540-6545	398.2043936	Folk literature, Afrikaans
			PT6545	839.361008	Afrikaans poetry
			PT6560	839.361008	Afrikaans poetry
			PT6590	839.36808	Afrikaans prose literature
			PT6570	839.36808	Afrikaans prose literature
PT1411-1418	831.03208	Epic poetry, German	PT6570	839.363008	Afrikaans fiction
			PT6570	839.362008	Afrikaans drama

LC	Dewey	Subject Heading	LC	Dewey	Subject Heading
PT7001-9999	839.5	Scandinavian literature	PT9460-9499	839.7808	Swedish prose literature
PT7035-7039	839.5071	Scandinavian literature—Study and teaching	PT9480-9492	839.73009	Swedish fiction
PT7088-7089	398.204395	Folk literature, Scandinavian	PT9509-9542	398.204397	Folk literature, Swedish
PT7101-7338	839.6	Old Norse literature	PT9580-9599	839.71008	Swedish poetry
PT7135-7139	839.6071	Old Norse literature—Study and teaching	PT9605-9625	839.72008	Swedish drama
PT7170-7175	839.61009	Old Norse Poetry	PT9626-9639	839.7808	Swedish prose literature
PT7177-7211	839.6808	Old Norse prose literature	PT9627-9630	839.73008	Swedish fiction
PT7181-7193	839.6309	Sagas	PZ1	823.00809287	English fiction—Women authors
PT7230-7252	839.61008	Old Norse poetry	PZ1-3	808.83872	Detective and mystery stories
PT7255-7262	839.6808	Old Norse prose literature	PZ1	813	American fiction
PT7261-7262	839.6308	Sagas	PZ5-90	808.068	Children's literature
PT7351-7550	839.69	Icelandic literature	PZ8	398.2	Fairy tales
PT7370-7373	839.69071	Icelandic literature—Study and teaching	PZ8.3	398.8	Nursery rhymes
PT7411	839.692009	Icelandic drama	Q	500.2	Physical sciences
PT7413	839.693009	Icelandic fiction	Q	500	Science
PT7420-7438	398.20439691	Folk literature, Icelandic	Q1-9	505	Science—Periodicals
PT7465-7467	839.691008	Icelandic poetry	Q10-99	506	Science—Societies, etc.
PT7470-7477	839.692008	Icelandic drama	Q105	507.4	Science—Exhibitions
PT7480-7495	839.69808	Icelandic prose literature	Q123	503	Science—Dictionaries
PT7485-7487	839.693008	Icelandic fiction	Q124.95	509.01	Science, Ancient
PT7601-8260	839.81	Danish literature	Q124.97	509.02	Science, Medieval
PT7640-7644	839.81071	Danish literature—Study and teaching	Q124.6-127.2	509	Science—History
PT7721-7737	839.8109001	Danish literature—To 1500	Q125.2	509.0(24-31)	Science, Renaissance
			Q127-.2	509.(4-9)	Science—[By region or country]
PT7741-7747	839.810900(4-5)	Danish literature—18th century	Q141-143	509.2	Scientists—Biography
PT7751-7756	839.8109006	Danish literature—19th century	Q145	502.5	Scientists—Directories
			Q148-149	508	Scientific surveys
PT7760	839.8109007	Danish literature—20th century	Q172.5.S95	539.725	Symmetry
			Q174-175.32	501	Science—Philosophy
PT7770-7795	839.811009	Danish poetry	Q174-175.32	501	Science—Methodology
PT7800-7832	839.812009	Danish drama	Q175.5	303.483	Science—Social aspects
PT7835-7862	839.81808	Danish prose literature	Q179	501.4	Science—Terminology
PT7835-7862	839.813009	Danish fiction	Q179	501.4	Science—Nomenclature
PT7866	839.816009	Danish letters	Q180	507.2	Research
PT7900-7930	398.2043981	Folk literature, Danish	Q180.55.G7	001.40681	Endowment of research
PT7975-7994	839.811008	Danish poetry	Q181-183.4	507.1	Science—Study and teaching
PT7999-8020	839.812008	Danish drama	Q182.3	507.8	Science projects
PT8021-8024	839.81808	Danish prose literature	Q183-.4	507.2	Laboratories
PT8022-8024	839.813008	Danish fiction	Q183.9	502.85	Science—Data processing
PT8030	839.816008	Danish letters	Q184-185.7	502.84	Scientific apparatus and instruments
PT8301-9155	839.82	Norwegian literature	Q222	502.2	Scientific illustration
PT8340-8344	839.82071	Norwegian literature—Study and teaching	Q295	003.01	System theory
PT8460-8490	839.821009	Norwegian poetry	Q300-390	003.5	Cybernetics
PT8500-8534	839.822009	Norwegian drama	Q304	003.503	Cybernetics—Dictionaries
PT8540-8567	839.82808	Norwegian prose literature	Q305	003.509	Cybernetics—History
PT8555-8567	839.823009	Norwegian fiction	Q316	003.5071	Cybernetics—Study and teaching
PT8600-8635	398.2043982	Folk literature, Norwegian			
PT8675-8695	839.821008	Norwegian poetry	Q317-321	003.5	Bionics
PT8699-8718	839.822008	Norwegian drama	Q325-390	003.7	Self-organizing systems
PT8719-8722	839.82808	Norwegian prose literature	Q325.5-.78	006.31	Machine learning
PT8720-8722	839.823008	Norwegian fiction	Q325.6	006.31	Reinforcement learning (Machine learning)
PT9000-9094	839.83	Norwegian literature (Nynorsk)	Q327	006.4	Pattern perception
PT9201-9999	839.7	Swedish literature	Q334-342	006.3	Artificial intelligence
PT9375-9405	839.71009	Swedish poetry	Q350-390	003.54	Information theory
PT9415-9449	839.72009	Swedish drama			

LC	Dewey	Subject Heading
Q387-.5	006.332	Knowledge representation (Information theory)
QA	510	Mathematics
QA1	510.5	Mathematics—Periodicals
QA5	510.3	Mathematics—Dictionaries
QA8-10.5	510.1	Mathematics—Philosophy
QA9-10.3	511.3	Logic, Symbolic and mathematical
QA9	510.1	Metamathematics
QA9	515.24	Infinite
QA9.4-.5	511.3	Nonclassical mathematical logic
QA9.5	511.3	Lambda calculus
QA9.54	511.3	Proof theory
QA9.65	511.3	Decidability (Mathematical logic)
QA9.7	511.801	Forcing (Model theory)
QA9.7	511.801	Model theory
QA10-.3	511.324	Algebraic logic
QA10.3	511.324	Algebra, Boolean
QA11-20	510.71	Mathematics—Study and teaching
QA21-27	510.9	Mathematics—History
QA22	510.901	Mathematics, Ancient
QA22	510.935	Mathematics, Babylonian
QA22	510.938	Mathematics, Greek
QA23	510.902	Mathematics, Medieval
QA27	510.9(4-9)	Mathematics—[By region or country]
QA27.C	510.931	Mathematics, Chinese
QA28-29	510.92	Mathematicians
QA32	510.902	Mathematics, Medieval
QA49	513.23	Square root
QA51	513.23021	Factor tables
QA55-59	512.922	Logarithms
QA55	516.24021	Trigonometry—Tables
QA71-90	510.284	Mathematical instruments
QA73	510.284	Slide-rule
QA75	513.0284	Abacus
QA75	510.284	Calculators
QA75.5-.95	004	Computers
QA76.9.D3	005.74	Database management
QA76.15	004.03	Computers—Dictionaries
QA76.17	004.09	Computers—History
QA76.5	005.13	EGPS (Computer program language)
QA76.5	004.35	Multiprocessors
QA76.5	004.35	Parallel computers
QA76.54-.545	004.33	Real-time data processing
QA76.55-.57	005.7	Online data processing—Downloading
QA76.575	006.7	Multimedia systems
QA76.6-.66	004.1	Electronic digital computers—Programming
QA76.6-.66	005.1	Programming (Electronic computers)
QA76.6	005.452	Interpreters (Computer programs)
QA76.6	005.112	Modular programming
QA76.6	005.45	Macro processors

LC	Dewey	Subject Heading
QA76.6.U84	005.43	Utilities (Computer programs)
QA76.63	005.115	Logic programming
QA76.64	005.117	Object-oriented programming (Computer science)
QA76.7-.73	005.13	Programming languages (Electronic computers)
QA76.75-.9	005.3	Computer software
QA76.758	005.1	Software engineering
QA76.76.A65	005.3	Application software
QA76.76.C64	005	Software compatibility
QA76.76.C65	005.453	Compilers (Computer programs)
QA76.76.C68	005.84	Computer viruses
QA76.76.D63	005.3	Software documentation
QA76.76.E95	006.33	Expert systems (Computer science)
QA76.76.I59	006.7	Interactive multimedia
QA76.76.O63	005.43	Operating systems (Computers)
QA76.76.O63	005.4476	Distributed operating systems (Computers)
QA76.76.P76	005.8	Software protection
QA76.76.S46	005.3	Shareware (Computer software)
QA76.76.S64	005.16	Software maintenance
QA76.76.S95	005.43	Systems software
QA76.85	004.1	Fifth generation computers
QA76.87	006.32	Neural computers
QA76.87	006.32	Neural networks (Computer science)
QA76.88	004.11	Supercomputers
QA76.89	004.16	Pen-based computers
QA76.9.A25	005.8	Computer security
QA76.9.A43	005.1	Computer algorithms
QA76.9.A73	004.22	Computer architecture
QA76.9.B32	005.86	Electronic data processing—Backup processing alternatives
QA76.9.C65	003.3	Computer simulation
QA76.9.D26	005.74	Database design
QA76.9.D3	005.758	Distributed databases
QA76.9.D3	005.74	Database management
QA76.9.D314	005.8	Database security
QA76.9.D32	005.74	Databases
QA76.9.D32	006.33	Deductive databases
QA76.9.D33	005.746	Data compression (Computer science)
QA76.9.D337	005.72	Electronic data processing—Data entry
QA76.9.D345	005.72	Electronic data processing—Data preparation
QA76.9.D348	005.86	Data recovery (Computer science)
QA76.9.D5	004.36	Electronic data processing—Distributed processing
QA76.9.D6	004	Electronic data processing documentation

LC	Dewey	Subject Heading	LC	Dewey	Subject Heading
QA76.9.F5	005.741	File organization (Computer science)	QA221-224	512.924	Approximation theory
			QA241-247.5	512.7	Number theory
QA76.9.F53	005.74	File processing (Computer science)	QA242	512.72	Diophantine equations
			QA242	512.74	Diophantine analysis
QA76.9.H85	004.019	Human-computer interacton	QA242	512.72	Numbers, Divisibility of
QA76.9.N38	006.35	Natural language processing (Computer science)	QA242	512.923	Factors (Algebra)
			QA242	513.26	Decimal fractions
QA76.9.T48	005	Text processing (Computer science)	QA242-244	512.72	Congruences and residues
			QA243	512.944	Forms (Mathematics)
QA76.9.U83	005.437	User interfaces (Computer systems)	QA244	512.74	Fermat's theorem
			QA245	512.942	Equations, Binomial
QA90	511.5	Nomography (Mathematics)	QA246	515.52	Euler's numbers
QA101-141.8	513	Arithmetic	QA246	512.72	Numbers, Prime
QA113	513.211	Counting	QA246	512	Numerical functions
QA115	513.211	Addition	QA247-.45	512.3	Algebraic fields
QA115	513.212	Subtraction	QA247	512.4	Ideals (Algebra)
QA115	513.214	Division	QA247	512.4	Rings (Algebra)
QA115	513.213	Multiplication	QA247.35	513.6	Modular arithmetic
QA117	513.26	Fractions	QA247.4	512.56	Difference algebra
QA119	513.23	Roots, Numerical	QA247.45	512.3	Division algebras
QA119	513.23	Square root	QA248-.5	513	Arithmetic—Foundations
QA135-139	513.26071	Fractions—Study and teaching	QA251	512	Algebra, Universal
			QA251.3	512.4	Dedekind rings
QA141-.8	513.5	Numeration	QA252.3	512.55	Lie algebras
QA141.15	512.7	Number concept	QA267-268.5	511.3	Machine theory
QA141.5	513.56	Duodecimal system	QA269-272.5	519.3	Game theory
QA141.8.S4	513.57	Sexadecimal system	QA273	519.2	Games of chance (Mathematics)
QA150-272.5	512	Algebra			
QA159	512.0071	Algebra—Study and teaching	QA273-274.8	519.2	Chance
			QA273-274.8	519.2	Probabilities
QA161	512.942	Equations, Quadratic	QA273-281	519.537	Correlation (Statistics)
QA161.B5	512.942	Binomial theorem	QA273.6	519.24	Distribution (Probability theory)
QA161.F3	512.923	Factors (Algebra)			
QA162	512.02	Algebra, Abstract	QA274-.8	519.23	Stochastic processes
QA164-167.2	511.6	Combinatorial analysis	QA274.7-.76	519.233	Markov processes
QA164.8	515.55	Generating functions	QA274.75	519.233	Diffusion processes
QA165	512.925	Combinations	QA274.8	519.82	Queuing theory
QA165	511.64	Magic squares	QA275	511.43	Error analysis (Mathematics)
QA165	512.925	Permutations	QA275	511.42	Least squares
QA165	512.73	Partitions (Mathematics)	QA276-280	519.5	Mathematical statistics
QA166-.24	511.5	Graph theory	QA276.17	310.92	Statistical consultants
QA171	512.4	Group extensions (Mathematics)	QA276.6	519.52	Sampling (Statistics)
			QA276.8	519.544	Estimation theory
QA171	512.3	Infinite groups	QA278.5	519.5354	Factor analysis
QA171	512.3	Galois theory	QA278.6	519.535	Latent structure analysis
QA171.5	512.7	Lattices, Distributive	QA278.65	519.535	Discriminant analysis
QA171.5	511.33	Lattice theory	QA278.8	519.5	Nonparametric statistics
QA174-183	512.2	Group theory	QA279-.2	519.538	Analysis of variance
QA176	512.2	Representations of groups	QA279.4-.7	519.542	Decision-making
QA188-196	512.9434	Matrices	QA280	519.55	Time-series analysis
QA190-201	512.5	Substitutions, Linear	QA295	515.26	Inequalities (Mathematics)
QA191	512.9432	Determinants	QA295	515.243	Partial sums (Series)
QA199.5	512.5	Multilinear algebra	QA295	515.24	Processes, Infinite
QA201	512.944	Forms (Mathematics)	QA295	515.243	Series, Infinite
QA211	512.3	Galois theory	QA297-299.4	515	Numerical analysis
QA211-218	512.94	Equations, Theory of	QA297	519.4	Numerical calculations
QA211-218	512.94	Equations	QA299.3-.4	515.624	Numerical integration
QA214	512.3	Galois theory	QA299.82	515	Nonstandard mathematical analysis
QA215	512.942	Equations, Quartic			
QA215	512.2	Equations, Abelian	QA303-316	515	Calculus
QA215	512.942	Equations, Cubic	QA306	511.66	Maxima and minima

LC	Dewey	Subject Heading	LC	Dewey	Subject Heading
QA308-311	515.4	Integrals	QA482	516.15	Triangle
QA312	515.4	Integrals, Generalized	QA484	516.15	Circle
QA313	515.42	Ergodic theory	QA485	516.15	Parabola
QA315-316	515.64	Calculus of variations	QA491	516.23	Geometry, Solid
QA319-329.9	515.7	Functional analysis	QA491	516.15	Prisms
QA321.5	515.7248	Nonlinear functional analysis	QA501-521	516.6	Geometry, Descriptive
QA322	515.73	Linear topological spaces, Ordered	QA501-521	516.5	Projection
			QA531-538	516.24	Trigonometry
QA324	515.7	Theory of distribution (Functional analysis)	QA533	516.242	Plane trigonometry
			QA535	516.244	Spherical trigonometry
QA326	512.55	Operator algebras	QA551-563	516.3	Geometry, Analytic
QA329.42	515.7242	Partial differential operators	QA564-609	516.35	Geometry, Algebraic
QA331-355	515.25	Functions	QA571-573	516.352	Surfaces
QA331	515.73	Analytic functions	QA601-608	516.1	Transformations (Mathematics)
QA331.5	515.8	Functions of real variables			
QA331.7	515.9	Functions of complex variables	QA608	516.2	Congruences (Geometry)
			QA608	516.183	Line geometry
QA333-337	515.93	Riemann surfaces	QA611-614.97	514	Topology
QA341	512.74	Algebraic functions	QA611.234	514.3	Hewitt-Nachbin spaces
QA343	515.983	Elliptic functions	QA611.28	514.3	Metric spaces
QA351	515.56	Functions, Zeta	QA611.5	514	Ergodic theory
QA353.G3	515.52	Gamma functions	QA612.3-.77	514.23	Homology theory
QA353.G44	515.55	Generating functions	QA613.6-.66	514.72	Differential topology
QA355	515.623	Numerical differentiation	QA613.62	514.72	Foliations (Mathematics)
QA360	515.9	Conformal mapping	QA614-.97	514.74	Global analysis (Mathematics)
QA370-380	515.35	Differential equations			
QA372	515.354	Differential equations, Linear	QA614.83	514.74	Hamiltonian systems
			QA614.92	514.74	Index theorems
QA372.5	512.56	Differential-algebraic equations	QA615-639	516.36	Geometry, Infinitesimal
			QA631-638	516.36	Surfaces
QA373	515.38	Differential-difference equations	QA641-672	516.36	Surfaces
			QA641-672	516.36	Geometry, Differential
QA374-377	515.353	Differential equations, Partial	QA646	515.9	Conformal mapping
			QA689	514.3	Generalized spaces
QA381	515.37	Differential invariants	QA689	516.375	Finsler spaces
QA381	515.37	Differential forms	QA689	516.375	G-spaces
QA387	512.55	Lie groups	QA801-871	531.01515	Mechanics, Analytic
QA402-.37	003	System analysis	QA801-935	531.11	Motion
QA402	003.83	Discrete-time systems	QA821-835	531.12	Statics
QA402.2	519.4	Decomposition method	QA839	531.12	Moments of inertia
QA402.3-.37	515.64	Control theory	QA841-842	531.112	Kinematics
QA402.35	515.64	Nonlinear control theory	QA845-871	531.11	Dynamics
QA402.5	519.7	Programming (Mathematics)	QA851-855	531.16	Dynamics of a particle
QA403-.3	515.2433	Harmonic analysis	QA861-863	531.11	Dynamics, Rigid
QA403.3	515.2433	Wavelets (Mathematics)	QA862.G9	531.34	Gyroscopes
QA403.5-404.5	515.2433	Fourier analysis	QA862.P4	531.324	Pendulum
QA405	515.53	Harmonic functions	QA865-867.5	531.32	Oscillations
QA405	515.54	Mathieu functions	QA871	515.35	Perturbation (Mathematics)
QA408	515.53	Hankel functions	QA871	515.35	Stability
QA431	515.625	Difference equations	QA901-930	532	Fluids
QA432	515.723	Laplace transformation	QA907	532.25	Floating bodies
QA433	515.63	Vector analysis	QA911-930	530.42	Fluid dynamics
QA440-699	516	Geometry	QA911-930	532.5	Hydrodynamics
QA451-485	516.22	Geometry, Plane	QA913	532.593	Wakes (Fluid dynamics)
QA451-469	516.2	Euclid's Elements	QA913	532.59	Turbulence
QA457	516.23	Geometry, Solid	QA913	532.051	Boundary layer
QA465	516.15	Mensuration	QA913	532.5	Kinematics
QA473-475	516.04	Geometry, Modern	QA913	532.5	Rotating masses of fluid
QA473	516.9	Inversions (Geometry)	QA925	532.59	Vortex-motion
QA482	516.15	Polygons	QA927	532.593	Nonlinear wave equations
			QA927	532.593	Wave-motion, Theory of

LC	Dewey	Subject Heading	LC	Dewey	Subject Heading
QA927	532.59	Gravity waves	QB155-156	522.9	Refraction, Astronomical
QA929	532.0525	Laminar flow	QB163	522.9	Aberration
QA930	533.62	Aerodynamics	QB165	521.9	Nutation
QA930	533.2	Gas dynamics	QB175-185	523.99	Eclipses
QA931-939	531.381	Strains and stresses	QB175-185	523.9	Transits
QA931-939	531.382	Elasticity	QB201-205	526.6	Geodetic astronomy
QA931-939	531.385	Plasticity	QB207	526.63	Azimuth
QA935-939	531.32	Vibration	QB209-224	529	Time
QA935	531.382	Elastic solids	QB213	529.7	Time measurements
QA935	531.382	Elastic plates and shells	QB214	529.7	Hour-glasses
QA935	531.382	Elastic waves	QB215	529.7	Dialing
QA935	531.33	Wave-motion, Theory of	QB215	529.7	Sundials
QB	520	Astronomy	QB216	525.317	Sun—Rising and setting
QB1	520.5	Astronomy—Periodicals	QB217	529.1	Time, Equation of
QB4-.9	522.1	Astronomy—Observations	QB223	529.0218	Time—Systems and
QB6	520.216	Astrographic catalog and			standards
		chart	QB225-229.5	526.62	Longitude
QB6	523.80216	Stars—Catalogs	QB231-237	526.61	Latitude
QB6	523.8	Stars—Observations	QB275-343	526.1	Geodesy
QB7-9	528	Ephemerides	QB279	526.103	Geodesy—Encyclopedias
QB8	528	Nautical alamancs	QB280.5	526.109	Geodesy—History
QB14	520.3	Astronomy—Encyclopedias	QB291	526.30287	Arc measures
QB14.5	520.1	Astronomy—Philosophy	QB297	526.10285	Geodesy—Computer
QB15-34	520.9	Astronomy—History			programs
QB15-26	523	Zodiac	QB301-328	526.3	Surveys
QB16-22	520.901	Astronomy, Ancient	QB303	526.3	Base measuring
QB17	520.931	Astronomy, Chinese	QB311	526.33	Triangulation
QB19	520.935	Astronomy, Assyro-	QB330-339	526.7	Gravity
		Babylonian	QB331	526.0284	Gravimeters (Geophysical
QB21	520.938	Astronomy, Greek			instruments)
QB23-26	520.902	Astronomy, Medieval	QB341	526.7	Gravitation
QB25-26	520	Astrology	QB349-421	521	Celestial mechanics
QB29	520.90(23-31)	Astronomy, Renaissance	QB355-357	521.3	Orbits
QB35-36	520.92	Astronomers—Biography	QB357	523.63	Comets—Orbits
QB47	520.151	Astronomy—Mathematics	QB361-407	521.4	Perturbation (Astronomy)
QB51.3.I45	522	Imaging systems in	QB361-389	523.4	Planetary theory
		astronomy	QB362.F47	521.4	Few-body problem
QB54	999	Life on other planets	QB362.M3	521.4	Many-body problem
QB61-62.7	520.71	Astronomy—Study and	QB362.T9	521.4	Two-body problem
		teaching	QB371	523.41	Mercury (Planet)
QB63	523.1	Constellations	QB372	523.423	Venus (Planet)—Orbit
QB65	529.223	Astronomy—Charts,	QB372	523.42	Venus (Planet)
		diagrams, etc.	QB374	523.7021	Sun—Tables
QB65	520.223	Stars—Atlases	QB376	523.43	Mars (Planet)
QB67	520.228	Astronomical models	QB377-379	523.44	Asteroids
QB81-84	522.29	Astronomical observatories	QB384	623.263	Saturn (Planet)—Orbit
QB84.5-115	522.2	Astronomical instruments	QB384	523.45	Jupiter (Planet)
QB84.5-135	522	Lenses	QB384	523.46	Saturn (Planet)
QB88	522.2	Reflecting telescopes	QB387	523.47	Uranus (Planet)
QB88	522.2	Telescopes	QB388	523.481	Neptune (Planet)
QB105	522	Solar compass	QB391-399	523.3	Lunar theory
QB105	522.4	Quadrant	QB399	523.3021	Moon—Tables
QB107	522.5	Chronometers	QB401-407	523.98	Satellites
QB107	522.5	Astronomical clocks	QB405	523.986	Saturn (Planet)—Ring
QB121-.5	522.63	Astronomical photography			system
QB121	523.87	Stars—Photographic	QB407	523.9881	Neptune (Planet)—
		measurements			Satellites
QB135	522.62	Astronomical photometry	QB420-499	552	Petrology
QB136	520	Space astronomy	QB421	523.841	Double stars
QB140-237	522.7	Spherical astronomy	QB450-.5	523.02	Cosmochemistry
QB149	520.21	Statistical astronomy	QB460-466	523.01	Astrophysics

LC	Dewey	Subject Heading	LC	Dewey	Subject Heading
QB462.6	523.019	Molecular astrophysics	QB799-903	523.8	Stars
QB462.7-.72	523.019	Plasma astrophysics	QB802	523	Zodiac
QB463-464.2	523.019	Nuclear astrophysics	QB806	523.88	Stars—Formation
QB465	522.67	Astronomical spectroscopy	QB806	523.88	Stars—Evolution
QB470	522.683	Infrared astronomy	QB807	522	Astrometry
QB471.7.B85	522.6862	Gamma ray bursts	QB810	523.83	Stars—Rotation
QB472-473	522.6863	X-ray astronomy	QB812	523.83	Stellar oscillations
QB475-479.55	522.682	Radio astronomy	QB814	523.81	Stars—Masses
QB479.2	522.682	Radio telescopes	QB817	523.82	Stars—Radiation
QB480	522.68	Radar in astronomy	QB821-830	523.841	Multiple stars
QB495-500.268	500.5	Space sciences	QB821-830	523.841	Double stars
QB500.267-.268	522.29	Orbiting astronomical observatories	QB833-841	523.844	Variable stars
			QB835.E4	523.8444	Eclipsing binaries—Orbits
QB500.5-785	523.2	Solar system	QB841	523.88	Stars, New
QB509-513	523.423	Venus (Planet), Transit of	QB843.B55	523.8875	Black holes (Astronomy)
QB516	523.44	Asteroids	QB843.B55	523.8875	Kerr black holes
QB516.F6	523.75	Solar flares	QB843.D85	523.8446	Dwarf Novae
QB520-545	523.7	Sun	QB843.D9	523.88	Dwarf stars
QB523	523.73	Sun—Rotation	QB843.E2	523.88	Early stars
QB524-526	523.72	Solar activity	QB843.N12	523.88	N stars
QB525	523.75	Sunspots	QB843.N4	523.8874	Neutron stars
QB526.C9	523.73	Solar cycle	QB843.R4	523.88	Red dwarfs
QB529	523.58	Solar wind	QB843.R42	523.88	Red giants
QB529	523.75	Sun—Corona	QB843.W5	523.887	White dwarfs
QB531	523.72	Solar radiation	QB851-855.9	523.85	Stars—Clusters
QB539.I5	523.76	Sun—Internal structure	QB855.5	523.1135	Planetary nebulae
QB539.M23	523.72	Solar magnetic fields	QB856-858.8	523.112	Galaxies
QB539.N6	523.72	Solar noise storms	QB860	523.115	Quasars
QB541-545	523.78	Solar eclipses	QB895	523.88	Stars, New
QB551	523.73	Sun—Rotation	QB980-991	523.1	Cosmology
QB579	523.38	Lunar eclipses	QB980-991	523.12	Cosmogony
QB580-595	523.3	Moon	QB991.B54	523.18	Big bang theory
QB591	523.3	Moon—Surface	QB991.E53	523.19	End of the universe
QB592	523.3	Lunar geology	QB991.I54	523.18	Inflationary universe
QB592	523.3	Lunar soil	QC	530	Physics
QB600-701	523.4	Planets	QC1	530.06	Physics—Congresses
QB603.R55	523.4	Planetary rings	QC5	530.03	Physics—Encyclopedias
QB611	523.41	Mercury (Planet)	QC5.56-6.4	530.01	Physics—Philosophy
QB621	523.42	Venus (Planet)—Surface	QC6.9-9	530.09	Physics—History
QB621	523.42	Venus (Planet)	QC15-16	530.092	Physicists
QB630-638.8	525	Earth	QC19.2-20.85	530.15	Mathematical physics
QB630-638.8	525	Astronomical geography	QC20.8-.82	530.15071	Mathematical physics—Study and teaching
QB632	523.12	Earth—Origin			
QB633	525.35	Earth—Rotation	QC29	530.071	Physics—Vocational guidance
QB637.2-.8	525.5	Seasons			
QB641	523.43	Mars (Planet)	QC30-48	530.071	Physics—Study and teaching
QB651	523.44	Asteroids			
QB661	523.45	Jupiter (Planet)	QC35-37	530.078	Physics—Laboratory manuals
QB671	523.46	Saturn (Planet)			
QB681	523.47	Uranus (Planet)	QC51	530.072	Physical laboratories
QB691	523.481	Neptune (Planet)	QC53-55	530.7	Physical instruments
QB701	523.482	Pluto (Planet)	QC53	530.7	Recording instruments
QB717-732	523.6	Comets	QC72-73.8	531.6	Force and energy
QB723.H2	523.642	Halley's comet	QC81-114	530.81	Weights and measures
QB738	523.51	Meteoroids	QC83-86	530.8109	Weights and measures—History
QB740-753	523.51	Meteors			
QB754.8-759	523.51	Meteorites	QC90.8-94	530.812	Metric system
QB754.8-759	551.397	Meteorite craters	QC90.8-94	530.812	Decimal system
QB790-792	523.1125	Interstellar matter	QC100-111	530.8	Testing
QB791	523.1125	Cosmic dust	QC100.5-.8	530.7	Measuring instruments
QB791.3	523.1126	Dark matter (Astronomy)			

LC	Dewey	Subject Heading
QC107	530.7	Scales (Weighing instruments)
QC107	530.7	Weighing-machines
QC111-114	531.14	Specific gravity
QC115-116	543.0871	Electrochemical analysis
QC120-168.86	530	Mechanics
QC122-168	531.11	Motion
QC138-168.86	532	Fluids
QC141-159	532	Liquids
QC147	532.25	Floating bodies
QC150-159	532.5	Fluid dynamics
QC150-159	532.5	Hydrodynamics
QC157	532.593	Waves
QC159	532.595	Vortex-motion
QC161-166.5	533	Pneumatics
QC161-166.5	533.6	Air
QC161-166.5	533	Gases
QC164	536.412	Expansion of gases
QC166-.5	533.5	Vacuum
QC166	533.50284	Vacuum-gages
QC167.5-168.86	533.2	Gas dynamics
QC168	533.61	Aerostatics
QC168.85.D46	532.593	Detonation waves
QC170-197	530	Matter
QC173	539.7	Atoms
QC173	539.6	Molecules
QC173	530.7217	Photon beams
QC173.4.A87	539.14	Atomic structure
QC173.5-.65	530.11	Relativity (Physics)
QC173.59.S65	530.11	Space and time
QC173.68-.75	530.14	Field theory (Physics)
QC173.96-174.52	530.12	Quantum theory
QC174.1	530.416	Tunneling (Physics)
QC174.17.B6	530.12	Bound states (Quantum mechanics)
QC174.17.D44	530.122	Density matrices
QC174.17.H4	530.122	Heisenberg uncertainty principle
QC174.17.P7	530.14	Few-body problem
QC174.17.P7	530.144	Many-body problem
QC174.17.S9	530.1423	Supergravity
QC174.17.S9	539.725	Symmetry (Physics)
QC174.2-.26	530.124	Wave mechanics
QC174.3-.35	530.122	Matrix mechanics
QC174.4-.43	530.133	Quantum statistics
QC174.45-.52	530.143	Quantum field theory
QC174.52.D43	530.143	Degree of freedom
QC174.7-175.36	530.13	Statistical mechanics
QC175-.16	533.7	Kinetic theory of gases
QC175.16.P5	530.474	Phase transformations (Statistical physics)
QC175.2-.25	530.138	Transport theory
QC175.3-.36	532.5	Kinetic theory of liquids
QC175.4-.47	530.42	Superfluidity
QC176-.9	531	Solid state physics
QC176.8.E9	530.416	Exciton theory
QC176.8.L3	530.411	Lattice dynamics
QC176.82-.9R37	530.4175	Thin films
QC178	531.14	Gravitational fields
QC178	531.14	Gravitation
QC179	539.6	Molecules
QC183	530.475	Brownian movements
QC183	530.427	Surface tension
QC185	530.475	Diffusion
QC189-.2	531.1134	Viscosity
QC191	531.382	Elastic solids
QC191	531.382	Elasticity
QC191	531.385	Plasticity
QC191	531.382	Elastic waves
QC197	531.1134	Friction
QC220-246	534	Sound
QC228.3	534.0284	Sound—Equipment and supplies
QC231	534.5	Kinematics
QC233	534.208	Absorption of sound
QC233	534.204	Echo
QC235-241	534.5	Vibration
QC235	534.208	Sound-waves—Damping
QC242-.5	534.23	Underwater acoustics
QC243	534.0287	Sound—Measurement
QC243	534.208	Sound-waves—Damping
QC244	534.55	Ultrasonic waves
QC251-338.5	536	Heat
QC270-278.6	536.50287	Temperature measurements
QC270-278.6	536.50287	Thermometers
QC276-277	536.57	High temperatures
QC277	536.520287	Pyrometers
QC277.9-278.6	536.56072	Low temperature research
QC281.5.E9	536.41	Expansion (Heat)
QC290-297	536.6	Calorimeters
QC303	536.42	Fusion
QC303	536.42	Solidification
QC304	536.44	Evaporation
QC310.15-319	536.7	Thermodynamics
QC318.M3	530.475	Mass transfer
QC319.8-338.5	536.2	Heat—Transmission
QC350-467	535	Light
QC350-467	535	Optics
QC367	535.0284	Optical measurements
QC370.5-379	535.028	Optical instruments
QC375	666.156	Glass, Optical
QC385	535.323	Reflection (Optics)
QC385	535.324	Lenses
QC391	535.220287	Photometry
QC392-449.5	535.2	Physical optics
QC402	535.12	Light, Corpuscular theory of
QC403	535.2	Coherence (Optics)
QC403	535.13	Light, Wave theory of
QC411	535.47	Interference (Light)
QC414.8-417	535.4	Diffraction
QC425	535.420284	Prisms
QC425	535.323	Reflection (Optics)
QC425	535.324	Refraction, Double
QC431-435	535.4	Dispersion
QC437	535.326	Absorption of light
QC440-446	535.52	Polarization (Light)
QC446.15-.3	535.2	Nonlinear optics
QC447.9-448.2	621.3692	Fiber optics
QC449-.3	774.0153	Holography
QC450-467	543.0858	Spectrum analysis

LC	Dewey	Subject Heading	LC	Dewey	Subject Heading
QC451	535.840284	Spectrum analysis—Instruments	QC660.5-665	537.534	Electric waves
			QC661	621.381331	Wave guides
QC454.A8	535.84	Atomic absorption spectroscopy	QC665.D5	539.2	Electromagnetic waves—Diffraction
QC454.E46	535.84	Emission spectroscopy	QC665.E4	539.2	Electromagnetic fields
QC454.L63	535.843	Light beating spectroscopy	QC665.P6	537.534	Radio waves—Polarization
QC454.R36	535.846	Raman effect	QC665.T7	539.2	Electromagnetic waves—Transmission
QC457	535.842	Infrared spectra			
QC457	535.842	Infrared spectroscopy	QC669-675.8	537	Electromagnetic theory
QC459-.5	535.014	Ultraviolet radiation	QC676-678.6	537.534	Radio waves
QC459-.5	535.844	Ultraviolet spectroscopy	QC679-680.5	537.67	Quantum electrodynamics
QC459.5	535.014	Far ultraviolet radiation	QC685-689.55	537.5	Quantum electronics
QC465	535.84	Spectroscope	QC701.7-702.7	530.444	Ionization
QC474-492	539.2	Radiation	QC702-721	530.44	Ionization of gases
QC476.4-480.2	535.35	Luminescence	QC702.7.H42	539.7234	Heavy ions
QC476.S6	539.2	Radiation sources	QC703.7	537.5	Exploding wire phenomena
QC477-.4	535.352	Fluorescence	QC705	537.52	Electric arc
QC480-482.3	539.7222	X-rays	QC715.15	537.54	Photoemission
QC480	535.357	Electroluminescence	QC717-.8	530.44	Plasma (Ionized gases)
QC482.S6	537.5352	X-ray spectroscopy	QC718.5.M36	538.6	Magnetohydrodynamics
QC484.3	539.7222	Bremsstrahlung	QC750-776	538	Magnetism
QC484.8-485.9	539.7223	Cosmic rays	QC754.2.M33	538.4	Magnetic induction
QC485	539.7223	Solar cosmic rays	QC757	538.4	Magnets
QC494-496.9	535.6	Colors	QC759.6-761.3	537	Electromagnetism
QC494-496.9	535.6	Color	QC760-.3	538	Electromagnets
QC501-721	537	Electricity	QC761	538.0287	Magnetic measurements
QC514-515	537.092	Electricians	QC762	538.362	Nuclear magnetic resonance
QC527	537.0724	Electricity—Experiments	QC762	538.362	Deuteron magnetic resonance spectroscopy
QC533-534	537.0724	Electricity—Experiments			
QC535-537	537.0287	Electric measurements	QC763	538.364	Electron paramagnetic resonance
QC541-543	541.372	Electrolytes			
QC541	537.072	Electric laboratories	QC770-798	539.7	Nuclear physics
QC543-544	537.0284	Electric apparatus and appliances	QC771	538.42	Diamagnetism
			QC783.3-.4	621.4830285	Nuclear reactors—Computer programs
QC570-596.9	537.2	Electrostatics			
QC581.E4	537.21	Electric charge and distribution	QC785.5-787	539.770284	Radioactivity—Instruments
			QC786.4-786.8	621.483	Nuclear reactors
QC584-585.8	537.24	Dielectrics	QC787.C6	539.77	Neutron counters
QC584	537.240287	Dielectric measurements	QC787.C6	539.77	Nuclear counters
QC596-.9	537.2448	Ferroelectricity	QC787.E39	539.73	Electron accelerators
QC601-641	537.6	Electric currents	QC787.E4	539.732	Electrostatic accelerators
QC610.3-635	537.62	Electric conductivity	QC787.G4	539.774	Geiger-Muller counters
QC610.9-611.8	537.6226	Semiconductors	QC787.I6	539.772	Ionization chambers
QC611	537.62	Electric resistance	QC787.L5	539.733	Linear accelerators
QC611	537.54	Photoelectricity	QC787.P3	539.73	Particle accelerators
QC611.8.D66	537.6223	Doped semiconductors	QC787.S34	539.775	Scintillation counters
QC611.8.M25	537.6223	Diluted magnetic semiconductors	QC787.S83	539.736	Superconducting Super Collider
QC611.8.N35	537.6223	Narrow gap semiconductors	QC787.S9	539.735	Synchrotrons
QC611.8.O7	537.6223	Organic semiconductors	QC789.7-790.8	539.762	Nuclear fission
QC611.8.W53	537.6223	Wide gap semiconductors	QC790.95-791.8	539.764	Nuclear fusion
QC611.9-.98	537.623	Superconductivity	QC791.7-.775	539.764	Controlled fusion
QC612.H3	537.6	Hall effect	QC791.9-792.8	539.7	Nuclear energy
QC612.P5	537.54	Photoconductivity	QC793-.5	539.72	Particles (Nuclear physics)
QC615	621.3743	Voltameter	QC793.3.B4	539.73	Particle beams
QC621-625	537.65	Thermoelectricity	QC793.3.D4	539.752	Decay schemes (Radio activity)
QC623	537.6	Electric currents—Heating effects			
			QC793.3.F5	530.1435	Gauge fields (Physics)
QC630-648	537.6	Electrodynamics	QC793.3.S8	539.74	Nuclear structure
QC641	537.6	Electric currents, Alternating	QC793.3.S9	539.725	Symmetry (Physics)

LC	Dewey	Subject Heading	LC	Dewey	Subject Heading
QC793.5.A22-.A229	539.7232	Alpha rays	QC835	538.744	Magnetic storms
			QC845	538.748	Earth currents
QC793.5.E462-.E4629	539.72112	Electrons	QC851-999	551.5	Atmosphere
			QC851-999	551.6	Climatology
QC793.5.E62-.E629	537.56	Electron optics	QC851-999	551.5	Meteorology
			QC851	551.505	Meteorology—Periodicals
QC793.5.E628	539.72112	Electrons—Polarization	QC854.2	551.5014	Meteorology—Terminology
QC793.5.F42-.F429	539.721	Fermions	QC855-857	551.509	Meteorology—History
			QC858	551.5092	Meteorologists—Biography
QC793.5.G322	539.7222	Gamma ray sources	QC875	551.63	Automatic meteorological stations
QC793.5.H32-.H329	539.7216	Hadrons			
			QC875	354.37	Meteorological services
QC793.5.L42-.L429	539.7211	Leptons (Nuclear physics)	QC875	551.63	Meteorological stations
			QC875.5-876.7	551.50284	Meteorological instruments
QC793.5.M42-.M429	539.72162	Mesons	QC877.5	551.632	Weather reporting, Radio
			QC877.5	551.632	Weather broadcasting
QC793.5.M42-.M429	539.72162	Kaons	QC877.5	551.632	Television weathercasting
			QC879-.59	551.514	Atmosphere, Upper
QC793.5.N42-.N429	539.7215	Neutrinos	QC879	551.514	Atmosphere, Upper—Radiosonde observations
QC793.5.N462-.N4622	539.7213	Neutrons			
			QC879	551.5145	F region
QC793.5.N4629	539.7213	Neutron sources	QC879.6-.85	551.511	Atmospheric chemistry
QC793.5.P42-.P429	539.7217	Photons	QC880	551.50284	Densitometer (Meteorological instrument)
QC793.5.P72-.P729	539.72123	Antiprotons			
			QC880.4.A5	551.5512	Air masses
QC793.5.P72-.P729	539.72123	Antiprotons	QC880.4.A8	551.517	Atmospheric circulation
QC880.4.F7	551.5512	Fronts (Meteorology)			
QC793.5.Q252-.Q2529	539.72167	Quarks	QC880.4.F7	551.5512	Occluded fronts (Meteorology)
QC793.5.S72-.S729	539.7216	Strange particles	QC880.4.S65	551.55	Squall lines
			QC880.4.S65	551.55	Squalls
QC794	539.75	Annihilation reactions	QC880.4.T5	551.52	Atmospheric thermodynamics
QC794.6.C6	539.757	Collisions (Nuclear physics)			
QC794.6.E9	539.725	Spin excitations	QC880.4.T8	551.55	Atmospheric turbulence
QC794.6.G7	530.142	Grand unified theories (Nuclear physics)	QC881.2.E2	551.5145	E region
			QC881.2.I6	551.5145	Ionosphere
QC794.6.S3	539.758	Scattering amplitude (Nuclear physics)	QC881.2.O9	551.5142	Ozone layer
			QC881.2.T75	551.513	Troposphere
QC794.6.S3	539.758	Scattering (Physics)	QC882	363.7392	Smaze
QC794.8.E4	539.7546	Electromagnetic interactions	QC882.4-.46	363.7392	Aerosols
			QC882.5	551.5113	Dust
QC794.8.P4	539.756	Photonuclear reactions	QC882.6	363.7392	Smoke plumes
QC794.8.W4	539.7544	Weak interactions (Nuclear physics)	QC883-.2	551.5	Weather, Influence of the moon on
			QC883.2.S6	551.5276	Cosmic physics
QC794.95-798	539.752	Radioactivity	QC883.2.A8	551.4708	Atmospheric tides
QC795.8.D4	539.752	Decay schemes (Radioactivity)	QC883.7-.86	551.66	Micrometeorology
			QC884-.2	551.69	Paleoclimatology
QC795.8.E5	539.725	Energy levels (Quantum mechanics)	QC885-896	551.54	Atmospheric pressure
			QC886-887	551.540284	Barometers
QC795.8.H3	539.752	Half-life (Nuclear physics)	QC901-912.2	551.525	Atmospheric temperature
QC801-809	550	Cosmic physics	QC910.2-913.2	551.5271	Sunshine
QC801-809	550	Geophysics	QC910.2-911.82	551.5271	Solar radiation
QC809.M25	538.7	Cosmic magnetic fields	QC912.3	551.5273	Atmospheric radiation
QC809.M3	538.6	Magnetohydrodynamics	QC913-.2	551.5276	Atmospheric radioactivity
QC809.M35	538.766	Magnetosphere	QC915-929	551.57	Moisture
QC809.T4	551.5272	Terrestrial radiation	QC915-917	551.572	Evaporation (Meteorology)
QC809.V3	538.766	Van Allen radiation belts	QC915-917	551.571	Humidity
QC811-849	538.7	Geomagnetism	QC915	551.57	Moisture index
QC818-849	538.0287	Magnetic measurements	QC915.5-.7	551.572	Evapotranspiration
QC818	538.79	Geomagnetic observatories	QC920	551.57	Water
QC822	538.70223	Geomagnetism—Maps			

LC	Dewey	Subject Heading	LC	Dewey	Subject Heading
QC920.7-924	551.576	Clouds	QC989	551.694	Europe—Climate
QC921.6.C6	551.574	Condensation (Meteorology)	QC990	551.695	Asia—Climate
QC921.6.C6	551.5741	Atmospheric nucleation	QC991	551.696	Africa—Climate
QC924.5-926.2	551.577	Rain and rainfall	QC992	551.6994	Australia—Climate
QC926	551.5770284	Rain gauges	QC993.5	551.6913	Tropics—Climate
QC926	551.5770284	Precipitation gauges	QC993.6	551.69143	Mountain climate
QC926.6-928.74	551.68	Weather control	QC993.7	551.69154	Arid regions climate
QC926.5-.57	551.5771	Acid precipitation (Meteorology)	QC993.83-994.9	551.65162	Marine meteorology
			QC994.95-999	551.63	Weather forecasting
QC928.6	551.68	Rain-making	QC996	551.634	Numerical weather forecasting
QC929	551.577	Precipitation (Meteorology)			
QC929.2-.28	551.5773	Droughts	QC996.5	551.633	Statistical weather forecasting
QC929.A8	551.307	Avalanches			
QC929.D5	551.5744	Dew	QC997	551.6365	Long-range weather forecasting
QC929.F7	551.575	Ice fog			
QC929.F7	551.575	Fog	QC997.75	551.6362	Nowcasting (Meteorology)
QC929.H15	551.5787	Hail	QC999	551.6365	Almanacs
QC929.H15	551.554	Hailstorms	QD	540	Chemistry
QC929.H6	551.38	Frost	QD1	540.6	Chemistry—Societies, etc.
QC929.S7	551.5784	Snow	QD4-5	540.3	Chemistry—Dictionaries
QC930.5-959	551.518	Winds	QD7	540.14	Chemistry—Nomenclature
QC931	551.6418	Wind forecasting	QD11-18	540.9	Chemistry—History
QC935	551.5183	Jet stream	QD13	540.112	Alchemy
QC935	551.518	Winds aloft	QD21-22	540.92	Chemists
QC939.L37	551.5185	Sea breeze	QD23.3-26.5	540.112	Alchemy
QC939.M7	551.5184	Monsoons	QD40-49	540.71	Chemistry—Study and teaching
QC939.M8	551.5185	Mountain wave			
QC939.T7	551.5183	Trade winds	QD43	540.724	Chemistry—Experiments
QC940.6-959	551.5513	Cyclones	QD51-64	540.72	Chemical laboratories
QC940.6-959	551.55	Storms	QD53-54	542	Chemical apparatus
QC944-948	551.552	Hurricanes	QD54.C4	542	Centrifuges
QC948	551.552	Typhoons	QD63.D6	542.4	Distillation
QC948	551.68	Typhoon modification	QD63.F5	542.6	Filters and filtration
QC951	551.64513	Cyclone forecasting	QD63.O9	541.393	Electrolytic oxidation
QC955-.5	551.553	Tornadoes	QD63.R4	541.393	Electrolytic reduction
QC957	551.553	Waterspouts	QD63.R4	541.393	Reduction (Chemistry)
QC958-959	551.559	Dust storms	QD71-142	543	Chemistry, Analytic
QC960.5-969	551.563	Atmospheric electricity	QD71	543.005	Chemistry, Analytic—Periodicals
QC966-.7	551.5632	Lightning			
QC966.7.A84	551.561	Atmospheric ionization	QD79.C45	543.0896	Gas chromatography
QC968-.2	551.554	Thunderstorms	QD79.E44	541.372	Electrophoresis
QC970-972.5	538.768	Auroras	QD79.T38	544.2	Thermal analysis
QC972.6-973.8	551.635	Radio meteorology	QD81-98	544	Chemistry, Analytic—Qualitative
QC973.4.R35	551.51	Atmospheric radio refractivity			
			QD87	542.4	Blowpipe
QC973.4.M33	551.514	Magnetospheric radio wave propagation	QD95-96	544.6	Spectrum analysis
			QD101-117	545	Chemistry, Analytic—Quantitative
QC973.45-.8	551.6353	Radar meteorology			
QC973.8.W	551.6353	Weather radar networks	QD111	545.2	Volumetric analysis
QC974.5-976	551.56	Meteorological optics	QD117.C515	545.896	Gas chromatography
QC976.R2	551.567	Rainbow	QD117.E45	541.372	Electrophoresis
QC980-999	551.6	Weather	QD117.T4	545.4	Thermal analysis
QC980	551.605	Weather—Periodicals	QD142	546.22	Water—Analysis
QC981.7.U7	551.691732	Urban climatology	QD146-197	546	Chemistry, Inorganic
QC981.8.A5	551.5512	Cold waves (Meteorology)	QD146	546.06	Chemistry, Inorganic—Societies, etc.
QC981.8.G56	363.73874	Global warming			
QC983-984	551.6973	United States—Climate	QD169.W3	546.22	Water
QC985-.5	551.6971	Canada—Climate	QD161-169	546.7	Nonmetals
QC986	551.6972	Mexico—Climate	QD165	546.73	Halogen compounds
QC987	551.69729	West Indies—Climate	QD167	546.24	Inorganic acids
QC988	551.698	South America—Climate	QD171-172	546.3	Metals

LC	Dewey	Subject Heading
QD172.A4	546.38	Alkalies
QD172.R2	546.41	Earths, Rare
QD172.R2	546.41	Rare earth metals
QD172.T6	546.6	Transition metal compounds
QD181.C1	546.6812	Carbon dioxide
QD181.F1	546.731	Fluorine
QD181.H1	546.212	Deuterium
QD181.H1	546.2	Hydrogen
QD181.H4	546.751	Helium
QD181.H6	546.663	Mercury
QD181.I1	546.734	Iodine
QD181.N1	546.711	Nitrogen
QD181.N5	546.752	Neon
QD181.O1	546.721	Oxygen
QD181.O1	546.721	Active oxygen
QD181.P1	546.712	Phosphorus
QD181.R2	546.756	Radon
QD181.S3	546.716	Antimony
QD181.T7	546.678	Thallium
QD181.U7	546.431	Uranium
QD181.X1	546.755	Xenon
QD189-193	546.34	Salts
QD191	546.343	Double salts
QD241-441	547	Chemistry, Organic
QD241	547.005	Chemistry, Organic—Periodicals
QD262	547.2	Organic compounds—Synthesis
QD272.E43	541.372	Electrophoresis
QD273	541.37	Electrochemistry
QD281.O9	547.23	Electrolytic oxidation
QD281.O9	547.23	Oxidation
QD281.P6	547.28	Addition polymerization
QD281.P6	547.28	Polymerization
QD281.R4	547.23	Electrolytic reduction
QD305.H5-.H9	547.41	Hydrocarbons
QD305.H8	547.413	Acetylene compounds
QD305.H8	547.413	Acetylene
QD320-327	547.78	Carbohydrates
QD320-327	547.781	Sugars
QD321	547.7813	Fructose
QD321	547.7813	Dextrose
QD321	547.7813	Glucose
QD330-341	547.6	Aromatic compounds
QD341	547.28	Condensation products (Chemistry)
QD341.H9	547.611	Benzene
QD341.H9	547.61	Hydrocarbons
QD341.P5	547.632	Phenols
QD380-388	547.7	Polymers
QD399-406	547.59	Heterocyclic compounds
QD410-412.5	547.05	Organometallic compounds
QD412	547.62	Halogen compounds
QD415-436	572	Biochemistry
QD419-.7	547.8434	Gums and resins
QD421-.7	547.72	Alkaloids
QD431-.7	547.75	Proteins
QD431-.7	547.75	Amino acids
QD431-.7	547.756	Peptides
QD450-801	541	Chemistry, Physical and theoretical
QD450	541.06	Chemistry, Physical and theoretical—Societies, etc.
QD461	541.2	Atomic theory
QD461	541.22	Molecular structure
QD462-464	541.28	Quantum chemistry
QD463-464	541.242	Atomic weights
QD463-464	541.222	Molecular weights
QD466	541.242	Atomic mass
QD466.5	541.388	Isotopes
QD467	541.24	Periodic law
QD471	541.224	Radicals (Chemistry)
QD471	541.2252	Tautomerism
QD471	541.224	Free radicals (Chemistry)
QD461	541.2	Molecular theory
QD478	541.0421	Organic solid state chemistry
QD478	541.0421	Solid state chemistry
QD501-505.5	541.39	Chemical reaction, Conditions and law of
QD503	541.392	Phase rule and equilibrium
QD505	541.395	Phase-transfer catalysts
QD505	541.395	Catalysis
QD506-509	541.33	Surface chemistry
QD510-536	541.36	Thermochemistry
QD515	541.3686	Cryochemistry
QD516	541.361	Combustion
QD516	541.361	Explosions
QD516	541.361	Flame
QD517	541.364	Dissociation
QD535	542	Dewar flasks
QD536	541.3686072	Low temperature research
QD541-549	541.34	Solution (Chemistry)
QD541-543	541.34	Activity coefficients
QD543	541.342	Solubility
QD543	541.3415	Osmosis
QD549	541.372	Electrolytes
QD551-575	541.37	Electrochemistry
QD553-585	541.372	Electrolytes
QD561-562	541.3722	Ionization
QD561-562	541.372	Ions
QD562.I63	541.3723	Ion exchange
QD562.I65	541.3722	Dissociation
QD565	541.372	Electrolytes—Conductivity
QD571-572	541.3724	Electrodes
QD581	541.0424	Plasma chemistry
QD601-608	541.38	Nuclear chemistry
QD601-608	541.38	Radiochemistry
QD625-655	541.382	Radiation chemistry
QD701-731	541.35	Photochemistry
QD901-999	548	Crystallography
QD901-999	548.5	Crystallization
QD911-919	548.7	Crystallography, Mathematical
QD911-919	548.7	Lattice theory
QD921-926	548.5	Crystal growth
QD945	548.842	Dislocations in crystals
QE	551	Geology
QE1	551.06	Geology—Societies, etc.
QE7	551.014	Geology—Terminology
QE11-13	551.09	Geology—History
QE21-22	551.092	Geologists
QE28.2	551	Physical geology

LC	Dewey	Subject Heading	LC	Dewey	Subject Heading
QE28.3	551.09	Historical geology	QE456.5	552.09989	Petrology—Antarctic regions
QE36	551.0223	Geology—Maps	QE461-462	552.1	Rocks, Igneous
QE39	551.4608	Submarine geology	QE461-462	552.23	Volcanic ash, tuff, etc.
QE40-48	551.071	Geology—Study and teaching	QE461	552.22	Lava
QE43	551.0228	Geological modeling	QE462.D56	552.3	Diorite
QE48.8	551.0285	Geology—Computer programs	QE462.G7	552.3	Granite
			QE471-.15	552.5	Rocks, Sedimentary
QE49.5	550.284	Earth science instruments	QE471-.15	552.5	Sedimentology
QE51	551.074	Geological museums	QE471.15.C3	552.58	Rocks, Carbonate
QE61-350.62	551.0723	Geological surveys	QE471.15.D6	552.58	Dolomite
QE61-350	551.0723	Surveys	QE471.15.S25	552.5	Sandstone
QE70	559.8(1/2)	Geology—Arctic regions	QE471.15.S5	552.5	Shale
QE71-217	557	Geology—North America	QE471.3	552.5	Clay
QE72-182	557.3	Geology—United States	QE472	552.5	Sedimentary structures
QE81-182	557.(4-9)	Geology—[United States, By state]	QE475	552.4	Rocks, Metamorphic
			QE475.A2	552.4	Metamorphism (Geology)
QE185-199	557.1	Geology—Canada	QE500-639.5	551.(2-3)	Geodynamics
QE201-203	557.2	Geology—Mexico	QE500-511.7	550	Geophysics
QE210-217	557.28	Geology—Central America	QE501.4.P3	551.7	Paleogeography
QE220-226	557.29	Geology—West Indies	QE501.4.P35	538.727	Paleomagnetism
QE230-251	558	Geology—South America	QE508	551.701	Earth—Age
QE260-288	554	Geology—Europe	QE508	551.701	Geological time
QE289-319	555	Geology—Asia	QE508	551.701	Radioactive dating
QE320-339	556	Geology—Africa	QE509	551.11	Earth—Internal structure
QE340-348	559.4	Geology—Australia	QE509	551.12	Earth temperature
QE350	559.89	Geology—Antartica	QE511.4-.48	551.8	Plate tectonics
QE351-399.2	549	Mineralogy	QE511.7	551.136	Sea-floor spreading
QE351	549.05	Mineralogy—Periodicals	QE514-516.5	551.9	Geochemistry
QE364.2.R3	549.528	Radioactive substances	QE521.5-527.5	551.21	Volcanoes
QE367-369	549.1	Mineralogy, Determinative	QE528	551.23	Hot springs
QE371	549.13	Mineralogical chemistry	QE531-541	551.22	Seismology
QE388	549.012	Minerals—Classification	QE531-541	551.22	Earthquakes
QE389.1	549.2	Native element minerals	QE539	551.22	Elastic waves
QE389.4	549.4	Halide minerals	QE541	551.220287	Seismometry
QE389.64	549.72	Phosphate minerals	QE545	551.23	Volcanic gases
QE390.2.T85	549.74	Tungsten ores	QE565-566	551.424	Coral reefs and islands
QE391.D6	549.782	Dolomite	QE570	551.302	Weathering
QE391.F3	549.68	Feldspar	QE571-597	551.302	Erosion
QE391.G37	549.62	Garnet	QE571-597	551.303	Sedimentation and deposition
QE391.I7	546.621	Iron	QE575-579	551.313	Glacial erosion
QE391.Q2	549.68	Quartz	QE597	551.372	Wind erosion
QE391.T6	549.62	Topaz	QE598-600.3	551.307	Earth movements
QE394.07	549.68	Opals	QE598-600.3	551.307	Mass-wasting
QE394.T8	549.72	Turquoise	QE599	551.307	Debris avalanches
QE420-499	552	Petrology	QE599	551.307	Landslides
QE420-499	552	Rocks	QE599	551.307	Rockslides
QE420	552.005	Petrology—Periodicals	QE604	551.8	Rock deformation
QE444-445	552.00973	Petrology—United States	QE606-.5	551.872	Faults (Geology)
QE445.5-446	552.00971	Petrology—Canada	QE606-.5	551.875	Folds (Geology)
QE446.5-.6	552.00972	Petrology—Mexico	QE611-.5	551.88	Dikes (Geology)
QE447	552.09728	Petrology—Central America	QE611-.5	551.88	Necks (Geology)
QE448	552.09729	Petrology—West Indies	QE611-.5	551.88	Intrusions (Geology)
QE449	552.098	Petrology—South America	QE611-.5	551.88	Veins (Geology)
QE451	552.0094	Petrology—Europe	QE640-699	551.7	Geology, Stratigraphic
QE452	552.095	Petrology—Asia	QE654-674	551.72	Geology, Stratigraphic—Paleozoic
QE453	552.096	Petrology—Africa			
QE453.5-454	552.0994	Petrology—Australia	QE675-688	551.76	Geology, Stratigraphic—Mesozoic
QE454.5-.6	552.0993	Petrology—New Zealand			
QE455	552.099(5-6)	Petrology—Oceania	QE690-699	551.78	Geology, Stratigraphic—Cenozoic
QE456	552.09981	Petrology—Arctic regions			

LC	Dewey	Subject Heading	LC	Dewey	Subject Heading
QE697-698	551.792	Glacial epoch	QH	508	Natural history
QE701-996.5	560	Paleontology	QH1-7	508.06	Natural history—Periodicals
QE701	560.5	Paleontology—Periodicals	QH13	508.03	Natural history—Dictionaries
QE718	560.75	Fossils—Collection and preservation	QH26-35	508.092	Naturalists
			QH26-31	570.92	Biologists
QE721.2.E97	576.84	Extinction (Biology)	QH46	508.0222	Natural history—Pictorial works
QE724	560.171	Paleontology—Precambrian			
QE725-730	560.172	Paleontology—Paleozoic	QH46.5	508.022	Natural history illustration
QE726	560.1723	Paleontology—Cambrian	QH51-58	508.071	Natural history—Study and teaching
QE728	560.174	Paleontology—Devonian			
QE731-734	560.176	Paleontology—Mesozoic	QH51-58	508.071	Nature study
QE733	560.1766	Paleontology—Jurassic	QH68	635.9824	Terrariums
QE734	560.177	Paleontology—Cretaceous	QH70	508.074	Natural history museums
QE735-741.3	560.178	Paleontology—Cenozoic	QH75-77	508.072	Research natural areas
QE737	560.1784	Paleontology—Eocene	QH75-77	333.95	Biological diversity conservation
QE738	560.1785	Paleontology—Oligocene			
QE739	560.1787	Paleontology—Miocene	QH75-77	333.95	Biosphere reserves
QE744	560.9981	Paleontology—Arctic regions	QH75-77	333.7816	Nature conservation
QE746-747	560.973	Paleontology—United States	QH75-77	333.91816	Wetland conservation
QE748	560.971	Paleontology—Canada	QH75-77	578.68	Endangered species
QE749	560.972	Paleontology—Mexico	QH78	576.84	Extinction (Biology)
QE750	560.9729(9)	Paleontology—West Indies	QH83	508.014	Natural history—Terminology
QE751	560.9728	Paleontology—Central America	QH84-198	578.09	Biogeography
			QH84.8	578.757	Soil biology
QE752	560.98	Paleontology—South America	QH87.3	578.768	Wetlands
			QH87.3	578.768	Marshes
QE753-755	560.94	Paleontology—Europe	QH87.3	578.768	Swamps
QE756	560.95	Paleontology—Asia	QH87.5	578.738	Moors and heaths
QE757	560.96	Paleontology—Africa	QH87.7	578.748	Savannas
QE758	560.994	Paleontology—Australia	QH88	578.754	Desert biology
QE760	560.9989	Paleontology—Antarctic regions	QH88	578.754	Deserts
			QH90-100	578.76	Aquatic biology
QE760.8-899.2	560	Animals, Fossil	QH90.8.P5	578.776	Plankton
QE770-832	562	Invertebrates, Fossil	QH91-95.59	578.77	Marine biology
QE815-832	565	Arthropoda, Fossil	QH91.6-.65	578.77072	Marine laboratories
QE841-899	566	Vertebrates, Fossil	QH91.75	578.77	Marine parks and reserves
QE862.D5	567.9	Dinosaurs	QH92-93.9	578.773	Marine biology—Atlantic Ocean
QE881-882	569	Mammals, Fossil			
QE882.C5	569.5	Dolphins, Fossil	QH94-.7	578.775	Marine biology—Indian Ocean
QE882.P7	569.8	Primates, Fossil			
QE934	561.1998(1-8)	Paleobotany—Arctic regions	QH95-.55	578.774	Marine biology—Pacific Ocean
QE936-937	561.1973	Paleobotany—United States			
QE938	561.1971	Paleobotany—Canada	QH95.58	578.777	Marine biology—Antarctic Ocean
QE939	561.1972	Paleobotany—Mexico			
QE940	561.19729	Paleobotany—West Indies	QH95.8	578.7789	Coral reef biology
QE941	561.19728	Paleobotany—Central America	QH95.9	578.77	Brackish water biology
			QH96-100	578.76	Freshwater biology
QE942	561.198	Paleobotany—South America	QH98	578.763	Lakes
			QH101-199	578.09(4-9)	Natural history—[By region or country]
QE943-945	561.194	Paleobotany—Europe			
QE946	561.195	Paleobotany—Asia	QH104-105	578.0973	Natural history—United States
QE947	561.196	Paleobotany—Africa			
QE948	561.1994	Paleobotany—Australia	QH106-.2	578.0971	Natural history—Canada
QE948.2	561.1993	Paleobotany—New Zealand	QH107	578.0972	Natural history—Mexico
QE949	561.199(5-6)	Paleobotany—Oceania	QH108	578.09728	Natural history—Central America
QE950	561.19989	Paleobotany—Antarctic regions	QH109	578.09729	Natural history—West Indies
QE975-978	561.5	Gymnosperms, Fossil	QH111-130	578.098	Natural history—South America
QE980-983	561	Angiosperms, Fossil			
QE983	561.3	Dicetyledons, Fossil	QH135-178	578.094	Natural history—Europe
QE991	561.16	Petrified forests	QH179-193	578.095	Natural history—Asia

LC	Dewey	Subject Heading	LC	Dewey	Subject Heading
QH194-195	578.096	Natural history—Africa	QH517	572.437	Electrophysiology
QH197	578.0994	Natural history—Australia	QH521	572.4	Metabolism
QH201-278.5	570.282	Microscopy	QH527	571.77	Biological rhythms
QH211-212	570.282	Microscopes	QH540-549.5	591.7	Animal ecology
QH212.E4	570.2825	Electron microscopy	QH540-549.5	577	Ecology
QH212.E4	570.2825	Electron microscopes	QH541.15.M64	363.7063	Environmental monitoring
QH236.2	570.2827	Freeze fracturing	QH541.2-.264	577.071	Environmental education
QH237	570.2827	Stains and staining (Microscopy)	QH541.3	577.15	Biological productivity
			QH541.5.B63	577.687	Bog ecology
QH301-705	570	Biology	QH541.5.C6	577.56	Urban ecology (Biology)
QH305-.2	570.9	Biology—History	QH541.5.C7	577.789	Coral reef ecology
QH315-320	570.72	Biology—Research	QH541.5.D35	577.7	Deep-sea ecology
QH315-320	570.71	Biology—Study and teaching	QH541.5.D4	577.54	Desert ecology
QH321-323.2	570.72	Biological laboratories	QH541.5.E8	577.786	Estuarine ecology
QH323.5	570.151	Biomathematics	QH541.5.F6	577.3	Forest ecology
QH324	570.284	Biological apparatus and supplies	QH541.5.F7	577.6	Freshwater ecology
			QH541.5.G37	577.554	Garden ecology
QH324.2	570.285	Biology—Data processing	QH541.5.H67	577.554	Household ecology
QH324.8	570.228	Biological models	QH541.5.L27	577.63	Lagoon ecology
QH324.9.C7	571.4645	Cryobiology	QH541.5.L3	577.63	Lake ecology
QH325-349	570.1	Life (Biology)	QH541.5.M3	577.68	Wetland ecology
QH325	576.83	Spontaneous generation	QH541.5.M4	577.46	Meadow ecology
QH327-328	571.0919	Space biology	QH541.5.M6	577.38	Moor ecology
QH331	570.1	Biology—Philosophy	QH541.5.P7	577.4	Grasslands
QH332	174.957	Bioethics	QH541.5.P7	577.4	Grassland ecology
QH343.7-344	577.14	Biogeochemistry	QH541.5.P7	577.48	Savanna ecology
QH345	572	Biochemistry	QH541.5.P7	577.44	Prairie ecology
QH351	571.3	Morphology	QH541.5.R27	577.34	Rain forest ecology
QH352	577.88	Population biology	QH541.5.R3	577.4	Range ecology
QH353	577.18	Biological invasions	QH541.5.R62	577.55	Roadside ecology
QH359-425	576.8	Evolution (Biology)	QH541.5.S22	577.639	Salt lake ecology
QH372	576.87	Coevolution	QH541.5.S26	577.583	Sand dune ecology
QH375	576.82	Natural selection	QH541.5.S35	577.69	Seashore ecology
QH401-411	576.54	Variation (Biology)	QH541.5.S35	577.69	Tide pool ecology
QH426-470	576.5	Genetics	QH541.5.S55	577.38	Shrubland ecology
QH442-.6	660.65	Genetic engineering	QH541.5.S6	577.57	Soil ecology
QH442.2	660.65	Cloning	QH541.5.S7	577.64	Stream ecology
QH442.2	660.65	Molecular cloning	QH541.5.S87	577.78	Sublittoral ecology
QH443-450.6	572.877	Genetic recombination	QH541.5.S9	577.68	Swamp ecology
QH445.2	572.8633	Gene mapping	QH541.5.W3	577.6	Aquatic ecology
QH447-.8	572.86	Genes	QH543-.2	577.22	Bioclimatology
QH447	572.86	Genomes	QH543.2	578.42	Acclimatization
QH450-.6	572.865	Genetic regulation	QH543.5-.6	577.277	Radioecology
QH450.2	572.8845	Genetic transcription	QH544	578.42	Phenology
QH450.5	572.645	Genetic translation	QH546	578.4	Adaptation (Biology)
QH455	576.58	Population genetics	QH546.3	577.83	Competition (Biology)
QH460-468	576.549	Mutation (Biology)	QH548.3	577.852	Mutualism (Biology)
QH465-.5	576.549	Mutagens	QH573-671	571.6	Cytology
QH471-489	571.8	Reproduction	QH573-671	571.6	Cells
QH475-479	571.89	Reproduction, Asexual	QH583-.2	571.6072	Cytology—Research
QH485	571.864	Fertilization (Biology)	QH585.2-.45	571.638	Cell culture
QH489	571.884	Generations, Alterating	QH595	571.66	Cell nuclei
QH499	571.889	Regeneration (Biology)	QH601-602	571.64	Cell membranes
QH504	154.72	Biomagnetism	QH603.R5	571.658	Ribosomes
QH505	571.4	Biophysics	QH605-.3	571.844	Cell division
QH506	572.8	Molecular biology	QH605	571.845	Meiosis
QH508	571.7	Biological control systems	QH605.2	571.844	Mitosis
QH509	571.64	Biological transport	QH607	571.835	Cell differentiation
QH511	571.8	Growth	QH613	572	Histochemistry
QH513	571.43	Biomechanics	QH631-647	571.6	Cell physiology
QH514.15.E27	577	Ecotones	QH633	572.47	Cell respiration

LC	Dewey	Subject Heading	LC	Dewey	Subject Heading
QH634.5	572.4	Cell metabolism	QK494.5.P66	585.2	Fir
QH641	572.4358	Bioluminescence	QK494.5.T3	585.5	Dawn redwood
QH651	571.63455	Light—Physiological effect	QK495	580	Angiosperms
QH652-.7	571.6345	Cells—Effect of radiation on	QK495.A12	583	Dicotyledons
QH657	571.63435	Gravity	QK495.A26	584.352	Agave
QH671	571.939	Cell death	QK495.A484	584.34	Daffodils
QH671	571.936	Death	QK495.A6853	583.84	Ginseng
QK	580	Botany	QK495.C74	583.99	Dandelions
QK	580	Plants	QK495.C74	583.99	Daisies
QK	582.13	Flowers	QK495.C98	583.94	Dodder
QK1	580.6	Botany—Societies, etc.	QK495.E92	583.79	Coca
QK9	580.3	Botany—Dictionaries	QK495.F14	583.46	Durmast oak
QK10	580.14	Botany—Terminology	QK495.F14	583.46	English oak
QK26-31	580.92	Botanists	QK495.G4	583.95	African violets
QK51-57	580.71	Botany—Study and teaching	QK495.G74	584.9	Deepwater rice
QK61	580.75	Plants—Collection and preservation	QK495.G74	584.9	Durum wheat
			QK495.G74	584.9	Fescue
QK62	580.723	Vegetation surveys	QK495.G74	584.9	Grasses
QK63	580.223	Vegetation mapping	QK495.I75	584.38	Dwarf irises
QK71-73	580.73	Botanical gardens	QK495.L72	584.32	Daylilies
QK75-77	580.74	Herbaria	QK495.L72	584.32	Easter lily
QK79-.5	580.74	Botany—Exhibitions	QK495.M27	583.685	Hibiscus
QK86-.4	333.953	Plant conservation	QK495.M73	583.45	Fig
QK86	581.68	Endangered plants	QK495.M9	583.766	Eucalyptus
QK91-97	580.12	Botany—Classification	QK495.M9	583.765	Guava
QK96	580.14	Botany—Nomenclature	QK495.P17	584.5	Date palm
QK98	580.222	Botany—Pictorial works	QK495.97	583.952	Eggplant
QK98.4	581.63	Plants, Useful	QK495.U48	583.849	Dill
QK98.5	581.632	Wild plants, Edible	QK495.V84	583.86	Grapes
QK98.5	581.632	Plants, Edible	QK504-635	586	Cryptogams
QK98.7	581.636	Dye plants	QK520-532	587	Pteridophyta
QK99	581.634	Botany, Medical	QK532.4-563.87	588	Bryophytes
QK99	581.634	Medicinal plants	QK564-580.5	579.8	Algae
QK100	581.659	Poisonous plants	QK580.7-597.7	579.7	Lichens
QK101-474.5	581.9	Phytogeography	QK600-635	579.5	Fungi
QK102-105	581.76	Aquatic plants	QK600-635	579.6	Mushrooms, Hallucinogenic
QK105	581.76	Freshwater plants			
QK108-474.5	583	Dicotyledons	QK602	579.5135	Fungi—Genetics
QK108-474.5	581.7786	Estuarine plants	QK617	579.6	Mushrooms, Edible
QK108-474.5	581.73	Forest plants	QK617	581.659	Mushrooms, Poisonous
QK115-195	580.973	Botany—United States	QK641-707	575	Botany—Anatomy
QK145-195	580.97(4-9)	Botany—[United States, By state]	QK644	575.54	Roots (Botany)
			QK645-650	575.49	Shoots (Botany)
QK201-203	580.971	Botany—Canada	QK649	575.57	Leaves
QK211	580.972	Botany—Mexico	QK653-661	575.633	Flowers—Anatomy
QK215-222	580.9728	Botany—Central America	QK653-661	575.633	Flowers—Morphology
QK225-231	580.9729	Botany—West Indies	QK653	575.6	Double flowers
QK241-274	580.98	Botany—South America	QK658-659	575.6	Plants, Sex in
QK281-339	580.94	Botany—Europe	QK658	571.845	Pollen
QK341-379	580.95	Botany—Asia	QK710-899	575	Plant physiology
QK353	580.956	Botany—Middle East	QK725	571.7236	Plant cells and tissues
QK360-368	580.959	Botany—Asia, Southeastern	QK725	571.7236	Plant cell development
QK381-424	580.96	Botany—Africa	QK725	571.72366	Plant chromosomes
QK431-461	580.994	Botany—Australia	QK728	572.82	Plant molecular biology
QK474-.3	580.998	Botany—Arctic regions	QK731-745	571.82	Growth (Plants)
QK474.4	580.9989	Botany—Antarctica	QK740	571.862	Germination
QK474.8-494	582.16	Trees	QK750-751	577.27	Plants, Effect of pollution on
QK494-.5	585	Gymnosperms	QK751	577.2752	Plants, Effect of acid precipitation on
QK494.5.C975	585.4	Eastern redcedar			
QK494.5.P66	585.2	Douglas fir	QK751	577.276	Plants, Effect of air pollution on
QK494.5.P66	585.2	Eastern hemlock			

LC	Dewey	Subject Heading	LC	Dewey	Subject Heading
QK756	632.11	Plants—Frost resistance	QL78-79	597.073	Aquariums, Public
QK761	571.772	Biological rhythms in plants	QL78.5	597.073	Marine aquariums, Public
QK761	571.782	Dormancy in plants	QL81.5-84.7	333.95416	Wildlife conservation
QK776	581.498	Roots (Botany)	QL81.5-84.77	578.68	Endangered species
QK825-830	575.6	Plants—Reproduction	QL83.2	636.0832	Wildlife rescue
QK827-830	575.6	Plants, Sex in	QL83.4	333.95416	Wildlife reintroduction
QK828	571.8642	Fertilization of plants	QL88-.15	560	Extinct animals
QK828	575.65	Pollination	QL89.2.S2	001.944	Sasquatch
QK830	575.6	Plants, Flowering of	QL100	591.65	Dangerous animals
QK830	575.6	Double flowers	QL100	591.65	Poisonious animals
QK840	571.8892	Regeneration (Botany)	QL101-345	590.9(3-9)	Zoogeography
QK845	572.4372	Electrophysiology of plants	QL105	590.98	Zoology—Arctic regions
QK861-899	572.2	Botanical chemistry	QL112	591.73	Forest animals
QK867-898	572.42	Plants—Nutrition	QL115.3-.5	591.74	Grassland fauna
QK871	575.76	Plants—Absorption of water	QL116	591.754	Desert animals
QK871	575.75	Plants, Motion of fluids in	QL120-149	591.77	Aquatic animals
QK873	575.8	Evapotranspiration	QL126	591.7732	Aquatic animals—Arctic Ocean
QK876	575.8	Gases from plants	QL126.5	591.777	Aquatic animals—Antarctic Ocean
QK881-897	572.42	Plants—Metabolism			
QK882	572.46	Photosnythesis	QL127-135	591.773	Aquatic animals—Atlantic Ocean
QK891	572.472	Plants—Respiration			
QK898.E58	572.72	Plant enzymes	QL137	591.775	Aquatic animals—Indian Ocean
QK898.H67	571.742	Plant hormones			
QK898.P7	572.592	Plant pigments	QL138	591.774	Aquatic animals—Pacific Ocean
QK900-938	577	Plants—Habitat			
QK900-938	581.7	Plant ecology	QL141-149	591.76	Freshwater animals
QK911	577.83	Plant competition	QL155-339	590.9	Zoology—[By region or country]
QK917	583.75	Carnivorous plants			
QK922	581.754	Desert plants	QL360-599	592	Invertebrates
QK926	571.8642	Fertilization of plants by insects	QL366-369.2	579.4	Protozoa
			QL368.A5	579.432	Amoeba
QK926	571.8642	Pollination	QL368.F5	579.82	Flagellata
QK929	571.847	Spores (Botany)—Dispersal	QL370.7-374.2	593.4	Sponges
QK930-935	581.76	Aquatic plants	QL375-379	593.5	Coelenterata
QK932-.7	581.76	Freshwater plants	QL380-.8	593.8	Ctenophora
QK936	581.748	Tropical plants	QL381-385.2	593.9	Echinodermata
QK937	581.7538	Mountain plants	QL386-394	592.3	Worms
QK938.D4	581.754	Desert plants	QL391.A6	592.64	Earthworms
QK938.E	581.7786	Estuarine plants	QL401-445.2	594	Shellfish
QK938.F6	581.73	Timberline	QL401-432	591.477	Shells
QK938.F6	581.73	Forest ecology	QL401-432	594	Mollusks
QK938.F6	581.73	Forest plants	QL430.5.H34	594.32	Abalones
QK938.M4	581.746	Meadow plants	QL434-599.82	595	Arthropoda
QK938.P7	581.74	Grasslands	QL435-445.2	595.3	Crustacea
QK938.P7	581.744	Prairies	QL444.M33	595.38	Decapoda (Crustacea)
QK980-989	581.38	Plants—Evolution	QL449.6-.65	595.66	Millipedes
QK981.3	581.35	Plant biochemical genetics	QL451-459.2	595.4	Arachnida
QK981.4	581.35	Plant genetic regulation	QL461-599.82	595.7	Insects
QL	590	Zoology	QL468.5	595.7072	Entomology—Research
QL1	590.6	Zoology—Societies, etc.	QL508.A2	595.726	Desert locust
QL10	590.14	Zoology—Terminology	QL508.A2	595.726	Migratory locust
QL26-31	590.92	Ethologist	QL520-.42	595.733	Damselflies
QL26-31	591.5092	Zoologists	QL520-.42	595.733	Dragonflies
QL46	590.222	Zoology—Pictorial works	QL541-562.4	595.789	Butterflies
QL51-58	590.71	Zoology—Study and teaching	QL561.L3	595.78139	Eastern tent caterpillar
QL52.6	590.724	Zoology—Experiments	QL561.S2	595.78	Ailanthus moth
QL63	590.752	Taxidermy	QL561.T55	595.78	Clothes moths
QL71	590.74	Zoological museums	QL563-569.4	595.799	Bees
QL73	590.73	Menageries	QL568.A6	595.799	Honeybee
QL76-77.5	590.73	Petting zoos	QL568.A6	595.799	Africanized honeybee
QL76-77.5	590.73	Zoos			

LC	Dewey	Subject Heading	LC	Dewey	Subject Heading
QL568.F7	595.796	Ants	QL698.8	573.87	Bird navigation
QL568.F7	595.796	Fire ants	QL700-739.8	599	Mammals
QL596.S3	595.7649	Dung beetles	QL706.8-.83	599.168	Rare mammals
QL596.S35	595.76	Douglas fir beetle	QL707	569	Extinct mammals
QL605-739.8	596	Vertebrates	QL708.6	599.1788	Mammal populations
QL614-639.8	597	Fishes	QL737.C2	599.7	Carnivora
QL618	597.012	Fishes—Classification	QL737.C2	599.77	Dogs
QL618.3	597.1788	Fish populations	QL737.C22	599.775	Foxes
QL618.5-.55	597.072	Fishes—Research	QL737.C23	599.756	Tigers
QL618.7	597.165	Dangerous fishes	QL737.C432	599.53	Dolphins
QL618.7	597.165	Poisonous fishes	QL737.C434	599.53	Dall Porpoise
QL619-637	597.09(4-9)	Fishes—Geographical distribution	QL737.M242	599.336	Elephant shrews
QL638.9	597.36	Dogfish	QL737.P63	599.79	Eared seals
QL638.95.S7	597.3	Hammerhead sharks	QL737.P64	599.794	Elephant seals
QL638.99	597.135	Fishes—Genetics	QL737.P9-.P968	599.8	Primates
QL638.P4	597.75	Darters (Fishes)	QL737.P93	599.83	Demidoff's galago
QL638.S9	597.6798	Dwarf sea horse	QL737.P96	599.88	Apes
QL639	597.1479	Fins	QL737.P96	599.884	Gorilla
QL639	597.1477	Scales (Fishes)	QL737.P98	599.674	African elephant
QL639.2	597.562	Fishes—Spawning	QL737.P98	599.67	Elephants
QL639.4	597.1479	Fishes—Locomotion	QL737.R6	599.35	Dancing mice
QL639.5	597.1568	Fishes—Migration	QL737.R634	599.3592	Guinea pigs
QL641-669	597.9	Reptiles	QL737.R666	599.356	Hamsters
QL645.7	597.9165	Dangerous reptiles	QL737.R638	599.356	Dwarf hamsters
QL666.C584	597.92	Desert tortoise	QL737.R656	599.3596	Dormice
QL666.C925	597.98	Alligators	QL737.R656	599.3596	Edible dormouse
QL666.C925	597.98	Crocodiles	QL737.R656	599.35097	Desert kangaroo rat
QL666.O6-.694	597.96	Snakes	QL737.R68	599.36	Abent squirrel
QL666.O64	597.96	Cobras	QL737.R68	599.364	Eastern chipmunk
QL666.O69	597.96	Eastern diamondback rattlesnake	QL737.T8	599.31	Aardvark
QL668.E2-.E275	597.89	Frogs	QL737.U5	599.642	Elands
QL671-699	598	Ornithology	QL737.U53	599.642	African buffalo
QL671-699	598	Birds	QL737.U53	599.64	Antelopes
QL676.5-.57	639.978	Bird attracting	QL737.U53	599.643	American bison
QL676.5-.57	333.958	Bird refuges	QL737.U55	599.65	Deer
QL676.7	597.168	Rare birds	QL737.U55	599.657	Elk
QL676.8	597.168	Extinct birds	QL737.U56	599.638	Giraffe
QL677.75	598.165	Dangerous birds	QL737.U62	599.665	African wild ass
QL677.8	598.073	Aviaries	QL750-795	591.5	Animal behavior
QL678-695.5	598.(4-9)	Birds—Geographical distribution	QL752	591.788	Animal populations
QL696.A52	598.41	Ducks	QL755	591.565	Hibernation
QL696.A52	598.415	Eider	QL756-.15	591.564	Animals—Habitations
QL696.C34	598.53	Emus	QL756.15	591.5648	Animal burrowing
QL696.C63	598.65	Eared dove	QL756.5-.57	591.5(3-4)	Animals—Food
QL696.C67	598.65	Dodo	QL756.57	591.53	Cannibalism in animals
QL696.F32	598.942	African fish eagle	QL757	591.65	Parasitology
QL696.F32	598.942	Eagles	QL757	591.65	Parasites
QL696.F34	598.96	Falcons	QL759	591.47	Animal defenses
QL696.G27	598.625	Pheasants	QL761	591.562	Sexual behavior in animals
QL696.P235	598.832	Dippers (Birds)	QL761	591.562	Sexual selection in animals
QL696.P2438	598.883	Dusky seaside sparrow	QL761.5	591.563	Familial behavior in animals
QL696.P288	598.842	Eastern bluebird	QL762	591.563	Parental behavior in animals
QL696.P7	598.71	African gray parrot	QL763.2	591.563	Imprinting (Psychology)
QL696.S473	598.47	Adelie penguin	QL763.5	591.563	Play behavior in animals
QL696.S473	598.47	Emperor penguin	QL765	591.594	Animal sounds
QL697	598.147	Feathers	QL765	591.594	Sound production by animals
QL698.5	598.1594	Birdsongs	QL765	591.594	Voice
QL698.7	598.1479	Birds—Flight	QL767	591.472	Protective coloration (Biology)
			QL768	591.479	Animal tracks
			QL775	591.56	Social hierarchy in animals

LC	Dewey	Subject Heading	LC	Dewey	Subject Heading
QL776	591.59	Animal communication	QL940	591.47	Animal weapons
QL776	591.59	Human-animal communication	QL941-943	573.5	Dermis
			QL941-943	573.5	Epidermis
QL781	591.512	Instinct	QL941-943	573.5	Skin
QL782	573.87	Animal navigation	QL942	573.58	Hair
QL785-.27	591.5	Animal psychology	QL942	573.59	Nails (Anatomy)
QL785	591.513	Cognition in animals	QL942	573.59	Toenails
QL785	591.513	Animal intelligence	QL944	573.679	Mammary glands
QL785.3	591.5	Extrasensory perception in animals	QL945-949	573.87	Sense organs
			QL946	573.357	Tongue
QL799-.5	571.3	Morphology (Animals)	QL948	573.89	Ear, External
QL801-950.9	571.3	Anatomy, Comparative	QL948	573.89	Ear
QL807	571.5	Histology	QL948	573.89	Eustachian tube
QL821-831	573.7	Musculoskeletal system	QL948	573.89	Middle ear
QL821-827	573.76	Skeleton	QL948	579.89	Labyrinth (Ear)
QL821	573.76	Bones	QL949	573.88	Eye
QL825	573.78	Joints	QL949	573.88	Eyelids
QL827	573.78356	Ligaments	QL949	573.88	Optic nerve
QL831	573.75	Muscles	QL949	573.88	Pupil (Eye)
QL835-841	573.1	Cardiovascular system	QL949	573.88	Retina
QL835	573.18	Blood-vessels	QL950.7	573.79	Leg
QL835	573.185	Arteries	QL951-991	571.86	Embryology
QL835	573.186	Veins	QL961	571.860724	Embryology, Experimental
QL838	573.17	Heart—Anatomy	QL981	571.876	Metamorphosis
QL841	573.16	Lymphatics	QM	611	Human anatomy
QL845-855	573.2	Respiratory organs	QM24	599.94	Human anatomy—Variation
QL848	573.22	Lungs	QM25	611.0022	Human anatomy—Atlases
QL856-867	573.3	Digestive organs	QM34	611.0078	Human anatomy—Laboratory manuals
QL857	573.35	Mouth			
QL857	573.355	Lips	QM51	611.0074	Anatomical museums
QL858	573.356	Teeth	QM100-170	611.7	Musculoskeletal system
QL861	573.359	Esophagus	QM101-117	611.71	Human skeleton
QL862	573.36	Stomache	QM101-117	611.71	Skeleton
QL863	573.378	Duodenum	QM101-117	573.76	Bones
QL863	573.37	Intestines	QM101	611.717	Clavicle
QL865-868	573.4	Glands	QM105	611.716	Jaws
QL866	573.377	Pancreas	QM105	611.715	Skull
QL867	573.38	Gallbladder	QM111	611.711	Spinal canal
QL867	573.38	Liver	QM111	611.711	Vertebrae
QL868	573.4	Endocrinology, Comparative	QM111	611.711	Spine
QL868	573.4	Endocrine glands	QM113	611.712	Ribs
QL868	573.45	Pituitary gland	QM117	611.718	Femur
QL868	573.1555	Spleen	QM131-142	611.72	Joints
QL872-881	573.49	Urinary organs	QM141	611.72	Ligaments
QL872-875	573.49	Excretory organs	QM151-170	611.73	Muscles
QL872	573.49	Bladder	QM170	611.74	Tendons
QL873	573.496	Kidneys	QM178-197	611.1	Cardiovascular system
QL876-881	573.6	Generative organs	QM181	611.12	Heart—Anatomy
QL878	573.65	Generative organs, Male	QM181	611.11	Pericardium
QL878	573.658	Prostate	QM181	611.12	Myocardium
QL881	573.66	Generative organs, Female	QM191	611.13	Aorta
QL881	573.665	Ovaries	QM191	611.13	Blood-vessels
QL881	573.667	Uterus	QM191	611.13	Arteries
QL921-939	573.8	Nervous system	QM191	611.13	Pulmonary artery
QL933-937	573.86	Medulla oblongata	QM191	611.14	Veins
QL933-937	573.86	Meninges	QM197	611.42	Lymphatics
QL937	573.86	Cerebellum	QM251-265	611.2	Respiratory organs
QL938.H56	573.86	Hippocampus (Brain)	QM255	611.22	Epiglottis
QL938.S6	573.869	Spinal cord	QM255	611.22	Glottis
QL939	573.85	Nerves	QM255	611.22	Larynx
QL939	573.85	Sympathetic nervous system	QM261	611.24	Lungs

LC	Dewey	Subject Heading	LC	Dewey	Subject Heading
QM301-367	611.3	Alimentary canal	QM507	611.85	Labyrinth (Ear)
QM301-367	611.3	Digestive organs	QM511	611.84	Eye
QM301-367	611.3	Gastrointestinal system	QM511	611.84	Eyelids
QM306	611.317	Lips	QM511	611.84	Optic nerve
QM306	611.31	Mouth	QM511	611.84	Pupil (Eye)
QM311	611.314	Teeth	QM511	611.84	Retina
QM325-371	611.316	Salivary glands	QM531-549	611.9	Anatomy, Surgical and topographical
QM325-371	611.4	Glands			
QM331	611.32	Esophagus	QM535	611.92	Chin
QM331	611.32	Pharnyx	QM535	611.91	Head
QM331	611.32	Tonsils	QM535	611.93	Neck
QM341	611.33	Stomache	QM535	611.92	Face
QM345	611.347	Colon (Anatomy)	QM535	611.32	Throat
QM345	611.345	Appendix (Anatomy)	QM540	612.9	Back
QM345	611.341	Duodenum	QM543	611.95	Abdomen
QM345	611.34	Intestines	QM548-549	611.9(7-8)	Extremities (Anatomy)
QM351	611.36	Liver	QM548	611.97	Arm
QM352	611.36	Gallbladder	QM548	611.97	Hand
QM353	611.37	Pancreas	QM548	611.97	Forearm
QM367	611.38	Peritoneum	QM548	611.97	Fingers
QM371	611.45	Adrenal glands	QM549	611.98	Toes
QM371	611.4	Endocrine glands	QM549	611.98	Foot
QM371	611.47	Pituitary gland	QM549	611.98	Leg
QM371	611.41	Spleen	QM550-577.8	611.018	Histology
QM371	611.44	Thyroid gland	QM551-575	611.018	Tissues
QM401-413	611.61	Urinary organs	QM561	611.77	Epidermis
QM401	611.61	Kidneys	QM562	611.74	Connective tissues
QM411	611.62	Bladder	QM563	611.0182	Elastic tissue
QM416-421	611.6	Generative organs	QM563	611.74	Fasciae (Anatomy)
QM416	611.64	Penis	QM563	611.72	Ligaments
QM416	611.63	Prostate	QM565	611.0182	Adipose tissues
QM416	611.63	Generative organs, Male	QM567	611.0183	Cartilage
QM421	611.65	Fallopian tubes	QM569	611.0184	Bone marrow
QM421	611.65	Generative organs, Female	QM571	611.73	Muscles
QM421	611.65	Ovaries	QM575	611.0188	Nerve tissue
QM421	611.66	Uterus	QM576	611.4	Endocrine glands
QM451-471	611.8	Nervous system	QM601-695	611.013	Embryology, Human
QM455	611.81	Cerebellum	QP	571	Physiology
QM455	611.81	Hippocampus (Brain)	QP1	571.05	Physiology—Periodicals
QM455	611.81	Hypothalamus	QP13	571.014	Physiology—Terminology
QM455	611.81	Medulla oblongata	QP31-33	571.1	Physiology, Comparative
QM465	611.82	Spinal cord	QP34-38	612	Human physiology
QM469	611.81	Meninges	QP34-38	612	Human biology
QM471	611.83	Nerves	QP39-47	571.071	Physiology—Study and teaching
QM471	611.83	Sympathetic nervous system			
QM481-484	611.77	Skin	QP55	571.0284	Physiological apparatus
QM484	611.77	Dermis	QP81-87	570.1	Life (Biology)
QM484	611.77	Epidermis	QP82-.2	578.4	Adaptation (Physiology)
QM488	611.78	Eyelashes	QP82.2.A4	571.49	Altitude, Influence of
QM488	611.78	Hair	QP82.2.C5	571.49	Weather—Physiological effect
QM488	611.78	Nails (Anatomy)			
QM495	611.49	Breast	QP82.2.C6	571.464	Cold—Physiological effect
QM495	611.49	Mammary glands	QP82.2.G7	571.435	Gravity
QM501-511	611.8	Sense organs	QP82.2.N6	571.444	Noise—Physiological effect
QM503	611.313	Tongue	QP82.2.N64	571.45	Nonionizing radiation
QM505	611.21	Frontal sinus	QP82.2.P6	571.49	Pollution—Physiological effect
QM505	611.21	Nasopharynx			
QM507	611.85	Ear	QP82.2.P7	571.437	Atmospheric pressure—Physiological effect
QM507	611.85	Ear, External			
QM507	611.85	Eustachian tube	QP84	612.6	Human growth
QM507	611.85	Middle ear	QP84	612.6	Growth

LC	Dewey	Subject Heading	LC	Dewey	Subject Heading
QP84.4	612.661	Puberty	QP193	612.32	Stomache—Secretions
QP84.6	571.77	Biological rhythms	QP195	612.34	Pancreas—Secretions
QP84.6	571.77	Sleep-wake cycle	QP211	612.46	Excretion
QP85	612.68	Longevity	QP221	612.7921	Perspiration
QP86	612.67	Old age	QP246	612.664	Lactation
QP87	571.939	Death	QP247-250.8	612.46	Urinary organs
QP88-.6	611.018	Tissues	QP249	612.463	Kidneys
QP88.5	573.5	Dermis	QP251-285	612.6	Generative organs
QP88.5	573.5	Epidermis	QP251-285	612.6	Reproduction
QP90.4	571.75	Homeostasis	QP251-285	612.6	Human reproduction
QP91-99.5	612.11	Blood	QP251-281	612.63	Conception
QP91	612.115	Fibrin	QP253-257	612.61	Generative organs, Male
QP93.5-.7	612.115	Blood—Coagulation	QP255	612.61	Semen
QP93.5-.7	612.115	Blood coagulation factors	QP259-281	612.62	Generative organs, Female
QP96.5	612.1111	Hemoglobin	QP301-336	612.7	Musculoskeletal system
QP98	612.11825	Blood groups	QP301-336	612.76	Human mechanics
QP99	612.116	Blood plasma	QP301-336	612.76	Locomotion
QP101	612.14	Pulse	QP301-336	613.71	Exercise
QP105-.4	612.14	Blood pressure	QP301-310	612.76	Animal locomotion
QP107	612.2	Pulmonary circulation	QP301-310	612.044	Exercise—Physiological
QP108	612.17	Coronary circulation			aspects
QP109	612.18	Vasomotor system	QP303	613.7	Kinesiology
QP111-114	612.17	Heart	QP306	612.2	Larynx
QP113.2	612.17	Myocardium	QP306	612.78	Voice
QP115	612.42	Lymphatics	QP306	612.78	Speech
QP121-125	612.2	Lungs	QP310.F5	573.798	Animal flight
QP121-125	612.2	Respiratory organs	QP311	612.92	Jaws
QP121-125	612.2	Respiration	QP321-322	612.74	Muscles
QP135	612.01426	Body temperature	QP321	612.744	Fatigue
QP139	612.391	Thirst	QP330	612.83	Spine
QP141-185.3	612.3	Nutrition	QP341	572.437	Electrophysiology
QP141	612.391	Hunger	QP351-430	612.81	Nervous system
QP145-159	612.3	Digestion	QP356.3	612.8042	Neurochemistry
QP146	612.315	Esophagus	QP360	152.1423	Pattern perception
QP146	612.312	Tonsils	QP361-375.5	612.81	Nerves
QP151-156	612.3	Gastrointestinal system	QP370-375	612.83	Spinal cord
QP151	612.32	Stomache	QP376-430	612.82	Brain
QP156	612.33	Duodenum	QP377	612.828	Medulla oblongata
QP156	612.33	Intestines	QP379	612.827	Cerebellum
QP159	612.46	Excretion	QP383-.17	612.825	Cerebral cortex
QP165	612.38	Absorption (Physiology)	QP401	612.88	Pain
QP165	612.38	Intestinal absorption	QP406	612.82	Memory
QP171-177	612.39	Metabolism	QP425-427	612.821	Sleep
QP185	612.35	Gallbladder	QP431-495	612.8	Senses and sensation
QP185	612.35	Liver	QP451	612.88	Touch
QP187-.6	612.4	Endocrinology, Comparative	QP455-458	612.86	Chemical senses
QP187-.6	612.4	Endocrinology	QP456	612.87	Taste
QP187-.6	612.4	Endocrine glands	QP458	612.86	Odors
QP187	612.41	Spleen	QP458	612.86	Nose
QP187.7	612.4	Exocrine glands	QP458	612.86	Smell
QP188.A28	612.45	Adrenal cortex	QP460-471.2	612.85	Ear
QP188.A3	612.45	Adrenal glands	QP460-469.3	612.85	Hearing
QP188.M3	612.664	Mammary glands	QP461	612.854	Eustachian tube
QP188.P26	612.34	Pancreas	QP461	612.854	Middle ear
QP188.P3	612.44	Parathyroid glands	QP471-.2	612.858	Labyrinth (Ear)
QP188.P58	612.492	Pituitary gland	QP471	612.858	Vestibular apparatus
QP186-246	612.4	Glands	QP474-495	612.84	Vision
QP190-246.5	612.4	Secretion	QP475-495	612.84	Eye
QP191	612.313	Saliva	QP476	612.84	Pupil (Eye)
QP188.S2	612.313	Salivary glands	QP477.5	612.846	Eye—Movements
QP193	612.32	Gastric juice	QP479	612.843	Retina

LC	Dewey	Subject Heading	LC	Dewey	Subject Heading
QP501-801	572	Biochemistry	QR12	579.012	Microbiology—Classification
QP517.P45	572.435	Photobiochemistry	QR13	579.138	Microorganisms—Evolution
QP527	541.224	Free radicals (Chemistry)	QR21-22	579.09	Microbiology—History
QP531-535	572.51	Bioinorganic chemistry	QR30-31	579.092	Microbiologists
QP532	572.52	Metals in the body	QR46-48	616.01	Body, Human—Microbiology
QP533	572.51	Minerals in the body	QR46	616.014	Medical bacteriology
QP534	572.515	Trace elements in the body	QR46	616.01	Medical microbiology
QP535.01	572.53	Active oxygen in the body	QR53-.5	660.62	Industrial microbiology
QP535.C2	572.516	Calcium in the body	QR54	579.0222	Microbiology—Pictorial
QP535.C2	572.516	Calcium			works
QP535.H1	572.539	Water in the body	QR61-63	579.072	Microbiology—Research
QP535.N1	572.54	Nitrogen in the body	QR64-.8	579.3072	Bacteriological laboratories
QP550-801	572	Bioorganic chemistry	QR65-69	579.3028	Bacteriology—Technique
QP551	572.633	Amino acid sequence	QR65-69	579.028	Microbiology—Technique
QP552.C34	572.69	Carrier proteins	QR75-99.5	579.3	Bacteria
QP552.P4	572.65	Peptides	QR77.35	571.629	Bacteria cell surfaces
QP561-563	572.65	Amino acids	QR78	571.672	Flagella (Microbiology)
QP561	613.282	Amino acids in human	QR81.7	579.3138	Bacteria—Evolution
		nutrition	QR82.B3	579.362	Bacillus (Bacteria)
QP572.H9	612.8262	Hypothalamic hormones	QR82.P78	579.332	Pseudomonas
QP572.I5	612.34	Insulin	QR82.S78	579.355	Streptococcus
QP572.M44	612.02	Melatonin	QR89.5	579.3149	Anaerobic bacteria
QP572.P4	572.65	Peptide hormones	QR100-130	576.15	Microbial ecology
QP572.P7	612.405	Progesterone	QR105.5	579.176	Freshwater microbiology
QP572.P74	612.405	Prolactin	QR106-.5	579.177	Marine microbiology
QP572.S4	612.405	Hormones, Sex	QR111-113	579.1757	Soil microbiology
QP572.T4	612.405	Testosterone	QR111	579.31755	Bacteriology, Agricultural
QP572.V28	572.65	Vasoactive intestinal	QR115-129	664.001579	Food—Bacteriology
		peptides	QR115-129	664.001579	Food—Microbiology
QP601-619	572.7	Enzymes	QR130	579.17	Space microbiology
QP616.D56	572.86	DNA topoisomerase I	QR151	579.562	Yeast
QP616.D56	572.86	DNA topoisomerase II	QR177	616.01	Drug resistance in
QP619.D53	572.86	DNA Ligases			microorganisms
QP620-625	572.8	Nucleic acids	QR180-189.5	571.96	Immunology
QP623-.5	572.88	RNA	QR180-183.5	571.960724	Experimental immunology
QP623.5.M47	572.88	Messenger RNA	QR184-.4	571.9648	Immunogenetics
QP623.5.T73	572.886	Transfer RNA	QR184.2	616.0796	Human immunogenetics
QP624-.75	572.86	DNA	QR185.2	571.96	Natural immunity
QP625.N89	572.8633	Nucleotide sequence	QR185.8.T2	571.966	T cells
QP670-671	572.59	Pigments (Biology)	QR186-.3	571.964	Immune response
QP701-702	572.56	Carbohydrates	QR186.5-.6	571.9645	Antigens
QP702.S85	572.565	Sugar in the body	QR186.7-.85	971.967	Immunoglobulins
QP702.S85	572.565	Sugars	QR186.82-.83	571.973	Autoantibodies
QP751-752	572.57	Lipids	QR187-.3	571.9677	Antigen-antibody reactions
QP752.E84	572.57	Essential fatty acids	QR187.5	571.9644	Interferon inducers
QP752.F35	572.57	Fatty acids in human	QR187.5	571.9644	Interferon
		nutrition	QR188	571.972	Allergy
QP752.F35	572.57	Fatty acids	QR188.3	571.973	Autoimmunity
QP801.A48	572.548	Amines in the body	QR188.35	571.974	Immunodeficiency
QP801.H7	573.44	Hormones	QR189-.5	615.372	Vaccines
QP801.P38	571.49	Pesticides—Physiological	QR189.5.B33	615.372	Bacterial vaccines
		effect	QR189.5.E53	615.372	Enterobacterial vaccines
QP913.C1	612.22	Carbon dioxide—	QR201	579.165	Pathogenic microorganisms
		Physiological effect	QR201	579.3	Pathogenic bacteria
QP913.N2	572.5238224	Salt—Physiological effect	QR201.A72	571.992562	Arbovirus infections
QP913.01	572.53	Oxygen—Physiological effect	QR201.B34	571.993	Bacterial diseases
QR	579.3	Bacteriology	QR201.E75	571.992	Epstein-Barr virus diseases
QR	579	Microbiology	QR201.P26	571.992445	Papillomavirus diseases
QR	579	Microorganisms	QR201.P33	571.99247	Parvovirus infections
QR1	579.05	Microbiology—Periodicals	QR201.S68	571.99353	Staphylococcal infections
QR11	579.014	Microbiology—Terminology	QR245-248	571.995	Pathogenic fungi

LC	Dewey	Subject Heading	LC	Dewey	Subject Heading
QR251-255	616.96	Medical parasitology	R608.2-.5	610.95493	Medicine—Sri Lanka
QR342-.2	579.26	Bacteriophages	R609-612	610.959(3-7)	Medicine—Indochina
QR343	579.27	Fungal viruses	R614-617	610.9598	Medicine—Indonesia
QR351	579.28	Plant viruses	R618-621	610.9599	Medicine—Philippines
QR351	579.31755	Bacteriology, Agricultural	R623-626	610.952	Medicine—Japan
QR353.5.R4	571.99327	Rickettsia	R627-630	610.9519	Medicine—Korea
QR355-502	579.2	Viruses	R631-634	610.955	Medicine—Iran
QR372.058	579.2569	Oncogenic DNA viruses	R635-638	610.957	Medicine—Asiatic Russia
QR395	579.25	RNA viruses	R640-643	610.9561	Medicine—Turkey
QR398	579.2562	Arboviruses	R651-654	610.96	Medicine—Africa
QR406-.2	579.2445	Papovaviruses	R671-674	610.994	Medicine—Australia
QR408-.2	579.247	Parvoviruses	R675-678	610.993	Medicine—New Zealand
QR414.5-.6	579.2569	Retroviruses	R681-684	610.99(5-6)	Medicine—Oceania
QR414.6.H58	616.979201	HIV (Viruses)	R692	610.82	Women physicians
R	610	Medicine	R695	610.8996073	Afro-Americans in medicine
R5-101	610.5	Medicine—Periodicals	R695	610.8996073	Blacks in medicine
R10-99.7	610.6	Medicine—Societies, etc.	R702	616.009	Diseases and history
R106	610.6	Medicine—Congresses	R707-.4	610.6952	Physicians
R119.8	026.61	Archives, Medical	R711-713.97	610.25	Physicians—Directories
R120	610.222	Medicine—Pictural works	R723-.5	610.1	Medicine—Philosophy
R121	610.3	Medicine—Dictionaries	R724-726	174.2	Medical ethics
R123	610.14	Medicine—Terminology	R726	179.7	Assisted suicide
R131-684	610.9	Medicine—History	R726	179.7	Euthanasia
R134-.5	610.92	Physicians—Biography	R726.5-.8	601.9	Medicine and psychology
R135-138.5	610.901	Medicine, Ancient	R726.8	362.1756	Hospices (Terminal care)
R135	610.935	Medicine, Persian	R726.8	616.029	Terminally ill
R141-144	610.902	Medicine, Medieval	R726.8	616.029	Terminal care
R143	610.089927	Medicine, Arab	R727.3-.45	610.696	Physician and patient
R151-363	610.973	Medicine—United States	R727.43	615.5	Patient compliance
R155-363	610.97(4-9)	Medicine—[United States, by state]	R727.5	362.172	Medical referral
			R729.5	610.6	Medicine—Practice
R461-464	610.971	Medicine—Canada	R728	651.3741	Medical secretaries
R465-468	610.972	Medicine—Mexico	R728	610.6	Medical offices
R469-472	610.9728	Medicine—Central America	R728.8	610.737	Medical assistants
R473-476	610.9729	Medicine—West Indies	R733	615.5	Alternative medicine
R480-483	610.98	Medicine—South America	R735-845	610.711	Medical colleges
R484-575	610.94	Medicine—Europe	R735-845	610.71	Medicine—Study and teaching
R486-498.4	610.941	Medicine—Great Britain			
R498.6-.9	610.9415	Medicine—Ireland	R837.E9	616.075	Medicine—Examinations
R499-502	610.9436	Medicine—Austria	R850-854	619	Medicine, Experimental
R504-507	610.944	Medicine—France	R853.H8	619.98	Human experimentation in medicine
R509-512.5	610.943	Medicine—Germany			
R513-516	610.9495	Medicine—Greece	R856-858	610.284	Medical instruments and apparatus
R517-520	610.945	Medicine—Italy			
R521-524	610.9493	Medicine—Belgium	R856-857	610.28	Biomedical engineering
R526-529	610.9492	Medicine—Netherlands	R857.U48	616.07543	Ultrasonics in medicine
R531-534	610.947	Medicine—Russia	R858-859.7	610.285	Medical informatics
R535-538	610.9438	Medicine—Poland	R860-862	610.72	Medical laboratories
R539-542	610.9489	Medicine—Denmark	R895-920	616.07575	Nuclear medicine
R543-546	610.94912	Medicine—Iceland	RA	614	Public health
R547-550	610.9481	Medicine—Norway	RA10-388	353.605	Health boards
R551-554	610.9485	Medicine—Sweden	RA11-182	353.6097305	Health boards—United States
R555-558	610.946	Medicine—Spain			
R559-562	610.9469	Medicine—Portugal	RA13	353.6097(4-9)05	Health boards—[United States, cities]
R563-566	610.9494	Medicine—Switzerland			
R581-644	610.95	Medicine—Asia	RA15-182	353.6097(4-9)05	Health boards—[United States, by state]
R581	610.95	Medicine, Oriental			
R591-594	610.9538	Medicine—Saudi Arabia	RC141.E6	614.832	Epidemic encephalitis
R601-604	610.951	Medicine—China	RA184-186	353.6097105	Health boards—Canada
R604.2-.5	610.95491	Medicine—Pakistan	RA187-188	353.6097205	Health boards—Mexico
R605-608	610.954	Medicine—India			

LC	Dewey	Subject Heading	LC	Dewey	Subject Heading
RA191	353.60972805	Health boards—Central America	RA639-641	614.43	Animals as carriers of disease
RA198-235	353.609805	Health boards—South America	RA639.3	614.43	Vector control
			RA639.5	614.432	Insects as carriers of disease
RA239-299	353.609405	Health boards—Europe			
RA303-340	353.609505	Health boards—Asia	RA640	614.4323	Mosquitoes as carriers of disease
RA345-352	353.609605	Health boards—Africa			
RA371-372	353.6099405	Health boards—Australia	RA640	614.4323	Mosquitoes—Control
RA390-392	362.1	Missions, Medical	RA641.D6	614.56	Dogs as carriers of disease
RA404	614.4	Diseases—Reporting	RA641.M5	614.433	Mites as carriers of disease
RA405	353.596	Death—Proof and certification	RA641.T5	614.433	Tick-borne diseases
			RA641.T7	614.4322	Tsetse-flies
RA407-409.5	610.21	Medical statistics	RA643-644	614.5	Communicable diseases
RA407.3-408	614.42	Health surveys	RA643-644	614.55	Parasitic diseases
RA410-415	338.473621	Medical economics	RA644.A25	614.599392	AIDS-related complex
RA413-.7	362.104258	Health maintenance organizations	RA644.A57	614.516	Amebiasis
			RA644.C3	614.514	Cholera
RA413-.5	362.104258	Managed care plans (Medical care)	RA644.D4	614.571	Dengue
			RA644.D6	614.5123	Diphtheria—Prevention
RA418.5.F3	613.04	Family—Health and hygiene	RA644.E52	614.59832	Epidemic encephalitis
RA421-790	613	Medicine, Preventive	RA644.F5	614.5552	Filariasis
RA424.4-.5	613.092	Hygienists	RA644.H45	614.547	Herpes genitalis
RA427.5-.6	362.177	Medical screening	RA644.I6	614.518	Influenza
RA427.8	613	Health promotion	RA644.M2	614.532	Malaria
RA440.85-.87	614.072	Public health—Research	RA644.M5	614.523	Measles
RA441.5	614.091724	Public health—Developing countries	RA644.P7	614.5732	Plague—Vaccination
			RA644.P8	614.59241	Pneumonia
RA442-558	614.09(4-9)	Public health—[By region or country]	RA644.R3	614.563	Rabies
			RA644.R8	614.524	Rubella
RA443-450	614.097	Public health—North America	RA644.T7	614.542	Tuberculosis—Vaccination
			RA644.T7	614.542	Tuberculosis
RA445-448.5	614.0973	Public health—United States	RA644.T8	614.5112	Typhoid fever—Vaccination
RA448.5.N4	362.108996073	Afro-Americans—Medical care	RA644.T8	614.5112	Typhoid fever
			RA644.V4	614.547	Sexually transmitted diseases—Prevention
RA448.5.N4	613.08996073	Afro-Americans—Health and hygiene	RA644.V4	614.547	Sexually transmitted diseases
RA449-450	614.0971	Public health—Canada			
RA451-452	614.0972	Public health—Mexico	RA644.V55	614.57	Virus diseases
RA453-454	614.09728	Public health—Central America	RA644.W6	614.543	Whooping cough
			RA644.Y4	614.541	Yellow fever
RA455-456	614.09729	Public health—West Indies	RA645.3-.37	362.14	Home care services
RA457-482	614.098	Public health—South America	RA645.5-.7	616.025	Emergency medical technicians
RA483-523	614.094	Public health—Europe	RA645.5-.9	362.18	Emergency medical services
RA525-541	614.095	Public health—Asia	RA645.5-.8	616.025	Emergency medical personnel
RA545-552	614.096	Public health—Africa			
RA566.7	613.091732	Urban health	RA645.A44	614.5993	Allergy
RA571	614.59	Soil pollution	RA645.C47	614.59836	Cerebral palsy
RA576	614.59	Smog	RA645.D5	614.59462	Diabetes
RA577	615.91	Gases, Asphyxiating and poisonous	RA645.M82	614.59834	Multiple sclerosis
			RA645.N87	614.5939	Nutrition disorders
RA601.5	614.5	Foodborne diseases	RA645.N87	614.5939	Nutritionally induced diseases
RA615.2	629.1344	Aeronautics—Sanitation			
RA619-640	614.6	Dead	RA645.N87	614.5939	Malnutrition
RA622-623.6	363.75	Undertakers and undertaking	RA648.5-654	614.4	Epidemics
			RA648.5-654	614.4	Epidemiology
RA625-630	614.6	Burial	RA650-650.9	614.42(4-9)	Epidemics—[By region or country]
RA626-630	363.75	Cemeteries			
RA631-636.7	614.6	Cremation	RA650-.55	614.42(7-8)	Epidemics—America
RA638	614.47	Vaccination	RA650.6	614.424	Epidemics—Europe
RA639-641	614.56	Zoonoses	RA650.7	614.425	Epidemics—Asia

LC	Dewey	Subject Heading	LC	Dewey	Subject Heading
RA650.8	614.426	Epidemics—Africa	RA813-814	614.42728	Medical geography—Central America
RA650.9.A8	614.4294	Epidemics—Australia			
RA652.2.P82	614.42	Public health surveillance	RA815-816	614.42729	Medical geography—West Indies
RA655-758	614.46	Quarantine			
RA664-758	614.4609(4-9)	Quarantine—[By region or country]	RA817-844	614.428	Medical geography—South America
RA664-677	614.46097	Quarantine—North America	RA845-887	614.424	Medical geography—Europe
RA665-667	614.460973	Quarantine—United States	RA891-934	614.425	Medical geography—Asia
RA671	614.460971	Quarantine—Canada	RA943-949	614.426	Medical geography—Africa
RA673	614.460972	Quarantine—Mexico	RA951-952	614.4294	Medical geography—Australia
RA675	614.4609728	Quarantine—Central America			
RA677	614.4609729	Quarantine—West Indies	RA952.5	614.4293	Medical geography—New Zealand
RA678-699	614.46098	Quarantine—South America	RA953-954	614.429(5-6)	Medical geography—Oceania
RA700-737	614.46094	Quarantine—Europe			
RA738-751	614.46095	Quarantine—Asia	RA960-996	362.11	Hospitals
RA753-755	614.46096	Quarantine—Africa	RA960-996	362.11	Public hospitals
RA756	614.460994	Quarantine—Australia	RA960-993	362.12	Dispensaries
RA758	614.46099(5-6)	Quarantine—Oceania	RA960-993	362.16	Sanatoriums
RA761-767	614.48	Fumigation	RA964	362.110902	Hospitals, Medieval
RA766.G6	614.48	Glycerin	RA964.5	362.11072	Hospitals—Research
RA766.H9	614.48	Hydrogen peroxide	RA966	362.12	Clinics
RA766.R2	614.48	Radiation sterilization	RA971-.8	362.11068	Hospitals—Administration
RA766.S8	614.48	Steam as a disinfectant	RA972	610.6952	Interns (Medicine)
RA770.5	613	Hygiene	RA972	610.6952	Residents (Medicine)
RA771-.7	613.091734	Rural health	RA974-.5	362.12	Hospitals—Outpatient services
RA772.T7	363.125	Traffic accidents			
RA773-790	613	Health	RA974-.5	362.12	Public hospitals—Outpatient services
RA776.75	612.68	Longevity			
RA780	613	Hygiene	RA975	614.45	Isolation (Hospital care)
RA780	613.41	Baths	RA975.5.E5	362.18	Hospitals—Emergency service
RA780.5	615.822	Massage			
RA781-.85	613.71	Exercise	RA975.5.I56	362.174	Intensive care units
RA781.15	613.71	Aerobic exercises	RA975.5.T83	362.18	Trauma centers
RA781.15	613.71	Low impact aerobic exercises	RA975.R87	362.11091734	Rural hospitals
			RA980-993	362.1109(4-9)	Hospitals—[By region or country]
RA781.17	613.71	Aquatic exercises			
RA781.5	613.78	Posture	RA981-982	362.110973	Hospitals—United States
RA782	613.192	Breathing exercises	RA983	362.110971	Hospitals—Canada
RA784	613.2	Diet	RA985-989	362.11094	Hospitals—Europe
RA784	613.2	Nutrition	RA986-988	362.110941	Hospitals—Great Britain
RA785	613.79	Relaxation	RA990	362.11095	Hospitals—Asia
RA785	613.79	Rest	RA990.5	362.1109174927	Hospitals—Arab countries
RA786-.3	613.79	Sleep	RA991	362.11096	Hospitals—Africa
RA788	613.95	Hygiene, Sexual	RA992-.3	362.110994	Hospitals—Australia
RA790-.95	362.2	Mental health services	RA992.5-.7	362.110993	Hospitals—New Zealand
RA790-.95	362.2	Mental health	RA993	362.11099(5-6)	Hospitals—Oceania
RA790.55	362.22	Community psychology	RA995-996	362.188	Ambulance service
RA791-954	616.988	Medical climatology	RA996.5	362.188	Airplane ambulances
RA791-954	614.42	Medical geography	RA997-999	362.16	Long-term care facilities
RA793-954	613.287	Mineral waters	RA997-999	362.16	Nursing homes
RA794-954	613.122	Health resorts	RA997-998	362.16092	Volunteer workers in long-term care facilities
RA801-954	614.42(3-9)	Medical geography—[By region or country]			
			RA1001-1171	614.1	Medical jurisprudence
RA804-807	614.4273	Medical geography—United States	RA1018.5-.56	614.1021	Medical jurisprudence—Statistics
RA809-810	614.4271	Medical geography—Canada	RA1021-1022	614.109	Medical jurisprudence—History
RA811-812	614.4272	Medical geography—Mexico	RA1027-.5	614.107	Medical jurisprudence—Study and teaching

LC	Dewey	Subject Heading	LC	Dewey	Subject Heading
RA1056.5	344.0411	Medical personnel—Malpractice	RB128	616.8491	Headache
			RB128	616.8491	Tension headache
RA1057	614.1	Chemistry, Forensic	RB129	616.047	Fever
RA1062	614.1	Dental jurisprudence	RB131-.5	571.9379	Suppuration
RA1063-.5	616.078	Death	RB140-.5	616.47	Growth disorders
RA1063	614.1	Death—Causes	RB144-.5	616.1	Blood circulation disorders
RA1063	614.1	Death, Apparent	RB144-.5	616.047	Edema
RA1063.3	614.1	Brain death	RB144-.5	616.157	Hemorrhage
RA1063.4	614.10973	Forensic pathology	RB145	616.15027	Hematology, Experimental
RA1063.4	614.1	Autopsy	RB147	616.3992	Acidosis
RA1071-1082	617.18	Asphyxia	RB147	616.39	Metabolism—Disorders
RA1076	617.18	Drowning	RB150.C6	616.849	Coma
RA1085	617.11	Fires—Casualties	RB150.F37	616.0478	Chronic fatigue syndrome
RA1091	617.122	Electrical injuries	RB150.S5	616.047	Shock
RA1116	616.39	Starvation	RB152	616.98	Environmentally induced diseases
RA1121	617.14	Wounds and injuries			
RA1136-1137	616.858445	Suicide	RB153-154	616.047	Infection
RA1146	616.8582	Self-mutilation	RB155-.8	616.042	Medical genetics
RA1148	614.1	Psychology, Forensic	RB155.5-.8	616.042	Human chromosome abnormalities
RA1151-1152	614.1	Forensic psychiatry			
RA1190-1270	615.9	Poisons	RB155.5-.8	616.042	Genetic disorders
RA1190-1270	615.9	Toxicology	RB155.8	616.042	Gene therapy
RA1190-1270	615.9	Poisoning	RB156	616.044	Chronic diseases
RA1198-.3	615.90071	Toxicology—Study and teaching	RB170	541.224	Free radicals (Chemicals)
			RC	616	Internal medicine
RA1199-.5	615.90072	Toxicology—Research	RC31-80	616	Clinical medicine
RA1199-.5	615.907	Toxicity testing	RC41	616.003	Internal medicine—Dictionaries
RA1199.4.A38	615.907	Acute toxicity testing			
RA1221-1223	615.907	Analytical toxicology	RC48.6	618	Women—Diseases
RA1224.5	615.908	Toxicological emergencies	RC49-52	616.08	Medicine, Psychosomatic
RA1225	615.90083	Poisoning, Accidental, in children	RC65	616.0751	Medical history taking
			RC69	616.047	Symptomatology
RA1229-.5	615.902	Industrial toxicology	RC71-78.7	616.075	Diagnosis
RA1231.R2	616.9897	Radioactive substances—Toxicology	RC71.5	616.075	Diagnosis, Differential
			RC71.6	616.075	Diagnosis, Noninvasive
RA1242.S48	615.954	Seafood poisoning	RC73-.2	616.0472	Pain
RA1242.S53	615.942	Poisonous snakes—Venom	RC73.2	615.892	Acupuncture points
			RC75	610.284	Medical thermometers
RA1245-1247	615.91	Gases, Asphyxiating and poisonous	RC75	616.0754	Body temperature
			RC76-.5	616.0754	Physical diagnosis
RA1247.C17	615.91	Carbon monoxide	RC76.3	616.0754028	Stethoscopes
RA1247.M8	615.91	Mustard gas	RC77-.5	616.07547	Electrodiagnosis
RA1258-1260	615.954	Food—Toxicology	RC78-.5	616.0757	Diagnosis, Radioscopic
RB	616.07	Pathology	RC78-.5	616.07572	Radiography, Medical
RB1	616.0705	Pathology—Periodicals	RC78.7.D53	616.0754	Diagnostic imaging
RB3	616.0706	Pathology—Congresses	RC78.7.D86	616.07543	Duplex ultrasonography—Diagnostic use
RB15-.2	616.0709	Pathology—History			
RB37-56.5	616.075	Diagnosis, Laboratory	RC78.7.E5	616.07545	Endoscopy
RB43-.6	616.0758	Medical microscopy	RC78.7.F5	616.07572	Diagnosis, Fluoroscopic
RB45-15	616.07561	Blood—Analysis	RC78.7.N83	616.07548	Magnetic resonance imaging
RB46.7	616.0758	Electron microscopic immunocytochemistry			
			RC78.7.T6	616.0757	Tomography
RB48.5	616.047	Endocrine manifestations of general diseases	RC78.7.U4	616.07543	Diagnosis, Ultrasonic
			RC80	616.075	Prognosis
RB52	616.0756	Body fluids—Analysis	RC86-88.9	616.028	Critical care medicine
RB57	616.0759	Autopsy	RC86-88.9	616.025	Emergency medicine
RB112.5	616.0756	Clinical biochemistry	RC86-88.9	616.0252	First aid in illness and injury
RB113	571.9	Physiology, Pathological			
RB123-124	616.07071	Pathology—Study and teaching	RC86-88.9	616.025	Medical emergencies
			RC87	615.8043	Resuscitation
RB127	616.0472	Pain	RC87	617.14	Wounds and injuries

LC	Dewey	Subject Heading	LC	Dewey	Subject Heading
RC87.3	617.18	Asphyxia	RC254-282	616.992	Tumors
RC87.9	617.1806	Artificial respiration	RC254-282	616.994	Oncology
RC90	615.5	Iatrogenic diseases	RC261-282	616.994	Cancer
RC103.A4	616.9893	Mountain sickness	RC280.M6	616.99431	Mouth—Cancer
RC103.C3	616.9894	Decompression sickness	RC266	610.73698	Cancer—Nursing
RC103.M6	616.9892	Motion sickness	RC267	616.9940072	Cancer—Research
RC106	616.91	Exanthemata	RC268-.15	616.99405	Cancer—Prevention
RC108	616.044	Chronic diseases	RC268.4-.44	616.994042	Cancer—Genetic aspects
RC109-216	616.9(01-6)	Communicable diseases	RC268.48	616.994071	Cancer—Etiology
RC113.5	616.959	Zoonoses	RC268.5-.7	616.994071	Carcinogenesis
RC114-.7	616.92	Virus diseases	RC268.55	616.992	Radiation carcinogenesis
RC114.6	616.925	Slow virus diseases	RC268.57	616.994071	Viral carcinogenesis
RC115-116	616.92	Bacterial diseases	RC268.6-.7	616.994071	Carcinogens
RC116.M8	616.92	Mycobacterial diseases	RC270.8-271	616.99406	Cancer—Treatment
RC116.S8	616.92	Staphylococcal infections	RC271.C5	616.99406	Antineoplastic agents
RC117	616.969	Mycoses	RC271.D68	616.994061	Doxorubicin
RC118.7	616.936	Protozoan diseases	RC271.H55	616.99406	Cancer—Hormone therapy
RC119-.7	616.96	Parasitic diseases	RC271.I45	616.99406	Cancer—Immunotherapy
RC119.5	616.968	Ectoparasitic infestations	RC271.P54	616.99406	Plasma exchange (Therapeutics)
RC121.A5	616.936	Amebiasis	RC280.A2	616.99495	Abdomen—Tumors
RC121.A6	616.956	Anthrax	RC280.A2	616.99495	Abdomen—Cancer
RC124	616.82	Meningitis	RC280.B6	616.9947	Osteosarcoma
RC125	616.914	Chickenpox	RC280.B7	616.99481	Brain—Cancer
RC126-134	616.932	Cholera	RC280.C6	616.994347	Colon—Cancer
RC137	616.921	Dengue	RC280.D5	616.99434	Digestive organs—Cancer
RC138-.9	616.9313	Diphtheria	RC280.E2	616.99485	Ear—Tumors
RC140	616.935	Dysentery	RC280.E8	616.99432	Esophagus—Cancer
RC141.5	616.925	Epstein-Barr virus diseases	RC280.E8	616.99432	Esophagus—Tumors
RC142.5	616.9652	Elephantiasis	RC280.H47	616.99419	Hematological oncology
RC142.5	616.9652	Filariasis	RC280.L8	616.99424	Lungs—Cancer
RC144.G3	616.047	Gas gangrene	RC280.M37	616.99477	Melanoma
RC147.G6	616.925	Mononucleosis	RC280.N4	616.9948	Neuroblastoma
RC148	616.953	Rabies	RC280.S5	616.99477	Basal cell carcinoma
RC150-.9	616.203	Influenza	RC280.S5	616.99477	Skin—Cancer
RC150	616.203	Asian flu	RC306-320.5	616.995	Tuberculosis
RC154-.9	616.998	Leprosy	RC309-.5	362.196995	Tuberculosis—Hospitals
RC156-166	616.936	Malaria	RC311.2	616.995075	Tuberculin test
RC168.M4	616.915	Measles	RC311.3.C45	616.995061	Tuberculosis—Chemotherapy
RC168.M8	616.313	Mumps			
RC171-179	616.9232	Black death	RC311.D5	616.9950654	Tuberculosis—Diet therapy
RC171-179	616.9232	Plague	RC346-429	616.8(1-4)	Neurology
RC180-181	616.835	Poliomyelitis	RC346-429	616.8(1-4)	Nervous system—Diseases
RC180.8	610.73699	Poliomyelitis—Nursing			
RC182.R3	616.9244	Relapsing fever	RC348-349	616.804075	Neurologic examination
RC182.R4	616.991	Rheumatic fever	RC350.5	610.7368	Neurological nursing
RC182.R8	616.916	Rubella	RC350.N48	616.806	Neural stimulation
RC182.S12	616.927	Salmonellosis	RC350.N49	616.8028	Neurological intensive care
RC182.S2	616.917	Scarlatina	RC372-374.5	616.853	Epilepsy
RC183-.9	616.912	Smallpox	RC374.5	616.853	Petit mal epilepsy
RC184.T6	616.964	Echinococcosis	RC376	616.82	Meningitis
RC185	616.9318	Tetanus	RC377	616.834	Multiple sclerosis
RC186.T82	616.9363	African trypanosomiasis	RC382	616.833	Parkinsonism
RC187-197	616.9272	Typhoid fever	RC382	616.833	Parkinsonism, Symptomatic
RC199-.9	616.9222	Typhus fever	RC386-395	616.8(1-4)	Brain—Diseases
RC200-203	616.951	Sexually transmitted diseases	RC386.6.A45	616.8047547	Ambulatory electroencephalography
RC201-.9	616.9513	Syphilis	RC386.6.E43	616.8047547	Electroencephalography
RC203.H45	616.9518	Herpes genitalis	RC386.6.U45	616.8047543	Ultrasonic encephalography
RC204	616.204	Whooping cough	RC388	616.836	Cerebral palsied
RC206-216	616.928	Yellow fever	RC388.5	616.81	Cerebrovascular disease
RC226-248	616.96	Blood—Parasites			

LC	Dewey	Subject Heading	LC	Dewey	Subject Heading
RC391	616.858843	Hydrocephalus	RC475-489	616.8914	Psychotherapy
RC392	616.8491	Cluster headache	RC480.52	616.891	Psychiatry—Differential
RC392	616.8491	Headache			therapeutics
RC394.A5	616.85232	Amnesia	RC480.55	616.8914	Single-session
RC394.C77	616.845	Convulsions			psychotherapy
RC394.D35	616.8	Brain—Degeneration	RC480.6	616.89025	Psychiatric emergencies
RC394.I5	616.81	Cerebral infarction	RC480.6	362.2881	Psychiatric hospitals—
RC394.M46	616.84	Memory disorders			Emergency service
RC394.W6	616.8553	Dyslexia	RC480.7	616.8910028	Interviewing in psychiatry
RC400-406	616.87	Spinal cord—Diseases	RC481	616.8914	Client-centered
RC406.P3	616.837	Paraplegics			psychotherapy
RC416	616.87	Neuritis	RC487	616.89165	Occupational therapy
RC420	616.87	Sciatica	RC488-.6	616.89152	Group psychotherapy
RC422.C26	616.87	Carpal tunnel syndrome	RC488.5-.6	616.89156	Marital psychotherapy
RC423-428.8	616.855	Speech disorders	RC488.5-.6	616.89156	Family psychotherapy
RC423-428.8	616.85506	Speech therapy	RC488.6	616.89156	Divorce therapy
RC423-428.8	616.855	Communicative disorders	RC489.A7	616.891656	Art therapy
RC423-428.5	616.855	Language disorders	RC489.A77	158.2	Assertiveness training
RC424	616.8554	Stuttering	RC489.B4	616.89142	Behavior therapy
RC424.7	616.855	Articulation disorders	RC489.B4	616.89142	Aversion therapy
RC425-.7	616.8552	Aphasia	RC489.C6	616.89142	Cognitive-analytic therapy
RC425.5	616.8552	Agrammatism	RC489.C63	616.89142	Cognitive therapy
RC435-571	616.89	Psychology, Pathological	RC489.C68	616.8914	Countertransference
RC439.2	616.891	Psychiatric day treatment			(Psychology)
RC439.4	362.21	Violence in psychiatric	RC489.D3	616.891655	Dance therapy
		hospitals	RC489.E24	616.8914	Eclectic psychotherapy
RC440	610.7300	Psychiatric nursing	RC489.E03	616.8014	Existential psychotherapy
RC440.5	616.890092	Psychiatric aides	RC489.F27	616.8914	Psychotherapy—Failure
RC440.7	616.89	Mental health care teams	RC489.I45	616.8914	Impasse (Psychotherapy)
RC451.4.A5	362.20846	Aged—Mental health	RC489.M85	616.8914	Multiple psychotherapy
		services	RC489.N3	616.8918	Narcotherapy
RC451.4.A5	618.9789	Geriatric psychiatry	RC489.O24	616.8917	Object constancy
RC451.5.N4	616.89008996073	Afro-Americans—Mental			(Psychoanalysis)
		health	RC489.O25	616.8917	Object relations
RC455	362.22	Community psychiatry			(Psychoanalysis)
RC455.2.A28	616.89140092	Psychotherapy patients—	RC489.P68	616.8914	Problem-solving therapy
		Abuse of	RC489.P7	616.891523	Psychodrama
RC455.2.C4	616.89075	Mental illness—	RC489.R4	616.891653	Recreational therapy
		Classification	RC489.S86	616.8914	Supportive psychotherapy
RC455.2.E8	616.8914	Psychotherapy—Moral and	RC489.T45	616.8914	Psychotherapy—Termination
		ethical aspects	RC489.T7	616.89145	Transactional analysis
RC455.2.E8	174.2	Psychotherapists—	RC489.T73	154.24	Transference (Psychology)
		Professional ethics	RC490-499	616.89162	Therapeutics, Suggestive
RC455.2.E8	174.2	Psychiatric ethics	RC490-499	154.7	Hypnotism
RC455.2.M4	616.89001	Psychiatry—Methodology	RC499.D7	154.63	Dreams
RC455.2.R43	362.172	Psychiatric referral	RC499.S92	153.736	Subliminal perception
RC455.4.C6	616.89	Psychiatry, Comparative	RC500-510	616.8917	Psychoanalysis
RC455.4.L67	155.93	Loss (Psychology)	RC510	616.8917	Group psychoanalysis
RC455.4.S67	302.14	Social adjustment	RC512-528	616.892	Psychoses
RC455.4.S87	155.24	Adjustment disorders	RC514	616.898	Schizophrenia
RC466-.3	158.3	Mental health counseling	RC514	616.898	Paranoid schizophrenia
RC466.8-467.95	616.89	Clinical psychology	RC516	616.895	Manic-depressive psychoses
RC469-473	616.89075	Psychodiagnostics	RC521-524	616.8983	Dementia
RC473.D43	155.2	Defense Mechanisms	RC523-.2	616.831	Alzheimer's disease
		Inventory	RC524	616.8983	Senile dementia
RC473.E36	154.22	Ego Function Assessment	RC525-527	616.861	Alcoholic psychoses
RC473.G7	155.282	Graphology	RC526	616.861	Delirium tremens
RC473.M5	616.89075	Minnesota Multiphasic	RC530-552	616.852	Neuroses
		Personality Inventory	RC531	616.85223	Anxiety
RC473.P7	616.890028	Projective techniques	RC532	616.8524	Hysteria
RC473.R6	616.89075	Rorschach Test	RC533	616.8584	Compulsive behavior

LC	Dewey	Subject Heading	LC	Dewey	Subject Heading
RC533	616.85227	Obsessive-compulsive disorders	RC569.5.B67	616.85852	Borderline personality disorder
RC535	616.85225	Phobias	RC569.5.C55	616.858223	Child abuse
RC535	616.85223	Panic disorders	RC569.5.C63	616.8619	Codependency
RC537-545	616.8527	Affective disorders	RC569.5.C68	154.24	Complexes (Psychology)
RC537-545	616.8527	Depression, Mental	RC569.5.D47	155.232	Dependency (Psychology)
RC537.5	616.852700846	Depression in old age	RC569.5.E5	616.849	Enuresis
RC547-549	616.8498	Sleep disorders	RC569.5.F3	616.85822	Family violence
RC548-.5	616.8498	Insomnia	RC569.5.F3	616.85822	Wife abuse
RC549	616.8498	Narcolepsy	RC569.5.G35	616.85841	Compulsive gambling
RC552.A44	616.85225	Agoraphobia	RC569.5.I46	616.8584	Impulsive personality
RC552.A5	616.85262	Anorexia nervosa	RC569.5.M8	616.85236	Multiple personality
RC552.B84	616.85263	Bulimia	RC569.5.P75	616.858223	Psychological child abuse
RC552.C65	616.8526	Compulsive eating	RC569.5.P9	616.85843	Pyromania
RC552.E18	616.8526	Eating disorders	RC569.5.S45	616.8582	Self-destructive behavior
RC552.N5	616.8528	Neurasthenia	RC569.5.S48	616.8582	Self-injurious behavior
RC552.O3	616.8521	Occupational neuroses	RC569.5.V55	616.8582	Violence
RC552.P67	616.8521	Post-traumatic stress disorder	RC569.7-571	616.8588	Mental retardation
RC552.S4	616.8582	Self-mutilation	RC571	616.858842	Down's syndrome
RC552.S66	616.8524	Somatization disorder	RC583-598	616.97	Allergy
RC553.A88	616.8982	Autism	RC588.C45	616.97	Antiallergic agents
RC553.D5	616.8523	Dissociative disorders	RC588.D53	616.9750654	Food allergy—Diet therapy
RC553.H3	616.8634	Hallucinations and illusions	RC589-596	616.202	Respiratory allergy
RC553.M36	616.85835	Masochism	RC590	616.202	Hay fever
RC553.N36	616.8585	Narcissism	RC591	616.238	Asthma
RC554-569.5	616.858	Personality disorders	RC596	616.975	Food allergy
RC555	616.858	Antisocial personality disorders	RC598.D7	616.9758	Drug allergy
RC556-560	616.8583	Psychosexual disorders	RC600	616.978	Autoimmune diseases
RC558-.5	616.8583	Homosexuality	RC606-607	616.979	Immunological deficiency symdromes
RC558.5	616.8583	Lesbianism	RC607.A26	616.9792	AIDS (Disease)
RC560.A97	616.8583	Autoerotic asphyxia	RC620-627	616.39	Nutrition disorders
RC560.C46	616.85836	Child sexual abuse	RC622	616.39	Nutritionally induced diseases
RC560.I45	616.85832	Impotence	RC623	616.39	Malnutrition
RC560.I53	618.9285836	Incest victims	RC623.5-627	616.39	Deficiency diseases
RC560.I53	616.85836	Incest	RC623.7	616.39	Avitaminosis
RC560.R36	616.8521	Rape trauma syndrome	RC627.5-632	616.39	Metabolism—Disorders
RC560.R36	362.883	Rape victims	RC627.8	616.39043	Metabolism, Inborn errors of
RC560.S23	616.85835	Sadomasochism	RC628-.5	616.398	Obesity
RC560.S43	616.8583	Sex addiction	RC629-.5	616.3999	Gout
RC560.S45	616.8583	Sexual aversion disorders	RC630	616.3992	Water-electrolyte imbalances
RC560.V68	616.8583	Voyeurism	RC632.L33	616.3998	Lactose intolerance
RC563-568	616.86	Substance abuse	RC633-647.5	616.15	Blood—Diseases
RC564.7-565.9	616.861	Alcoholism	RC636	616.15027	Hematology, Experimental
RC566	616.8632	Narcotic habit	RC641-.7	616.152	Anemia
RC567	616.865	Tobacco—Physiological effect	RC641.7.F36	616.152	Fanconi's anemia
RC567	616.865	Nicotine	RC641.7.R44	616.152	Renal anemia
RC567	616.865	Smoking	RC642	616.1572	Hemophilia
RC567	616.865	Tobacco habit	RC643	616.99419	Acute leukemia
RC567.5	616.8526	Coffee habit	RC643	616.99419	Chronic lymphocytic leukemia
RC568.C2	616.8635	Hashish			
RC568.C2	616.8635	Cannabis	RC643	616.99419	Leukemia
RC568.C6	616.8647	Cocaine habit	RC643	616.99419	Lymphocytic leukemia
RC568.O58	616.8632	Opioid habit	RC644	616.99446	Hodgkin's disease
RC568.O6	616.8632	Morphine habit	RC647.B5	616.15	Blood platelet disorders
RC568.O6	616.8632	Opium habit	RC647.C55	616.157	Blood coagulation disorders
RC569	616.858445	Suicide	RC647.D5	616.157	Disseminated intravascular coagulation
RC569	616.858445	Suicidal behavior			
RC569.5.A53	152.47	Anger	RC648-665	616.4	Endocrine glands—Diseases

LC	Dewey	Subject Heading	LC	Dewey	Subject Heading
RC648-665	616.4	Endocrinology	RC691.5-.6	616.13075	Blood-vessels—Diseases—Diagnosis
RC655-657	616.44	Thyroid gland—Diseases			
RC656-.3	616.442	Goiter	RC691.6.A53	616.1307572	Angiography
RC657	616.858848043	Cretinism	RC691.6.D87	616.1307543	Duplex ultrasonography—Diagnostic use
RC657	616.444	Hypothyroidism			
RC657.5.G7	616.443	Graves' disease	RC693	616.133	Aneurysms
RC658-.7	616.47	Pituitary gland—Diseases	RC693	616.138	Aortic aneurysms
RC658.3	616.47	Acromegaly	RC693	617.413059	Dissecting aortic aneurysms
RC658.5	616.462	Diabetes	RC694	616.131	Peripheral vascular diseases
RC659	616.45	Adrenal glands—Diseases	RC694.5.I53	616.13	Arteritis
RC659	616.45	Addison's disease	RC694.5.I53	616.131	Vasculitis
RC660-662.18	616.462	Non-insulin-dependent diabetes	RC695-697	616.143	Varicose veins
			RC695-697	616.14	Veins—Diseases
RC660-662.4	616.462	Diabetes	RC696	616.142	Phlebitis
RC660.7	362.12	Diabetes clinics	RC701	616.1043	Cardiovascular system—Abnormalities
RC666-701	616.1	Cardiovascular system—Diseases	RC705-779	616.2	Respiratory organs—Diseases
RC666.7-.72	616.10092	Cardiologists	RC734.P84	616.2075	Pulmonary function tests
RC670-.5	616.1075	Cardiovascular system—Diagnosis	RC735.5	610.73692	Respiratory organs—Diseases—Nursing
RC674	610.73691	Cardiovascular system—Diseases—Nursing	RC735.H54	616.206	High-frequency ventilation (Therapy)
RC681-688	616.12	Heart—Diseases	RC735.I5	615.836	Respiratory therapy
RC683.5.A43	616.132075	Ambulatory blood pressure monitoring	RC737-.5	616.2	Apnea
RC683.5.A45	616.1207547	Ambulatory electrocardiography	RC740	616.2	Respiratory infections
			RC746	616.201	Croup
RC683.5.A5	616.1207572	Angiocardiography	RC751	616.25	Pleurisy
RC683.5.B63	616.12075	Body surface mapping	RC756-776	616.24	Lungs-Diseases
RC683.5.E5	616.1207547	Electrocardiography	RC771-772	616.241	Pneumonia
RC683.5.E94	616.12075	Treadmill exercise tests	RC776.E5	616.248	Emphysema, Pulmonary
RC683.5.U5	616.1207543	Doppler echocardiography	RC776.F33	616.24	Farmer's lung
RC683.5.U5	616.1207543	Two-dimensional echocardiography	RC776.O3	616.24	Respiratory organs—Obstructions
RC683.5.U5	616.1207543	Echocardiography	RC776.P85	616.249	Pulmonary embolism
RC684.A34	616.1206	Adrenergic alpha blockers	RC778	616.234	Bronchitis
RC684.A35	616.1206	Adrenergic beta blockers	RC799-869	616.3	Digestive organs—Diseases
RC684.E4	616.120645	Electric countershock	RC799-869	616.33	Gastrointestinal system
RC684.P3	617.4120645	Cardiac pacing	RC804.A5	616.307572	Digestive organs—Radiography
RC684.P3	617.4120645	Pacemaker, Artificial (Heart)	RC804.G3	616.3307545	Gastroscopy
RC685.A6	616.122	Angina pectoris	RC804.D79	616.3407545	Duodenoscopy
RC685.A65	616.128	Arrhythmia	RC804.R6	616.3407572	Duodenum—Radiography
RC685.A65	616.128	Palpitation	RC811	616.31	Gastrointestinal system—Motility—Disorders
RC685.C173	616.123025	Cardiac arrest			
RC685.C18	616.12	Cardiogenic shock	RC815-.6	616.31	Mouth—Diseases
RC685.C6	616.123	Coronary heart disease	RC815-.6	616.31	Oral medicine
RC685.E5	616.11	Endocarditis	RC815.2	616.332	Indigestion disorders
RC685.H8	616.132	Hypertension	RC815.7	616.32	Esophagus—Diseases
RC685.H8	616.132	Essential hypertension	RC815.7	616.32	Esophageal varices
RC685.H93	616.13	Hypotension	RC815.7	616.32043	Esophagus—Abnormalities
RC685.I6	616.1237	Myocardial infarction	RC816-840	616.33	Stomache—Diseases
RC685.M9	616.124	Myocardium—Diseases	RC821	616.343	Peptic ulcer
RC685.M92	616.124	Myocarditis	RC827	616.332	Indigestion
RC685.P5	616.11	Pericardium	RC831	616.333	Gastritis
RC685.V2	616.125	Heart valves—Diseases	RC840.G3	616.33	Gastroenteritis
RC685.V2	616.125	Mitral valve insufficiency	RC845-848	616.362	Liver—Diseases
RC685.V43	616.128	Ventricular fibrillation	RC847-.5	616.3362075	Liver function tests
RC687	616.12043	Congenital heart disease	RC848.A42	616.3624	Alcoholic liver diseases
RC691-701	616.13	Blood-vessels—Diseases	RC848.C4	616.3623	Chronic active hepatitis
RC691-697	616.13	Arteries—Diseases	RC848.H42	616.3623	Hepatitis
RC691	616.138	Aorta—Diseases			

LC	Dewey	Subject Heading	LC	Dewey	Subject Heading
RC849-853	616.365	Gallbladder—Diseases	RC944	617.55	Abdomen—Diseases
RC851	616.3625	Jaundice	RC946	617.55	Pelvis—Diseases
RC857-858	616.37	Pancreas—Diseases	RC951	617.585	Foot—Diseases
RC858.C95	616.37	Cystic fibrosis	RC951	617.58	Extremities (Anatomy)—
RC860-862	616.34	Colon—Diseases			Diseases
RC861	616.3428	Constipation	RC952-954.6	618.97	Aged—Diseases
RC862.C6	616.3447	Colitis	RC952-954.6	618.97	Geriatrics
RC862.E5	616.344	Enteritis	RC953.7	615.10846	Geriatric pharmacology
RC862.M3	616.3423	Malabsorption syndromes	RC953.8.E93	615.820846	Exercise therapy for the
RC864-866	616.35	Proctology			aged
RC865	616.35	Hemorrhoids	RC954	610.7365	Geriatric nursing
RC866.D43	616.342	Fecal incontinence	RC955-958	616.9881	Circumpolar medicine
RC866.D43	616.342	Defecation disorders	RC960-962	616.9883	Tropical medicine
RC867.5	618.73	Peritonitis	RC963-969	616.9803	Work environment
RC870-923	616.6	Urology	RC963-969	616.9803	Medicine, Industrial
RC875-899.5	616.65	Andrology	RC963	613.62092	Industrial hygienists
RC881.5-883.5	616.65043	Generative organs—	RC965.P46	616.0088791	Entertainers—Diseases
		Abnormalities	RC967	613.62	Industrial hygiene
RC883	616.694	Hermaphroditism	RC967.5	158.7	Industrial psychiatry
RC884	616.693	Climacteric, Male	RC968-969	613.62	Occupational health services
RC889	616.692	Infertility, Male	RC970-971	616.98023	Medicine, Military
RC889	616.692	Infertility	RC981-986	616.98024	Medicine, Naval
RC889	616.692	Impotence	RC1000-1020	616.98022	Submarine medicine
RC892	616.62	Urethra—Diseases	RC1030-1035	616.9802	Transportation medicine
RC896	616.66	Penis—Diseases	RC1040-1045	613.69	Traffic accidents
RC897	616.67	Scrotum—Diseases	RC1050-1097	616.980213	Aviation medicine
RC899	616.65	Prostate—Diseases	RC1076.J48	616.980213	Jet lag
RC900-923	616.6	Urinary organs—Diseases	RC1120-1160	616.980214	Space medicine
RC901	616.6075	Urinary organs—	RC1150-1151	612.0145	Space flight—Physiological
		Examination			effect
RC901.75	616.6	Urination disorders	RC1151.B54	612	Biological rhythms—Effect
RC901.8	616.6	Urinary tract infections			of space flight on
RC902-918	616.61	Kidneys—Diseases	RC1200-1245	617.1027	Sports medicine
RC902	616.61	Nephrology	RD96.15	617.1	Blunt trauma
RC904-.5	616.61075	Kidneys—Diseases—	RD96.3	617.145	Gunshot wounds
		Diagnosis	RD96.4-.55	617.11	Burn care teams
RC907	616.612	Bright's disease	RD96.4-.55	617.11	Burns and scalds
RC915	616.635	Uremia	RD96.45	617.11	Chemical burns
RC916	616.622	Urinary organs—Calculi	RD96.5	617.122	Electrical burns
RC918.R38	616.132	Renal hypertension	RD98-.4	617.01	Surgery—Complications
RC918.R4	616.614	Chronic renal failure	RD98.3	617.01	Surgical wound infections
RC919-921	616.62	Bladder—Diseases	RD98.4	617.01	Postoperative pain
RC924-.5	616.77	Connective tissues—	RD99-.35	610.73677	Surgical nursing
		Diseases	RD101-104	617.15	Fractures
RC925-935	616.7	Muscles—Diseases	RD101	617.15	Fractures, Spontaneous
RC927-.5	616.723	Rheumatism	RD103.B65	617.471	Bone wiring (Orthopedics)
RC927.3	616.723	Fibromyalgia	RD103.E88	617.471059	External skeletal fixation
RC927.5.N65	616.723	Nonarticular rheumatism			(Surgery)
RC930-931	616.71	Bones—Diseases	RD104.A95	617.15	Avulsion fractures
RC931.F5	616.71	Fibrous dysplasia of bone	RD104.S77	617.15	Stress fractures
RC931.064	616.712	Osteitis			(Orthopedics)
RC931.067	616.7223	Osteoarthritis	RD106	617.16	Dislocations
RC931.073	616.716	Osteoporosis	RD110-.5	617.024	Ambulatory surgery
RC933	616.722	Arthritis	RD111-114	617.024	Surgery, Minor
RC933	616.7227	Rheumatoid arthritis	RD113-.4	617.93	Bandages and bandaging
RC935.A8	616.74	Muscular atrophy	RD113-.4	617.93	Surgical dressings
RC935.B8	616.76	Bursitis	RD118-120.5	617.95	Surgery, Plastic
RC935.T4	616.76	Tendinitis	RD119.5.F33	617.520592	Facelift
RC936	617.51	Head—Diseases	RD120.6-129.8	617.95	Transplantation of organs,
RC941	617.54	Chest pain			tissues, etc.
RC941	617.54	Chest—Diseases	RD121	617.4770592	Skin-grafting

197

LC	Dewey	Subject Heading
RD123	617.4710592	Bone-grafting
RD123.5	617.440592	Bone marrow—Transplantation
RD127-128.5	362.1783	Tissue banks
RD128	362.1783	Musculoskeletal banks
RD129.5	362.1783	Donation of organs, tissues, etc.
RD129.5	362.1783092	Organ donors
RD130	617.95	Prosthesis
RD137-139	617.98	Children—Surgery
RD137	616.244	Respiratory organs—Foreign bodies
RD139	617.960083	Pediatric anesthesia
RD145	617.97	Aged—Surgery
RD145	617.9600846	Geriatric anesthesia
RD151-498	617.99	Surgery, Military
RD151-498	617.99	Surgery, Naval
RD153	616.047	Gangrene
RD156	617.044	War wounds
RD200-214	617.990973	Surgery, Military—United States
RD216	617.990971	Surgery, Military—Canada
RD221	617.990972	Surgery, Military—Mexico
RD224-225	617.9909728	Surgery, Military—Central America
RD231-232	617.9909729	Surgery, Military—West Indies
RD235-267	617.99098	Surgery, Military—South America
RD268-441	617.99094	Surgery, Military—Europe
RD445-476	617.99095	Surgery, Military—Asia
RD481-489	617.99096	Surgery, Military—Africa
RD493	617.990994	Surgery, Military—Australia
RD493.5	617.990993	Surgery, Military—New Zealand
RD498	617.99099(5-6)	Surgery, Military—Oceania
RD523-527	617.52059	Face—Surgery
RD523	617.52044	Face—Wounds and injuries
RD529	617.155	Skull—Fractures
RD529	617.514	Craniotomy
RD533	617.482044	Spine—Wounds and injuries
RD539.5	617.548044	Esophagus—Wounds and injuries
RD539.5	617.548059	Esophagus—Surgery
RD539.5	617.548	Esophagectomy
RD539.8	618.190592	Augmentation mammaplasty
RD539.8	618.19059	Mammaplasty
RD540-548	617.55	Acute abdomen
RD540-548	617.55059	Abdomen—Surgery
RD540-548	617.55044	Abdomen—Wounds and injuries
RD540-547	617.55059	Digestive organs—Surgery
RD540.5-.57	617.553059	Gastrectomy
RD540.5-.57	617.553059	Stomache—Surgery
RD540.5	617.553059	Gastrostomy
RD542	617.5545	Appendectomy
RD546-547	617.5565	Gallbladder—Surgery
RD549-.5	617.158	Pelvic bones—Fractures
RD549	617.4720592	Artificial hip joints
RD549	617.4720592	Total hip replacement
RD551-563	617.158	Extremities (Anatomy)—Fractures
RD551-563	617.58059	Extremities (Anatomy)—Surgery
RD551-563	617.580592	Extremities (Anatomy)—Transplantation
RD551-563	617.58044	Extremities (Anatomy)—Wounds and injuries
RD553	617.58059	Amputation
RD553	617.58	Phantom limb
RD557.5	617.16	Shoulder joint—Dislocation
RD557	617.574059	Arm—Amputation
RD558	617.157	Elbow—Fractures
RD561	617.5820592	Artificial knee
RD561	617.5820592	Total knee replacement
RD562	617.584059	Excision of ankle
RD563	617.5850592	Foot—Amputation
RD563	617.5850592	Foot—Reimplantation
RD563	617.585075	Foot—Examination
RD563	617.585044	Foot—Wounds and injuries
RD563	617.585059	Foot—Surgery
RD563	616.547	Nails, Ingrowing
RD563	617.585	Podiatry
RD572	617.463059	Castration
RD580-581	617.462059	Bladder—Surgery
RD585	618.145	Sterilization reversal
RD585.5	617.463	Sterilization reversal
RD585.5	617.463	Vasectomy
RD590	617.463	Circumcision
RD592.5-596	617.48059	Nervous system—Surgery
RD592.5-596	617.48044	Nervous system—Wounds and injuries
RD594-.15	617.481059	Brain—Surgery
RD594-.15	617.481044	Brain—Wounds and injuries
RD594-.15	617.481	Psychosurgery
RD594.3	617.482059	Spinal cord—Surgery
RD596	610.7368	Neurological nursing
RD597-598.7	617.41	Cardiovascular system—Surgery
RD598-.35	617.412	Heart—Surgery
RD598.35.A78	617.4120592	Heart, Artificial
RD598.35.C35	617.412	Cardiac catheterization
RD598.35.C37	617.412	Cardiomyoplasty
RD598.35.C67	617.413	Coronary artery bypass
RD598.35.T7	617.4120592	Heart—Transplantation
RD598.5-.7	617.413	Blood-vessels—Surgery
RD598.5	617.413	Angioplasty
RD598.5	617.413	Arterial catheterization
RD598.5	617.413	Dissecting aortic aneurysms
RD599.5.A37	617.44	Adrenalectomy
RD599.5.P58	617.440592	Pituitary gland—Transplantation
RD621-626	617.559059	Hernia
RD628	616.047	Gangrene
RD641	616.047	Abscess
RD651-678	616.994059	Cancer—Surgery
RD651-678	616.992	Tumors
RD663	616.9948	Nervous system—Tumors
RD663	616.99481	Brain—Tumors

LC	Dewey	Subject Heading	LC	Dewey	Subject Heading
RD667.5	616.99449059	Mastectomy	RE73	617.700284	Ophthalmology—Instruments
RD680-688	617.47044	Musculoskeletal system—Wounds and injuries	RE73	616.700284	Optical instruments
RD684	617.471059	Bones—Surgery	RE75-79	617.7075	Eye—Examination
RD688	616.74	Muscles—Diseases	RE79.E39	617.707547	Electroculography
RD701-811	616.7	Orthopedics	RE79.E4	617.707547	Electroretinography
RD701-789	617.47	Orthopedic surgery	RE79.R3	617.707572	Eye—Radiography
RD705-706	362.11	Orthopedic hospitals	RE80-87	617.7059	Eye—Surgery
RD705.5	362.110973	Orthopedic hospitals—United States	RE88	610.73677	Ophthalmic nursing
RD711	616.7005	Orthopedics—Periodicals	RE89	362.1783	Eye banks
RD725-726	616.709	Orthopedics—History	RE91-95	617.75	Vision disorders
RD727-728	616.70232	Orthopedists	RE91-95	617.712	Blindness
RD733.2	617.300222	Orthopedics—Pictorial works	RE91	617.712	Low vision
RD734-.5	616.70754	Orthopedics—Diagnosis	RE95	617.712	Vision, Monocular
RD736.M25	615.82	Manipulation (Therapeutics)	RE96	617.74	Eye—Infections
RD736.T7	617.9	Orthopedic traction	RE96	617.74	Eye—Inflammation
RD750	616.7025	Orthopedic emergencies	RE121-155	617.771	Eyelids—Diseases
RD753	610.73677	Orthopedic nursing	RE201-216	617.764	Lacrimal apparatus—Diseases
RD755-757	617.9	Orthopedic apparatus	RE310-326	617.773	Conjunctiva—Diseases
RD755.5-.7	617.470592	Orthopedic implants	RE320	617.773	Acute hemorrhagic conjunctivitis
RD756-.42	617.58	Artificial limbs			
RD756	617.9	Crutches	RE321	617.773	Conjunctivitis
RD756.2-.22	617.574	Artificial arms	RE328	617.719	Sclera—Diseases
RD757.S45	616.70284	Orthopedic shoes	RE336-340	617.719	Cornea—Diseases
RD757.S5	617.9	Orthopedic slings	RE336	617.7190592	Artificial corneas
RD757.W4	617.9	Wheelchairs	RE350-355	617.72	Uvea—Diseases
RD762	616.7	Posture disorders	RE401-461	617.742	Crystalline lens—Diseases
RD763	616.71043	Skull—Abnormalities	RE451	617.742	Cataract
RD768-771	616.73043	Spine—Abnormalities	RE501	617.746	Vitreous body—Diseases
RD771.B217	617.564	Backache	RE551-661	617.735	Retina—Diseases
RD771.I58	616.73	Spine—Instability	RE603	617.735	Retinal detachment
RD772	617.71043	Hip joint—Dislocation, Congenital	RE651	617.74	Thrombosis
			RE661.D5	617.735	Diabetic retinopathy
RD775-789	616.71043	Extremities (Anatomy)—Abnormalities	RE711	617.78	Eye-sockets—Diseases
			RE725-780	617.732	Neuroophthalmology
RD778-.5	617.575059	Hand—Surgery	RE731-780	617.762	Eye—Muscles
RD779-789	616.71043	Leg—Abnormalities	RE731-780	617.762	Eye—Movement disorders
RD781-789	617.585043	Foot—Abnormalities	RE738	617.762	Diplopia
RD781	617.585044	Foot—Dislocation	RE760	617.762	Eye—Paralysis
RD786-789	617.585043	Toes—Abnormalities	RE831-840	617.713	Eye—Wounds and injuries
RD925-927	616.74	Muscles—Diseases	RE835	617.74	Eye—Foreign bodies
RE	617.7	Ophthalmology	RE871	617.741	Glaucoma
RE1	617.7006	Ophthalmology—Societies, etc.	RE906	617.7043	Eye—Abnormalities
			RE918-921	617.759075	Color vision—Testing
RE6	617.7005	Ophthalmology—Periodicals	RE921	617.759	Color blindness
RE11	617.7006	Ophthalmology—Congresses	RE925-939	617.755	Eye—Refractive errors
			RE925-939	617.755	Eye—Accomodation and refraction
RE20	617.70014	Ophthalmology—Terminology			
RE22	617.70025	Ophthalmologists—Directories	RE932	617.755	Astigmatism
			RE940-981	681.4092	Opticians
RE26-30	617.709	Ophthalmology—History	RE940-981	617.75	Optometry
RE31-36	617.70232	Ophthalmologists	RE940-981	617.7522	Eyeglasses
RE48	617.755	Eyestrain	RE961-962	617.7522	Ophthalmic lenses
RE48	617.7026	Ophthalmologic emergencies	RE977.C6	617.7523	Contact lenses
			RE986-988	617.79	Eyes, Artificial
RE48.2.C5	618.920977	Pediatric ophthalmology	RE988	617.7524	Intraocular lenses
RE51	617.75	Eyestrain	RE994	617.7061	Ophthalmic drugs
RE56	617.70071	Ophthalmology—Study and teaching	RE994	617.7061	Ocular pharmacology
			RF	617.51	Otolaryngology

LC	Dewey	Subject Heading	LC	Dewey	Subject Heading
RF1	617.51006	Otolaryngology—Societies, etc.	RG1	618.1006	Gynecology—Societies, etc.
RF5-6	362.11	Hospitals, Ophthalmic and aural	RG12-16	362.11	Hospitals, Gynecologic and obstetric
RF6	362.1109(4-9)	Hospitals, Ophthalmic and aural—[By region or country]	RG26	618.1005	Gynecology—Periodicals
			RG31	618.1006	Gynecology—Congresses
RF11	617.51005	Otolaryngology—Periodicals	RG32-33	618.10025	Gynecologists—Directories
RF16	617.51006	Otolaryngology—Congresses	RG47	618.10014	Gynecology—Terminology
			RG51-67	618.1009	Gynecology—History
RF25-26	617.5109	Otolaryngology—History	RG71-76	618.1092	Gynecologists
RF28	617.510025	Otolaryngologists—Directories	RG77	618.07	Gynecologic pathology
			RG103.5	618.10019	Gynecology—Psychological aspects
RF37-38	617.51092	Otolaryngologists			
RF48-.5	617.51075	Otolaryngology—Diagnosis	RG104-.7	618.145	Generative organs, Female—Surgery
RF48-.5	617.51075	Otolaryngologic examination	RG104.5	618.1059	Gynoplasty
RF50	617.51044	Otolaryngology—Wounds and injuries	RG105	610.73678	Gynecologic nursing
			RG107-.5	618.1075	Gynecologic examination
RF51-52	617.51059	Otolaryngology, Operative	RG107.5.E48	618.107543	Endoscopic ultrasonography
RF52.5	610.736	Otolaryngological nursing	RG107.5.L34	618.107545	Laparoscopy
RF62	617.80071	Otolaryngology—Study and teaching	RG133	618.2	Conception
			RG133.5-135	618.178	Human reproductive technology
RF110-320	617.8	Ear—Diseases			
RF110-320	617.8	Otology	RG134	618.178	Artificial insemination, Human
RF126-127	617.8059	Ear—Surgery			
RF210	617.85	Tympanic membrane—Diseases	RG135	618.178059	Fertilization in vitro, Human
RF220-229	617.84	Middle ear—Diseases	RG136-137.6	613.94	Contraception
RF230	617.86	Eustachian tube—Diseases	RG136.5	613.9434	Natural family planning
RF235	617.87	Mastoid process—Diseases	RG137-.6	613.9432	Contraceptives
RF260-275	617.882	Labyrinth (Ear)—Diseases	RG137.2	613.9435	Contraceptives, Vaginal
RF286-320	617.8	Audiology	RG137.2	613.9432	Spermicides
RF286-320	617.8	Deafness	RG137.3	613.9435	Intrauterine contraceptives
RF286-320	617.8	Hearing disorders	RG136.85	613.9432	Antifertility vaccines
RF286	617.8006	Audiology—Societies, etc.	RG137.4-.6	613.9432	Contraceptive drugs
RF293.5	617.8	Deafness, Noise induced	RG137.5	613.9432	Oral contraceptives
RF294-.5	612.85	Audiometry	RG138	618.12059	Sterilization of women
RF298-310	617.800284	Audiology—Instruments	RG138	618.12059	Sterilization reversal
RF300-310	617.89	Hearing aids	RG155	618.20072	Obstetrics—Research
RF305	617.8820592	Cochlear implants	RG158	618.1025	Gynecologic emergencies
RF341-437	616.212	Nose—Diseases	RG159-208	618.17	Endocrine gynecology
RF341	616.87	Smell disorders	RG161-186	618.172	Menstrual cycle
RF345	616.21207545	Nasoscopy	RG161-186	618.172	Menstruation disorders
RF361	616.205	Cold (Disease)	RG165	618.172	Premenstrual syndrome
RF460-547	616.31	Throat—Diseases	RG181	618.172	Dysmenorrhea
RF476	616.31075	Throat—Examination	RG186	618.175	Menopause
RF481-499	616.32	Tonsils—Diseases	RG201-205	618.178	Infertility, Female
RF481-499	616.32	Pharnyx—Diseases	RG261-266	618.16	Vulva—Diseases
RF484.5	617.531059	Tonsillectomy	RG268-272	618.15	Vagina—Diseases
RF485	616.32	Pharyngitis	RG301-391	618.14	Uterus—Diseases
RF491	616.314	Tonsillitis	RG304-.5	618.1075	Uterus—Diseases—Diagnosis
RF510-540	616.855	Voice disorders			
RF514-.5	616.2207545	Laryngoscopy	RG310-315	618.14	Cervix uteri—Diseases
RF516-517	617.533059	Larynx—Surgery	RG314	618.143	Cervix erosion
RF517	617.533059	Tracheotomy	RG316	618.1	Endometrium—Diseases
RF526	616.22	Vocal cords—Diseases	RG361	618.14	Uterus—Rupture
RF545	616.32	Esophagus—Foreign bodies	RG391	618.1453	Hysterectomy
RF547	617.531044	Throat—Wounds and injuries	RG411	618.142	Pelvic inflammatory disease
			RG421-433	618.12	Fallopian tubes—Diseases
RG	618.1	Gynecology	RG483.P44	618.1	Pelvic pain
RG	618.2	Obstetrics	RG484-485	616.62	Bladder—Diseases

LC	Dewey	Subject Heading	LC	Dewey	Subject Heading
RG491-499	618.19	Breast—Diseases	RG661.5	618.4	Childbirth at home
RG504-505	618.20025	Obstetricians—Directories	RG662	618.4	Active childbirth
RG509-510	618.2092	Obstetricians	RG663	618.4	Underwater childbirth
RG511-518	618.209	Obstetrics—History	RG671-693	618.42	Fetal presentation
RG519-520	618.2	Uterus, Pregnant	RG696-698	618.25	Multiple birth
RG527.5.U48	618.207543	Ultrasonics in obstetrics	RG701-721	618.5	Labor (Obstetrics)—
RG529	618.209	Obstetrics—Case studies			Complications
RG545	618.200284	Obstetrics—Apparatus and	RG711	618.54	Uterine hemorrhage
		instruments	RG715	618.56	Placenta praevia
RG551-591	618.2	Pregnancy	RG719	618.58	Umbilical cord—Prolapse
RG556.5	618.200835	Teenage pregnancy	RG725-791	618.8	Obstetrics—Surgery
RG559	618.24	Pregnancy—Nutritional	RG732-733	617.9682	Anesthesia in obstetrics
		aspects	RG734-.5	363.46	Abortion services
RG560	618.20019	Pregnancy—Psychological	RG734	618.4	Labor, Induced (Obstetrics)
		aspects	RG734	618.172	Menstrual regulation
RG563-564	618.2075	Pregnancy—Signs and	RG739	618.20284	Obstetrical forceps
		diagnosis	RG741	618.82	Obstetrical extraction
RG567	618.25	Multiple pregnancy	RG761	618.86	Cesarean section
RG571-591	618.3025	Obstetrical emergencies	RG781	618.83	Craniotomy
RG575-576	618.75	Toxemia of pregnancy	RG801-871	618.7	Puerperal disorders
RG576	618.75	Eclampsia	RG801-871	618.7	Postnatal care
RG580.A44	618.3	AIDS (Disease) in	RG821	618.54	Uterine hemorrhage
		pregnancy	RG831	618	Puerperal convulsions
RG580.D5	618.326	Diabetes in pregnancy	RG850-852	618.76	Postpartum psychiatric
RG580.D76	618.3268	Drug abuse in pregnancy			disorders
RG580.E64	618.3268	Epilepsy in pregnancy	RG851	618.76	Puerperal psychoses
RG580.H47	618.3261	Blood diseases in	RG852	618.76	Postpartum depression
		pregnancy	RG861-866	618.71	Lactation disorders
RG580.H5	618.54	Uterine hemorrhage	RG950	618.2	Midwives
RG580.M34	618.3	Malnutrition in pregnancy	RG951	610.73678	Maternity nursing
RG580.S75	618.3268	Substance abuse in	RJ	618.92	Children—Diseases
		pregnancy	RJ	618.92	Pediatrics
RG586	618.31	Ectopic pregnancy	RJ1	618.920006	Pediatricians—Societies,
RG591	618.34	Placenta			etc.
RG600-650	618.32	Fetus	RJ16	618.920005	Pediatrics—Periodicals
RG600-650	618.32	Perinatology	RJ21	618.920006	Pediatrics—Congresses
RG610-621	612.647	Fetus—Physiology	RJ27-28	362.12	Pediatric clinics
RG613	612.647	Fetus—Growth	RJ27.2-.3	362.110973	Pediatric clinics—United
RG613.7	618.32	Fetus—Immunology			States
RG615	618.326	Fetus—Metabolism	RJ29	618.9200025	Pediatricians—Directories
RG618	618.3261	Perinatal cardiology	RJ33.5-.8	618.920232	Pediatrics—Practice
RG620	618.4	Fetus—Respiration and cry	RJ36-42	618.920009	Pediatrics—History
RG626-629	618.32	Fetus—Diseases	RJ43	618.9200092	Pediatricians
RG626-629	618.32043	Fetus—Abnormalities	RJ47.3-.4	618.920042	Genetic disorders in
RG627.6.D79	618.32	Fetus—Effect of drugs on			children
RG627.6.M34	618.32	Fetal malnutrition	RJ47.5-.53	618.9200019	Pediatrics—Psychosomatic
RG628-.3	618.32075	Prenatal diagnosis			aspects
RG628-.3	618.32075	Fetal monitoring	RJ52-53	615.542	Children—Diseases—
RG628.3.A48	618.3204275	Amniocentesis			Treatment
RG628.3.E34	618.326107543	Echocardiography	RJ53.A27	615.892083	Acupuncture for children
RG628.3.H42	618.3261075	Fetal heart rate monitoring	RJ53.A27	615.822083	Acupressure for children
RG628.3.U58	618.3207543	Fetus—Ultrasonic imaging	RJ53.D53	618.9200654	Diet therapy for children
RG629.G75	618.32	Fetal growth disorders	RJ53.E95	618.920062	Exercise therapy for
RG629.G76	618.32	Fetal growth retardation			children
RG631-633	618.32	Perinatal death	RJ53.F5	618.9200653	Fluid therapy for children
RG631-633	618.4	Stillbirth	RJ61	618.9201	Infants—Care
RG631-633	618.32	Fetal death	RJ91	618.24	Prenatal influences
RG648	618.392	Miscarriage	RJ101-103	649.122	Infants—Care
RG649	618.397	Labor, Premature	RJ125-137	612.0083	Children—Physiology
RG651-791	618.4	Labor (Obstetrics)	RJ128	618.92716	Children—Metabolism
RG661-662	618.45	Natural childbirth	RJ131-137	612.65	Child development

LC	Dewey	Subject Heading	LC	Dewey	Subject Heading
RJ131-137	612.65	Children—Growth	RJ431-436	618.922	Pediatric respiratory diseases
RJ134	612.654	Infants—Development	RJ434	615.542	Respiratory therapy for children
RJ135	618.92	Failure to thrive syndrome	RJ436.A8	618.92238	Asthma in children
RJ140-145	612.661	Youth—Physiology	RJ446-456	618.9233	Pediatric gastroenterology
RJ140	612.661	Teenagers—Growth	RJ456.E83	618.9232	Esophagus—Atresia
RJ145	612.662	Menarche	RJ456.F43	618.92342	Fecal incontinence in children
RJ206-235	612.3	Children—Nutrition	RJ460-463	618.9231	Pediatric oral medicine
RJ216	613.269	Breast feeding	RJ466-478.5	618.926	Pediatric urology
RJ240	613.0432	Immunization of children	RJ476.5-478.5	618.92098	Sexual disorders in children
RJ245-247	610.7362	Pediatric nursing	RJ476.E6	618.92849	Enuresis
RJ250-.3	618.92011	Infants (Premature)	RJ476.R46	618.92614	Acute renal failure in children
RJ251-325	618.9201	Neonatology	RJ478-.5	618.92098	Adolescent gynecology
RJ253.5	618.9201	Neonatal emergencies	RJ482.B65	618.9271	Bone diseases in children
RJ253.5	618.9201	Neonatal intensive care	RJ482.C65	618.9277	Connective tissue diseases in children
RJ256	618.922	Asphyxia neonatorum	RJ482.D78	618.92748	Duchenne muscular dystrophy
RJ267	618.9233	Colic	RJ486-496	618.928	Pediatric neurology
RJ268.8	618.9201	Neonatal gastroenterology	RJ496.A5	618.928553	Dyslexic children
RJ269	618.3261043	Fetal heart—Abnormalities	RJ496.B7	618.928043	Brain-damaged children
RJ269.5-271	618.9215	Neonatal hematology	RJ496.C4	618.92836	Cerebral palsied children
RJ272	618.923623	Hepatitis, Neonatal	RJ496.C7	618.92845	Febrile convulsions
RJ274	618.922	Hyaline membrane disease	RJ496.E6	618.92967	Epilepsy in children
RJ275	618.929	Neonatal infections	RJ496.E6	616.85300835	Epilepsy in adolescence
RJ276	618.923625	Jaundice, Neonatal	RJ496.P2	618.92842	Paralysis
RJ281	618.9201	Birth weight, Low	RJ496.S8	618.928554	Stuttering in children
RJ290-.5	618.928043	Nervous system—Abnormalities	RJ499-520	618.9289	Child psychiatry
RJ290	010.02007770	Conjunctivitis, Infantile	RJ499-520	618.9289	Child psychopathology
RJ301	618.92842	Paralysis	RJ500.2	618.9289027	Child psychopathology—Research
RJ312	618.922	Respiratory insufficiency in children	RJ502.3	610.7368	Adolescent psychiatric nursing
RJ320.S93	618.92	Sudden infant death syndrome	RJ502.5	616.890932	Infant psychiatry
RJ370	618.920025	Pediatric emergencies	RJ503	616.8900835	Adolescent psychopathology
RJ370	618.920028	Pediatric intensive care	RJ503	618.928917	Adolescent analysis
RJ386-.5	618.9297	Allergy in children	RJ503	616.891400835	Adolescent psychotherapy
RJ386.5	618.92975	Food allergy in children	RJ503	616.8900835	Adolescent psychiatry
RJ386.5	618.92975	Food allergy in infants	RJ504-505	618.928914	Child psychotherapy
RJ387.A25	618.929792	AIDS (Disease) in children	RJ504.2	618.928917	Child analysis
RJ387.A25	616.979200835	AIDS (Disease) in adolescence	RJ505.D3	615.85155083	Dance therapy for children
RJ387.A25	618.929792	AIDS (Disease) in infants	RJ505.T47	616.891400835	Adolescent psychotherapy—Termination
RJ396	618.92395	Rickets	RJ506.A58	618.9285223	Anxiety in children
RJ399.M26	618.9239	Malnutrition in children	RJ506.A9	618.928982	Autism in children
RJ401-406	618.92925	Virus diseases in children	RJ506.B44	618.92858	Behavior disorders in children
RJ406.B32	618.9292	Bacterial diseases in children	RJ506.C48	616.85836	Child sexual abuse
RJ411-416	618.9215	Pediatric hematology	RJ506.C65	618.9289	Conduct disorders in children
RJ416.A25	618.9299419	Acute myelocytic leukemia in children			
RJ418-420	618.924	Pediatric endocrinology	RJ506.D4	618.928527	Depression in infants
RJ420.A27	618.9245	Adrenal glands	RJ506.D4	618.928527	Depression in children
RJ420.D5	618.92462083	Diabetes in youth	RJ506.D4	616.852700835	Depression in adolescence
RJ420.D5	618.92462083	Diabetes in children	RJ506.D68	618.92858842	Down's syndrome
RJ420.D5	616.46200835	Diabetes in adolescence	RJ506.E18	616.852600835	Eating disorders in adolescence
RJ420.G65	618.92442	Endemic goiter in children			
RJ420.P58	618.9247	Dwarfism, Pituitary			
RJ421-426	618.9212	Pediatric cardiology			
RJ423.5.D54	618.92107572	Digital subtraction angiography			
RJ423.5.U46	618.921207543	Echocardiography	RJ506.F73	618.928588	Fragile X syndrome

LC	Dewey	Subject Heading	LC	Dewey	Subject Heading
RJ506.H9	618.928589	Attention-deficit hyperactivty disorder	RK328	617.6	Dental plaque
			RK328	617.6	Dental deposits
RJ506.M4	618.9285884	Mental retardation	RK331	617.67	Dental caries
RJ506.P38	618.9285225	Phobias in children	RK340-341	617.634	Dental enamel—Diseases
RJ506.S39	618.928582	Self-destructive behavior in children	RK351-356	617.6342	Endodontics
			RK351	617.63	Focal infection, Dental
RJ506.D4	618.928527	Affective disorders in children	RK361-450	617.645	Periodontics
			RK361-450	617.632	Periodontal disease
RJ507.F47	155.4567	Feral children	RK401-410	617.632	Gums—Diseases
RJ507.S49	618.9285836	Sexually abused children	RK410	617.632	Gingivitis
RJ516.E35	618.92521	Eczema in children	RK450.P4	617.632	Periodontitis
RJ520.C64	618.9277	Collagen diseases in children	RK490-493	617.6044	Teeth—Wounds and injuries
			RK501-519	617.605	Dentistry, Operative
RJ550	616.00835	Adolescent medicine	RK503	617.605	Dentistry, Operative—Positioning
RJ560-570	615.1083(2-4)	Pediatric pharmacology			
RK	617.6	Dentistry	RK513	617.605	Dentistry, Operative—Complications
RK	617.60232	Dentists			
RK1	617.6006	Dentistry—Societies, etc.	RK515	617.672	Dental drilling
RK3-.5	362.11	Dental clinics	RK515	617.672	Dental cavity preparation
RK3.5	362.1109(4-9)	Dental clinics—[By region or country]	RK517-519	617.675	Fillings (Dentistry)
			RK519.A4	617.675	Dental amalgams
RK16	617.6005	Dentistry—Periodicals	RK520-528	617.643	Orthodontics
RK21	617.6006	Dentistry—Congresses	RK523	617.643	Malocclusion
RK28	617.60014	Dentistry—Terminology	RK527-528	617.643	Orthodontics, Corrective
RK29-34	617.60901	Dentistry—History	RK527-528	617.64300284	Orthodonic appliances
RK31	617.60901	Dentistry, Ancient	RK529-535	617.605	Mouth—Surgery
RK37	617.60025	Dentists—Directories	RK531-.5	617.66	Teeth—Extraction
RK52-.45	617.600723	Dental surveys	RK533	617.60592	Teeth—Transplantation
RK52-.45	614.5996	Dental public health	RK641-667	617.69	Prosthodontics
RK52.7	174.2	Dental ethics	RK652.5-655	617.695	Dental materials
RK53	617.60019	Dentistry—Psychological aspects	RK652.7-.8	617.695	Dental cements
			RK652.7-.8	617.695	Dental adhesives
RK55.C5	617.645	Pedodontics	RK652.7-.8	617.69	Dental bonding
RK57	617.60076	Dentistry—Examinations, questions, etc.	RK653	617.675	Dental metallurgy
			RK653	617.675	Gold alloys
RK58-59.3	617.6023	Dentistry—Practice	RK653.5	617.675	Dental ceramic metals
RK60-.5	617.60023	Dentistry—Vocational guidance	RK655	617.675	Dental ceramics
			RK656	617.69	Denture attachments
RK60.45	617.6008996073	Afro-Americans in dentistry	RK656-666	617.692	Dentures, Immediate
RK60.5	617.60233	Dental auxiliary personnel	RK656-666	617.692	Overlay dentures
RK60.7-.8	617.601	Dental Prophylaxis	RK656-666	617.692	Dentures
RK60.7-.8	617.601	Preventive dentistry	RK664-666	617.692	Partial dentures
RK60.7	617.601	Teeth—Polishing	RK665	617.692	Partial dentures, Removable
RK60.8	617.60071	Dental health education	RK666	617.692	Bridges (Dentistry)
RK61	617.601	Teeth—Care and hygiene	RK666	617.692	Crowns (Dentistry)
RK71-231	617.60071	Dentistry—Study and teaching	RK667.I45	617.6920592	Implant dentures
			RK667.T57	617.69	Tissue-integrated prostheses
RK80	617.60072	Dentistry—Research	RK681-686	617.600284	Dental instruments and apparatus
RK86-231	617.600710(4-9)	Dentistry—Study and teaching—[By region and country]			
			RK701-715	617.606	Dentistry—Formulae, receipts, prescriptions
RK91-97	617.6071073	Dentistry—Study and teaching—United States	RL	616.5	Dermatology
			RL1	616.5006	Dermatology—Societies, etc.
RK301-493	617.63	Teeth—Diseases			
RK305	617.63	Focal infection, Dental	RL26	616.5005	Dermatology—Periodicals
RK308-310	617.630754	Teeth—Diseases—Diagnosis	RL31	616.5006	Dermatology—Congresses
			RL39	616.50014	Dermatology—Terminology
RK318-320	617.606	Dental therapeutics	RL43	616.50025	Dermatologists—Directories
RK320.E53	617.634	Dental enamel microabrasion	RL46	616.5009	Dermatology—History
			RL46.2-.3	616.50092	Dermatologists
RK328	617.6	Dental calculus			

LC	Dewey	Subject Heading	LC	Dewey	Subject Heading
RL55	616.500284	Dermatology—Apparatus and instruments	RM177	615.39	Blood platelets—Transfusion
RL77	616.50071	Dermatology—Study and teaching	RM182-190	617.414059	Veins—Puncture
			RM184-.5	615.892	Acupuncture
RL79	616.5027	Dermatology, Experimental	RM214-258	615.854	Dietetics
RL87	613.4	Skin—Care and hygiene	RM214-258	615.854	Diet therapy
RL91	616.546	Dandruff	RM214-258	615.854	Diet in disease
RL91	616.546	Beard	RM222.2	613.25	Low-calorie diet
RL94	646.727	Manicuring	RM222.2	613.25	Reducing diets
RL125	610.736	Dermatologic nursing	RM226-228	613.25	Fasting
RL131	616.53	Acne	RM232	613.26	Egg-free diet
RL155-.5	616.546	Baldness	RM234.5	613.26	Milk-free diet
RL221	616.523	Carbuncle	RM236	613.262	Vegetarianism
RL221	616.523	Furuncle	RM237.5	613.26	Raw food diet
RL231-241	616.51	Skin—Inflammation	RM237.56	613.285	High-calcium diet
RL241	616.5	Occupational dermatitis	RM237.58	613.283	Complex carbohydrate diet
RL242-249	616.521	Atopic dermatitis	RM237.59	613.283	High-carbohydrate diet
RL244	616.51	Contact dermatitis	RM237.6	613.263	High-fiber diet
RL247	616.5	Photosensitivity disorders	RM237.65	613.282	High-protein diet
RL251	616.521	Eczema	RM237.7	613.284	Low-fat diet
RL283	616.524	Impetigo	RM237.73	613.283	Low-carbohydrate diet
RL321	616.526	Psoriasis	RM237.75	613.284	Low-Cholesterol diet
RL431	616.546	Hupertrichosis	RM237.8	613.285	Salt-free diet
RL435	616.544	Keratosis	RM237.85	613.26	Sugar-free diet
RL435	616.544	Ichthyosis	RM237.87	613.26	Wheat-free diet
RL451	616.544	Scleroderma (Disease)	RM259	615.328	Vitamin therapy
RL471	616.544	Warts	RM260-263	615.58	Chemotherapy
RL675	616.545	Bedsores	RM265-267	615.329	Antibiotics
RL701-751	616.5	Neurocutaneous disorders	RM270-282	615.37	Immunotherapy
RL764.S28	616.57	Scabies	RM270-282	615.37	Serotherapy
RL780	616.57	Ringworm	RM278	615.375	Antitoxins
RL793	616.(042/55)	Mole (Dermatology)	RM281	615.372	Vaccination
RM	615.5	Therapeutics	RM282.T7	615.37	Transfer factor (Immunology)
RM1	615.506	Therapeutics—Societies, etc.	RM283-298	615.36	Hormone therapy
			RM298.P5	615.39	Placental extracts
RM16	615.505	Therapeutics—Periodicals	RM300-671.5	615.1	Pharmacology
RM21	615.506	Therapeutics—Congresses	RM300-671.5	615.1	Drugs
RM38	615.5014	Therapeutics—Terminology	RM301.25-.27	615.1072	Pharmacology, Experimental
RM40	616.0756	Clinical chemistry	RM301.27	615.1901	Drugs—Testing
RM41-47	615.509	Therapeutics—History	RM301.5	615.7	Pharmacokinetics
RM108-.5	615.5071	Therapeutics—Study and teaching	RM302-.4	615.7045	Drug interactions
			RM302.5	615.7042	Drugs—Side effects
RM111	615.5072	Therapeutics, Experimental	RM312	615.773	Musculoskeletal system—Effect of drugs on
RM138	615.14	Drugs—Prescribing			
RM139	615.14	Prescription writing	RM312	615.773	Neuromuscular blocking agents
RM147-180	615.6	Drugs—Administration			
RM149	615.855	Parenteral therapy	RM315-334	615.78	Neuropsychopharmacology
RM149	615.855	Parenteral solutions	RM315-334	615.788	Psychotropic drugs
RM161	615.836	Respiratory therapy	RM315-334	615.78	Psychopharmacology
RM162	615.6	Oral medication	RM315-334	615.78	Neuropharmacology
RM163-176	615.6	Injections	RM316	616.86	Designer drugs
RM169	615.6	Injections, Hypodermic	RM319	615.783	Analgesics
RM170-180	615.855	Intravenous therapy	RM324.8	615.7883	Hallucinogenic drugs
RM171-174	615.39	Blood—Transfusion	RM325	615.782	Barbiturates
RM171.4-.45	615.39	Blood products	RM325	615.782	Hypnotics
RM171.4	615.39	Recombinant blood proteins	RM325	615.782	Sedatives
RM171.5	615.39	Blood coagulation factors	RM328	615.7822	Narcotics
RM171.7	615.39	Blood plasma substitutes	RM330	615.788	Central nervous system depressants
RM172	362.1784	Blood banks			
RM175-176	615.39	Plasma exchange (Therapeutics)	RM332-.3	615.788	Antidepressants
			RM332-.3	615.785	Stimulants

LC	Dewey	Subject Heading
RM333	615.7882	Tranquilizing drugs
RM345-349	615.71	Cardiovascular agents
RM347	615.716	Myocardial depressants
RM349	615.71	Cardiotonic agents
RM355-365	615.73	Gastrointestinal agents
RM357	615.732	Laxatives
RM359	615.731	Emetics
RM365	615.73	Antacids
RM370-373	615.37	Immunopharmacology
RM373	615.37	Immunosuppressive agents
RM377	615.761	Diuretics
RM386	615.766	Aphrodisiacs
RM388-.7	615.72	Pulmonary pharmacology
RM388-.7	615.72	Respiratory agents
RM390	615.72	Expectorants
RM409	615.329	Antibacterial agents
RM666.A4	615.321	Alkaloids
RM666.A82	615.3137	Aspirin
RM666.B2	615.329	Bacitracin
RM666.C266	615.7827	Cannabis
RM666.C375	615.32369	Castor oil
RM666.D5	615.711	Digitalis
RM666.H33	615.321	Herbs—Therapeutic use
RM666.L88	615.788	LSD (Drug)
RM666.M8	615.7822	Morphine
RM666.O8	615.836	Oxygen therapy
RM666.P35	615.3295654	Penicillin
RM666.T2	615.731	Tartar emetic
RM666.T6	616.865	Tobacco—Physiological effect
RM671-.5	615.1	Drugs, Nonprescription
RM671-.5	615.886	Patent medicines
RM695-951	615.82	Medicine, Physical
RM695-931	615.82	Therapeutics, Physiological
RM695-893	615.82	Physical therapy
RM695	615.8206	Physical therapy—Societies, etc.
RM696	615.8206	Physical therapy—Congresses
RM697	615.82025	Physical therapists—Directories
RM699.5-.7	615.82092	Physical therapists
RM706-707	615.82071	Physical therapy—Study and teaching
RM719-727	615.822	Mechanotherapy
RM721-723	615.822	Massage
RM723.A27	615.822	Acupressure
RM724	615.82	Manipulation (Therapeutics)
RM725-727	615.82	Exercise therapy
RM735-.7	615.8515	Occupational therapy
RM735.7.H35	615.85156	Handicraft—Therapeutic use
RM736.7	615.85153	Recreational therapy
RM801-822	615.853	Hydrotherapy
RM824-827	615.836	Aerotherapy
RM827	615.836	Compressed air—Therapeutic use
RM835-844	615.831	Phototherapy
RM835-844	615.831	Light, Colored
RM838	615.831	Light—Physiological effect
RM840	615.831	Color—Therapeutic use
RM843	613.193	Sun-baths
RM845-862.5	615.842	Radiotherapy
RM845-862.5	615.842	Radiation—Dosage
RM859	615.8423	Radium—Therapeutic use
RM862.7	615.83	Ultrasonic waves—Therapeutic use
RM862.E4	615.845	Electron beams—Therapeutic use
RM865-868.5	615.832	Thermotherapy
RM868-.5	615.8325	Fever therapy
RM869-890	615.845	Electrotherapeutics
RM874	615.8323	Diathermy
RM886	615.845	Electrolysis in medicine
RM889	610.284	Electric apparatus and appliances
RM930-950	617.03	Medical rehabilitation
RM950	617.03	Rehabilitation technology
RS	615.1	Pharmacy
RS1	615.106	Pharmacy—Societies, etc.
RS3	615.106	Pharmacy—Congresses
RS21	615.105	Pharmacy—Periodicals
RS55	615.1014	Pharmacy—Terminology
RS57	615.10151	Pharmaceutical arithmetic
RS61-68	615.109	Pharmacy—History
RS71-73	615.1092	Pharmacists
RS74-76	615.1025	Pharmacists—Directories
RS93	615.1078	Pharmacy—Laboratory manuals
RS100-.4	615.1068	Pharmacy management
RS100.5	174.2	Pharmaceutical ethics
RS101-121	615.1071	Pharmacy—Study and teaching
RS110-121	615.10710(4-9)	Pharmacy—Study and teaching—[By region or country]
RS122	615.1072	Pharmacy—Research
RS122.5	615.108996073	Afro-American pharmacists
RS122.95	615.1092	Pharmacy technicians
RS123	615.1074	Pharmaceutical museums
RS125-131.9	615.13	Medicine—Formulae, receipts, prescriptions
RS139-141.9	615.11	Pharmacopoeias
RS151.2-.9	615.13	Dispensatories
RS153-185	615.1	Materia medica
RS159	615.18	Drugs—Preservation
RS159.5	615.18	Drugs—Packaging
RS160-167	615.321	Pharmacognosy
RS165.C3	633.88393	Quinine
RS165.C5	615.32379	Coca
RS165.D5	615.711	Digitalis
RS165.H3	633.79	Hashish
RS165.P38	615.3295654	Penicillin
RS189-190	615.1901	Drugs—Analysis
RS189	615.10128	Drugs—Standards
RS192-210	615.19	Pharmaceutical technology
RS199.5-210	615.6	Drug delivery systems
RS200-201	615.14	Drugs—Dosage forms
RS201.B54	615.6	Bioadhesive drug delivery systems
RS201.C3	615.43	Capsules (Pharmacy)
RS201.C64	615.6	Drugs—Controlled release
RS201.E4	615.42	Elixirs

LC	Dewey	Subject Heading	LC	Dewey	Subject Heading
RS201.E5	615.45	Emulsions (Pharmacy)	RV211	616.04706	Fever—Eclectic treatment
RS201.O3	615.45	Ointments	RV241-246	616.806	Nervous system—Diseases—Eclectic treatment
RS201.P37	615.6	Parenteral solutions			
RS201.P5	615.43	Pills			
RS201.P8	615.43	Powders (Pharmacy)	RV251-256	616.106	Cardiovascular system—Diseases—Eclectic treatment
RS201.S6	615.42	Solutions (Pharmacy)			
RS201.S8	615.42	Syrups			
RS201.T2	615.43	Tablets (Medicine)	RV261-266	616.206	Respiratory organs—Diseases—Eclectic treatment
RS201.V43	615.6	Drugs—Vehicles			
RS210	615.6	Drug delivery devices			
RS400-431	615.19	Pharmaceutical chemistry	RV271-276	616.306	Digestive organs—Diseases—Eclectic treatment
RS424	615.18	Drug stability			
RS431.D58	615.761	Diuretics			
RS431.E73	615.321	Exgot alkaloids	RV291	617.5106	Head—Diseases—Eclectic treatment
RT	610.73	Nursing			
RT1	610.7306	Nursing—Societies, etc.	RV293	617.5406	Chest—Dieases—Eclectic treatment
RT3	610.7306	Nursing—Congresses			
RT4-17	610.7309(4-9)	Nursing—[By region or country]	RV297	617.5506	Pelvis—Diseases—Eclectic treatment
RT25	610.73025	Nurses—Directories	RV321-331	617.706	Eye—Diseases—Eclectic treatment
RT31	610.7309	Nursing—History			
RT34-37	610.73092	Nurses	RV341-347	617.52306	Nose—Diseases—Eclectic treatment
RT48-.6	610.73069	Nursing assessment			
RT48.6	610.73069	Nursing diagnosis	RV361-365	618.206	Obstetrics, Eclectic
RT50.5	610.730285	Nursing—Data processing	RV375-377	618.9206	Children—Diseases—Eclectic treatment
RT62	610.730693	Practical nursing			
~~RT71-81~~	~~610.730711~~	~~Nursing schools~~	~~RV391-394~~	~~616.506~~	~~Dermatology~~
RT71-81	610.73071	Nursing—Study and teaching	RV431	615.53	Dispensatories, Eclectic
			RX	615.532	Homeopathy
RT81.5	610.73072	Nursing—Research	RX1	615.53206	Homeopathy—Societies, etc.
RT82.8	610.730692	Nurse practitioners			
RT83.5	615.7308996073	Afro-American nurses	RX6-.5	362.11	Homeopathy—Hospitals and dispensaries
RT84	610.730698	Nurses' aides			
RT84.5	610.7301	Nursing—Philosophy	RX11	615.53205	Homeopathy—Periodicals
RT85	174.2	Nursing ethics	RX21	615.53206	Homeopathy—Congresses
RT86	610.73019	Nursing—Psychological aspects	RX46	615.532025	Homeopathic physicians—Directories
RT86.3	610.730699	Nurse and patient	RX51	615.53209	Homeopathy—History
RT86.4	610.730699	Nurse and physician	RX61-66	615.532092	Homeopathic physicians—Biography
RT86.7-.75	610.73069	Nursing—Practice			
RT87.T45	610.7361	Hospice care	RX81	615.532	Homeopathy—Attenuations, dilutions, and potencies
RT87.T45	610.7361	Terminal care			
RT90-.3	615.507	Patient education	RX91-101	615.532071	Homeopathy—Study and teaching
RT90.5	610.73028	Team nursing			
RT90.7	610.733	Primary nursing	RX211	616.04706	Fever—Homeopathic treatment
RT97	610.734	Public health nursing			
RT98	610.7343	Visiting nurses	RX261.C3	616.99406	Cancer—Homeopathic treatment
RT104	610.732	Private duty nursing			
RT108	610.7349	Disaster nursing	RX281-301	616.806	Nervous system—Diseases—Homeopathic treatment
RT120.E4	610.7361	Emergency nursing			
RT120.I5	610.7361	Intensive care nursing			
RV1-9	615.53	Medicine, Botanic	RX311-316	616.106	Cardiovascular system—Diseases—Homeopathic treatment
RV11-431	615.53	Medicine, Eclectic			
RV15	615.5305	Medicine, Eclectic—Periodicals	RX321-326	616.206	Respiratory organs—Diseases—Homeopathic treatment
RV21	615.5306	Medicine, Eclectic—Congresses			
RV61	615.5309	Medicine, Eclectic—History	RX331-336	616.306	Digestive organs—Diseases—Homeopathetic treatment
RV100-181	615.53071	Medicine, Eclectic—Study and teaching			

206

LC	Dewey	Subject Heading	LC	Dewey	Subject Heading
RX360	617.5406	Chest—Diseases— Homeopathic treatment	S421-431	630.901	Agriculture, Prehistoric
RX366-376	617	Surgery, Homeopathic	S431	630.945632	Agriculture—Rome
RX410-431	617.706	Eye—Diseases— Homeopathic treatment	S439-481	630.11	Agricultural systems
			S439-481	630.9(4-9)	Agricultural geography
RX451	617.52306	Nose—Diseases— Homeopathic treatment	S439-481	333.7316	Green Revolution
			S441-482	577.55	Agricultural ecology
RX476	618.206	Obstetrics, Homeopathic	S441-451	630.723	Agricultural surveys
RX501-531	618.9206	Children—Diseases— Homeopathic treatment Dermatology	S494	636.082	Breeding
			S494	636.082	Inbreeding
RX561-581	616.506		S494.5.A4	630.23	Agriculture—Vocational guidance
RX601-675	615.532	Homeopathy—Materia medica and therapeutics	S494.5.A45	634.99	Agroforestry
			S494.5.A47	630	Agropastoral systems
RX671-675	615.532	Pharmacy, Homeopathic	S494.5.E5	631.37	Agriculture and energy
RZ201-275	615.534	Chiropractic	S494.5.E8	630.723	Agricultural surveys
RZ201	615.53406	Chiropractic—Societies, etc.	S494.5.P47	631.58	Permaculture
RZ211	615.53405	Chiropractic—Periodicals	S494.5.U72	630.91732	Urban agriculture
RZ213	615.53406	Chiropractic—Congresses	S521	390.463	Farm life
RZ221-225	615.53409	Chiropractic—History	S530-539	630.7	Agricultural education
RZ231-232	615.534092	Chiropractors—Biography	S531-539	630.71	Agriculture—Study and teaching
RZ233	615.534025	Chiropractors—Directories			
RZ237-238	615.534071	Chiropractic—Study and teaching	S533-534	630.715092	County agricultural agents
			S533.F66	630.6	4-H clubs
RZ242	362.12	Chiropractic clinics	S537-539	630.711	Agricultural colleges
RZ260-275	615.534	Diseases—Chiropractic treatment	S539.5-542	630.72	Agriculture—Research
			S541-543	630.724	Agricultural experimental stations
RZ265.S64	616.73062	Spinal adjustment			
RZ270-275	617.1062	Wounds and injuries— Chiropractic treatment	S544-545	630.715	Agricultural extension work
			S549	630.74	Agricultural museums
RZ301-397.5	615.533	Osteopathic medicine	S550-559	630.74	Agricultural exhibitions
RZ301	615.53306	Osteopathic medicine— Societies, etc.	S560-575	630	Farms
			S560-572	630.68	Farm management
RZ302-304	362.11	Osteopathic hospitals	S565	630.289	Agriculture—Safety measures
RZ311	615.53305	Osteopathic medicine— Periodicals			
			S571-.5	380.141	Farm produce—Marketing
RZ313	615.53306	Osteopathic medicine— Congresses	S571.5	380.141	Roadside marketing
			S583-587.5	631.41	Agricultural chemistry
RZ321-325	615.53309	Osteopathic medicine— History	S587.45	631.86	Natural products in agriculture
RZ331-332	615.533092	Osteopathic physicians— Biography	S587.5.N5	631.84	Nitrogen in agriculture
			S589-.6	631.43	Agricultural physics
RZ333	615.533025	Osteopathic physicians— Directories	S589.8-.85	631.4	Potting soils
			S589.8	631.4	Plant growing media
RZ336	615.533023	Osteopathic medicine— Vocational guidance	S590-599.9	631.4	Soils
			S590-599.9	631.4	Soil science
RZ337-338	615.5330711	Osteopathic schools	S590-599.9	631.4	Land capability for agriculture
RZ337-338	615.533071	Osteopathic medicine— Study and teaching			
			S590-592	631.4	Soil management
RZ400-408	615.851	Mental healing	S592.14-.147	631.47	Soil surveys
RZ403.S56	615.851	Silva Mind Control	S592.17.A73	631.49154	Arid soils
RZ407-408	615.851092	Healers	S592.17.D47	631.49154	Desert soils
RZ414	615.53	Medicine, Chronothermal	S592.5-.6	631.41	Soil chemistry
RZ414.6	615.831	Color—Therapeutic use	S592.57-.575	631.42	Acid soils
RZ420	615.532	Electrohomeopathy	S592.575	631.42	Acid sulphate soils
RZ422	615.845	Magnetic healing	S592.575	631.42	Soil acidity
RZ433-445	615.535	Naturopathy	S592.6.A34	631.41	Soils—Agricultural chemical content
RZ440	615.535092	Naturopaths			
S1-954	630-638	Agriculture	S592.7-.85	631.417	Soil biochemistry
S1-19	630.5	Agriculture—Periodicals	S592.85	631.826	Peat soils
S20	630.6	Agriculture—Societies, etc.	S593	631.4	Soils—Analysis
S419-481	630.9	Agriculture—History	S594	631.62	Drain-gages

LC	Dewey	Subject Heading	LC	Dewey	Subject Heading
S594	631.432	Moisture index	S715.C64	631.37	Cotton-picking machinery
S594	631.432	Soil moisture	S723	631.27	Gates
S595	631.42	Alkali lands	S790-.3	631.27	Fences
S599-.9	631.49154	Desert soils	S900-954	333.72/631.45	Conservation of natural resources
S599-.9	631.587	Soils, Irrigated			
S600	630.2515	Meteorology, Agricultural	S946	333.72071	Environmental education
S600.7.H37	631.55	Harvesting time	SB1-317	630	Crops
S600.7.P53	631.53	Planting time	SB1-13	630.5	Crops—Periodicals
S602.87	631.5818	Shifting cultivation	SB16	630.6	Crops—Congresses
S603	631.582	Crop rotation	SB45.65	630	Crop science literature
S603.5	631.58	Intercropping	SB51-56	630.72	Crops—Research
S603.7	631.58	Double cropping	SB106.B56	631.5233	Plant biotechnology
S603.7	631.58	Multiple cropping	SB106.I47	631.52	Crop improvement
S604	631.5814	No-tillage	SB106.O74	631.52	Crops—Evolution
S604	631.51	Tillage	SB107-109	338.1	Botany, Economic
S604.33	630.911	Cold regions agriculture	SB108-109	631.523	Plant introduction
S604.5-.64	631.451	Agricultural conservation	SB109.7	630.911	Cold regions agriculture
S604.8-621.5	631.6	Reclamation of land	SB110	631.586	Dry farming
S605.5	631.584	Organic farming	SB111	631.913	Tropical crops
S612-619	630.9154	Arid regions agriculture	SB113.2-118.45	631.521	Seeds
S612-619	631.587	Irrigation	SB113.2-118.45	631.521	Seed technology
S612-619	631.6	Desert reclamation	SB114	631.521	Seed adulteration and inspection
S612-619	631.587	Irrigation farming			
S621	631.62	Drainage	SB118.48-.75	635	Nurseries (Horticulture)
S621.5.P59	631.64	Plants for land reclamation	SB119-124	631.52	Plant propagation
S621.5.S3	631.64	Sand dune planting	SB121	631.53	Planting (Plant culture)
S622-627	631.45	Soil conservation	SB121	631.536	Seedlings—Transplanting
S627.H5	631.455	Hillside planting	SB121	631.531	Sowing
S627.P55	631.45	Plants for soil conservation	SB123-.25	631.52	Selection (Plant breeding)
S627.P76	631.45	Soil conservation projects	SB123-.5	631.52	Plant breeding
S631-667	631.8	Fertilizers	SB123.57	631.5233	Crops—Genetic engineering
S633	631.8	Garden fertilizers	SB123.57	631.5233	Transgenic plants
S647	631.85	Phosphatic fertilizers	SB123.57	631.5233	Plant genetic engineering
S651-.3	631.84	Nitrogen fertilizers	SB123.65	631.54	Grafting
S651-.3	631.842	Nitrates	SB125	631.54	Disbudding
S654	631.86	Organic fertilizers	SB126.5-.57	631.585	Hydroponics
S654	631.86	Organic wastes as fertilizer	SB129	631.55	Harvesting
S655	631.861	Manures	SB170-171	634.99	Tree crops
S654.5	631.847	Biofertilizers	SB172	634.99	Multipurpose trees
S655	631.861	Farm manure	SB175-177	635	Food crops
S657	631.869	Sewage	SB183-187	633	Seed crops
S659	631.85	Bone-meal	SB185.8	631.53	Planting time
S661	631.874	Green manuring	SB185.8	631.55	Harvesting time
S661	631.875	Compost	SB188-192	633.1	Winter grain
S661.2.M3	631.87	Marine algae as fertilizer	SB189-192	633.1	Grain
S661.5	631.451	Mulching	SB191.P64	635.677	Popcorn
S662-.5	631.8	Liquid fertilizers	SB191.W5	633.11	Durum wheat
S671-760	631.3	Agricultural machinery	SB193-207	633.2	Forage plants
S671-760	631	Agricultural engineering	SB193-.55	633.202	Rangelands
S671-760	631.3	Farm equipment	SB195	633.2	Silage
S675.3	631.3	Agricultural mechanics	SB197-202	633.2	Grasses
S676-.3	631.3	Agricultural implements	SB199	633.202	Meadows
S676.5	631.3	Agricultural instruments	SB199	633.202	Pastures
S683-685	631.3	Plows	SB201.K4	633.21	Kentucky bluegrass
S687-689	631.3	Drill (Agricultural implement)	SB203-205	633.3	Legumes
S695-697	631.3	Sickles	SB205.F3	633.3	Faba bean
S695-697	631.3	Mowing machines	SB209-211	635.1	Root crops
S699-701	631.3	Threshing machines	SB215-239	633.6	Sugar
S711-713	631.373	Farm trucks	SB241-261	633.5	Fiber plants
S711-713	631.372	Power transmission	SB261.M3	633.571	Abaca (Fiber)
S711-713	631.372	Farm tractors	SB267	633.74	Cacao

LC	Dewey	Subject Heading	LC	Dewey	Subject Heading
SB269	633.73	Coffee	SB415	635.9823	Greenhouse gardening
SB273-278	633.71	Tobacco	SB415	635.986	Plants, Potted
SB281-283	633.58	Matwork plants	SB418-.4	635.986	Container gardening
SB285-287	633.86	Dye plants	SB418-.4	635.986	Hanging baskets
SB289-291	633.8952	Rubber plants	SB419-.3	635.965	Indoor gardening
SB289-291	633.895	Gums and resins	SB419-.3	635.9678	Window gardening
SB292	633.898	Pesticidal plants	SB419-.3	635.965	Indoor gardens
SB293-295	633.88	Mushrooms, Hallucinogenic	SB419-.3	635.965	House plants
SB293-295	633.88	Medicinal plants	SB419.5	635.9671	Balcony gardening
SB295.E63	633.8858	Ephedra	SB419.5	635.9671	Roof gardening
SB295.G5	633.88384	Ginseng	SB422	635.9312	Annuals (Plants)
SB295.06	633.75	Opium	SB423	635.9674	Water gardens
SB295.065	633.75	Opium poppy	SB427.5	635.9525	Desert gardening
SB298-299	633.85	Oilseed plants	SB427.5	635.9525	Desert plants
SB299.S9	635.93399	Sunflowers	SB428.5	635.973	Everlasting flowers
SB301-303	633.81	Aromatic plants	SB429	635.9373	Ferns, Ornamental
SB305-307	633.8(3-4)	Spice plants	SB431	635.975	Foliage plants
SB317.5-319.77	635	Horticultural crops	SB431.7	635.9	Ornamental grasses
SB320-353.5	635	Vegetable gardening	SB432.7	635.93375	Carnivorous plants
SB320-353.5	635	Vegetables	SB433-.34	635.9647	Lawns
SB339	635.61	Melons	SB433-.34	635.9642	Turfgrasses
SB341	635.25	Onions	SB433.5	635.9772	Bonsai
SB349	635.642	Tomatoes	SB433.5	635.9772	Gardens, Miniature
SB351.E5	635.646	Eggplant	SB434	635.932	Perennials
SB351.H5	635.7	Herb gardens	SB434.7	635.9543	Gardening in the shade
SB351.H5	635.7	Herbs	SB434.7	635.9543	Shade-tolerant plants
SB351.R65	635.1	Root crops	SB435-437	635.97713	Flowering woody plants
SB353-.5	635.8	Fungi, Edible	SB435-437	635.977	Ornamental trees
SB354-399	634	Fruit	SB435-437	635.977	Tree planting
SB354-402	634	Orchards	SB435-.8	635.9772	Dwarf trees
SB364	634.62	Date	SB435	635.97715	Ornamental evergreens
SB364	634.62	Date palm	SB435	635.9775	Evergreens
SB365	634.37	Fig	SB436	635.977	Trees in cities
SB369	634.3	Citrus fruits	SB437	635.976	Hedges
SB370.G7	634.32	Grapefruit	SB439-.26	719	Natural landscaping
SB386.B6	634.713	Blackberries	SB439-.26	635.951	Native plant gardening
SB386.B7	634.737	Blueberries	SB439.8	635.9525	Drought-tolerant plants
SB387-399	634.8	Grapes	SB441-.75	635.9074	Flower shows
SB401	634.57	Cashew nut	SB442.8-445	380.14159	Florists
SB401	634.5	Nuts	SB447	635.973	Everlasting flowers
SB401.M32	634.5	Macadamia nut	SB449-450.87	745.92	Flower arrangement
SB403-450.87	635.9	Flower gardening	SB449.5.W4	745.926	Wedding decorations
SB403-450.87	635.9	Floriculture	SB450.9-467.8	635	Gardening
SB403-450.87	635.9	Plants, Ornamental	SB450.9-467	635	Gardens
SB403-450	635.9	Flowers	SB453.5	635.0484	Organic gardening
SB409	635.9344	Dendrobium	SB454.3.P7	635.043	Planting time
SB410.9-411.7	635.933734	Roses	SB454.8	635.0284	Garden tools
SB411	635.933734	Rose gardens	SB459	635.9528	Alpine gardens
SB413.D	635.93399	Daisies	SB459	635.9672	Rock gardens
SB413.D12	635.93434	Daffodils	SB469-476.4	712	Landscape architecture
SB413.D13	635.93399	Dahlias	SB472.45	712	Landscape design
SB413.D4	635.93334	Delphinium	SB473	635	Backyard gardens
SB413.E27	635.97752	Eastern hemlock	SB473.2	635.9671	Patio gardening
SB413.G35	635.93379	Dwarf pelargoniums	SB473.5	645.8	Garden ornaments and furniture
SB413.H6	635.933685	Hibiscus			
SB413.I8	635.93438	Dwarf irises	SB475.8	714	Water in landscape architecture
SB413.P17	635.9345	Palms			
SB413.R43	633.28	Red fescue	SB475.9.F67	719.33	Forest landscape design
SB414.6-416.3	635.9823	Greenhouse plants	SB476	621.3229	Garden lighting
SB415-416.3	631.583	Greenhouses	SB481-485	363.68068	Parks—Management
SB415-416.3	631.583	Solar greenhouses	SB481-485	363.68	Parks

209

LC	Dewey	Subject Heading	LC	Dewey	Subject Heading
SB481-484	363.68	National parks and reserves	SD	634.9	Forests and forestry
SB482-483	363.680973	Parks—United States	SD1	634.906	Forests and forestry—Societies, etc.
SB484-485	363.6809(4-9)	Parks—[Other countries or regions]	SD11-115	634.909(4-9)	Forests and forestry—[By region or country]
SB599-1100	632.(6-7)	Pests	SD11-12	634.90973	Forests and forestry—United States
SB599-989	632.3	Plant diseases			
SB599-999	632.(6-7)	Agricultural pests	SD12	634.9097(4-9)	Forests and forestry—[United States, By state]
SB599.2	632.(6-7)06	Agricultural pests—Congresses			
SB601	632	Plant parasites	SD250-381.5	634.9071	Forestry schools and education
SB603.5	635.92	Garden pests			
SB605	632.09(4-9)	Garden pests—[By region or country]	SD356-.54	634.9072	Forests and forestry—Research
SB610-615	632.5	Weeds	SD387.C58	634.92	Clearcutting
SB610-615	632.5	Weeds—Control	SD387.043	333.75	Old growth forests
SB610-615	632.52	Parasitic plants	SD387.S52	634.92	Short rotation forestry
SB733	632.4	Fungal diseases of plants	SD387.W6	634.99	Woodlots
SB733	632.4	Fungi in agriculture	SD388	634.90284	Forest machinery
SB741.D68	632.446	Downy mildew diseases	SD391-535	634.9	Trees
SB741.M65	632.43	Mildew	SD391	634.9565	Tree planting
SB745	632.19	Crops—Effect of air pollution on	SD392	634.95	Silvicultural systems
			SD396.5	634.953	Forest thinning
SB745	632.19	Crops—Effect of acid precipitation on	SD397.D37	634.9758	Dawn redwood
			SD397.D7	634.9754	Douglas fir
SB745	632.19	Plants, Effect of air pollution on	SD397.D87	634.9721	Durmast oak
			SD397.E27	634.9753	Eastern hemlock
SB745	632.19	Plants, Effect of acid precipitation on	SD397.E54	634.9721	English oak
			SD397.E8	634.973766	Eucalyptus
SB750	632.95042	Plants—Disease and pest resistance	SD397.F5	634.9754	Fir
			SD397.R3	634.9758	Redwood
SB761	634.96	Forest insects	SD399.5	634.956	Forest genetics
SB767	632.2	Galls (Botany)	SD409	634.956	Afforestation
SB818-945	632.7	Insect pests	SD409	634.956	Reforestation
SB922-998	591.6	Zoology, Economic	SD411-428	634.93	Forest protection
SB939	632.752	Scale insects	SD411-428	333.75/634.9	Forest conservation
SB950-989	632.9	Pests—Control	SD411	634.93	Forests and forestry—Safety measures
SB950-989	632.9	Plants, Protection of			
SB950.9-970.4	632.95	Pesticides	SD420.5-421.5	634.9618	Forest fires
SB951.145.N37	632.95	Natural pesticides	SD421	634.9618	Forest fire detection
SB951.3	632.952	Fungicides	SD421	634.9618	Forest fires—Prevention and control
SB951.4	632.954	Herbicides			
SB951.5-.54	632.9517	Insecticides	SD421.375	634.93	Fire lookout stations
SB952.8-955	632.94	Pesticides—Application	SD421.43	634.9618	Aeronautics in wildfire control
SB953	632.94	Spraying and dusting in agriculture			
			SD425	634.9617	Floods
SB955	632.94	Fumigation	SD426-428	333.75	Forest reserves
SB957	632.95042	Pesticide resistance	SD430-557	338.17498	Timber
SB970-.4	344.04633	Pesticides—Government policy	SD537-538.83	634.98	Logging
			SD538-557	634.98	Lumbering
SB975-989	632.96	Pests—Biological control	SF	636	Animal culture
SB975	632.96	Biological pest control agents	SF	636	Small animal culture
			SF1-140	636	Livestock
SB979.5-985	632.93	Plant quarantine	SF41	636.082	Domestication
SB993.3-.34	591.609(4-9)	Zoology, Economic—[By region or country]	SF180	636.0882	Draft animals
			SF84-.45	591.6	Zoology, Economic
SB993.3-32	591.60973	Zoology, Economic—United States	SF84.82-85.6	636.0845	Rangelands
			SF84.82-98	636.0845	Range management
SB993.34	591.609(4-9)	Zoology, Economic—[Other regions or countries]	SF94.5-99	636.085	Animal nutrition
			SF94.5-99	636.0855	Feeds
SB993.5-994	632.69	Mammal pests	SF94.5-99	636.084	Animal feeding
SB995	632.68	Bird pests	SF97.7	636.0855	Feeds—Flavor and odor

LC	Dewey	Subject Heading	LC	Dewey	Subject Heading
SF98.A2	636.08557	Feed additives	SF290-291	636.1	Horse farms
SF98.A5	636.08557	Antibiotics in animal nutrition	SF293.M56	636.109	Miniature horses
			SF293.P5	636.13	Pinto horse
SF98.F	636.0852	Fiber in animal nutrition	SF293.S72	636.13	Standardbred horse
SF98.F	636.0855	Feeds—Fiber content	SF294.2-294.35	798	Horse sports
SF98.M4	636.08557	Medicated feeds	SF294.5-297.7	636.10811	Horse shows
SF98.P46	636.0855	Pesticide residues in feeds	SF295.185-.187	636.10811	Show horses
SF99	636.0855	Bone-meal	SF295.2	798.24	Show riding
SF99.A37	636.08556	Agricultural wastes as feed	SF295.65	799.23	Hunt riding
SF99.D5	636.0855	Distillers feeds	SF295.7	636.10811	Event horses
SF99.F37	636.0855	Feathers as feed	SF296.R4	798.2028	Reining (Horsemanship)
SF99.F5	636.0855	Fish meal as feed	SF296.T75	798.23	Trick riding
SF99.M33	636.0855	Marine algae as feed	SF296.V37	798.25	Vaulting (Horsemanship)
SF99.W34	636.0855	Organic wastes as feed	SF304.5-307	388.341	Driving of horse-drawn vehicles
SF99.Y4	636.0855	Yeast as feed			
SF101-103.5	636.20812	Livestock brands	SF304.5-307	388.341	Coaching
SF101-103.5	636.20812	Cattle brands	SF309	798.2	Horsemanship
SF105-109	636.082	Animal breeding	SF309.27	798.23	Sidesaddle riding
SF105	636.082	Inbreeding	SF309.28	798.23	Trail riding
SF105.27-.275	636.082	Rare breeds	SF309.3	798.23	Western riding
SF105.5	636.08245	Artificial insemination	SF309.48-.658	798.23	Dressage
SF140.B54	636.0821	Animal biotechnology	SF309.65-.653	636.13	Dressage horses
SF140.P38	636.0845	Pastoral systems	SF309.9	636.10837	Bits (Bridles)
SF170-180	636.0886	Working animals	SF309.9	636.10837	Bridles
SF191-219	636.2	Cattle	SF309.9	636.13037	English saddles
SF191-219	636.2	Cows	SF309.9	636.13037	Western saddle
SF198-199	636.2(2-8)	Cattle breeds	SF310-.5	798.2306	Riding clubs
SF199.A3	636.28	Africander cattle	SF310.4	798.23071	Riding schools
SF199.D38	636.226	Devon cattle	SF311-.3	636.15	Draft horses
SF199.D4	636.225	Dexter cattle	SF312	636.14	Coach horses
SF199.E2	636.23	East Prussian cattle	SF315	636.16	Ponies
SF199.G8	636.224	Guernsey cattle	SF315.2.C4	636.16	Chincoteague pony
SF207	636.213	Beef cattle	SF321-359.7	798.4	Horse racing
SF208	636.2142	Dairy cattle	SF324-.4	798.40068	Racetracks (Horse-racing)
SF211	636.226	Dual-purpose cattle	SF338.7-345	798.46	Harness racing
SF221-250	636.2142	Dairy farming	SF343	636.12	Harness racehorses
SF221-250	636.2142	Dairy farms	SF357.K4	798.400976944	Kentucky Derby, Louisville, Ky.
SF221-250	636.2142	Dairying			
SF241-245	636.21420711	Dairy schools	SF359-.7	798.45	Steeplechasing
SF241-245	636.2142071	Dairying—Study and teaching	SF359.7.G7	798.450942753	Grand National Handicap Steeplechase
SF247	636.21420284	Dairying—Equipment and supplies	SF360.6-361.75	636.1	Domestic asses
			SF361	636.182	Donkeys
SF247	637.1240284	Milking machines	SF361	636.182092	Donkey breeders
SF250	637.124	Milking	SF362	636.183	Mules
SF250.5-275	637.14	Dairy processing	SF371-379	636.3	Sheep
SF250.5-275	637	Dairy products	SF376.5	636.3	Lambs
SF251-262.5	636.2142	Milk	SF379	636.30833	Sheep-shearing
SF255	363.1929064	Dairy inspection	SF380-388	636.39	Goats
SF259	637.143	Dairy products—Drying	SF391-397.4	636.4	Swine
SF259	637.143	Dried milk	SF393.D9	636.483	Duroc Jersey swine
SF259	637.141	Milk—Pasteurization	SF401.A45	636.292	American bison
SF259	637.141	Milk—Sterilization	SF401.D3	636.29401	Deer farming
SF259	636.2142	Homogenized milk	SF401.E4	636.965701	Elk farming
SF261	636.21420681	Dairying—Accounting	SF401.G85	636.93592	Guinea pigs
SF261	636.21420688	Dairy products—Marketing	SF402-405	636.9701	Fur farming
SF263-269.5	637.2	Butter	SF403-405	636.97	Fur-bearing animals
SF270-274	637.3	Cheese	SF405.5-407	636.0885	Laboratory animals
SF272.P3	637.354	Parmesan cheese	SF405.M6	636.97662701	Mink farming
SF277-359.7	636.101	Foals	SF411-459	636.0887	Pets
SF277-359.7	636.1	Horses	SF411.5	636.0811	Pet shows

LC	Dewey	Subject Heading
SF414.2	636.0887	Pets—Housing
SF414.3	636.0887	Pet boarding facilities
SF421-440.2	636.7	Dogs
SF421-435	636.707	Puppies
SF423	636.70822	Dogs—Pedigrees
SF425-.8	636.70811	Dog shows
SF425.3	636.70811	Show dogs
SF425.7	636.70811	Dogs—Obedience trials
SF427.15	636.70837	Dog collars
SF427.46	636.7083	Dog walking
SF427.55	636.70833	Pet grooming salons
SF428	636.70831	Kennels
SF428.2	636.73	Working dogs
SF428.5	636.752	Bird dogs
SF428.55	636.70886	Rescue dogs
SF428.6	636.70886	Livestock protection dogs
SF428.7	636.70886	Sled dogs
SF428.73	636.70886	Search dogs
SF428.8	636.70886	Watchdogs
SF429.A4	636.7533	Afghan hounds
SF429.D25	636.7538	Dachshunds
SF429.D3	636.72	Dalmatian dog
SF429.D33	636.755	Dandie Dinmont terrier
SF429.D6	636.736	Doberman pinschers
SF429.E47	636.7524	English cocker spaniel
SF429.E7	636.7524	English springer spaniels
SF429.E8	636.73	Eskimo dogs
SF429.G75	636.73	Great Pyrenees
SF429.H6	636.753	Hounds
SF429.S39	636.7532	Scottish deerhound
SF429.S5	636.7526	Setters (Dogs)
SF431	636.70835	Dogs—Training
SF434.5-435	338.1767	Dog industry
SF439.5-440.2	798.8	Dog racing
SF440.15	798.83	Sled dog racing
SF441-450	636.8	Cats
SF443	636.80822	Cats—Pedigrees
SF449.A28	636.826	Abyssinian cat
SF449.P4	636.832	Persian cat
SF451-455	636.9322	Rabbits
SF455.D8	636.9322	Dutch rabbits
SF455.D85	636.9322	Dwarf rabbits
SF456-458.83	597.073	Aquariums
SF457.1	597.177073	Marine aquariums
SF459.H3	636.93560887	Dwarf hamsters as pets
SF461	636.68	Cage birds
SF461	636.6	Aviculture
SF481-513	636.5	Chickens
SF490-.8	636.5142	Eggs—Production
SF490-.8	636.5142	Eggs
SF492-493	636.5082	Poultry—Breeding
SF494	636.508(4-5)	Poultry—Feeding and feeds
SF495	636.5082	Eggs—Incubation
SF495-497	636.5082	Poultry—Hatcheries
SF502.8-503.52	636.63	Game fowl
SF504.7-505.63	636.597	Ducks
SF507	636.592	Turkeys
SF508-510	636.63082	Game bird culture
SF518	638	Insect rearing
SF521-539	638.1	Bee culture
SF521-539	638.12	Honeybee
SF539	638.16	Honey
SF539	638.16	Bee products
SF541-560	638.2	Sericulture
SF541-560	638.2	Silk
SF541-560	638.2	Silkworms
SF559.5-560	638.2	Silkworms, Non-mulberry
SF597.E3	639.75	Earthworm culture
SF600-1100	636.0896	Domestic animals—Diseases
SF600-1100	636.0893	Animal health
SF600-1100	636.0896	Animals—Diseases
SF600-1100	636.0896	Livestock—Diseases
SF600-1100	636.089	Veterinary medicine
SF600-604	636.08906	Veterinary medicine—Societies, etc.
SF604.4-.7	636.089	Veterinary hospitals
SF605	636.08906	Veterinary medicine—Congresses
SF610	636.089014	Veterinary medicine—Terminology
SF611	636.089025	Veterinarians—Directories
SF612-613	636.089092	Veterinarians
SF615-724	636.08909	Veterinary medicine—History
SF740	636.0894	Veterinary public health
SF740	636.089456	Animals as carriers of disease
SF740	636.0896959	Zoonoses
SF756.39	174.2	Veterinarians—Professional ethics
SF756.5	636.0821	Domestic animals—Genetic engineering
SF756.5	636.0821	Veterinary genetics
SF757.15	636.089448	Veterinary disinfection
SF761-767	636.0891	Veterinary anatomy
SF768-.2	636.0892	Veterinary physiology
SF769	636.08960759	Veterinary autopsy
SF771-774	636.0896075	Veterinary medicine—Diagnosis
SF774.5	636.089073	Veterinary nursing
SF756.3-.37	636.0890711	Veterinary colleges
SF778	636.0896025	Veterinary emergencies
SF778	636.0896028	Veterinary critical care
SF780.3	636.0896014	Veterinary bacteriology
SF780.4	636.08960194	Veterinary virology
SF780.9	636.08944	Veterinary epidemiology
SF781-809	636.08969	Communicable diseases in animals
SF787	636.0896956	Anthrax
SF799	636.089682	Meningitis
SF810	636.089696	Domestic animals—Parasites
SF810.H8	636.0896964	Echinococcosis
SF811	636.089612	Veterinary cardiology
SF851-855	636.089639	Nutrition disorders in animals
SF887	636.08982	Veterinary obstetrics
SF910.5	636.08967	Veterinary orthopedics
SF910.T8	636.0896992	Veterinary oncology
SF911-914.4	636.0897	Veterinary surgery
SF914	636.089796	Veterinary anesthesia

LC	Dewey	Subject Heading	LC	Dewey	Subject Heading
SF914.3	636.08960252	First aid for animals	SH285-286	639.20946	Fisheries—Spain
SF914.4	636.089715	Fractures in animals	SH287-288	639.209485	Fisheries—Sweden
SF914.5	636.0895892	Veterinary acupuncture	SH291-292	639.209561	Fisheries—Turkey
SF915-918	636.08951	Pharmacy	SH295-307	639.2095	Fisheries—Asia
SF916.5	636.08951	Veterinary prescriptions	SH297-298	639.20951	Fisheries—China
SF918.A5	636.0895329	Antibiotics in veterinary medicine	SH301-302	639.20952	Fisheries—Japan
			SH302.5-.7	639.209519	Fisheries—Korea
SF918.V32	636.0895372	Veterinary vaccines	SH317-318	639.20994	Fisheries—Australia
SF961-967	636.20886	Cattle—Diseases	SH318.5	639.20993	Fisheries—New Zealand
SF961-967	636.208969	Cattle—Infections	SH319	639.2099(5-6)	Fisheries—Oceania
SF962	636.208969	Blackleg in cattle	SH327.5	333.7	Fishery resources
SF967.E3	636.208969	East Coast fever	SH327.7	639.977	Fishery conservation
SF969.E	636.308969	Epizootic catarrh in sheep	SH328-329	639.2068	Fishery management
SF977.P5	636.408969	Swine plague	SH332-.2	639.2071	Fishery schools
SF991.D5	636.70896	Distemper	SH332-.2	639.2072	Fishery research stations
SF991-992	636.70896	Dogs—Diseases	SH334	338.3727	Fisheries subsidies
SF995-.4	636.50896	Poultry—Diseases	SH334.5-344.8	639.2028	Fishery technology
SF996.45	333.95416	Wildlife rehabilitation	SH334.9-336.5	664.94	Fishery processing
SH	639.2	Fisheries	SH335-337	664.94(1-8)	Fishery products—Preservation
SH1	639.305	Fisheries—Periodicals			
SH3	639.206	Fisheries—Congresses	SH335	363.1929064	Fish inspection
SH11	639.20973	Fisheries—United States	SH337.5	387.1	Fishing ports
SH20	639.2092	Fish culturists	SH343.4	338.372072	Fishery research vessels
SH20.5-191	639.8	Aquaculture	SH343.5	639.2072	Exploratory fishing
SH21	639.809	Aquaculture—History	SH343.8	623.89	Fisheries navigation
SH34-133	639.809(4-9)	Aquaculture—[By region or country]	SH343.9	639.20289	Fisheries—Safety measures
			SH344-.8	639.20284	Fisheries—Equipment and supplies
SH138	639.8	Mariculture			
SH151-179	639.3	Fish-culture	SH344.6.T67	639.20284	Fish traps
SH153	639.92	Fishways	SH344.8.H6	639.20284	Fishhooks
SH157.8-.85	639.92	Fish habitat improvement	SH344.8.N4	639.20284	Fishing nets
SH157.85.A7	639.92	Artificial reefs	SH351.E4	639.2743	Eel fisheries
SH171-179	639.964	Fishes—Pathogens	SH351.S3	639.2745	Sardine fisheries
SH171-179	639.96	Fish kills	SH360-363	639.29	Sealing
SH171-179	639.964	Fishes—Diseases	SH364	639.2	Sea otter
SH171-179	639.964	Fishes—Infections	SH365-380.92	639.4	Shellfish culture
SH175	639.96	Fishes—Parasites	SH365-367	639.409(4-9)	Shellfish culture—[By region or country]
SH177.R4	639.964	Red tide			
SH177.R4	615.954	Paralytic shellfish poisoning	SH371-374.52	639.42	Mussel fisheries
SH185	639.3789	Frog culture	SH371	639.41	Oyster fisheries
SH211	639.209	Fisheries—History	SH371.5-.52	639.4832	Abalone fisheries
SH213-.77	639.209163	Fisheries—Atlantic Ocean	SH371.5-.52	639.4832	Abalone culture
SH214-215	639.209164	Fisheries—Pacific Ocean	SH372.5-.52	639.42	Mussels
SH216-.55	639.209165	Fisheries—Indian Ocean	SH375-377	639.412	Pearl fisheries
SH221-222	639.20973	Fisheries—United States	SH377.5	639.412	Mother-of-pearl
SH223-229	639.20971	Fisheries—Canada	SH379.5	639.41	Oyster shell
SH231	639.20972	Fisheries—Mexico	SH380.4-.45	639.56	Crab culture
SH232	639.209728	Fisheries—Central America	SH381-385	639.28	Whaling
SH233	639.209729	Fisheries—West Indies	SH393	639.89	Seagrasses
SH234-251	639.2098	Fisheries—South America	SH399.C6	639.32	Coral fisheries
SH253-293	639.2094	Fisheries—Europe	SH399.T9	639.392	Turtle fisheries
SH255-260	639.20941	Fisheries—Great Britain	SH400-.8	639.22	Seafood gathering
SH261-262	639.209415	Fisheries—Ireland	SH400.4-.8	639.4	Shellfish gathering
SH267-268	639.209489	Fisheries—Denmark	SH401-691	799.12	Fishing
SH268.G83	639.209982	Fisheries—Greenland	SH401	799.1205	Fishing—Periodicals
SH273-274	639.209495	Fisheries—Greece	SH403	799.1206	Hunting and fishing clubs
SH275-276	639.209492	Fisheries—Netherlands	SH414-415	799.1092	Fishers
SH277-278	639.20945	Fisheries—Italy	SH421	799.109	Fishing—History
SH279-280	639.209481	Fisheries—Norway	SH447-453	799.10284	Fishing tackle
SH281-282	639.209469	Fisheries—Portugal	SH447-453	799.10284	Fishing—Equipment and supplies
SH283-284	639.20947	Fisheries—Russia			

LC	Dewey	Subject Heading	LC	Dewey	Subject Heading
SH448	799.10284	Bait	SK321	799.232	Falconry
SH451.3	799.10284	Fish decoys	SK323-325	799.246	Upland game bird shooting
SH452-.2	799.10284	Fishing rods	SK324	799.24609(4-9)	Upland game bird shooting—[By region or country]
SH452.9.H	799.10284	Fishhooks			
SH452.9.K6	799.1028	Fishing knots			
SH454-.9	799.124	Casting (Fishing)	SK325.P5	799.246	Pheasant shooting
SH454.2	799.124	Fly casting	SK331-335	799.244	Waterfowl
SH455.4	799.122	Bait fishing	SK333.D8	799.244	Duck shooting
SH455.6	799.122	Bottom fishing	SK335	799.2028	Decoys (Hunting)
SH456-.2	799.124	Fly fishing	SK341.H3	799.259328	Hare hunting
SH457-.5	799.16	Saltwater fishing	SK351-579	639.9	Wildlife management areas
SH457.5	799.12	Big game fishing	SK351-579	333.95816	Birds, Protection of
SH462	799.1097	Fishing—North America	SK352	639.906	Wildlife management—Congresses
SH463-565	799.10973	Fishing—United States			
SH571-572	799.10971	Fishing—Canada	SK354	639.9092	Wildlife managers
SH577-578	799.1209729	Fishing—West Indies	SK357	639.95	Game reserves
SH681	799.1758	Bass fishing	SK361-579	639.909(4-9)	Wildlife management areas—[By region or country]
SH684-686.7	799.1755	Salmon fishing			
SH687-688	799.1755	Trout fishing			
SH691.E4	799.1743	Eel fishing	SK361-465	639.909(4-9)	Wildlife management areas—United States
SK	799.2	Hunting			
SK1	799.206	Hunting—Societies, etc.	SK470-471	639.90971	Wildlife management areas—Canada
SK3	799.206	Hunting and fishing clubs			
SK7	799.205	Hunting—Periodicals	SK473	639.90972	Wildlife management areas—Mexico
SK12	799.292025	Hunters—Directories			
SK15-17	799.2092	Hunters	SK475	639.909728	Wildlife management areas—Central America
SK21	799.209	Hunting—History			
SK36	799.215	Bowhunting	SK477	639.909729	Wildlife management areas—West Indies
SK36.2	799.24	Game and game-birds, Dressing of	SK479-501	639.9098	Wildlife management areas—South America
SK36.7	799.2028	Poaching			
SK37-39.5	799.21	Shooting	SK503-543	639.9094	Wildlife management areas—Europe
SK39.3	799.213	Handgun hunting			
SK40-267	799.29(4-9)	Hunting—[By region or country]	SK505-511	639.90941	Wildlife management areas—Great Britain
SK40-157	799.297	Hunting—North America	SK553-567	639.9095	Wildlife management areas—Asia
SK41-145	799.2973	Hunting—United States			
SK43	799.2975	Hunting—Southern States	SK571-575	639.9096	Wildlife management areas—Africa
SK45	799.2978	Hunting—West (U.S.)			
SK47-145	799.297(4-9)	Hunting—[United States, By state]	SK577	639.90994	Wildlife management areas—Australia
SK251-255	799.296	Hunting—Africa	T	600	Technology
SK273-275	799.2028	Hunting—Equipment and supplies	T1-5	605	Technology—Periodicals
			T6	606	Technology—Congresses
SK274	799.20283	Hunting guns	T8	601.48	Technology—Abbreviations
SK274	799.20283	Sporting guns	T9-10	601.4	Technology—Terminology
SK274.2-.4	799.202832	Rifles	T9-10	603	Technology—Dictionaries
SK274.5	799.202834	Shotguns	T11-.3	601.4	Technology—Language
SK276	799.2074	Hunting—Museums	T11.8	602.2	Technical illustration
SK283-.6	799.2	Trapping	T11.9	026.6	Archives, Technical
SK283-.6	799.2597	Fur-bearing animals	T13	620.00284	Engineering—Supplies
SK284-287	799.259775	Fox hunting	T14	601	Technology—Philosophy
SK293	799.23	Ferreting	T14.5	303.483	Technology—Social aspects
SK295-305	799.26	Big game hunting	T14.7-33	609	Technology—History
SK301	799.2765	Deer hunting	T15-31	609	Inventions—History
SK303	799.27657	Elk hunting	T37	930.1	Industrial archaeology
SK305.A	799.2798	Alligator hunting	T39-40	609.2	Inventors
SK305.E3	799.2767	Elephant hunting	T50-51	530.8	Mensuration
SK311-335	799.24	Fowling	T54	363.11	Hazardous occupations
SK317	799.206	Shooting preserves	T55-.3	363.11	Industrial safety
SK319	799.258	Bird trapping	T55.3.H3	604.7	Hazardous substances

LC	Dewey	Subject Heading	LC	Dewey	Subject Heading
T55.4-60.8	670	Industrial engineering	TA30-31	620.009728	Engineering—Central America
T55.4-60.8	658	Management science	TA32-33	620.009729	Engineering—West Indies
T55.6	670.9	Industrial engineering—History	TA36-37	620.00982	Engineering—Argentina
T56	658.5	Production control	TA38-39	620.00984	Engineering—Bolivia
T56.3	670.92	Industrial engineers	TA41-42	620.00981	Engineering—Brazil
T57.35	670.21	Industrial engineering—Statistical methods	TA43-44	620.00983	Engineering—Chile
T57.72	658.544	Fatigue	TA45-46	620.009861	Engineering—Colombia
T57.74-.79	519.72	Linear programming	TA47	620.009866	Engineering—Ecuador
T57.8-.825	519.76	Nonlinear programming	TA48	620.009881	Engineering—Guyana
T57.85	658.4032	Network analysis (Planning)	TA49	620.009883	Engineering—Surinam
T57.9	658.4034	Queuing theory	TA50	620.009882	Engineering—French Guiana
T57.92	519.3	Game theory	TA51	620.009892	Engineering—Paraguay
T57.95	658.5036	Decision-making	TA52	620.00985	Engineering—Peru
T58.8	658.515	Industrial efficiency	TA53	620.009895	Engineering—Uruguay
T58.7-.8	338/670.42	Industrial capacity	TA54	620.00987	Engineering—Venezuela
T59-.2	658.562	Standardization	TA57-64	620.00941	Engineering—Great Britain
T59.5	670.427	Automation	TA65-.2	620.009436	Engineering—Austria
T60.4-.47	658.5421	Time study	TA65.3-.4	620.009437	Engineering—Czechoslovakia
T60.7	658.542	Motion study	TA65.5-66	620.009439	Engineering—Hungary
T61-173	607.1	Technical education	TA67-68	620.009493	Engineering—Belgium
T65	607.2	Research	TA69-70	620.009489	Engineering—Denmark
T71-170	607.10(4-9)	Technical education—[By region or country]	TA71-72.5	620.00944	Engineering—France
T174	601.12	Technological forecasting	TA73-74.5	620.00943	Engineering—Germany
T174.3	338.926	Technology transfer	TA75-76	620.009495	Engineering—Greece
T174.5	303.483	Technology assessment	TA77-78	620.009492	Engineering—Netherlands
T174.7	620.5	Nanotechnology	TA79-80	620.00945	Engineering—Italy
T175-178	607.2	Research, Industrial	TA81-82	620.009481	Engineering—Norway
T201-342	608	Patents	TA83-84.5	620.009469	Engineering—Portugal
T201-339	608	Inventions	TA85-86	620.00947	Engineering—Russia
T221-323.7	608.7	Patents—History	TA87-88	620.00946	Engineering—Spain
T324	608.0228	Models (Patents)	TA88.5	620.00948	Engineering—Scandinavia
T325	602.75	Trademarks	TA89-90	620.009485	Engineering—Sweden
T351-385	604.2	Mechanical drawing	TA91-92	620.009494	Engineering—Switzerland
T352	604.2068	Drawing-room management	TA95.A2	620.009496	Engineering—Balkan Peninsula
T352	604.24	Drawing-room practice	TA95.F5	620.0094897	Engineering—Finland
T355	604.2	Structural drawing	TA95.Y8	620.009497	Engineering—Yugoslavia
T359	604.2	Freehand technical sketching	TA101-102	620.00951	Engineering—China
T362-369	604.245	Projection	TA103-104	620.00954	Engineering—India
T369	604.245	Perspective	TA104.5-.6	620.0095491	Engineering—Pakistan
T375-377	604.20284	Drawing instruments	TA104.7-.8	620.0095493	Engineering—Sri Lanka
T379	604.25	Blueprints	TA105-106	620.00952	Engineering—Japan
T385	006.6	Computer graphics	TA107-108	620.00955	Engineering—Iran
T391-999	607.34	Exhibitions	TA109-110	620.00957	Engineering—Asiatic Russia
TA	620	Engineering	TA111-112	620.009561	Engineering—Turkey
TA1-4	620.005	Engineering—Periodicals	TA113.I55	620.009598	Engineering—Indonesia
TA5	620.006	Engineering—Congresses	TA113.I7	620.009567	Engineering—Iraq
TA9	620.003	Engineering—Dictionaries	TA113.I75	620.0095694	Engineering—Israel
TA11	620.00148	Engineering—Notation	TA113.P6	620.009599	Engineering—Philippines
TA12	620.0025	Engineering firms—Directories	TA115-119	620.0096	Engineering—Africa
TA15-19	620.009	Engineering—History	TA117-118	620.00962	Engineering—Egypt
TA21-127	620.009(4-9)	Engineering—[By region or country]	TA121-122	620.00994	Engineering—Australia
TA23-25	620.00973	Engineering—United States	TA122.5-.6	620.00993	Engineering—New Zealand
TA26-27	620.00971	Engineering—Canada	TA123-124	620.0099(5-6)	Engineering—Oceania
TA28-29	620.00972	Engineering—Mexico	TA125-.5	620.00998	Engineering—Arctic regions
			TA139-140	620.0092	Engineers—Biography
			TA157-158.3	620.0023	Engineers
			TA157	620.008996073	Afro-American engineers
			TA157	174.962	Engineering ethics

215

LC	Dewey	Subject Heading	LC	Dewey	Subject Heading
TA157	620.006	Engineering firms	TA439	620.136	Expansive concrete
TA160-.6	620.0072	Engineering—Research	TA439-446	620.136	Concrete
TA165	629.8	Automatic control	TA447	620.14	Drain-tiles
TA165	620.00284	Engineering instruments	TA450	620.144	Glass
TA167	621.3984	Man-machine systems	TA455.F5	620.143	Fire-clay
TA168	620.001171	Systems engineering	TA455.P5-.P55	620.1923	Plastics
TA174	620.0042	Engineering design	TA455.P58	620.192	Polymers
TA177	620.00228	Engineering models	TA459-492	620.160287	Metals—Testing
TA177.4-185	620.00681	Engineering economy	TA460	620.166	Metals—Fatigue
TA180-182	620.00212	Engineering—Specifications	TA473	620.176	Steel—Fatigue
TA180-181	620.00212	Specifications	TA472-473	620.17	Steel, Galvanized
TA191	620.0044	Engineering inspection	TA478	620.18	Nonmetallic steel
TA190-194	620.0068	Engineering—Management	TA479.3	620.18	Nonferrous metals
TA213-215	620.00284	Engineering—Equipment and supplies	TA479.S7	620.16	Steel, Stainless
TA216-217	620.006	Engineering firms	TA480.A6	620.186	Aluminum, Structural
TA329-348	620.00151	Engineering mathematics	TA480.A6	620.186	Aluminum alloys
TA337-338	620.00728	Engineering—Graphic methods	TA480.C7	620.182	Copper
			TA480.N6	620.188	Nickel
TA340	620.00727	Engineering—Statistical methods	TA480.S5	620.18923	Silver
			TA480.T5	620.185	Tin
			TA480.T54	620.18932	Titanium
TA347.D45	515.35	Differential equations	TA486	620.16	Corrosion resistant alloys
TA347.F5	620.00151535	Finite element method	TA492.G5	624.17723	Girders
TA350-359	620.1	Mechanics, Applied	TA492.S25	624.1779	Sandwich construction
TA354.5	620.1126	Penetration mechanics	TA501-625	526.9	Surveying
TA357-359	620.106	Fluid dynamics	TA515-531	526.9	Surveyors
TA357.5.C38	620.1064	Cavitation	TA535-538	526.9071	Surveying—Study and teaching
TA357.5.M43	620.10640287	Fluid dynamic measurements	TA562-581	526.90284	Surveying—Instruments
TA357.5.M59	620.1064	Mixing	TA579-581	526.90284	Measuring-tapes
TA357.5.M84	620.1064	Multiphase flow	TA579	526.90284	Surveyors' chains
TA357.5.U57	620.1064	Unsteady flow (Fluid dynamics)	TA583	526.33	Triangulation
			TA590	526.3	Topographical surveying
TA365-367	620.2	Acoustical engineering	TA592-593.9	526.982	Photographic surveying
TA368	620.00218	Standards, Engineering	TA593	526.982	Photogrammetry
TA401-492	620.11	Materials	TA597	526.63	Azimuth
TA401-492	620.110287	Testing	TA611	526.9	Surveys—Plotting
TA401-492	620.1(2-9)	Building materials	TA616	526.98	Topographical drawing
TA401	620.1105	Materials—Periodicals	TA625	526.9	Route surveying
TA402	620.1103	Materials—Dictionaries	TA630-901	624.1	Structural engineering
TA404.2	620.11072	Materials—Research	TA630	624.105	Structural engineering—Periodicals
TA405	620.112	Strength of materials			
TA409	620.1126	Fracture mechanics	TA638.2	624.1072	Structural engineering—Research
TA410-417.7	620.112	Strength of materials			
TA410	620.112	Buckling (Mechanics)	TA641	624.10285	Structural engineering—Computer programs
TA413-.5	620.11260287	Fatigue testing machines			
TA413-.5	620.11260287	Testing-machines	TA645-656.5	624.171	Structural analysis (Engineering)
TA416-417	620.0072	Engineering experiment stations	TA648.2	624.172	Dead loads (Mechanics)
TA416-417	620.0072	Engineering laboratories	TA652	620.11233	Plastic analysis (Engineering)
TA417.2-.55	620.1127	Non-destructive testing			
TA417.4	620.11274	Ultrasonic testing	TA654-656.5	624.176	Structural dynamics
TA417.6	620.11232	Deformations (Mechanics)	TA654.4	624.172	Snow loads
TA418.12	620.11295	Photoelasticity	TA654.6	624.1762	Earthquake engineering
TA418.22	620.11233	Materials—Creep	TA656.5	624.10289	Safety factor in engineering
TA418.42	620.1126	Hardness	TA658-.8	624.1771	Structural design
TA418.45	620.1126	Hard materials	TA658.44	624.1762	Earthquake resistant design
TA418.58	620.1121	Thermal stresses	TA660.F7-.F73	624.1773	Structural frames
TA418.74-.76	620.11223	Corrosion and anti-corrosives	TA660.S6	624.1772	Slabs
TA418.76	667.9	Protective coatings	TA660.S67	624.17723	Steel I-beams
TA419-424.6	620.12	Timber	TA660.T8	624.1773	Trusses

LC	Dewey	Subject Heading	LC	Dewey	Subject Heading
TA665	624.183412	Prestressed construction	TC1	621.205	Hydraulic engineering—Periodicals
TA668	624.18923	Plastics in building	TC9	621.203	Hydraulic engineering—Dictionaries
TA670-683.94	624.183	Masonry			
TA680-683.94	624.1834	Concrete construction	TC15-20	621.209	Hydraulic engineering—History
TA680-683.94	624.1833	Portland cement			
TA683-683.94	624.18341	Reinforced concrete construction	TC21-127	621.109(4-9)	Hydraulic engineering—[By region or country]
TA683.5.S4	624.1834	Shells, Concrete	TC139-140	621.2092	Hydraulic engineers—Biography
TA683.5.W34	624.1834	Concrete walls			
TA683.9-.94	624.183412	Prestressed concrete construction	TC147	621.20422	Tidal power
			TC147	621.20422	Ocean wave power
TA684-695	624.182	Building, Iron and steel	TC147	621.20422	Water-power
TA684-695	624.1821	Steel, Structural	TC157-.5	621.1071	Hydraulic engineering—Study and teaching
TA703-705.4	624.151	Engineering geology			
TA705.2-.4	624.15109(3-4)	Engineering geology—[By region or country]	TC158	621.2072	Hydraulic laboratories
			TC160-179	532	Hydraulics
TA710-711.5	624.15136	Soil mechanics	TC167	627.4	Flood dams and reservoirs
TA712	624.19	Underground construction	TC167	627.86	Reservoirs
TA715-772	624.152	Earthwork	TC171-179	532.5	Hydrodynamics
TA725	624.1520284	Earthmoving machinery	TC172	532.59	Wave makers
TA725	624.1520284	Scrapers (Earthmoving machinery)	TC172	532.59	Water waves
			TC173	532.52	Water jets
TA730-748	624.152	Excavation	TC173	532.52	Nozzles
TA740-747	624.152	Rock excavation	TC174	620.1064	Water hammer
TA745-747	621.952	Rock-drills	TC175-.2	532.54	Channels (Hydraulic engineering)
TA748	624.152	Blasting			
TA760-772	624.162	Embankments	TC175.2	551.353	Sediment transport
TA760-772	624.164	Retaining walls	TC177	532.510284	Flow meters
TA775-787	624.15	Foundations	TC187-188	627.73	Dredging
TA780-787	624.154	Piling (Civil engineering)	TC187	627.73	Dredging spoil
TA800-820	624.19	Tunneling	TC188	627.73	Dredges
TA1001-1280	629.04	Transportation engineering	TC193	627.75	Underwater drilling
TA1001-1004	629.0405	Transportation engineering—Periodicals	TC195-201	627.7	Underwater construction
			TC198	624.157	Coffer-dams
TA1015	629.0409	Transportation engineering—History	TC201	594.4	Shipworms
			TC203-327	387.1	Harbors
TA1021-1127	629.0409(3-9)	Transportation engineering—[By region or country]	TC328	627.38	Marinas
			TC330-340	627.24	Shore protection
			TC333	627.24	Breakwaters
TA1023-1025	629.040973	Transportation engineering—United States	TC335	627.24	Sea-walls
			TC337	627.24	Dikes (Engineering)
TA1163	629.04071	Transportation engineering—Study and teaching	TC337	627.24	Levees
			TC337	627.24	Embankments
TA1205-1207	388.4	Urban transportation	TC343-345	627.54	Reclamation of land
TA1225	388.47	Terminals (Transportation)	TC353-365	627.2	Harbors
TA1250	629.040289	Signal lights	TC355-365	627.31	Docks
TA1501-1820	621.36	Photonics	TC357	627.31	Piers
TA1570	621.362	Infrared technology	TC357	627.31	Warves
TA1570	621.362	Infrared sources	TC361	627.31	Dry docks
TA1637	621.367	Image processing	TC363	623.83	Floating harbors
TA1660	621.3693	Integrated optics	TC375-381	627.922	Lighthouses
TA1671-1715	621.366	Lasers	TC401-558	628.112	River engineering
TA1690	621.3664	Dye lasers	TC401-558	628.112	Rivers
TA1693	621.366	Free electron lasers	TC401-558	627	Water resources development
TA1695	621.3663	Gas lasers			
TA1705	621.366	Ruby lasers	TC415-527	628.109(4-9)	River engineering—[By region or country]
TA1750	623.7314	Electrooptical devices			
TA1770	621.3828	Acoustooptical devices	TC533	627.42	Embankments
TC	621.2	Hydraulic engineering	TC533	627.42	Levees
			TC540-558	627.8	Dams

LC	Dewey	Subject Heading
TC540-558	627.8	Flood dams and reservoirs
TC540	627.8	Dams—Design and construction
TC542.5	627.8	Dams—Earthquake effects
TC543	627.83	Earth dams
TC547	627.8	Arch dams
TC547	627.82	Concrete dams
TC553	627.882	Sluice gates
TC555	627.883	Spillways
TC601-791	623.89229	Inland navigation
TC601-791	627.13	Canals
TC601-791	627.1	Canals, Interoceanic
TC615-727	627.109(4-9)	Inland navigation—[By region or country]
TC759	627.133	Embankments
TC763	627.1353	Canals—Lifts
TC765	623.829	Canal-boats
TC769	623.89229	Canals—Steam-navigation
TC771-772	625.39	Ship-railroads
TC791	627.1370962	Suez Canal (Egypt)
TC801-957	333.736153	Desert reclamation
TC801-937	627.5	Reclamation of land
TC815-927	627.509(4-9)	Reclamation of land—[By region or country]
TC930-933	627.52	Irrigation canals and flumes
TC933	627.52	Flumes
TC970-978	627.5	Reclamation of land
TC970-978	627.54	Drainage
TC970	627.54	Ditches
TC975	627.54	Marshes
TC1501-1800	620.4162	Ocean engineering
TC1501	620.416205	Ocean engineering—Periodicals
TC1505	620.416206	Ocean engineering—Congresses
TC1662	623.8205	Remote submersibles
TC1800	627.7	Underwater pipelines
TD	628	Sanitary engineering
TD1-4	628.05	Sanitary engineering—Periodicals
TD12	628.025	Sanitary engineers—Directories
TD15-20	628.09	Sanitary engineering—History
TD21-127	628.09(4-9)	Sanitary engineering—[By region or country]
TD139-140	628.092	Sanitary engineers—Biography
TD159-168	628	Municipal engineering
TD169-171.8	628	Environmental protection
TD172-193.5	628.5	Pollution
TD178.5-.7	628.5072	Pollution—Research
TD179	628.509	Pollution—History
TD179.5-191	628.509(4-9)	Pollution—[By region or country]
TD180-181	628.50973	Pollution—United States
TD182-.4	628.50971	Pollution—Canada
TD182.6-.7	628.50972	Pollution—Mexico
TD185-.5	628.5098	Pollution—South America
TD186-.5	628.5094	Pollution—Europe
TD187-.5	628.5095	Pollution—Asia
TD188-.5	628.5096	Pollution—Africa
TD189.5.A8	628.5099(3-6)	Pollution—[New Zealand/ Australia/Oceania]
TD190-.5	628.50998	Pollution—Arctic regions
TD192	628.5028	Pollution control equipment
TD193-.5	577.14	Environmental chemistry
TD194.5-.58	363.7	Environmental impact statements
TD194.6	363.7	Environmental impact analysis
TD195.A34	577.273	Agricultural pollution
TD196.C45	628.16836	Chemical spills
TD201-500	628.1	Municipal water supply
TD201-500	628.1	Water-supply
TD215-220	628.109	Water-supply—History
TD221-327	628.109(4-9)	Water-supply—[By region or country]
TD365-.5	628.16	Water quality management
TD370-375	628.16	Water quality
TD388-.5	628.13	Water conservation
TD388-.5	628.13	Water conservation projects
TD395-397	628.132	Reservoirs
TD395	628.13	Dew-ponds
TD396	628.132	Reservoir sedimentation
TD398	628.15	Aqueducts
TD405-414	628.114	Wells
TD412	628.114	Boring
TD412	628.114	Percussion drilling
TD418	628.11	Rain-water (Water-supply)
TD419-428	628.168	Water—Pollution
TD426-.8	628.168	Groundwater—Pollution
TD427.D4	628.1682	Detergent pollution of rivers, lakes, etc.
TD427.O7	628.1682	Organic water pollutants
TD427.P4	628.16833	Oil pollution of water
TD427.R3	628.1685	Radioactive substances in rivers, lakes, etc.
TD427.R3	628.1685	Radioactive pollution of water
TD427.V55	628.168	Viral pollution of water
TD429	628.162	Water reuse
TD429.5-477	628.162	Water—Purification
TD434	628.162	Water treatment plants
TD441-449	628.164	Filters and filtration
TD458	628.165	Water—Aeration
TD478-480.7	628.167	Saline water conversion
TD479.6	628.16723	Nuclear saline water conversion plants
TD479.7	628.16725	Solar saline water conversion plants
TD480.4	628.16744	Saline water conversion—Reverse osmosis process
TD480.5	628.1674	Saline water conversion—Electrodialysis process
TD481-493	628.144	Water—Distribution
TD485-487	628.144	Pumping stations
TD489	628.13	Water towers
TD491	628.15	Water-pipes
TD491	628.15	Electrolytic corrosion
TD511-780	628.3	Sewerage
TD515-520	628.309	Sewerage—History

LC	Dewey	Subject Heading	LC	Dewey	Subject Heading
TD521-627	628.309(4-9)	Sewerage—[By region or country]	TD927	628.72	Water-supply, Rural
			TD929-930.4	628.742	Sewerage, Rural
TD657-.5	628.21	Urban runoff	TD929-930.4	628.744	Refuse and refuse disposal, Rural
TD665	628.212	Storm sewers			
TD678-688	628.2	Sewer design	TD929-930.4	628.742	Sewage disposal, Rural
TD682	628.2	Sewers, Concrete	TD929	628.742	Drainage, House
TD730-737	628.3	Sewage	TE	625.7	Highway engineering
TD741-780	628.36	Sewage disposal	TE	625.7	Roads
TD745-758.5	628.3	Sewage—Purification	TE1-4	625.705	Roads—Periodicals
TD746.5	628.351	Sewage lagoons	TE5	625.706	Roads—Congresses
TD760	628.3623	Sewage irrigation	TE15-19	625.709	Roads—History
TD769.7	628.364	Sewage sludge—Conditioning	TE21-127	625.709(4-9)	Roads—[By region or country]
TD770-.3	628.37	Sewage sludge—Incineration	TE175	625.725	Roads—Design and construction
TD778	628.742	Septic tanks	TE176.5	625.7	Traffic circles
TD785-812.5	628.44	Refuse and refuse disposal	TE177	625.77	Roadside improvement
TD788-.4	628.440973	Refuse collection—United States	TE178.8	625.77	Roadside rest areas
			TE180	625.70212	Roads—Specifications
TD789	628.4409(3-9)	Refuse collection—[Other countries]	TE191	625.7071	Roads—Study and teaching
			TE200-205	625.8	Road materials
TD793.3	628.44072	Refuse and refuse disposal—Research	TE206-209.5	625.7	Roads—Location
			TE208-.5	625.732	Soil surveys
TD793.95	628.44	Source reduction (Waste management)	TE209-.5	625.723	Roads—Surveying
			TE210-212	625.733	Roads—Foundations
TD794	628.442	Refuse collection	TE210.5.B5	625.85	Bitumen
TD794.5	628.4458	Recycling (Waste, etc.)	TE213	625.7342	Culverts
TD795-.7	628.44564	Sanitary landfills	TE215	625.734	Road drainage
TD796-.2	628.4457	Incineration	TE220-.63	625.76	Roads—Maintenance and repair
TD796.5	363.728	Compost			
TD800	628.16837	Petroleum waste	TE221	625.85	Bituminous materials
TD930.2	628.16846	Feedlot runoff	TE223-227	625.70284	Road machinery
TD812-.4	628.42	Radioactive waste disposal	TE223-227	625.70284	Road-rollers
TD813-870	628.44	Litter (Trash)	TE228	625.794	Electronic traffic controls
TD813-870	628.46	Street cleaning	TE229-.9	625.7091734	Rural roads
TD815-849	628.4609(3-9)	Street cleaning—[By region or country]	TE229.5	625.709152	Forest roads
			TE229.8	625.709143	Mountain roads
TD860	628.460284	Street cleaning—Equipment and supplies	TE230	625.74	Roads, Earth
			TE233	625.82	Roads, Gravel
TD868-870	625.763	Snow removal	TE243	625.86	Roads, Macadamized
TD878-880	363.7396	Soil pollution	TE245	625.83	Roads, Plank
TD878-880	628.5	Soil protection	TE250-278.8	625.8	Pavements
TD879.P37	628.55	Soils—Pesticide content	TE253	625.83	Pavements, Wooden
TD879.P4	628.55	Oil pollution of soils	TE255	625.82	Roads, Brick
TD881-890	628.53	Air—Pollution	TE266-276	625.85	Pavements, Asphalt
TD883	628.53	Air quality	TE278-.8	625.84	Pavements, Concrete
TD884	614.59	Smoke	TE278-.8	625.84	Roads, Concrete
TD884	628.532	Smoke prevention	TE279.3	625.889	Driveways
TD885	628.532	Flue gases	TE280-295	625.88	Sidewalks
TD885.5.G73	628.532	Greenhouse gases	TE298	625.888	Curbs
TD887.H3	628.532	Halocarbons	TE301	625.88	Bicycle trails
TD887.R3	628.535	Radioactive pollution of the atmosphere	TE303	625.88	Trails
			TE304	625.88	Trails
TD891-893.6	620.23	Noise pollution	TE305	796.72068	Racetracks (Automobile racing)
TD892	620.23	Noise barriers			
TD893.6.T7	620.23	Transportation noise	TF	625.1	Railroad engineering
TD895	628.51	Factory sanitation	TF	625.1	Railroads
TD896-899	628.51	Factory and trade waste	TF1-4	625.1005	Railroads—Periodicals
TD899.M5	628.42	Acid mine drainage	TF5	625.1006	Railroads—Congresses
TD899.P4	628.16836	Petroleum waste	TF6	625.10074	Railroad museums
TD920-931	628.7	Sanitation, Rural	TF12	625.10025	Railroads—Directories

LC	Dewey	Subject Heading	LC	Dewey	Subject Heading
TF15-20	625.1009	Railroads—History	TF920-952	625.2	Electric railroads—Cars
TF16	625.1	Horse railroads	TF920-952	621.330284	Electric railroads—Equipment and supplies
TF21-127	625.1009(4-9)	Railroads—[By region or country]	TF930	621.33	Electric controllers
TF139-140	625.10092	Railroad engineers	TF935	621.33	Electric railway motors
TF171-183	625.10072	Railroads—Research	TF949.B7	625.25	Electric railroads—Brakes
TF193	625.11299	Railroads—Design and construction—Costs	TF970	385.24	Electric railroads—Freight
TF195	625.100212	Railroads—Specifications	TF975	625.263	Electric locomotives
TF197	625.19	Railroads—Models	TF980	625.263	Electro-diesel locomotive
TF200-320	625.1	Railroads—Design and construction	TF1021-1127	621.3309(4-9)	Electric railroads—[By region or country]
TF205	625.10021	Railroad engineering—Tables	TF1600	625.4	Magnetic levitation vehicles
TF210-217	625.11	Railroads—Surveying	TG	624.2	Bridges
TF220-226	625.12	Railroads—Earthwork	TG1-4	624.205	Bridges—Periodicals
TF240-268	385.312	Railroads—Track	TG5	624.206	Bridges—Congresses
TF258-262	625.15	Railroads—Rails	TG15-20	624.209	Bridges—History
TF262	625.15	Railroads—Continuous rails	TG21-127	624.209(3-9)	Bridges—[By region or country]
TF263	625.163	Railroads—Crossings	TG260-270	624.25	Structural analysis (Engineering)
TF300-308	625.18	Railroad terminals	TG260	624.257	Structural frames
TF340-499	625.100284	Railroads—Equipment and supplies	TG265-267	624.252	Strains and stresses
TF371-499	625.2	Railroads—Cars	TG265-267	624.25	Moments of inertia
TF413	625.21	Draft-gear	TG265	624.252	Flexure
TF420-430	625.25	Air-brakes	TG265	624.252	Buckling (Mechanics)
TF455-461	625.23	Railroads—Passenger-cars	TG300-304	624.25	Bridges—Design and construction
TF457	625.23	Pullman cars	TG304	624.252	Snow loads
TF459	625.23	Sleeping-cars (Railroads)	TG313	624.250299	Bridges—Design and construction—Estimates
TF470-481	625.24	Railroads—Freight-cars	TG315	624.20288	Bridges—Maintenance and repair
TF477	625.24	Refrigerator cars			
TF485	625.22	Cabooses (Railroads)	TG320	624.284	Bridges—Foundations and piers
TF530-548	625.100288	Railroads—Maintenance and repair	TG325	624.28	Bridges—Abutments
TF542	625.100288	Railroads—Snow-plows	TG325	624.284	Retaining walls
TF542	625.22	Snow removal	TG325.6	624.283	Bridges—Floors
TF590-593	625.18	Railroads—Yards	TG327-340	624.6	Bridges, Arched
TF592	625.163	Railroads—Switching	TG330	624.63	Bridges, Brick
TF610	625.100289	Railroads—Safety measures	TG330	624.63	Bridges, Stone
TF615-640	625.165	Railroads—Signaling	TG335-340	624.63	Bridges, Concrete
TF653	385.22	Railroads—Passenger traffic	TG350-362	624.37	Girders
TF656	625.23	Railroads—Baggage handling	TG355	624.33	Girders, Continuous
TF662-667	625.24	Railroads—Freight	TG365-370	624.32	Trestles
TF670-1124	385.5/625.(4-6)	Railroads, Local and light	TG365	624.32	Bridges, Wooden
TF675	385.52	Railroads, Narrow-gage	TG375-380	624.38	Bridges, Truss
TF677	385.54	Railroads, Industrial	TG375	624.38	Bridges, Wooden
TF694	625.103	Monorail railroads	TG385	624.35	Bridges, Cantilever
TF701-1124	625.66	Street-railroads	TG400	624.5	Suspension bridges
TF830	625.66	Horse railroads	TG413-416	624.33	Bridges, Continuous
TF835	625.5	Railroads, Cable	TG420	624.8	Drawbridges
TF840-841	625.44	Railroads, Elevated	TG450	624.87	Pontoon bridges
TF845-851	625.42	Subways	TH	690	Building
TF857	625.19	Electric railroads, Miniature	TH1-4	690.05	Building—Periodicals
TF858-859	621.33	Railroads—Electrification	TH5	690.06	Building—Congresses
TF863-952	621.33	Electric railroads—Design and construction	TH12-13	690.025	Building—Directories
			TH15-19	690.09	Building—History
TF872	625.15	Electric railroads—Rails	TH21-127	690.09(3-9)	Building—[By region or country]
TF880-900	621.33	Electric railroads—Wires and wiring			
TF890	625.15	Electric railroads—Third rail	TH23-25	690.0973	Building—United States

LC	Dewey	Subject Heading	LC	Dewey	Subject Heading
TH165-213	690.071	Building—Study and teaching	TH3401-3411	690.24	Buildings—Remodeling for other use
TH425	692.3	Buildings—Specifications	TH3401-3411	690.24	Buildings—Repair and reconstruction
TH434-437	692.5	Building—Estimates	TH4224	690.61	Pagodas—Design and construction
TH443	690.22	Building—Accidents			
TH845-895	690.21	Strains and stresses	TH4311-4315	690.52	Commercial buildings—Design and construction
TH895	690.21	Snow loads	TH4451-4499	690.535	Warehouses—Design and construction
TH900-915	690.0284	Construction equipment			
TH915	690.0284	Building—Equipment and supplies	TH4461	690.53	Granaries—Design and construction
TH1061-1093	693.82	Building, Fireproof	TH4511-4591	690.54	Factories
TH1061-1093	693.82	Fireproofing	TH4511-4591	690.54	Factories—Design and construction
TH1065	693.82	Fire resistant materials			
TH1077-1083	693.3	Tile construction	TH4532	690.54	Distilleries
TH1095	693.852	Buildings—Earthquake effects	TH4541	690.54	Drug factories
TH1097	693.854	Building, Bombproof	TH4581-4591	690.54	Power-plants
TH1097	690.5	Air raid shelters	TH4805-4890	690.8	House construction
TH1098	729.2	Modular construction	TH4805-4890	690.8	Dwellings
TH1098	693.97	Buildings, Prefabricated	TH4816.2	690.24	Buildings—Additions
TH1199-1301	693.1	Masonry	TH4818.A3	690.8370473	Earth houses
TH1201	693.1	Building, Stone	TH4819.E27	690.8370473	Earth sheltered houses
TH1301	693.21	Building, Brick	TH4819.P7	643.2	Prefabricated houses
TH1421	690.8370473	Earth construction	TH4835	690.872	Vacation homes
TH1431	693.91	Building, Ice and snow	TH4840	690.873	Log cabins
TH1461-1501	693.5	Concrete construction	TH4911-4935	690.892	Farm buildings
TH1501	693.54	Reinforced concrete construction	TH4920	690.86	Farmhouses
TH1560	693.96	Glass construction	TH4930	690.8922	Dairy barns
TH1610-1635	693.71	Building, Iron and steel	TH4935	690.892	Silos
TH1715-1718	621.4024	Insulation (Heat)	TH4970	690.893	Decks (Architecture, Domestic)
TH1725	693.834	Factories—Soundproofing			
TH1725	693.834	Soundproofing	TH5101	624.152	Excavation
TH2025-3000	690.1	Building—Details	TH5201	690.11	Foundations
TH2060	690.1	Buildings—Joints	TH5281	624.152	Shoring and underpinning
TH2101	690.11	Foundations	TH5311-5701	693.1	Masonry
TH2170-.7	690.146	Domes	TH5401-5440	693.1	Stonemasonry
TH2180	690.15	Towers	TH5601-5695	694	Carpentry
TH2201-2251.5	690.12	Walls	TH5611	694.1	Carpentry drafting
TH2235-2238.7	690.12	Exterior walls	TH5618	694.0284	Miter-gages
TH2245	690.12	Concrete walls	TH5640-5695	694.6	Finish carpentry
TH2249	690.12	Stone walls	TH5662-5663	694.6	Joinery
TH2252-2253	690.13	Columns	TH5667-5680	690.1832	Staircases
TH2261-2276	690.1823	Windows	TH6010-6013	696-697	Building fittings
TH2274	628.922	Fire-escapes	TH6014-7696	648	Sanitation, Household
TH2276	690.182	Blinds	TH6014-6085	697	Buildings—Environmental engineering
TH2278	690.1822	Fire doors			
TH2278	690.1822	Screen doors	TH6025	648	Electronics in sanitary engineering
TH2278	690.1822	Doors			
TH2279	690.1822	Door fittings	TH6057.T23	690	Tall buildings
TH2279	683.32	Locks and keys	TH6101-6729	696.1	Plumbing
TH2281-2288	697.8	Flues	TH6485-6500	696.182	Bathrooms
TH2281-2288	690.15	Chimneys	TH6492	696.182	Showers (Plumbing fixtures)
TH2301-2311	694.2	Framing (Building)	TH6493	696.182	Bathtubs
TH2391-2495	690.15	Roofs	TH6498	696.182	Toilets
TH2409	690.15	Flat roofs	TH6551-6568	696.6	Hot-water supply
TH2416-2417	690.15	Roofs, Shell	TH6561	696.6	Water heaters, Gas
TH2431-2459	690.15	Roofing	TH6571-6675	696.13	Drainage, House
TH2521-2529	690.16	Flooring	TH6681-6685	696.10288	Plumbing—Repairing
TH2531-2533	690.17	Ceilings	TH6703-6729	696.2	Pipe fitting
TH3351-3361	690.24	Buildings—Maintenance	TH6880	696.2	Gas-burners

LC	Dewey	Subject Heading	LC	Dewey	Subject Heading
TH6840	696.2	Gas-fitting	TJ	621	Mechanical engineering
TH7005-7699	697	Heating	TJ	621.8	Machinery
TH7140	697.07	Fluidized-bed furnaces	TJ	621.4	Motors
TH7400	697.07	Furnaces	TJ1-4	621.05	Mechanical engineering—Periodicals
TH7413-7414	697.78	Solar heating			
TH7414	697.78	Solar houses	TJ5	621.06	Mechanical engineering—Congresses
TH7421-7434.7	697.1	Fireplaces			
TH7435-7458	697.22	Stoves	TJ11-13	621.025	Mechanical engineers—Directories
TH7437-7441	697.22	Stoves, Wood			
TH7443-7446	697.22	Stoves, Coal	TJ14	621.01	Mechanical engineering—Philosophy
TH7450.5	697.24	Kerosene heaters			
TH7453-7457	697.043	Gas—Heating and cooking	TJ15-20	621.09	Mechanical engineering—History
TH7454-7457	697.043	Stoves, Gas			
TH7461	697.03	Heating plants	TJ21-127	621.09(4-9)	Mechanical engineering—[By region or country]
TH7466.06	697.044	Oil burners			
TH7480-7495	697.507	Radiators	TJ139-140	621.092	Mechanical engineers—Biography
TH7511-7549	697.4	Hot-water heating			
TH7538	697.07	Boilers	TJ148	621.80287	Machinery—Testing
TH7561-7599	697.5	Steam-heating	TJ158-159	621.071	Mechanical engineering—Study and teaching
TH7570-7578	697.5	Steam-heating, Low pressure			
			TJ163.6-.95	621	Power (Mechanics)
TH7588	697.507	Boilers	TJ164	621.3121	Power-plants
TH7601-7635	697.3	Hot-air heating	TJ177	621.81	Machinery—Vibration
TH7638	697.3	Heat pumps	TJ181-210	621.81	Mechanical movements
TH7647-7699	697.92	Ventilation	TJ181.5	621.837	Wheels
TH7684.F2-.F3	697.9354	Factories—Air conditioning	TJ184-204	621.833	Gearing
TH7687-7688	697.93	Air conditioning	TJ192	621.8333	Gearing, Spiral
TH7688.H6	697.938	Dwellings—Air conditioning	TJ193-196	621.8332	Gearing, Bevel
TH7700-7975	621.32	Lighting	TJ200	621.8333	Gearing, Worm
TH7703	729.28	Lighting, Architectural and decorative	TJ210	621.824	Springs (Mechanism)
			TJ210.2-211.49	629.892	Robots
TH7910-7970	621.324	Gas-lighting	TJ210.2-211.49	629.892	Robotics
TH7960-7967	621.3240284	Gas-fixtures	TJ212.2-225	629.8	Automatic machinery
TH8135-8139	693.6	Plaster	TJ216	629.83	Feedback control systems
TH8251-8275	698.5	Glazing	TJ217.5	629.89	Intelligent control systems
TH8441	698.6	Paperhanging	TJ227-240	621.815	Machine design
TH8461-8463	676.2848	Wallpaper	TJ250-255	621.4	Engines
TH9031	693.892	Dampness in buildings	TJ254.7	621.43	Combustion chambers
TH9031	693.892	Waterproofing	TJ255-265	621.4025	Heat-engines
TH9057-9092	693.898	Lightning protection	TJ262	621.4025	Heat pumps
TH9057-9092	693.898	Lightning-conductors	TJ265	621.4021	Thermodynamics
TH9111-9599	693.82	Fire prevention	TJ266-267.5	621.406	Turbines
TH9111-9599	628.925	Fire extinction	TJ266-267.5	621.406	Turbomachines
TH9120	628.922072	Fire prevention—Research	TJ268-748	621.1	Steam engineering
TH9128	363.37092	Fire fighters—Physical training	TJ268-280.7	621.1	Steam
			TJ281-393	621.183	Steam-boilers
TH9271-9275	628.9225	Fire alarms	TJ290-291	621.194	Boiler-plates
TH9271	628.9225	Fire detectors	TJ320-358	621.183	Furnaces
TH9311-9334	628.9252	Fire extinction—Water-supply	TJ350-357	621.1830289	Steam-boilers—Safety appliances
TH9332-9334	628.9252	Water towers			
TH9336	628.9252	Fire sprinklers	TJ370-372	621.185	Pressure gages
TH9338	628.9254	Fire extinction—Chemical systems	TJ395-444	621.312132	Steam power plants
			TJ415-444	621.185	Steam-pipes
TH9362	628.9254	Fire extinguishers	TJ427	621.185	Steam-pipe coverings
TH9365	628.9252	Hydrants	TJ461-740	621.1	Steam-engines
TH9371-9377	628.9259	Fire engines	TJ533	621.84	Pistons
TH9391	628.9259	Fireboats	TJ603-695	625.26	Locomotives
TH9448-9449	628.92	Fires	TJ619-.7	625.266	Diesel locomotives
TH9701-9745	643.16	Burglary protection	TJ735-740	621.165	Steam-turbines
TH9735	683.32	Locks and keys	TJ751-805	621.43	Internal combustion engines
TH9739	643.16	Burglar alarms	TJ778	621.433	Gas-turbines

LC	Dewey	Subject Heading	LC	Dewey	Subject Heading
TJ779	621.4335	Free piston engines	TJ1376	621.8676	Escalators
TJ787	621.437	Carburetors	TJ1385-1418	621.867	Conveying machinery
TJ807-830	621.042	Renewable energy sources	TJ1435	621.2	Hydraulic jacks
TJ809-812.8	621.47	Solar energy	TJ1465	621.98	Pneumatic presses
TJ811-.5	621.47072	Solar energy—Research	TJ1480-1496	631.3	Agricultural machinery
TJ812	621.472	Solar collectors	TJ1501-1519	646.2044	Sewing machines
TJ812.5	621.473	Solar engines	TJ1560	629.82	Vending machines
TJ820-828	621.45	Wind power	TJ1570	688.752	Slot machines
TJ823-828	621.453	Windmills	TK	621.3	Electric engineering
TJ836-935	621.2	Hydraulic machinery	TK1-4	621.305	Electric engineering—Periodicals
TJ840-890	621.21	Water-power			
TJ843	621.20424	Oil hydraulic machinery	TK5	621.306	Electric engineering—Congresses
TJ844	621.20424	Hydraulic fluids			
TJ855-857	621.2	Hydraulic motors	TK6	621.3074	Electric engineering—Museums
TJ859	621.21	Water mills			
TJ860-880	621.21	Water-wheels	TK9	621.303	Electric engineering—Dictionaries
TJ898.5	388.57	Coal slurry pipelines			
TJ899-927	621.69	Pumping machinery	TK12	621.3025	Electric engineering—Directories
TJ901	621.6	Ejector pumps			
TJ915	621.65	Reciprocating pumps	TK15-18	621.309	Electric engineering—History
TJ917	621.66	Rotary pumps			
TJ930-934	621.8672	Pipelines	TK21-127	621.309(4-9)	Electric engineering—[By region or country]
TJ940-.5	621.55	Vacuum technology			
TJ940.5	621.55	Vacuum pumps	TK139-140	621.31924092	Electricians
TJ950-1030	621.51	Pneumatic machinery	TK153	621.31	Electric power factor
TJ981-1009	621.51	Compressed air	TK165-213	621.3071	Electric engineering—Study and teaching
TJ990-992	621.51	Air-compressors			
TJ990-992	621.51	Compressors	TK275-399	621.37	Electric measurements
TJ1005-1007	621.904	Pneumatic tools	TK301-399	621.373	Electric meters
TJ1045-1119	621.85	Power transmission	TK321	621.3743	Voltmeter
TJ1061-1073.7	621.822	Bearings (Machinery)	TK331	621.3744	Voltameter
TJ1071	621.822	Roller bearings	TK393	621.373	Recording instruments
TJ1073.R8	621.822	Rubber bearings	TK401	621.37	Electric testing
TJ1075-1081	621.89	Lubrication and lubricants	TK431	621.30221	Electric drafting
TJ1081	621.890284	Oil filters	TK454.2	621.3192	Electric networks, Active
TJ1100-1119	621.852	Belts and belting	TK454.2	621.3192	Electric network topology
TJ1103	621.85	Pulleys	TK454.2	621.3192	Electric networks, Passive
TJ1165	670.420151	Shop mathematics	TK1001-1841	621.3121	Electric power production
TJ1180-1313	621.902	Machine-tools	TK1001-1841	621.31	Electric power
TJ1180-1313	621.9	Tools	TK1041-1078	621.3121	Cogeneration of electric power and heat
TJ1201.H3	621.973	Hammers			
TJ1205-1210	621.91	Planing-machines	TK1078	621.483	Nuclear power plants
TJ1218-1222	621.942	Lathes	TK1081-1083	621.312134	Hydroelectric power plants
TJ1225-1227	621.91	Milling-machines	TK1081	621.312134	Tidal power-plants
TJ1230-1240	621.93	Cutting machines	TK1085-1087	621.31244	Solar power plants
TJ1233-1255	621.93	Saws	TK1141-1168	621.31913	Electric currents, Alternating
TJ1233	621.93	Hacksaws	TK1191-1841	621.3121	Electric power-plants
TJ1260-1270	621.952	Drilling and boring	TK1545	621.31244	Solar power plants
TJ1260	621.952	Drill presses	TK1751	621.3126	Electric substations
TJ1280-1298	621.92	Grinding and polishing	TK1831	621.31210287	Electric power-plants—Testing
TJ1290	621.923	Emery-wheels			
TJ1320-1340	621.88	Fasteners	TK2000-2891	621.31042	Electric machinery
TJ1330-1333	621.882	Bolts and nuts	TK2271	621.31042	Eddy currents (Electric)
TJ1335	621.984	Taps and dies	TK2411-2491	621.313	Electric generators
TJ1338-1340	621.882	Screws	TK2435	621.46	Electric motors—Design and construction
TJ1345	621.914	Crushing machinery			
TJ1350-1383	621.862	Hoisting machinery	TK2441	621.3132	Gramme dynamos
TJ1363-1365	621.87	Cranes, derricks, etc.	TK2477	621.316	Armatures
TJ1363-1365	621.873	Electric cranes	TK2484	621.316	Brushes, Carbon
TJ1365	621.873	Gantry cranes	TK2511-2541	621.46	Electric motors
TJ1370-1380	621.877	Elevators	TK2551	621.314	Electric transformers

LC	Dewey	Subject Heading	LC	Dewey	Subject Heading
TK2611-2699	621.3132	Electric machinery—Direct current	TK4383	621.3275	Neon lamps
TK2681	621.46	Electric motors	TK4386	621.3273	Fluorescent lamps
TK2699	621.3815322	Electric inverters	TK4399.S6	621.3229	Electric signs
TK2711-2799	621.3133	Electric machinery—Alternating current	TK4601-4661	621.402	Electric heating
			TK4601	621.4028	Induction heating
TK2781-2789	621.46	Electric motors, Alternating current	TK4601	621.4028	Microwave heating
			TK4660	671.521	Electroslag welding
TK2781-2789	621.46	Electric motors	TK4660	671.521	Electric welding
TK2796	621.313	Electric current converters	TK5101-5105.9	621.382	Telecommunication
TK2796	621.313	Rotary converters	TK5101	621.38224	Random noise theory
TK7872.R35	621.3137	Electric current rectifiers	TK5103.59	621.3827	Optical communications
TK2821-2846	621.317	Electric switchgear	TK5103.7-.8	621.382	Digital communications
TK2842	621.317	Electric circuit-breakers	TK5104-.2	621.3825	Artificial satellites in telecommunication
TK2851	629.8043	Electric controllers	TK5105-.42	621.38216	Data transmission systems
TK2851	621.317	Electric rheostats	TK5105	621.38216	Packet switching (Data transmission)
TK2861	621.317	Electric contactors			
TK2861	621.317	Differential relays	TK5105.5-.9	004.6	Computer networks
TK2896-2986	621.31242	Electric batteries	TK5105.7-.85	004.68	Local area networks (Computer networks)
TK2896	621.3124	Direct energy conversion			
TK2931	621.312429	Fuel cells	TK5105.87-.888	004.67	Wide area networks (Computer networks)
TK2941	621.31242	Storage batteries			
TK2960	621.31244	Solar cells	TK5105.875.I57	004.678	Internet (Computer network)
TK3001-3521	621.3192	Electric circuits	TK5105.9	005.3	Communications software
TK3001-3521	621.319	Electric power distribution	TK5105-5865	621.383	Telegraph
TK3001-3521	621.319	Electric power transmission	TK5107	621.38305	Telegraph—Periodicals
TK3001-3511	621.31	Electric power	TK5301-5481	384.15	Telegraph lines
TK3091	621.319	Electric power failures	TK5601-5681	384.1	Cables, Submarine
TK3111	621.31912	Electric power distribution—Direct current	TK5700-5865	621.3842	Telegraph, Wireless
			TK5811-5865	621.3842	Telegraph, Wireless—Marconi system
TK3141-3171	621.31913	Electric power transmission—Alternating current			
			TK5981-5990	621.3828	Electro-acoustics
			TK5984	621.38234	Magnetic tapes
TK3141-3171	621.31913	Electric power distribution—Alternating current	TK5986	621.38284	Electrostatic microphone
			TK6001-6571.5	621.385	Telephone
TK3144	621.31913	Electric power distribution—High tension	TK6001	621.38505	Telephone—Periodicals
			TK6011	621.385025	Telephone—Directories
TK3201-3261	621.3192	Electric lines	TK6201-6285	621.38784	Telephone lines
TK3201-3285	621.31933	Electric wiring	TK6381-6383	621.38784	Telephone wire
TK3226	621.3192	Electric networks	TK6381-6383	621.38784	Telephone cables
TK3226	621.31921	Transients (Electricity)	TK6391-6397	621.385	Telephone switchboards
TK3242-3243	621.3192	Electric lines—Poles and towers	TK6397	621.3857	Telephone switching systems, Electronic
TK3251-3261	621.31923	Underground electric lines	TK6401-6505	621.387	Telephone systems
TK3271-3285	621.31933	Electric wiring, Interior	TK6540-6571.5	621.384(1-5)	Radio
TK3301-3351	537.62	Electric conductors	TK6540	621.38405	Radio—Periodicals
TK3301-3351	621.31934	Electric cables	TK6553	621.38411	Radio—Interference
TK3301-3351	621.31933	Electric wire	TK6553	621.384 (1-5)0288	Radio—Repairing
TK4001-9971	621.31	Electric power			
TK4058-4059	629.2293	Electric driving	TK6560-6565	621.384 (1-5)0284	Radio—Equipment and supplies
TK4125-4399	621.32	Electric lighting			
TK4134-4156	621.3209(4-9)	Electric lighting—[By region or country]	TK6561-6562	621.384131	Radio—Transmitters and transmission
TK4188	621.3229	Exterior lighting	TK6563-6564	621.38418	Radio—Receivers and reception
TK4198	621.320284	Electric light fixtures			
TK4311-4335	621.325	Electric lighting, Arc	TK6565.A55	621.38412	Amplifiers (Electronics)
TK4321-4335	621.325	Electric lamps, Arc	TK6565.A6	621.384135	Radio—Antennas
TK4341-4367	621.326	Electric lighting, Incandescent	TK6565.07	621.38412	Oscillators, Electric
			TK6565.R426	621.384133	Electric resistors
TK4351-4367	621.326	Incandescent lamps	TK6565.V3	621.384132	Vacuum-tubes
TK4383	621.3275	Neon tubes	TK6570.C5	621.38454	Citizens band radio

LC	Dewey	Subject Heading	LC	Dewey	Subject Heading
TK6573-6595	621.3848	Radar	TK7876	621.3813	Microwave devices
TK6587	621.38483	Radar transmitters	TK7876	621.38131	Microwave transmission lines
TK6592.D6	621.3848	Doppler radar			
TK6592.M67	621.3848	Moving target indicator radar	TK7878-7879.4	621.3810287	Electronic measurements
TK6630-6720	621.388	Television	TK7878.7	621.3815483	Cathode ray oscilloscope
TK6630.A1	621.388005	Television—Periodicals	TK7881.6	621.38932	Magnetic recorders and recording
TK6650-6655	621.38800284	Television—Equipment and supplies	TK7881.65	621.3883	Digital audiotape recorders and recording
TK6655.V5	621.38833	Video cassette recorders			
TK6655.V5	621.38833	Videocassette recorders	TK7882.C56	621.3976	Compact discs
TK6670	621.38804	Color television	TK7882.E2	621.38928	Electronic surveillance
TK6676	621.38835	Television, Master antenna	TK7882.S65	621.399	Speech synthesis
TK6680	384.556	Closed-circuit television	TK7885-7895	621.39	Computer engineering
TK6685	384.558	Videodisc players	TK7885-7895	621.39	Computers
TK6687	006.7	Interactive video	TK7887	621.390288	Computers—Maintenance and repair
TK6710-7620	621.38235	Facsimile transmission			
TK7018-7301	643.6	Household appliances, Electric	TK7887.5	621.398	Computer interfaces
			TK7887.55	621.3976	Data tape drives
TK7241	621.38928	Electric alarms	TK7887.6	621.39814	Analog-to-digital converters
TK7800-8360	621.381	Electronics	TK7887.8.M63	621.39814	Modems
TK7800	621.38105	Electronics—Periodicals	TK7887.8.T4	621.3985	Computer terminals
TK7801	621.38106	Electronics—Congresses	TK7888	621.3919	Electronic analog computers
TK7825	621.3810728	Electronics—Graphic methods	TK7888.3-.4	621.39	Electronic digital computers
TK7855	621.381072	Electronics—Research	TK7888.4	621.395	Electronic digital computers—Circuits
TK7866	621.3810221	Electronic drafting			
TK7866	621.3810223	Electronics—Charts, diagrams, etc.	TK7888.4	621.395	Logic circuits
			TK7895.M4	621.397	Cache memory
TK7867-7868	621.3815	Electronic circuits	TK7895.M4	621.39767	Optical storage devices
TK7868.I58	621.3981	Interface circuits	TK7895.M4	621.3973	Random access memory
TK7868.P7	621.381531	Printed circuits	TK7895.M4	621.3973	Read-only memory
TK7868.S9	621.381537	Switching circuits	TK7895.M4	621.39732	Semiconductor storage devices
TK7869-7872	621.3810284	Electronic apparatus and appliances			
			TK8300-8360	621.381542	Photoelectric cells
TK7870	621.3810284	Electronic instruments	TK8314	621.381542	Photoelectric multipliers
TK7870	621.381	Electronic systems	TK9001-9401	621.48	Nuclear engineering
TK7870	621.3810228	Miniature electronic equipment	TK9001-9401	621.48	Nuclear energy
			TK9001	621.4805	Nuclear engineering—Periodicals
TK7871.2-.58	621.381535	Transistor amplifiers			
TK7871.2-.58	621.381535	Amplifiers (Electronics)	TK9151.6-.7	621.4835	Remote handling (Radioactive substances)
TK7871.7-.84	621.38151	Electron Tubes			
TK7871.75	621.381334	Magnetrons	TK9152-.16	621.480289	Radiation—Safety measures
TK7871.8-.84	621.381513	Gas tubes	TK9152-.16	621.480289	Nuclear engineering—Safety measures
TK7871.85-.99	621.38152	Semiconductor wafers			
TK7871.89.A94	621.381522	Diodes, IMPATT	TK9178-9183	621.480284	Nuclear power plants—Instruments
TK7871.89.S95	621.381522	Diodes, Switching			
TK7871.92	621.3815282	Junction transistors	TK9202-9230	621.483	Nuclear reactors
TK7871.96.B55	621.381528	Bipolar transistors	TK9203.B6	621.4834	Boiling water reactors
TK7871.99.M4	621.38152	Metal insulator semiconductors	TK9203.B7	621.4834	Liquid metal fast breeder reactors
TK7872.F44	537.2448	Ferroelectric devices	TK9203.H4	621.4834	Heavy water reactors
TK7872.I65	621.3815322	Electric inverters	TK9203.H4	621.483	Steam generating heavy water reactors
TK7872.L56	621.3815422	Liquid crystal displays			
TK7872.L64	621.395	Logic devices	TK9203.S65	621.4834	Solid fuel reactors
TK7872.M25	621.39763	Magnetic bubble devices	TK9203.S86	621.4834	Superheating reactors
TK7872.O7	621.381533	Feedback oscillators	TK9204	621.484	Fusion reactors
TK7872.S5	621.381548	Signal generators	TK9207	621.4833	Nuclear fuel rods
TK7872.T7	621.314	Electronic transformers	TK9212	621.48336	Nuclear reactors—Cooling
TK7872.V3	621.381512	Vacuum-tubes	TK9230	621.485	Nuclear propulsion
TK7874-.8	621.395	Digital integrated circuits	TK9340	539.73	Particle accelerators
TK7874	621.395	Linear integrated circuits	TK9360	621.4833	Nuclear fuels
			TK9360	621.4838	Reactor fuel reprocessing

LC	Dewey	Subject Heading	LC	Dewey	Subject Heading
TK9360	621.48335	Spent reactor fuels	TL475-480	629.295	Roving vehicles (Astronautics)
TK9360	621.484	Thermonuclear fuels			
TK9956	621.38416	Amateur radio stations	TL480	629.295	Lunar surface vehicles
TL	629.2	Motor vehicles	TL500-4050	629.1	Aerospace engineering
TL1-230.5	629.222	Automobiles	TL500-830	629.13	Aeronautics
TL1-5	629.22205	Automobiles—Periodicals	TL500-504	629.13006	Aeronautics—Societies, etc.
TL6	629.22206	Automobiles—Congresses	TL505	629.13006	Aeronautics—Congresses
TL7	629.222074	Automobiles—Museums	TL506	629.130074	Aeronautical museums
TL9	629.22203	Automobiles—Encyclopedias	TL509	629.1300148	Aeronautics—Abbreviations
TL12	629.2220294	Automobiles—Catalogs	TL513	629.1300272	Aeronautics—Patents
TL15	629.22209	Automobiles—History	TL515-532	629.13009	Aeronautics—History
TL21-127	629.22209(4-9)	Automobiles—[By region or country]	TL521-532	629.13009(4-9)	Aeronautics—[By region or country]
TL23-25	629.2220973	Automobiles—United States	TL539-540	629.130092	Aeronautics—Biography
TL57-64	629.2220941	Automobiles—Great Britain	TL549	629.1300222	Aeronautics—Pictorial works
TL71-72.5	629.2220944	Automobiles—France	TL553.5	629.1300289	Aeronautics—Safety measures
TL73-74.5	629.2220943	Automobiles—Germany			
TL85-86	629.2220947	Automobiles—Russia	TL553.7	613.69	Survival after airplane accidents, shipwrecks, etc.
TL105-106	629.2220952	Automobiles—Japan			
TL139-140	629.222092	Automobile engineers—Biography	TL553.8	363.3481	Search and rescue operations
TL152-.2	629.287	Automobiles—Maintenance and repair	TL556-558	629.1324	Meteorology in aeronautics
			TL557.F6	629.1324	Fog—Control
TL152.2	629.287	Automobiles—Conservation and restoration	TL557.V5	629.136	Airports—Visibility
			TL566-568	629.130072	Aeronautical laboratories
TL152.5-.55	629.283	Automobile driving	TL567.R47	629.130072	Research aircraft
TL152.5-.55	629.283092	Automobile drivers	TL570-578	629.13	Flight
TL153	629.286	Service stations	TL570-574	629.1323	Aerodynamics
TL154	629.283	Automobile parking	TL571.5	629.132306	Aerodynamics, Hypersonic
TL200	629.2292	Automobiles, Steam	TL573	629.13230287	Aerodynamic measurements
TL210-.7	629.252	Automobiles—Motors	TL574.B6	629.13237	Boundary layer
TL214.P6	629.25	Automobiles—Pollution control devices	TL574.F6	629.132362	Flutter (Aerodynamics)
			TL574.M6	629.132364	Rolling (Aerodynamics)
TL214.P6	629.25	Motor vehicles—Pollution control devices	TL574.M6	629.132364	Yawing (Aerodynamics)
			TL574.N6	629.1323	Aerodynamic noise
TL230-.5	629.224	Trucks	TL574.S7	629.13236	Stability of airplanes
TL230	629.2234	Vans	TL574.U5	629.13232	Unsteady flow (Aerodynamics)
TL230	629.224	Dump trucks			
TL230.3	629.224092	Truck drivers	TL574.V5	629.132362	Vibration (Aeronautics)
TL232	629.22233	Trolley buses	TL570-578	629.132	Flight
TL232.3	629.22233092	Bus drivers	TL586-589	629.13251	Navigation (Aeronautics)
TL233-.8	629.2252	Traction-engines	TL589-.5	629.1300284	Aeronautical instruments
TL233-.8	629.2252	Farm tractors	TL589.2.A3	629.1352	Accelerometers
TL235.8	629.22234	Ambulances	TL589.2.C58	629.1352	Gyro compass
TL236	629.228	Automobiles, Racing	TL589.2.O6	681.753	Optical gyroscopes
TL236.7	629.222	Dune buggies	TL589.5	629.1326	Automatic pilot (Airplanes)
TL237-.2	629.221	Automobiles—Models	TL609-639	629.13322	Balloons
TL240-278	629.23	Automobiles—Design and construction	TL620	629.13322	Balloon ascensions
			TL638	629.13322	Hot air balloons
TL245	629.231	Automobiles—Aerodynamics	TL650-668.1	629.13324	Airships
TL255-256.5	629.26	Automobiles—Bodies	TL670-724	629.13334	Flying-machines
TL271-.5	629.2772	Automobiles—Heating and ventilation	TL670-723	629.13334	Airplanes
			TL671.6	629.13431	Airframes
TL272	629.2548	Automobiles—Electric equipment	TL671.7	629.13453	Airplanes—Flight testing
			TL671.7	629.13452	Airplanes—Inspection
TL272.5-.55	629.2549	Motor vehicles—Electronic equipment	TL672-673	629.13432	Airplanes—Wings
			TL673.F6	629.13433	Flaps (Airplanes)
TL285-295	629.282	Automobiles—Testing	TL673.S9	629.13432	Airplanes—Wings, Swept-back
TL410-438	629.2272	Bicycles			
TL439-448	629.2275	Motorcycles	TL677.E6	629.13433	Elevators (Airplanes)
TL443	629.2275	Minibikes	TL681.A5	629.13442	Airplanes—Air conditioning

LC	Dewey	Subject Heading	LC	Dewey	Subject Heading
TL681.C3	629.13445	Aircraft cabins	TL726.15	629.136	International airports
TL681.P7	629.13442	Airplanes—Pressurization	TL750-758	629.134386	Parachuting
TL682-683	629.134381	Airplanes—Landing gear	TL750-758	629.134386	Parachutes
TL684-.3	629.133347	Seaplanes	TL753	629.134386	Parachutes—Rigging
TL685	629.13335	Vertically rising aircraft	TL760-769	629.13333	Gliders (Aeronautics)
TL685.3	623.746	Airplanes, Military	TL778	745.592	Paper airplanes
TL685.3	358.4383	Fighter planes	TL780-785.8	629.475	Rockets (Aeronautics)
TL685.7	358.44	Jet transports	TL783.5	629.4753	Nuclear rockets
TL685.7	358.44	Supersonic transport planes	TL783.54-.63	629.4755	Electric rocket engines
TL686.G	629.133340422	Lear jet aircraft	TL783.57	629.4754	Photon rockets
TL690-691	629.1354	Electricity in aeronautics	TL783.6	629.4755	Plasma rockets
TL692-696	629.135	Aeronautics—Communication systems	TL783.63	629.4755	Ion rockets
			TL784.C63	629.47522	Liquid propellant rockets—Control systems
TL693.R2	629.1355	Airplanes—Radio equipment			
TL693-696	629.1355	Airplanes—Electronic equipment	TL784.C63	629.433	Rockets (Aeronautics)—Guidance systems
TL693-696	629.1355	Radio in aeronautics	TL785	629.47524	Solid propellants
TL694.T35	629.437	Aerospace telemetry	TL787-4050	629.4	Astronautics
TL695-696	629.135	Avionics	TL789-790	629.455	Interplanetary voyages
TL695-696	629.1352	Aids to air navigation	TL789-.6	001.942	Unidentified flying objects
TL696.B4	621.384191	Radio beacons	TL789.8	629.409(4-9)	Astronautics—[By region or country]
TL696.C7	629.1352	Radio compass			
TL696.D5	629.1352	Radio direction finders	TL790	629.41	Space flight
TL696.L3	629.1351	Landing aids (Aeronautics)	TL794.3	629.40724	Astronautics—Experiments
TL696.L33	629.1325213	Ground controlled approach	TL795-.5	629.47	Space ships
TL697.08	629.1344	Airplanes—Oxygen equipment	TL795.7	629.442	Space colonies
			TL796-798	629.46	Artificial satellites
TL701-704.7	629.13435	Airplanes—Motors	TL797	629.442	Space stations
TL704.7	629.134351	Airplanes—Fuel	TL797	338.0919	Space industrialization
TL705-708	629.13436	Propellers, Aerial	TL798.G4	629.46	Geodetic satellites
TL708	629.134355	Airplanes—Nuclear power plants	TL799.J8	629.4555	Space flight to Jupiter
			TL799.M3	629.4553	Space flight to Mars
TL709-.5	629.134353	Airplanes—Jet propulsion	TL799.M6	629.454	Space flight to the moon
TL709.3.T8	629.1343532	Airplanes—Turbine-propeller engines	TL799.V45	629.4552	Space flight to Venus
			TL759-.7	629.13332	Kites
TL709.3.T83	629.1343533	Airplanes—Turbojet engines	TL844	621.43560228	Rockets (Aeronautics)—Models
TL709.5.C55	629.134353	Aircraft gas-turbines—Combustion chambers			
			TL845-848	629.4071	Astronautics—Study and teaching
TL709.5.I5	629.134353	Airplanes—Turbojet engines—Air intakes	TL867	363.124	Space vehicle accidents
TL710-713.5	629.13252	Airplanes—Piloting	TL869	629.40212	Space vehicles—Specifications
TL712-.8	629.1325071	Flight training			
TL711.B6	629.1325214	Instrument flying	TL943	629.455	Planetary quarantine
TL711.H65	629.13252	Holding patterns (Aeronautics)	TL945	629.4774	Space vehicles—Sterilization
			TL950-954	629.472	Space vehicles—Materials
TL711.L3	629.1325213	Airplanes—Landing	TL1050-1060	629.4	Astrodynamics
TL711.N5	629.1325214	Night flying	TL1065-1080	629.453	Navigation (Astronautics)
TL711.S8	629.1325071	Student flying	TL1070	629.453	Astronautical charts
TL711.T3	629.1325212	Airplanes—Take-off	TL1082	629.474	Astronautical instruments
TL712	629.13252	Air pilots	TL1085	629.45071	Space flight training
TL716-.9	629.133352	Helicopters	TL1090-1095	629.458	Space vehicles—Piloting
TL720.7	387.744	Aeronautics, Commercial—Freight	TL1098	629.450284	Space tools
			TL1100-1102	629.474	Space vehicles—Electric equipment
TL721	629.13	Aeronautics—Flights			
TL725-733	629.136	Airports	TL1102.B3	629.47445	Space vehicles—Batteries
TL725-733	387.72	Airways	TL1500-1575	629.477	Life support systems (Space environment)
TL725.3.B8	629.136	Airport buildings			
TL725.3.C64	629.1366	Airport control towers	TL1530	629.477	Space cabin atmospheres
TL725.3.R8	629.1363	Runways (Aeronautics)	TL1550	629.4772	Space suits
TL725.3.T7	629.1366	Air traffic control			
TL725.6	629.1361	Seaplane bases			

LC	Dewey	Subject Heading	LC	Dewey	Subject Heading
TL1565	629.4773	Space vehicles—Water-supply	TN57-64	622.0941	Mines and mineral resources—Great Britain
TL3000-3285	629.474	Space vehicles—Electronic equipment	TN65-.2	622.09436	Mines and mineral resources—Austria
TL4000-4050	629.478	Ground support systems (Astronautics)	TN65.3-.4	622.09437	Mines and mineral resources—Czechoslovakia
TL4030	629.(437/457)	Space vehicles—Tracking	TN65.5-66	622.09439	Mines and mineral resources—Hungary
TN	622	Mining engineering			
TN	622	Mines and mineral resources	TN69-70	622.09489	Mines and mineral resources—Denmark
TN1-4	338.205	Mineral industries—Periodicals	TN71-72.5	622.0944	Mines and mineral resources—France
TN5	338.206	Mineral industries—Congresses	TN73-74.5	622.0943	Mines and mineral resources—Germany
TN6	338.2074	Mineral industries—Exhibitions	TN75-76	622.09495	Mines and mineral resources—Greece
TN9-10	338.203	Mineral industries—Dictionaries	TN77-78	622.09492	Mines and mineral resources—Netherlands
TN12	338.2025	Mineral industries—Directories	TN79-80	622.0945	Mines and mineral resources—Italy
TN15-124	338.209	Mineral industries—History	TN81-82	622.09481	Mines and mineral resources—Norway
TN21-127	622.09(4-9)	Mines and mineral resources—[By region or country]	TN83-84.5	622.09469	Mines and mineral resources—Portugal
TN23-25	622.0973	Mines and mineral resources—United States	TN85-86	622.0947	Mines and mineral resources—Russia
TN26-27	622.0971	Mines and mineral resources—Canada	TN87-88	622.0946	Mines and mineral resources—Spain
TN28-29	622.0972	Mines and mineral resources—Mexico	TN88.5	622.0948	Mines and mineral resources—Scandinavia
TN30-31	622.09728	Mines and mineral resources—Central America	TN89-90	622.09485	Mines and mineral resources—Sweden
TN32-33	622.09729	Mines and mineral resources—West Indies	TN91-92	622.09494	Mines and mineral resources—Switzerland
TN36-37	622.0982	Mines and mineral resources—Argentina	TN95.A2	622.09496	Mines and mineral resources—Balkan Peninsula
TN38-39	622.0984	Mines and mineral resources—Bolivia	TN95.F5	622.094897	Mines and mineral resources—Finland
TN41-42	622.0981	Mines and mineral resources—Brazil	TN95.Y8	622.09497	Mines and mineral resources—Yugoslavia
TN43-44	622.0983	Mines and mineral resources—Chile	TN101-102	622.0951	Mines and mineral resources—China
TN45-46	622.09861	Mines and mineral resources—Colombia	TN103-104	622.0954	Mines and mineral resources—India
TN47	622.09866	Mines and mineral resources—Ecuador	TN104.5-.6	622.095491	Mines and mineral resources—Pakistan
TN48	622.09881	Mines and mineral resources—Guyana	TN104.7-.8	622.095493	Mines and mineral resources—Sri Lanka
TN49	622.09883	Mines and mineral resources—Surinam	TN105-106	622.0952	Mines and mineral resources—Japan
TN50	622.09882	Mines and mineral resources—French Guiana	TN107-108	622.0955	Mines and mineral resources—Iran
TN51	622.09892	Mines and mineral resources—Paraguay	TN109-110	622.0957	Mines and mineral resources—Asiatic Russia
TN52	622.0985	Mines and mineral resources—Peru	TN111-112	622.09561	Mines and mineral resources—Turkey
TN53	622.09895	Mines and mineral resources—Uruguay	TN113.I55	622.09598	Mines and mineral resources—Indonesia
TN54	622.0987	Mines and mineral resources—Venezuela	TN113.I7	622.09567	Mines and mineral resources—Iraq

LC	Dewey	Subject Heading	LC	Dewey	Subject Heading
TN113.I75	622.095694	Mines and mineral resources—Israel	TN400-409	622.341	Iron mines and mining
TN113.P6	622.09599	Mines and mineral resources—Philippines	TN410-439	622.342	Precious metals
			TN410-429	622.3422	Gold mines and mining
TN115-119	622.096	Mines and mineral resources—Africa	TN420-429	622.3422	Gold ores
			TN422	622.3422	Gold dredging
TN117-118	622.0962	Mines and mineral resources—Egypt	TN430-439	622.3423	Silver mines and mining
			TN450-459	622.344	Lead ores
TN121-122	622.0994	Mines and mineral resources—Australia	TN470-479	622.3453	Tin mines and mining
			TN470-479	622.3453	Tin ores
TN122.5-.6	622.0993	Mines and mineral resources—New Zealand	TN490.B6	622.347	Bismuth ores
			TN490.C6	622.3483	Cobalt ores
TN123-124	622.099(5-6)	Mines and mineral resources—Oceania	TN530	622.77	Magnetic separation of ores
			TN550-580	669.92	Assaying
TN125-.5	622.0998	Mines and mineral resources—Arctic regions	TN565	669.92	Metallurgical analysis
			TN600-799	669	Metallurgy
TN139-140	622.092	Mining engineers	TN600-605	669.05	Metallurgy—Periodicals
TN165-213	622.071	Mining schools and education	TN615-620	669.09	Metallurgy—History
			TN621-655	669.09(4-9)	Metallurgy—[By region or country]
TN260	553	Geology, Economic	TN672	669.8	Precipitation hardening
TN263.5	333.79	Energy minerals	TN675.3	669.071	Metallurgy—Study and teaching
TN264	333.8509162	Marine mineral resources			
TN270-271	622.18	Prospecting	TN677-.5	669.0282	Smelting furnaces
TN271.P4	622.1828	Petroleum—Prospecting	TN677-.5	669.0282	Blast furnaces
TN273	622.14	Mine surveying	TN677-.5	669.0282	Metallurgical furnaces
TN277	622.8	Quarries and quarrying—Safety measures	TN681-687	669.0284	Electrometallurgy
			TN686.5.E4	669.0284	Electroslag process
TN277	622.292	Quarries and quarrying	TN688	669.0283	Hydrometallurgy
TN278	622.2927	Hydraulic mining	TN689-693	669.95	Metallography
TN279-281	622.23	Rock-drills	TN690	669.9	Physical metallurgy
TN279	622.23	Percussion drilling	TN690	669.95	Alloys
TN279	622.23	Blasting	TN695-697	671.37	Powder metallurgy
TN281	622.24	Boring	TN713-718	669.1413	Blast furnaces
TN281.5	622.23	Rotary drilling	TN736-738	669.1423	Bessemer process
TN283	622.25	Shaft sinking	TN740-742	669.1422	Open-hearth furnaces
TN285	622.26	Tunneling	TN755	669.142	Steel-works
TN289	622.28	Mine timbering	TN756-757	669.141	Iron alloys
TN291	622.292	Strip mining	TN758-799	669.(2-7)	Nonferrous metals
TN295	622.8	Coal mines and mining—Safety measures	TN760-769	669.22	Gold—Metallurgy
			TN775	669.722	Aluminum—Metallurgy
TN297	622.89	Mine rescue work	TN780	669.3	Copper—Metallurgy
TN297	622.80284	Gas masks	TN799.9-844.7	622.334	Coal
TN301-306	622.42	Mine ventilation	TN799.9-844.7	622.334	Coal mines and mining
TN305-306	622.82	Firedamp	TN820-823	622.335	Anthracite coal
TN305-306	622.82	Mine gases	TN850	622.33	Bitumen
TN307	622.473	Safety-lamps	TN853	622.337	Asphalt
TN307	622.473	Electric lamps, Portable	TN858-859	662.3383	Oil-shales
TN306.5-309	622.47	Mine lighting	TN860-879	622.3382	Petroleum
TN311-320	622.8	Coal mine accidents	TN870	622.338	Oil fields—Production methods
TN311-320	622.8	Mine accidents			
TN313-315	622.82	Combustion, Spontaneous	TN871	622.3382	Gushers
TN313	622.82	Mine explosions	TN871	622.3382	Oil reservoir engineering
TN315	622.82	Mine fires	TN871.2-.3	622.3381	Oil well drilling
TN318	622.5	Mine water	TN871.3	622.33819	Oil well drilling, Submarine
TN336	622.66	Mine railroads	TN871.37	622.3382	Secondary recovery of oil
TN338	622.66	Gasoline locomotives	TN871.5	622.3381	Oil well drilling rigs
TN342	622.6	Shuttle cars (Mine haulage)	TN879.5-.6	665.544	Petroleum pipelines
TN343	622.48	Electricity in mining	TN880-884	622.3385	Gas wells
TN345-347	622.0284	Mining machinery	TN880-884	622.3385	Gas engineering
TN400-580	622.34	Metals	TN880-884	622.3385	Natural gas
TN400-580	622.34	Ores	TN880.5	665.744	Natural gas pipelines

LC	Dewey	Subject Heading	LC	Dewey	Subject Heading
TN885	622.339	Amber	TP240	661.63	Sulphites
TN890	622.3668	Sulphur	TP242-244	665.(7-8)	Gases
TN895-897	669.725	Alkalies	TP245.C4	661.0681	Carbon
TN900-909	622.3632	Salt mines and mining	TP245.F6	661.0731	Fluorine
TN900-909	622.3632	Salt	TP245.H4	665.822	Helium
TN911	622.364	Nitrates	TP245.09	661.0721	Oxygen
TN913-914	622.364	Phosphate mines and mining	TP245.U7	661.0431	Uranium
TN917	622.3633	Borax	TP247-248	661.8	Organic compounds
TN919	622.3636	Potassium salts	TP247.2	661.86	Organic acids
TN923-929.7	622.373	Mineral waters	TP247.5	661.807	Solvents
TN930	622.3672	Asbestos	TP248.13-.65	660.6	Biotechnology
TN933	622.3674	Mica	TP248.25.M45	660.28424	Membrane reactors
TN939	622.3622	Sand and gravel plants	TP248.25.M46	660.28424	Membrane separation
TN939	622.3622	Sand	TP248.27.M53	660.6	Microbial biotechnology
TN941-943	622.367	Fire-clay	TP248.3	660.63	Biochemical engineering
TN945	622.368	Cement	TP248.6	660.65	Genetic engineering
TN946	622.3635	Gypsum	TP248.65.F66	664.024	Food—Biotechnology
TN948.D5	622.36	Diatomaceous earth	TP250-261	660.297	Electrochemistry, Industrial
TN948.P5	622.3662	Pigments	TP265-267	660.2961	Fire
TN950-997	622.35	Stone	TP267.5-301	662.2	Explosives
TN957	622.353	Sandstone	TP268-299	623.452	Explosives, Military
TN967	622.3516	Dolomite	TP272	662.26	Gunpowder
TN970	622.352	Granite	TP276	662.26	Guncotton
TN980-997	622.38	Precious stones	TP285	662.27	Dynamite
TN997.A35	622.387	Agates	TP297	662.20289	Explosives—Safety measures
TN997.E5	622.386	Emeralds	TP300-301	662.1	Firecrackers
TN997.G3	622.387	Garnet	TP300-301	662.1	Fireworks
TN997.S24	622.384	Sapphires	TP310	662.5	Matches
TP	660	Chemistry, Technical	TP315-360	662.6	Fuel
TP1	660.05	Chemistry, Technical—Periodicals	TP323	662.65	Briquets (Fuel)
			TP324	662.65	Fuelwood
TP5	660.06	Chemistry, Technical—Congresses	TP331	662.74	Charcoal
			TP343	665.5384	Diesel fuels
TP9	660.03	Chemistry, Technical—Encyclopedias	TP345-350	665.75	Gas as fuel
			TP350	665.7	Natural gas
TP15-20	660.09	Chemistry, Technical—History	TP355	665.5	Petroleum as fuel
			TP358	662.6692	Alcohol as fuel
TP149	660.2804	Chemicals—Safety measures	TP358	662.6692	Gasohol
			TP359.B48	665.776	Biogas
TP155-156	660	Chemical engineering	TP371.44	664.024	Fermented foods
TP155.5-.6	660.28	Chemical plants	TP371.8	664.0288	Radiation preservation of food
TP155.7-.75	660.281	Chemical processes			
TP156.C57	667.9	Coating processes	TP372.2	664.02852	Cold storage
TP156.D5	660.28425	Distillation	TP372.3	664.02853	Frozen foods
TP156.E6	660.294514	Emulsions	TP375-414.5	664.1	Sugar—Manufacture and refining
TP156.E8	660.284248	Extraction (Chemistry)			
TP156.F5	660.284245	Filters and filtration	TP375-414.5	664.1	Syrups
TP156.F65	660.284292	Fluidization	TP390-391	664.123	Beet sugar
TP156.P6	668.92	Polymerization	TP415-416	664.2	Starch
TP157-159	660.283	Chemical engineering—Equipment and supplies	TP434-435	664.756	Cereals, Prepared
			TP443-444	664.805	Vegetables—Drying
TP165-183	660.072	Chemical engineering laboratories	TP480-482	621.56	Low temperature engineering
			TP490-497	621.56	Refrigeration and refrigerating machinery
TP187-197	660.072	Research, Industrial—Laboratories			
			TP496-497	621.57	Refrigerators
TP200-248	661	Chemicals	TP500-660	663	Beverages
TP213-217	661.2	Acids	TP544-559	663.2	Wine and wine making
TP213-217	661.2	Inorganic acids	TP555	663.224	Champagne (Wine)
TP222-223	661.03	Alkalies	TP559.P8	663.223	Madeira wine
TP237-238	661.65	Nitrates	TP559.P8	663.223	Port wine

LC	Dewey	Subject Heading	LC	Dewey	Subject Heading
TP568-587	663.42	Beer	TP958-959	661.806	Essence and essential oils
TP589-618	663.5	Liquors	TP967-970	668.3	Glue
TP593	663.1	Alcohol	TP967-970	668.3	Adhesives
TP599	663.53	Brandy	TP973	668.2	Glycerin
TP605	663.52	Whiskey	TP977-979.5	665.332	Turpentine
TP607.R9	663.59	Rum	TP977-979.5	668.374	Gums and resins, Synthetic
TP611	663.55	Liqueurs	TP977-979.5	668.37	Gums and resins
TP628-636	663.62	Carbonated beverages	TP983-986	668.55	Cosmetics
TP645	663.93	Coffee	TP990-992.5	668.12	Soap
TP669-699	664.3	Oils and fats	TP995-996	658.567	Waste products
TP669-695	665.1	Waxes	TP1101-1185	668.4	Plastics
TP676	664.34	Lard oil	TP1101	668.406	Plastics—Societies, etc.
TP676	665.2	Fish oils	TP1103	668.405	Plastics—Periodicals
TP678	638.17	Beeswax	TP1105	668.406	Plastics—Congresses
TP680-684	665.3	Vegetable oils	TP1110	668.403	Plastics—Encyclopedias
TP684.C275	665.353	Castor oil	TP1114	668.4027	Plastics—Patents
TP684.C7	665.355	Coconut oil	TP1116-1118	668.409	Plastics—History
TP684.M3	664.32	Margarine	TP1127-1129	668.4071	Plastics—Study and teaching
TP685-699	665.4	Mineral oils			
TP690-692.5	665.53	Petroleum—Refining	TP1135	668.41	Plastics machinery
TP690-692.5	665.5	Petroleum	TP1150	668.412	Plastics—Molding
TP690-692.5	665.5	Petroleum products	TP1160	668.415	Plastics—Welding
TP690.4	665.533	Cracking process	TP1175.E9	668.413	Plastics—Extrusion
TP692.2	662.66	Gasoline, Synthetic	TP1180.A33	668.423	Acetal resins
TP692.2	665.53827	Gasoline	TP1180.C5	668.44	Celluloid
TP692.4.K4	665.5383	Kerosene	TP1180.C6	668.44	Cellulose
TP692.5	665.542	Oil storage tanks	TP1180.E6	668.374	Epoxy resins
TP692.5	665.542	Petroleum—Storage	TP1180.P57	668.423	Polycarbonates
TP700-764	665.7	Gas manufacture and works	TP1180.P6	668.4225	Polyesters
TP700	665.7	Gas	TP1180.S7	668.4233	Styrene
TP751-764	665.7	Gas	TP1183.F6	668.493	Plastic foams
TP757	665.744	Gas distribution	TP1183.L3	668.492	Laminated plastics
TP757	665.744	Gas-pipes	TR	770	Photography
TP759	665.772	Coal gasification	TR1	770.5	Photography—Periodicals
TP759	665.773	Oil gasification	TR5	770.6	Photography—Congresses
TP785-842	666.3	Pottery	TR6	770.74	Photography—Exhibitions
TP812	666.427	Glazes	TR9	770.3	Photography—Encyclopedias
TP823	666.427	Glazes	TR15	770.9	Photography—History
TP826-833	666.737	Brickmaking	TR21-127	770.9(4-9)	Photography—[By region or country]
TP839	666.733	Drain-tiles			
TP841-842	666.43	Kilns	TR22-25	770.973	Photography—United States
TP845-869	666.1	Glass manufacture	TR26-27	770.971	Photography—Canada
TP859	666.122	Glass blowing and working	TR28-29	770.972	Photography—Mexico
TP865-868	666.19	Glassware	TR30-31	770.9728	Photography—Central America
TP866	666.192	Bottles			
TP867	681.428	Mirrors	TR32-33	770.9729	Photography—West Indies
TP870	666.86	Artificial minerals	TR36-37	770.982	Photography—Argentina
TP873-.5	666.88	Precious stones, Artificial	TR38-39	770.984	Photography—Bolivia
TP890-933	677	Textile chemistry	TR41-42	770.981	Photography—Brazil
TP890-929	667.2	Dyes and dyeing—Chemistry	TR43-44	770.983	Photography—Chile
TP894-895	667.14	Bleaching	TR45-46	770.9861	Photography—Colombia
TP897-929	667.2	Dyes and dyeing	TR47	770.9866	Photography—Ecuador
TP901	686.2316	Silk-printing	TR51	770.9892	Photography—Paraguay
TP990-992.5	667.1	Cleaning compounds	TR52	770.985	Photography—Peru
TP932-.6	667.12	Dry cleaning	TR53	770.9895	Photography—Uruguay
TP934-945	677.02825	Finishes and finishing	TR54	770.987	Photography—Venezuela
TP934-937.5	667.6	Paint	TR55-95	770.94	Photography—Europe
TP934-937.5	667.29	Pigments	TR57-64	770.941	Photography—Great Britain
TP940	667.72	Polishes	TR59-60	770.9415	Photography—Ireland
TP946-950	667.4	Ink	TR65-.2	770.9436	Photography—Austria
TP953	661.803	Coal-tar	TR71-72.5	770.944	Photography—France

LC	Dewey	Subject Heading	LC	Dewey	Subject Heading
TR73-74.5	770.943	Photography—Germany	TR590-620	778.72	Photography—Lighting
TR75-76	770.9495	Photography—Greece	TR593	778.37	Photography, High-speed
TR77-78	770.9492	Photography—Netherlands	TR600	778.72	Photography—Artificial light
TR79-80	770.945	Photography—Italy			
TR81-82	770.9481	Photography—Norway	TR610	778.719	Night photography
TR85-86	770.947	Photography—Russia	TR640-688	770	Photography, Artistic
TR87-88	770.946	Photography—Spain	TR656.5	778.935	Still-life photography
TR89-90	770.9485	Photography—Sweden	TR659	778.94	Architectural photography
TR91-92	770.9494	Photography—Switzerland	TR659.5	778.71	Outdoor photography
TR99-113	770.95	Photography—Asia	TR660-.5	778.936	Landscape photography
TR101-102	770.951	Photography—China	TR661	778.36	Photography, Panoramic
TR103-104	770.954	Photography—India	TR670-.5	778.937	Marine photography
TR105-106	770.952	Photography—Japan	TR680-681	778.92	Portrait photography
TR107-108	770.955	Photography—Iran	TR693-696	526.982	Photogrammetry
TR109-110	770.957	Photography—Asiatic Russia	TR713	778.35	Space photography
TR111-112	770.9561	Photography—Turkey	TR721-733	778.93	Nature photography
TR115-119	770.96	Photography—Africa	TR729.W54	778.932	Wildlife photography
TR117-118	770.962	Photography—Egypt	TR755	778.34	Infrared photography
TR121-122	770.994	Photography—Australia	TR785	623.72	Photography, Military
TR122.5-.6	770.993	Photography—New Zealand	TR800	778.73	Underwater photography
TR123-124	770.99(5-6)	Photography—Oceania	TR810	778.35	Aerial photography
TR139-140	770.92	Photography—Biography	TR818	371.897	School photography
TR139	770.92	Photographers	TR820	070.49	Photojournalism
TR148	778.8	Trick photography	TR821	070.49796	Photography of sports
TR151	770.21	Photography—Tables	TR824-835	686.4	Photocopying
TR161	770.71	Photography—Study and teaching	TR835	302.23	Microfilm readers
TR183	770	Photography, Artistic	TR845-899.5	778.53	Cinematography
TR196-199	771	Photography—Equipment and supplies	TR855	778.53	Wide-screen processes (Cinematography)
TR210-212	771.5	Photographic chemistry	TR858	778.5345	Cinematography—Special effects
TR212	771.5	Photographic chemicals	TR882.3	384.558	Camcorders
TR225	771.47	Photography—Wastes, Recovery of	TR893.5	778.53859	Wildlife cinematography
			TR897.5-.75	778.5347	Animation (Cinematography)
TR250-265	771.3	Cameras	TR899-.5	778.535	Motion pictures—Editing
TR262	771.32	35mm cameras	TR905	771.44	Photography—Enlarging
TR268	771	Photography, Pinhole	TR920-923	686.4	Photographic reproduction of plans, drawings, etc.
TR269	770	Instant photography			
TR270-271	771.352	Photographic lenses	TR921	686.42	Blueprinting
TR281	771.5322	Photography—Plates	TR925-997	686.232	Photomechanical processes
TR283	771.5324	Photography—Films	TR930-937	686.2325	Collotype
TR287-500	772.774	Photography—Processing	TR940-950	686.2325	Photolithography
TR290-312	771.43	Photography—Negatives	TR970-977	686.2327	Photoengraving
TR295	771.49	Photography—Developing and developers	TR975	686.2327	Photoengraving—Halftone process
TR330-333	772.774	Photography—Printing processes	TR980	686.2327	Photogravure
			TR1010	686.22544	Phototypesetting
TR340	771.44	Photographs—Trimming, mounting, etc.	TR1035-1050	686.44	Electrophotography
			TS	670	Manufactures
TR365	772.12	Daguerreotype	TS23-25	670.973	United States—Manufactures
TR400	772.16	Kallitype			
TR415	686.42	Blueprinting	TS26-27	670.971	Canada—Manufactures
TR465	779.0288	Photographs—Conservation and restoration	TS28-29	670.972	Mexico—Manufactures
			TS30-31	670.9728	Central America—Manufactures
TR470	686.45	Photostat			
TR475	771.44	Photography—Enlarging	TS32-33	670.9729	West Indies—Manufactures
TR504-508	778.2	Slides (Photography)	TS36-37	670.982	Argentina—Manufactures
TR510-545	778.6	Color photography	TS38-39	670.984	Bolivia—Manufactures
TR550-581	771.1	Photography—Studios and dark rooms	TS41-42	670.981	Brazil—Manufactures
			TS43-44	670.983	Chile—Manufactures
TR575-581	778.92	Portrait photography	TS45-46	670.9861	Colombia—Manufactures

LC	Dewey	Subject Heading	LC	Dewey	Subject Heading
TS47	670.9866	Ecuador—Manufactures	TS214	363.7288	Scrap metals
TS48	670.9881	Guyana—Manufactures	TS225	671.332	Forging
TS49	670.9883	Surinam—Manufactures	TS215	671.0284	Metal-working machinery
TS50	670.9882	French Guiana—Manufactures	TS227-228.96	671.52	Welding
			TS228.9	671.529	Pressure welding
TS51	670.9892	Paraguay—Manufactures	TS228.97-239	671.2	Founding
TS52	670.985	Peru—Manufactures	TS228.99-240	671.2	Founding
TS53	670.9895	Uruguay—Manufactures	TS250	671.823	Sheet-metal
TS54	670.987	Venezuela—Manufactures	TS253	621.984	Dies (Metal-working)
TS57-64	670.941	Great Britain—Manufactures	TS283	681.76041	Pressure vessels
TS65-.2	670.9436	Austria—Manufactures	TS300-360	672	Steel-works
TS65.3-.4	670.9437	Czechoslovakia—Manufactures	TS320	671.36	Tempering
			TS340	671.32	Roll-mill
TS65.5-66	670.9439	Hungary—Manufactures	TS380-.4	683.82	Cutlery
TS67-68	670.9493	Belgium—Manufactures	TS400-455	683	Hardware
TS69-70	670.9489	Denmark—Manufactures	TS519-531	683.3	Locksmithing
TS71-72.5	670.944	France—Manufactures	TS519-531	683.32	Locks and keys
TS73-74.5	670.943	Germany—Manufactures	TS532-537.5	683.4	Firearms
TS75-76	670.9495	Greece—Manufactures	TS535-.4	683.4	Gunsmithing
TS77-78	670.9492	Netherlands—Manufactures	TS536.6.B6	683.422	Rifles, Bolt action
TS79-80	670.945	Italy—Manufactures	TS537	683.436	Revolvers
TS81-82	670.9481	Norway—Manufactures	TS540-549	681.11(3-4)	Horology
TS83-84.5	670.9469	Portugal—Manufactures	TS540-549	681.11(3-4)	Clock and watch making
TS85-86	670.947	Russia—Manufactures	TS551-552	669.72	Light metals
TS87-88	670.946	Spain—Manufactures	TS564-589	673.3	Brass
TS88.5	670.948	Scandinavia—Manufactures	TS570	673.3	Bronze
TS89-90	670.9485	Sweden—Manufactures	TS653-719	671.7	Metals—Finishing
TS91-92	670.9494	Switzerland—Manufactures	TS662-693	671.732	Plating
TS95.A2	670.9496	Balkan Peninsula—Manufactures	TS670-693	671.732	Electroplating
			TS720-770	739.2782	Rings
TS95.F5	670.94897	Finland—Manufactures	TS740-770	739.27	Jewelry making
TS95.Y8	670.9497	Yugoslavia—Manufactures	TS747-770	739.27	Gems
TS101-102	670.951	China—Manufactures	TS800-915	674	Lumber
TS103-104	670.954	India—Manufactures	TS850-851	674.0284	Saws
TS104.5-.6	670.95491	Pakistan—Manufactures	TS850	674.2	Sawmills
TS104.7-.8	670.95493	Sri Lanka—Manufactures	TS869	674.835	Laminated wood
TS105-106	670.952	Japan—Manufactures	TS870	674.834	Plywood
TS107-108	670.955	Iran—Manufactures	TS870	674.83	Veneers and veneering
TS109-110	670.957	Asiatic Russia—Manufactures	TS880	684.14	Desks
			TS880	684.13	Tables
TS111-112	670.9561	Turkey—Manufactures	TS880	684.13	Chairs
TS113.I55	670.9598	Indonesia—Manufactures	TS880-889	684.1	Furniture
TS113.I7	670.9567	Iraq—Manufactures	TS880-889	684.1	Furniture making
TS113.I75	670.95694	Israel—Manufactures	TS890	674.82	Coopers and cooperage
TS113.P6	670.9599	Philippines—Manufactures	TS932-934	674.386	Wood—Chemistry
TS115-119	670.96	Africa—Manufactures	TS940-1047	675	Leather
TS117-118	670.962	Egypt—Manufactures	TS940-1047	675.23	Tanning
TS121-122	670.994	Australia—Manufactures	TS967	675.2	Hides and skins
TS122.5-.6	670.993	New Zealand—Manufactures	TS989-1025	685.31	Shoes
			TS989-1025	685.31	Boots
TS123-124	670.99(5-6)	Oceania—Manufactures	TS1030-1035	685.1	Saddlery
TS155-194	658.5	Factory management	TS1060-1070	675.3	Fur
TS155-194	658.5	Production management	TS1080-1268	676	Papermaking
TS156-.6	658.562	Quality control	TS1080-1268	676	Paper
TS161	658.7	Materials management	TS1080-1268	676	Paper products
TS192	670.288	Plant maintenance	TS1090-1096	676.09	Papermaking—History
TS195-198.8	688.8	Packaging	TS1118.F5	676.235	Paper coatings
TS197.5	688.8	Containers	TS1118.F5	676.234	Paper finishing
TS200-770	671	Metal-work	TS1171-1177	676.12	Wood-pulp
TS200	671.05	Metal-work—Periodicals	TS1228-1268	676.2823	Stationery
TS213	671.732	Plating	TS1262-1266	681.6	Pens

LC	Dewey	Subject Heading	LC	Dewey	Subject Heading
TS1300-1865	677	Textile fabrics	TT154-.5	688.1	Models and modelmaking
TS1480-1487	677.02822	Spinning	TT161-170.7	373.246	Manual training
TS1485-1487	676.02821	Carding	TT174-.5	745.592	Toys
TS1488	677.028	Sizing (Textile)	TT175-.7	745.59221	Dolls
TS1490-1500	677.028242	Weaving	TT175.3	745.5923	Dollhouses
TS1493	677.02854	Looms	TT175.5	745.5923	Doll furniture
TS1510	677.02825	Textile finishing	TT175.7	745.5922	Doll clothes—Patterns
TS1520	677.682	Waterproofing of fabrics	TT180-203.5	745.51	Woodwork
TS1540-1549	677	Textile fibers	TT194-199.4	684.1	Furniture making
TS1542	677.21	Cotton	TT194-199.4	684.104	Furniture
TS1546	677.39	Silk	TT197	684.16	Cabinetwork
TS1547	677.31	Wool	TT197	684.16	Chests
TS1548.7.P58	677.4743	Polyester fibers	TT197.5.D4	684.14	Desks
TS1550-1590	677.02862	Yarn	TT197.5.D5	684.13	Dining room furniture
TS1590	677.02862	Thread	TT197.5.09	684.18	Outdoor furniture
TS1600-1631	677.02862	Yarn	TT197.5.T3	684.13	Tables
TS1600-1631	677.31	Woolen and worsted manufacture	TT199	684.00288	Furniture—Repairing
			TT199.75	745.5936	Decoys (Hunting)
TS1640-1688	677.39	Satin	TT205-273	745.56	Metal-work
TS1640-1688	677.39	Silk	TT270-273	745.73	Stencil work
TS1675	677.617	Velvet	TT273	686.2316	Screen process printing
TS1680	677.617	Plush	TT288	745.58	Bone carving
TS1688	677.46	Rayon	TT290	745.531	Leatherwork
TS1688	677.4	Synthetic fabrics	TT297-.5	745.572	Plastics craft
TS1700-1735	677.11	Flax	TT300-380	667.6	Painting, Industrial
TS1760-1770	677	Dry-goods	TT310	667.0283	Paint mixing
TS1772 1770.5	677.043	Carpets	TT320-324	698.1	House painting
TS1780	677.64	Tapestry	TT360	667.6	Sign painting
TS1784-1787	677.71	Cordage	TT360	745.61	Lettering
TS1784-1787	677.71	Rope	TT390	646.21	Drapery
TS1825	677.6(2/3)	Felt	TT490-695	687	Clothing trade
TS1828	677.6	Nonwoven fabrics	TT490	646.05	Clothing trade—Periodicals
TS1870-1935	678.2	Rubber industry and trade	TT498	687	Clothing factories
TS1891	678.24	Vulcanization	TT500-560	687.112	Dressmaking
TS1912	678.32	Tires, Rubber	TT507	687	Clothing and dress
TS1920	678.35	Rubber bands	TT509	741.672	Fashion drawing
TS1925-1927	678.72	Rubber, Articifical	TT520	687.043	Garment cutting
TS1927.S55	668.4227	Silicone rubber	TT525	685.24	Fur garments
TS1950-1982	664.9	Animal products	TT530-535	687.147	Cloaks
TS1960-1967	664.9029	Slaughtering and slaughter-houses	TT530	687.142	Coats
			TT550	646.408	Clothing and dress—Alteration
TS1980-1981	664.34	Lard			
TS2001-2035	688.6	Carriage and wagon-making	TT570-630	687.044	Tailoring
TS2120-2159	664.7207	Flour-mills	TT570-630	646.402	Men's furnishing goods
TS2120-2159	664.7207	Meal	TT583	648.1	Pressing of garments
TS2120-2159	664.7207	Flour	TT590	687.043	Garment cutting
TS2158	664.76	Feed mills	TT595-600	687.141	Coats
TS2160	685.4	Gloves	TT603	646.40608341	Boy's clothing
TS2220-2283	679.7	Tobacco industry	TT605	687.113	Trousers
TS2255	679.7	Nicotine	TT616	687.19	Neckties
TS2260	679.72	Cigars	TT626	687.16	Livery
TS2270	688.42	Tobacco-pipes	TT635-645	646.406	Children's clothing
TS2301.T7	688.7221	Dolls	TT637	646.4060832	Layettes
TT	745.5	Handicraft	TT650-665	687.42	Millinery
TT1	745.505	Handicraft—Periodicals	TT657	687.19	Kerchiefs
TT6	745.5074	Handicraft—Exhibitions	TT669-678	687.2	Underwear
TT9	745.503	Handicraft—Encyclopedias	TT669-670	687.22	Lingerie
TT15-127	745.509(4-9)	Handicraft—[By region or country]	TT675	687.21	T-shirts
			TT677	687.22	Foundation garments
TT151	745.50288	Repairing	TT679-695	687.3	Hosiery
TT152-153.7	684.08	Workshops	TT699-854.5	746	Textile crafts

LC	Dewey	Subject Heading	LC	Dewey	Subject Heading
TT700-845	746.4	Needlework	TX335	640.73	Consumer education
TT700-715	646.2	Sewing	TX340	646.3	Clothing and dress
TT713	646.2044	Machine sewing	TX341-641	641.3	Food
TT720-730	646.2	Clothing and dress—Repairing	TX341-641	363.8	Nutrition
			TX341-357	641	Groceries
TT740-897	746.4	Fancy work	TX356	641.31	Marketing (Home economics)
TT778.C65	746.442	Counted thread embroidery			
TT800-810	746.22	Lace and lace making	TX364-365	363.8071	Nutrition—Study and teaching
TT819-829	746.432	Knitting			
TT820-829	746.434	Crocheting	TX369	641.302	Natural foods
TT835	746.46	Quilting	TX371-389	641.36	Meat
TT835	746.46	Coverlets	TX385-388	641.392	Seafood
TT840.S66	746.44	Smocking	TX385	641.392	Fish as food
TT840.T38	746.436	Tatting	TX391	641.35	Vegetable juices
TT847	746.12	Hand spinning	TX392-.8	613.262	Vegetarianism
TT848-849.2	746.14	Hand weaving	TX393	641.331	Flour
TT850	746.73	Rugs, Braided	TX393	641.331	Cereals as food
TT850.2	746.3	Wall hangings	TX394.5	641.822	Pasta products
TT852.5	746.662	Batik	TX395	641.331	Cereals, Prepared
TT853-854.5	746.6	Dyes and dyeing	TX401.2.S69	641.35655	Tofu
TT860	745.582	Beadwork	TX406-407	641.3383	Spices
TT862	745.55	Shellcraft	TX406-407	641.657	Herbs
TT870	736.982	Origami	TX415	641.357	Herbal teas
TT877.5	746.41	Palm frond weaving	TX415	641.3373	Coffee
TT879.B3	746.412	Basket making	TX501-597	363.192064	Food adulteration and inspection
TT890-894	745.5943	Artificial flowers			
TT896.7	745.5944	Egg decoration	TX551-560	641.563	Diet
TT900.E2	745.5941	Easter decorations	TX551-560	641.563	Dietaries
TT900.P3	745.5941	Party decorations	TX551	613.23	Food—Caloric content
TT900.V34	745.5941	Valentine decorations	TX552	641.612	Canned foods
TT950-979	646.724	Barbering	TX553.A3	641.3	Food additives
TT950-979	646.7042	Beauty culture	TX553.C28	613.283	Food—Carbohydrate content
TT967	646.724	Electric shavers	TX553.C43	613.284	Food—Cholesterol content
TT967	646.7240284	Razors	TX553.F53	613.263	Fiber in human nutrition
TT969	646.7240284	Hair preparations	TX553.S8	613.283	Sugars in human nutrition
TT969	646.7240284	Shampoos	TX553.V5	613.286	Vitamins
TT970	646.724	Shaving	TX555-556	641.36	Meat
TT973	646.724	Hair—Dyeing and bleaching	TX556.M5	641.37143	Dried skim milk
TT975	646.724	Braids (Hairdressing)	TX558.L4	641.6565	Legumes as food
TT975	646.724	Hairweaving	TX558.R5	641.3318	Rice
TT975	646.7248	Wigs	TX560.H7	641.38	Honey
TT980-999	648.1	Laundries	TX599-613	641.4	Food—Preservation
TX	640	Home economics	TX599-612	641.4	Canning and preserving
TX1	640.5	Home economics—Periodicals	TX599-612	641.47	Food preservatives
			TX609	641.44	Drying apparatus—Food
TX5	640.6	Home economics—Congresses	TX609	641.44	Dried foods
			TX609	641.44	Food—Drying
TX11	640.3	Home economics—Encyclopedias	TX610	641.453	Frozen foods
			TX612.F5	641.494	Fishery products—Preservation
TX15-19	640.9	Home economics—History			
TX21-127	640.9(4-9)	Home economics—[By region or country]	TX631-641	641.013	Gastronomy
			TX642-840	641.5	Cookery
TX147	647	Institution management	TX645	641.509	Cookery—History
TX151-162	641.5	Recipes	TX649	641.5092	Cooks
TX165-286	640.71	Home economics—Study and teaching	TX653-655	643.3	Kitchens
			TX657.064	641.5882	Microwave ovens
TX298-299	640.284	Home economics—Equipment and supplies	TX657.S3-.S8	641.5028	Stoves
			TX661-669	641.5071	Cookery—Study and teaching
TX311-317	645	Interior decoration			
TX324	648.5	House cleaning	TX685	641.73l	Boiling (Cookery)
TX331-334	640.46	Domestics	TX687	641.76	Broiling

235

LC	Dewey	Subject Heading	LC	Dewey	Subject Heading
TX689.5	641.77	Stir frying	TX837-838	641.5636	Vegetarianism
TX690	641.71	Roasting (Cookery)	TX840.B3	641.5784	Barbecue cookery
TX691	641.73	Steaming (Cookery)	TX840.C65	641.58	Convection oven cookery
TX693	641.821	Casserole cookery	TX840.F6	641.589	Food processor cookery
TX693	641.73	Stews	TX840.P7	641.587	Pressure cookery
TX716.M4	641.5972	Cookery, Mexican	TX840.W65	641.589	Wok Cookery
TX719-.2	641.5944	Cookery, French	TX851-885	642.(6-8)	Entertaining
TX721	641.5943	Cookery, German	TX855-859	643.4	Dining rooms
TX724.5.C	641.589	Wok cookery	TX871-885	642	Table
TX724.5.J3	641.5952	Cookery, Japanese	TX871-885	642.7	Table setting and decoration
TX727-739.2	642	Menus	TX885	642.6	Carving (Meat, etc.)
TX731-739	642.4	Entertaining	TX901-946.5	658.383	Food service
TX733	641.52	Breakfasts	TX901-946	647.94	Hotels
TX735	641.53	Luncheons	TX901-941	647.94	Tourist camps, hostels, etc.
TX737	641.54	Dinners and dining	TX901-921	642.4	Caterers and catering
TX739-.2	641.568	Holiday cookery	TX901-910	642.5	Coffeehouses
TX739.2.C45	641.568	Christmas cookery	TX907-910	647.94	Youth hostels
TX739.2.E37	641.568	Easter cookery	TX911.3.M27	658.383068	Food service management
TX739.2.H35	641.5676435	Hanukkah cookery	TX911.3.P4	647.940683	Hotels—Personnel
TX739.2.P37	641.5676437	Passover cookery			management
TX739.2.T45	641.568	Thanksgiving cookery	TX911.3.P4	647.950683	Restaurants—Personnel
TX740	641.812	Appetizers			management
TX740	641.82	Entrees (Cookery)	TX945-.5	647.95	Restaurants
TX740	641.83	Salads	TX951	641.874	Bartending
TX740.5	641.81	Garnishes (Cookery)	TX951	641.874	Cocktails
TX743-759.5	641.36	Food of animal origin	TX951	641.874	Martinis
TX747	641.092	Cookery (Fish)	TX951	641.2	Beverages
TX747	641.692	Cookery (Seafood)	TX955	647	Building management
TX749-.5	641.66	Cookery (Meat)	TX957-959	647.92	Apartment houses
TX750-.5	641.665	Cookery (Poultry)	TX1100-1105	643.2	Mobile home living
TX761-799	664.02	Bakers and bakeries	U	355.02	War
TX769-770	641.815	Bread	U	355	Military art and science
TX770.B55	641.815	Biscuits	U1-145	355.0092	Soldiers
TX770.B55	641.815	Scones	U7	355.006	Military art and science—
TX770.M83	641.815	Muffins			Congresses
TX770.P34	641.815	Pancakes, waffles, etc.	U11	355.309730216	United States. Army—
TX770.P56	641.815	Pita bread			Registers
TX771-.2	641.8653	Cake	U13	355.0074	Military art and science—
TX771	641.8659	Coffee cakes			Exhibitions
TX772	641.8654	Cookies	U13	355.0074	Military museums
TX773	641.86	Desserts	U21	355.0213	Militarism
TX773	641.8659	Pastry	U22	355.123	Morale
TX773	641.864	Puddings	U24-26	355.003	Military art and science—
TX783-793	641.853	Candy			Dictionaries
TX783-799	641.853	Confectionery	U27-43	355.009	Military art and science—
TX795	641.86(2-3)	Ice cream, ices, etc.			History
TX801-807	641.65	Cookery (Vegetables)	U29-35	355.00901	Military art and science—
TX807	641.83	Salads			History—To 500
TX809.N65	641.822	Noodles	U51-55	355.0092	Military art and science—
TX815-817	641.87	Beverages			Biography
TX817.C5	641.877	Cocoa	U51-55	355.0092	Generals
TX818	641.84	Sandwiches	U56-59	355.3460973	United States—Armed
TX819	641.814	Sauces			Forces—Officers' clubs
TX819	641.3382	Condiments	U110-115	355.5	Military art and science—
TX819.S27	641.814	Salad dressing			Soldiers' handbooks
TX820	641.57	Quantity cookery	U113	355.5470973	United States. Army—
TX821	641.612	Cookery (Canned foods)			Handbooks, manuals, etc.
TX823	641.578	Outdoor cookery	U130-135	355	Military art and science—
TX827	641.586	Stoves, Electric			Officers' handbooks
TX832	641.5882	Microwave cookery	U161-163	355.4	Operational art (Military
TX837-838	641.5636	Vegetarian cookery			science)

LC	Dewey	Subject Heading	LC	Dewey	Subject Heading
U161-163	355.42	Strategy	U390-395	355.07	Military research
U162.6	355.0217	Deterrence (Strategy)	U400-714	355.0071	Military education
U164-167.5	355.42	Tactics	U407-714	355.00710(4-9)	Military education—[By region or country]
U167	355.422	Amicicide (Military science)	U408-439	355.0071073	Military education—United States
U167.5.A35	355.4	Advanced guard (Military science)	U408.3	355.50973	Experimental Volunteer Army Training Progam
U167.5.E57	355.422	Envelopment (Military science)	U409	355.007107(4-9)	Military education—[United States, By state]
U167.5.H3	355.824	Flexible weapons (Hand-to-hand fighting)	U410.E9	355.0071073	Hazing
U167.5.J8	355.423	Jungle warfare	U440-444	355.0071071	Military education—Canada
U167.5.L5	355.422	Lightning war	U445-449	355.0071072	Military education—Mexico
U167.5.R34	355.422	Raids (Military science)	U450-454	355.00710728	Military education—Central America
U167.5.W5	355.423	Winter warfare	U455-459	355.00710729	Military education—West Indies
U168	355.411	Logistics			
U168	355.411	Integrated logistic support	U465-499	355.007108	Military education—South America
U173	355.350973	United States. Army—Field service	U505-630	355.007104	Military education—Europe
U173.5	355.350975	Confederate States of America. Army—Field service	U510-549.3	355.0071041	Military education—Great Britain
U190-195	355.422	Guard duty	U550-554	355.00710436	Military education—Austria
U190	355.413	Scouts and scouting	U570-574.54	355.0071043	Military education—Germany
U200	355.422	Landing operations	U635-660	355.007105	Military education—Asia
U205	355.423	Stream crossing, Military	U640-644	355.0071051	Military education—China
U210	355.422	Skirmishing	U645-649	355.0071054	Military education—India
U215	355.422	Rearguard action (Military science)	U650-654	355.0071052	Military education—Japan
U220	355.413	Military reconnaisance	U655-659	355.0071055	Military education—Iran
U230	355.351	Riots	U670-695	355.007106	Military education—Africa
U240	355.0218	Guerrilla warfare	U700-704	355.0071094	Military education—Australia
U241	355.0218	Counterinsurgency	U715-717	355.5071	Soldiers—Education, Non-military
U250-255	355.4	Military maneuvers			
U253	355.40973	United States. Army—Maneuvers	U750-773	355.0092	Soldiers
			U800-897	623.4409	Armor
U260	355.46	Combined operations (Military science)	U800-897	355.8	Weapons
			U804	623.441074	Armor—Exhibitions
U260	366.46	Unified operations (Military science)	U805	623.4410901	Armor, Ancient
			U818-823.5	623.44109(4-9)	Armor—[By region or country]
U261	355.46	Amphibious warfare			
U262	355.422	Commando troops	U825	355.81	Helmets
U263	355.0217	Nuclear warfare	U850-872	355.8241	Swords
U263	355.0217	Nuclear crisis stabililty	U850-863	355.8241	Sabers
U264	355.825119	Nuclear weapons	U865	355.4	Swordplay
U264	355.0217	No first use (Nuclear strategy)	U872	623.441	Lances
U280-285	355.4(8)	Staff rides	U875	355.8241	Ballista
U290-295	355.5	Military training camps	U875	355.8241	Catapult
U300-305	355.5	Bombing and gunnery ranges	U877-878	355.8241	Bow and arrow
U310	355.480285	Computer war games	UA	355.75	Armories
U310	355.48	War games	UA	355.31	Armies
U310	355.480285	AGATE (Computer war game)	UA10	355.0213	Militarism
U313	355.48	Imaginary wars and battles	UA10.7	355.45	Civilian-based defense
U320-325	355.5	Physical education and training, Military	UA11	355.0335	Military policy
			UA11.5	355.0215	Limited war
U323	355.50973	United States. Army—Physical training	UA12	355.031	Mutual security program, 1951-
U350-365	355.17	Military ceremonies, honors, and salutes	UA12.5	327.1747	Disarmament—Inspection
			UA12.8	355.35	Guard troops
U350-355	355.17	Weddings, Military	UA13	355.37	Militia
U370-375	355.35	Garrisons	UA14	355.352	Armies, Colonial

LC	Dewey	Subject Heading	LC	Dewey	Subject Heading
UA16	355.032	Military missions	UA330-339	355.3709742	New Hampshire—National Guard
UA17	355.622	Armies, Cost of			
UA17	355.622	War, Cost of	UA340-349	355.3709749	New Jersey—National Guard
UA17.5	355.22	Manpower	UA350-359	355.3709789	New Mexico—National Guard
UA18	355.26	Industrial mobilization			
UA19	355.0021	Military statistics	UA360-369	355.3709747	New York (State)—National Guard
UA23.2-.6	355.60973	United States. Dept. of Defense	UA370-379	355.3709756	North Carolina—National Guard
UA24-39	355.30973	United States. Army			
UA23-25	355.30973	United States. Army—History	UA380-389	355.3709784	North Dakota—National Guard
UA23	355.450973	United States—Defenses	UA390-399	355.3709771	Ohio—National Guard
UA24-39	355.30973	United States. Army	UA400-409	355.3709766	Oklahoma—National Guard
UA24.A7	355.30973	United States. Army—Appropriations and expenditures	UA410-419	355.3709795	Oregon—National Guard
			UA420-429	355.3709748	Pennsylvania—National Guard
UA28-29	356.10973	United States. Army. Infantry	UA430-439	355.3709745	Rhode Island—National Guard
UA30-31	357.10973	United States. Army. Cavalry			
UA32-33	358.120973	United States. Army—Artillery	UA440-449	355.3709757	South Carolina—National Guard
UA42-560	355.370973	United States—National Guard	UA450-459	355.3709783	South Dakota—National Guard
UA42-560	355.370973	United States—Militia	UA460-469	355.3709768	Tennessee—National Guard
UA42-560	355.370973	United States—Armed Forces—Reserves	UA470-479	355.3709764	Texas—National Guard
			UA480-489	355.3709792	Utah—National Guard
UA45	355.3480973	United States—Armed Forces—Women's reserves	UA490-499	355.3709743	Vermont—National Guard
			UA500-509	355.3709755	Virginia—National Guard
UA50-549	355.37097(4-9)	United States—Armed Forces—Reserves [By state]	UA510-519	355.3709797	Washington (State)—National Guard
			UA520-529	355.3709754	West Virginia—National Guard
UA50-59	355.3709761	Alabama—National Guard			
UA60-69	355.3709798	Alaska—National Guard	UA530-539	355.3709775	Wisconsin—National Guard
UA70-79	355.3709791	Arizona—National Guard	UA540-549	355.3709787	Wyoming—National Guard
UA80-89	355.3709767	Arkansas—National Guard	UA580-585	355.30975	Confederate States of America. Army
UA90-99	355.3709794	California—National Guard			
UA100-109	355.3709746	Connecticut—National Guard	UA580-585	355.450975	Confederate States of America—Defenses
UA110-119	355.3709751	Delaware—National Guard			
UA120-129	355.3709753	Washington (D.C.)—National Guard	UA830	355.03305	East Asia—Strategic aspects
UA140-149	355.3709759	Florida—National Guard	UA910-915	355.28	Armed forces—Mobilization
UA150-159	355.3709758	Georgia—National Guard	UA926-929	363.35	Civil defense
UA159.1-.9	355.3709969	Hawaii—National Guard	UA940-945	355.85/623.73	Communications, Military
UA160-169	355.3709796	Idaho—National Guard	UA985-997	355.47	Military geography
UA170-179	355.3709773	Illinois—National Guard	UA985-997	355.47	Maps, Military
UA180-189	355.3709772	Indiana—National Guard	UB	355.6	Military administration
UA190-199	355.3709777	Iowa—National Guard	UB1	355.605	Military administration—Periodicals
UA200-209	355.3709781	Kansas—National Guard			
UA210-219	355.3709769	Kentucky—National Guard	UB15	355.609	Military administration—History
UA220-229	355.3709763	Louisiana—National Guard			
UA230-239	355.3709741	Maine—National Guard	UB23-25	355.60973	United States—Armed Forces—Management
UA240-249	355.3709752	Maryland—National Guard			
UA250-259	355.3709744	Massachusetts—National Guard	UB73-74	355.60943	Germany—Armed Forces—Management
UA260-269	355.3709774	Michigan—National Guard	UB85-86	355.60947	Russia—Armed Forces—Management
UA270-279	355.3709776	Minnesota—National Guard			
UA280-289	355.3709762	Mississippi—National Guard	UB101-102	355.60951	China—Armed Forces—Management
UA290-299	355.3709778	Missouri—National Guard			
UA300-309	355.3709786	Montana—National Guard	UB105-106	355.60952	Japan—Armed Forces—Management
UA310-319	355.3709782	Nebraska—National Guard			
UA320-329	355.3709793	Nevada—National Guard			

LC	Dewey	Subject Heading	LC	Dewey	Subject Heading
UB163	355.60973	United States. Army—Records and correspondence	UB640-644	343.4501	Military law—Italy
			UB650-654	343.46901	Military law—Portugal
			UB655-659	343.4701	Military law—Russia
UB210	355.33041	Command of troops	UB660-664	343.4601	Military law—Spain
UB210	355.33041	Leadership	UB685-710	343.501	Military law—Asia
UB233	355.306073	United States—Armed Forces—Headquarters	UB690-694	343.5101	Military law—China
			UB695-699	343.5401	Military law—India
UB240-245	355.685	Military inspectors general	UB700-704	343.5201	Military law—Japan
UB243	355.6850973	United States. Army—Inspection	UB715-729	343.601	Military law—Africa
			UB730-734	343.9401	Military law—Australia
UB250-271	355.3432	Military intelligence	UB735-736	343.9(5-6)01	Military law—Oceania
UB270-271	355.3432092	Spies	UB780-789	355.1334	Military offenses
UB275-277	355.3434	Psychological warfare	UB787	355.1334	Mutiny
UB280-285	355.113	Military passes	UB788	355.1334	Desertion, Military
UB320-345	355.223	Recruiting and enlistment	UB789	355.1334	Insubordination
UB320-338	355.2236	Advertising—Recruiting and enlistment	UB790-795	343.014	Military discipline
			UB800-805	365.48	Military prisons
UB320-325	355.22362	Military service, Voluntary	UB810-815	355.13325	Corporal punishment
UB323	355.2230973	United States. Army—Recruiting, enlistment, etc. Draft	UB820-825	355.13323	Military police
			UB850-857	343.0143	Courts-martial and courts of inquiry
UB340-355	355.22363	Conscientious objectors	UB880	394.(7-8)	Courts of honor
UB341-342	355.224	Draft	UC15	355.28	Requisitions, Military
UB350-355	355.225	Veterans	UC40-44	355.620973	United States. Army—Commissariat
UB356-375	362.1608697	Veterans—Employment			
UB356-359	331.52	Veterans—Education	UC70-75	355.640973	United States. Army—Pay, allowances, etc.
UB356-359	371.82697	Veterans, Disabled			
UB360-366	362.408697	Veterans—Medical care	UC85-86	355.620975	Confederate States of America. Army—Commissariat
UB368-369.5	362.108697	Military pensions			
UB370-375	331.25291355	Soldiers' homes			
UB380-385	362.1608697	Military reservations	UC90-93	355.80971	Canada—Armed forces—Supplies and stores
UB390-395	355.7	Military dependents			
UB400-405	355.12	United States—Armed Forces—Warrant officers	UC94-97	355.80972	Mexico—Armed forces—Supplies and stores
UB408-.5	355.3320973				
			UC98-99	355.809728	Central America—Armed Forces—Supplies and stores
UB410-415	355.332	Armies—Officers			
UB412-414	355.3320973	United States. Army—Officers	UC106-154	355.8098	South America—Armed Forces—Supplies and stores
UB418.B69	355.3308351	Boys as soldiers			
UB430-435	355.134	Military decorations	UC158-233	355.8094	Europe—Armed Forces—Supplies and stores
UB430-435	355.1342	Decorations of honor			
UB433	355.13420973	Distinguished Service Cross (U.S.)	UC180-183	355.80943	Germany—Armed Forces—Supplies and stores
			UC184-187	355.80941	Great Britain—Armed Forces—Supplies and stores
UB433	355.13420973	Medal of Honor			
UB435.G	355.13420941	Distinguished Conduct Medal (Great Britain)	UC234-245	355.8095	Asia—Armed Forces—Supplies and stores
UB461-736	343.(3-9)01	Military law—[By region and country]	UC241	355.80952	Japan—Armed Forces—Supplies and stores
UB505-509	343.7101	Military law—Canada	UC247-253	355.8096	Africa—Armed Forces—Supplies and stores
UB510-514	343.7201	Military law—Mexico			
UB515-519	343.72801	Military law—Central America	UC255-256	355.80994	Australia—Armed Forces—Supplies and stores
UB520-524	343.72901	Military law—West Indies			
UB530-589	343.801	Military law—South America	UC260-267	355.62137	Surplus military property
UB530-534	343.8201	Military law—Argentina	UC260-267	355.8	Military supplies
UB545-549	343.8301	Military law—Chile	UC260-267	355.62120973	United States—Armed Forces—Procurement
UB550-554	343.86101	Military law—Colombia			
UB585-589	343.8701	Military law—Venezuela	UC260	355.6212	Armed forces—Procurement
UB590-684	343.401	Military law—Europe	UC263	355.62120973	United States. Army—Procurement
UB615-619	343.4401	Military law—France			
UB620-624	343.4301	Military law—Germany	UC270-360	358.25	Transportation, Military
UB630-634	343.49501	Military law—Greece			

239

LC	Dewey	Subject Heading	LC	Dewey	Subject Heading
UC273	358.250973	United States. Army—Transporation	UE21-124	357.09(4-9)	Cavalry—[By region or country]
UC300-305	358.25	Pack transportation	UE23-25	357.0973	Cavalry—United States
UC320-325	355.83	Transports	UE26-27	357.0971	Cavalry—Canada
UC330-335	355.83	Airlift, Military	UE28-29	357.0972	Cavalry—Mexico
UC330-335	355.83	Airdrop	UE30-31	357.09728	Cavalry—Central America
UC340-345	355.83	Motorization, Military	UE32-33	357.09729	Cavalry—West Indies
UC400-440	355.71	Barracks	UE34-54	357.098	Cavalry—South America
UC410	355.71	Soldiers—Billeting	UE36-37	357.0982	Cavalry—Argentina
UC460-465	355.81	Armies—Equipment	UE43-44	357.0983	Cavalry—Chile
UC480-485	355.14	Military uniforms	UE45-46	357.09861	Cavalry—Colombia
UC523	355.80973	United States. Army—Equipment	UE54	357.0987	Cavalry—Venezuela
UC530-535	355.14	Insignia	UE55-95	357.094	Cavalry—Europe
UC533	355.13420973	United States. Army—Medals, badges, decorations, etc.	UE57-64	357.0941	Cavalry—Great Britain
			UE71-72	357.0944	Cavalry—France
			UE73-74	357.0943	Cavalry—Germany
			UE75-76	357.09495	Cavalry—Greece
UC570-575	355.81	Tents	UE79-80	357.0945	Cavalry—Italy
UC590-595	355.15	Standards, Military	UE83-84	357.09469	Cavalry—Portugal
UC590-595	355.15	Guidons	UE85-86	357.0947	Cavalry—Russia
UC590-595	355.15	Flags	UE86.5	357.0948	Cavalry—Scandinavia
UC600-695	357.2	Horses	UE87-88	357.0946	Cavalry—Spain
UC600-695	357.2	Remount service	UE99-113	357.095	Cavalry—Asia
UC700-780	355.62	Armies—Commissariat	UE101-102	357.0951	Cavalry—China
UC720-735	641.57	Cookery, Military	UE103-104	357.0954	Cavalry—India
UC723	355.3410973	United States—Armed Forces—Messes	UE105-106	357.0952	Cavalry—Japan
			UE115-119	357.096	Cavalry—Africa
UD	356.1	Infantry	UE121-122	357.0994	Cavalry—Australia
UD1	356.106	Infantry—Societies, etc.	UE123-124	357.099(5-6)	Cavalry—Oceania
UD15	356.109	Infantry—History	UE157-302	357.184	Cavalry drill and tactics
UD23	356.10973	United States. Army. Infantry	UE420-425	357.0482	Sabers
UD157-302	356.1154	Infantry drill and tactics	UE420-425	357.048241	Swords
UD310-315	356.114	Marching	UE440-445	357.04144	Cavalry—Uniforms
UD330-335	356.114	Sharpshooting (Military science)	UE460-475	357.2	War horses
			UE460-475	357.2	Horses
UD330-335	356.114	Sniping (Military science)	UE460-475	357.2	Horsemanship
UD330-335	356.11547	Shooting, Military	UF	358.12	Artillery
UD340-345	356.118241	Bayonets	UF1	358.12006	Artillery—Societies, etc.
UD370-375	356.118	Infantry—Equipment	UF6	358.12074	Military museums
UD380-415	356.1182	Firearms	UF9	358.1203	Artillery—Dictionaries
UD383.5	355.82420975	Confederate States of America. Army—Firearms	UF15	358.1209	Artillery—History
			UF21-124	358.1209(4-9)	Artillery—[By region or country]
UD390-395	356.1182425	Assault rifles			
UD390-395	356.1182425	Rifles	UF23-25	358.120973	Artillery—United States
UD390	356.1182	Firearms—Sights	UF23	358.120973	United States. Army—Artillery
UD395.M17	356.11824250973	M1 carbine			
UD400	356.118241	Bayonets	UF26-27	358.120971	Artillery—Canada
UD410-415	356.1182432	Pistols	UF28-29	358.120972	Artillery—Mexico
UD410-415	356.1182436	Revolvers	UF30-31	358.1209728	Artillery—Central America
UD420-425	356.118241	Swords	UF32-33	358.1209729	Artillery—West Indies
UD460-465	356.164	Mountain warfare	UF34-54	358.12098	Artillery—South America
UD460-465	356.4	Military maneuvers	UF36-37	358.120982	Artillery—Argentina
UD470-475	356.164	Ski troops	UF43-44	358.120983	Artillery—Chile
UD480-485	356.166	Parachute troops	UF45-46	358.1209861	Artillery—Colombia
UD483	356.1660973	United States—Armed Forces—Airborne troops	UF54	358.120987	Artillery—Venezuela
			UF55-95	358.12094	Artillery—Europe
UD483	356.1660973	United States—Armed Forces—Parachute troops	UF57-64	358.120941	Artillery—Great Britain
			UF71-72	358.120944	Artillery—France
UE	357	Cavalry	UF73-74	358.120943	Artillery—Germany
UE1	357.06	Cavalry—Societies, etc.	UF75-76	358.1209495	Artillery—Greece
UE15	357.09	Cavalry—History	UF79-80	358.120945	Artillery—Italy

LC	Dewey	Subject Heading	LC	Dewey	Subject Heading
UF83-84	358.1209469	Artillery—Portugal	UG21-124	358.2209(4-9)	Military engineering—[By region or country]
UF85-86	358.120947	Artillery—Russia			
UF86.5	358.120948	Artillery—Scandinavia	UG127-128	358.22092	Tank engineers
UF87-88	358.120946	Artillery—Spain	UG157	358.22071	Military engineering—Study and teaching
UF99-113	358.12095	Artillery—Asia			
UF101-102	358.120951	Artillery—China	UG330	623.62	Military roads
UF103-104	358.120954	Artillery—India	UG335	623.67	Military bridges
UF105-106	358.120952	Artillery—Japan	UG335	623.67	Pontoon bridges
UF115-119	358.12096	Artillery—Africa	UG340	623.68	Tunneling
UF121-122	358.12099 (3/4)	Artillery—[New Zealand/ Australia]	UG345	623.63	Armored trains
			UG345	623.63	Military railroads
UF123-124	358.12099(5-6)	Artillery—Oceania	UG360-390	358.22	Military field engineering
UF157-302	358.124	Artillery drill and tactics	UG370	358.23	Demolition, Military
UF160-162	358.1240973	United States. Army—Artillery—Drill and tactics	UG375	358.22	Obstacles (Military science)
			UG400-442	623.1	Fortification
UF340-345	358.125	Target practice	UG403	623.1	Fortification, Field
UF400-445	358.12	Artillery, Field and mountain	UG403	623.1	Intrenchments
UF450-455	358.16	Artillery, Coast	UG443-449	355.44	Siege warfare
UF470-475	358.12822	Howitzers	UG446	355.44	Intrenchments
UF520-780	358.1282	Ordnance	UG446.5	358.1883	M1 (Tank)
UF523-563	355.80973	United States. Army—Ordnance and ordnance stores	UG446.5	358.1883	Armored personnel carriers
			UG446.5	358.1883	Half-track vehicles, Military
			UG446.5	358.1883	Tanks (Military science)
UF540-545	355.7	Arsenals	UG447-.5	358.34	Gases, Asphyxiating and poisonous—War use
UF560-565	358.128	Ordnance, Rapid-fire			
UF560-565	358.1282	Howitzers	UG447-.65	358.34	Chemical warfare
UF563.A77	358.1282	Trench mortars	UG447.5.M8	358.34	Mustard gas
UF620	358.1282	Machine-guns	UG447.7	355.41	Smoke screens
UF625	358.1382	Antiaircraft guns	UG447.8	358.38	Biological warfare
UF625	358.174	Surface-to-air missiles	UG448	358.16	Coast defenses
UF628	358.12	Antitank weapons	UG449	355.41	Camouflage (Military science)
UF656	358.1282	Recoilless rifles			
UF700-770	358.1282	Ammunition	UG470-474	623.71	Maps, Military
UF740-745	358.128255	Cartridges	UG476	623.72	Photographic interpretation (Military science)
UF750-770	358.1282513	Projectiles			
UF765	358.1282	Grenades	UG480	623.76	Electricity in military engineering
UF767	358.128251	Projectiles, Aerial			
UF767	358.1282356	Rockets (Ordnance)	UG485	623.043	Electronic counter-countermeasures
UF780	358.1282	Electric detonators			
UF800-805	623.55	Gunnery	UG485	623.043	Electronic countermeasures
UF820-840	623.51	Ballistics	UG485	623.043	Electronics in military engineering
UF820	623.51021	Ballistics—Tables			
UF830	623.510284	Ballistic instruments	UG487	623.042	Infrared radiation—Military applications
UF845	358.128	Telescopes			
UF848-856	623.558	Fire control (Gunnery)	UG490	623.45115	Mines (Military explosives)
UF849	623.5580284	Fire control (Gunnery)—Optical equipment	UG570-613.5	358.24	Signals and signaling
			UG582.H4	623.7312	Heliograph
UF850-857	623.46	Range-finding	UG590-613.5	623.732	Military telegraph
UF853	623.46	Position-finders	UG590-610.5	623.73 (2-3)	Military telecommunication
UF854	623.46	Firearms—Sights	UG611-.5	623.7341	Radio, Military
UF855	623.46	Telescopic sights	UG612-.5	623.7348	Radar—Military applications
UF860-880	623.452	Military fireworks	UG615-620	623.7472	Automobiles, Military
UF890	358.1280287	Ordnance testing	UG615-620	623.7472	Tracked landing vehicles
UG	358.22092	Military engineers	UG622-1425	358.4	Air forces
UG	358.22	Military engineering	UG622	358.4006	Air forces—Societies, etc.
UG1	358.2206	Military engineering—Societies, etc.	UG623	358.4006	Air forces—Congresses
			UG625	358.4009	Air forces—History
UG5	358.2206	Military engineering—Congresses	UG626-.2	358.40092	Air pilots, Military
			UG626-.2	358.43092	Fighter pilots
UG15	358.2209	Military engineering—History	UG630-670	358.4	Aeronautics, Military
			UG630-635	623.746	Airplanes, Military—Turrets

LC	Dewey	Subject Heading	LC	Dewey	Subject Heading
UG630	358.4	Air warfare	UH257-264	355.3450941	Medicine, Military—Great Britain
UG633-634.5	358.400973	United States. Air Force			
UG635	358.4009(4-9)	Air forces—[Other countries]	UH271-272	355.3450944	Medicine, Military—France
UG700-705	358.434	Fighter plane combat	UH273-274	355.3450943	Medicine, Military—Germany
UG700	358.41422	Air interdiction	UH275-276	355.34509495	Medicine, Military—Greece
UG730-735	358.414	Air defenses	UH279-280	355.3450945	Medicine, Military—Italy
UG760-765	358.45	Aerial reconnaissance	UH283-284	355.34509469	Medicine, Military—Portugal
UG763	358.450973	Aerial reconnaissance, American	UH285-286	355.3450947	Medicine, Military—Russia
			UH286.5	355.3450948	Medicine, Military—Scandinavia
UG765.G	358.450941	Aerial reconnaissance, British			
			UH287-288	355.3450946	Medicine, Military—Spain
UG1180-1185	358.414	Air forces—Insignia	UH299-313	355.345095	Medicine, Military—Asia
UG1230-1235	358.4383	Attack helicopters	UH301-302	355.3450951	Medicine, Military—China
UG1240-1242	358.4183	Airplanes, Military	UH303-304	355.3450954	Medicine, Military—India
UG1240	385.4183	Stealth aircraft	UH305-306	355.3450952	Medicine, Military—Japan
UG1242.A25	358.4283	Antisubmarine aircraft	UH315-319	355.345096	Medicine, Military—Africa
UG1242.A28	358.4283	Dive bombers	UH321-322	355.345094	Medicine, Military—Australia
UG1242.A28	358.43	Attack planes	UH323-324	355.345099(5-6)	Medicine, Military—Oceania
UG1242.A28	358.42	Dauntless (Dive bomber)	UH341-347	355.345092	Medicine, Military—Biography
UG1242.B6	358.42830973	B-52 bomber			
UG1242.F5	358.4303	Night fighter planes	UH398-399	355.345071	Medicine, Military—Study and teaching
UG1242.F5	358.4383	Fighter planes			
UG1242.R4	358.45	Reconnaissance aircraft	UH400	355.345092	Physicians
UG1282.N48	358.428251	Neutron bomb	UH420-425	355.345	Pharmacy, Military
UG1312.C7	358.428251	Cruise missiles	UH440-445	355.88	Medical supplies
UG1312.I2	358.175482	Intercontinental ballistic missiles	UH460-485	355.72	Military hospitals
			UH490-495	355.345	Military nursing
UG1500-1530	358.8	Space surveillance	UH500-505	355.83	Transportation, Military
UG1530	358.8	Space warfare	UH535-537	361.77	Red Cross
UH20-25	355.347	Chaplains	UH600-629.5	355.345	Military hygiene
UH40-45	781.599	Music in the army	UH650-655	355.345	Veterinary service, Military
UH40-45	781.599	Military calls	UH750-769	306.27	Military social work
UH40-45	781.599	Trumpet-calls	V	359	Naval art and science
UH80-85	355.693	Postal service	V	359	War
UH87-100	355.424	Animals—War use	V1-5	359.005	Naval art and science—Periodicals
UH201-551	355.345	War—Relief of sick and wounded			
			V7	359.006	Naval art and science—Congresses
UH201-515	355.345	Medicine, Military			
UH205	355.34506	Medicine, Military—Congresses	V13	359.0074	Naval museums
			V23-24	359.003	Naval art and science—Dictionaries
UH215-325	355.345021	War—Casualties (Statistics, etc.)			
			V23-24	359.003	Naval art and science—Terminology
UH215-324	355.34509	Medicine, Military—History			
UH223-224	355.3450973	Medicine, Military—United States	V25-55	359.009	Naval art and science—History
			V46	359.3220948	Viking ships
UH226-227	355.3450971	Medicine, Military—Canada	V61-65	359.0092	Naval biography
UH228-229	355.3450972	Medicine, Military—Mexico	V123	359.3320973	United States. Navy—Petty officers' handbooks
UH230-231	355.34509728	Medicine, Military—Central America			
			V133	359.3320973	United States. Navy—Officers' handbooks
UH232-233	355.34509729	Medicine, Military—West Indies			
			V143-144	359.3380973	United States. Navy—Sailors' handbooks
UH234-254	355.345098	Medicine, Military—South America			
UH236-237	355.3450982	Medicine, Military—Argentina	V160-165	359.42	Naval strategy
			V167-178	359.42	Naval tactics
UH243-244	355.3450983	Medicine, Military—Chile	V175	359.350973	United States. Navy—Field service
UH245-246	355.34509861	Medicine, Military—Colombia			
			V179	359.411	Logistics, Naval
UH254	355.3450987	Medicine, Military—Venezuela	V190	359.413	Naval reconnaissance
			V210-214.5	359.93	Submarine warfare
UH255-295	355.345094	Medicine, Military—Europe	V214.5	359.93	Submarine boat combat

242

LC	Dewey	Subject Heading	LC	Dewey	Subject Heading
V215	359.41	Warships—Camouflage	V857-859	359.933	Submarines (Ships)
V215	359.41	Camouflage (Military science)	V857-859	359.9383	Submarine boats
			V857.5	359.93834	Nuclear submarines
V230	359.7	Navy-yards and naval stations	V858	359.9330973	United States. Navy—Submarine forces
V245	359.41	Naval maneuvers	V865	359.985	Naval auxiliary vessels
V245	359.410973	United States. Navy—Maneuvers	V874-875	359.9435	Aircraft carriers
			V880	359.3220973	United States. Navy—Boats
V250	359.48	War games, Naval	V880	359.83	Motor vehicles, Amphibious
V253	359.48	Imaginary wars and battles	V880	359.82	Steel boats
V263	359.50973	United States. Navy—Physical training	V890	359.32	Floating batteries
			V990-995	359.981782	Fleet ballistic missile weapons systems
V280-285	623.8561	Signals and signaling			
V300-305	359.15	Flags	VA	359	Naval districts
V303-304	359.150973	Flags—United States	VA20-25	359.6229	Navies, Cost of
V305	359.1509(4-9)	Flags—[Other countries]	VA37-42	359	Navies
V310	359.17	Naval ceremonies, honors, and salutes	VA45	359.37	Naval reserves
			VA49-395	359.30973	United States. Navy—Organization
V383	359.00289	United States. Navy—Safety measures	VA53	359.6220973	United States. Navy—Appropriations and expenditures
V390-395	359.07	Naval research			
V396-.5	359.8	Military oceanography	VA66	359.70973	Navy-yards and naval stations—United States
V400-695	359.0071	Naval education			
V411-695	359.00710(4-9)	Naval education—[By region or country]	VA393-395	359.30975	Confederate States of America. Navy—Organization
V411-437	359.0071073	Naval education—United States	VA402	359.370971	Naval militia—Canada
V415	359.0071073	Midshipmen	VA460	359.370941	Navy-yards and naval stations—Great Britain
V435-436	359.50973	Training-ships			
V437	359.9709073	United States. Coast Guard	VB	359.6	Naval art and science
V438	973.0071075	Naval education—Confederate States of America	VB21-124	359.609(4-9)	Naval art and science—[By region or country]
			VB23-25	359.60973	Naval art and science—United States
V440-444	359.0071071	Naval education—Canada	VB26-27	359.60971	Naval art and science—Canada
V445-449	359.0071072	Naval education—Mexico			
V450-453	359.00710728	Naval education—Central America	VB28-29	359.60972	Naval art and science—Mexico
V455-458	359.00710729	Naval education—West Indies	VB30-31	359.609728	Naval art and science—Central America
V465-496	359.007108	Naval education—South America	VB32-33	359.609729	Naval art and science—West Indies
V500-623	359.007104	Naval education—Europe	VB34-54	359.6098	Naval art and science—South America
V510-530	359.0071041	Naval education—Great Britain	VB36-37	359.60982	Naval art and science—Argentina
V570-574.54	359.0071043	Naval education—Germany			
V625-650	359.007105	Naval education—Asia	VB43-44	359.60983	Naval art and science—Chile
V630-634	359.0071051	Naval education—China	VB45-46	359.609861	Naval art and science—Colombia
V635-639	359.0071054	Naval education—India			
V640-644	359.0071052	Naval education—Japan	VB55-96	359.6094	Naval art and science—Europe
V645-649	359.0071055	Naval education—Iran	VB57-64	359.60941	Naval art and science—Great Britain
V660-680	359.007106	Naval education—Africa			
V690-694	359.0071094	Naval education—Australia	VB71-72	359.60944	Naval art and science—France
V750-995	359.32	Warships			
V795	358.32	Ships of the line	VB73-74.5	359.60943	Naval art and science—Germany
V799-800	359.32	Armored vessels			
V810	623.888	Damage control (Warships)	VB75-76	359.609495	Naval art and science—Greece
V820-.5	359.3253	Battle cruisers			
V825-.5	359.3254	Destroyers (Warships)	VB79-80	359.60945	Naval art and science—Italy
V830-840	359.3258	Torpedo-boats			
V850-855	359.82517	Torpedoes			
V856-.5	623.26	Mines and minelaying			

LC	Dewey	Subject Heading	LC	Dewey	Subject Heading
VB83-84	359.609469	Naval art and science—Portugal	VC530-535	359.985	Military sealift
			VC550-580	359.985	Transportation, Military
VB85-86	359.60947	Naval art and science—Russia	VC553	359.9850973	United States. Navy—Transportation
VB87-88	359.60946	Naval art and science—Spain	VD	359.0092	Sailors
			VD15	359.0092	Sailors—History
VB99-113	359.6095	Naval art and science—Asia	VD21-124	359.0092	Sailors—[By region or country]
VB101-102	359.60951	Naval art and science—China			
VB105-106	359.60952	Naval art and science—Japan	VD23-25	359.009	Sailors—United States
			VD150-155	359.3380973	United States. Navy—Sailors' handbooks
VB115-119	359.6096	Naval art and science—Africa	VD360-390	359.824	Firearms
VB121-122	359.60994	Naval art and science—Australia	VD360-390	359.8240973	United States. Navy—Firearms
VB123-124	359.6099(5-6)	Naval art and science—Pacific Islands	VD370	359.82425	Rifles
			VD390	359.82432	Pistols
VB190	359.331	Admirals	VD390	359.82436	Revolvers
VB223	359.6850973	United States. Navy—Inspection	VD403	359.310973	United States. Navy—Small-boat service
VB230-250	359.3432	Intelligence service	VE	359.96	Marines
VB250	359.3432092	Spies	VE15	359.9609	Marines—History
VB258	359.610973	United States. Navy—Personnel management	VE21-124	359.96309(4-9)	Marines—[By region or country]
VB260-275	359.2236	Recruiting and enlistment	VE23-25	359.9630973	United States. Marine Corps
VB263	359.22360973	United States. Navy—Recruiting, enlistment, etc.	VE26-27	359.9630971	Marines—Canada
			VE28-29	359.9630972	Marines—Mexico
			VE30-31	359.96309728	Marines—Central America
VB280-285	362.86	Military pensions	VE32-33	359.96309729	Marines—West Indies
VB308	359.3320973	United States—Armed Forces—Warrant officers	VE34-54	359.963098	Marines—South America
			VE55-96	359.963094	Marines—Europe
VB310-315	359.332	Navies—Officers	VE57-64	359.9630941	Marines—Great Britain
VB313-314	359.3320973	United States. Navy—Officers	VE71-72	359.9630944	Marines—France
			VE73-74.5	359.9630943	Marines—Germany
VB330-335	359.1342	Military decorations	VE79-80	359.9630945	Marines—Italy
VB333	355.13420973	Navy Cross (Medal)	VE85-86	359.9630947	Marines—Russia
VB350-785	343.019	Naval law	VE86.5	359.9630948	Marines—Scandinavia
VB800-807	343.0143	Courts-martial and courts of inquiry	VE87-88	359.9630946	Marines—Spain
			VE99-113	359.963095	Marines—Asia
VB840-845	343.014	Naval discipline	VE105-106	359.9630952	Marines—Japan
VB850-880	359.1334	Naval offenses	VE115-119	359.963096	Marines—Africa
VB860-867	359.1334	Mutiny	VE121-122	359.9630994	Marines—Australia
VB870-875	359.1334	Desertion, Naval	VE122.5	359.9630993	Marines—New Zealand
VB880	359.1334	Insubordination	VE150-155	359.9633	Marines—Handbooks, manuals, etc.
VB890-895	365.48	Military prisons			
VB910	359.13325	Corporal punishment	VE160-162	359.9650973	United States. Marine Corps—Drill and tactics
VB920-925	359.13323	Military police			
VC20-65	359.80973	United States. Navy	VE345	359.961342	Marines—Insigna
VC50-65	359.80973	United States. Navy—Pay, allowances, etc.	VE350-390	359.96824	Marines—Firearms
			VE400-405	359.9614	Marines—Uniforms
VC184-187	359.80941	Great Britain. Royal Navy	VE420-425	359.9671	Marines—Barracks and quarters
VC260-267	359.62120973	United States. Navy—Procurement			
			VE430-435	359.965	Military training camps
VC263	359.80973	United States. Navy—Supplies and stores	VF	359.82	Ordnance, Naval
			VF1	359.82/ 623.82510 + 6	Ordnance, Naval—Societies, etc.
VC300-345	359.81	Military uniforms			
VC345	359.1342	Insignia	VF6	359.82/ 623.8251 + (074)	Naval museums
VC370-375	641.57	Cookery, Marine			
VC423	359.710973	United States. Navy—Barracks and quarters	VF15	359.82/ 623.8251 + (09)	Ordnance, Naval—History
VC503	359.6220973	United States. Navy—Accounting			

LC	Dewey	Subject Heading	LC	Dewey	Subject Heading
VF21-124	359.82/ 623.8251 + 09 (4-9)	Ordnance, Naval—[By region or country]	VF105-106	359.82/ 623.8251 + (0952)	Ordnance, Naval—Japan
VF23-25	359.82/ 623.8251 + (0973)	Ordnance, Naval—United States	VF111-112	359.82/ 623.8251 + (09561)	Ordnance, Naval—Turkey
VF26-27	359.82/ 623.8251 + (0971)	Ordnance, Naval—Canada	VF115-119	359.82/ 623.8251 + (096)	Ordnance, Naval—Africa
VF28-29	359.82/ 623.8251 + (0972)	Ordnance, Naval—Mexico	VF121-122	359.82/ 623.8251 + (0994)	Ordnance, Naval—Australia
VF30-31	359.82/ 623.8251 + (09728)	Ordnance, Naval—Central America	VF122.5	359.82/ 623.8251 + (0993)	Ordnance, Naval—New Zealand
VF32-33	359.82/ 623.8251 + (09729)	Ordnance, Naval—West Indies	VF310-315	359.547	Target practice
			VF347	359.820973	United States. Navy—Weapons systems
VF34-54	359.82/ 623.8251 + (098)	Ordnance, Naval—South America	VF347	359.98170973	AEGIS (Weapons system)
			VF347	359.98170973	United States. Navy—Fire control technicians (Missile)
VF36-37	359.82/ 623.8251 + (0982)	Ordnance, Naval—Argentina	VF350-420	359.8240973	United States. Navy—Firearms
VF43-44	359.82/ 623.8251 + (0983)	Ordnance, Naval—Chile	VF353-420	359.80973	United States. Navy—Ordnance and ordnance stores
VF45-46	359.82/ 623.8251 + (09861)	Ordnance, Naval—Colombia	VF410	359.82424	Machine-guns
			VF410.G2-.G24	359.82424	Gardner machine-gun
			VF410.G3-.G34	359.82424	Gatling guns
VF55-96	359.82/ 623.8251 + (094)	Ordnance, Naval—Europe	VF440	359.32	Warships—Turrets
			VF440	359.820973	Ridgway's revolving battery
			VF480-500	359.8251	Projectiles
			VF509	359.8251	Depth charges
VF57-64	359.82/ 623.8251 + (0941)	Ordnance, Naval—Great Britain	VF520-530	359.422	Fire control (Naval gunnery)
			VF540	359.80287	Ordnance testing
			VF550	623.51021	Ballistics—Tables
VF71-72	359.82/ 623.8251 + (0944)	Ordnance, Naval—France	VF550	359.422	Range-finding
			VG20-25	359.347	Chaplains, Military
			VG23	359.3470973	United States. Navy—Chaplains
VF73-74.5	359.82/ 623.8251 + (0943)	Ordnance, Naval—Germany	VG30-35	781.599	Military music
			VG33	781.599/ 784.84(0973)	United States. Navy—Songs and music
VF79-80	359.82/ 623.8251 + (0945)	Ordnance, Naval—Italy	VG53	359.970973	United States. Coast Guard
			VG60-65	359.34	Postal service
VF83-84	359.82/ 623.8251 + (09469)	Ordnance, Naval—Portugal	VG63	359.340973	United States. Navy—Postal service
			VG70-85	623.8567	Communications, Military
VF85-86	359.82/ 623.8251 + (0947)	Ordnance, Naval—Russia	VG73	359.9830973	United States. Navy—Communication systems
VF86.5	359.82/ 623.8251 + (0948)	Ordnance, Naval—Scandinavia	VG86-88	359.984	Underwater demolition teams
			VG87	359.9840973	Underwater demolition teams—United States
VF87-88	359.82/ 623.8251 + (0946)	Ordnance, Naval—Spain	VG90-95	359.94	Naval aviation
			VG90-95	359.94834	Airplanes, Military—Turrets
			VG93	359.940973	United States. Navy—Aviation
VF101-113	359.82/ 623.8251 + (095)	Ordnance, Naval—Asia	VG100-475	359.345	Medicine, Naval
			VG121-224	359.34509(4-9)	Medicine, Naval—[By region or country]

LC	Dewey	Subject Heading	LC	Dewey	Subject Heading
VG123-125	359.3450973	Medicine, Naval—United States	VK139-140	387.5092	Merchant mariners—Biography
VG126-127	359.3450971	Medicine, Naval—Canada	VK149	387.54044	Seafaring life
VG128-129	359.3450972	Medicine, Naval—Mexico	VK160	387.5023	Merchant marine—Vocational guidance
VG130-131	359.34509728	Medicine, Naval—Central America	VK200	623.890289	Navigation—Safety measures
VG132-133	359.4509729	Medicine, Naval—West Indies	VK200	623.888	Merchant marine—Safety measures
VG134-154	359.345098	Medicine, Naval—South America	VK205	387.5092	Ship captains
VG155-196	359.345094	Medicine, Naval—Europe	VK221	359.32092	Ships—Manning
VG157-164	359.3450941	Medicine, Naval—Great Britain	VK221	387.5092	Merchant marine—Officers
VG171-172	359.3450944	Medicine, Naval—France	VK235-237	387.245	Ships—Cargo
VG173-174.5	359.3450943	Medicine, Naval—Germany	VK235	387.544	Cargo handling
VG179-180	359.3450945	Medicine, Naval—Italy	VK235	387.544	Stowage
VG185-186	359.450947	Medicine, Naval—Russia	VK237	387.544	Load-line
VG186.5	359.3450948	Medicine, Naval—Scandinavia	VK321-369.8	387.1	Harbors
VG187-188	359.3450946	Medicine, Naval—Spain	VK321	387.12	Roadsteads
VG199-213	359.345095	Medicine, Naval—Asia	VK361-365	387.54044	Mooring of ships
VG205-206	359.3450952	Medicine, Naval—Japan	VK361-365	387.15	Docks
VG215-219	359.345096	Medicine, Naval—Africa	VK361	387.54044	Coaling
VG221-222	359.3450994	Medicine, Naval—Australia	VK369-.8	387.1	Harbors of refuge
VG222.5	359.3450993	Medicine, Naval—New Zealand	VK369-.8	387.15	Marinas
			VK371-378	623.8884	Collisions at sea—Prevention
VG226-228	359.345092	Medicine, Naval—Biography	VK371	623.8884	Rule of the road at sea
VG230-235	359.345071	Medicine, Naval—Study and teaching	VK381-397	623.8561	Signals and signaling
			VK381-397	387.54	Merchant marine—Signaling
VG270-275	359.345	Pharmacy, Military	VK388	623.8938	Sonar
VG280-285	359.345	Dentistry, Naval	VK397	623.85642	Telegraph, Wireless—Installation on ships
VG290-295	359.88	Medical supplies	VK397	623.8932	Radio—Installation on ships
VG410-450	359.72	Hospitals, Naval and marine	VK397	623.8932	Radio in navigation
VG457	361.77	Red Cross	VK401-529	623.89071	Navigation—Study and teaching
VG470-475	359.345	Naval hygiene	VK525-529	623.880971	Nautical training-schools
VG500-505	359.342	Journalism, Military	VK541-547	623.88	Seamanship
VG503	359.3420973	Journalism, Military—United States	VK543	623.88203	Sailing
			VK549-587	527	Nautical astronomy
VG803	359.3380973	United States. Navy—Machinist's mates	VK560-561	623.8932	Loran
			VK560	623.89	Hyperbolic navigation
VG903	359.3380973	United States. Navy—Yeomen	VK560	623.89	Decca navigation
			VK560	623.893	Electronics in navigation
VG913	359.3380973	United States. Navy—Draftsmen	VK560	623.8938	Sonar
VG953	359.3380973	United States. Navy—Boatswains	VK562	623.893	Artificial satellites in navigation
VG1020	359.34320973	United States. Navy—Intelligence specialists	VK563-567	527.021	Navigation—Tables
			VK563-567	523.3021	Moon—Tables
VK	387.5	Merchant marine	VK563	527	Azimuth
VK	551.46	Hydrography	VK565-567	527.2	Longitude
VK	623.82	Ships	VK565	527.1	Latitude
VK1-4	387.505	Merchant marine—Periodicals	VK570	387.52	Optimum ship routing
			VK571	387.52	Great circle sailing
VK5	387.506	Merchant marine—Congresses	VK572	527.015308	Mile, Nautical
			VK573-587	623.89(2-3)	Nautical instruments
VK15-20	387.509	Merchant marine—History	VK577	623.8932	Radio compass
VK21-124	387.509(4-9)	Merchant marine—[By region or country]	VK577	623.8932	Gyro compass
			VK577	623.8932	Compass
VK23-25	387.50973	Merchant marine—United States	VK581	623.890284	Logs (Nautical instruments)
			VK583	623.890284	Sextant
			VK583	623.890284	Quadrant

LC	Dewey	Subject Heading	LC	Dewey	Subject Heading
VK583.5	623.89	Inertial navigation systems	VM17	623.821	Ships, Medieval
VK584.A7	527.0284	Artificial horizons (Nautical instruments)	VM101	623.810951	Junks
			VM142-144	623.8184	Ships, Wooden
VK584.S6	623.8938	Echo sounding	VM146-147	623.81821	Ships, Iron and steel
VK584.S6	623.8938	Sounding and soundings	VM146	623.81821	Marine steel
VK588-597	551.4607	Hydrographic surveying	VM148	623.81833	Ships, Concrete
VK798-997	623.8922	Pilot guides	VM155	623.810287	Ships—Measurement
VK798	623.8922	Notices to mariners	VM157	623.81	Displacement (Ships)
VK804-997	623.892216 (3-7)	Pilot guides—[By body of water]	VM159	623.81	Stability of ships
			VM165-276	623.81071	Naval architecture—Study and teaching
VK810-880	623.89223	Pilot guides—Atlantic Ocean			
VK815-818	623.8922336	Pilot guides—North Sea	VM298	623.8201	Ship models
VK819-821.8	623.8922334	Pilot guides—Baltic Sea	VM298	623.8201043	Sailing ships—Models
VK839-844	623.8922336	Pilot guides—English Channel	VM298.3	745.5928	Ship models in bottles
			VM298.5-301	338.4762382	Shipbuilding industry
VK853-874	623.892238	Pilot guides—Mediterranean Sea	VM299.5-.7	623.820681	Shipbuilding subsidies
			VM308	623.84	Figureheads of ships
VK885-901	623.89225	Pilot guides—Indian Ocean	VM311.C3	623.822	Catamarans
VK915-956	623.89224	Pilot guides—Pacific Ocean	VM317	623.8728	Nuclear ships
VK917	623.892244	Pilot guides—North Pacific Ocean	VM320-361	623.843	Steel boats
			VM320-361	623.82	Boatbuilding
VK925	623.892248	Pilot guides—South Pacific Ocean	VM325	623.85641	Radio on boats
			VM325	623.8504	Boats and boating—Electronic equipment
VK947-948	623.89223(4/6)	Pilot guides—United States			
VK1000-1249	623.8944	Beacons	VM331-333	623.82023	Yachts
VK1000-1246	623.8943	Lightships	VM331	623.8226	Skipjacks
VK1000-1246	623.8942	Lighthouses	VM335	728.78	Houseboats
VK1000-1246	623.8944	Buoys	VM340-349	623.81	Motorboats
VK1015	623.894209	Lighthouses—History	VM340-349	623.81	Launches
VK1021-1124	623.894209 (4-9)	Lighthouses—[By region or country]	VM341-349	623.84	Planing hulls
			VM345-347	623.8726	Electric boats
VK1023-1025	623.89420973	Lighthouses—United States	VM351-361	623.8223	Sailboats
VK1025.D	623.89420916347	Drum Point Lighthouse (Md.)	VM352	623.8202	Rafts
VK1025.H	623.894209751	Harbor of Refuge Lighthouse (Del.)	VM353	623.8202	Dugout canoes
			VM362	623.8204	Hydrofoil boats
VK1026-1027	623.89420971	Lighthouses—Canada	VM365-367	623.8257	Submarines (Ships)
VK1150-1246	623.8944	Buoys—[By region or country]	VM371	623.8226	Dhows
			VM381-383	623.8243	Passenger ships
VK1250-1299	363.123	Steamboat disasters	VM391-395	623.8245	Cargo ships
VK1250-1299	363.123	Shipwrecks	VM393.B7	623.8245	Bulk carrier cargo ships
VK1250-1294	623.8886	Ships—Fires and fire prevention	VM393.R64	623.8245	Roll-on/roll-off ships
			VM396	623.82436	Inland waterway vessels
VK1259	363.3481	Refloating of ships	VM451	623.828	Ice-breaking vessels
VK1265	363.123	Submarine disasters	VM453	623.8226	Oceanographic research ships
VK1270-1294	363.12309(4-9)	Shipwrecks—[By region or country]			
			VM453	623.828	Deep-sea drilling ships
VK1300-1481	623.8887	Life-saving	VM455	623.8245	Tankers
VK1315	623.888709	Life-saving—History	VM455.3	623.8(1245/245)	Chemical carriers (Tankers)
VK1321-1424	623.888709 (4-9)	Life-saving—[By region or country]	VM457	623.8245	Ore carriers
			VM459	623.8245	Refrigerator ships
VK1460-1481	623.8887	Life-saving apparatus	VM460	623.82436	Lake steamers
VK1473	387.29	Life-boats	VM461-.5	623.82436	River boats
VK1477	623.865	Life-preservers	VM461-.5	623.82436	River steamers
VK1479	623.865	Line-throwing rockets	VM464	623.8232	Tugboats
VK1481.L55	623.865	Line-throwing guns	VM464	623.8232	Towboats
VK1491	387.55	Salvage	VM466.B3	623.829	Barges
VK1500-1661	623.8922	Pilots and pilotage	VM466.035	623.826	Offshore support vessels
VK1515	623.892209	Pilots and pilotage—History	VM471-479	623.8503	Ships—Electric equipment
VK1521-1624	623.892 (2-9) + (4-9)	Pilots and pilotage—[By region or country]	VM480-.5	623.8504	Ships—Electronic equipment
			VM481-482	623.853	Ships—Heating and ventilation
VM	623.81	Ships			

247

LC	Dewey	Subject Heading	LC	Dewey	Subject Heading
VM485	623.8535	Marine refrigeration	Z244	686.2	Print finishing processes
VM485	623.8535	Cold storage on shipboard	Z245	686.20299	Printing industry—Estimates
VM491-493	623.852	Ships—Lighting	Z246	686.2252	Printing—Layout
VM493	623.852	Search-lights	Z247	676	Paper
VM503-505	623.8542	Ships—Water-supply	Z247	667.4	Printing ink
VM505	623.854	Seawater—Distillation	Z249-.4	681.62	Printing-press
VM505	623.854	Distilled water	Z249	686.20284	Paper-cutting machines
VM531-533	623.862	Masts and rigging	Z250	686.224	Printing—Specimens
VM531-533	623.88	Marlin spike seamanship	Z252	686.221	Electrotyping
VM532	623.862	Sails	Z252.5.N46	686.233	Nonimpact printing
VM533	623.8882	Knots and splices	Z253	686.22542	Monotype
VM595-989	623.87	Marine engineering	Z253	686.22542	Linotype
VM600-881	623.8	Marine engineering	Z253.5	686.2252	Magazine design
VM615-619	623.809	Marine engineering—History	Z253.53-.532	686.22544416	Desktop publishing
VM621-724	623.809(4-9)	Marine engineering—[By region or country]	Z254	686.2255	Proofreading
			Z256	686.20284	Rollers (Printing)
VM725-728	623.8071	Marine engineering—Study and teaching	Z258	686.23042	Color-printing
			Z265-.5	686.43	Documents on microfilm
VM731-779	623.87	Marine engines	Z265	686.43	Micrographics
VM741-750	623.8722	Steam-boilers, Marine	Z266-276	686.3	Bookbinding
VM753-757	623.873	Propellers	Z269-.3	686.30092	Bookbinders
VM770	623.87236	Marine diesel motors	Z272	686.3	Endpapers
VM774-777	623.8728	Nuclear ships	Z278-550	381.45002	Booksellers and bookselling
VM774-777	623.8728	Marine nuclear reactor plants	Z278-550	070.5	Publishers and publishing
			Z286.D47	686.22544416	Desktop publishing
VM779	623.874	Ships—Fuel	Z286.S37	070.594	Scholarly publishing
VM781-881	623.86	Ships—Equipment and supplies	Z280-550	070.509(1-9)	Publishers and publishing, [By region or country]
VM781	623.86	Deck machinery	Z549	070.5	Book clubs
VM791	623.862	Anchors	Z551-656	351.824	Copyright
VM801	623.86	Davits	Z649.T7	346.0482	Copyright—Transfer
VM811	621.864	Windlasses	Z657-659	323.445	Book burning
VM811	621.864	Capstan	Z662-664	027	Libraries
VM815	623.852	Ships' lights	Z665-720	020	Library science
VM821	623.8501	Marine compressors	Z674.2-.5	025.52	Information services
VM831	623.86	Davits	Z674.7-.83	021.65	Library information networks
VM841-845	623.862	Steering-gear	Z675.A2	026	Special libraries
VM965	623.8432	Underwater welding and cutting	Z675.A5	026.62913	Aeronautical libraries
			Z675.B8	027.69	Business libraries
VM987	623.827	Diving bells	Z675.C5	027.67	Church libraries
Z4-8	002.09	Books—History	Z675.C8	027.5	Public libraries
Z40-104.5	652.1	Writing	Z675.D28	026.3046	Demographic libraries
Z41-42	929.88	Signatures (Writing)	Z675.D3	026.6176	Dental libraires
Z41-42.5	929.88	Autographs	Z675.D4	025.26	Depository libraries
Z43-45	745.61	Caligraphy	Z675.G7	027.5	Government libraries
Z43-45	652.1	Penmanship	Z675.G7	027.5	Libraries, Governmental, administrative, etc.
Z48	686.4	Copying processes			
Z48	686.4	Fluid copying processes	Z675.H7	027.662	Hospital libraries
Z49-50.5	652.3	Typewriters	Z675.P8	027.665	Prison libraries
Z53-104.5	653	Shorthand	Z675.P85	027.2	Proprietary libraries
Z102.5-104.5	652.8	Cryptography	Z675.R4	027.3	Rental libraries
Z105-115.5	411.7	Paleography	Z675.S3	027.8	School libraries
Z116.A2-265.5.A5	686.2	Printing	Z675.U5	027.7	Academic libraries
			Z675.V7	027.091734	Rural libraries
Z122-.5	686.071	Printing—Study and teaching	Z678-.88	025.1	Library administration
Z124-242	686.09	Printing—History	Z678.9-.93	025.3132	Libraries—Automation
Z231-234	686.2092	Printers	Z678.93.D85	025.3132	Dynix (Computer system)
Z231.5.L5	070.592	Small presses	Z682-.4	023.2	Librarians
Z235-236	686.20278	Printers' marks	Z682.4.A45	023.4	Library administrators
Z240-241.5	092	Block books	Z682.4.C65	023.2	Library consultants
Z242.9-264	686.225	Printing	Z683-.2	025.11	Library finance

LC	Dewey	Subject Heading	LC	Dewey	Subject Heading
Z683	027.0021	Library statistics	Z1365-1401	015.71	Bibliography, National—Canada
Z688.A7	025.277	Acquisition of art catalogs			
Z688.M4	025.2761	Acquisition of medical literature	Z1411-1431	015.72	Bibliography, National—Mexico
Z689-.5	025.21	Book selection	Z1501-1595	015.729	Bibliography, National—West Indies
Z689-.8	025.2	Acquistions (Libraries)			
Z692.D38	025.284	Acquisition of databases	Z1601-1939	015.8	Bibliography, National—South America
Z692.M3	025.286	Acquisition of maps			
Z692.S5	025.28305	Acquisition of serial publications	Z2000-2959	015.4	Bibliography, National—Europe
Z693-695.83	025.32	Descriptive cataloging	Z3013-3028	015.56	Bibliography, National—Middle East
Z695.83	025.31	Catalogs, Union			
Z699-.5	025.3132	Machine-readable bibliographic data	Z3126-3415	015.5	Bibliography, National—Asia
Z700.9-701.5	025.7	Books—Conservation and restoration	Z3221-3415	015.59	Bibliography, National—Asia, Southeastern
Z701.3.D4	025.84	Books—Deacidification	Z3366-3370	015.55	Bibliography, National—Iran
Z702	025.82	Book thefts			
Z704	025.56	Library rules and regulations	Z3401-3409	015.47	Bibliography, National—Asiatic Russia
Z710	025.31	Library catalogs			
Z711	028.7	Reference books	Z3461-3465	015.4756	Bibliography, National—Armenia
Z711.2	025.56	Library orientation			
Z711.3	027.0021	Library statistics	Z3466-3470	015.5692	Bibliography, National—Lebanon
Z711.3	025.58	Library use studies			
Z720	020.92	Librarians	Z3476-3480	015.5694	Bibliography, National—Israel
Z721-871	027.009	Libraries—History			
Z987-997.2	026.1	Book collecting	Z3481-3485	015.5691	Bibliography, National—Syria
Z998-1000.5	017.4	Catalogs, Booksellers'			
Z1001-9000	010	Bibliography	Z3501-3975	015.6	Bibliography, National—Africa
Z1003-.5	028	Books and reading			
Z1008	070.5	Book clubs	Z4001-4439	015.94	Bibliography, National—Australia
Z1030	096.2	Vellum printed books			
Z1201-4980	015	Bibliography, National			
Z1215-1363	015.73	Bibliography, National—United States			